RELIGION
IN
LATIN AMERICA

RELIGION
IN
LATIN AMERICA

A Documentary History

*Edited with Introductions, Commentary,
and Select Translations by*

LEE M. PENYAK
WALTER J. PETRY

ORBIS BOOKS
Maryknoll, New York 10545

Founded in 1970, Orbis Books endeavors to publish works that enlighten the mind, nourish the spirit, and challenge the conscience. The publishing arm of the Maryknoll Fathers and Brothers, Orbis seeks to explore the global dimensions of the Christian faith and mission, to invite dialogue with diverse cultures and religious traditions, and to serve the cause of reconciliation and peace. The books published reflect the views of their authors and do not represent the official position of the Maryknoll Society. To learn more about Maryknoll and Orbis Books, please visit our website at www.maryknoll.org.

Library of Congress Cataloging-in-Publication Data

Religion in Latin America: a documentary history / edited with introductions, commentary, and select
    translations by Lee M. Penyak and Walter J. Petry.
        p. cm.
    Includes bibliographical references and index.
    ISBN-13: 978-1-57075-679-5 (pbk.)
    1. Latin America—Religion. I. Penyak, Lee M. II. Petry, Walter J.
    BL2540.R45 2006
    200.98—dc22

                                                                    2006010823

Dedicated to the memory of

Oscar Arnulfo Romero (1917-1980),

*archbishop of San Salvador and
strident defender of human rights,
a true shepherd to his flock,
assassinated by members of El Salvador's
military establishment while celebrating Mass.*

Contents

CONTENTS

CONTENTS

Contents

CONTENTS

XIV. THE TROUBLED TWENTIETH CENTURY • 239

XV. PROTO–LIBERATION THEOLOGY • 263

XVIII. CRITIQUES OF LIBERATION THEOLOGY · 313

XIX. DIVERSE RESPONSES TO AND BY THE CATHOLIC CHURCH · 321

XX. LATINO JEWS, AFRO-LATINOS, AND AMERINDIANS · 329

Contents

Preface

Though designed for undergraduate and graduate students of Latin American history, politics, religion, culture, and society, this anthology should be useful for members of church groups, grassroots organizations, and others concerned with issues of peace and justice. As academics convinced of the importance of utilizing primary documents to help students think critically and write analytically, we chose sources that force readers to grapple with the realities of imperialism, racism, poverty, and injustice, via eyewitness accounts of the dynamic religious currents in Latin American history. As a result, many of our documents are not found in standard anthologies because they focus on marginalized members of society, highlight Catholic differences over revolution and political participation, and pay significant attention to recent movements such as liberation theology, Pentecostalism, Santería and Candomblé, and Catholic charismatic renewal.

Troubled by the growing trend for editors of anthologies to write such thoroughly descriptive introductions that render the documents almost superfluous, we chose to write contextual introductions that place documents in historical perspective and force students to think and analyze on their own. Each introduction, therefore, ends with questions that should help the general reader make connections to major themes and other readings, and which should foster discussion.

Scholars familiar with H. McKennie Goodpasture's anthology entitled *Cross and Sword: An Eyewitness History of Christianity in Latin America* (Maryknoll, N.Y.: Orbis Books, 1989) will find few similarities with our work. Some primary documents are indispensable for any understanding of Latin American history and are included here as well as in Goodpasture's anthology. We, however, expanded these documents and incorporated many new ones that more closely relate religion to the themes of race, class, and, whenever possible, gender. In addition, our new introductions will enable the reader to understand the status and mentality of the writer and the specific context in which he or she wrote. We have also traced all documents back to their original source in order to eliminate errors in punctuation and typography. Some authors and presses insisted that we incorporate excerpts exactly as printed in the original, even if they contained mistakes in punctuation, spelling, and accents. We usually did not write *sic* after these errors so as not to interrupt the flow of the reading. We are all too aware of inconsistencies in the usage of accents and commas. Publication dates in the introductions and in the table of contents correspond to the original publication, typically in Spanish or Portuguese, and not to the publication of an English translation. The editors' ellipses are placed in brackets; ellipses not contained within brackets are from the original source. Most footnotes in original documents have been eliminated.

The editors gratefully acknowledge assistance from reference librarians at Scranton's Harry and Jeanette Weinberg Memorial Library, especially Katie Duke, Clara Hudson, Betsey Moylan, and Kevin Norris, as well as from the interlibrary loan department, especially Sheila Ferraro and Magdalene Restuccia. Margaret Robinson requested and organized interlibrary loan materials. Bonnie

Strohl walked Penyak through the intricate maze of copyright permissions. Sarah Malcolm helped to contact copyright holders. Orbis's Doris Goodnough supervised the process of obtaining permissions. Aileen McHale facilitated the scanning of excerpts, an activity carried out by David Grizzanti, Joe Casabono, and Matt Pfahl. Eric J. Ledesma and Sarah Malcolm helped to check scanned materials for accuracy. Jane Wesloski and Hillel Arnold assisted with numerous clerical activities. The editors benefited from friendly correspondence with Mrs. Ellen Goodpasture and with Philip Goodpasture, Esq. Ralph Coury, Paul Lakeland, and Melissa Nash Coury gave valuable assistance on select documents. Robert A. Parsons, Consuelo García-Devesa, and Germán A. Zárate Sández made recommendations on certain translations from the Spanish. Linda Ledford-Miller helped to translate phrases originally in Portuguese. William M. Abbott meticulously critiqued introductions to units and excerpts and saved the editors from some embarrassment. Susan Perry, editor at Orbis, assisted us during every step of the process, maintained constant email correspondence, and offered invaluable recommendations.

The following students in Scranton's faculty-student research program accumulated materials for individual excerpts: Johan Balbuena, Andrew A. Cammarano, Kelly Jackson, Emily Kocis, Christopher Konopka, Jeffrey W. Marx, Megan Niedbala, Kali Racavich, Maureen Redington, Katherine Robinson, and David A. Taylor. Timothy P. McVeigh provided research assistance and helped undergraduate students locate materials.

Despite immeasurable assistance and guidance from friends, colleagues, and students, the editors assume full responsibility for interpretations and analyses in introductions, as well as for any errors in translation and transcription.

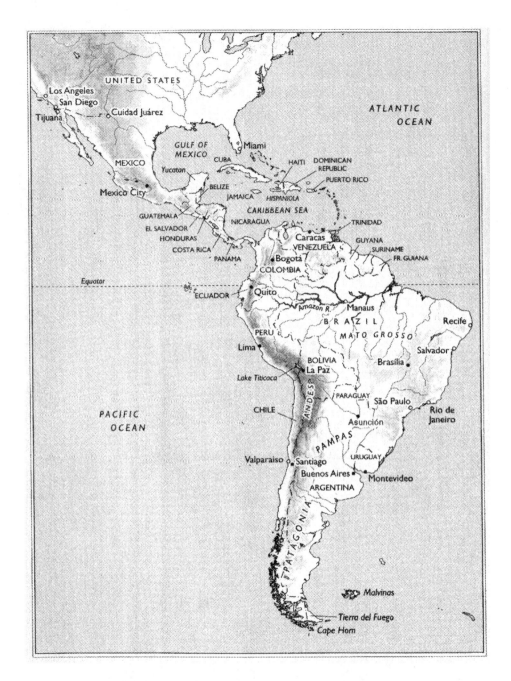

Source: Map by William Nelson in Peter Winn, *Americas: The Changing Face of Latin America and the Caribbean,* 3rd ed. (Berkeley: University of California Press, 2006), x. Reprinted by permission of Peter Winn.

Table 1: Religious Affiliation by Country: CIA Fact Books: 2005 (1990)

	Roman Catholic	Protestant	Other	None	Evangelical	Other Protestant	Jehovah's Witnesses
Argentina 2005	92% (90%)	2% (2%)	4% (6%)				
Belize 2005	49.6% (60%)	27% (40%)	14%	9.4%			
Bolivia 2005	95% (95%)	5% (present)					
Brazil 2005	80% (90%)		20%				
Chile 2005	89% (89%)	11% (11%)					
Colombia 2005	90% (90%)		10%				
Costa Rica 2005	76.3% (95%)		4.8%	3.2%	13.7%	4.8%	1.3%
Cuba 2005	85% (85%)	present					present
Dominican Republic 2005	95% (95%)						
Ecuador 2005	95% (95%)		5%				

SOURCE: Percentages in parentheses are derived from the *1990 CIA Factbook*. Percentages without parentheses are derived from the *2005 CIA Factbook*. See, *The World Factbook 1990* (Washington, D.C.: Central Intelligence Agency, 1990), and *The World Factbook 2005* (Washington, D.C.: Central Intelligence Agency, 2005. Present = a sizeable population but not quantifiable.

	Roman Catholic	Protestant	Other	None	Evangelical	Other Protestant	Jehovah's Witnesses
El Salvador 2005	83% (97%)	present (present)	17%				
Guatemala 2005	present (present)	present (present)					
Haiti 2005	80% (75-80%)	16% (10%)	3%	1%			
Honduras 2005	97% (97%)	3% (present)					
Mexico 2005	89% (97%)	6% (3%)	5%				
Nicaragua 2005	85% (95%)	15% (5%)					
Panama 2005	85% (93%)	15% (6%)					
Paraguay 2005	90% (90%)					10% (present)	
Peru 2005	90% (present)		10%				
Puerto Rico 2005	85% (85%)	15% (15%)	present (present)				
Uruguay 2005	66% (66%)	2% (2%)	31% (30%)				
Venezuela 2005	96% (96%)	2% (2%)	2%				

Table 2: Percentage of Catholics in Select Archdioceses in Latin America

The percentages of Catholics in the following twenty-seven archdioceses, which include all the capitals of Latin American countries and a few other large cities, have been calculated from statistics printed in the official yearbook of the Roman Catholic Church, the *Annuario Pontificio*. Each year this Vatican publication gives a statistical profile of every diocese and archdiocese in the world that includes the total population of the diocese/archdiocese and the number of baptized Catholics therein. The statistics demonstrate clearly the decline of the Catholic population throughout Latin America.

	Percentages by year		
	1979	1987	2003
Asunción	90.0	90.0	—
Bogotá	96.8	96.0	85.3
Brasília	91.7	85.4	77.0
Buenos Aires	90.0	92.6	91.5
Caracas	88.0	84.0	74.0
Guadalajara	94.0	94.7	90.7
Guatemala	99.4	85.0	70.1
La Paz	92.0	90.2	87.5
Lima	96.0	96.0	92.3
Managua	99.0	89.0	81.5
Medellín	95.3	97.5	90.1
Mexico	95.0	94.0	90.5
Montevideo	75.8	68.0	63.0
Panama	90.0	89.5	90.0
Port-au-Prince	93.5	82.5	71.4
Quito	90.3	90.0	90.0
San Cristóbal de la Habana	48.3	47.0	—
San José de Costa Rica	97.5	90.0	85.2
San Juan de Puerto Rico	80.2	78.6	68.5
San Salvador	84.4	85.0	69.8
Santiago de Chile	81.8	78.4	73.8
Santiago de Cuba	—	24.7	22.6
Santo Domingo	93.9	94.2	95.0
São Paulo	87.0	87.0	75.0
São Salvador da Bahia	94.8	93.0	73.8
São Sebastião do Rio de Janeiro	88.0	86.5	68.6
Tegucigalpa	95.0	94.8	82.1

SOURCE: *Annuario Pontificio* (Città del Vaticano: Libreria Editrice Vaticana, 1979, 1987, 2003).

PART I
Indigenous Religions

Amerindians created sophisticated and elaborate religious systems prior to European contact. Though significant differences existed among nonsedentary, semisedentary, and fully sedentary peoples, most cultures rendered tribute to many gods and attempted to abide by the laws of nature and to respect spirits who resided within nature. Pre-Hispanic peoples, notes William B. Taylor, did not distinguish the sacred from the profane, and "stone, wood, clay, seeds, and maize pith were not simply inert materials to be shaped into images that symbolized or evoked divinity . . . [they]—and all others—were alive with the sacred. . . ."[1] Gods usually represented specific attributes, sometimes associated with natural phenomena. Priests, in communion with the gods, regulated political and religious activities, which gave meaning to people's lives and helped them to understand their place in the cosmos. Amerindians recorded information in the form of pictographic images on paper, stone, and pottery, sometimes used hieroglyphics, built temples and pyramids to demonstrate devotion, and passed down oral histories of their beliefs. Immediately after the conquest they related their vision of the world to Catholic missionaries. It is not surprising that most information on pre-Hispanic religious traditions centers on the Mexica, Maya, and Inca, because Spaniards eagerly imposed their political and religious control on these wealthy and large populations, and recorded information as a vehicle to expose "heathen" practices, titillate the small but growing European literate populace, and justify the military conquest.[2]

The Mexica, or Aztecs, dominated most of Mesoamerica when Hernán Cortés and his fellow Spaniards arrived at the mainland in 1519. The inheritors of the rich and complex polytheistic religious system shared by previous cultures, such as the peoples of Teotihua-

---

1. William B. Taylor, *Magistrates of the Sacred: Priests and Parishioners in Eighteenth-Century Mexico* (Stanford, Calif.: Stanford University Press, 1996), 49.

2. David J. Weber, *The Spanish Frontier in North America* (New Haven, Conn.: Yale University Press, 1992), 22; John E. Kizca, *Resilient Cultures: America's Native Peoples Confront European Colonization, 1500-1800* (Upper Saddle River, N.J.: Prentice Hall, 2003), 13; Enrique Dussel, ed., *The Church in Latin America, 1492-1992* (Maryknoll, N.Y.: Orbis Books, 1992), 2; Inga Clendinnen, *Aztecs: An Interpretation* (Cambridge: Cambridge University Press, 1991), 218-19.

can and Tula, the Mexica venerated Quetzalcoatl, the god of culture, Tlaloc, the god of rain, Tezcatlipoca, a war god, and Tonatiuh, the sun-god and protector of warriors, among others. They gave special homage to Huitzilopochtli, a war god associated with the sun, whom they credited with having led them to the promised land of Tenochtitlan in 1325 after having identified his symbol: an eagle on a cactus devouring a snake. Huitzilopochtli's beneficence, they believed, allowed the Mexica empire to expand and its people to benefit from the tribute paid by subordinate tribes. But celestial favor simultaneously implied earthly sacrifice. Just as Mexicas expected their gods to provide them with bountiful harvests and military success, the gods expected their devotees to observe proper religious observance and offer sacrifices. Mexica leaders accepted their responsibilities enthusiastically and sacrificed thousands of victims each year. On rare occasions they ate the cooked flesh of valiant captive warriors to absorb their qualities. As long as Mexica faithful maintained this equilibrium, all could reasonably expect the fifth and final sun to continue to rise each morning. But "failures in important aspects of life," notes John E. Kizca, "would cause the devotees first to question whether they had followed proper ceremonies, and then even to doubt the effectiveness of the god being beseeched."[3]

Though certain Spaniards, such as Bishop Diego de Landa in the Yucatan, attempted to erase the memory of pre-Hispanic religions and destroyed dozens of Maya codices and hundreds of religious images, surviving sacred books such as the *Popul Vuh*, together with recently deciphered hieroglyphics, accounts by indigenous peoples themselves, and Landa's own *Account of the Things of Yucatan*, provide important clues to Maya religious practices. Hunab Ku was the creator god of the Maya, whose various city-states dominated the Yucatan and Central America from approximately 1000 B.C. to A.D. 1300. Itzamná, god of the sky, helped Kinich Ahao, the sun god, and Ixchel, the moon god, regulate celestial and earthly time. Chac, the god of rain, provided essential nourishment to sustain cities and outlying agricultural communities. Other gods, such as Ah Puch, the god of death, lorded over the underworld, said to consist of thirteen layers, each with its own deity. Consistent with a belief shared by other Mesoamerican peoples, the Maya held that human beings occupied the fifth and final world created by the gods, and that calamity would befall humans eventually. Outstanding mathematicians and astrologers, Maya elites created solar (365 day) and lunar (260 day) calendars and accurately predicted eclipses (sometimes to frighten the populace into submission). Theocratic rulers promoted religious ceremonies that included ritualized fasting, bloodletting, and human sacrifice, the latter apparently increasing after A.D. 1000.[4]

---

3. Kizca, *Resilient Cultures*, 13; Kay Almere Read, *Time and Sacrifice in the Aztec Cosmos* (Bloomington and Indianapolis: Indiana University Press, 1998), 5, 197-98; Kay A. Read, "Mesoamerica: Religion," in *Encyclopedia of Mexico: History, Society & Culture*, vol. 2, ed. Michael S. Werner (Chicago and London: Fitzroy Dearborn Publishers, 1997), 825-26; Mark A. Burkholder and Lyman L. Johnson, *Colonial Latin America*, 5th ed. (New York and Oxford: Oxford University Press, 2004), 17.

4. Burr C. Brundage, "Maya," in *Encyclopedia of Latin America*, ed. Helen Delpar (New York: McGraw-Hill, 1974), 363; Benjamin Keen and Keith Haynes, eds., *A History of Latin America*, vol. 1, 7th ed. (Boston and New York: Houghton Mifflin, 2004), 17-18, 20.

Inca state religion fostered belief in a creator god, Viracocha, whose special devotees consisted primarily of members of the royal family. The emperor, or Sapi Inca, traced his lineage directly to the sun god, Inti, who became a powerful symbol of Inca dominance and to whom temples were dedicated in conquered provinces. Other gods included Mama Quilla, associated with the moon; Pachamama, the earth mother; and Huanacauri, the god of war. Inca deities were enshrined in a temple in the imperial capital of Cuzco, as were the most important gods of subjugated peoples—which created a vehicle to incorporate them within the Inca pantheon and a way to control potentially dangerous and competing deities and their followers. Members of individual communities, or *ayllu*, also venerated their own divine ancestors from whom local leaders, or *kuraka*, claimed to have descended. Male priests, assisted by virgin holy women, or *mamacona*, presided over religious ceremonies that included prayer, confession, divination, and occasional human sacrifice to commemorate feats or acknowledge setbacks. Andean peoples generally believed that men descended from male gods associated with activities such as hunting and warfare and that women descended from female gods associated with activities such as weaving and childrearing. Andean peoples, notes Kenneth J. Andrien, "believed that the sacred permeated every aspect of their world and deeply influenced everyday life [and that] inanimate natural objects such as mountains or trees represented or evoked divine ancestors."[5]

1. The Place Where One Becomes Deified

Both readings 1 and 2 are taken from the Codex Matritensis (Madrid Codex), manuscripts compiled between 1562 and 1575 by the friar/anthropologist Bernadino de Sahagún (see reading 19). It consisted of the poetry, legends, stories, myths, and history of the Mexica (Aztecs) as dictated by informants in their native Nahuatl language to scribes working under the direction of Sahagún whose aim was to record as much as possible of Mexica culture to aid the missionaries in their task of converting the conquered to Christianity. Sahagún's work remains the repository for almost all that is known about Aztec culture.

Teotihuacan (Nahua-Aztec for "the place where one becomes deified"), a site some thirty miles northeast of today's Mexico City, reached its greatest development around A.D. 500 (long before the Aztecs appeared in Mesoamerican history). At its height it contained some 200,000 inhabitants and is considered the first true city in the Americas. The text below is at pains to express historical, political, social, and religious concepts that were vital parts of

5. Kenneth J. Andrien, ed., *The Human Tradition in Colonial Latin America* (Wilmington, Del.: Scholarly Resources, 2002), 22, 25; Burr C. Brundage, "Incas," in *Encyclopedia of Latin America*, ed. Helen Delpar (New York: McGraw-Hill, 1974), 294-95; Keen and Haynes, *History of Latin America*, 33.

SOURCE: Miguel León-Portilla, Alfredo Barrera Vásquez, Luis Gonzáles et al., eds., "La fundación de Teotihuacan," in *Historia documental de México*, vol. 1 (Mexico City: Universidad Nacional Autónoma de México, 1984), 14-15. Translated from the Spanish by Lee M. Penyak.

Mexica tradition and culture. To determine those teachings it is necessary to identify the "we" and "us" and the "they" in the final two verses. Why the vivid description of sunrise?

They set out immediately,
they all set out in motion:
the little children, the elders,
the young girls, the old women.
They left very slowly, very gradually,
there they came together to meet in Teotihuacan.
There they were given the orders,
there the dominion was established.
Those who became lords
were the learned ones,
the experts in things of the occult,
the holders of tradition.
Later principalities were established there . . .

And all the people built pyramids there,
to the Sun and to the Moon;
later they built many smaller pyramids.
There they worshipped
and there the high priests established themselves
over all of the people.
Thus they named it Teotihuacan,
because when the lords died, there they were
    buried.
Later they built pyramids on top of them,
that are still there now.
A pyramid is like a small hill,
but made by man.
There are quaries
from where they took the stones,
to build the pyramids,
and in that way they enlarged
the one to the Sun and the one to the Moon.

They are like hills
and it is not unbelievable
to say that they were built by hand,
because there were still giants
in many places back then. . . .

And they called it Teotihuacan,
because it was the place where
the lords were buried.
For, as they say:
"When we die,
we don't truly die,
because we live, we come back to life,
we continue living, we awaken.
This makes us happy."

In this way, they made their journey
at the time of death.
If a man, they spoke to him,
they helped him to become divine,
with the name of pheasant,
if a woman, with the name of owl.
They said:
"Awake, the sky is already turning red,
dawn has already arrived,
the pheasants are already singing with the color of
burning passion,
the swallows with the color of fire,
butterflies now soar."
For this reason the elders said
he who has died has returned as a god.
They said: "he became a god there,
which means that he died."

2. Our Grandfathers, Our Grandmothers

Archeologists have not been able to locate the site of Tamoanchan, the legendary place of the mythical first great culture in Mexico. Mysterious immigrants from the Gulf coast apparently brought superior cultural forms, which were adopted by the simpler farmers and pottery makers who had lived for many years at the site.

SOURCE: Miguel León-Portilla, Alfredo Barrera Vásquez, Luis Gonzáles et al., eds., "Llegada de los antiguos pobladores portadores de cultura superior," in *Historia documental de México*, vol. 1 (Mexico City: Universidad Nacional Autónoma de México, 1984), 12-13. Translated from the Spanish by Lee M. Penyak.

Popol Vuh

The first long verse is a geographical account of the place where the ancestors originated. The brief verse makes clear the divine plan for a special people. Who are these people? What is the message of the last verse, which suggests that Tamoanchan did not represent the ultimate ideal master culture? Is this message merely a historical account or does it represent a larger cosmological one?

Here is the story
that the ancients used to tell:
In a certain time
that no one can now recount,
and which no one is now able to remember . . .
of those who came here to plant
our grandfathers, our grandmothers,
these, they say,
arrived, came,
continued on their journey,
they came to end it
to govern here on this land,
which was mentioned by only one name,
as if it had become a small world.
They came on water by their boats,
in many groups,
and there they arrived on the water's shore,
at the northern coast,
and there where their boats came to rest,
is called Panutla,
which means, where one passes above the water,
and now is called Panutla (Pánuco).
Right away they followed the water's shore,
Looking for the mountains
Some the white mountains
And others the smoking mountains,
they arrived to Quauhtemalla (Guatemala),
following the water's shore.

Moreover they didn't go
because they wanted to
but rather under the guidance of their priests,
and their God showed the way.
Later they came,
there they arrived,
to the place that is called Tamoanchan,
which means "we are looking for our home."

And in the place called Tamoanchan
their dominion lasted a long time:
then dominion passed
to a place called Xomiltepec
and there in Xomiltepec
the lords, the ancients, and the priests convened.
They said:
"The Master of near and far has called us,
He has called each one who acknowledges him as God."
They said:
"Because we are not going to live here
we will not remain here,
let us look for a new land.
There we will meet
the one who is Night and Wind,
the Master of near and far."

3. Popol Vuh

The Popol Vuh *(Book of the Council) was probably formulated in the late pre-Classic period (no later than A.D. 200) and written in the 1550s by Maya noblemen based on a glyphic text and oral tradition. The nobles had been taught by the friars to write the Maya language in European script.*

The tiny excerpt below contains the Maya creation story (1b), an initial statement of Maya cosmology (1c, 1d, 1e), and a moral parable (2a). Compare the Maya and Hebrew creation stories in the Bible. Is it possible to discern any physical characteris-

Source: Thomas Ballantine Irving, ed., *The Maya's Own Words* (Culver City, Calif.: Labrinthos, 1985), 13-16.

tics of Central America in 1b? Why do 1c, 1d, and 1e begin the delineation of a whole cosmology? What does the insistence of the creators on "say[ing] the names of us," being "invoked and remembered," and [being] "perfect worshipers" suggest about this cosmology? How does the description of earth in 1e relate to that in 1b? The twin boy gods decide to poison Vucub-Cakish. Who might the latter be? Is there any indication that the Maya writers were influenced, consciously or unconsciously, by the Christian beliefs or formulations promoted by the friars?

1. Creation

a. Preamble

This is the beginning of the ancient history of the Kiché land; we are going to record the traditions of all that the Kiché nation did, and reveal what has been hidden up till now. We are bringing this forth under Christianity, for the *Popol-Vuh* as our Book of the Council was called, is no longer to be seen.

b. The Earth

This is the story of how everything was in suspense, everything at rest, everything silent. All was motionless, hushed; and empty was the vastness of Heaven.

Here is our first document, the first account we have. There were still no men nor animals; there were no birds, fish nor crabs, no trees, stones nor caves, no ravines, grass nor woods. Only Heaven existed; the face of Earth had not yet appeared. Only the calm sea and Heaven's expanse were spread out everywhere. Nothing made a sound, nor did anything move. There was nothing which stood erect; only the water spread out peacefully, the calm and tranquil sea. There was only motionlessness and silence in the darkness of the night. Only the Creator and Fashioner, Tepeu and Gucumatz,[1] lived in the water surrounded by radiance. They lay hidden by the green and blue feathers of great sages; in this way existed the Heart of Heaven, which means God.

Then the Word was;[2] Tepeu and Gucumatz came and spoke to each other amid the darkness, consulting and meditating. They reached an agreement; they put their words and thoughts on life and light together in an effort to decide what to do when it should dawn. They finally resolved that man should appear, and thus they arranged for life to commence and men to be created. Tepeu and Gucumatz pronounced in unison:

"May the void be filled! May this water withdraw so Earth may arise! May it dawn on Heaven and Earth!"

This is how they planned the creation of Earth.

"*Earth!*" they said, and it was formed at once. Like the mist, like clouds, mountains rose from the water; through a miracle—a stroke of magic—hills and valleys were formed; at the same time cedars and pines sprang up in clusters. So Gucumatz of the green feathers was filled with joy and exclaimed:

"Welcome, Heart of Heaven, O Hurricane!"

Thus while Heaven was still in suspense, Earth was created so it could rise easily from the waters. This is how the gods accomplished their task after they had considered how to bring it to a successful conclusion.

c. The Animals

Then the wild animals, the guardians of the woods and spirits of the forest, were created: deer, birds, lions, jaguars, large serpents, harmless smaller snakes, and more deadly vipers. The Creators thought matters over again and came to this decision:

---

1. Here and elsewhere I [Irving] am omitting the names of several other deities. Notice how gods and kings tend to appear in pairs in the Mayan culture, although this couple is associated with a third being, Hurricane, the Heart of Heaven. Gucumatz is Kiché for "Feathered Snake," and is a translation of Quetzalcoatl in Aztec and of Kukulcan in Yucatecan (Yucatan Mayan). His green feathers are mentioned in the next sentence, and in the play *Warrior of Rabinal*, the princess is distinguished by her emerald plumes, which were a symbol of deity or of royalty.

2. Compare the beginning of the Gospel of John; this may be Christian influence.

"Must there be only silence and stillness under the trees and beneath the vines? Someone should be guarding them."

So they spoke again, and at once deer and birds were created. They assigned them their dwellings as follows:

"You, O deer, will sleep along the river flats and in ravines; you will increase and feed in the meadows and woods, and walk on four feet."

As it was said, so it was done. Then they assigned the birds their homes; they told them what to do, and each flew to its nest. When the four-footed animals and the birds had been created, the Creator and Fashioner said to them:

"*Cry! Shout! Warble! Howl!* Each of you should speak according to your kind."

Yet it was impossible for them to speak like man—they only squealed, cackled, or brayed. Their language was meaningless, for each one cried out in a different manner. When the Creator and Fashioner saw it was impossible for them to speak, they remarked to each other:

"They cannot say the names of us, their Creator and Fashioner! That is not right."

So they announced: "You will be transformed; we have changed our minds because you do not speak. You will eat and live in the ravines and woods, for you do not call upon us, and we are going to make other creatures who will be more attentive. You must accept your fate, which is to have your flesh chewed and eaten."

Thus the Forerunners made their will known to every animal on Earth; but as these did not speak a common tongue they could not do a thing about it. In this way, the animals which exist on the face of the Earth were condemned to be killed and eaten.

d. The Men of Clay and Wood

Then the Creator and Fashioner wanted to try their luck again. They made another attempt to form a man who would worship them.

"Let's try again! What shall we do to be invoked and remembered on Earth? We have already tried with our first creatures, but could not get them to praise and venerate us. Let us make obedient and respectful beings. Dawn and sunrise are approaching; let us form someone to sustain and nourish us."

Thus they spoke, and then they started making fresh creations. From Earth, from plain mud, they made man's flesh—but this fell apart, for it was soft and limp and had no strength. It could not move its head, its face fell towards one side, its neck was so stiff it could not look backward. It soaked up water and would not hold together. Then the Creator and Fashioner talked things over once more.

"Let us consult an omen, since our men cannot walk nor multiply. Let us ask for some advice on this matter."

So they knocked their handiwork apart, complaining:

"What shall we do for perfect worshipers? We must find a way so the man we fashion will sustain and feed us. He must invoke and call upon us!"

Hurricane, Tepeu, and Gucumatz went off to ask the magic pair of grandparents for help, since these were soothsayers.

"Talk matters over, grandmother and grandfather: toss lots with your corn and beans, and find out if we should make a man from wood."

In order to cast a spell the old woman and old man threw lots with corn and beans:

"Get together! Speak so we can hear you! Say whether the Creator and Fashioner should make a man from wood; and whether this man will feed and nourish us. Corn! Beans! Fate! Unite! *Get together!*"

This is how the old couple talked to the corn and beans, and then they declared:

"Your figures will turn out fine if they are made of wood, and they will speak upon the face of the Earth."[3]

"*So be it!*" answered the Forerunners.

Immediately the Creator and Fashioner made their figures out of wood. They resembled men, they spoke like men, and they peopled the face of the Earth. These were the first men who existed in large numbers in the world.

---

3. This was Ish-Mucanch and Ish-Piyacoc [. . .]. The beans, bright red in color, were from the tzite or coral tree, which also furnished the wood for the first men.

e. Destruction of the Wooden Men

The wooden dolls existed and had daughters and sons; but they had no soul or understanding. They did not remember who their Creator and Fashioner were, and limped around aimlessly. At first they spoke, but their faces soon withered and their feet and hands had no consistency. They quickly forgot about the Heart of Heaven, and therefore fell into disgrace. They had no blood nor moisture nor stoutness; their cheeks were hollow, their hands and feet were shriveled, and their flesh was yellowish. They were only a sample—an attempt at making man.

Since they no longer remembered the Creator and Fashioner who had given them their being and cared for them, they were destroyed. The Heart of Heaven who is called Hurricane caused a great flood to overwhelm the wooden dolls, while a shower of pitch fell from Heaven into their eyes. It cut off their heads and gnawed their flesh; it shattered their nerves and ground their bones.

The wooden men ran around in desperation; they tried to climb up on their houses, but these collapsed and tossed them to the ground. They tried to climb the trees, and were shaken off; they wanted to crawl into the caves and were chased out of them. This was their punishment for not remembering the Heart of Heaven: the face of Earth was darkened and a black rain began to fall that lasted day and night.

Then the animals both great and small started to eat them, and even the trees and stones struck them in the face. Their jars, dishes, and pots began to murmur and their dogs, turkeys, and grindstones rose up against them.

"On your account our faces are being worn away," said the grindstones; "day after day, at nightfall and at dawn, you make us groan—'Holee! holee! Hukee! hukee!'[4] That was our duty toward you; but now you are no longer men; we'll see how strong we are! We will grind you and reduce your flesh to dust!" the grindstones warned them.

The dogs in turn addressed the wooden men as follows: "Why haven't you fed us? We've just looked at you from a distance, while you were eating, and you chased us away. You always had a stick handy to beat us with; this is how you treated us when we couldn't speak to you. Why shouldn't we sink our teeth into you now?"

Thus spoke the dogs, and the wooden men, attacked by their animals and utensils, perished. They say their only descendants are the monkeys in the forest; and for this reason monkeys look like men and remind us of a race who were made from wood.

2. How Pride Was Punished

a. Vucub-Cakish, the Proud

At the time when the flood overwhelmed the wooden dolls, Heaven and Earth already existed, but the Sun and Moon were hidden. There was little light on the face of Earth since there was still no Sun, but a proud creature called Vucub-Cakish went about saying:

"These men who were drowned prove clearly that I am the greatest creature on Earth. I am the light of the Sun and Moon!" he exclaimed. "Great is my splendor! Through me men will move and hold sway. My eyes glow like emeralds; my teeth shine like precious stones; and my nose can be seen from a distance like the Moon. My throne is made of silver, and the face of Earth lights up whenever I come to sit on it. Thus I am both the Sun and Moon!"

This is how Vucub-Cakish talked, even though he was not the Sun; he was only boasting of his feathers and other wealth. His sight did not take in all the Earth, but was limited to wherever he was looking at the moment. Since dawn still had not come, the Sun could not be seen, nor could the Moon and Stars. Therefore Vucub-Cakish went around as proud as if he really were the Sun and Moon, and his ambition was to become powerful and go around giving orders.

He had two sons, Zipacna and Cabracane. Zupacna played with mountains, which he tossed up overnight. Cabracane moved them around, making great mountains and little hills shake. Both sons of Vucub-Cakish had the same urge for glory as their father.

---

4. These sounds imitate the noise of the grindstone or metate when corn is being ground on it.

Now two youths called Hunahpu and Ish-Bal-ankeh had noticed the harm that Vucub-Cakish and his two sons were causing through their pride, and when the father started annoying the Heart of Heaven they decided to put an end to him.

"This isn't right. Let's shoot him with our blow-guns while he's eating; we'll make him ill and put an end to his wealth, his jade and precious metals, and all the emeralds and other jewels on which he prides himself. Neither power nor wealth should turn one's head like this."

The boys were really gods. Each picked up his blowgun—and that meant Vucub-Cakish was doomed right there.

4. Maya Religiosity

There is a real problem in using accounts of the Amerindians written by Spaniards, especially those written in the immediate or near aftermath of the conquest. This becomes even more problematical when the authors are missionary friars who have an agenda and usually possess no anthropological sense (major exceptions: Bartolomé de Las Casas and Bernardino de Sahagún; see readings 10 and 19).

Diego de Landa (1524-1579), Franciscan zealot and author of the excerpt below, arrived in Yucatan in 1549, only seven years after the conquest of that province. Since the Maya "Christo-Europeanization" had just begun, Landa would have been able to observe firsthand many of their traditional practices. His Relación de las cosas de Yucatán (1566) *[translated as "Yucatan before and after the Conquest"] is based on years of meticulous observation and research. Upon discovering that the converts still maintained their old practices, Landa initiated a ferocious inquisition, which resulted in the imprisonment, torture, and deaths of hundreds of Maya as well as the burning of twenty-seven of the hieroglyphic rolls, which contained their religious, philosophical, and scientific teachings. Sent to Spain to stand trial for his excesses by the new bishop of Yucatan, Francisco Toral, O.F.M. (Landa was exonerated), he wrote the invaluable* Relación, *which, until the recent discovery of the technique for deciphering Maya glyphs, was virtually the sole source of information about the Maya.*

What does the reading reveal about the nature of Maya religious beliefs, their priesthood, the social status of the clergy, their learning, Maya festivals and ceremonies, and the nature, frequency, and ritual of human and animal sacrifice? Note that while Landa is highly informative, he uses inflammatory and judgmental terms in his detailed descriptions: he may have been tempted to emphasize the dramatic or the exotic rather than the mundane. What is the purpose of the Maya ceremony of gathering men together to bleed by drawing rope through their penises? What is the relation between the anointment of the "idol" with the blood of that ritual and the anointment of the "idol" with the much more copious blood of sacrificed humans? Does Landa's writing, which frequently refers to Christian practices to explain Maya ones, reveal the superzealous missionary that Landa actually was? If so, how often?

The people of Yucatan were as attentive to matters of religion as of government, and had a High Priest whom they called Ahkin May, or also Ahaucan May, meaning the Priest May, or the High Priest May. He was held in great reverence by the chiefs, and had no allotment of Indians for him-

SOURCE: Diego de Landa, *Yucatan before and after the Conquest*, trans. William Gates (New York: Dover Publications, 1978), 12-13, 46-48, 49-50.

self, the chiefs making presents to him in addition to the offerings, and all the local priests sending him contributions. He was succeeded in office by his sons or nearest kin. In him lay the key to their sciences, to which they most devoted themselves, giving counsel to the chiefs and answering their inquiries. With the matter of sacrifices he rarely took part, except on great festivals or business of much moment. He and his disciples appointed the priests for the towns, examining them in their sciences and ceremonies; put in their charge the affairs of their office, and the setting of a good example to the people; he provided their books and sent them forth. They in turn attended to the service of the temples, teaching their sciences and writing books upon them.

They taught the sons of the other priests, and the second sons of the chiefs, who were brought to them very young for this purpose, if they found them inclined toward this office. The sciences which they taught were the reckoning of the years, months and days, the festivals and ceremonies, the administration of their sacraments, the omens of the days, their methods of divination and prophecies, events, remedies for sicknesses, antiquities, and the art of reading and writing by their letters and the characters wherewith they wrote, and by pictures that illustrated the writings.

They wrote their books on a long sheet doubled in folds, which was then enclosed between two boards finely ornamented; the writing was on one side and the other, according to the folds. The paper they made from the roots of a tree, and gave it a white finish excellent for writing upon. Some of the principal lords were learned in these sciences, from interest, and for the greater esteem they enjoyed thereby; yet they did not make use of them in public. [. . .]

The Yucatecans had a great number of temples, sumptuous in their style; besides these temples in common the chiefs, priest and principal men also had their oratories and idols in their house, for their private offerings and prayers. They held Cozumel and the well at Chichén Itzá in as great veneration as we have in our pilgrimages to Jerusalem and Rome; they visited them to offer gifts, especially at Cozumel, as we do at our holy places; and when they did not visit they sent offer-

ings. When traveling also, and passing an abandoned temple, it was their custom to enter for prayers and burn incense.

So many idols did they have that their gods did not suffice them, there being no animal or reptile of which they did not make images, and these in the form of their gods and goddesses. They had idols of stone (though few in number), others more numerous of wood, but the greatest number of terracotta. The idols of wood were especially esteemed and reckoned among their inheritances as objects of great value. They had no metal statues, there being no metals in the country. As regards the images, they knew perfectly that they were made by human hands, perishable, and not divine; but they honored them because of what they represented and the ceremonies that had been performed during their fabrication, especially the wooden ones.

The most idolatrous of them were the priests, the chilanes, the sorcerers, the physicians, the chacs and the nacones. It was the office of the priests to discourse and teach their sciences, to indicate calamities and the means of remedying them, preaching during the festivals, celebrating the sacrifices and administering their sacraments. The chilanes were charged with giving to all those in the locality the oracles of the demon, and the respect given them was so great that they did not ordinarily leave their houses except borne upon litters carried on the shoulders. The sorcerers and physicians cured by means of bleeding at the part afflicted, casting lots for divination in their work, and other matters. The chacs were four old men, specially elected on occasion to aid the priest in the proper and full celebration of the festivals. There were two of the nacones; the position of one was permanent and carried little honor, since it was his office to open the breasts of those who were sacrificed; the other was chosen as a general for the wars, who held office for three years, and was held in great honor; he also presided at certain festivals. [. . .]

At times they sacrificed their own blood, cutting all around the ears in strips which they let remain as a sign. At other times they perforated their cheeks or the lower lip; again they made cuts in parts of the body, or pierced the tongue cross-ways and passed stalks through, causing extreme pain; again they cut away the superfluous part of the member, leaving the flesh in the form of ears. It was this custom which led the historian of the Indies to say that they practised circumcision.

At other times they practised a filthy and grievous sacrifice, whereby they gathered in the temple, in a line, and each made a pierced hole through the member, across from side to side, and then passed through as great a quantity of cord as they could stand; and thus all together fastened and strung together, they anointed the statue of the demon with the collected blood. The one able to endure the most was considered most valiant, and their sons of tender age began to accustom themselves to this suffering; it is frightful to see how much they were dedicated to this practice. [. . .]

Apart from the festivals which they solemnized by the sacrifices of animals, on occasions of great tribulation or need the priests or chilanes ordained the sacrifice of human beings. For this purpose all contributed, for the purchase of slaves. Some out of devotion gave their young sons. The victims were feted up to the day of the sacrifice, but carefully guarded that they might not run away, or defile themselves by any carnal acts; then while they went from town to town with dances, the priests, the chilanes and the celebrants fasted.

When the day of the ceremony arrived, they assembled in the court of the temple; if they were to be pierced with arrows their bodies were stripped and anointed with blue, with a miter on the head. When they arrived before the demon, all the people went through a solemn dance with him around the wooden pillar, all with bows and arrows, and then dancing raised him upon it, tied him, all continuing to dance and look at him. The impure priest, vestured, ascended and whether it was man or woman wounded the victim in the private parts with an arrow, and then descended and anointed the face of the demon with the blood he had drawn; then making a sign to the dancers,

they began in order as they passed rapidly, dancing, to shoot an arrow to the victim's heart, shown by a white mark, and quickly made of his chest a single point, like a hedgehog of arrows.

If his heart was to be taken out, they conducted him with great display and concourse of people, painted blue and wearing his miter, and placed him on the rounded sacrificial stone, after the priest and his officers had anointed the stone with blue and purified the temple to drive away the evil spirit. The chacs then seized the poor victim and swiftly laid him on his back across the stone, and the four took hold of his arms and legs, spreading them out. Then the nacon executioner came, with a flint knife in his hand, and with great skill made an incision between the ribs on the left side, below the nipple; then he plunged in his hand and like a ravenous tiger tore out the living heart, which he laid on a plate and gave to the priest; he then quickly went and anointed the faces of the idols with that fresh blood.

At times they performed this sacrifice on the stone situated on the top step of the temple, and then they threw the dead body rolling down the steps, where it was taken by the attendants, was stripped completely of the skin save only on the hands and feet; then the priest, stripped, clothed himself with this skin and danced with the rest. This was a ceremony with them of great solemnity. The victims sacrificed in this manner were usually buried in the court of the temple; but it occurred on occasions that they ate the flesh, distributing portions to the chiefs and those who succeeded in obtaining a part; the hands, feet and head went to the priests and celebrants; and these sacrificial victims they then regarded as sainted. If they were slaves captured in war, their masters kept the bones, and displayed them in the dances, as a mark of victory. At times they threw the victims alive into the well at Chichén Itzá, believing that they would come forth on the third day, even though they never did see them reappear.

5. Huitzilopochtli and Tlaloc

Spaniard Diego Durán (1537-c. 1588) was at the age of six brought to New Spain where he learned Nahuatl. As an ordained Dominican priest he became aware of the need for the friars to understand Mexica (Aztec) religion so that the conversion process could be effective. Between 1576 and 1581 he wrote a three-part Historia de las Indias de Nueva España islas de tierra firme *on pre-Columbian history, religion, and the Mexica calendar, based on indigenous manuscripts and interviews with older Mexica and Spaniards who had witnessed Mexica religious practices before they were eliminated by the ongoing conquest (1521 and afterward).*

Huitzilopochtli (Hummingbird-Left) was the god of war, patron of the Mexica, and the focus of their major cult.

Tlaloc was the god of rain, fertility, and agriculture, second in veneration only to Huitzilopochtli.

Durán did not witness any of the ceremonies he describes so minutely and vividly. Aside from his use of the term "idol," is his writing judgmental? What does the manner in which the Mexica portray Tlaloc reveal about their cosmology? What does the sacrifice of a child reveal?

When we spoke of the god named Huitzilopochtli, in whose honor the Mexicas celebrated a most solemn feast, I wrote that next to the chamber where he stood, within the same temple, was a companion of his, [Tlaloc], who was no less honored or revered than [Huitzilopochtli]. [Tlaloc] was also held to be a god like the others, and he was honored with as many sacrifices and ceremonies as any. [...]

First of all, it must be noted that the idol is known as Tlaloc and was venerated and feared throughout the entire land. The whole country was dedicated to his service—lords, kings, noblemen, and the common people. [...]

His statue was carved of stone, representing a frightful monster. Its horrendous face was like that of a serpent with huge fangs; it was bright and red like a flaming fire. This was a symbol of the brilliance of the lightning and rays cast from the heavens when he sent tempests and thunderbolts; to express the same thing, he was clad totally in red. [...]

This same name of the god [Tlaloc] was given to a lofty mountain which is bounded by Coatlichan and Coatepec on one side and by Huexotzinco on the other. [...]

On the summit of the mountain stood a great square courtyard surrounded by a finely built wall about eight feet high, crowned with a series of merlons and plastered with stucco. [...]

The feast of this god fell on the twenty-ninth of April, and it was celebrated in such a solemn way that men came from all parts of the land to commemorate it, to the point that no king or lord great or small failed to bring his offerings. [...]

Just after dawn these kings and lords with their followers left [their shelters]. They took a child of six or seven years and placed him within an enclosed litter so that he would not be seen. This was placed on the shoulders of the leaders. All in order, they went in the form of a procession to the courtyard, which was called Tetzacualco. When they arrived before the image of the god Tlaloc, the men slew the child within the litter, hidden [from those present]. He was slain by this god's own priests, to the sound of many trumpets, conch shells, and flutes.

At dawn the lords celebrated the Feast of Tlaloc on the mountain (this Mountain of Tlalocan) with the solemnity and lavishness I have mentioned, in great haste, since they wished to be present at the sacrifice of the waters. [While these rites

SOURCE: Fray Diego Durán, *Book of the Gods and Rites and the Ancient Calendar*, trans. and ed. Fernando Horcasitas and Doris Heyden (Norman: University of Oklahoma Press, 1971), 154-57, 160-61. Reprinted by permission of University of Oklahoma Press © 1971.

were being performed], those who had remained in the city [of Mexico], where the image of the god, sumptuously and richly adorned, was kept in the temple of Huitzilopochtli, prepared for the same feast of the waters. This was especially true of the priests and dignitaries of the temples and of all the youths and boys who lived in seclusion and in the schools. [All of them] donned new ornaments and performed many different dances, farces, and games. They wore various disguises as if it were their principal feast day, very much the way [our] students celebrate the Feast of Saint Nicholas. All these games and festivities were carried out in an [artificial] forest set up in the courtyard of the temple in front of the image of the god Tlaloc. In the middle of this forest was placed a very large tree. It was the tallest that could be found in the woods, and it was called Tota, which means Our Father. This indicated that the idol was the god of the woods, forests, and waters. When the news arrived [that the lords who had been on Mount Tlaloc] were descending from the mountains and drawing close to the waters to embark in the canoes which awaited them, this solemnity and feast ended in the lagoon.

6. Maya Afterlife

Since immortality of the soul is a fundamental Christian belief, the fact that the Maya shared it suggests that Landa's account, in the reading below, may have been based on many conversations and interviews with Maya whom Landa would want to draw out on a subject so central to Christian teaching. He must have been relieved that both religions shared a vital belief, but he would have had to verify how much the Maya version accorded with Christian teaching.

How would he have responded to the Maya description of the afterlife as recorded below? Would he correct or modify their understanding of the afterlife? What would he have said about their attitude toward suicide?

These people have always believed more in the immortality of the soul than have other nations, though they haven't been vigilant as such because they believed that after death there would be an even more excellent life for the soul to enjoy when departing the body.

They said that this future life was divided into good and bad, and into a life of arduous labor and one of complete rest. The bad and the arduous, they said, was reserved for the depraved persons, and the good and delightful for those who had lived well in life. The rest that they said was to be achieved, if they were good, was by going to a delightful place where nothing would cause sorrow and where there would be abundance of sweet foods and drinks, and a tree that they call *Yaxche*; very cool and with great shade is the ceiba, under whose branches and shade they all rest and relax forever.

They said that the bad ones had to be punished in the bad life for their evil ways by going to a place far below the other which they called *Mitnal*, which means Hell and in which they are tormented by devils and by great need of hunger and by cold, exhaustion, and sadness.

They held that for them in this place there was a devil, the prince of all devils, whom all obeyed and called in their tongue *Hunhau*, and they said that these lives neither had a good nor a bad purpose because they did not have souls.

They also said and they held as very true that those who hanged themselves went to their glory,

SOURCE: Miguel León-Portilla, Alfredo Barrera Vásquez, Luis Gonzáles, "La vida futura," in *Historia documental de México* (Mexico City: Universidad Nacional Autónoma de México, 1984), 1:81-82. Translated from the Spanish by Lee M. Penyak.

and in this way there were many who hanged themselves for minor causes such as sadness, travails, or illnesses in order to get out from under them and rest in glory where they said the goddess of the hanged named *Ixtab* would take them.

7. Ilya-Tiqsi Viracocha Pachayacachiq

Bernabé Cobo, S.J. (1580-1657), arrived in Lima from Spain in 1599. He spent the rest of his life in New Spain and Peru doing missionary work, especially in remote Andean communities of the Inca. He taught and also conducted research. From personal observation, interviews with Inca informants, and study of chronicles, he produced a forty-three-book Historia del Nuevo Mundo *(1653) of which seventeen books exist. The Spanish abbreviated the Inca Ilya-Tiqsi Viracocha Pachayacachiq (Ancient Foundation, Lord, Instructor of the World) to "Viracocha," the creator of all the other Inca gods as well as of men and animals.*

In the reading below, Cobo describes the great temple of the Sun in Cuzco, the ruins of which stand today. Is Cobo's account objective? What does Cobo's account of this aspect of Inca religion reveal about Inca perception, values, and culture in general?

The god most respected by them after Viracocha was that most excellent of material creations, the sun; and the Inca, who boasted that they were the Children of the Sun, bent all their efforts toward exalting its authority and endowing it with a magnificent ritual, numerous priests, and frequent offerings and sacrifices. Not that much had to be done to inspire esteem for the sun among their people; they respected the objects of Nature in accord with the benefits that they obtained from them, and since the beneficial effects produced by this planet were so manifest and excellent, they held it in great regard. The authority and example of the Inca only served to make the external displays of worship more costly and elaborate. They believed that the Pachayachachic [*sic*] had given the sun power to create all the foods, together with the earth, whence came their regard for it as the greatest guaca of all after the Viracocha; and so they called it *Apu-Inti*, which means "My Lord Sun": they visualized it in the likeness of a man, and consequently they used to say that the moon was his wife and the stars their children.

They held the sun in such reverence throughout this kingdom of the Inca that I question whether in any other part of the world there ever prevailed a cult so respected and well served. This may be seen from the fact that to no other god did they dedicate so many and such magnificent temples; for there was not an important town where the sun did not have a temple with numerous priests and *mamaconas* and ample revenues for its maintenance. And the wealthiest and most sumptuous temple of all was that which the Inca kings had erected to the sun in their court, the temple called Coricancha, where they kept their principal and most venerated idol. It was an impressive image, called *Punchau*, which means "the day," all worked in finest gold with a wealth of precious stones, in the likeness of a human face, surrounded by rays, as we depict the sun; they placed it so that it faced the east, and when the sun rose its rays fell on it; and since it was a sheet of finest metal the rays were reflected from it so brightly that it actually seemed to be the sun. The Indians were wont to say that the sun lent this image both its light and its power. From the spoils which the Spaniards obtained in the beautiful temple of Coricancha there fell to the lot of a soldier this splendid sheet of gold, and since at that time gambling was the popular pastime he lost it one night at play; from this came the saying used in

SOURCE: Bernabé Cobo, *Historia del Nuevo Mundo*, 3:324-27. Excerpt translated by Benjamin Keen, *Latin American Civilization: The Colonial Origins*, 3rd ed. (Boston: Houghton Mifflin, 1974), 1:63-64.

Peru about heavy gamblers: "He gambles the sun away before it rises." This soldier was named Manso Serra; he later became a leading citizen of Cuzco, where I came to know a son of his, named Juan Serra. . . .

They regarded the eclipse of the sun as a grave matter, and when it occurred they consulted the diviners about its meaning; and having been told what it denoted, they made great and costly sacrifices, offering up various gold and silver figures, and killing a large number of sheep as well as many boys and girls. The sorcerers commonly asserted that the eclipse portended the death of some prince, and that the sun had gone into mourning for the loss that the world would suffer; when this happened all the women dedicated to the sun fasted for many days, wore mourning garments, and offered frequent sacrifices. The Inca [emperor] retired to a secret spot, and there, having dealings with none, he fasted many days; during all this time no fire was lighted in the whole city.

PART II

Encounter, Conquest, Empire

Militant Catholic Spaniards began imposing their religion in the Americas at the moment of occupation, 1492. The dynastic rule of Ferdinand (1452-1516) and Isabella (1451-1504) was geared to create a unified nation-state, which gave Spain a head start in European imperialist expansion. The seven-hundred-year crusade against the Moors, the forced conversion of Jews (into "New Christians"), the establishment of the Inquisition by the "Catholic monarchs" in 1479, and the expulsion of the Jews in 1492 all testify to the militant Catholicism infusing Spanish culture. Spanish Catholics firmly believed that St. James of Compostela (St. James Matamoros or "the Killer of Moors"), patron saint of Spain, was behind them in every battle against the infidel and the heathen and was helping Spain to become a nation of one people with one religion subject to one ruling family. Columbus's landing in the New World only nine months after the defeat of the Moors in Granada may well have been considered divine invitation to continue Christian conquest. Indeed, Columbus's entourage included many veterans of the *reconquista* who carried the mentality and methods of this holy war to the Western hemisphere. Their efforts received papal blessing in 1493 when Pope Alexander VI issued the bull *Inter Caetera,* which neatly established two spheres of influence for the competing maritime rivals in the Iberian peninsula. Spain received all of the New World save the easternmost tip of South America, which later became Portuguese Brazil, and Portugal received the right to exploit unfettered its interests in Africa and Asia.

Thus, as with the Aztecs, who associated their greatness and success with Huitzilopochtli, Spanish conquerors in the New World firmly believed that God had provided them with the means to subjugate and convert pagans to Christianity. Spaniards committed every excess imaginable in newly conquered lands. Almost immediately upon Spanish contact, natives on the islands of Hispaniola and Cuba were enslaved on *encomiendas* (lands and Amerindians given to Spaniards) though the Crown insisted that the Amerindians be regarded as free. Unused to the strenuous and incessant labor, the Amerindians perished at catastrophic rates. Diseases easily spread among peoples who had developed in virtual isolation over millennia and did not possess antibodies to fight off smallpox, influenza, and measles. Caribbean Arawak and Taino populations numbering tens and even hundreds of thousands were totally obliterated within fifty years of European contact. Amerindian populations on the mainland—in today's Mexico and Peru—declined by roughly 90 percent. Spaniards, having no sense that they themselves were carriers of the diseases, concluded that God was punishing the Amerindians for their resistance to conversion. Virginia Garrard-Burnett places the drama of the Christian conquest into its proper historical perspective: "To cynical modern eyes, it is difficult to reconcile the zealous Christian rhetoric of the conquistadors with the more peaceful sensibilities that we now associate with the ideal ethic of 'Christian behavior.' But ... Spaniards of the sixteenth century ... believed that it was their destiny and duty to show the Amerindians the single path ... to eternal salvation."[1]

An early example of clerical outrage at Spanish abuse came from the Dominican Antonio de Montesinos in Hispaniola, who, during a homily at Mass shortly before Christmas in 1511, vehemently denounced the attitude and behavior of the Spaniards toward the Amerindians and pleaded with the Spaniards to end their excesses. It is not surprising that Montesinos became a pariah on the island before unsuccessfully defending himself at court in Spain. Nonetheless, Bartolomé de Las Casas (1484-1566), the first ordained priest in the Americas, heeded Montesinos's call and deservedly received the title of "Defender of the Indians." He promoted Amerindian welfare for the next fifty years, ultimately becoming bishop of Chiapas but resigning his post out of frustration and returning to Spain to fight for the Amerindian. Las Casas's efforts may have inspired the writing of the New Laws of 1542, which forbade the enslavement of Amerindians, and Pope Paul III's bull *Sublimis Deus* (The Sublime God, 1537), which had previously acknowledged that the Amerindians possessed souls and were perfectly capable of becoming true Catholics. Unfortunately, individual heroics, royal dictates, and papal decrees proved insufficient to curb abuse.[2]

"[M]oved by sincere religious conviction and shrewd calculation of self-interest," notes Nancy M. Farriss, the Spanish monarchy carefully wedded the interests of the church and state. During nearly three centuries of colonial rule, she continues, "priests and bishops constantly impressed upon the people their duty to render obedience and devotion to their temporal sovereign as well as to God."[3] In recognition of Spain's military triumphs over

---

1. Virginia Garrard-Burnett, "Introduction," in *On Earth as It Is in Heaven: Religion in Modern Latin America*, ed. Virginia Garrard-Burnett (Wilmington, Del.: Scholarly Resources, 2000), xiv, xvi; David J. Weber, *The Spanish Frontier in North America* (New Haven, Conn.: Yale University Press, 1992), 20; María Elena Martínez, "Limpieza de Sangre," in *Encyclopedia of Mexico: History, Society & Culture*, vol. 2, ed. Michael S. Werner (Chicago and London: Fitzroy Dearborn Publishers, 1997), 750.

2. Enrique Dussel, ed., *The Church in Latin America, 1492-1992* (Maryknoll, N.Y.: Orbis Books, 1992), 4-5; John F. Schwaller, "Introduction," in *The Church in Colonial Latin America*, ed. John F. Schwaller (Wilmington, Del.: Scholarly Resources, 2000), xv-xviii; George Sanderlin, ed., *Witness: Writings of Bartolomé de Las Casas* (Maryknoll, N.Y.: Orbis, 1992), 1-17; Margaret E. Crahan, "Catholic Church (Colonial Period)," in *Encyclopedia of Latin America*, ed. Helen Delpar (New York: McGraw-Hill, 1974), 121.

3. Nancy M. Farriss, *Crown and Clergy in Colonial Mexico, 1759-1821: The Crisis of Ecclesiastical Privilege* (London: Athlone Press, 1968), 1, 3.

potential new converts to the faith, papal decrees granted extraordinary powers to the crown. Beginning as early as 1501, for example, the state received permission to collect church tithes, usually a 10 percent tax on mining and agriculture, so that it could offset the costs of evangelization. Later, in 1508, Pope Julius II granted royal patronage or *patronato real* to the monarchy in his bull *Universalis Ecclesiae*, which enabled the Crown to establish the demarcation of dioceses and gave it the right to present the names of ecclesiastical candidates to the papacy for final consideration. With these privileges came responsibilities, which Habsburg monarchs took seriously; they used tithe revenues to build churches, monasteries, hospitals, and orphanages, and to supplement clerical income when necessary.[4]

8. Imperialism Triumphant

A perpetual problem for students of the conquest is determining the role that religion, that is, Roman Catholicism, played in the motivation of the proponents and participants — the Spanish monarchs, conquistadors, friars, soldiers, adventurers—in that conquest, especially at its inception.

Christopher Columbus's letter (recorded by Bartolomé de Las Casas [see readings 10 and 12], acknowledging the commission granted to him by Ferdinand and Isabella to "discover and acquire certain islands and mainland," is permeated with the same fervent religious rhetoric used by Pope Alexander VI when he bestowed the title of reyes católicos *upon the two monarchs in 1495.*

Is it possible to determine the genuineness of this apparent religiosity? Is it merely a commonplace formula in an age when the church was a strong presence in society? Is it rhetoric useful for advancement in society? Or is it part of Spanish identity—of the Spain that had recently established the Holy Office of the Inquisition, the Spain that had just completed the Reconquista, *and expelled the Jews? Is it all of the above?*

"In the name of the Lord Jesus Christ, the Most Christian, the most high, the most excellent and most powerful princes, King and Queen of the Spains. . . . In this present year 1492, after Your Highnesses had brought to an end the war against the Moors who reigned in Europe, and *after Your Highnesses had terminated this war in the very great city of Granada*, where, in this present year, on the 2nd of the month of January, I saw, by force of arms, the royal banners of Your Highnesses planted on the towers of the Alhambra, the citadel of the said city, and where I saw the Moorish king

4. Sarah L. Cline, "Church and State: Habsburg New Spain," in *Encyclopedia of Mexico: History, Society & Culture*, vol. 1, ed. Michael S. Werner (Chicago and London: Fitzroy Dearborn Publishers, 1997), 248-50; Kenneth Medhurst, "The Church in Latin America: Politics and Society," in *The Cambridge Encyclopedia of Latin America and the Caribbean*, 2nd ed., ed. Simon Collier, Thomas Skidmore, and Harold Blakemore (Cambridge: Cambridge University Press, 1992), 358; Schwaller, "Introduction," xi; Crahan, "Catholic Church (Colonial Period)," 120.

SOURCE: Christopher Columbus's diary, as recorded by Bartolomé de Las Casas, *Historia de las Indias,* quoted in Louis Bertrand and Charles Petrie, *The History of Spain: From the Visigoths to the Death of Phillip II*, part 1, 2nd ed. (New York: Collier Books, 1971), 163-64.

come out of his gates and kiss the royal hands of Your Highnesses;

"And *immediately afterwards, in this same month*, in consequence of information which I had given Your Highnesses on the subject of India and of the Prince who is called the 'Great Khan,' which, in our Roman, means 'the King of Kings'—namely, that many times he and his predecessors had sent ambassadors to Rome to seek doctors of our holy faith, to the end that they should teach it in India, and that never has the Holy Father been able so to do, so that accordingly so many peoples were being lost, through falling into idolatry and receiving sects of perdition among them;

"Your Highnesses, as good Christian and Catholic princes, devout and propagators of the Christian faith, as well as enemies of the sect of Mahomet and of all idolatries and heresies, *conceived the plan of sending me, Christopher Columbus, to this country of the Indies*, there to see the princes, the peoples, the territory, their disposition and all things else, and the way in which one might proceed to convert these regions to our holy faith.

"And Your Highnesses have ordered that I should go, not by land, towards the East, which is the accustomed route, but by the way of the West, whereby hitherto nobody to our knowledge has ever been. *And so, after having expelled all the Jews from all your kingdoms and lordships*, in this same month of January, Your Highnesses ordered me to set out, with a sufficient fleet, for the said country of India, and, to this end, Your Highnesses have shown me great favour. . . ."

9. Labor Policy in Hispaniola

In light of the heady achievements of Ferdinand and Isabella's reign of nearly thirty years, and considering the Crown's need of monetary resources for its political and military programs, the Crown's concerns for a productive labor force are understandable.

The passage below reveals a number of concerns of Isabella: cultural, religious, economic, and moral. Elaborate upon those concerns. Are they reconcilable? Does Isabella have priorities?

Medina del Campo, Dec. 20, 1503. Isabella, by the Grace of God, Queen of Castile, etc. In as much as the King, my Lord, and I, in the instruction we commanded given to Don Fray Nicolás de Ovando, Comendador mayor of Alcántara, at the time when he went to the islands and mainland of the Ocean Sea, decreed that the Indian inhabitants and residents of the island of Española, are free and not subject . . . and as now we are informed that because of the excessive liberty enjoyed by the said Indians they avoid contact and community with the Spaniards to such an extent that they will not even work for wages, but wander about idle, and cannot be had by the Christians to convert to the Holy Catholic Faith; and in order that the Christians of the said island . . . may not lack people to work their holdings for their maintenance, and may be able to take out what gold there is on the island . . . and because we desire that the said Indians be converted to our Holy Catholic Faith and taught in its doctrines; and because this can better be done by having the Indians living in community with the Christians of the island, and by having them go among them and associate with them, by which means they will help each other to cultivate and settle and increase the fruits of the island and take the gold which may be there and bring profit to my kingdom and subjects:

SOURCE: Cédula of Isabella to Ovando, December 20, 1503, in D.I.I., XXXI, 209-12 (*Colección de documentos inéditos relativos al descubrimiento, conquista y organización de las antiguas posesiones españolas*. 42 vols., ed. Joaquín F. Pacheco, Francisco de Cárdenas, Luis Torres de Mandoga, Madrid, 1864-89), quoted and translated by Lesley Byrd Simpson, *The Encomienda in New Spain: Forced Native Labor in the Spanish Colonies, 1492-1550* (Berkeley: University of California Press, 1929), 30-31.

I have commanded this my letter to be issued on the matter, in which I command you, our said Governor, that beginning from the day you receive my letter you will compel and force the said Indians to associate with the Christians of the island and to work on their buildings, and to gather and mine the gold and other metals, and to till the fields and produce food for the Christian inhabitants and dwellers of the said island; and you are to have each one paid on the day he works the wage and maintenance which you think he should have . . . and you are to order each cacique to take charge of a certain number of the said Indians so that you may make them work wherever necessary, and so that on feast days and such days as you think proper they may be gathered together to hear and be taught in matters of the Faith. . . . This the Indians shall perform as free people, which they are, and not as slaves. And see to it that the said Indians are well treated, those who become Christians better than the others, and do not consent or allow that any person do them any harm or oppress them. . . .

I, the Queen

10. Bartolomé de Las Casas

Bartolomé de Las Casas (1484-1566), Dominican friar, historian, anthropologist, ardent missionary to and defender of the natives of the Caribbean isles and Mesoamerican mainland, began his History of the Indies *in 1527 and worked on it for the next thirty-five years, though it was published only in 1875-79 (in six volumes).*

History written by an eyewitness and advocate such as Las Casas presents difficulties for the reader in determining which of those two qualities, if either, dominates any given moment in the narrative.

Does Las Casas present an accurate picture of the status of the evangelical component in the everyday life of the colony of Hispaniola?

Note that the comendador *(no. 1 below) is Fray Nicolás de Ovando, of the military order of Alcántara, with whom the Crown replaced the lax administration of Francisco de Bobadilla, who was sent home for trial. "This order" (no. 8 below) refers to Queen Isabella's warrant (Reading 9) in which she emphasized the importance of the conversion of indigenous peoples and her desire for Spaniards and Amerindians to live and work harmoniously for their own "prosperity" and that of the Crown of Castile.*

1. I have already said and I repeat, the truth is that in the nine years the comendador governed the island, no measures were taken for the conversion of Indians and no more was done about the matter nor any more thought given to it than if the Indians were sticks, stones, cats or dogs. This applies not only to the comendador and those who owned Indians but also to the Franciscan friars who had come with him. These were good people but they lived religiously in their houses here and in La Vega and had no other aspiration. One thing they did was brought to my knowledge: they asked permission to have the sons of some caciques (few of them to be sure), perhaps four, and taught them to read and write and I suppose their good example taught Christian doctrine, for they were good and lived virtuously.

2. He disrupted villages and distributed Indians at his pleasure, giving fifty to one and a hundred to another, according to his preferences, and these

SOURCE: Bartolomé de Las Casas, *History of the Indies*, trans. and ed. Andrée Collard (New York: Harper & Row, 1971), 109-15, passim. Copyright © 1971 by Andrée M. Collard, renewed 1999 by Joyce J. Contrucci. Reprinted by permission of Joyce Contrucci.

numbers included children, old people, pregnant women and nursing mothers, families of high rank as well as common people. They called this system "Indian grants" (*repartimientos*) and the King had his grant and his manager in each town who worked his land and mined his part of the gold. The wording of the comendador's Indian grants read like this: "Mr. X, I grant you fifty or a hundred Indians under the cacique X so that you may avail yourself of their services and teach them our holy Catholic Faith," by which was meant, "Mr. X, I grant you fifty or a hundred Indians together with the person of the cacique X, so that you may use them in your lands and your mines and teach them our holy Catholic Faith." And this was the same as to condemn them all to an absolute servitude which killed them in the end, as we shall see. This, then, was the nature of their freedom.

3. The men were sent out to the mines as far as eighty leagues away while their wives remained to work the soil, not with hoes or plowshares drawn by oxen, but with their own sweat and sharpened poles that were far from equaling the equipment used for similar work in Castile. [. . .] Thus husbands and wives were together only once every eight or ten months and when they met they were so exhausted and depressed on both sides that they had no mind for marital communication and in this way they ceased to procreate. As for the newly born, they died early because their mothers, overworked and famished, had no milk to nurse them, and for this reason, while I was in Cuba, 7,000 children died in three months. Some mothers even drowned their babies from sheer desperation, while others caused themselves to abort with certain herbs that produced stillborn children. [. . .] If this concatenation of events had occurred all over the world, the human race would have been wiped out in no time.

4. [. . .] Our own eyes have seen such inhuman conduct several times and God is witness that whatever is said of it falls short of reality.

5. "Moderate labor" turned into labor fit only for iron men: mountains are stripped from top to bottom and bottom to top a thousand times; they dig, split rocks, move stones and carry dirt on their backs to wash it in rivers, while those who wash gold stay in the water all the time with their backs bent so constantly it breaks them; and when water invades the mines, the most arduous task of all is to dry the mines by scooping up pansful [*sic*] of water and throwing it up outside. [. . .]

6. The comendador arranged to have wages paid as follows, which I swear is the truth: in exchange for his life of services, an Indian received 3 *maravedís* every two days, less one-half a *maravedí* in order not to exceed the yearly half gold peso, that is, 225 *maravedís*, paid them once a year as pin money or *cacona*, as Indians call it, which means bonus or reward. This sum bought a comb, a small mirror and a string of green or blue glass beads, and many did without that consolation for they were paid much less and had no way of mitigating their misery, although in truth, they offered their labor up for nothing, caring only to fill their stomachs to appease their raging hunger and find ways to escape from their desperate lives. [. . .]

7. I believe the above clearly demonstrates that the Indians were totally deprived of their freedom and were put in the harshest, fiercest, most horrible servitude and captivity which no one who has not seen it can understand. Even beasts enjoy more freedom when they are allowed to graze in the fields. [. . .]

8. This order was difficult or impossible and not designed to bring Indians to the Faith; indeed, it was pernicious and deadly and designed to destroy all Indians. Obviously, the Queen had not intended the destruction but the edification of the Indians, and the comendador would have done well to consider this, as well as the fact that, had the Queen been alive to see the results of her order, she would have revoked and abominated it. It is amazing how this prudent man did not realize what a deadly pestilence his order was when, at the end of each shift, he found out how many Indians were missing and how the rest suffered.

As I said, the Queen died shortly after sending her warrant and therefore never found out about this cruel decimation. Philip and Juana succeeded her, but Philip died before he could appraise the situation in the Indies and Castile was two years without the presence of a King. Thus, the decimation of these poor Indians had begun and could be kept silent, and when King Hernando came to rule Castile they kept it from him too. About eight years passed under the comendador's rule and this disorder had time to grow; no one gave it a thought and the multitude of people who originally lived on this island, which, according to the admiral, was infinite, as we said in Book I, was consumed at such a rate that in those eight years 90 percent had perished. From here this sweeping plague went to San Juan, Jamaica, Cuba and the continent, spreading destruction over the whole hemisphere [. . .]

11. Human Rights in 1511?

It apparently took some eighteen years after Columbus's return to Spain from his initial voyage for the first remonstrances to be made against the harsh treatment of the natives. Regular clergy were present in the New World (always referred to as "The Indies" by the Crown) since at least 1503, but it was not until 1511 that three Dominican friars newly arrived on Hispaniola made formal, public denunciation of such treatment. Las Casas reports what happened on the third Sunday in Advent that year.

Again the reader must distinguish between Las Casas the historian (he was not an eyewitness) and Las Casas the advocate, the "Protector of the Indian" (the title given him by Francisco Cardinal Ximénes de Cisneros, O.F.M., regent of Spain, in 1516).

What meaning did Catholicism have for the colonists in Hispaniola?

Sunday having arrived, and the time for preaching, Father Antonio Montesino rose in the pulpit, and took for the text of his sermon, which was written down and signed by the other friars, "I am the voice of one crying in the wilderness." Having made his introduction and said something about the Advent season, he began to speak of the sterile desert of the consciences of the Spaniards on this isle, and of the blindness in which they lived, going about in great danger of damnation and utterly heedless of the grave sins in which they lived and died.

Then he returned to his theme, saying: "In order to make your sins known to you I have mounted this pulpit, I who am the voice of Christ crying in the wilderness of this island; and therefore it behooves you to listen to me, not with indifference but with all your heart and senses; for this voice will be the strangest, the harshest and hardest, the most terrifying that you ever heard or expected to hear."

He went on in this vein for a good while, using cutting words that made his hearers' flesh creep and made them feel that they were already experiencing the divine judgment. . . . He went on to state the contents of his message.

"This voice," said he, "declares that you are in mortal sin, and live and die therein by reason of the cruelty and tyranny that you practice on these innocent people. Tell me, by what right or justice do you hold these Indians in such cruel and horrible slavery? By what right do you wage such detestable wars on these people who lived mildly and peacefully in their own lands, where you have consumed infinite numbers of them with unheard-of murders and desolations? Why do you so greatly oppress and fatigue them, not giving them enough to eat or caring for them when they fall ill from excessive labors, so that they die or rather are slain by you, so that you may extract and acquire gold every day? And what care do you take that they receive religious instruction and

SOURCE: Bartolomé de Las Casas, *Historia de las Indias* [1565], 2:441-42, trans. Benjamin Keen, in Robert Buffington and Lila Caimari, eds., *Keen's Latin American Civilization: History and Society, 1492 to the Present*, 8th ed. (Boulder, Colo.: Westview Press, 2004), 77-78. Copyright © by Westview Press. Reprinted by permission of Westview Press, a member of Perseus Books, L.L.C.

come to know their God and creator, or that they be baptized, hear mass, or observe holidays and Sundays?

"Are they not men? Do they not have rational souls? Are you not bound to love them as you love yourselves? How can you lie in such profound and lethargic slumber? Be sure that in your present state you can no more be saved than the Moors or Turks who do not have and do not want the faith of Jesus Christ."

Thus he delivered the message he had promised, leaving his hearers astounded. Many were stunned, others appeared more callous than before, and a few were somewhat moved; but not one, from what I could later learn, was converted.

When he had concluded his sermon he descended from the pulpit, his head held high, for he was not a man to show fear, of which indeed he was totally free; nor did he care about the displeasure of his listeners, and instead did and said what seemed best according to God. With his companion he went to their straw-thatched house, where, very likely, their entire dinner was cabbage soup, unflavored with olive oil. . . . After he had left, the church was so full of murmurs that . . . they could hardly complete the celebration of the mass.

12. Las Casas on Empire

Bartolomé de Las Casas O.P. (1484-1566) played many roles during his long life: lay cate-chist, encomendero, *priest, missionary friar, historian, and anthropologist. In his* Very Brief Account of the Destruction of the Indies *(1542; published in 1552) he plays the role of moralist, that is, prophet. Why does this writing not qualify as history yet remain a major source for understanding the Conquest (in this case of the Caribbean in general and Cuba in particular)?*

The Indies were discovered in the year 1492. The year following, Spanish Christians went to inhabit them, so that it is since forty-nine years that numbers of Spaniards have gone there. [. . .]

They [Amerindians] are likewise of a clean, unspoiled, and vivacious intellect, very capable, and receptive to every good doctrine; most prompt to accept our Holy Catholic Faith, to be endowed with virtuous customs.

Among these gentle sheep . . . the Spaniards entered . . . like wolves, tigers, and lions which had been starving for many days, and since forty years they have done nothing else; nor do they other-wise at the present day, than outrage, slay, afflict, torment, and destroy them. . . . To such extremes has this gone that, whereas there were more than 3 million souls, whom we saw in Hispaniola, there are today, not 200 of the native population left. [. . .]

The reason why the Christians have killed and destroyed such infinite numbers of souls is solely because they have made gold their ultimate aim, seeking to load themselves with riches in the shortest time. . . . These lands, being so happy and so rich, and the people so humble, so patient, and so easily subjugated, they have . . . taken no more account of them . . . than—I will not say of ani-mals, for would to God they had considered and treated them as animals—but as even less than the dung in the streets.

In this way have they cared for their lives—and for their souls: and therefore, all the millions above mentioned have died without faith and without sacraments. And it is . . . admitted . . . by

SOURCE: Bartolomé de Las Casas, *Bartolomé de Las Casas: A Selection of His Writings,* trans. and ed. George Sanderlin (New York: Alfred A. Knopf, 1971), 165-69. From *Bartolomé de Las Casas: A Selection of His Writings,* by Bartolomé de Las Casas, trans. Geo. Sanderlin, copyright © 1971 by Alfred A. Knopf, a division of Random House, Inc. Used by permission of Alfred A. Knopf, a division of Random House, Inc.

all . . . that the Indians throughout the Indies never did any harm to the Christians: they even esteemed them as coming from heaven, until they and their neighbors had suffered the same many evils, thefts, deaths, violence, and visitations at their hands. [. . .]

A very high prince and lord, named Hatuey, who had fled with many of his people from Hispaniola to Cuba, to escape the calamity and inhuman operations of the Christians, having received news from some Indians that the Christians were crossing over, assembled many or all of his people and addressed them thus.

"You already know that it is said the Christians are coming here; and you have experience of how they have treated the lords so and so and those people of Hayti (which is Hispaniola); they come to do the same here. Do you know perhaps why they do it?"

The people answered no; except that they were by nature cruel and wicked.

"They do it," said he, "not alone for this, but because they have a God whom they greatly adore and love; and to make us adore Him they strive to subjugate us and take our lives." He had near him a basket full of gold and jewels and he said, "Behold here is the God of the Christians, let us perform *Areytos* before Him, if you will (these are dances in concert and singly); and perhaps we shall please Him, and He will command that they do us no harm." [. . .]

This prince and lord continued retreating before the Christians when they arrived at the island of Cuba, because he knew them, but when he encountered them he defended himself; and at last they took him. And merely because he fled from such iniquitous and cruel people and defended himself . . . with all his people and offspring until death, they burnt him alive.

When he was tied to the stake, a Franciscan friar, a holy man who was there, spoke as much as he could to him, in the little time that the executioner granted them, about God and some of the teachings of our faith. . . . He told him that if he would believe what was told him, he would go to heaven where there was glory and eternal rest; and if not, that he would go to hell, to suffer perpetual torments and punishment.

After thinking a little, Hatuey asked the friar whether the Christians went to heaven; the friar answered that those who were good went there. The prince at once said, without any more thought, that he did not wish to go there, but rather to hell so as not to be where Spaniards were, nor to see such cruel people.

This is the renown and honor that God and our faith have acquired by means of the Christians who have gone to the Indies. . . .

13. The *Requerimiento*

The requerimiento, *drafted by Dr. Palacios Rubios by royal order in 1513, was to be proclaimed to natives present at the initial incursion of the Spaniards on their land (excepting those natives practicing ritual cannibalism, who were deemed beyond respect and subject to immediate conquest). The document's language, its Castilian wording, and its terminology expressing the political ideology of the "Catholic monarchs" would obviously have no meaning for its Amerindian audience.*

In attempting to come to grips with what it reveals about the religious component of the Conquest, it might help to consider how the French or English monarchs might respond to its religious as opposed to its political aspects.

SOURCE: Arthur Helps, *The Spanish Conquest in America and Its Relation to the History of Slavery and to the Government of Colonies*, 4 vols., ed. M. Oppenheim (London and New York: John Lane, 1900), 1:264-67.

"On the part of the King, Don Fernando, and of Doña Juana, his daughter, Queen of Castille and León, subduers of the barbarous nations, we their servants notify and make known to you, as best we can, that the Lord our God, Living and Eternal, created the Heaven and the Earth, and one man and one woman, of whom you and we, and all the men of the world, were and are descendants, and all those who come after us. But, on account of the multitude which has sprung from this man and woman in the five thousand years since the world was created, it was necessary that some men should go one way and some another, and that they should be divided into many kingdoms and provinces, for in one alone they could not be sustained.

"Of all these nations God our Lord gave charge to one man, called St. Peter, that he should be Lord and Superior of all the men in the world, that all should obey him, and that he should be the head of the whole human race, wherever men should live, and under whatever law, sect, or belief they should be; and he gave him the world for his kingdom and jurisdiction.

"And he commanded him to place his seat in Rome, as the spot most fitting to rule the world from; but also he permitted him to have his seat in any other part of the world, and to judge and govern all Christians, Moors, Jews, Gentiles, and all other sects. This man was called Pope, as if to say, Admirable Great Father and Governor of men. The men who lived in that time obeyed that St. Peter, and took him for Lord, King, and Superior of the universe . . . so also they have regarded the others who after him have been elected to the pontificate, and so has it been continued even till now, and will continue till the end of the world.

"One of these Pontiffs, who succeeded that St. Peter as Lord of the world, in the dignity and seat which I have before mentioned, made donation of these isles and Tierra-firme to the aforesaid King and Queen and to their successors, our lords, with all that there are in these territories, as is contained in certain writings which passed upon the subject as aforesaid, which you can see if you wish.

"So their Highnesses are kings and lords of these islands and land of Tierra-firme by virtue of this donation: and some islands, and indeed almost all those to whom this has been notified, have received and served their Highnesses, as lords and kings, in the way that subjects ought to do, with good will, without any resistance, immediately, without delay, when they were informed of the aforesaid facts. And also they received and obeyed the priests whom their Highnesses sent to preach to them and to teach them our Holy Faith; and all these, of their own free will, without any reward or condition, have become Christians, and are so, and their Highnesses have joyfully and benignantly received them, and also have commanded them to be treated as their subjects and vassals; and you too are held and obliged to do the same. Wherefore, as best we can, we ask and require you that you consider what we have said to you, and that you take the time that shall be necessary to understand and deliberate upon it, and that you acknowledge the Church as the Ruler and Superior of the whole world (por Señora y Superiora del universo mundo), and the high priest called Pope, and in his name the King and Queen Doña Juana our lords, in his place, as superiors and lords and kings of these islands and this Tierra-firme by virtue of the said donation, and that you consent and give place that these religious fathers should declare and preach to you the aforesaid.

"If you do so, you will do well, and that which you are obliged to do to their Highnesses, and we in their name shall receive you in all love and charity, and shall leave you your wives, and your children, and your lands, free without servitude, that you may do with them and with yourselves freely that which you like and think best, and they shall not compel you to turn Christians, unless you yourselves, when informed of the truth, should wish to be converted to our Holy Catholic Faith, as almost all the inhabitants of the rest of the islands have done. And, besides this, their Highnesses award you many privileges and exemptions . . . and will grant you many benefits.

"But, if you do not do this, and maliciously make delay in it, I certify to you that, with the help of God, we shall powerfully enter into your country, and shall make war against you in all ways and manners that we can, and shall subject you to the yoke and obedience of the Church and of their Highnesses; we shall take you and your wives and your children, and shall make slaves of them, and as such shall sell and dispose of them as their Highnesses may command; and we shall take away your goods, and shall do you all the mischief and damage that we can, as to vassals who do not obey, and refuse to receive their lord, and resist and contradict him; and we protest that the deaths and losses which shall accrue from this are your fault, and not that of their Highnesses, or ours, nor of these cavaliers who come with us. And that we have said this to you and made this Requisition, we request the notary here present to give us his testimony in writing, and we ask the rest who are present that they should be witnesses of this Requisition."

14. Initiating International Law

Francisco de Vitoria, O.P. (c. 1486-1546), was professor of sacred theology at the great university of Salamanca and was one of the primary thinkers in the renewal of the Dominican order's humanist philosophical tradition associated with St. Thomas Aquinas. The discovery of a culture (Vitoria apparently conceived of all Amerindians as having one undifferentiated culture, the same as that found among the indigenous inhabitants of Hispaniola) with institutions, laws, and practices completely alien to those of Christian Europe, constituted a dramatic test of the integrity of the commitment of those Dominicans whose vocations were academic. They rose magnificently to the challenge. Vitoria's colleague, Domingo de Soto (1494-1560) summed up the position of the order, stating that "those who are in the grace of God are not a whit better off than the sinner or the pagan in what concerns natural rights."[1]

Vitoria recognized the material interests that the Crown and powerful Spanish elites had in the New World's wealth, which resulted from forced Amerindian labor. The Crown and elites believed that the requerimiento *permitted them to subject Amerindian peoples at will. Vitoria and the Dominicans, therefore, advocated positions that were contrary to the economic interests of the conquistadors. Vitoria had to be prepared to face hostile criticism when he wrote* Reflections on the Indies and the Right of War, *from which the excerpt comes and which was published posthumously in 1557.*

The Dutch Protestant Hugo Grotius (1583-1645) is usually considered, perhaps erroneously, the father of international law. Could that father instead be Vitoria? What do the propositions in the excerpt, which were well publicized at the time, reveal about sixteenth-century Spanish culture?

On the illegitimate titles for the reduction of the aborigines of the New World into the power of the Spaniards.

1. The Emperor [Charles I (V)] is not the lord of the whole world.
2. Even if the Emperor were the lord of the world, that would not entitle him to seize the provinces of the Indian aborigines and to erect new lords and put down the former lords or to levy taxes.
3. The Pope is not civil or temporal lord of the whole world, in the proper sense of civil lordship and power.
4. Even if the Supreme Pontiff had secular

SOURCE: Francisci de Victoria, *De Indis et de iure Belli relectiones* [1557], ed. Ernest Nys; trans. John Pawley Bate (Washington, D.C.: Carnegie Institution of Washington, 1917), 129.

1. Domingo de Soto, quoted in *Bartolomé de las Casas in History: Toward an Understanding of the Man and His Work,* ed. Juan Friede and Benjamin Keen (DeKalb: Northern Illinois University Press, 1971), 253.

power over the world, he could not give that power to secular princes.

5. The Pope has temporal power, but only so far as it subserves things spiritual.

6. The Pope has no temporal power over the Indian aborigines or over other unbelievers.

7. A refusal by these aborigines to recognize any dominion of the Pope is no reason for making war on them and for seizing their goods.

8. Whether these aborigines were guilty of the sin of unbelief, in that they did not believe in Christ, before they heard anything of Christianity.

9. What is required in order that ignorance may be imputed to a person as, and be, sin, that is, vincible ignorance. And what about invincible ignorance?

10. Whether the aborigines are bound to hearken to the first messengers of Christianity so as to commit mortal sin in not believing Christ's Gospel merely on its simple announcement to them.

11. If the faith were simply announced and proposed to them and they will not straightway receive it, this is no ground for the Spaniards to make war on them or to proceed against them under the law of war.

12. How the aborigines, if they refuse when asked and counseled to hear peaceably preachers of religion, can not be excused from mortal sin.

13. When the aborigines would be bound to receive Christianity under penalty of mortal sin.

14. In the author's view it is not sufficiently clear whether Christianity has been so proposed and announced to these aborigines that they are bound to believe it under the penalty of fresh sin.

15. Even when Christianity has been proposed to them with never so much sufficiency of proof and they will not accept it, this does not render it lawful to make war on them and despoil them of their possessions.

16. Christian princes can not, even on the authority of the Pope, restrain these aborigines from sins against the law of nature or punish them therefor.

15. Indians Are Truly Men

The term "bull" derives from the huge lead seal, bulla *in Latin, that denoted a major papal document.* Sublimis Deus, *promulgated in 1537 by Paul III (1534-1549) is the most important statement by the Vatican on the conquest of "pagan Indians" by Catholic Spain. Where does the Vatican stand?*

The Spanish Crown suppressed the bull: that is, refused its promulgation. Why did it do so while it supported the work of the Dominicans at the University of Salamanca (see previous reading)?

Paul III Pope. To all faithful Christians to whom this writing may come, health in Christ our Lord and the apostolic benediction.

The sublime God so loved the human race that He created man in such wise that he might participate, not only in the good that other creatures enjoy, but endowed him with capacity to attain to the inaccessible and invisible Supreme Good and behold it face to face; and since man, according to the testimony of the sacred scriptures, has been created to enjoy eternal life and happiness, which none may obtain save through faith in our Lord Jesus Christ, it is necessary that he should possess the nature and faculties enabling him to receive

SOURCE: Francis Augustus MacNutt, *Bartholomew de Las Casas: His Life, His Apostolate, and His Writings, with Portraits and Maps* (New York and London: G. P. Putnam's Sons, 1909), 427-31.

that faith; and that whoever is thus endowed should be capable of receiving that same faith. Nor is it credible that any one should possess so little understanding as to desire the faith and yet be destitute of the most necessary faculty to enable him to receive it. Hence Christ, who is the Truth itself, that has never failed and can never fail, said to the preachers of the faith whom He chose for that office "Go ye and teach all nations." He said all, without exception, for all are capable of receiving the doctrines of the faith.

The enemy of the human race, who opposes all good deeds in order to bring men to destruction, beholding and envying this, invented a means never before heard of, by which he might hinder the preaching of God's word of Salvation to the people: he inspired his satellites who, to please him, have not hesitated to publish abroad that the Indians of the West and the South, and other people of whom We have recent knowledge should be treated as dumb brutes created for our service, pretending that they are incapable of receiving the catholic faith.

We, who, though unworthy, exercise on earth the power of our Lord and seek with all our might to bring those sheep of His flock who are outside, into the fold committed to our charge, consider, however, that the Indians are truly men and that they are not only capable of understanding the catholic faith but, according to our information,

they desire exceedingly to receive it. Desiring to provide ample remedy for these evils, we define and declare by these our letters, or by any translation thereof signed by any notary public and sealed with the seal of any ecclesiastical dignitary, to which the same credit shall be given as to the originals, that, notwithstanding whatever may have been or may be said to the contrary, the said Indians and all other people who may later be discovered by Christians, are by no means to be deprived of their liberty or the possession of their property, even though they be outside the faith of Jesus Christ; and that they may and should, freely and legitimately, enjoy their liberty and the possession of their property; nor should they be in any way enslaved; should the contrary happen, it shall be null and of no effect.

By virtue of our apostolic authority We define and declare by these present letters, or by any translation thereof signed by any notary public and sealed with the seal of any ecclesiastical dignitary, which shall thus command the same obedience as the originals, that the said Indians and other peoples should be converted to the faith of Jesus Christ by preaching the word of God and by the example of good and holy living.

Given in Rome in the year of our Lord 1537. The fourth of June and of our Pontificate, the third year.

PART III

"Conversion"

Systematic conversion of New World peoples to Catholicism commenced during and immediately following military conquests. Priests accompanied Columbus, Cortés, Pizarro, and other *conquistadores* throughout the Americas. Pedro de Arenas may have celebrated the first Mass in the Bahamas in 1492, though some scholars credit Franciscan Fray Bernardo Buil for having done so in Hispaniola on the feast of the Epiphany (January 6), 1494. Bartolomé de Olmedo went with Cortés to Mexico in 1519, and Vicente de Valverde accompanied Pizarro to Peru in 1532. Twelve Franciscans, under the leadership of friar Martín de Valencia, arrived in Mexico less than three years after the fall of Tenochtitlan. Dominicans came two years later, followed by Augustinians in 1533. Franciscans established monasteries in Quito and Lima in 1534 and 1535. Twelve Dominicans, under the leadership of friar Francisco Toscano, undertook missionary activities in Peru in 1540. Mercedarian fathers established monasteries shortly thereafter. Secular clergy organized parishes in Brazil in 1532. Six Jesuits, under the leadership of Manuel de Nóbrega, initiated missionary activities in Brazil in 1549. Ultimately, Spain divided its overseas possessions into ten archdioceses and thirty-eight dioceses, Santo Domingo becoming the first in 1511. Franciscan Juan de Zumárraga became the first bishop of New Spain in 1530 and Dominican Vicente de Valverde the first bishop of Cuzco in 1537. The Portuguese established the diocese of Brazil in 1551.[1]

Many early missionaries convinced themselves that this fortuitous opportunity to convert millions of Amerindians to Christianity surely signaled Christ's imminent second coming. This millenarian spirit and awesome responsibility, states John F. Schwaller, made it more practical "to baptize the masses and concentrate later on their spiritual prepara-

---

1. Enrique Dussel, ed., *The Church in Latin America, 1492-1992* (Maryknoll, N.Y.: Orbis Books, 1992), 5; Margaret E. Crahan, "Catholic Church (Colonial Period)," in *Encyclopedia of Latin America*, ed. Helen Delpar (New York: McGraw-Hill, 1974), 120; John F. Schwaller, "Catholic Church: Colonial Period," in *Encyclopedia of Latin American History and Culture*, vol. 2, ed. Barbara A. Tenenbaum (New York: Charles Scribner's Sons, 1996), 29.

tion."[2] Priests learned native languages and wrote catechisms and confessionals to teach church doctrine. They used songs, plays, and dances as vehicles to instill Christian values. Parishes were organized in already-existing Amerindian population centers. Because of the shortage of priests, they generally administered the sacraments in outlying communities only once or twice a year. In their absence, native community leaders called *fiscales* oversaw daily church operations. Each community usually established a *cofradía,* or lay brotherhood, whose dues-paying members sponsored annual festivals, venerated the local saint in a public procession, and received proper Christian burials at death.[3]

Some scholars question the depth of Amerindian conversion to Christianity and, instead, emphasize that syncretism was in fact the real result of the process. Peter Bakewell, for example, explains how Christianity was "absorbed into earlier beliefs, just as the deities of native invaders have typically been added to a conquered people's pantheon of gods in pre-Colombian times."[4] During the first century of Spanish rule, Amerindians in Peru continued to make offerings to *huacas,* or stones carved into human and animal form, and to practice ancestor worship of mummies preserved in caves. Maya peoples worshiped "idols" and guarded sacred writings. Others offered gifts of cacao, maize, guinea pigs, or chickens to images of saints. Some even hid ancient religious objects in Christian altars. But, by the end of the colonial period, according to Bakewell, most Amerindians came to accept and acknowledge Catholicism as their religion and as a powerful symbol of their own identity. As William B. Taylor suggests, colonial priests had learned to be flexible; if they "had no intention of compromising on fundamental matters of doctrine such as monotheism and the Trinity… [they had] learned to live with the local sorcery and spirits," thereby sanctioning a syncretism characterized by a dominant Catholic veneer or ethos.[5]

Spanish and Portuguese monarchs considered priests, friars, and monks of regular religious orders especially apt to undertake evangelization during the first decades of colonialism. As men who took special vows and lived according to a rule of life, *regula* in Latin, they already possessed the type of internal structure needed to convert millions of Amerindians in a methodical and organized fashion. Pope Adrian VI permitted members of regular orders to serve as parish priests by virtue of the bull *Exponi Nobis Omnimoda* of 1522. The earliest and most powerful orders included the Franciscans, Dominicans, Augustinians,

---

2. Schwaller, "Catholic Church: Colonial Period," 29.

3. James Lockhart, *The Nahuas after the Conquest: A Social and Cultural History of the Indians of Central Mexico, Sixteenth through Eighteenth Centuries* (Stanford: Stanford University Press, 1992), 218; Virginia Garrard-Burnett, "Introduction," in *On Earth as It Is in Heaven: Religion in Modern Latin America,* ed. Virginia Garrard-Burnett (Wilmington, Del.: Scholarly Resources, 2000), xvi; John E. Kizca, *Resilient Cultures: America's Native Peoples Confront European Colonization, 1500-1800* (Upper Saddle River, N.J.: Prentice Hall, 2003), 87-89; John F. Schwaller, "Introduction," in *The Church in Colonial Latin America,* ed. John F. Schwaller (Wilmington, Del.: Scholarly Resources, 2000), xxi.

4. Peter Bakewell, *A History of Latin America,* 2nd ed. (Malden, Mass.: Blackwell Publishing, 2004), 253.

5. Inga Clendinnen, *Ambivalent Conquests: Maya and Spaniard in Yucatan, 1517-1570* (Cambridge: Cambridge University Press, 1987), 69, 73; Bakewell, *History of Latin America,* 253; Kizca, *Resilient Cultures,* 87-89; William B. Taylor, *Magistrates of the Sacred: Priests and Parishioners in Eighteenth-Century Mexico* (Stanford: Stanford University Press, 1996), 51. See also Martin Austin Nesvig, ed., *Local Religion in Colonial Mexico* (Albuquerque: University of New Mexico, 2006).

and Mercedarians. Each tended to predominate in different urban areas, though all had churches, monasteries, and schools in viceregal capitals. New expeditions into hostile Amerindian areas usually included at least one or two regular clergy to minister to the spiritual needs of the conquerors and to commence evangelization. Many other orders such as the Hieronymites, Carmelites, and Bethlehemites became numerous with time. The latter, founded by Rodrigo de Arias Maldonado (1637-1716), was the only order founded in Spanish colonial America, receiving papal confirmation and royal approval in 1687 and 1696, respectively. Ordinary parish priests, or "secular" priests, served under the direction of the local bishop and were considered to live in "the world," or *saeculum*. These seculars grew in importance during the second half of the colonial period at the expense of the regulars.[6]

The Society of Jesus, founded by the Spaniard Ignatius Loyola (1491-1556) and recognized by Pope Paul III in 1540, arrived as missionaries to Brazil in 1549, Florida in 1565, and to other regions of Spanish America in 1572. As with other regulars, Jesuit priests and lay brothers took vows of poverty, chastity, and obedience, but they also made an additional vow of obedience to the pope. Worldwide membership in this highly centralized and energetic order grew from 936 in 1556 to more than 15,000 in 1626. By the second half of the eighteenth century there were approximately 2,600 in Portuguese and Spanish America. They gained prominence as missionaries to Amerindians on the fringes of empire (most notably in Paraguay); owned many lucrative haciendas, cattle ranches, textile mills, and sugar plantations; and became the teachers of wealthy male youth in cities.[7]

As the colonial period matured, the Habsburg monarchs of Spain sought to curb the influence of the regular orders. The Crown had needed the organizational skills and dedication of the regulars during the initial, precarious phase of colonialism, but once royal authority was firmly established it feared their strong presence and growing influence. In addition, the Crown could more easily control secular priests by virtue of its Royal Patronage, whereas members of the regular orders reported to their prior, abbot, provincial, and ultimately to their head in Rome. In 1574 Philip II issued the *Ordenanza del Patronazgo*, which firmly placed members of religious orders under episcopal authority and began the long and sometimes bitter process of replacing regulars with seculars in parishes.[8]

Most curates preferred the excitement and refinement of the city, and few sought posts in the countryside. In the seventeenth century, fortunate prelates might hold Mass in magnificent baroque churches, whose interiors radiated with gold-plated altars, frescos and

6. Schwaller, "Introduction," xi, xiii; Margaret E. Crahan, "Religious Orders (Colonial Period)," in *Encyclopedia of Latin America*, ed. Helen Delpar (New York: McGraw-Hill, 1974), 525-26; Schwaller, "Catholic Church: Colonial Period," 28-29, 32; Sarah L. Cline, "Church and State: Habsburg New Spain," in *Encyclopedia of Mexico: History, Society & Culture*, vol. 1, ed. Michael S. Werner (Chicago and London: Fitzroy Dearborn Publishers, 1997), 249.

7. Nicholas P. Cushner, "Jesuits," in *Encyclopedia of Latin American History and Culture*, vol. 3, ed. Barbara A. Tenenbaum (New York: Charles Scribner's Sons, 1996), 316-17.

8. Crahan, "Religious Orders (Colonial Period)," 525; Cline, "Church and State: Habsburg New Spain," 249; Schwaller, "Catholic Church: Colonial Period," 32.

paintings, and silver chalices, monstrances, and candelabra. Wealthy parishioners demonstrated, as Pamela Voekel states, "unrestrained ostentation" at every opportunity.[9]

The ethnic and racial composition of priests changed slowly. While Spaniards usually received the highest positions, Creoles (children of Spaniards born in the New World) joined religious orders and became a majority by 1700. Income requirements kept mixed-blood peoples from entering the priesthood, and caste laws prevented blacks and Amerindians from doing so during most of the colonial period. Young men needed to secure a guaranteed income or sufficient education for a benefice prior to ordination. Some mestizos and mulattoes acquired dispensations to join the priesthood, but, once there, their ancestry stymied their mobility.[10]

University professors incorporated the ideas of the Enlightenment into their lectures, began to teach in Spanish and Portuguese rather than in Latin, and offered classes in physics, chemistry, and mathematics, in addition to the traditional ones in arts, theology, canon law, civil law, and medicine. By the beginning of the nineteenth century, there were fifty *colegios,* or high schools, and twenty-three universities in Spanish America, seven of which were public institutions. Though it can be said that all students received a Catholic education, all institutions were under royal authority. The Jesuits in Spanish America staffed thirty-five of the *colegios* and eight universities, such as those in Córdoba, Lima, and Mexico City. The Brazilian *colegios* of the Jesuits in Bahia and Rio de Janeiro prepared students for possible future study at the great Jesuit University of Coimbra in Portugal. In all, notes John Tate Lanning, more than 150,000 students received academic degrees in Spanish America between 1550 and 1821. It is not surprising that wealthy white males received most of the formal educational opportunities, though poorer and even illegitimate boys who showed aptitude might be accepted, especially into Jesuit institutions, during the waning years of colonial rule.[11]

16. "Converting" the Conquered

This account of the events preceding the second and ultimately successful Spanish assault upon Tenochtitlan (the stronghold of the Mexica/Aztecs, now Mexico City) was written by a native in Nahuatl and subsequently translated into Spanish. Fragments are preserved in the Codex Ramírez, the original Nahuatl account being lost.

---

9. Pamela Voekel, *Alone before God: The Religious Origins of Modernity in Mexico* (Durham, N.C.: Duke University Press, 2002), 24-26.

10. John Frederick Schwaller, *The Church and Clergy in Sixteenth-Century Mexico* (Albuquerque: University of New Mexico Press, 1987), 193-95; John Frederick Schwaller, *Origins of Church Wealth in Mexico: Ecclesiastical Revenues and Church Finances, 1523-1600* (Albuquerque: University of New Mexico Press, 1985), 167-69.

11. John Tate Lanning, "The Church and the Enlightenment in the Universities," *The Americas* 15, no. 4 (April 1959): 334-38, 337; Schwaller, "Catholic Church: Colonial Period," 31; Cushner, "Jesuits," 317.

Several problems arise from a study of this dramatic account: Does the hostility of Tex-coco to Tenochtitlán color the account and make it suspect? Since this indigenous account was written after the conquest, how reliable would it be, as it was done under the aegis of Spanish Catholic overlords? Does the depiction of Cortés as a fervent Catholic, deeply and personally committed to the conversion of the Texcocans, ring true or might it be obsequious propaganda? Does Prince Ixtlilxachitl's instantaneous conversion make sense? Would not his mother's reaction be more understandable? Why would the writer include the mother's hostile reaction to Catholicism when the account is so well disposed to Christian evange-lism? For what effect was the author striving in his account of Moctezuma's rejection of his brother Cuitlahuac's hostile but ultimately correct view of Spanish imperialism?

The Arrival at the City

At the request of Ixtlilxochitl, Cortés and his men ate the gifts of food that had been brought out from Tezcoco. Then they walked to the city with their new friends, and all the people came out to cheer and welcome them. The Indians knelt down and adored them as sons of the Sun, their gods, believing that the time had come of which their dear king Nezahualpilli had so often spoken. The Spaniards entered the city and were lodged in the royal palace.

Word of these events was brought to the king, Motecuhzoma, who was pleased by the reception his nephews had given Cortés. He was also pleased by what Cohuamacotzin and Ixtlilxochitl had said to the Captain, because he believed that Ixtlilxo-chitl would call in the garrisons stationed on the frontiers. But God ordered it otherwise.

Cortés was very grateful for the attentions shown him by Ixtlilxochitl and his brothers; he wished to repay their kindness by teaching them the law of God, with the help of his interpreter Aguilar. The brothers and a number of the other lords gathered to hear him, and he told them that the emperor of the Christians had sent him here, so far away, in order that he might instruct them in the law of Christ. He explained the mystery of the Creation and the Fall, the mystery of the Trin-ity and the Incarnation and the mystery of the Passion and the Resurrection. Then he drew out a crucifix and held it up. The Christians all knelt, and Ixtlilxochitl and the other lords knelt with them.

Cortés also explained the mystery of Baptism. He concluded the lesson by telling them how the Emperor Charles grieved that they were not in God's grace, and how the emperor had sent him among them only to save their souls. He begged them to become willing vassals of the emperor, because that was the will of the pope, in whose name he spoke.

Ixtlilxochitl Becomes a Christian

When Cortés asked for their reply, Ixtlilxochitl burst into tears and answered that he and his brothers understood the mysteries very well. Giv-ing thanks to God that his soul had been illu-mined, he said that he wished to become a Christian and to serve the emperor. He begged for the crucifix, so that he and his brothers might worship it, and the Spaniards wept with joy to see their devotion.

The princes then asked to be baptized. Cortés and the priest accompanying him said that first they must learn more of the Christian religion, but that persons would be sent to instruct them. Ixtlilxochitl expressed his gratitude, but begged to receive the sacrament at once because he now hated all idolatry and revered the mysteries of the true faith.

Although a few of the Spaniards objected, Cortés decided that Ixtlilxochitl should be baptized immediately. Cortés himself served as godfather, and the prince was given the name Hernando, because that was his sponsor's name. His brother Cohuamacotzin was named Pedro because his godfather was Pedro de Alvarado, and Tecocoltzin was named Fernando, with Cortés sponsoring him also. The other Christians became godfathers to the other princes, and the baptisms were performed with the greatest solemnity. If it had been possible, more than twenty thousand persons would have been baptized that very day, and a great number of them did receive the sacrament.

The Reactions of Yacotzin

Ixtlilxochitl went to his mother, Yacotzin, to tell her what had happened and to bring her out to be baptized. She replied that he must have lost his mind to let himself be won over so easily by that handful of barbarians, the conquistadors. Don Hernando said that if she were not his mother, he would answer her by cutting off her head. He told her that she would receive the sacrament, even against her will, because nothing was important except the life of the soul. Yacotzin asked her son to leave her alone for the time being. She said she would think about what he had told her and make her decision the next day. He left the palace and ordered her rooms to be set on fire (though others say that he found her in a temple of idolatry).

Finally she came out, saying that she wanted to become a Christian. She went to Cortés and was baptized with a great many others. Cortés himself was her godfather, naming her Doña María because she was the first woman in Tezcoco to become a Christian. Her four daughters, the princesses, were also baptized, along with many other women. And during the three or four days they were in the city, the Spaniards baptized a great multitude of people.

Motecuhzoma's Final Decision

When Motecuhzoma learned what had happened in Tezcoco, he called together his nephew Cacama, his brother Cuitlahuac and the other lords. He proposed a long discussion in order to decide whether they should welcome the Christians when they arrived, and if so, in what manner. Cuitlahuac replied that they should not welcome them in any manner, but Cacama disagreed, saying that it would show a want of courage to deny them entrance once they were at the gates. He added that it was not proper for a great lord like his uncle to turn away the ambassadors of another great prince. If the visitors made any demands which displeased Motecuhzoma, he could punish their insolence by sending his hosts of brave warriors against them.

Before any one else could speak, Motecuhzoma announced that he agreed with his nephew. Cuitlahuac warned him: "I pray to our gods that you will not let the strangers into your house. They will cast you out of it and overthrow your rule, and when you try to recover what you have lost, it will be too late." With this the council came to an end. The other lords all showed by their gestures that they approved of this last opinion, but Motecuhzoma was resolved to welcome the Christians as friends. He told his nephew Cacama to go out to meet them and sent his brother Cuitlahuac to wait for them in the palace at Ixtapalapa.

17. Palm Sunday, Tabasco, 1519

Bernal Díaz del Castillo (c. 1495-c. 1584) arrived in the Americas in 1514, took part in the conquest of Mexico, and was an effective common soldier who was awarded an encomienda in 1522. In the 1560s he wrote the most complete account of the conquest—the "true" history—recounting Cortés's brilliance, bravery, and daring but also emphasizing Cortés's continual consultation with his soldiers in all his decisions.

At this point, March 1519, the Spaniards have successfully prevailed against a native host

---

SOURCE: Bernal Díaz del Castillo, *The True History of the Conquest of New Spain*, ed. Genaro García; trans. Alfred Percibal Maudslay (London: Hakluyt Society, 1908), 1:128-30.

in the area today called Tabasco. Cortés convinced the caciques of the region to meet with the victorious Spaniards, the results of which Bernal describes in this excerpt.

That the natives were intimidated by the Spaniards and did not want them as enemies is understandable; hence the caciques' presentation of the twenty women to the Spaniards (an insight into the place of women in that society). But would they immediately convert to Catholicism?

What might be the various motives for the Spaniards celebrating Palm Sunday in so fervent and demonstrative a manner and for commissioning the chiefs to maintain the shrine of the cross?

So the talk ceased until the next day when the sacred image of Our Lady and the Cross were set up on the altar and we all paid reverence to them, and Padre Fray Bartolomé de Olmedo said mass and all the caciques and chiefs were present and we gave the name of Santa María de la Victoria to the town, and by this name the town of Tabasco is now called. The same friar, with Aguilar as interpreter, preached many good things about our holy faith to the twenty Indian women who had been given us, telling them not to believe in the Idols which they had been wont to trust in, for they were evil things and not gods, and that they should offer no more sacrifices to them for they would lead them astray, but that they should worship our Lord Jesus Christ, and immediately afterwards they were baptized. One Indian lady who was given to us here was christened Doña Marina, and she was truly a great chieftainess and the daughter of great caciques and the mistress of vassals, and this her appearance clearly showed. [...]

Cortés then ordered the caciques to come with their women and children early the next day, which was Palm Sunday, to the altar, to pay homage to the holy image of Our Lady and to the Cross, and at the same time Cortés ordered them to send six Indian carpenters to accompany our carpenters to the town of Cintla where our Lord God was pleased to give us victory in the battle which I have described, there to cut a cross on a great tree called a ceiba which grew there, and they did it so that it might last a long time, for as the bark is renewed the cross will show there forever. When this was done he ordered the Indians to get ready all the canoes that they owned to help us to embark, for we wished to set sail on that holy day because the pilots had come to tell Cortés that the ships ran a great risk from a *Norther* which is a dangerous gale.

The next day, early in the morning, all the caciques and chiefs came in their canoes with all their women and children and stood in the court where we had placed the church and cross, and many branches of trees had already been cut ready to be carried in the procession. Then the caciques beheld us all, Cortés, as well as the captains, and every one of us marching together with the greatest reverence in a devout procession, and the Padre de la Merced and the priest, Juan Díaz, clad in their vestments, said mass, and we paid reverence to and kissed the Holy Cross, while the caciques and Indians stood looking on at us.

When our solemn festival was over the chiefs approached and offered Cortés ten fowls, and baked fish and vegetables, and we took leave of them, and Cortés again commended to their care the Holy image and the sacred crosses and told them always to keep the place clean and well swept and to deck the cross with garlands and to reverence it, and then they would enjoy good health and bountiful harvests.

18. Señor Moctezuma Discusses Religion with Señor Malinche

It is now November 1519 and the Spaniards have advanced to the very heart of Tenochtitlan. Cortés is addressing Moctezuma in the name of the Spanish king and Holy Roman Emperor Charles.

Why does Cortés's discourse center on Catholic (Christian) doctrine? Why does Cortés belittle the gods "as devils ... of little worth"?

Cortés, of course, speaks through doña Marina, a.k.a. Malinche, who knows the Aztec language (Nahuatl). Hence, Moctezuma addresses him as "Señor Malinche" when he rejects the aggressive proselytization of the Spaniards (though he recognizes they both understand creation in the same manner).

Why might the friar be less anxious than Cortés about building a church?

In the final part of the excerpt Bernal gives a vivid description of the great cue *(a sacred precinct) with richly ornamented gods and votive "candles" consisting of human hearts burning.*

Is Cortés's suddenly low-key reaction surprising? What must be going through his mind as he begs Moctezuma's pardon?

[T]he Emperor having heard of him and what a great prince he was, had sent us to these parts to see him, and to beg them to become Christians, the same as our Emperor and all of us, so that his soul and those of all his vassals might be saved. Later on he would further explain how and in what manner this should be done, and how we worship one only true God, and who He is, and many other good things which he should listen to. [...]

But what he chiefly came to say on behalf of our Lord God had already been brought to his [Montezuma's] knowledge through his ambassadors, Tendile, Pitalpitoque and Quintalbor, at the time when he did us the favour to send the golden sun and moon to the sand dunes; for we told them then that we were Christians and worshipped one true and only God, named Jesus Christ, who suffered death and passion to save us, and we told them that a cross (when they asked us why we worshipped it) was a sign of the other Cross on which our Lord God was crucified for our salvation, and that the death and passion which He suffered was for the salvation of the

whole human race, which was lost, and that this our God rose on the third day and is now in heaven, and it is He who made the heavens and the earth, the sea and the sands, and created all the things there are in the world, and He sends the rain and the dew, and nothing happens in the world without His holy will. That we believe in Him and worship Him, but that those whom they look upon as gods are not so, but are devils, which are evil things, and if their looks are bad their deeds are worse, and they could see that they were evil and of little worth, for where we had set up crosses such as those his ambassadors had seen, they dared not appear before them, through fear of them, and that as time went on they would notice this. [...]

Montezuma replied—"Senor Malinche, I have understood your words and arguments very well before now, from what you said to my servants at the sand dunes, this about three Gods and the Cross, and all those things that you have preached in the towns through which you have come. We have not made any answer to it because here throughout all time we have worshipped our own

Source: Bernal Díaz del Castillo, *The True History of the Conquest of New Spain*, ed. Alfred Percival Maudslay (London: Hakluyt Society, 1910), 2:54, 56-58, 75-79.

gods, and thought they were good, as no doubt yours are, so do not trouble to speak to us any more about them at present. Regarding the creation of the world, we have held the same belief for ages past, and for this reason we take it for certain that you are those whom our ancestors predicted would come from the direction of the sunrise. [. . .]

Let us leave this, and return to our Captain, who said to Fray Bartolomé de Olmedo, who has often been mentioned by me, and who happened to be nearby him: "It seems to me, Señor Padre, that it would be a good thing to throw out a feeler to Montezuma, as to whether he would allow us to build our church here;" and the Padre replied that it would be a good thing if it were successful, but it seemed to him that it was not quite a suitable time to speak about it, for Montezuma did not appear to be inclined to do such a thing. [. . .]

Montezuma replied that he must first speak with his high priests, and when he had spoken to them he said that we might enter into a small tower and apartment, a sort of hall, where there were two altars, with very richly carved boardings on the top of the roof. On each altar were two figures, like giants with very tall bodies and very fat, and the first which stood on the right hand they said was the figure of Huichilobos their god of War; it had a very broad face and monstrous and terrible eyes, and the whole of his body was covered with precious stones, and gold and pearls, and with seed pearls stuck on with a paste that they make in this country out of a sort of root, and all the body and head was covered with it, and the body was girdled by great snakes made of gold and precious stones, and in one hand he held a bow and in the other some arrows. And another small idol that stood by him, they said was his page, and he held a short lance and a shield richly decorated with gold and stones. Huichilobos had round his neck some Indians' faces and other things like hearts of Indians, the former made of gold and the latter of silver, with many precious blue stones.

There were some braziers with incense which they call copal, and in them they were burning the hearts of the three Indians whom they had sacrificed that day, and they had made the sacrifice with smoke and copal. All the walls of the oratory

were so splashed and encrusted with blood that they were black, the floor was the same and the whole place stank vilely. Then we saw on the other side on the left hand there stood the other great image the same height as Huichilobos, and it had a face like a bear and eyes that shone, made of their mirrors which they call *Tezcat*, and the body plastered with precious stones like that of Huichilobos, for they say that the two are brothers; and this Tezcatepuca was the god of Hell and had charge of the souls of the Mexicans, and his body was girt with figures like little devils with snakes' tails. The walls were so clotted with blood and the soil so bathed with it that in the slaughter houses in Spain there is not such another stench.

They had offered to this Idol five hearts from that day's sacrifices. In the highest part of the Cue there was a recess of which the woodwork was very richly worked, and in it was another image half man and half lizard, with precious stones all over it, and half the body was covered with a mantle. They say that the body of this figure is full of all the seeds that there are in the world, and they say that it is the god of seed time and harvest, but I do not remember its name, and everything was covered with blood, both walls and altar, and the stench was such that we could hardly wait the moment to get out of it.

They had an exceedingly large drum there, and when they beat it the sound of it was so dismal and like, so to say, an instrument of the infernal regions, that one could hear it a distance of two leagues, and they said that the skins it was covered with were those of great snakes. In that small place there were many diabolical things to be seen, bugles and trumpets and knives, and many hearts of Indians that they had burned in fumigating their idols, and everything was so clotted with blood, and there was so much of it, that I curse the whole of it, and as it stank like a slaughter house we hastened to clear out of such a bad stench and worse sight. Our Captain said to Montezuma through our interpreter, half laughing: "Señor Montezuma, I do not understand how such a great Prince and wise man as you are has not come to the conclusion, in your mind, that these idols of yours are not gods, but evil things that are called devils, and so that you may know it and all your priests may see it clearly, do me the favour to approve of my placing a cross here on the top of this tower, and that in one part of these oratories where your Huichilobos and Tezcatepuca stand we may divide off a space where we can set up an image of Our Lady (an image which Montezuma had already seen) and you will see by the fear in which these Idols hold it that they are deceiving you."

Montezuma replied half angrily, (and the two priests who were with him showed great annoyance,) and said: "Señor Malinche, if I had known that you would have said such defamatory things I would not have shown you my gods, we consider them to be very good, for they give us health and rains and good seed times and seasons and as many victories as we desire, and we are obliged to worship them and make sacrifices, and I pray you not to say another word to their dishonour."

When our Captain heard that and noted the angry looks he did not refer again to the subject, but said with a cheerful manner: "It is time for your Excellency and for us to return," and Montezuma replied that it was well, but that he had to pray and offer certain sacrifices on account of the great *tatacul*, that is to say sin, which he had committed in allowing us to ascend his great Cue, and being the cause of our being permitted to see his gods, and of our dishonouring them by speaking evil of them, so that before he left he must pray and worship.

Then Cortés said, "I ask your pardon if it be so," and then we went down the steps.

19. Our Ancestors Did Not Speak in This Manner

This stubborn and stunning affirmation by Mexica tlamatinime (wisemen and priests of the Mexica) was reported by a Franciscan friar who may be described as the greatest ethnographer of the Americas, Bernardino de Sahagún (c. 1499–c. 1590). His monumental Historia de las cosas de Nueva España (begun in 1547 and finished in 1585 but not published in his lifetime) is Sahagún's own translation of and added commentary upon the Florentine Codex, a compilation in Nahuatl of three sets of responses by native informants to questions about Mexica culture, especially religion. The questions were devised by Sahagún and administered by young native nobles who had been educated by the friars.

A dialogue between the newly arrived Twelve Franciscans and some of the tlamatinime took place in 1524. Some forty years later Sahagún gathered the following text (here translated from the Nahuatl) from notes in Spanish but translated into Nahuatl literary style. Note that "our lords" refers to the victorious Spanish overlords; "Him" refers to "the Lord of the Near and . . . Surrounding."

What kind of argument do the tlamatinime use to explain their refusal to accept Christianity? Is their argument theological, or even religious? Would the friars understand their argument? How might they respond?

Our Lords, very esteemed lords:

You have endured hardships to arrive in this land. Here before you, we ignorant people contemplate you. . . . And now, what shall we say? What shall we raise to your ears? We are merely common people. . . .

Source: Bernardino de Sahagún quoted in Miguel León-Portilla, *Endangered Cultures*, trans. Julie Goodson-Lawes (Dallas: Southern Methodist University Press, 1990), 68-70. Reprinted by permission of Southern Methodist University Press.

Through an interpreter we respond, we return the breath and the word of the Lord of the Near and of the Surrounding (Tloque Nahuaque). . . .

Because of Him we put ourselves at risk, for Him we put ourselves into danger. . . . Perhaps we are to be taken to our ruin, perhaps to our destruction. (But) where are we to go now? We are common people, we are destructible, we are mortal. Let us die now, let us perish, since our gods have already died.

Calm your hearts and your flesh, our lords! Because we will break open a little now, we will open the secret a little, the ark of the Lord, our (god). You said that we know not the Lord of the Near and of the Surrounding (Tloque Nahuaque), the One to whom the heavens and the earth belong. You said that our gods are not real gods. This word that you speak is a new one, and because of it we are distressed, because of it we are frightened. Indeed, our ancestors, those who came to be, those who came to live on the earth, did not speak in this manner. They gave us their ways of life; they believed them truly, they worshiped them, they honored them, the gods. They taught us all their forms of worship, their ways of honoring (the gods). Thus, before them we eat earth (kiss earth to make an oath), for them we bleed ourselves, we fulfill our promises, we burn *copal* (incense), and we offer sacrifices.

It was the doctrine of our elders that we give thanks to our gods, that they merited us (with their sacrifice they gave us life). In what way? When? Where? When it is still night.

It was their doctrine that they grant us our sustenance, all that we drink and eat, all that which maintains life: corn, beans, wild amaranth, sage. They are the ones from whom we request the water, the rain, from which the things of the earth are made. They themselves are rich, they are happy, they possess things; in such a way that always and forever things germinate there, and grow green there, in their house . . . there, where somehow there is life, in the place of Tlalocan (the paradise of the Rain God). Never is there hunger there, never is there sickness, there is no poverty. They give courage and authority to the people. . . . And in what way? When? Where were the gods invoked, beseeched, accepted as such, revered? It has already been a very long time: it was there in Tula, it was there in Huapalcalco, it was there in Xuchitlapan, it was there in Tlamohuanchan, it was there in Yohualichan, it was there in Teotihuacán. . . .

And now, are we the ones who will destroy the ancient rule of life? That of the Chichimes, the Toltecs, the Acolhuas, the Tepanecs? We know to whom life is owed, to whom birth is owed, to whom conception is owed, to whom growth is owed; how we must pray.

Listen, our lords, do nothing to our people that would bring about their disgrace, that would cause them to perish. . . . Peacefully and calmly consider, our lords, what is necessary. We cannot be tranquil, and certainly we still do not believe, we do not accept your words to be true, even though we may offend you. Here are the Lords, those who govern, those who carry, who have in their charge the whole world. It is enough that we have already lost it, that it has been taken from us, that our governance has been impeded. If we were to stay in this place, we would be but prisoners. Do with us what you will. This is all that we respond, that we answer, to your breath, to your word, Oh, our lords!

20. Tupi Innocence?

Pero Vaz de Caminha (c. 1437-1500), secretary for Pedro Alvarez Cabral's fleet, which stumbled upon Brazil in 1500, writes an account of the first glimpse and evaluation by the Portuguese of the inhabitants of the New World. What does this account reveal about European cultures and values in this era?

SOURCE: Quoted in Charles R. Boxer, *The Portuguese Seaborne Empire, 1415-1825* (New York: Alfred A. Knopf, 1969), 85. Boxer, C. R., *Portuguese Society in the Tropics.* © 1965. Reprinted by permission of The University of Wisconsin Press.

They seem to me to be people of such innocence that, if we could understand them and they us, they would soon become Christians, because they do not seem to have or to understand any form of religion. . . . For it is certain that this people is good and of pure simplicity, and there can easily be stamped upon them whatever belief we wish to give them. And furthermore, Our Lord gave them fine bodies and good faces as to good men, and He who brought us here, I believe, did not do so without purpose . . . there were among them three or four girls, very young and very pretty, with very dark hair, long over the shoulders, and their privy parts so high, so closed and so free from hair that we felt no shame in looking hard at them . . . one of the girls was all painted from head to foot with that [bluish-black] paint, and she was so well built and so rounded, and her lack of shame was so charming, that many women of our own land seeing such attractions, would be ashamed that theirs were not like hers.

21. Jesuits and Tupi

Arriving in Brazil in 1553, José de Anchieta, S.J. (1534-1597), became a schoolmaster in the newly established colegio *(school), São Paolo, which ultimately gave its name to that town and province. In response to a complaint against the Jesuits to the* Mesa de Conciencia *(the royal council in Lisbon with responsibility for religious affairs in Brazil) by Portuguese colonizers for the Jesuits' "enslaving" of Amerindians, Anchieta gave a detailed description (c. 1560) of the Jesuit* aldeias, *the Amerindian villages in which the Jesuits implemented their program of religious instruction and acculturation.*

What did that program of acculturation entail? What were some reactions of the Amerindians to its demands? Keep in mind the nature of the Tupi Amerindians, who were wandering and warring hunters and gatherers when the Portuguese arrived.

Every day, in the morning, the Fathers teach the Indians doctrine and say mass for those who want to hear it before going to their fields; after that the children stay in school, where they learn reading and writing, counting, and other good customs pertaining to the Christian life; in the afternoon they conduct another class especially for those who are receiving the sacred sacraments. Daily the Fathers visit the sick with certain Indians assigned for this purpose, and if they have some special needs they attend to them, and always administer to them the necessary sacraments. All this they do purely for love of God and for no other interest or profit, for the Fathers get their food from the *colegio*, and they live with the Indians solely because of love of their souls, which have such great need of them. The Fathers make no use of them on plantations, for if the *colegio* needs them for certain tasks, and they come to help, they work for wages . . . and not through force but of their own free will, because they need clothing or implements. For although it is their natural tendency to go about naked, all those who have been raised in the Jesuit schools now wear clothes and are ashamed to go about naked. It is not true, as some say, that the Fathers are the lords of the villages.

When the Portuguese come to the villages in search of Indian labor, the Fathers help them all they can, summoning one of the Indian headmen to take the Portuguese to the houses of the natives

SOURCE: *Cartas, Informaçoes, Fragmentos Históricos e Sermões do Padre Joseph de Anchieta, S.J.* (1554-1594) (Rio de Janeiro, 1933), 377-78, trans. Benjamin Keen, in Robert Buffington and Lila Caimari, eds., *Keen's Latin American Civilization: History and Society, 1492 to the Present*, 8th ed. (Boulder, Colo.: Westview Press, 2004), 148-49. Copyright © by Westview Press. Reprinted by permission of Westview Press, a member of Perseus Books, L.L.C.

to show them the goods they have brought, and those who wish to go they permit to leave without impediment. If the Fathers object at times, it is because the Indians have not finished their farm work, and they have to do this for the sake of their wives and children. In other cases, the Indians are not getting along with their wives, and once they leave for the homes of the Portuguese they never return; such Indians the Father also restrains from going, so that they may continue living with their wives. . . .

The Indians are punished for their offenses by their own magistrates, appointed by the Portuguese governors; the only chastisement consists in being put in the stocks for a day or two, as the magistrate considers best; they use no chains or other imprisonment. If some Indian who went to work for the Portuguese returns before completing his time, the Father compels him to return to work out his time, and if the Indian cannot go for some good reason the Father arranges matters to the satisfaction of his employer.

The Fathers always encourage the Indians to cultivate their fields and to raise more provisions than they need, so that in case of necessity they might aid the Portuguese by way of barter; in fact, many Portuguese obtain their food from the villages. Thus one could say that the Fathers are truly the fathers of the Indians, both of their souls and of their bodies.

22. Rigorous Evangelization of Adult Amerindians

Despite the reference to himself in the third person (in the third paragraph) the following letter was probably written by António Pires, S.J., in September 1558 to the Jesuit father general in Rome. This letter may be regarded as a more straightforward account than Anchieta's necessarily defensive one of 1560 refuting unfounded accusations against the Jesuits (see previous reading). The letter provides an excellent insight into the manner in which the Portuguese, lay and clerical, perceived their mission in Brazil, the measures this mission mandated for the Amerindians, and the responses of the latter.

Pires writes approvingly of the provincial governor's using "fear" to "subjugate" Amerindians to "the law and servitude." This "fear" will allow the Amerindians to learn of Christ and the "kindness [of] Our Lord," enabling them "to remain a strong and stable people." This language allows the reader to understand the Jesuit technique in evangelizing adult Amerindians and their optimism about its effects. It is important that the reader enter into and understand the European mind of the era without judging it with twenty-first-century sensibilities.

Why were these Portuguese so confident in their rigorous treatment of the adult Amerindians? Why would they be so optimistic about the effects of that treatment? They are even more optimistic about the effects of their program on Amerindian children. Why are they so sanguine? What may they have not considered?

Since the letter written on July 19, 1558, from Bahia, the Governor has continued zealously in his efforts and Our Lord has given him rewards for his efforts.

He continued to punish the wrongdoers with such prudence and temperance that he builds up the community and does not destroy it, and for that reason he has been able to subjugate all to the law and servitude whom he wanted.

Thus, from far away they [the Indians] send

SOURCE: E. Bradford Burns, "Introduction to the Brasilian Jesuit Letters," *Mid-America: An Historical Review* 44, no. 3 (July 1962): 184-85. Reprinted by permission of *Mid-America: An Historical Review.*

requests for priests to indoctrinate them because they want friendship with Christians and to change their habits for ours. In this way four large settlements are already constructed for them; but for the present only two of us reside among them in the newly constructed churches because there are only three of us in this Captaincy who can say mass and we are scattered in the following three areas: in the College of Bahia resides João Conçalves with a few Brothers, Father Nóbrega is in São Paulo, and Antônio Pires is in São João. The other two settlements are awaiting aid.

Besides these, other settlements are being prepared in more remote parts where the Christians never imagined it possible to enter and subjugate, and we are taking care of this slowly until there are enough Fathers to reap the great harvest there. It is certain that if there were enough people to teach and to maintain them, we could easily establish 20 or 30 churches around which we could settle all the Indians from an area many leagues square.

All these are losing their habit of eating human flesh; and if we learn that some are about to eat flesh, we order them to send it to us. They send it, as they did several days ago, and they bring it to us from a long distance so that we can bury or burn it. In this way they all tremble with fear of the Governor, a fear which, although it may not last a lifetime, is enough so that we can teach them; it serves us so that we can tell them of Christ, and the kindness which Our Lord will show them will cause all human fear to flee so that they will remain a strong and stable people. This fear makes them more capable of being able to hear the word of God. Their children are instructed; the innocent ones about to die are all baptized; they are

forgetting their habits and exchanging them for good ones. Proceeding in this way a noble Christianity will be inculcated at least among the youngsters.

With much diligence the children are being taught good habits, reading, and writing, and there are some very intelligent ones among them. From these we hope to have some good students, because, since they can no longer wander around and now remain among us, they will not be able to forget what they have learned. Those of São Paulo, the first settlement built, are all Christians, that is the children up to 14 years of age, and every day more are baptized because those who are born again bring others for baptism and there are more than two hundred of these. We do not baptize the older ones who may already have committed some mortal sins unless they confess and live in a manner acceptable to Our Lord, and of these older ones many are living orderly lives so that already we have baptized and married a large number. This good order is encountered throughout the other Indian settlements we have created.

There are a great many things which I could tell your Paternity and all the Brothers which would please you very much, but I will concentrate only on two things. The first is that one of the boys whom we brought up some years ago and taught to weave is in São Paulo with his loom and is making cloth. The concern which before they all had for their feasts of human flesh and for their wars and ceremonies has been converted to the planting of cotton. They weave it and thus dress themselves. This now is their principal concern. All have begun to clothe themselves and many of them go around dressed now.

23. Brazilian Slavers and Jesuit Missionaries

Some seventy years after the auspicious start of Jesuit evangelization (1630) comes this shocking report by two Jesuits about the actual status of the aldeias *and the "heathen" Amerindians who were positively disposed to the Jesuits. The account is so specific and*

SOURCE: Jaime Cotesão, ed., *Jesuítas e bandeirantes no Guairá, 1549-1640* (Rio de Janeiro: Biblioteca Nacional, 1951), 310-38, trans. and ed. Richard M. Morse in *The Bandeirantes: The Historical Role of the Brazilian Pathfinders* (New York: Alfred A. Knopf, 1965), 82-91.

detailed that exaggeration is unlikely. Arrogance, wanton cruelty, massive kidnappings, incineration of Indian villages, brazen collusion by magistrates—how is it possible that these entradas *(the term given to such raids against the Amerindians) could have character- ized the growing Portuguese colony?*

Most disturbing to the two Jesuit authors is the image of their order in Amerindian eyes—an image of the Jesuits in collusion with the brutal bandeirantes *(the raiders in the* entradas*) to enslave the entire Amerindian population—which would preclude the possi- bility of any further successful evangelization of the Amerindians. Does this depiction of the maturing colony suggest the actual reality of the colonization process, whether Portuguese or Spanish? How would that, in turn, affect the process of "conversion"?*

For forty years the inhabitants of São Paulo have flaunted the laws of the King Our Lord with no regard for them, nor for their great offense against God, nor for the punishment which they deserve. In their raids they continually capture and carry off by force of arms the free and emanci- pated Indians whom they keep for their own slaves or sell. Lately their boldness has been even greater than in years past, and for two principal reasons: first, this time they have gone out in greater numbers than ever, emboldened by the lit- tle or no punishment inflicted on them for their continual and unjust entradas in the past; second, they have assaulted the reductions of the Fathers of the Company of Jesus of the Province of Paraguay and taken all the people whom we were instructing.

With regard to the first point: In the beginning of the month of August, 1628, some nine hundred Portuguese left the town of São Paulo with mus- kets, swords, cotton armor, bucklers, machetes, and much ammunition of shot and powder, and other arms. They were accompanied by two thou- sand two hundred Indians, unjustly taken captive on previous occasions, and also among them were the two judges of the same town of São Paulo, Sebastião Fernandes Camacho and Francisco de Paiva; two aldermen, Maurício de Castilho and Diogo Barbosa; the Procurator of the Town Council, Cristóvão Mendes; and the son, son-in- law, and brother of Amador Bueno, the senior judge of the town. [. . .]

With regard to the second point: The men of the company of Antônio Rapôso Tavares who committed these injuries which we are recording here had said many times before setting out from São Paulo that they had decided to plunder and destroy our settlements, and thus they purposely took the route to the Plains of the Iguaçu. Here, far removed from the towns of the Spaniards and isolated in these lonely regions, where twelve reductions or Indian settlements have already been built and others, for lack of priests, merely planned, we were settling and instructing the Indi- ans in their own lands with infinite toil and lack of necessities, being content to carry on for the love of God and for the salvation of those heathen. We suffered the poverty of the land in food and dress, planting vineyards and sowing wheat so as to have the host and wine for saying Mass.

When these bandits, then, had crossed the River Tibajiva on the 8th of September of that same year 1628, they built their palisade or fort of wooden stakes close by our villages. And—to show clearly the intention they had from the beginning—Antônio Pedroso, Captain of the advance guard of this Company, as soon as he arrived in these parts chanced upon some seven- teen Christian Indians from our settlement of Encarnación on the Ñatingui, who had left their wives and children in the village under the protec- tion of the Fathers and gone to the woods to col- lect mate, which they drink with warm or cold water after grinding it into powder. Pedroso seized them and carried them all off. . . .

Thereafter, although they continued most cru- elly to capture the heathen who, for lack of Fathers, had not yet been settled in reductions, wounding, killing, and mangling many old caciques and unbaptized children, they left us in peace with our wards for four months; and we treated them with friendliness, for in this way, although we could not arrest the many evils they were committing, we at least protected our reductions as best we could and those Indians who were again coming to us. And when it was necessary to dispatch some Indians of our village elsewhere we simply gave them a note begging the Portuguese to let them pass as our own sons; thus we treated the thief as a loyal friend, and they let them pass. Furthermore the Fathers went now and again to their palisade and baptized the children and the sick (for there were many afflicted with pox) to save them from eternal captivity since they could not be saved from the temporal one. The Portuguese themselves also sent for Father Pedro [Mola], who was in the village of San Antonio a day's journey from their palisade, to confess a Portuguese who was dying, although God would not allow it, depriving him of speech and reason the whole time the Father remained with him.

This false peace lasted until a very great cacique called Tatabrana who had many vassals—and whom Simão Álvares, a citizen of São Paulo, had unjustly captured a few years previously but who, desiring his freedom, soon fled and returned to his lands—came to deliver himself with all his people to the same Father Mola. They were Christians whom we had won over, shortly before the Portuguese entered those parts, by gifts and celebrations given in their honor when they entered our villages to see us, attracted by the good word which had gone forth concerning the peace and contentment enjoyed by the Indians who lived in them with us.

Then the Portuguese, thinking that they now had some pretext to carry out their wicked intention, sent to ask the Father for Tatabrana. And as the Father replied that he could not be turned over to them since he was free and in his own lands, they advised Captain Major Antônio Rapôso Tavares requesting his approval, and then, on the 30th of January, 1629, they came to take by force not only Tatabrana but also all the others whom the Father was instructing in the village of San Antonio. Thus, as they themselves admit, they took from it four thousand Indians or burden bearers along with a crowd of others, and they destroyed the entire village burning many houses, plundering the church and the Father's house, and desecrating an image of Our Lady. With great violence they removed the Indian men and women who had taken refuge in the Father's house, and they killed an Indian at the very door of the house, as well as another ten or twelve persons in the same village. They took most of the Father's meager belongings, including a few shirts, two blankets, shoes, hats, napkins, tablecloths, spoons, knives, ten or twelve iron wedges, and six or seven chickens that he had. They killed one of three cows they found, and took other small things. . . .

What is of gravest concern in this whole affair is that the Holy Gospel is now so disesteemed and its Preachers so discredited that—with the door now completely closed to the preaching of the Gospel among all those heathen—the Indians imagine and repeat that we did not gather them to teach them the law of God, as we told them, but to deliver them by this subterfuge to the Portuguese. They also say that we tricked them by telling them so often that they were safe with us and that the Portuguese, being Christians and vassals of the same king, would not touch nor harm those who were with the Fathers, for they were then Christians and children of God. Therefore, since an action so atrocious goes unpunished and with no effective remedy, it seems to me that we shall be forced to abandon all these heathen, whom year after year we have been gathering together and instructing by order of His Holiness and His Majesty with so much labor and hardship. . . .

And so that the multitude of the infidels which was already disposed to settle with the Fathers and embrace the Holy Faith may be better appreciated: In the village of Jesús María alone, Father Concovado had almost five thousand warriors not counting their crowd of women and little ones. Besides this, the caciques of Caayu . . . saw that because of the lack of Fathers (who, in villages as densely populated as those, were almost all distributed one by one) they could not achieve their good hopes of having priests in their lands to instruct them; so they themselves with their vassals went to the village of San Antonio, just recently plundered, to be there with the Father. They had not known of the shameless action of the Portuguese there, but when they saw the village destroyed, the houses burned and so many killed, they returned to their lands and now, from what they have seen, imagine that we are traitors and deceivers, and that we have secret intelligence with these Portuguese. And therefore, as some Indians who met these people on a journey have affirmed to us, many of them are now traveling in a band looking for Fathers to kill them. . . .

What we saw along the route [to São Paulo] was the inhumanity and cruelty with which [the Portuguese] treated the Indians. For the poor creatures were overworked and sick at heart to find themselves slaves with little hope of regaining their liberty. Against their will and resistance they were leaving their lands where they had lived most contentedly and amid great plenty; and they now had to cross many rivers, swamps, lakes, and mountains, making this long march on forty consecutive days from the palisade to São Paulo, carrying their little ones on their backs, seeing them turn sick and die from hunger, cold, exertions, the maltreatment of the Portuguese, and the rigors of the journey. They ate only the little that the Portuguese sometimes gave them, stolen from their own farms and plots, or else what they themselves had to search for in the forests and woods, fatigued from the day's journey—although not all were permitted to do this for fear they would escape. Besides all this, the Portuguese loaded them with their burdens, and many caciques as well as vassals (especially those from our reductions) were taken in chains to São Paulo. All day they were scolded and at night the Portuguese kept them from sleeping, wearing them out with constant shouting and sermonizing which they themselves did or ordered their Tupi to do, or else some of the recently captured caciques. The latter were on the one hand promised, to discourage their escaping, that they would have a very good life, both temporal and spiritual, with their houses and lands in São Paulo (as if perpetual captivity could be designated a life), and, on the other hand, the Indians were threatened that if they fled they would be killed, and in fact when someone did run away they sent their Tupi after him and when he was brought back he was cruelly whipped. . . .

Two Indians whom the Portuguese released to us after persistent importunities assert that when the Portuguese left the palisade they set fire to the huts and settlements, burning with them some of the aged and infirm, and, if some did manage to escape so as not to die in the flames, the Tupi in the presence of their masters forced them to return to the fire to expire in it. In this regard we might say here that the cruelty of the Tupi was no less than that of their masters and that they no less deserve to be punished than the Portuguese. . . .

But let us return to the Portuguese and consider the wiles they employ to deceive the courts and avoid the punishment which they deserve. This does not require much effort, for they have as companions in crime not only all the people of São Paulo but also the very judges and administrator of the council of this same town. However, so that they might have a way of deceiving the higher magistrates of the state (if it can be called deceit, against persons who witness enough cases of the constant entradas, carried out with so many wrongs and cruelties, to have no illusions about such clear and open deceits) they requested I know not what sort of legal writs. [. . .]

What we aspire to and came to seek on such long and wearying journeys by land and sea, with such toil and hardship, is some effective remedy for the past and for what is to come. For the past, we feel that there can be no proper satisfaction unless all the captured Indians are given their freedom, and unless all or most of them are returned to their lands and the reductions. In this way they can bear witness to those of their lands that we are innocent, that we did not deliver them to the Portuguese, and that we took measures here to try and secure their freedom. And moreover they can remove the bad opinion which the infidels not yet in reductions have already formed of us of the Company, that we are traitors and deceivers, and thus we would regain the credit which we enjoyed with them and without which it seems impossible to convert them to Our Holy Faith. As for the future, let some very exemplary punishment be fixed, or in some other fashion let an order be given that extortions and enslavements such as the men of São Paulo have carried on for so many years be henceforth prevented. . . .

It is said that simply the band of Antônio Rapôso Tavares which plundered our villages carried away as many as twenty thousand souls, and it is therefore certain that if a very genuine remedy is not supplied in the briefest time, they will soon destroy everything and depopulate these populous lands as they have done in most of the state of Brazil. . . .

There were those who for five, and others . . . who for seven continuous years, and even those who for eighteen years neglected their salvation and remained in those wilds capturing Indians and living in concubinage with as many Indian women as they wished. [. . .]

In this City of Salvador Bahia de Todos os Santos, October 10, 1629.

SIMÓN MACETA—JUSTO MANSILLA

24. António Vieira Promotes Human Rights

António Vieira, S.J. (1608-1697), may be considered the most remarkable Portuguese personality, public servant, writer, orator, and "human rights" advocate of the early modern era. Amerindians, Jews, Africans—all were subjects of his concern and compassion despite his nation's and era's images of them.

In this Lenten sermon of 1653, Father Vieira plays the roles of both prophet and pastor and apparently demonstrates their incompatibility. The prophetic Vieira celebrates human freedom in the first two-thirds of the reading (up to the paragraph ending "your own sweat than from the blood of others"). The final third reveals Vieira's attempt, as pastor to the Portuguese colonizers as well as defender of the Amerindians, to lure the former into salvation. But to achieve success in this endeavor, what does Vieira have to do? Are the prophetic and the pastoral indeed incompatible? Again, how would Vieira's "solution" affect the Amerindians' understanding and reception of "conversion"?

Christians, nobles, and people of Maranhão, do you know what God wants of you during this Lent? That you break the chains of injustice and let free those whom you have captive and oppressed. These are the sins of Maranhão; these are what God commanded me to denounce to you. Christians, God commanded me to clarify these matters to you and so I do it. All of you are in mortal sin; all of you live in a state of condemnation; and all of you are going directly to Hell. Indeed, many are there now and you will soon join them if you do not change your life.

Is it possible that an entire people live in sin, that an entire people will go to hell? Who questions thus does not understand the evil of unjust captivity. The sons of Israel went down into Egypt, and after the death of Joseph, the Pharaoh seized them and made slaves of them. God wanted to liberate those miserable people, and He sent Moses there with no other escort than a rod. God knew that in order to free the captives a rod was sufficient, even though He was dealing with a ruler as tyrannical as Pharaoh and with a people as cruel as the Egyptians. When Pharaoh refused to free the captives, the plagues rained down upon him. The land was covered with frogs and the air clouded with mosquitoes; the rivers flowed with blood; the clouds poured forth thunder and lightning. All Egypt was dumbfounded and threatened with death. Do you know what brought those plagues to the earth? Unjust captivity. Who brought to Maranhão the plague of the Dutch? Who brought the smallpox? Who brought hunger and drought? These captives. Moses insisted and pressed the Pharaoh to free the people, and what did Pharaoh respond? He said one thing and he did another.

Source: Afrânio Peixoto, ed., *Vieira Brazileiro* (Paris: Ailland et Bertrand, 1921), 1:203-21, trans. and ed. E. Bradford Burns in *A Documentary History of Brazil* (New York: Alfred A. Knopf, 1966), 83-88.

What he said was, I do not know God and I do not have to free the captives. However, it appears to me proper and I do declare them free. Do you know why you do not give freedom to your illicitly gotten slaves? Because you do not know God. Lack of Faith is the cause of everything. If you possessed true faith, if you believed that there was an eternal Hell, then you would not take so lightly the captivity of a single Tapuya. [. . .]

Any man who deprives others of their freedom and being able to restore that freedom does not do so is condemned. All or nearly all are therefore condemned. You will say to me that even if this were true they did not think about it or know it and that their good faith will save them. I deny that. They did think about it and know it just as you think of it and know it. If they did not think of it nor know it, they ought to have thought of it and to have known it. Some are condemned by their knowledge, others by their doubt, and still others by their ignorance. . . . If only the graves would open and some who died in that unhappy state could appear before you, and in the fire of their misery you could clearly read this truth. Do you know why God does not permit them to appear before you? It is exactly as Abraham said to the rich miser when he asked him to send Lazarus to this world: *Habent Moysen et Prophetas* (Luc. 16.29). It is not necessary for one to appear on earth from Hell to tell you the truth because you already have Moses and the Law, you have the prophets and learned men. My brothers, if there are any among you who doubt this, here are the laws, here are the learned men, question them. There are in this State, three religious orders which have members of great virtue and learning. Ask them. Study the matter and inform yourselves. But it is not necessary to question the religious: go to Turkey, go to Hell, because there is no Turk so Turkish in Turkey nor no devil so devilish in Hell who will tell you that a free man can be a slave. Is there one among you with natural intelligence who can deny it? What do you doubt?

I know what you are going to tell me . . . our people, our country, but government cannot be sustained without Indians. Who will fetch a pail of water for us or carry a load of wood? Who will grind our manioc? Will our wives have to do it? Will our sons? In the first place, this is not the state into which I am placing you as you soon will see. But when necessity and conscience require such a thing, I answer yes and repeat again yes. You, your wives, your sons, all of us are able to sustain ourselves with our own labor. It is better to live from your own sweat than from the blood of others! [. . .]

I have studied the matter carefully and in accordance with the most lenient and favorable opinions and have come to a conclusion by which, with only minor worldly losses, all the inhabitants of this state can ease their consciences and build for a better future. Give me your attention.

All the Indians of this State are either those who serve as slaves or those who live as free inhabitants in the King's villages, or those who live in the hinterlands in their natural or free condition. These latter are the ones you go upriver to buy or "to rescue" (as they say), giving the pious verb "to rescue" to a sale so involuntary and violent that at times it is made at pistol point. These are held, owned, and bequeathed in bad faith: therefore they will be doing no small task if they forgive you for their past treatment. However, if after you have set them free, they, particularly those domestics whom you raised in your house and treated as your children, spontaneously and voluntarily wish to continue to serve you and remain in your home, no one will or can separate them from your service. And what will happen to those who do not wish to remain in your service? These will be obliged to live in the King's villages where they also will serve you in the manner which I shall mention. Each year you will be able to make your expeditions into the interior during which time you can really rescue those who are prisoners ready to be eaten. Those justly saved from death will remain your slaves. Also, all those captured in just wars will be made slaves. Upon this matter the proper judges will be the Governor of the State, the Chief Justice of the State, the Vicars of Maranhão or of Pará, and the Prelates of the four orders: Carmelite, Franciscan, Mercedarian, and the Company of Jesus. All of these who after judgment are qualified to be true captives, will be returned to the inhabitants. And what will happen to those captured in a war not classified as just? All of them will be placed in new villages or divided among the villages which exist today. There, along with the other village Indians they will be hired out to the inhabitants of this State to work for them for six months of every year alternating two months of hired work with two months devoted to their own labors and families. Thus, in this manner, all the Indians of this State will serve the Portuguese either as legitimate slaves, that is those rescued from death or captured in a just war, or those former slaves who freely and voluntarily wish to serve their old masters, or those from the King's villages who will work half the year for the good and growth of the State. It only remains to set the wages of those village Indians for their labor and service. It is a subject which would make any other nation of the world laugh and only in this land is not appreciated. The money of this land is cloth and cotton, and the ordinary price for which the Indians work and will work each month is seven feet of this cloth which has a market value of about twenty cents. An Indian will work for less than a penny a day. It is an insignificant amount and it is unworthy of a man of reason and of Christian faith not to pay such a slight price to save his soul and to avoid Hell.

Could there be anything more moderate? Could there be anything more reasonable than this? Whoever is dissatisfied or discontent with this proposal either is not a Christian or has no understanding.

25. Competing Missionary Perspectives

So far this anthology has concentrated on the incursions of the Spaniards into the Caribbean, the Portuguese into Brazil, and the religious commitments of such conquistadors as Cortés. Now the early missionary friars in New Spain will speak.

Motolinía ("poor little one" in Nahuatl), Toribio de Benavente, O.F.M. (c. 1495-c. 1569), one of the original twelve Franciscans to arrive in New Spain (Mexico) in 1524, was both a fervent pastor to and educator of the Amerindians and author of History of the Indians of New Spain *(c. 1540). In this passage he describes the situation of one group of Amerindians in central Mexico.*

His contemporary, the Dominican friar Tomás Ortiz, describes in 1524 another group of Amerindians who are located near Santa Marta on the northern coast of today's Colombia. Obviously there is no reason why both descriptions cannot be true despite their clear contradictions of each other. But can either be taken at face value? Does each description reveal as much about the author as about the Amerindians? Why might these descriptions help in understanding the nature of the missionary vocation? ". . . if they wish to take the discipline"; what does this phrase suggest about the "conversion" process?

[Motolinía]

There is hardly anything to hinder the Indians from reaching heaven, nothing like the obstacles which hinders us Spaniards and which submerge us. The Indians live in contentment, though what they possess is so little that they have hardly enough to clothe and nourish themselves. Their meal is extremely poor and the same is true of their clothing; for sleep the majority of them have

SOURCE: Francis Borgia Steck, O.F.M., trans., *Motolinía's History of the Indians of New Spain* (Washington, D.C.: Academy of American Franciscan History, 1951), 148-49. Reprinted by permission of American Academy of Franciscan History. Quoted by Germán Arciniegas, *Latin America: A Cultural History,* trans. Joan MacLean (New York: Alfred A. Knopf, 1967), 149-50.

not even a whole mat. They lose no sleep over acquiring and guarding riches, nor do they kill themselves trying to obtain ranks and dignities. They go to bed in their poor blanket and on awakening are immediately ready to serve God; and if they wish to take the discipline, they are neither troubled nor embarrassed with dressing and undressing. They are patient, exceedingly long-suffering, meek as lambs. I do not recall having ever seen them nurturing an injury. They are humble, obedient to all, either of necessity or voluntarily; all they know is to serve and work. They all know how to build a wall and erect a dwelling, to twist a rope, and to engage in such crafts as do not require much skill. Great is their patience and endurance in time of sickness. Their mattress is the hard and bare ground. At most, they have only a ragged mat to sleep on and for a pillow a stone or a piece of wood, while some have no other pillow than the bare earth. Their dwellings are very small, some with a very low roof, others with a roof of straw, while some dwellings resemble the cell of that holy abbot Hilarion, looking more like a grave than a dwelling. The riches that suffice to fill such dwellings show what treasures the Indians have! These Indians live in their little houses—the parents, the children, and the grandchildren. They eat and drink without much noise and talking. They spend their days peacefully and amicably. They seek only what is necessary to sustain life.

[Ortiz]

The men on the mainland of the Indies eat human flesh and are more sodomistic than any generation. There is no justice among them, they go about naked, they feel neither love nor shame, they are asses, stupid, mad, insane; to kill or be killed is all the same to them; they have no truth in them unless it be to their advantage; they are inconstant; they do not know what counsel is; they are ingrates and fond of novelties; they boast of their drunkenness; they distill wine from various herbs, fruits, roots, and grain; they also get drunk on smoke and on certain herbs that steal away their brains; they are bestial in their vices; neither obedience nor courtesy do the young boys show to the old, nor sons to their father; nor are they capable of learning from doctrine and punishment; they are treacherous, cruel, vengeful, for they never forgive; extremely inimical toward religion, idlers, thieves, liars, and poor and mean in judgment; they keep neither faith nor order; men do not stay faithful to their wives, nor wives to their husbands; they are sorcerers, soothsayers, and necromancers; they are as cowardly as rabbits, as dirty as pigs; they eat lice, spiders, and raw worms wherever they find them; they have neither the art nor the dexterity of men; when they forget the matters of faith they have learned, they say that such things are for Castile and not for them, and they wish not to change customs or gods; they are beardless, and if some beard hairs sprout, they pull them out; they treat the sick with no pity at all; even though they be neighbors and kinsmen they leave them helpless at the moment of death; or else they carry them into the wilderness to die with a sup of bread and water; the older they grow the worse they are; up to the age of ten or twelve years, it seems to me they come forth with some breeding or virtue; from then on they become as brute beasts. In short, I say that God never created people so steeped in vices and bestiality, with no leaven of goodness or politeness.

26. The Franciscan Method

Andrés de Moguer, a young but learned theologian educated at Salamanca, arrived in New Spain in 1533, rapidly acquired the Nahua language, and commenced active missionary life.

Source: Published in Spanish in *Cartas de Indias*, 123-24. Cited, translated, and edited by James Lockhart and Enrique Otte, *Letters and Peoples of the Spanish Indies: Sixteenth Century* (Cambridge: Cambridge University Press, 1976), 216-17. Reprinted with the permission of Cambridge University Press.

"Conversion"

He eventually became confessor of Viceroy Mendoza and a judge of the Inquisition. He died as a result of caring for victims of plague.

His 1554 letter reveals much about the reality of the "conversion" process in the thirty years since the famous "Twelve" Franciscans arrived in 1524. Moguer wants the Council of the Indies, the ministry in Spain responsible for determining and enforcing policy in the colonies, to compel the Franciscans to give up their near monopoly on "converting" the Amerindians so that other orders, with better techniques, may join in the process.

What is that Franciscan approach? How do Amerindians apparently react to it? Might not the archbishop's action be deemed a revelation? If so, of what?

Very powerful lords:

To the glory of our God and Lord and His honor and with royal favor, we have here in New Spain nineteen houses of friars in Indian towns, with four to six friars in each one, and even in the smallest one two friars, not counting three other houses that we have in the Spanish towns, which are here in Mexico City, in Puebla and in Oaxaca; in these three houses the friars are numerous and there is higher instruction in the necessary sciences, and we teach the faith and good customs that are necessary to instruct and indoctrinate the natives. In these houses we also treat the friars who fall ill in the Indian towns, and punish those who are delinquent because, with our weaknesses, everything is necessary.

Following the counsel of the oldest and wisest, that those who have taken the habit in this country should be taught before they teach, it has been necessary to occupy ourselves in that effort for some time, and during that time the very reverend Franciscan fathers, imitating the holy apostles, have taken and occupied three fourths of the country, though they do not have enough friars for it, because in towns where ten or twelve ministers are needed they content themselves with having one or two. In most places they are content to say a mass once a year; consider what sort of indoctrination they can give them! His lordship the archbishop, wishing as pastor to remedy the situation and give ministers to his flock, has given some towns to others, but the natives have not

been willing to obey them or give them food, on the advice, it is said, of a fray Pedro de Gante, lay brother of the order of St. Francis, and the archbishop in annoyance had four or five of them given a lashing in jail, but even then they will not obey him.

We wish you to know that existing, as indeed there exist, such high abilities in the order of Saint Augustine, and in ours of Saint Dominic, and desire to learn these languages, the friars of Saint Francis have occupied a land as large as the Mexican using only one language, where more than two hundred languages are necessary, and they prevent the entry of other friars; this is clear, because the Indians say they want no others than the fathers of Saint Francis, and will not feed those whom the archbishop sends. As it concerns the royal conscience, they should be ordered not to intrude in more than they can accomplish, since we all preach one God and one faith, and not to permit so many souls to go to perdition because they cannot give them sufficient instruction, and to obey his lordship the archbishop as prelate and pastor that he is of all, and for the ministers his lordship assigns to be received, since he was given their governance. And you should write to the provincial superior of Saint Francis who resides here in New Spain, giving him these orders. From Mexico City, 10th of December, 1554.

Your highness' servant and chaplain,
Fray Andrés de Moguer

27. Motolinía Attacks Las Casas

Motolinía's letter to Charles I (1555) is useful for five different concerns: the status of Spanish-Amerindian relations some thirty-four years after the conquest of Tenochtitlan (see A, C, D); the status of the "conversion" of the Amerindians (A); problems facing missionaries venturing into unknown territories (B); the conflict between pastor and prophet (E); and fifth, the last sentence of (D).

[A]   Your majesty, when the Marqués del Valle [Cortés] entered this land, God our Lord was very offended with it; people suffered the cruelest of deaths, and our adversary the demon was very pleased with the greatest idolatries and most cruel homicides there ever were, because the predecessor of Moctezuma, lord of Mexico, called Ahuitzotzin, offered to the idols in a single temple and in one sacrifice that lasted three or four days, 80,400 men, whom they brought along four streets, in four lines, until they reached the sacrificial block before the idols. And at the time when the Christians entered New Spain, more than ever before there was sacrificing and killing of men before the idols in all the towns and provinces. Every day and every hour they offered human blood to the demons, in all the towns and districts of all this country, aside from many other sacrifices and services to the demons that they performed, not only in the demons' temples, of which almost the whole country was full, but on all the roads and in all the houses; all the people were devoted to the service of the demons and the idols. Now these and many other abominations, sins, and offenses made publicly to God and neighbors have been prevented and removed, our holy Catholic faith implanted, the cross of Jesus Christ and the confession of his holy name raised everywhere, and God has brought about a great conversion of people, in which many souls have been saved and are being saved every day; and many churches and monasteries have been built, with more than fifty monasteries inhabited by Franciscan friars alone, not to speak of our monasteries in Guatemala and Yucatán, and this whole country is in peace and justice. If your majesty could only see how the church festivals are celebrated all over New Spain and with what devotion the rites of Holy Week are observed, and all the Sundays and holidays, you would give praise and thanks to God a thousand times. This Las Casas is wrong in what he says, writes, prints and urges. It will be necessary that I tell where his zeal and works lead and what they end in, and whether he aided the Indians or vexed them. [...]

For the love of God, your majesty, take pity on those souls, have compassion and sorrow for the offenses against God being committed there, and prevent the idolatries and sacrifices being performed there to the demons; order, with the greatest speed and in the best way available to you as the anointed of God and captain of his holy church, that the holy gospel be preached to those Indian infidels.

[B]   Not in the way ordered by Las Casas, who gained nothing more than 2,000 or 3,000 pesos in costs to your majesty for providing and outfitting a ship in which some Dominican fathers went to preach to the Indians of Florida with the instructions he gave them. The moment they touched land half of them were killed, right at the port, before reaching the town; the others went fleeing back to the ship and came here to tell how they had escaped. But your majesty need not spend much, nor send much from Spain, beyond your order, and then I trust in God that a great spiritual and temporal gain will ensue. Here in New Spain

SOURCE: *Colección de documentos inéditos relativos al descubrimiento, conquista y colonización de las antiguas posesiones españoles (sic) en América y Oceanía*, 7:254-89, in *Letters and Peoples of the Spanish Indies: Sixteenth Century*, trans. and ed. James Lockhart and Enrique Otte (London, New York, Melbourne: Cambridge University Press, 1976), 221-23, 224, 230-31, 232, 237-38. Reprinted with the permission of Cambridge University Press.

are all the means required, because there are experienced friars who, given orders, will obediently go and expose themselves to all risks to help in the salvation of those souls; also there are many Spaniards here, and horses and livestock. All the survivors of Soto's company who came here, and there are quite a few of them, wish to go back there because of the goodness of the country. [. . .]

[C]   And so that what he says or prints may be better understood, may your majesty know that about five or six years ago I was ordered by your majesty and your Council of the Indies to collect certain confessionals that Las Casas left here in New Spain, handwritten, among the friars. I sought out all those to be found among the Franciscans and gave them to don Antonio de Mendoza, your viceroy, and he burned them, because they contained false and scandalous statements. Now, in the last ships to reach New Spain, there have arrived the same confessionals in print, which has caused a great outcry and scandal throughout the land, because many times he gives the conquerors, encomenderos and merchants the names of tyrants, robbers, violators, ravishers and thieves. He says that always and every day they are oppressing the Indians; he also says that all the tributes from the Indians have been and are being taken evilly, unjustly and tyrannically. If that were so, a fine state your majesty's conscience would be in, since your majesty draws from half or more of the most important towns and provinces of New Spain, and the encomenderos and conquerors have only what your majesty orders them to be given. And as far as the Indians receiving moderate tribute quotas, and being well treated and looked after, through the goodness of God today they almost all are; and as to justice and religion being administered to them, that is what is being done. Even so, this Las Casas maintains what he has said, and more; his principal insult or insults are to your majesty, and he condemns the learned men of your councils, often calling them unjust and tyrannical. And he also insults and condemns all the men of the law that there are and have been in all New Spain, whether ecclesiastic or secular, and your majesty's Audiencias and their regents.

[D]   Las Casas also says that of everything the Spaniards have, there is nothing that is not stolen; in this he insults your majesty and everyone who has come here, those who brought property with them as well as those who have bought and acquired it justly, and he dishonors them in writing and in print. Are the Spanish nation and its prince then to be thus insolently defamed, so that tomorrow the Indians and other nations may read it? And he also says that in all these years there has never been a just conquest or war against Indians. God provides the things to come, and he alone knows them, or such persons as his divine majesty should wish to reveal them to; now Las Casas in the things he says wants to be a soothsayer or prophet, but he will not be a true prophet, for the Lord says: this gospel will be preached in all the universe before the end of the world. Thus it is your majesty's mission to give haste to the preaching of the holy gospel through all these lands, and with those who will not willingly hear the holy gospel of Jesus Christ, let it be by force, for here one can apply the proverb 'better good forced on you than bad you desire.' [. . .]

[E]   I would like to see Las Casas persevere for fifteen or twenty years in confessing ten or twelve sick, ailing Indians daily, and an equal number of healthy old ones who never confessed before and see to many other things, many of them spiritual, concerning the Indians. A fine thing it is that there in Spain, to show his zeal, he says to your majesty and those of your councils: So-and-so is no friend of the Indians, he is a friend of the Spaniards; do not believe him. May it please God that he manages to be a friend of God and of his own soul. What he is concerned about there is harm done to the Indians, or lands the Spaniards request here in New Spain, or livestock rights granted them prejudicial to the Indians. This is no longer the time that was, because now he who does harm worth two pesos pays four, and he who does harm worth five pays eight. [. . .]

If the things Las Casas writes were true, certainly your majesty would have great reason to complain of all those you have sent here, and they would be worthy of great punishments, the bishops and prelates, who would all be obliged to lay down their responsibilities and appeal to God and king to conserve their flocks. Yet we see that the good bishops of New Spain persevere in working at their tasks and duties, hardly resting day or night. And your majesty would have grounds to complain of the judges and presiding officers that you have appointed to Audiencias everywhere, with high salaries; in New Spain alone there are Audiencias in Mexico City, New Galicia, and Guatemala, and all of these sleep soundly, content to have resting on their consciences so many sins of others as Las Casas says.

28. Mission Zeal Declines

The first reading below makes clear the kinds of problems faced by Alonso de Montúfar (c. 1489-1572), second archbishop of Mexico. (The archbishopric was a large region in the valley of Mexico, which included Mexico City.) What were the problems Montúfar faced during his eighteen-year tenure as archbishop? What categories do they fall into? What does this suggest about the "conversion" process?

The second reading is by Jerónimo de Mendieta, O.F.M. (1525-1604), missionary, mystic, historian, anthropologist, and scourge of Jews, Muslims, heretics, and idolaters. He spent some forty-five years in New Spain. By 1596 he had completed a vast account of the conversion and current religious state of the Amerindians, the famous Historia Ecclesiastica Indiana.

Does Mendieta confirm, refute, or modify Montúfar's account of the status of the church in the archdiocese of Mexico? Compare the two accounts of the reality of the conversion process by these highly committed friars, Dominican and Franciscan, whose mentality was typical of Christian Europe at the time, with the accounts by Motolinía and Moguer. Compare them also with Motolinía's version of Las Casas's position on the correct procedure for conversion.

[Montúfar]

The state of the church is this. In some parts there are monasteries of two or three friars, more frequently two, who live in one center and visit the country within a radius of two to thirty or more leagues around. One priest remains in the monastery while the other visits sometimes twenty or more head towns to which still others are subordinate. So the two friars frequently have charge of over one hundred thousand souls. The towns are visited anywhere from once in two weeks to once in six months and in some cases not more than two or three times in five years; moreover, the visits are of necessity hurried. The priest arrives late, baptizes and marries those who are waiting, says mass and passes on. The people come in at times to the center of the circuit for mass and the sacraments. . . .

The friars do not like to go out of the monastery to confess the sick. They say it is not the practice of their Order and they only do it of their own free will and as an act of charity. . . .

Here in Mexico City we would not think it a small matter if as many as three or four thousand, out of the fifty or sixty thousand who are accustomed to confess at all, should make confession in a single year. The rest of the Indians never confess. . . . There are some who have not confessed in four, ten, or even twenty years, and others in their

SOURCE: Alonso de Montúfar, quoted in "Carta del arzobispo al Consejo Real," *Colección de documentos inéditos,* 4:494-99, excerpted and translated in Charles S. Braden, *Religious Aspects of the Conquest of Mexico* (Durham, N.C.: Duke University Press, 1930), 1:247-49; Gerónimo de Mendieta, quoted in García Icazbalceta, ed., *Nueva colección de documentos,* 4, excerpted and translated in Braden, *Religious Aspects,* 1:249.

whole lives have not done so; yet in the number of priests this is the best provided for of all the provinces, and the best Christians are here. If it is thus here, what is the case in other places where only once in a long time do they ever see a priest?

Herein is the great need for ministers. . . . Nearly all the people die without confession or other sacrament than baptism. . . .

There is great rivalry among the Orders. Even though there be but one monastery and two friars in an area where not even a dozen would suffice, one Order is unwilling that another come in to help. Each defends its territory as if the villages were its own property. There has been and is great feeling between the Orders, not about which can best care for the flock, but which can have the greatest number of places and provinces in its hands; and so they go, occupying the best centers, building monasteries close together (a league and a half apart) not wishing to live in the difficult and needy places. If we assign a priest to help them, they cause the Indians not to admit him. . . . So great is the fear which the Indians have of the friars because of the severe punishment they practice upon them that they do not dare to complain. And if this is true in the province of Mexico, what of the mountains?

Things being as I have described, and no priest will deny it, very little fruit, it may be suspected, has come of the gospel among the people. Taking out the children, how very few adults have been saved or will be saved? From what has been said and will be said you can easily conjecture. . . .

If the gospel consisted only of holy baptism, we might believe in the salvation of the majority of the people, but since it is true that it is necessary, besides being baptized, to believe and do and perform penance for sins, it would require some new theology to believe and say that some of these adults are saved.

With regard to belief, the fault which we find is that they do not believe those things which are commonly thought by theologians to be necessary, such as the articles of faith and the mysteries which the church celebrates. Many of the people know the articles of faith and the prayers of the church fairly well, though many do not know them, and, of those who do know them, many say them like parrots, without knowing what they mean.

With regard to works and penance, this people is much inclined to vices and carnal practices. Rare are the women who are chaste. They are inclined to drunkenness, stealing, lying, and taking usury. . . . There are few vices they will not commit, and so great is their lack of firmness in the faith that if any other great power, greater than the gospel should come along it would sweep them off their feet. [. . .]

[Mendieta]

From what we see and hear in our congregations, everywhere the superiors are resigning. In visiting the convents one hardly finds a single monk who is content and happy. Discontent is manifest everywhere; many are seeking leave to return to Spain. It is a miracle to find a friar who is seriously trying to learn the language, for those who know it use it with so little satisfaction and profit. . . . The old fervor and enthusiasm for the salvation of souls seems to have disappeared. The primitive spirit is dead. The newly converted Indians no longer throng the churches to hear the word, confess or receive the sacraments, etc.

29. Serpentine Prudence

In the prologue to book 4 of the Historia, *Sahagún makes the intriguing declaration printed below.*

SOURCE: Bernardino de Sahagún, quoted in Miguel León-Portilla, *Endangered Cultures*, trans. Julie Goodson-Lawes (Dallas: Southern Methodist University Press, 1990), 59-61. Reprinted by permission of Southern Methodist University Press.

SERPENTINE PRUDENCE

Does that "serpentine prudence" appear in the manner in which any of the four previous authors (Motolinía, Moguer, Montúfar, and Mendieta—readings 25, 26, 28) criticize the evangelization process? How do the four authors' criticisms compare with Sahagún's analysis of Mexica religious culture? Are they concerned with the same issues? What does the comparison reveal about Sahagún, whose sympathy for Mexica culture is evident in his meticulous description of all its aspects?

They (the first evangelists) did not forget in their preaching the warning that the Redeemer left his disciples and apostles when he told them: *estote prudentes sicut serpentes et simplices sicut columbae*: be prudent like serpents and simple as doves. And though they proceeded with caution in the second, they failed in the first, and even the idolaters themselves noticed, in that they (the first evangelists) lacked that serpentine prudence and thus with their sly humility they quickly offered themselves to receive the faith that was being preached to them. But they remained deceitful in that they did not detest or renounce all their gods with all their customs, and thus they were baptized not like perfect believers but as fictitious ones, who received that faith without leaving the false one they had of many gods. This cover-up was not understood in the beginning, and the main reason for this was the opinion that the above-mentioned preachers had of their perfect faith, and thus they affirmed it to all the ministers of the gospel who happened to preach to these people. . . .

All of us were told (as had already been told to the Dominican fathers) that this people had come to the faith so sincerely and were almost all baptized and so wholly in the Catholic faith of the Roman Church that there was no need to preach against idolatry because they had abandoned it so truly. We accepted this information as very true and miraculous, because in such a short time and with so little preaching and knowledge of the language, and without any miracles, so many people had been converted. . . . It was discovered after a few years very evidently the lack of serpentine prudence that there was in the founding of the new Church, because they were ignorant of the conspiracy that had been made among the principals and native priests, to receive Jesus Christ among their gods as one of them and to honor him like the Spaniards honor him, according to their ancient custom wherein when foreigners arrived to settle near those who were already settled, when it pleased them they would take as a god the one brought by the recently arrived and in this manner they say the Tezcatlipoca is the god of those from Tlalmanalco, because they brought him with them, and Huitzilopochtli is the god of the Mexicans because they brought him with them. . . .

In this fashion they easily accepted as a god the god of the Spaniards, but not in order to leave their ancient ones, and this they hid during the catechism when they were baptized, and during the catechism when they were asked if they believed in God the Father, the Son, and the Holy Spirit, along with the other articles of the faith, they would respond "*quemachca*," yes, in accordance with the conspiracy and custom that they had; and asked whether they disowned all the other gods they had adored, they would also respond "*quemachca*," yes, deceitfully and lying. . . . and thus this new Church was established over a false foundation, and even after having put some buttresses, it is still damaged and ruined.

30. The Unchanging Spanish Mission, 1600-1800

Alexander von Humboldt (1769-1859) was a Prussian Protestant scientist, very much the product of the European Enlightenment and, because of his intellectual curiosity, open-mindedness, and astute observations, one of its finest representatives.

The Spanish Crown granted him permission to travel through its American dominions from 1799 to 1804. His report on the remote Venezuelan missions, run by the Capuchin friars, represents a mixture of acute observation and insightful interpretation deeply sympathetic to the Amerindian yet mildly Eurocentric.

How does von Humboldt evaluate the Capuchins' approach? What does he suggest are the positive and negative factors in settling the nomadic Amerindians in villages and easing them into Spanish culture? Von Humboldt makes his observations during what will be the last years of the three-hundred-year-old Spanish empire in the New World (except for Cuba and Puerto Rico). Does his description of the Capuchins as missionaries, pastors, and authority figures resemble accounts by others? By whom? Is indeed von Humboldt only "mildly Eurocentric"?

[T]he Conquistadores, by the continuation of their incursions, prolonged the system of petty warfare, which diminished the American population, perpetuated national animosities, and during a long period crushed the seeds of rising civilization. At length the missionaries, under the protection of the secular arm, spoke words of peace. It was the privilege of religion to console humanity for a part of the evils committed in its name; to plead the cause of the natives before kings, to resist the violence of the commendataries, and to assemble wandering tribes into small communities called Missions.

But these institutions, useful at first in stopping the effusion of blood, and in laying the first basis of society, have become in their result hostile to its progress. The effects of this insulated system have been such that the Indians have remained in a state little different from that in which they existed whilst yet their scattered dwellings were not collected round the habitation of a missionary. Their number has considerably augmented, but the sphere of their ideas is not enlarged. They have progressively lost that vigour of character and that natural vivacity which in every state of society are the noble fruits of independence. By subjecting to invariable rules even the slightest actions of their domestic life, they have been rendered stupid by the effort to render them obedient. Their subsistence is in general more certain, and their habits more pacific, but subject to the constraint and the dull monotony of the government of the Missions, they show by their gloomy and reserved looks that they have not sacrificed their liberty to their repose without regret.

On the 4th of September, at five in the morning, we began our journey to the Missions of the Chayma Indians and the group of lofty mountains, which traverse New Andalusia. [...]

This was the first Mission we saw in America. The houses, or rather the huts of the Chayma Indians, though separate from each other, are not surrounded by gardens. The streets, which are wide and very strait, cross each other at right angles. The walls of the huts are made of clay, strengthened by lianas. The uniformity of these huts, the grave and taciturn air of their inhabitants, and the extreme neatness of the dwellings, reminded us of the establishments of the Moravian Brethren. Besides their own gardens, every Indian family helps to cultivate the garden of the community, or, as it is called, the *conuco de la*

Source: Alexander von Humboldt and Aimé Bonpland, *Personal Narrative of Travels to the Equionctial Regions of America during the Years 1799-1804*, trans. and ed. Thomasina Ross (London: Henry G. Bohn, 1852), 1:201-2, 218-19, 245-46, 252, 296-97.

comunidad, which is situated at some distance from the village. In this conuco the adults of each sex work one hour in the morning and one in the evening. In the missions nearest the coast the garden of the community is generally a sugar or indigo plantation, under the direction of the missionary; and its produce, if the law were strictly observed, could be employed only for the support of the church and the purchase of sacerdotal ornaments. The great square of San Fernando, in the centre of the village, contains the church, the dwelling of the missionary, and a very humble-looking edifice pompously called the king's house (Casa del Rey). This is a caravanserai, destined for lodging travellers; and, as we often experienced, infinitely valuable in a country where the name of an inn is still unknown. [. . .]

The missionary of San Fernando was a Capuchin, a native of Aragon, far advanced in years, but strong and healthy. His extreme corpulency, his hilarity, the interest he took in battles and sieges, ill accorded with the ideas we form in northern countries of the melancholy reveries and the contemplative life of missionaries. Though extremely busy about a cow which was to be killed next day, the old monk received us with kindness, and permitted us to hang up our hammocks in a gallery of his house. Seated, without doing anything, the greater part of the day, in an armchair of red wood, he bitterly complained of what he called the indolence and ignorance of his countrymen. Our missionary, however, seemed well satisfied with his situation. He treated the Indians with mildness; he beheld his Mission prosper, and he praised with enthusiasm the waters, the bananas, and the dairy-produce of the district. The sight of our instruments, our books, and our dried plants, drew from him a sarcastic smile; and he acknowledged, with the naïveté peculiar to the inhabitants of those countries, that of all the enjoyments of life, without excepting sleep, none was comparable to the pleasure of eating good beef (carne de vaca): thus does sensuality obtain an ascendancy, where there is no occupation for the mind. [. . .]

Towards evening we reached the Mission of Guanaguana, the site of which is almost on a level with the village of San Antonio. The missionary received us cordially; he was an old man, and he

seemed to govern his Indians with great intelligence. The village has existed only thirty years on the spot it now occupies. Before that time it was more to the south, and was backed by a hill. It is astonishing with what facility the Indians are induced to remove their dwellings. There are villages in South America which in less than half a century have thrice changed their situation. The native finds himself attached by ties so feeble to the soil he inhabits, that he receives with indifference the order to take down his house and to rebuild it elsewhere. A village changes its situation like a camp. Wherever clay, reeds, and the leaves of the palm or heliconia are found, a house is built in a few days. These compulsory changes have often no other motive than the caprice of a missionary, who, having recently arrived from Spain, fancies that the situation of the Mission is feverish, or that it is not sufficiently exposed to the winds. Whole villages have been transported several leagues, merely because the monk did not find the prospect from his house sufficiently beautiful or extensive.

Guanaguana has as yet no church. The old monk, who during thirty years had lived in the forests of America, observed to us that the money of the community, or the produce of the labour of the Indians, was employed first in the construction of the missionary's house, next in that of the church, and lastly in the clothing of the Indians. He gravely assured us that this order of things could not be changed on any pretence, and that the Indians, who prefer a state of nudity to the slightest clothing, are in no hurry for their turn in the destination of the funds. The spacious abode of the *padre* had just been finished, and we had remarked with surprise, that the house, the roof of which formed a terrace, was furnished with a great number of chimneys that looked like turrets. This, our host told us, was done to remind him of a country dear to his recollection, and to picture to his mind the winters of Aragon amid the heat of the torrid zone. The Indians of Guanaguana cultivate cotton for their own benefit as well as for that of the church and the missionary. [. . .]

We were received with great hospitality by the monks of Caripe. The building has an inner court, surrounded by an arcade, like the convents in

Spain. This enclosed place was highly convenient for setting up our instruments and making observations. We found a numerous society in the convent. Young monks, recently arrived from Spain, were just about to settle in the Missions, while old infirm missionaries sought for health in the fresh and salubrious air of the mountains of Caripe. I was lodged in the cell of the superior, which contained a pretty good collection of books. I found there, to my surprise, the *Teatro Crítico* of Feijoó, the *Lettres Edifiantes*, and the *Traité d' Electricité* by abbé Nollet. It seemed as if the progress of knowledge advanced even in the forests of America. The youngest of the capuchin monks of the last Mission had brought with him a Spanish translation of Chaptal's Treatise on Chemistry, and he intended to study this work in the solitude where he was destined to pass the remainder of his days. During our long abode in the Missions of South America we never perceived any sign of intolerance. The monks of Caripe were not ignorant that I was born in the protestant part of Germany. Furnished as I was with orders from the court of Spain, I had no motives to conceal from them this fact; nevertheless, no mark of distrust, no indiscreet question, no attempt at controversy, ever diminished the value of the hospitality they exercised with so much liberality and frankness. [...]

Under the temperate zone, whether in the *provincias internas* of Mexico, or in Kentucky, the contact of European colonists has been fatal to the natives, because that contact is immediate.

These causes have no existence in the greater part of South America. Agriculture, within the tropics, does not require great extent of ground. The whites advance slowly. The religious orders have founded their establishments between the domain of the colonists and the territory of the free Indians. The Missions may be considered as intermediary states. They have doubtless encroached on the liberty of the natives; but they have almost everywhere tended to the increase of population, which is incompatible with the restless life of the independent Indians. As the missionaries advance towards the forests, and gain on the natives, the white colonists in their turn seek to invade in the opposite direction the territory of the Missions. In this protracted struggle, the secular arm continually tends to withdraw the reduced Indian from the monastic hierarchy, and the missionaries are gradually superseded by vicars. The whites, and the castes of mixed blood, favoured by the corregidors, establish themselves among the Indians. The Missions become Spanish villages, and the natives lose even the rememmbrance of their natural language. Such is the progress of civilization from the coasts toward the interior; a slow progress, retarded by the passions of man, but nevertheless sure and steady.

31. Tomás de Santa María or Thomas Gage?

The writings of Thomas Gage (c. 1603-1656), based on his extensive journals, present a fascinating problem for the reader. Here is an Englishman who, following the tradition of his Roman Catholic family, was so fervent a believer that he left his increasingly Puritan-oriented country to join the Dominican order in Spain, spent twelve years as missionary (friar Tomás de Santa María) to the Amerindians in New Spain, underwent a crisis of belief, returned to England, abjured his Catholicism, contributed directly to the execution of at least three former priest friends, and wrote one of the most valuable accounts of the state of religion (Christian and non-Christian) and of the religious orders in the New World.

The following selection comes from three widely separated sections of Gage's account:

SOURCE: Eric S. Thompson, ed., *Thomas Gage's Travels in the New World* (Norman: University of Oklahoma Press, 1958), 39, 42, 188-89, 191, 234-41. Reprinted by permission of University of Oklahoma Press © 1958.

(A) his first arrival in America; (B) his sojourn in Guatemala City; and (C) his lengthy ministry to the Amerindians in rural Guatemala.

The reader may ask as a general question: Does the self-serving nature—to convince Gage's compatriots of his complete repudiation of "popery" in all its manifestations—vitiate the document's worth?

In such phrases as "they honored us as Gods upon earth"; "to blind that simple people with Popish principles"; "submission of the poor Indians unto the priests"; "puff up some of our young friars' hearts"; "inhabitants as proud and vicious as are those of Mexico [City]" (all in section A), Gage presents actual events and actions and at the same time editorializes or assigns motivations. Perhaps people today would agree with his judgments, but would those Spaniards about whom he is writing see themselves as he does? Could they?

In section B, Gage describes the churches, cloisters, and nunneries in Guatemala City, which he saw later in his travels. If the excerpt is analyzed dispassionately, the reader will learn much about the institutions and workings of the Catholic Church in the increasingly stable and prosperous colony. Consider the nature and activities of those institutions rather than any venality that may characterize their individual members. (Convents in the seventeenth-century Catholic world could serve as places of refuge for daughters of wealthy families who would live relatively fulfilling lives reading, playing music, engaging in the arts, embroidering, praying, and entertaining guests, and had their needs taken care of by slaves and servants.)

In section C, is it possible to separate Gage's anti-Roman "spin" on Catholic beliefs and customs and determine how the clergy actually instructed and treated the Amerindians? Similarly, eliminate Gage's Puritan "spin" in his descriptions of the religious beliefs and practices of the Amerindians. Terms such as "idols," "witchcraft," and "deluded by the devil" were common to all Christians and cannot be used to understand the religious vision of the Amerindian. How does Gage's account contribute to a better understanding of the complex nature of "conversion"?

[A]   Here we began to discover the power of the priests and friars over the poor Indians, and their subjection and obedience unto them. The Prior of San Juan de Ulúa had writ a letter unto them the day before of our passing that way, charging them to meet us in the way, and to welcome us into those parts, and this the poor Indians gallantly performed. [...]

There was set up one long arbor with green bows, and a table ready furnished with boxes of conserves and other sweetmeats, and diet-bread to prepare our stomachs for a cup of chocolate, and while it was seasoning with the hot water and sugar, the chief Indians and officers of the town made a speech unto us, having first kneeled down and kissed our hands one by one. They welcomed us into their country, calling us the Apostles of Jesus Christ, thanked us for that we had left our own country, our friends, our fathers and mothers for to save their souls, they told us they honored us as gods upon earth, and many such compliments they used till our chocolate was brought. [...]

And thus we took our leaves, giving unto the chief of them some beads, some medals, some crosses of brass, some *Agnus Dei*, some relics brought from Spain, and to every one of the town an indulgence of forty years (which the Pope had granted unto us, to bestow where and upon whom, and as often as we would), wherewith we began to blind that simple people with Popish principles. As we went out of the arbor to take our mules, behold the market-place was full of Indian men and women, who, as they saw us ready to depart, kneeled upon the ground as adoring us for a blessing, which as we rid along we bestowed

61

upon them with lifted up hands on high, making over them the sign of the cross. And this submission of the poor Indians unto the priests in those parts, this vainglory in admitting such ceremonious entertainment and public worship from them, did so puff up some of our young friars' hearts that already they thought themselves better than the best bishops in Spain, who, though proud enough, yet never travel there with such public acclamations as we did. [. . .]

[B]   The churches, though they be not so fair and rich as those of Mexico, are for that place wealthy enough. There is but one parish church and a cathedral which standeth in the chief market-place. All the other churches belong to cloisters, which are of Dominicans, Franciscans, Mercenarians, Augustines, and Jesuits, and two of nuns, called the Concepción and Santa Catarina. The Dominicans, Franciscans, and Mercenarians are stately cloisters, containing near a hundred friars apiece, but above all is the cloister where I lived of the Dominicans, to which is joined in a great walk before the church, the University of the city. The yearly revenues which come into this cloister, what from the Indian towns belonging to it, what from a water-mill, what from a farm for corn, what from an *estancia* or farm for horses and mules, what from an *ingenio*, or farm of sugar, what from a mine of silver given unto it the year 1633, are judged to be (excepting all charges) at least thirty thousand ducats. Therewith those fat friars feast themselves, and have to spare to build, and enrich their church and altars. [. . .]

The other cloisters of the city are also rich; but next to the Dominicans is the cloister of nuns called the Concepción, in which at my time there were judged to live a thousand women, not all nuns, but nuns and their serving maids or slaves, and young children which were brought up and taught to work by the nuns. The nuns that are professed bring with them their portions, five hundred ducats the least, some six hundred, some seven, and some a thousand, which portions after a few years (and continuing to the cloister after the nuns' decease) come to make up a great yearly rent. They that will have maids within to wait on them may, bringing the bigger portion or allowing yearly for their servants' diet. [. . .]

Besides this one nun [Doña Juana de Maldonado y Paz, a young, beautiful, and accomplished wealthy woman upon whom lavish gifts were bestowed], there are many more, and also friars, who are very rich, for if the city be rich (as is this) and great trading in it, they will be sure to have a share. Great plenty and wealth hath made the inhabitants as proud and vicious as are those of Mexico. Here is not only idolatry, but fornication and uncleanness as public as in any place of the Indies. [. . .]

[C]   As for their [the Amerindians] religion, they are outwardly such as the Spaniards, but inwardly they are slow to believe that which is above sense, nature, and the visible sight of the eye. Many of them to this day do incline to worship idols of stocks and stones, and are given to much superstition concerning the observation of cross-ways and meeting of beasts in them, the flying of birds, and their appearing and singing near their houses at such and such times.

Many are given to witchcraft, and are deluded by the devil to believe that their life dependeth upon the life of such and such a beast (which they take unto them as their familiar spirit) and think that when that beast dieth, they must die. [. . .]

All Indians are much affected unto these Popish saints, but especially those which are given to witchcraft, and out of the smallness of their means they will be sure to buy some of these saints and bring them to the church, that there they may stand and be worshipped by them and others. The churches are full of them, and they are placed upon standers gilded or painted, to be carried in procession upon men's shoulders, upon their proper day. Upon such saints days, the owner of the saint maketh a great feast in the town, and presenteth unto the priest sometimes two or three, sometimes four or five, crowns for his Mass and sermon, besides a turkey and three or four fowls, with as much cacao as will serve to make him chocolate for all the whole octave or eight days following. So that in some churches, where there are at least forty of these saints, statues and images, they bring unto the priest at least forty pounds a year. [. . .]

But if you demand of these ignorant but zealous offerers, the Indians, an account of any point of faith, they will give you little or none. The mystery of the Trinity, and of the incarnation of Christ, and our redemption by him is too hard for them; they will only answer what they have been taught in a catechism of questions and answers. If you ask them if they believe such a point of Christianity, they will never answer affirmatively, but only thus: "Perhaps it may be so." They are taught there the doctrine of Rome, that Christ's body is truly and really present in the Sacrament, and no bread in substance, but only the accidents. Yet if the wisest Indian be asked whether he believes this, he will answer, "Perhaps it may be so." [...]

They are taught that they must remember the souls in Purgatory, and therefore that they must cast their alms into a chest, which stands for that purpose in their churches, the key of which the priest keeps, and opens it when he wants money. [...]

Christmas Day, with the rest of those holy days, is no less superstitiously observed by these Indians. [...]

Candlemas Day is no less superstitiously observed. [...]

Thus all the year are those priests and friars deluding the poor people for their ends, enriching themselves with their gifts, placing religion in mere policy. Thus the Indians' religion consists more in sights, shows, and formalities than in any true substance. But as sweet meat must have sour sauce, so this sweetness and pleasing delight of shows in the church hath its sour sauce once a year (besides the sourness of poverty which followeth to them by giving so many gifts unto the priest). For, to shew that in their religion there is some bitterness and sourness, they make the Indians whip themselves the week before Easter, like the Spaniards, which those simples, both men and women, perform with such cruelty to their own flesh that they butcher it, and mangle and tear their backs, till some swoon. Nay, some, to my own knowledge, have died under their own whipping, and have self murdered themselves.

Thus in religion they are superstitiously led on and blinded in the observance of what they have been taught more for the good and profit of their priests than for any good of their souls, for they do not perceive that their religion is a policy to enrich their teachers. But not only do the friars and priests live by them and eat the sweat of their brows, but also all the Spaniards not only grow wealthy and rich with their work and service (being themselves many given to idleness), but with needless offices and authority still fleece them, and take from them that little which they gain with much hardness and severity.

32. Zapotec Codices

Gonzalo de Balsalobre, a priest for twenty-two years in the diocese of Antequera (Oaxaca, Mexico), wrote a report to his bishop in 1654, which confirms the existence of religious documents written in the Zapotec language of the local Amerindians. These documents, called codices, preserved the beliefs and traditions of the preconquest Amerindians and were used by seventeenth-century Zapotec "elders" and "priests" to maintain the teachings and practices of the remote ancestors of the contemporary Zapotec.

Are the Amerindians described in this document motivated primarily by a negative resistance to Christianity, or by more positive adherence to traditional beliefs? Might these two simply be two sides of the same coin, or is it possible to accept Christian teachings and maintain traditional beliefs? Is it helpful to compare this lengthy account of Amerindian religious practices with Gage's brief account? Is it possible to define what constitutes "conversion"? Does this document help explain the character of fervent Catholic clergy?

SOURCE: Document translated and annotated by James H. Carmichael, "Balsalobre on Idolatry in Oaxaca," *Boletín de Estudios Oaxaqueños* 13 (September 1, 1959): 5-10, passim.

By order of the Most Illustrious and Reverend Lord, Maestro Don Fray Diego de Hevia y Valdés, Bishop of Antequera, Valley of Oaxaca, of the Council of His Majesty, Etc. This account is made by Bachiller Gonzalo de Balsalobre, Curate of the District of Zola [sic], of the cases of idolatries, sorceries, superstitions, rites and ceremonies of the heathen that he has attacked and inquired into among his parishioners, and of which many of them are confessed and convicted.

And concerning the common use, practice, and teaching about thirteen gods in the aforementioned district, as this appears through the testimony of several witnesses in the neighboring districts.

Most Illustrious and Reverend Sir:

Moved by the zeal of reverence for God Our Lord, and zealously concerned by the slight satisfaction which the natives of this kingdom give generally in things of the Faith, and to fulfill the obligations of my office, I have for some time had strong doubts regarding my parishioners and many of the natives of this bishopric. Although in public, whether forced by Ministers of the Doctrine, whether from habit, or whether to palliate the disobedience of their repeated and perfidious idolatries and superstitions that have continued from heathen times until now—with loss of many souls that have died and are dying disobedient and impenitent in that detestable crime, into which they are born, for they have inherited it from parents to children to grandchildren, by succession from one to the other (except those that die in the state of innocence preserved in Baptismal grace)—they perform acts suggestive of true faith, and pretend to appear as true Christians.

And by the experience that I have acquired from communication with them during *twenty-two years* as Minister of the Doctrine, desiring with tireless care by all roads to set them upon that of the State of Blessedness, I have always found them inwardly very far removed from it, although outwardly they show the contrary. And living among them with this sorrow and affliction, motivated by the causes referred to, Our Lord permitted that the falsity of their simulated faith commenced to show itself in a case of relapse that I prosecuted on the twenty-third of December of the past year, fifty-three, against Diego Luis, elder and teacher of these same Natives, and himself a native of a barrio under the Jurisdiction of my aforementioned district, whom a little more than nineteen years ago I punished for these same transgressions.

This and other teachers who are there, and who are called in the common language "wise men" and "teachers," have continually taught those same errors that they held during their heathenism, for which purpose they have had books and handwritten notebooks of which they avail themselves for this doctrine; and in them [are prescribed] the customs of and the teaching about thirteen gods, with names of men and women, to whom they attribute various effects [...]

From these [books], with sorceries, they take their different magical answers and prognostications, such as for all kinds of hunting, and for any fishing; for the harvest of maize, chile, and cochineal; for any sickness and for the superstitious medicine with which cures must be effected; and in order to ward off hardship and death, that these will not come to their houses; for success in pregnancy and childbirth among their wives, and that their children prosper; for [the interpretation of] the songs of birds and animals that to them are auguries; for dreams and their explanation, and for the outcome of one thing or another; and in order to counteract the omens which are predicted for them.

Finally, for any thing which they need they apply to one of these wise men or teachers, who, casting lots with thirteen grains of maize in honor of the aforementioned thirteen gods, teaches them to make horrendous idolatries and sacrifices to the Devil. [...]

And I specify this particularly: on collecting the first ears of green maize from their fields, on the day indicated by the teacher of these rites, they sacrifice a black native hen, sprinkling with its blood thirteen pieces of copal in memory of their thirteen gods, and burning this copal, and with the rest of the blood sprinkling the patio of the house.

This they offer to the god of maize and all food,

called in their language *Locucuy*, in thanksgiving for the good harvest that they have had; and on offering it they say certain words in a very low voice as when they pray. And they do the same on cutting the first chile, offering the sacrifice to the god of lightning called *Lociyo*, in the manner described above. [...]

For the same purpose [they sacrifice] to *Nocana*, [god] of their ancestors. In pregnancies and childbirths [they sacrifice] to the goddess *Nohuichana*, and to this same [goddess] on fishing for trout; to her they burn copal and light wax candles at the edge of the fishing hole at the river, for success in fishing. [...]

When a person expires, they wash the body and head with cold water; and if it is woman they comb her hair and tie it with a white cord of cotton, and they shroud her with the newest clothes that they have; they put on the body two or three pairs of skirts and *huipils*, more or less, depending upon the wealth of each one, and over this they usually put an ordinary shroud, placing inside of it a number of small stones tied in a cloth, in memory of the sacrifices that had been made in order to cure this dead person, or [in memory] of the superstitious remedies that the wise men applied to them, to no avail.

Before or after the burial, they again consult the wise men, or one of them, about this death; and the latter, casting lots with thirteen grains of maize in honor of their thirteen gods, orders them to do that penance which they have to do [...]

And [he orders them] to make ready, in the same way, little dogs, and native hens and cocks, and copal for the sacrifice that they have to make at the end of the last day of the fast, which having arrived, and the twenty-four hours having passed, the wise man comes to the house of the deceased,

taking with him one or two persons most closely related to the deceased.

And [with] these hens, or cocks, little dogs, copal and fire, he goes out of the town, and having come to a place which seems to him fitting, he digs one, two or three holes [...]

For offering alms in the church, they have good and bad days; and these are indicated to them by some counselor who judges of that, according to his computations from the book of their doctrine. If the day is good, although it be during the week, all or many of them come together to light candles or to bring other offerings, which, it is evident by their own declarations, they do in reverence of their thirteen gods.

For examples: if such a day is good for offering, and the counselor told them to perform it at the altar of the Virgin offering or lighting so many candles, they do it; and they offer them in reverence of the goddess *Nohuichaná*; and if at all of the altars they perform this sacrifice, it is done in reverence of all the thirteen gods; and the other offerings are made in the same respect.

They are accustomed to perform many other ceremonies and rites on burying the dead, upon getting married, on copulating with their wives, on building their houses, on sowing, and on gathering their harvest; and finally, all that they do in general is superstitious and so varied that only with difficulty can it be reduced to number and form.

Everything contained in this account is verified by a large number of witnesses, judicial confessions of many of the prisoners and statements of others. Either induced by fear of punishment or by the repentance which they claim to feel, they have accused themselves, asking for mercy and planning to make amends.

33. State and Church

It is impossible to understand the "conversion" process without considering the Crown's active role therein. King Philip II (1558-1598), a fervent Catholic and proponent of the

SOURCE: Emma Helen Blair and James Alexander Robertson, *The Philippine Islands, 1493-1898: Explorations by Early Navigators, Descriptions of the Islands and their Peoples* . . . , (1624), trans. and ed. Emma Helen Blair and James Alexander Robertson (Cleveland: Arthur H. Clark, 1905), 21:19-21, 27, 31, passim.

Counter Reformation was determined, however, to make clear his dominant position vis-à-vis the church and to establish the ground rules for continued "conquest"/"pacification" and "conversion" in the late sixteenth century, as the following two documents demonstrate.

The first selection from Royal Instructions (1574) *makes clear the Spanish Crown's right (conceded by the papacy in bulls of 1501 and 1508) to appoint all bishops and other church officers in the Indies. It also makes clear the duty of all government personnel, both secular and clerical—in the Spanish Philippines as in New Spain—to accept the Crown's orders and appointments. What important insight does it also reveal about Crown and church?*

Royal Instructions to Gómez Pérez Dasmariñas Regarding Ecclesiastical Affairs

The King. To Gómez Pérez Dasmariñas, my governor and captain-general of the Philipinas Islands, or the person or persons in charge of their government: I ordered a decree of various articles to be given to my viceroy of Nueva España, in regard to what was to be done and observed in that country for the preservation of my patronage, as is contained at length in the said decree, whose tenor is as follows:

The King. To our viceroy of Nueva España, or the person or persons who shall, for the time being, be exercising the government of that country: As you know, the right of the ecclesiastical patronage belongs to us throughout the realm of the Yndias—both because of having discovered and acquired that new world, and erected there and endowed the churches and monasteries at our own cost, or at the cost of our ancestors, the Catholic Sovereigns; and because it was conceded to us by bulls of the most holy pontiffs, conceded of their own accord. For its conservation, and that of the right that we have to it, we order and command that the said right of patronage be always preserved for us and our royal crown, singly and *in solidum*, throughout all the realm of the Yndias, without any derogation therefrom, either in whole or in part; and that we shall not concede the right of patronage by any favor or reward that we or the kings our successors may confer. [. . .]

We desire and order that no cathedral church, parish church, monastery, hospital, votive church, or any other pious or religious establishment be erected, founded, or constructed, without our express consent for it, or that of the person who

shall exercise our authority; and further, that no archbishopric, bishopric, dignidad, canonry, ración, media-ración, rectorial or simple benefice, or any other ecclesiastical or religious benefice or office, be instituted, or appointment to it be made, without our consent or presentation, or that of the person who shall exercise our authority; and such presentation or consent shall be in writing, in the ordinary manner.

The archbishoprics and bishoprics shall be appointed by our presentation, made to our very holy father [i.e., the Roman pontiff] who shall be at that time, as has been done hitherto.

The dignidades, canonries, racions and media-racions of all the cathedral churches of the Indias shall be filled by presentation made by our royal warrant, given by our royal Council of the Indias, and signed by our name [. . .]

The provincials of all the orders who are established in the Yndias, each one of them, shall always keep a list ready of all the monasteries and chief residences [maintained there by his orders] and of the members [resident in each] that fall in his province, and of all the religious in the province—noting each one of them by name, together with a report of his age and qualifications, and the office or ministry in which each one is occupied. He shall give that annually to our viceroy, Audiencia, or governor, or the person who shall have charge of the supreme government in the province, adding to or removing from the list the religious who shall be superfluous and those who shall be needed. Our viceroy, Audiencia, or governor, shall keep those general lists which shall thus be given, for himself, and in order that he may inform us by report of the religious that there are, and those of whom there is need of provision, by each fleet sent out. [. . .]

Therefore we strictly charge the diocesan prelates, and those superiors of the religious orders, and we order our viceroys, presidents, audiencias, and governors, that in the nominations, presentations, and appointments that they shall have to make there, as is said, in conformity [with this decree], they shall always prefer, in the first place, those who shall have been occupied, by life and example, in the conversion of the Indians, and in instruction and in administering the sacraments, and those who shall know the language of the Indians whom they have to instruct; and, in the second place, those who shall be the sons of Spaniards and who shall have served us in those regions. [...]

Accordingly we request and charge the very reverend father in Christ, the archbishop of that city, and member of our Council, and the reverend fathers in Christ, the archbishop of Nueva España, the venerable deans and cabildo of the cathedral churches of that country, and all the curas, beneficiaries, sacristans, and other ecclesiastical persons, the venerable and devout fathers provincial, guardians, priors, and other religious of the orders of St. Dominic, St. Augustine, St. Francis, and of all the other orders, that in what pertains to, and is incumbent on them, they observe and obey this decree, acting in harmony with you, for all that shall be advisable. Given in San Lorenzo el Real, June first, one thousand five hundred and seventy-four.

I THE KING
By order of his Majesty:
ANTONIO DE ERASO

34. Rationalizing Imperialism

This important ordenanza *(ordinance, statute) promulgated by Philip II in 1573 superseded all previous decrees concerning the nature and method of conquest in the Indies, vast areas of which still remained outside Spanish hegemony. There is much idealism, wiliness, underhandedness, and sensitivity in this royal decree. Is it possible, given those complex characteristics, to determine exactly the role that Philip envisages for Catholicism, the missionaries, and the church?*

Discoveries are not to be called conquests. Since we wish them to be carried out peacefully and charitably, we do not want the use of the term "conquest" to offer any excuse for the employment of force or the causing of injury to the Indians....

After a town has been laid out and its buildings constructed, but not before, the government and settlers are to attempt peacefully to win all the natives of the region over to the Holy Church and obedience to our rule. In this they are to show great diligence and holy zeal and to use the best means at their disposal, including the following:

They are to gather information about the various tribes, languages, and divisions of the Indians in the province and about the lords whom they obey. They are to seek friendship with them through trade and barter, showing them great love and tenderness and giving them objects to which they will take a liking. Without displaying any greed for the possessions of the Indians, they are to establish friendship and cooperation with the lords and nobles who seem most likely to be of assistance in the pacification of the land.

Once peace and amity with the Indians have been assured, the Spaniards will try to bring them

SOURCE: Ordenanzas de Su Magestad para los nuevos descubrimientos, conquistas y pacificaciones—Julio de 1573, "Colección de documentos inéditos relativos al descubrimiento, conquista y organización de las antiguas posesiones españolas de América y Oceanía, sacados de los archivos del reino y muy especialmente de Indias" (Madrid, 1864-1884), 16:142-87, passim. Trans. and ed. Lewis Hanke, *History of Latin American Civilization*, 2nd ed. (Boston: Little, Brown and Company, 1973), 1:111-14.

together in one spot. Then the preachers, with as much solemnity as possible, will start to teach our Holy Faith to those who wish to be instructed in it, using prudence and discretion and the gentlest methods possible. Accordingly, they are not to begin by rebuking the Indians for their vices and idolatry, nor by taking away their women and idols, so that they will not be shocked and form an aversion to Christian doctrine. Instead, it should be taught to them first, and after they have been instructed in it, they should be persuaded to give up of their own free will those things that are contrary to our Holy Catholic Faith and evangelical doctrine.

The Indians should be brought to an understanding of the position and authority which God has given us and of our zeal in serving Him by bringing to His Holy Catholic Faith all the natives of the Western Indies. They should also learn of the fleets and armies that we have sent and still send for this purpose, as well as of the many provinces and nations that have rendered us obedience and of the many benefits which they have received and are receiving as a result, especially that we have sent ecclesiastics who have taught them the Christian doctrine and faith by which they could be saved. Moreover, we have established justice in such a way that no one may aggravate another. We have maintained the peace so that there are no killings, or sacrifices, as was the custom in some parts. We have made it possible for the Indians to go safely by all roads and to peacefully carry on their civil pursuits. We have taught them good habits and the custom of wearing clothes and shoes. We have freed them from burdens and servitude; we have made known to them the use of bread, wine, oil, and many other foods, woolen cloth, silk, linen, horses, cows, tools, arms, and many other things from Spain; we have instructed them in crafts by which they live excellently. All these advantages will those Indians enjoy who embrace our Holy Faith and render obedience to us.

Even if the Indians are willing to receive the faith and the preachers in peace, the latter are to approach their villages with prudence and with precautions for their own safety. In this manner if the Indians should prove unruly, they will not be inclined to show disrespect to the preachers; otherwise, the guilty persons would have to be punished, causing great damage to the work of pacification and conversion. Although the preachers should keep this in mind when they visit the Indian settlements, it should be concealed from the natives so that they will not feel any anxiety. Difficulties may be avoided if the children of the caciques and nobles are brought to the Spanish settlements and are kept there as hostages under the pretext of entertaining them and teaching them to wear clothes. By means such as these is conversion to be undertaken in all the Indian communities which wish to receive the preachers in peace.

In areas where the Indians refuse to accept Christian doctrine peacefully, the following procedure may be used. An arrangement should be made with the principal lord who is a proponent of peace so that he will invite the belligerent Indians to his territory on one pretext or another. On this occasion the preachers, together with some Spaniards and friendly Indians, should be hidden nearby. At the opportune moment they should disclose themselves and begin teaching the faith with the aid of interpreters. In order that the Indians may hear the faith with greater awe and reverence, the preachers should carry the Cross in their hands and should be wearing at least albs or stoles; the Christians are also to be told to listen to the preaching with great respect and veneration, so that by their example the non-believers will be induced to accept instruction. If it seems advisable, the preachers may attract the attention of the non-believers by using music and singers, thereby encouraging them to join in. If the Indians seem inclined to be peaceful and request the preachers to go to their territory, the latter should do so, taking the precautions previously described. They should ask for their children under the pretext of teaching them and keep them as hostages; they should also persuade them to build churches where they can teach so that they may be safer. By these and other means are the Indians to be pacified and indoctrinated, but in no way are they to be harmed, for all we seek is their welfare and their conversion.

Once the region has been pacified and the

Indian lords and subjects have tendered us their fealty, the Governor, with their consent, is to distribute the land among the settlers who are to take charge of the natives in their parcels, defending and protecting them and providing them with clerics to teach them Christian doctrine and administer the sacraments. They should also teach them to live in an orderly fashion and fulfill all the obligations of encomenderos as set forth in the clauses dealing with this subject.

The Indians who offer us obedience and are distributed among Spaniards are to be persuaded to acknowledge our sovereignty over the Indies.

They are to give us tributes of local produce in moderate amounts, which are to be turned over to their Spanish encomenderos so that the latter may fulfill their obligations, reserving to us the tributes of the principal villages and the seaports, as well as an amount adequate to pay the salaries of our officials. If it appears that the pacification of the natives will be accomplished more easily by temporarily exempting them from tribute payments or by granting them other privileges, this should be done; and whatever is promised should be carried out. . . .

35. Franciscans in the Far-Flung Frontier

The following six documents enable the reader to follow the "conversion" process from the 1630s to the 1820s in the outlying areas of the Spanish empire.

In 1634, Fray Bernardino de Siena, O.F.M. (d. 1636), wrote a memorial to Pope Urban VIII (1623-1644) about the Franciscan missions in the new gobierno of New Mexico (1595). The account, emphasizing the hardships suffered by the friars, is clearly meant to elicit support from the pontiff. Compare the following account of friars in an isolated mission on the far-flung frontier with reading 42, a contemporaneous account of friars in urban centers.

Since the land is very remote and isolated and the difficulties of the long journeys require more than a year of travel, the friars, although there are many who wish to dedicate themselves to those conversions, find themselves unable to do so because of their poverty. Hence only those go there who are sent by the Catholic king at his own expense, for the cost is so excessive that only his royal zeal can afford it. This is the reason that there are so few friars over there and that most of the convents have only one religious each, and he ministers to four, six, or more neighboring pueblos, in the midst of which he stands as a lighted torch to guide them in spiritual as well as temporal affairs. More than twenty Indians, devoted to the service of the church, live with him in the con-

vent. They take turns in relieving one another as porters, sextons, cooks, bell-ringers, gardeners, refectioners, and in other tasks. They perform their duties with as much circumspection and care as if they were friars. At eventide they say their prayers together, with much devotion, in front of some image.

In every pueblo where a friar resides, he has schools for the teaching of praying, singing, playing musical instruments, and other interesting things. Promptly at dawn, one of the Indian singers, whose turn it is that week, goes to ring the bell for the Prime, at the sound of which those who go to school assemble and sweep the rooms thoroughly. The singers chant the Prime in the choir. The friar must be present at all of this and

SOURCE: Frederick Webb Hodge, George P. Hammond, and Agapito Rey, *Fray Alonso de Benavides' Revised Memorial of 1634, With Numerous Supplementary Documents Elaborately Annotated* (Albuquerque: University of New Mexico Press, 1945), 100-103. Reprinted by permission of University of New Mexico Press.

takes note of those who have failed to perform this duty, in order to reprimand them later. When everything is neat and clean, they again ring the bell and each one goes to learn his particular specialty; the friar oversees it all in order that these students may be mindful of what they are doing. At this time those who plan to get married come and notify him, so that he may prepare and instruct them according to our holy council; if there are any, either sick or healthy persons, who wish to confess in order to receive communion at mass, or who wish anything else, they come to tell him. After they have been occupied in this manner for an hour and a half, the bell is rung for mass. All go into the church, and the friar says mass and administers the sacraments. Mass over, they gather in their different groups, examine the lists, and take note of those who are absent in order to reprimand them later. After taking the roll, all kneel down by the church door and sing the *Salve* in their own tongue. This concluded, the friar says: "Praised be the most holy Sacrament," and dismisses them, warning them first of the circumspection with which they should go about their daily business.

At mealtime, the poor people in the pueblo who are not ill come to the porter's lodge, where the cooks of the convent have sufficient food ready, which is served to them by the friar; food for the sick is sent to their homes. After mealtime, it always happens that the friar has to go to some neighboring pueblo to hear a confession or to see if they are careless in the boys' school, where they learn to pray and assist at mass, for this is the responsibility of the sextons and it is their duty always to have a dozen boys for the service of the sacristy and to teach them how to help at mass and how to pray.

In the evening they toll the bell for vespers, which are chanted by the singers who are on duty for the week, and, according to the importance of the feast, they celebrate it with organ chants, as they do for mass. [. . .]

One of the weekdays which is not so busy is devoted to baptism, and all those who are to be baptized come to the church on that day, unless some urgent matter should intervene; in that case, it is performed at any time. With great care, their names are inscribed in a book; in another, those who are married; and in another, the dead.

One of the greatest tasks of the friars is to adjust the disputes of the Indians among themselves, for, since they look upon him as a father, they come to him with all their troubles, and he has to take pains to harmonize them. If it is a question of land and property, he must go with them and mark their boundaries, and thus pacify them.

For the support of all the poor of the pueblo, the friar makes them sow some grain and raise some cattle, because, if he left it to their discretion, they would not do anything. Therefore the friar requires them to do so and trains them so well, that, with the meat, he feeds all the poor and pays the various workmen who come to build the churches. With the wool he clothes all the poor, and the friar himself also gets his clothing and food from this source. All the wheels of this clock must be kept in good order by the friar, without neglecting any detail, otherwise all would be totally lost.

The most important thing is the good example set by the friars. This, aside from the obligation of their vows, is forced upon them because they live in a province where they concern themselves with nothing but God. Death stares them in the face every day! Today one of their companions is martyred, tomorrow, another; their hope is that such a good fortune may befall them while living a perfect life.

LIV
DEDICATION

This, Most Holy Father, is the state of that new and primitive church which the seraphic sons of Saint Francis, its only workers, have founded and watered with the blood and lives of ten of their brethren. In their name and in the name of all those who now continue to promote this work at the cost of so many hardships, but with a rich harvest of more than five hundred thousand souls converted to our most holy Catholic faith, I come to offer this church to the obedience, protection, and support of your Holiness, as its rightful prince and master. Likewise, in the name of all those nations, their princes and elders, who most urgently have begged me to do so, I offer their obedience to your Holiness, asking with all humility that you, here, bestow upon them your holy apostolic and paternal blessing, as on true sons of the church, of which they are duly proud. And again, in their name and in the name of all those who may be converted and baptized in the future, with all the humility I can command and which I owe, I kiss the foot of your Holiness.

36. A German Jesuit among the "Savage" Pima

Joseph Och, S.J. (1725-1773), arrived in Primería Alta (Sonora in northern Mexico) from Würzburg in 1756. For some years this area, inhabited by such hostile Amerindian nations as the Apache, Seri, and Pima, had been precarious territories for Jesuit missionaries. The Pima, however, had been calm for several years, and young Father Och commenced his evangelization among them.

Can Och's concept of evangelization be discerned in the excerpts below? Assuming that his account is accurate, how might the Pimas' reaction to his methods be explained?

In their customs the Indians are secretive toward the missionaries. Even among those who otherwise are good Christians there always clings something of the former odor of impiety. From fear of punishment they keep some things hidden, and possibly only during the absence of the father would they hold their secret assemblages. Here were observed always some of the customs inherited from their forebears, some of them amusing and some of them superstitious, which were kept by the obdurate old ones and passed on from them orally to their descendants.

Very frequently when they were contemplating a nocturnal dance and revelry they used all kinds of lies and subterfuges to get the father away from the village, so that he would not hinder them. They might trump up a story about a sick person whose circumstances were so perilous that the father would have to hear confession, all to get him to leave the village. As often as I rode away to a confession I was asked solicitously: "Father! when will you return? . . . how long will you be away?" The greatest vexation I could cause them occurred when I had them accompany me as guards for my protection on the journey, for then,

after they had taken me to the next village, they had to run back to be able to take part in their festivities.

The children are well built. They are born very large and strong, with hair as long as their arms, are quite chubby throughout, and of reddish color, one might well say *a matre rubet*. At baptism I might have taken them to be children of mulattoes, and the latter as Indian children, because the mulatto children were much browner and less well formed. The red color gradually changes within a year to a chestnut brown, resembling a piece of wet sole-leather.

At the tender age of six to twelve months these children must endure a cruel torture. All the hair is pulled from the child's eyebrows and the little holes or pores are enlarged with a thorn. Coal dust is then sprinkled on these bloody openings and rubbed in. The upper and lower lips are turned out as far as possible and pieced with sharp thorns as much as a hundred times. These wounds, too, are sprinkled with coal dust, or with a preparation from a pod, like our kidney bean, which is used instead of nutgall for the best ink. From this treatment the lips become swollen and blue-black, as

SOURCE: Theodore E. Treutlein, translator and annotator, *Missionary in Sonora: The Travel Reports of Joseph Och, S.J., 1755-1767* (San Francisco: California Historical Society, 1965), 124-31. Reprinted by permission of California Historical Society.

though the child had eaten large quantities of whortleberries, and they remain this way for life.

Temples, cheeks, the whole chin, the entire upper body, chest, arms and back, are pierced with many thousand different embroideries and figures, such as wheels, stars, roses, and all kinds of animals and snakes. The brown skin with these figures and the long, heavy hair hanging down from the head, make a fearsome sight. For performing this ugly ceremony there are, besides the one who does the pricking, a godfather and godmother who must hold the squirming, crying, and bleeding child during this torture. This devilish custom, which completely transforms a person and costs many children their lives, displeased me to the extent that I forbade it on pain of severe punishment. The first one who refused to obey and permitted his child to be so diabolically marked was disclosed to me by a faithful Indian. I had the father given twenty-five stripes, well laid-on with a braided leather whip by a powerful Indian; the mother received twelve, the godfather twenty-five, the godmother twelve, and the master of the ceremony twenty-five.

As often as a child died and was sewed in a palm mat and brought to me for burial, I cut open the mat in the churchyard to learn whether the child had died a natural death or from being tattooed. Whenever I learned that the child had succumbed to the torture, the parents and their assistants had to pay on the spot for their cruelty. These lashes made a greater impression than did my preachments. After but a few had received such a reward for their trouble they left off this barbarous ceremony, and the children grew up gay and healthy with their not badly formed physiognomies. [. . .]

Women far advanced in pregnancy are driven from the house and absolutely forbidden to give birth within it, for such women are looked upon as being poisoned. The Indians believe that a birth deprives arrows of their power so that they will never be able to hit a mark. More than once have I encountered a miserable woman in birth pangs hanging under a tree in the forest where some other old women had tied her with ropes passed under her arms so as to torment her until she delivered. This savage midwifery and banishment I corrected with whiplashes, and brought it to pass

that the women had to stay in their huts. They did this reluctantly, and the men fled elsewhere with their weapons. [. . .]

They also burned a house whenever anyone died in it. At first I did not understand what caused so many fire-damaged villages. But I learned the cause, for they explained to me they no longer desired to live in a certain place because the dead one had returned to it. They wanted to elude him so that he could no longer visit them in the house where he had lived. This constant changing of huts irked me greatly, for I never knew where they were living. They believed that the deceased always returned to his former dwelling. Since I forbade the burning of individual huts, and forced them to live in their old dwellings, they managed piece by piece to make over a house, even to the extent of digging out the floor deeply, to give it a different appearance and so to prevent the deceased from recognizing it. [. . .]

In warfare they drag out their slain enemies and let them lie unburied after they have torn the skin and hair from the crowns of their heads as victory trophies. For three nights in a row they hold a dance of celebration around a great fire, especially participated in by old women and children. On such occasions the scalps are held aloft on a pole, amid disagreeable singing and boastful speeches. The scalps are sent around from village to village by messenger to impress others with their bravery for having struck a blow against the enemy. The messenger brings back many congratulations, and in each village the tufts of hair are honored with dance and song. Eventually I succeeded in inducing them to cover their slain enemies with earth, and to deliver their captives to me alive.

Almost constantly they brought me captive children whom I baptized and sent elsewhere so that they would be raised in a Christian fashion by other padres. I took care of two such boys who turned out fairly well. One of them I wanted to take with me to the city of Mexico. But when we reached the first little town, which was more than one hundred hours from the mission and he saw the large churches and felt uncomfortable among none but Spaniards, he gave me the slip the next day, though he left without even one cent travel money.

37. Franciscans in California

Junípero Serra, O.F.M. (1713-1784), and his pupil, lifelong friend, and biographer Francisco Palou, O.F.M. (1723-1789), both natives of Majorca, worked together in founding and maintaining California missions between 1768 and 1784.

The first part of the reading below (May) contains excerpts from Palou's account of the expedition (1769) with Serra to Alta California. The brief second part quotes Father Serra rebuking Viceroy Bucareli (1771-1779), and a third part ("During the month of November") recounts the experience of Palou in 1775 in the area around the San Diego mission.

Describe the mind (depth of commitment, certitude, flexibility, curiosity, and expectations) of the Franciscans of California in the 1770s. How do Palou and Serra regard the Amerindians? Do these missionaries possess anthropological sensitivity? Do they have respect for the "gentile" and "pagan" Amerindians?

May 23. . . . According to my calculations, we traveled four and a half hours; and for more than half that time the road was all steep hills, rocky and tiresome, up hill and down dale, till we came to some level mesas where we found evident signs that the first division of the land expedition had stopped there. We did, likewise. As there was no water in sight, we dug a water hole for the animals to drink. May 24. We resumed our journey. It lasted three hours and a half, following half the time a dry ravine with much sand, making the going heavy. There were a few palm trees. Then came ugly steep hills, leading to a plain encircled by mountains. . . . Water had been brought in skins for the men, but the animals did not have any. . . . The blazing sun made the journey very painful.

For the last four nights a roaring lion [puma] quite close by kept us awake. May God guard us from it, as He has till now. [. . .]

All his [an Amerindian] talking seemed to be to excuse himself for having spied on us from the hill yesterday and today. . . . He told us he had been sent by his chief to spy upon us, the purpose being that, as we continued our march, the chief and all his *ranchería* [village] together with four other chiefs and their *rancherías* . . . lying in ambush behind the rocks, should surprise the Father and all accompanying him, and put them to death. . . . We pardoned him his murderous intentions, and

loading him down with presents, we let him go in order that he might tell his people how well we treated him . . . that they, too, might come to see us. But not one came, although some were seen this afternoon on the same ridge. . . .

May 28. Sunday. Before our departure, some gentiles approached us belonging to the group our soldiers had seen while keeping guard over the animals. Their huts were about twelve in number. Immediately our converts joined them to bring them to us. This only excited their hostile demonstrations, and, time and again, they made as if to shoot their arrows . . . so indignant were they that we could not calm them.

The time for Mass has come, and in order to hear it the soldiers made a circle and put them seated in the middle. . . . After Mass another large number of them came, and their shouting continued. . . . There was no way we could quiet them or disperse them. What they said, according to our interpreters, was that we should not go farther but go back, and that they wanted to fight. . . . We spent much time patiently trying to send them away in a friendly way. It was all in vain, no use whatever, and we feared bloodshed. By order of the governor, four soldiers mounted on horses, forming a line, forced them to retreat. But they again refused to go. At first one and then, a little later, a second shot was fired into the air by a soldier. On hearing it, they fled. . . .

SOURCE: Winifred E. Wise, *Fray Junípero Serra and the California Conquest* (New York: Charles Scribner's Sons, 1967), 34-37, 108-9, 113-17.

When we left today's stopping place, they followed us along the hills . . . so that during the whole day's trip we saw a great number of them continually running along the hills in the same direction as ourselves. However, to get near us they had to come down to level ground. . . . Matters were different, however, when the mountains came close together, and we had to pass between them through a narrow gully. All the soldiers then buckled on their leather jackets, and they and the mule drivers kept their arms ready for firing. We all kept on the alert, but the enemy did not show up. . . .

But as if to relieve us from the displeasure which they had caused us, Our Lord God sent us other Indians of a more pleasing character; and so one league before arriving at our camping grounds, twelve new gentiles came to us. Very politely, they said they would show us the place. . . . While we were busy with unloading . . . they retired to a nearby hillside and remained sitting there motionless. When we were free I sent them . . . an Indian interpreter, carrying presents of figs and meat, with an invitation to come and meet us without fear, since we were their friends. They replied showing they were highly delighted. . . . And so it happened that after we had taken our meal and some rest, they came with . . . all their weapons which they laid on the ground. They started in to explain their use in battle, one after another. They played all the parts both of the attacker and the attacked in such a vivid way . . . that it was a pleasant relaxation for all of us. . . .

So far we had not seen any woman among them, and, till now, I was anxious not to see them, because I feared they went as naked as the men. But when, in the midst of the entertainment, two women appeared—talking as rapidly and efficiently as that sex is accustomed to do—and when I saw them so decently covered that we would feel happy if no greater display of indecency were ever seen among the Christian women at our missions, I no longer regretted their arrival. [. . .]

[Viceroy Bucareli]

Because of the frequent meetings and lengthy conversations which His Excellency had with the fervent Fray Junípero during the seven months he remained in Mexico City, he [Bucareli] became deeply imbued with a religious zeal for the conversion of souls and the extension of our Holy Catholic Faith and the dominions of our King. This zeal animated him in such a manner that there was no slaking the thirst for souls which the continuous discussion with the Venerable Father on this delightful matter of converting the pagans caused him. . . . He disclosed . . . his desire to send a maritime expedition [farther north up the coast] . . . to discover if it was inhabited and if there might be a port around which to found new missions. . . .

On hearing this, the Venerable Father Junípero—who was insatiable in these matters, and whose thirst was never quenched when it came to extending the boundaries of Christendom, and who never considered any difficulty that might be placed in his way—not only praised the idea but tried to aid him in executing it. He told the Viceroy that with the frigate [*Santiago*] he had ordered completed, and with Captain Don Juan Pérez, His Excellency had exactly what he needed to carry out that enterprise, for the frigate could sail from Monterey as soon as it had unloaded the cargo of foodstuffs and supplies. Such was the impression which His Excellency had formed of the Venerable Fray Junípero that, without further consultation than the opinion given by His Reverence, he issued the corresponding orders for the expedition. [. . .]

When I hear that there is no possibility of sparing seven or eight men and a few animals to found a mission. . . . Your Excellency may well imagine how it disturbs me. That military men should move forward with caution is well and good; but for the kingdom of God some boldness is more in keeping that all these cautions they are forever urging on me. [**The San Diego Mission** . . .]

During the month of November of the year 1775, Venerable Father Lector Fray Luis Jayme . . . and Father Preacher Fray Vicente Fuster . . . were administering Mission San Diego with great joy of soul. . . . The mission constituted a populous town. . . .

Whilst the fathers and the new Christians [sixty recently baptized during the Feast of St.

Francis] were so happily and comfortably situated, the fury of the chief enemy of souls [Satan] increased. . . . To carry out his diabolical aims, he made use of two neophytes of the group baptized earlier. These . . . left the mission and traveled through the villages of the sierra. He incited those Indians to spread the report among the pagans . . . that the fathers wanted to uproot paganism entirely and forcibly make Christians of them all. . . . All who heard this were thrown into confusion—some believing it, others doubting it. . . . But the greater number believed the statement. . . . So when the enemy found them favorably disposed, he incited in them a passionate anger against the Fathers, which begot a cruel resolve to kill them as well as the soldiers who guarded them and to set fire to the mission and thus destroy everything.

Some groups invited others to participate, yet some towns held off, the natives declaring that the Fathers had done them no harm, nor did they force anyone to become a Christian. . . .

More than a thousand Indians gathered together. . . . They agreed to separate into two bodies, one to fall upon the mission, the other upon the presidio. The latter group . . . was to set fire to the presidio and kill the soldiers as soon as they saw the mission in flames. . . .

They arrived in the valley of the San Diego River on the night of November 4. There they separated. Half of them, assigned to attack the presidio, marched toward it [five or six miles away]. The others, without being detected, approached the huts where the neophytes lived at the mission . . . to prevent anyone from escaping [under threat of death] or giving the alarm. . . . The greater number of them went to the church and sacristy to rob clothing, church goods, and whatever else they could find. Others with fire brands which they found in the barracks of the soldiers—of whom there were only three and a corporal, and evidently they were asleep—began to set fire to the barracks and all the rooms. As a result of this and the terrifying cries of the pagans, all awoke. [. . .]

The soldiers sprang to arms while the Indians were already shooting their arrows. The priests were sleeping in separate rooms. . . . Father Fray

Luis . . . on hearing the noise of the shouts and the crackling of the fire, came out and, seeing a great number of Indians, approached them, greeting them in the accustomed manner: "Love God, my sons." The Indians . . . as wolves do to a young lamb, laid hold of him . . . They conducted him through the thickets of the arroyo, where they divested him of his holy habit. In his naked state, they began to strike the Venerable Father with their clubs and shot countless arrows through his body. Their furious anger was not satiated with taking his life with such great cruelty, for after he was dead they beat his face, head, and the rest of his body so that from head to foot there remained not a sound portion of him except his consecrated hands. . . .

The blacksmith was about to go outside with sword in hand, but . . . the Indians released a terrible volley of arrows and killed him. When the mission carpenter saw this, he seized a loaded rifle, fired, and shot down one of the pagans who were near the door. . . . The other carpenter from the presidio . . . who was sick in bed, was also shot with arrows and fatally wounded. . . .

The largest group of pagans was engaged in fighting the soldiers who were in the hut that served as their barracks. Here were also Father Fray Vicente Fuster, two small boys [son and nephew of the lieutenant in command of the presidio], and the carpenter who was not wounded. [. . .]

The small group of soldiers at the mission was able to defend itself against such a multitude of pagans with great bravery. . . . When the enemies saw their strong resistance and the casualties which our soldiers inflicted, they set fire to . . . the palings [surrounding the barracks]. In order not to be burned alive, our men came out bravely and took their positions in a little adobe room, the kitchen. For protection that structure had only three adobe walls. . . . Its roof consisted merely of some branches which the cook had placed there to protect himself from the sun. After our men took refuge in this kitchen, they showered continuous volleys of shots and defended themselves against the great crowd who harried them exceedingly from the unwalled side of the room, through which they shot arrows and hurled clubs.

Two of the soldiers were wounded and put out of action when they dared to rush out to one of the burning buildings and stagger back with bundles and boxes to build a fourth wall. For defense against hundreds of Indians, there remained only the corporal, one soldier, and the carpenter. The corporal, a good marksman, ordered the others to load and prime the guns while he did the shooting, killing or wounding every Indian who showed himself. The savages then set fire to the branches above the heads of the beleaguered Spaniards, causing fear that the sparks might fall into the gunpowder.

This would have happened had not the foresight of Father Fray Vicente caused him to cover the powder sack with the skirts of his habit, not minding the danger to which he himself was exposed. When the Indians saw that the fire on the roof did not cause the soldiers to come out, they tried to force them out by throwing lighted brands and pieces of adobe within. One of these latter struck the priest . . . although he did not suffer serious consequences.

Thus they kept on fighting until dawn, the beautiful light of which forced the pagans to flee in the fear that soldiers from the presidio would come. They went away, carrying with them their dead and wounded. . . .

When it dawned on that November 5, and after the great multitude of pagans had disappeared, the neophytes came out of their little houses and went immediately to see the father who was in the kitchen-fort with the corporal and three soldiers, all wounded. The corporal, though wounded, did not want to say so lest the rest lose courage. He [Fuster] asked them about Father Luis, about whom he had worried all night. . . . The soldiers tried to cheer him by saying that he had gone to hide in the willows. . . .

The Indians found the Venerable Father Fray Luis dead in the arroyo and so disfigured that they hardly recognized him. . . . When Father Fray Vicente beheld this sight, he was beside himself until the wailing of the neophytes who so heartily loved their deceased father made him break into tears.

38. Good and Bad Years in the Monterey Mission

Though Father Serra had earned a doctorate in theology in 1742 and taught in the University of Palma for seven years, he was at heart an inveterate missionary. Below are excerpts from his "Report on the Missions" completed shortly before he died in 1784. Did his childhood experience with his farming family on Majorca ultimately determine his vocation? What exactly is an inveterate missionary? Does Serra's account yield insight into the "conversion" process?

Year 1782

Towards the end of the past year, 31 fanegas of barley were sown and 53 of wheat. The barley was planted where the water could not reach it and as the drought was great, it was lost. This had never happened before in the case of this grain. We gathered only 107 fanegas.

The wheat which was irrigated did well but less was harvested than in the preceding year for the same reason and there were large stretches of sown land where [the major-domo] did not attempt to gather a single head. There was a task that they were completing in less than an hour and, to make it shorter, they gathered only the tall ears and even so it took them a long time. A great many of the people got sick and the [steward] asked permission to betake himself to Mission San Luis Obispo, because they had sent to tell him that he was needed there. Leaving the wheat in the

SOURCE: Antonine Tibesar, O.F.M., ed., *Writings of Junípero Serra* (Washington, D.C.: Academy of American Franciscan History, 1966), 4:269, 271, 273. Reprinted by permission of American Academy of Franciscan History.

fields and the people down, he departed and never returned.

The harvested wheat threshed out at 450 fanegas. There were 27 fanegas of garden vegetables and 160 of Indian corn. These are the results of the first year of irrigation and such an intelligent steward.

In things spiritual it was better. We had one hundred and one Baptisms and twenty-three marriages. The people gradually improved in health, even though some of them died. [...]

Year 1783

We can consider this the happiest year of the mission because the number of Baptisms was one hundred seventy-five and of marriages thirty-six.

The sowing of all grains amounted to 84 fanegas, 8 almuds. This included one fanega and a half of wheat, half a fanega of corn, and two almuds of beans, which were sown for the [Lower] California Indians, who had moved here and were married in this mission.

And the harvest [. . .] amounted to 2,613½ fanegas, that is, of measured barley 670 fanegas, 835 of wheat, only 200 according to our estimate are kept in the ear. There were 971 fanegas of corn of both kinds according to our estimate, 63 fanegas of peas, 16 fanegas of horse beans, 4 fanegas of lentils and 53 fanegas of various kinds of beans.

Today the new Christians of this mission number six hundred fourteen living persons, even though some of them take a leave of absence from time to time. They have been maintained and are maintained without any scarcity, and we supplied the quartermaster of the Presidio of San Carlos with 130 fanegas of Indian corn, because they did not ask for more, also with 30 fanegas of beans. [...]

The value of the food supplied to the presidio has been paid already in cloth, which now covers the Indians who grew the crops, but at that we are still distressed at the sight of so much nudity among them.

We do not get clothing now from the soldiers, as we did formerly, not even from those who have debts to us no matter how small. The wool, which in some of the missions is enough to cover Indian nakedness, here has not been any help to us so far, because the thefts of sheep are so numerous [...]

They [all the members of the mission] pray twice daily with the priest in the church. More than 120 of them confess in Spanish, and many who have died used to do it as well. The others confess as best they can. They work at all kinds of mission labor, such as farm hands, herdsmen, cowboys, shepherds, milkers, diggers, gardeners, carpenters, farmers, irrigators, reapers, blacksmiths, sacristans, and they do everything else that comes along for their corporal and spiritual welfare.

The work of cleaning the fields once, sometimes twice, or even three times a year, is considerable because the land is very fertile. When we clear new land great hardship is required. All together there is sufficient land cleared for sowing more than 100 fanegas of wheat, and it is sowed in that grain, barley, vegetables and corn. Every year we clear a little more.

To the seven months' work required to take water from the river for irrigation, as mentioned above, we must add the labor of bringing it to the lagoon near the mission residence. In some years, this lagoon used to be dry. Now it is always full, making it a great convenience and a delight to the mission. Some salmon have been placed in the pool and so we have it handy.

The timber palisade was inadequate to protect the seed grain because they steal the paling for firewood. So we dug a circular trench many thousands of veras long. This was a two years' labor and withal nothing sufficed to prevent losses every year.

39. Amerindian Survival in New Spain's Texas

How does this excerpt from the report (1809) of Manuel de Salcedo, governor of Texas, shed light on the problems of evangelizing the Amerindian?

The handling of the Indian nations that inhabit this province is also of the greatest importance. All of them at present are peaceful and the worst they are wont to do is to steal mules and horses. But, nonetheless, it would be advantageous for the King (which would be best) or for rich private individuals to establish trading posts or commercial houses to supply the Indians and to trade with them better or at least equally in kind and more abundantly than the Anglo-Americans do. Then we would be able to get out of them anything we proposed to, because the Indians develop and behave like those who trade with them according to the degree of recognized utility, convenience and advantages that are presented to them. New establishment of presidios among some of the Indian nations that desire it would be very useful.

At present this province has six missions, two of them without a missionary; and in all of them combined is the extremely small number of three hundred and forty-three souls. This system seems useful and good; but in my opinion it is much too slow and perhaps of little value. The Indians who come to the mission are not attracted because faith has entered through their ears but through their mouths by dint of gifts and food to eat. Those who are there hardly understand Spanish. They repeat the doctrine like automatons. It, therefore, would be better to bring them into missions with considerable population and with frequent friendly intercourse, for if one works only with the parents it is absolutely impossible to make them accomplished in our language and in the understanding of religious principles. Remedy is needed. [...]

This, in a nutshell, is what I have thought opportune to manifest as of absolute necessity in this province that merits all the consideration of our superior government to whose great acumen I commit my limited knowledge and my unalterable strong devotion and love of my religion and country to employ myself as may be best and to sacrifice my days in honor and defense of both such sublime causes.

Béxar, August 8, 1809. Manuel de Salcedo

40. The Late Missions in Mexico's California

Frederick William Beechey (1796-1856), of the British Royal Navy and a participant in the Arctic expedition of 1818, was appointed captain of a new expedition to explore the Bering Strait and the broad expanse of the Pacific Ocean. The three-year voyage commenced with a journey up the California coast. Captain Beechey spent considerable time in 1826 exploring the land area around San Francisco Bay and its presidio (garrison) where the newly independent Mexican government had implemented a policy that decreased governmental support of the friars in the missions.

SOURCE (39): Nettie Lee Benson, trans. and ed., "A Governor's Report on Texas in 1809," *Southwestern Historical Quarterly* 71 (April 1986): 614-15. © Texas State Historical Association. Used by permission.

SOURCE (40): Frederick William Beechy, *Narrative of a Voyage to the Pacific and Beering's (sic) Strait, Together with the Polar Expeditions: Performed in His Majesty's Ship Blossom . . . In the Years 1825, 26, 27, 28* (London: Henry Colburn and Richard Bentley, 1831), 2:11-14, 17-23.

THE LATE MISSIONS IN MEXICO'S CALIFORNIA

This report by a highly educated and well-traveled Englishman, excerpted below, demands an immediate comparison with von Humboldt's account (1804) of the Capuchin missions in Venezuela (reading 30). How does Beechey's slant on the missions compare with that of Thomas Gage (reading 31)? Does Beechey's portrait of the Christianized Amerindian differ from that of the previous two? What is the extent of his anthropological sensitivity as compared with theirs? Had the mentality of the friars in the 1820s changed from that described by the missionaries themselves?

The same feeling of discontent that was experienced by the garrison pervaded the missions, in consequence of some new regulations of the republican government, the first and most grievous of which was the discontinuance of a salary of 400 dollars per annum, heretofore allowed to each of the padres: the support the former government had given to the missions amounted, according to [George Heinrich von] Langsdorff, to a million piastres a year. Another grievance was, the requisition of an oath of allegiance to the reigning authorities, which these holy men considered so egregious a violation of their former pledge to the king of Spain, that, until he renounced his sovereignty over the country, they could not conscientiously take it; and, much as they were attached to the place in which they had passed a large portion of their lives, and though by quitting it they would be reduced to the utmost penury—yet, so much did they regard this pledge, that they were prepared to leave the country, and to seek an asylum in any other that would afford it them. Indeed, the Prefect, preferring his expulsion to renouncing his allegiance, had already received his dismissal, and was ready at the seaport of Monterey to embark in any vessel the government might appoint to receive him. A third grievance, and one which, when duly considered, was of some importance, not only to the missions but to the country in general, was an order to liberate all those converted Indians from the missions who bore good characters, and had been taught the art of agriculture, or were masters of a trade, and were capable of supporting themselves, giving them portions of land to cultivate, so arranged that they should be divided into parishes, with curates to superintend them, subservient to the clergy of the missions, who were to proceed to the conversion of the Indians as usual,

and to train them for the domesticated state of society in contemplation.

This philanthropic system at first sight appeared to be a very excellent one, and every friend to the rights of man would naturally join in a wish for its prosperity; but the Mexican government could not have sufficiently considered the state of California, and the disposition of the Indians, or they would have known it could not possibly succeed without long previous training, and then it would require to be introduced by slow degrees.

The Indians whom this law emancipated were essential to the support of the missions, not only for conducting their agricultural concerns, but for keeping in subordination by force and example those whom disobedience and ignorance would exempt from the privilege; and as a necessary consequence of this indulgence the missions would be ruined before the system could be brought into effect, even supposing the Indians capable of conducting their own affairs. So far from this being the case, however, they were known to possess neither the will, the steadiness, nor the patience to provide for themselves. Accustomed, many of them from their infancy, to as much restraint as children, and to execute, mechanically, what they were desired and no more, without even entertaining a thought for their future welfare, it was natural that such persons, when released from this discipline, should abandon themselves entirely to their favourite amusements, pastimes, and vices. Those also who had been converted in later life would return to their former habits, and having once again tasted the blessings of freedom, which confinement and discipline must have rendered doubly desirable, would forget all restraint, and then being joined by the wild discontented Indians, they would be more formidable enemies to the missions than before, inasmuch as they would be more enlightened. But I will not anticipate the result, which we had an opportunity of seeing on our return the following year; and from which the reader will be able to judge how the system worked.

The padres, however, dreading the worst, were very discontented, and many would willingly have quitted that country for Manilla. The government appeared to be aware of this feeling, as they sent some young priests from Mexico to supplant those who were disaffected, and desired that they should be trained up in the mission, and should make themselves acquainted with the language and usages of the Indians, in order that they might not promote discontent by any sudden innovation.

The missions have hitherto been of the highest importance to California, and the government cannot be too careful to promote their welfare, as the prosperity of the country in a great measure is dependent upon them, and must continue to be so until settlers from the mother country can be induced to resort thither. [. . .]

Whatever may be the system, and whether the Indians be really dragged from their homes and families by armed parties, as some assert, or not, and forced to exchange their life of freedom wandering for one of confinement and restraint in the missions, the change according to our ideas of happiness would seem advantageous to them, as they lead a far better life in the missions than in their forests, where they are in a state of nudity, and are frequently obliged to depend solely upon wild acorns for their subsistence.

Immediately the Indians are brought to the mission they are placed under the tuition of some of the most enlightened of their countrymen, who teach them to repeat in Spanish the Lord's Prayer and certain passages in the Romish litany; and also to cross themselves properly on entering the church. In a few days a willing Indian becomes a proficient in these mysteries, and suffers himself to be baptized, and duly initiated into the church. If, however, as it not unfrequently happens, any of the captured Indians show a repugnance to conversion, it is the practice to imprison them for a few days, and then to allow them to breathe a little fresh air in a walk round the mission, to observe the happy mode of life of their-converted countrymen; after which they are again shut up, and thus continue to be incarcerated until they declare their readiness to renounce the religion of their forefathers. [. . .]

A person acquainted with the language of the parties, of which there are sometimes several dialects in the same mission, is then selected to train them, and having duly prepared them takes his pupils to the padre to be baptized, and to receive the sacrament. Having become Christians they are put to trades, or if they have good voices they are taught music, and form part of the choir of the church. Thus there are in almost every mission weavers, tanners, shoemakers, bricklayers, carpenters, blacksmiths, and other artificers. Others again are taught husbandry, to rear cattle and horses; and some to cook for the mission: while the females card, clean, and spin wool, weave, and sew; and those who are married attend to their domestic concerns.

In requital of these benefits, the services of the Indian, for life, belong to the mission, and if any neophyte should repent of his apostacy from the religion of his ancestors and desert, an armed force is sent in pursuit of him, and drags him back to punishment apportioned to the degree of aggravation attached to his crime. It does not often happen that a voluntary convert succeeds in his attempt to escape, as the wild Indians have a great contempt and dislike for those who have entered the missions, and they will frequently not only refuse to re-admit them to their tribe, but will sometimes even discover their retreat to their pursuers. This animosity between the wild and converted Indians is of great importance to the missions, as it checks desertion, and is at the same time a powerful defense against the wild tribes, who consider their territory invaded, and have other just causes of complaint. The Indians, besides, from political motives, are, I fear, frequently encouraged in a contemptuous feeling towards their unconverted countrymen, by hearing them constantly held up to them in the degrading light of *bestias*! and in hearing the Spaniards distinguished by the appellation of *gente de razón*. [. . .]

In some of the missions much misery prevails,

while in others there is a degree of cheerfulness and cleanliness which shows that many of the Indians require only care and proper management to make them as happy as their dull senses will admit of under a life of constraint.

The two missions of San Francisco and San José are examples of the contrast alluded to. The former in 1817 contained a thousand converts, who were housed in small huts around the mission; but at present only two hundred and sixty remain— some have been sent, it is true, to the new mission of San Francisco Solano, but sickness and death have dealt with an unsparing hand among the others. The huts of the absentees, at the time of our visit, had all fallen to decay, and presented heaps of filth and rubbish; while the remaining inmates of the mission were in as miserable a condition as it was possible to conceive, and were entirely regardless of their own comfort. Their hovels afforded scarcely any protection against the weather, and were black with smoke: some of the Indians were sleeping on the greasy floor; others were grinding baked acorns to make into cakes, which constitute a large portion of their food. So little attention indeed had been paid even to health, that in one hut there was a quarter of beef suspended opposite a window, in a very offensive and unwholesome state, but its owners were too indolent to throw it out. San José, on the other hand, was all neatness, cleanliness, and comfort; the Indians were amusing themselves between the hours of labour at their games; and the children, uniformly dressed in white bodices and scarlet petticoats, were playing at bat and ball. Part of this difference may arise from the habits of the people, who are of different tribes. [...]

The children and adults of both sexes, in all the missions, are carefully locked up every night in separate apartments, and the keys are delivered into the possession of the padre; and as, in the daytime, their occupations lead to distinct places, unless they form a matrimonial alliance, they enjoy very little of each other's society. It, however, sometimes happens that they endeavour to evade the vigilance of their keepers, and are locked up with the opposite sex; but severe corporeal punishment, inflicted in the same manner as is practiced in our schools, but with a whip instead of a rod, is sure to ensue if they are discovered. Though there may be occasional acts of tyranny, yet the general character of the padres is kind and benevolent, and in some of the missions, the converts are so much attached to them that I have heard them declare they would go with them, if they were obliged to quit the country. It is greatly to be regretted that, with the influence these men have over their pupils, and with the regard those pupils seem to have for their masters, the priests do not interest themselves a little more in the education of their converts, the first step to which would be in making themselves acquainted with the Indian language. Many of the Indians surpass their pastors in this respect, and can speak the Spanish language, while scarcely one of the padres can make themselves understood by the Indians. They have besides, in general, a lamentable contempt for the intellect of these simple people, and think them incapable of improvement beyond a certain point. Notwithstanding this, the Indians are, in general, well clothed and fed; they have houses of their own, and if they are not comfortable, it is, in a great measure, their own fault; their meals are given to them three times a day, and consist of thick gruel made of wheat, Indian corn, and sometimes acorns, to which at noon is generally added meat. [...]

Having served ten years in the mission, an Indian may claim his liberty, provided any respectable settler will become surety for his future good conduct. A piece of ground is then allotted for his support, but he is never wholly free from the establishment, as part of his earnings must still be given to them. We heard of very few to whom this reward for servitude and good conduct had been granted; and it is not improbable that the padres are averse to it, as it deprives them of their best scholars.

PART IV
Ecclesiastical Realities

The church became the wealthiest institution and the largest landowner in Spanish and Portuguese America. Tithes paid to the state and reapportioned to the church plus fees charged for services represented important income. The *derrama*, or forced sale of goods to Amerindians, provided additional cash in select areas. But most income came from bequests or pious works. Wealthy individuals frequently endowed chantries, each of which guaranteed an income for the secular cleric in charge, for which he celebrated Masses for the souls of the founders and families. Others bequeathed lands and buildings in permanent *mortmain*, which allowed the church to rent but not sell. The church also acted as a bank and loaned money in return for monthly payments.[1]

Convents became powerful religious and economic institutions. As Jeffrey Klaiber, S.J., notes, their internal structure was "influenced by the society in which [they] functioned [and]... shared the same defects."[2] Women became nuns for myriad reasons, and convents became prevalent in every major colonial city, especially in the viceregal capitals of Mexico City and Lima. Young girls sometimes requested to join a convent out of true religious conviction and a desire to live in community. For others, conventual life became an enticing alternative to marriage. They could read and study or even apply entrepreneurial talents, since wealthier convents possessed considerable liquid capital and served as banks administered by the nuns. Just as elite fathers arranged marriages for their children, they sometimes compelled daughters to join a convent because they lacked sufficiently large dowries to attract suitable mates. Families gained prestige by having daughters in convents, which also ensured that they would realize the Marian ideal of purity and chastity. Nunneries catered to different clients based on race and class. With very few exceptions only white

---

1. John Frederick Schwaller, *Origins of Church Wealth in Mexico: Ecclesiastical Revenues and Church Finances, 1523-1600* (Albuquerque: University of New Mexico Press, 1985), 183-85; Virginia Garrard-Burnett, "Introduction," in *On Earth as It Is in Heaven: Religion in Modern Latin America*, ed. Virginia Garrard-Burnett (Wilmington, Del.: Scholarly Resources, 2000), xviii.

2. Jeffrey Klaiber, S.J., *The Catholic Church in Peru, 1821-1985: A Social History* (Washington, D.C.: Catholic University of America Press, 1992), 360.

women could become nuns during the first half of the colonial period. Mestizos and mulattoes joined in greater numbers in the eighteenth century. Luisa de Tapia (in religion, Sister Luisa del Espíritu Santo), an Amerindian woman from Querétaro, joined the Real Monasterio de Santa Clara de Jesús in 1607, but apparently no other Amerindian women in Mexico were permitted to take vows as professed nuns until 1724. Convents of Ursulines, Carmelites of St. Joseph, Poor Clares, and Conceptionists were established in Brazil in the eighteenth century. Nunneries were typically divided between those of the black veil and those of the white veil. Black-veiled nuns entered with sizable dowries and had a retinue of servants and black slaves so that they could continue to live in their sumptuous lifestyle. More modest white-veiled nuns were less pampered. Most convents also included *donadas*, or poorer women of mixed ancestry, who distinguished themselves by their piety or mysticism, such as the ability to "communicate" with souls in purgatory. Especially devout individuals in the baroque culture of the seventeenth century might wear hair shirts, partake in self-flagellation, or punish themselves in other ways; nuns and *donadas* were no exception. Since convents sometimes took in abandoned infant females, they too might form part of the cloistered community.[3]

41. A Letter from Potosí

The following frank letter (1577), written by Francisco de la Calzada, a parish priest, speaks for itself. Of what worth is it to the student of the church in the Indies? Compare it with the excerpt by Poma de Ayala (reading 43).

Dear Sister:

Since I have been in this realm of Peru I have written many letters, over fifteen of them, to you and to my nephew Próspero de Viso. And I have received only two from you, and one from my nephew, which I so prize and guard that they will accompany me when I return to Spain, if God permits.

I have always begged you to get my nephew Pedro de la Calzada started on his way here, since it would be greatly to my advantage and his. He has been so missed that if he had come I wouldn't be surprised to see us on the road to Spain within two years, because Potosí is more prosperous now than it has been since the world began. With this new invention of mercury, there are many men I know who less than three years ago were penniless and 3,000 or 4,000 pesos in debt, and now some of them have 50,000 pesos, others 40,000, and others who came only two years ago have 10,000 or 12,000 pesos.

The priests and friars who have a nephew whom they can trust are very rich, both groups of them. And those of us who have no one to trust have nothing but our parish salaries; there we spend more than we earn. [. . .]

---

3. Ann Miriam Gallagher, R.S.M., "The Indian Nuns of Mexico City's *Monasterio* of Corpus Christi, 1724-1821," in *Latin American Women: Historical Perspectives*, ed. Asunción Lavrin (Westport, Conn.: Greenwood Press, 1978), 152, 167 n. 9; Klaiber, *Catholic Church in Peru*, 3-4; Margaret E. Crahan, "Religious Orders (Colonial Period)," in *Encyclopedia of Latin America*, ed. Helen Delpar (New York: McGraw-Hill, 1974), 526-27.

SOURCE: Cited in James Lockhart and Enrique Otte, trans. and ed., *Letters and People of the Spanish Indies: Sixteenth Century* (Cambridge: Cambridge University Press, 1976), 254-55. Reprinted with the permission of Cambridge University Press.

Many [Spaniards] buy properties and possessions and marry here, intending not to see Spain
again. I don't know what I will do. Surely my
desire is to die not here, but where I was born. If I
am to go, it will be within three years, even if I take
only 4,000 or 5,000 pesos with me. If I decide to
stay, I will buy a very good farm or *chácara*, with a
vineyard of 10,000 or 12,000 stocks and many
trees, Castilian and local, that will support me
when I want to retire and rest, and not go about
instructing Indians, which is surely a great travail.
But, as I said, if I can I would rather go to Spain,
because I am very gray and fat, and this life is hard
on me.

42. Convents in the Maturing Colonies

*Antonio Vázquez de Espinosa (d. 1630), a Carmelite friar, theologian, missionary, and
inveterate traveler, wrote his last work,* Description of the Indies, *in 1620. It is an eyewitness catalogue of all that he saw in Peru and New Spain.*

    *What does his detailed and enthusiastic description of convents (here, men's friaries) and
nunneries in "Mexico" reveal to the reader about the lives, customs, and activities of religious in the maturing colonies?*

There are in Mexico City splendid and famous
convents of friars, with sumptuous temples, richly
and perfectly appointed, with large incomes and
charitable contributions which support them. All
of them maintain schools of Arts and Theology;
the chief one, Santo Domingo, is one of the best
and richest to be found in the Indies, and I doubt
whether there be its equal in Spain. It has over 200
friars, many of whom are highly educated and
great preachers. In this splendid convent they
teach Arts and Theology; the church has become a
glowing coal of gold, with great majesty of chapels
along its sides. Although the foundations have
sunk more than 5 feet below ground level, the convent is an excellent one, with large cloisters and
dormitories, well designed and carried out. [. . .]

[T]he largest with about 200 (*ex* 300) friars and
a school of Arts and Theology; the church is one of
the largest and finest in all the Indies, with many
handsome chapels and extensive cloisters and
dormitories, all beautifully done, with remarkable
paintings; the Seraphic Patriarch having founded
his order in poverty, it has been enriched with
virtue, membership, and buildings. The convent
of St. Joseph is connected with the large one; there

is a local superior there and friars with pastoral
circuits and Indians under instruction, in which
they administer the Holy Sacraments and teach
them the facts of our Holy Faith and virtue. [. . .]

Of the Order of the Glorious Doctor and Patriarch St. Augustine there are four convents; the
chief one contains over 150 friars; they teach Arts
and Theology; the church is one of the largest and
best designed and carried out, to be seen in Mexico; it is all one cluster of gold, with famous cloisters and dormitories and a great refectory. This
splendid convent receives every year from its
income and church contributions, not counting
other alms, over 100,000 pesos. The College of San
Pablo of the same Augustinian Order has about
100 friars; there they teach Arts and Theology with
great diligence and exactitude, and education
flourishes; from this distinguished order have
risen such remarkable men as Master Fray Juan
Zapata, Bishop of Guatemala, Master Fray Gabriel
de Ribera, a son of that splendid convent, and
many others whom I do not mention because
their virtue and learning are well known in that
kingdom and they have accomplished much
there. The convent of San Sebastián will have

SOURCE: Antonio Vázquez de Espinosa, *Descriptions of the Indies (c. 1620)*, trans. Charles Upson Clark (Washington, D.C.:
Smithsonian Institution Press, 1942), 157-62.

some 12 friars busied with pastoral visits and cate-chizing the Indians, and in administering the Holy Sacraments; these belonged to the friars of the Barefoot Carmelite Order. The Augustinians have another convent with some 8 friars, called Santa Cruz. [. . .]

Of the Order of the Company of Jesus there are four houses; the chief house, in the size of its church and dormitories and in its wealth, is one of the largest and finest in all the Indies, and has men remarkable for their virtue and education, in which this sainted order greatly excels. There is another fine college of the same order, in which they give lectures and instruction both in Latin and in the Mexican language, and in Arts and Theology. San Ildefonso is a Royal College of the same order; it is a kind of boarding school, in which there are three classes of students. The first is of students in Theology, limited to 12, all duly qualified, of good family, and poor; for their sup-port His Majesty as patron has assigned an income. Their gowns are dark gray with green sashes having at their tips or points a sort of circu-lar badge or crown. [. . .]

There are in this royal city 16 very strict nun-neries, of great virtue and sanctity; among them there are many handmaids of God who lead holy lives. The nunnery of Santa Inés ranks among the strictest and finest of all Christendom. This was founded by Diego Caballero with 33 nuns, in pious imitation of the number of years our Lord passed on earth; there may be neither more nor less, except that when one dies, another enters in her place, to keep the number full. They enter without dowry, for this noble knight, to whom God had given much wealth, and who had no heirs, established this nunnery with a total of 33 nuns and for their support he left an annual income of 33,000 pesos, together with 2,000 pesos of income for the patron or patroness of his fam-ily. They have excellent music in this nunnery.

452.   Mexico contains the nunneries of La Concepción, San Lorenzo, Santa Catalina de Sena, La Encarnación, Santa Clara, Santa Teresa, Jesús María, Regina Celi, San Jerónimo; Santa Mónica, with an annex where they bring up children under instruction; Santa Isabel of Franciscan barefoot nuns; Santa María de Gracia, which consists of two separate convents with one church and a boarding school for girls already novitiates; the nunnery of Las Recogidas is very wealthy; San Juan de Letrán is a boarding school in which they bring up orphan children.

453.   In this great city there are nine famous hospitals, in which they care for the indigent sick of various nationalities, and with different diseases. These are: The general hospital for the Indians, called the Royal Hospital, whose patron is His Majesty. This receives large revenues and charitable contributions; and the sainted Count of Monterrey when Viceroy of that kingdom gave it his favor and assistance by establishing a theatrical playhouse (corral de comedias) all the income from which he turned over to it for the care, maintenance, and comfort of the poor among the Indians.

454.   The Hospital of Los Desamparados (The Destitute) is run by the friars and brethren of the blessed San Juan de Dios; it is rich and sumptu-ous. It has a revolving dumb-waiter into which foundlings are dropped or put—they commonly call them children of the church door—and these friars care for these orphaned children and find women to nurse them and pay them out of the hospital's revenues and the large daily charitable contributions which they get from the city's vari-ous wards every day.

43. A "Letter" from Peru

Don Felipe Guaman Poma de Ayala (c. 1535-1615), son of a noble Inca mother and a Spanish father, wrote his enormous Nueva crónica y buen gobierno *(translated as "Letter*

SOURCE: Huamán Poma, *Letter to a King: A Peruvian Chief's Account of Life under the Incas and under Spanish Rule*, arranged, edited and translated by Christopher Dilke (New York: E. P. Dutton, 1978) 19, 144-49, 152, 155, 158, 160-61, 167, 169, 186-87.

A "LETTER" FROM PERU

*to a King. A Peruvian Chief's Account of Life under the Incas and under Spanish Rule")
between 1567 and 1615.*

*Poma clearly wants to avoid an entirely negative account of the Spanish empire and its
clerical and lay officials and so makes reference to the moral behavior and good deeds of
specifically named individuals. But his real concern is the relentless exploitation of the
Amerindians by imperial personnel, especially priests. If the reader considers the concerns of
the parish priest in Peru (reading 41), then the specific incidents recounted by Poma in Peru
become entirely credible. How did priests comport themselves vis-à-vis Amerindians in
early colonial Peru? Was this behavior typical of most of them?*

Your Majesty, I hesitated for a long while before writing this letter. Even after beginning, I wanted to retract my words. I decided that my intention was a rash one and that, once started upon my story, I would never be able to complete it in the way in which a proper history ought to be written. For I lacked all written evidence and had to rely on the coloured and knotted cords, on which we Indians of Peru used to keep our records. Among our people I also sought out the oldest and most intelligent, on whom I could rely as witnesses of the truth.

In weighing, cataloguing and setting in order the various accounts I passed a great number of days, indeed many years, without coming to a decision. At last I overcame my timidity and began the task which I had aspired to for so long. I looked for illumination in the darkness of my understanding, in my very blindness and ignorance. For I am no doctor or Latin scholar, like some others in this country. But I make bold to think myself the first person of Indian race able to render such a service to Your Majesty. [. . .]

The priesthood began with Jesus Christ and his Apostles, but their successors in the various religious orders established in Peru do not follow this holy example. On the contrary, they show an unholy greed for worldly wealth and the sins of the flesh and a good example would be set to everyone if they were punished by the Holy Inquisition.

These priests are irascible and arrogant. They wield considerable power and usually act with great severity towards their parishioners, as if they had forgotten that Our Lord was poor and humble and the friend of sinners. Their own intimate circle is restricted to their relations and dependants, who are either Spanish or half-caste.

They readily engage in business, either on their own or other people's account, and employ a great deal of labour without adequate payment. Often they say that the work is for ecclesiastical vestments, when really it is for the sale of ordinary clothing. [. . .]

The usual practice is for a priest to have a man and two girls in the kitchen, a groom, a gardener, a porter, and others to carry wood and look after the animals.

Sometimes there are as many as ten mules in the stables, not counting the beasts belonging to neighbours, and they all have to be sustained at the Indians' expense. Herds of 1,000 cattle, goats, pigs or sheep are a commonplace and there are often hundreds of capons, chickens and rabbits, all requiring their own special arrangements, as well as market gardens. If a single animal is lost, the Indian held responsible has to pay for it in full. Since the servants are not even properly fed, it is no wonder that they avoid work. But there are always pretty girls attached to the household, who have been corrupted by the priests and bear them children. This kind of showy establishment is of course enormously costly.

A favourite source of income of the priesthood consists in organising the porterage of wine, chillies, coca and maize. These wares are carried on the backs of Indians and llamas and in some cases need to be brought down from high altitudes. The descent often results in death for the Indians, who catch a fever when they arrive in a warm climate. Any damage to their loads during the journey has to be made good at their own expense.

The priests make a practice of confiscating property which really belongs to a church, a society or a hospital and putting it to their own uses. In the same way they often overcharge for Masses for the dead. For a sung Mass they charge 6 reales instead of 3; and for spoken Mass 4 reales instead of 1. Some of them go so far as to extort 10 or 20 reales and then fail to celebrate Mass at all. Although the giving of alms is supposed to be voluntary, they insist on a contribution of 4 reales from each person. This is robbery and our Indians should have their money refunded to them. When a priest officiates at a wedding, he wants 5 pesos to cover the earnest-money, the candles and the collection. Similarly the usual rate for a baptism is 4 pesos. It never seems to occur to the priest that he is paid his salary for performing these offices. [. . .]

Many of the priests live as grandly as our former rulers, offering banquets to their friends and wasting the substance of the people on these entertainments. If they have money to spare, it ought to be spent on the local hospital or church. At present, the church is often kept in worse condition than a stable for horses.

Our clergy, being obliged to provide wax candles, incense and soap, get the Indians to pay by confiscating the silver subscribed for charity. It would be more honest to use the fees from burials, weddings and baptisms, or the money left at the foot of the altars on holy days, to provide these stores. [. . .]

When they occasionally travel abroad, the priests insist on being welcomed home with a peal of bells. The villagers have to come out in procession with crosses and banners, just as if these clerics were Bishops, when in reality they are no better than the rest of humanity.

In setting down truthfully this account of the way of life of the priests, the goods which they possess and the evil which they do, I am hoping to bring it to the attention of Your Majesty and other important persons. Although I feel exhausted by the effort, I propose to continue with my task. [. . .]

It is true that many clerics begin as men of considerable learning, but pride is usually their downfall.

Among the few kind and charitable priests I have known were Father Benavides, Francisco de Padilla and Father Yñigo. These ones at least did not run after girls or beget bastards, and they treated people of all sorts with respect. [. . .]

Mass should be announced by ten peals of the big or little bells, followed by a single bell ringing for quarter of an hour. By this means all the people of consequence, as well as the old and sick who are only able to walk with difficulty, would get ample warning. It would also remove the necessity for town-criers and others to make a personal tour of the parishioners' houses, in the course of which they often find opportunities for theft and lechery. One way of punishing these offenders would be to get all the parishioners together in church, while a special party would lie in wait for clandestine prowlers and make them captive. These culprits might be allowed to get off with a caution the first time, but the second time they should be whipped behind the church. The same treatment would be appropriate for magicians who throw eggs at the church door. The surviving old people from Inca times are reaching the end of their lives and their children are all baptised Christians, so the whole population ought to respond to a summons to church.

Clerks and sacristans are inclined to exploit the Indians and particularly the girls. One of their tricks is to arrange services on Wednesday and Friday evenings when the priest is away, so as to arouse the interest of these young creatures and seduce them afterwards. When their priest leaves them in charge of the parish, they pay much less attention to matters such as ringing the bells for prayer, helping the sick to die well and burying the dead. [. . .]

Cristóbal de Albornoz, who held the office of Visitor-General, was fearless in his judgements and a stern opponent of arrogance on the part of the priests. He never accepted bribes or used physical violence. [. . .]

One of the Visitor's duties is to confiscate any arms carried by the priests, whether for self-defence or for aggressive purposes. Not only are such arms terrifying to the Indians, but they are unsuitable in the hands of men anointed and consecrated to the service of God, who should be performing works of compassion. [. . .]

In the year 1611 a Visitor-General was sent out by the Bishop of Cuzco to correct the arrogance of the clergy and it is worth relating what occurred as a lesson for the future. He punished some of the priests, but others he let off because he had become good friends with them. In contempt of his orders, he himself confiscated property and provisions from the Indians, insisted on unpaid service and assumed privileges which he was in no way entitled to. Over and above this he treated the Indians with manifest hatred, going to the limits of what the law permits. [...]

It is the Visitor's job to look out for any misdemeanour or oversight on the part of the priests: visit the church buildings and see that they are properly painted, check that the doors are provided with locks, notice whether the holy images have been treated with respect and whether the bells are in order, and inspect the stocks of wax, incense, soap and oil. The high cross for processions and the vestments of the sacristans and choirboys need to be inspected. The priest's house also deserves attention. Is it clean and proper, or is it full of women? Is the priest in the habit of roaming around at night, or visiting wine-shops during the day? Does he hoard food, own property or embezzle the funds encharged to him? If he has a pillar for flogging Indians in his back yard he is nothing but an executioner; and if his barns are stuffed with loot he is a thief. A large number of dependants and servants is bound to tell against him. [...]

Among the good Christians whom I have known in Peru were the following:

Don Pedro de Córdoba y Guzmán of the Order of St. James, Captain of Cavalry, was the principal landowner and employer of our Indians in Lucanas. Neither he nor his family visited the villages or sent stewards to them as a rule, but lived all the time in Lima. He left half the tribute due to him in the hands of the Indians. The administration was conducted for him by an Indian named Diego Chachapoya and no Spaniards were employed on the estate. Once, when complaints were made against his son Rodrigo, he sent the young man to Chile as a ship's Captain. He also opposed any exploitation by administrators, priests and others. He was charitable and never abusive, an honest man who did not engage in business himself or demand presents in the customary style. If any of the Indians ever brought him a gift, he returned it eightfold, for he was really sorry for their laborious life. It is a pleasure for me to record the good example which he set during his term of office.

The royal administrator of the province of Lucanas, Don Gregorio López de Puga, was a genuinely learned man whose influence was always exerted on the side of justice. He liked to travel alone, not even taking a clerk with him, and to judge cases and disputes on his own. Often his judgements reflected a sympathy with the native rulers and a distaste for vagabonds. On one occasion he sentenced two Spaniards, who held important positions, saying that Your Majesty had sent him to do justice and not to condone robbery and inhumanity. Such a person, mature and considerate, deserves to remain a long time in office. [...]

In this book I have set down both the good and the evil of life in my country, so that the next Government may be correspondingly improved. My hope is that my work will be preserved in the archives of the Cathedral in Rome. [...]

The Indians in our country are just as gifted as Castilians in their artistry and workmanship. Some of them are excellent singers and musicians. They make themselves masters of the organ, fiddle, flute, clarinet, trumpet and horn without any difficulty. They also become capable municipal clerks. It is quite usual for them to deputise for royal administrators and mayors and they sometimes perform the duties of constables and accountants. They can use a gun, a sword or a halberd as well as any Spaniard. Often they are first-rate horsemen and trainers of animals, with a special aptitude with bulls. Some of them know Latin and study literature. If they were allowed to, they could perfectly well be ordained as priests. Above all they are loyal and admirable servants of the Crown, with no taste for rebellion.

Indians are skilful at all the decorative arts such as painting, engraving, carving, gilding, metalwork and embroidery. They make good tailors, cobblers, carpenters, masons and potters. Also, by simply watching the Spaniards, they have learnt how to do well in trade.

In the same way the Indian girls learn reading, writing, music and needle-work at the convents which they attend. They are just as clever and accomplished as Spanish girls at the domestic skills.

The clever ones among the Indians get themselves jobs with the Church, either as singers or clerks. Because of the incompetence or absence of the priests they soon find themselves burying the dead with all the proper prayers and responses. They take vespers and look after the music and singing, as well as intoning the prayers. On Sundays and holy days they conduct the ceremonies as well as any Spaniard. In default of a priest they baptise the babies with holy water, reciting the proper form of words, and this is allowed by the authorities in order to avoid any of the small creatures going to limbo for lack of baptism. On Wednesdays and Fridays Indians conduct the early morning service, these being the obligatory days, and they say the prayers for the dead. However, they get nothing but interference from the priests themselves, who usually refer to them dismissively as 'clever children'.

44. Jesuit Labor Practices in Quito

The Jesuits, the last major order to arrive in the Spanish colonies, were experts at establishing themselves quickly and effectively in parish, missionary, and academic activity as they had done in Brazil commencing in 1549.

The following complaint of 1623 by Amerindian chieftains (principales) *from the vicinity of Quito, addressed to the king, suggests the intense Jesuit commitment—in this case rather extreme—to their work, and also their Eurocentric view of Amerindians. Does their Eurocentrism explain their zeal or their zeal their Eurocentrism?*

Principales of Sangolquí Complain of Unjust Treatment from Jesuit Estate Officials (1623)

Lord: By this memorial you will learn of the harmful treatment and extortions that the Indians of the town of Sangolquí receive from the fathers of the Society of Jesus. The said fathers own in the Valley of Chillo, a quarter of a league from Sangolquí, an estate where they sow 400 fanegas of wheat and harvest 5,000 or 6,000 fanegas. To work this farm the said fathers have 25 gañanes a year and because these 25 cannot do all the work of plowing, the fathers ask for replacements and additional laborers and to work for one month. Thus, ordinarily 50 Indians are employed and because of this we principales cannot comply with other requests for laborers. Also, supplies are diminishing, and a fanega of wheat and corn becomes dearer each year because the said fathers are the only ones who have a storehouse to keep the wheat. . . . So on their own authority, at times of plowing and harvest, the fathers, with their majordomos, lay brothers, and four or five blacks and mulattoes, come to the town and distribute silver to entice workers. And the Indian who does not want to go, because he must work on other farms, is carried by the said lay brothers and mulattoes, tied up, and placed in jail at night and made to work by day, being beaten, incarcerated, and the object of other wicked treatment.

Also the fathers have a church, with cross outside and bell; and the whole town [of Pintag] is gradually moving to the estate of the Jesuits, leav-

SOURCE: Excerpt from Archivo General de las Indias (Quito 10), Seville, Spain, "Principales of Sangolquí Complain of Unjust Treatment from Jesuit Estate Officials (1623)." Translated by and quoted in Nicholas P. Cushner, *Farm and Factory: The Jesuits and the Development of Agrarian Capitalism in Colonial Quito, 1600-1767* (Albany: State University of New York Press, 1982), 185.

ing the town empty; and for this reason we the caciques cannot fulfill our other obligations of supplying laborers.

Also, the said fathers have a tannery on the estate, where they cut and cure hides and leather. The garbage that comes from the tannery flows into the river near the town and this river supplies the town's drinking water. Thus, much sickness has been caused by this dumping.

In order to remedy those things we ask your Lordship to study this memorial and favor us with justice by sending someone, whoever he might be,

to investigate the charges we here make for, after God, you are our source of help, and in all we ask justice.

Also, the said fathers keep a gate shut on the Camino Real that passes through their estate, and guarding the gate continually are ferocious dogs, and this so that no one will use the said Camino Real. Don García Zangolquí. Don Domingo Humaná. Don Felipe Juali Zidemon, Don Felipe Sangolquí. Don Juan Zunno. Don Francisco Gualizanmi. Don Domingo Zangolquí. [Countersigned] Don Antonio de Morga. [AGI, Quito 10.]

45. Christian and "Pagan" Amerindians Confront Corrupt Clergy

Jorge Juan (1713-1773) and Antonio de Ulloa (1716-1795) were brilliant young naval officers and scientists chosen by Philip V (reigned 1700-1746) to accompany an expedition of French scientists to the New World. The two Spaniards traveled extensively between 1736 and 1744 in the Andean area of the empire and wrote reports on every aspect of its flora and fauna, politics, and culture. Excerpts follow from their secret report to the Crown, Discourse and Political Reflections on the Kingdoms of Peru.

How credible is Juan and Ulloa's description of clerical corruption in the mature Peruvian colony? If the account of that corruption, involving greed, cruelty, and illicit sex, is accurate, how might the Amerindians' desire for their own parish priest be explained? Not all Amerindians reacted in the same way to the corrupt Spaniards. What were some alternate responses?

A sad example of how a priest's bad behavior harms the Indians can be seen from what was told us in the village of Piniampiro in the corregimiento of the town of San Miguel de Ybarra in the province of Quito. According to extant accounts, its population was more than 5,000, all Indians. Unable to endure the great number of abuses heaped upon them, one night they revolted and fled to the mountains to join the heathen Indians and have remained with them ever since. The Indians live so close to the town that one can see clouds of smoke from their villages simply by climbing a nearby hill. Some of these Indians have appeared unexpectedly in the village of Mira, closest to the heathen settlements, but they have withdrawn to the mountains again very quickly. These abuses could also be the reason for the loss of the famous city of Logroño and the town of Guariboya, the main ones in the Macas district whose capital is Sevilla del Oro. Now completely in ruins, this city exists only as a sad reminder of the fate which the others met.

This area had so much gold that the capital received its name from the large amounts taken from it. In fact there is still a scale in the city to weigh the twenty percent due the royal treasury from gold and silver production. But the corregidores on the one hand and the clergy on the other demanded so much forced labor from the Indians that they drove them to revolt. Imitating what the

---

SOURCE: John J. TePaske, ed., *Discourse and Political Reflections on the Kingdoms of Peru* (Norman: University of Oklahoma Press, 1978), 110-13. Reprinted by permission of the University of Oklahoma Press © 1978.

Indians of Arauco, Tucapel, and Chile did to Pedro de Valdivia, the natives melted down a large portion of gold and poured it into the mouths, eyes, ears, and noses of the Spaniards. They killed the majority of the white males, seized their wives, and razed Logroño and the other villages. Only Sevilla del Oro and Zuña escaped, but both were decimated by frequent Indian raids. In fact the population of both became so small and poverty stricken that no money circulated in them. But in order to see how harmful the clergy's behavior can be, particularly the scandalous behavior of the regular clergy; in order to facilitate the permanent settlement of villages and tribes previously conquered; and even more important, in order to convert those areas not yet reduced, we shall refer here to a case which occurred a few years ago that bears out our views.

An Indian from the village of Guamboya appeared unexpectedly in the town of Riobamba, where he went directly to the house of the resident priest, a man of known virtue. The Indian told the cleric he was representing a number of Indians both from his own tribe and from neighboring villages, who wanted him to be their priest, to baptize them, and to say Mass. If he would accept, they would support him by giving him as much gold as he wished and by placing at his disposal any women he desired. But he would have to come alone, not in the company of other Spaniards, mestizos, or priests. Their reason for choosing him, said the Indian, was that he was not as greedy as other clerics. Fearing that the Indians intended to commit an atrocity against him, which was common for them, the priest replied that he could not give an answer at the moment but would respond shortly. The Indian seemed disconsolate but set the day for securing the priest's reply and designated a spot in the mountains for him to appear alone. He and some of his people agreed to meet the priest there and escort him to their territory in the event he accepted their proposal. Stipulating absolutely that the priest come alone, the Indian departed. Unable to make up his mind, the cleric went to Quito to consult with the bishop of that city, Don Andrés de Paredes (who had assumed this high office a little before we arrived in that province). A zealous Christian, the bishop encouraged the priest to accept the offer in order to convert as many heathen souls as wanted to receive the faith. Reinforced by the bishop's Catholic influence and Christian dedication, he returned to Riobamba, resolved to undertake the task. Becoming very diffident, he could not bring himself to go to the designated site at the appointed time. Meanwhile the Indian messenger and the others from his tribe did as they promised, remaining in hiding at the appropriate spot for a few days. When the priest failed to appear, the Indian representative unexpectedly entered Riobamba one night to visit the cleric. Although agreeing this time to become their priest, the cleric stipulated that for his own protection he must be accompanied by some secular clergymen. But this was what the Indians objected to most, and none of the entreaties, assurances, or simple guarantees that the Indian's limited capacity could provide persuaded the priest. Thus the emissary left Riobamba that same night very disheartened. Later, in the village, the priest divulged what the Indian told him on his second visit and provided information concerning the site where the Indians were to meet him. Some villagers then went out to reconnoiter the area and discovered signs that someone had been there. Although they claimed to have gone into the mountains trying to find the paths which the Indians had followed, they failed to find any of the natives. After a short distance they lost the trail completely.

This case created a considerable stir in that province. It is worth noting that even though the Indians had no close contact with civilized areas, they should still go directly to that particular priest and be fully aware of his good qualities. If the clergy fulfilled their obligations, this would not be so unusual, but oppressed by the corregidores and suffering bad treatment in the haciendas, many Indians flee to unconquered areas to live among the heathen. There they relate everything that occurs in areas under Spanish control and in the villages and they breed so much antagonism that reduction of the heathen becomes increasingly difficult. The agent who twice went into Riobamba was one of those who fled. Besides being acquainted with the priest, this Indian spoke the Inca tongue perfectly, a language which is not in use among the heathen Indians.

This example provides sufficient proof of the greed and scandalous behavior of the clergy and of the low opinion the Indians must have of them because of the abuses experienced at their hands. The Indian messenger made it clear that they wanted no other priest to teach catechism and give them spiritual guidance because he would not enslave them as other Spaniards had done. The emissary did not want any others to come into his territory with the chosen priest, for the Indians feared that once the Spaniards discovered the way into their domain, they would take the opportunity later to come in force to seize them and their land.

The most outrageous promise made to the priest by these unrefined, simple people serves to establish the Indians' view of the clergy: this was the offer of as many women as he wished. It stems from what the Indians learned about priests with female mates, living like laymen with wives and children. The Indians are convinced that this horrible sin is entirely licit and are both cowed and confused at being constant witnesses to repeated clerical sacrileges. Idealistic natives see the clergy indulge themselves in the most terrible evil and then go out to celebrate the greatest sacrifice imaginable (the Mass). Although this matter might better be kept quiet than exposed, our zeal and desire to correct such execrable abuses oblige us not to gloss over the situation. As proof of the clergy's excessively lewd behavior, we would like to cite a case well-known throughout the province of Quito, even though it occurred while we were not there. [...]

PART V
Roman Catholicism Triumphant?

Despite the continued decline of the Amerindian population in New Spain until the mid-seventeenth century and the increase in population of the marginalized castes, no widespread rebellion occurred in New Spain in the seventeenth century, and there were only two significant riots in Mexico City. The reforms of Viceroy Francisco de Toledo in late-sixteenth-century Peru also enabled that colony to escape any significant disturbances throughout the next century. So, despite the repressive character of most of the Spanish and Portuguese colonial institutions and the rigidity of the social order, many Amerindian communities and individuals from the castes were able to avoid a still harsher destiny; the former were able to maintain their traditions and the latter able to make some economic and social advancement. As the century wore on, the church's Holy Office of the Inquisition gradually relaxed its rigor, and the sacred mysteries of the church perhaps served as a soothing balm on society. The seventeenth century also witnessed such Catholic scholars and saints as Carlos de Sigüenza y Góngora, Juan Palafox y Mendoza, Sor Juana Inés de la Cruz, Toribio de Mongrovejo, Francisco Solano, Rosa de Lima, and Martín de Porres.

For New Spain and Peru, therefore, can the seventeenth century be considered a colonial "golden age," a time when Catholic culture flourished?[1]

---

1. Chester Lyle Guthrie, "Riots in Seventeenth-Century Mexico City," in *History of Latin American Civilization: Sources and Interpretations,* ed. Lewis Hanke (Boston: Little Brown, 1967), 302-13; Mariano Cuevas, S.J., *Historia de la Iglesia en México,* vol. 3 (El Paso, Tex., 1928), in *Colonial Spanish America: A Documentary History,* ed. Kenneth Mills and William B. Taylor (Wilmington, Del.: Scholarly Resources, 1998), 185-93.

46. Virgin of Guadalupe

The following narrative, translated from the original (1649) Nahuatl of Luis Lasso de la Vega, has been accepted as the authentic account of the story of the Virgin of Guadalupe popularized by Miguel Sánchez in his Spanish version (1648).

What does the narrative reveal about both the religious culture and the status of the Amerindian in New Spain?

Ten years after the capture of the city of Mexico, the wars came to an end, and there was peace in the land, and the faith began to spread, the knowledge of the true God in whom we live. About this time, in the year 1531, early in the month of December, there was a poor Indian, called Juan Diego, so it is said, a native of Cuautitlán. It was a Saturday, very early in the morning, and he was on his way to church and to do some errands. When he reached the hill known as Tepeyacac, day was breaking, and he heard the sound of singing on the hill; it was like the song of many sweet-voiced birds; at times the singers fell silent, and it seemed as though the hills were answering. The song, so sweet and pleasing, was lovelier than that of the *coyoltototl* and the *tziniz-can* and of other singing birds. Juan Diego stopped to look and said to himself: "Am I hearing right? Perhaps I am still asleep? Have I awakened? Where am I? Could I be in the earthly paradise our forefathers told of? Or could I be in heaven?" He was looking eastward, to the top of the hill, whence the heavenly music was coming, when it suddenly ceased, and there was a silence, and he heard someone calling to him from the summit of the hill and saying: "*Juanito, Juan Dieguito*." So he proceeded to where the voice came from; he was not at all frightened, on the contrary, very happy, and he climbed the hill to see who was calling him. When he reached the top he saw a lady standing there, who told him to come near her. When he approached her he was amazed at her superhuman grandeur: her raiment was resplendent like the sun; the rock on which her foot rested was shot through with radiance, and was like an anklet of precious stones, and the earth all around shone like the rainbow. The mesquites, cactus, and other little plants growing there were like emeralds, their foliage beautiful turquoise, and their branches and thorns gleamed like gold. He bent low before her and heard her speak, in a gentle, polite tone, as though to manifest her love and esteem: "Juanito, littlest of my sons, where are you going?" He answered: "Lady and *Niña mia*, I am on my way to your house in Mexico Tlatilolco, to follow the divine teachings given and taught us by our priests, the representatives of Our Lord." Then she spoke to him and revealed her holy desire. She said to him: "Know the Mother of the True God in whom we live, of the Creator in whom all exist, Lord of Heaven and Earth. I greatly desire that a temple be built me here, that in it I may manifest and give to all my love, pity, help, and defense, for I am your mother, yours and all the dwellers in this land and the others who love me and call upon me and trust in me; here I will listen to their pleas, and remedy their sufferings, griefs, and pains. And to carry out the desire of my clemency, go to the palace of the bishop of Mexico and tell him that I have sent you to reveal to him what I earnestly desire, that here on this spot a temple be erected to me. Describe to him carefully all that you have seen and admired, and what you have heard. Rest assured that I will be very grateful and will repay you, for I will make you happy, and you will deserve that I recompense the effort and the trouble you undergo to do what I ask of you. You have heard my bidding, littlest of

SOURCE: Harriet De Onís, ed. and trans., *The Golden Land: An Anthology of Latin American Folklore in Literature* (New York: Knopf, 1948), 72–78. From *The Golden Land*, trans. Harriet De Onís, copyright © 1948 and renewed 1976 by Harriet De Onís. Used by permission of Alfred A. Knopf, a division of Random House, Inc.

my sons; go now and do as I have said." At once he bowed low before her and said: "My Lady, I go to do your errand; for the present I take my leave of you, I, your humble servant." And he went down the hill to do as he was bid, and came out on the highway that follows a straight line into the city of Mexico.

When he reached the city he went without delay straight to the palace of the bishop, who had been appointed only a short while before, by name Fray Juan de Zumárraga, of the order of St. Francis. As soon as he got there he tried to see him; he begged the servants to announce him, and after a considerable time had elapsed, they came to call him, saying the bishop had said he should come in. As soon as he entered, he bowed and knelt before him, and proceeded to give him the message from the Lady of Heaven. He also told him of the wondrous thing he had seen and heard. After listening to all he had to say, the bishop seemed skeptical, and answered him: "Come again some other time, son, and we'll talk this over more slowly; I will hear all you have to say from the beginning, and consider the message and desire with which you have come." Juan Diego departed sadly, because he had in no wise accomplished his errand.

He went back the same day and climbed to the summit of the hill where he came upon the Lady of Heaven, who was waiting for him right where he had seen her the first time. [. . .]

["]I beg you, Lady and *Niña mia*, to pick out some important person who is known and respected to carry your message, so they will believe him. Because I am just a little man, a bit of rope, a frail wooden ladder, a fallen leaf, a nobody, and you, *Niña mia*, littlest of my daughters, My Lady, send me to a place where I am not in the habit of going and don't belong. Forgive me for causing you sorrow and arousing your anger, My Lady and Beloved." The Blessed Virgin answered: "Listen, oh littlest of my sons, know that my servants and messengers are many whom I could entrust to bear my message and do my will; but it is absolutely necessary that you, and you alone, solicit what I wish, and that my will be done through your mediation.["] [. . .]

The next day, which was Sunday, very early in the morning, he left his house and went straight to Tlatilolco, to hear the divine teachings, and to be there when they took the roll, and see the bishop afterwards. At about ten o'clock, after Mass had been said, and the roll taken, and the people had left, Juan Diego went to the palace of the bishop. After many difficulties he was admitted to his presence. He knelt at his feet, and grew sad and wept as he told him of the command of the Lady of Heaven, saying he hoped he would believe his message, and the will of the Immaculate, that a temple should be built to her in the place she desired. The bishop, to certify himself, asked him many things, where he had seen her, what she was like; and he carefully related everything to the bishop. He even described with great exactness how she looked, and all that he had seen and had wondered at, and in everything it was apparent that she was the ever Virgin Blessed Mother of the Saviour, Our Lord, Jesus Christ. Nevertheless the bishop did not believe him, and told him that not merely because of his talk and desire could his wish be fulfilled; that, in addition, he would have to have some sign to show that he was sent by the Queen of Heaven. As soon as he said this, Juan Diego replied to the bishop: "Sir, tell me the sign you want; and I will go at once and ask the Queen of Heaven, who sent me here, for it." When the bishop saw that he ratified all he had said without hesitating or retracting anything, he dismissed him. He immediately ordered some of the members of his household whom he could trust to follow him and watch carefully where he went and whom he met and talked with. And this was done. Juan Diego set straight out on the highroad; those who were following lost him near the bridge of Tepeyacac, where the ravine is, and although they looked everywhere for him, they could not find him. And they returned, angry at not having accomplished what they set out to do, but desirous of preventing Juan Diego from carrying out his plan. They went to see the bishop, to persuade him to pay him no heed; they told him that he was deceiving him, that he was inventing what he told him, or at any rate he had dreamed it. And they decided that if he came back again, they would punish him severely to teach him not to lie and deceive.

Meanwhile, Juan Diego was with the Blessed Virgin, telling her what the bishop had answered. After the Lady had heard him, she said: "It is well, my son. Tomorrow you will return here and take the bishop the sign he has asked for; with this he will believe you and will no longer doubt or distrust your word. And know, my son, that I will repay your diligence and the effort and fatigue you have endured for me. Go now, and I will be waiting for you here tomorrow." [. . .]

After the merciful Virgin had heard Juan Diego's words, she replied: "Listen and hearken to me, littlest of my sons. This that frightens and distresses you is nothing. Let not your heart be troubled. Have no fear of this sickness or of any other sickness or trouble. Am I, your mother, not here? Do you not stand in my shadow? Am I not your health? Are you not in my lap? What more do you need? Let nothing sadden or afflict you; have no concern for the illness of your uncle, who will not die now. Know that he is already cured." [. . .]

"Go up, littlest of my sons, to the top of the hill; there where you saw me and I gave you my orders you will find many flowers. Cut them, gather them up, and then come back to me with them." Juan Diego immediately climbed the hill, and when he reached the top he was amazed to see that many different roses of Castile had bloomed there before the season for them, because it was bitter cold at the time. [. . .]

When she saw them, she picked them up in her hand and then put them in his lap again, saying: "Littlest of my sons, these roses are the proof and token you will take to the bishop. Tell him in my name that they are evidence of my desire, which he must fulfill. You are my ambassador, worthy of confidence. I strictly order you not to open your blanket and reveal its contents to anyone but the bishop.["] [. . .]

When he reached the bishop's palace, the butler and the other servants of the prelate came to meet him. He told them to tell the bishop he wished to see him, but none of them would do it, pretending that they had not heard him, either because it was too early, or because they already knew him, and found him troublesome and

importunate; besides, their companions, who had lost sight of him when they tried to follow him, had already told them about him. For a long time he waited. Finally when they saw that he had been there a long time, standing, and with his head bowed, waiting patiently to see if he were sent for, and as it seemed that he was carrying something in his blanket, they drew near him to find out what it was and satisfy their curiosity. When Juan Diego saw that he could not hide what he was carrying, and that on this account they would upbraid him, or push him or beat him, he opened the blanket a little and showed the flowers. When they saw the different roses of Castile when it was not the season in which they bloomed, they marveled greatly to see them so fresh, so full-blown, so fragrant and so beautiful. They reached in to take some of them from him, but the three times they tried, they were unsuccessful, for when they went to touch them, they did not find real flowers, but they seemed painted or embroidered or worked in the blanket. They went at once to tell the bishop what they had seen, and to ask him to receive the little Indian who had come so many times and who had been waiting a long while to see him. When the bishop heard this, he realized that the Indian had come with the proof he had demanded. [. . .]

["]She told me why I was to give them to you; and I am doing so that you may see in them the sign you asked for and accomplish her will; and also that you may see the truth of my word and my message. Here they are; receive them." Then he unfolded his white blanket in which he was carrying the flowers. And as the different roses of Castile poured out on the floor, on the blanket there suddenly appeared the precious image of the ever Virgin Blessed Mary, Mother of God, as it is preserved today in her temple of Tepeyacac, which is called Guadalupe. When the bishop saw it, he and all those present knelt down; they marveled greatly at it; they arose to see it; they grew sad and grievous, showing that they were looking upon it with heart and mind. The bishop, with tears in his eyes, prayed and begged her forgiveness for not having carried out her wish and her command.

47. Artisans! Be Ready for Corpus Christi!

This decree, promulgated in 1673 by the officers of the municipality of São Salvador de Bahia, Brazil, stipulates both the participants and their duties for the celebration of the feast of Corpus Christi in 1674.

What does this decree reveal about such diverse aspects of colonial America as Catholicism, church-state relations, economic life and organizations, and daily life at the grassroots level?

On the 22 day of November of the year 1673 in the council chamber of this City of Salvador Bahia de Todos os Santos, present the ordinary judge, Manuel de Brito Lobo, and the aldermen, and the *Procurador do concelho*, and the *Juiz do Povo*, and the *mesteres* who have signed below, as also the judges of the workers' corporations of this city, the said aldermen moved and proposed that forasmuch as there were badly wanting in the processions the time-honoured insignia of the past, such as the dragon, hobby horses, and other old-time curiosities, which greatly enhanced the splendour and festivity which Christian piety renders to God and to his Saints, and that whereas this city had grown greatly in all the arts and crafts, some of which made no contribution of any sort or kind to the said processions—in view of all this, the said officers of the municipality resolved and agreed that the carpenters would supply the banner as they usually do, and likewise the wooden frame for the dragon, sharing this responsibility with the joiners and the turners. And the tailors would be obliged to supply their usual banner, and the cloth which covers the serpent, painted and fitted, it being their responsibility to keep and look after it always; and the carpenters would provide the wood whenever this was necessary, and all these various corporations would provide Negroes who would carry it in the processions. And the cobblers would provide their usual banner, and the dragon as they always have done. And the stonemasons will supply a banner which they will make forthwith at their own cost. The dyers, the hatters,

the harness-makers, the tinkers, and the coopers will provide a banner and four hobbyhorses [*cavalinhos fuscos*]. And the male and female bakers and the pastry-cooks will provide two giants and a giantess, and a dwarf which the common people call "Father of the Giants." And the blacksmiths, the locksmiths, the barbers, the sword-cutlers, and the saddlers, who all belong to the religious brotherhood of São Jorge will be obliged to provide a banner or a pennant, as they usually do, and the statue of the Saint on his bier, and likewise the statue of the same Saint seated and arrayed on horseback, together with a Page and an Ensign, a trumpet, and drummers, and six sergeants of the guard, all properly dressed and equipped. And the itinerant women who sell from door to door, and the male and female tavern-keepers will contribute with four dances, including that of the rope-makers — And thus the said aldermen decided that this regulation concerning the form of the insignia in the said processions would be mandatory from this day forward, and that the corporations whose representatives were present should be notified forthwith that a fine of 6,000 reis paid from prison for the public works of this municipality and the new prison, would be inflicted on any which failed entirely to fulfill the obligations hereby imposed on them. And the officers further ordered that all this should be entered in these minutes which they signed, and I, João Peixoto Viegas, Secretary of the municipality, wrote it. [Signed] *Manoel de Brita/ Pedro Borges Pacheco / Paulo Coelho de Vasconcellos / Sebastião*

SOURCE: Atas da Câmara de Bahia, vol. 1, 1669-1684, 114-15. Trans. C. R. Boxer, *Portuguese Society in the Tropics: The Municipal Councils of Goa, Macao, Bahia, and Luanda, 1510-1800* (Madison: University of Wisconsin Press, 1965), 181-82. Boxer, C. R., *Portuguese Society in the Tropics.* © 1965. Reprinted by permission of The University of Wisconsin Press.

de Araujo de Goes / João de Almeida Pinto / Sebastião de Lima.

[A marginal entry reads as follows:] And the officers of the municipal council further decided that the cattle-traders will provide three little barren cows. João Peixoto Viegas wrote it on the same day and it was signed by Lobo / Pacheco / Goes / Pinto.

[Another marginal entry, in a later hand, reads:] At a council meeting on the 20 October 1713 we have to declare that the button-makers should be added to the banner of the coopers.

48. A White Holy Woman in Seventeenth-Century Lima

The following is the testimony of don Gonzalo de la Maza (a Spanish bookkeeper who knew Isabel for sixteen years) in 1617 about Isabel Flores de Oliva (1586-1617), canonized Saint Rose of Lima in 1671. Only three weeks after her death don Gonzalo responded to thirty-two questions put to him by a tribunal of judges. What does her understanding of Christian piety and her rapid canonization reveal about the kind of Catholicism encouraged by the church in the colonial era?

Rosa told this witness of an incident that occurred when she was about five years old, while she was playing with one of her brothers, Hernando, who was two years older. Rosa [then Isabel] had grown beautiful blonde hair and [on this occasion] it had been handled roughly and soiled by her said brother. Once she saw the state of it, she started to cry. Her brother asked why she cried. Did she not know that on account of [worrying over] their hair many souls were in Hell? Knowing this, she should not be crying over her hair. [Rosa said] that this retort had so imprinted itself in her heart that in thinking about it she was seized by so great a fear in her soul that from that moment on she did not do a thing, not one thing, which she understood to be a sin and an offense to God Our Father. From this fear Rosa gained some knowledge of the divine goodness, which helped her [understand things about] her grandmother [who had died] and a sister, a little older than her, who died at the age of fourteen. [Rosa was now able to see them] as souls that, in her opinion, had been very pleasing to Our Lord, [and] whose deaths had been a great consolation to her because the things she had seen in them and been given to understand by His Divine Majesty convinced her that they had certainly gone to Heaven. [...]

To the sixth question ... Although they kept secret her mortifications of the flesh and penances until she died, this witness and his family knew of her way of life. This witness said that from a young age she was given to mortify herself with fasts, scourges, and other [self-inflicted] sufferings, and that from early on she had subsisted on bread and water for many days [at a time]. And, from the age of ten or eleven years she kept to her fasts of bread and water, especially on the days that her mother would excuse it, that is, on the Wednesdays, Fridays, and Saturdays of each week. At the age of fifteen and sixteen years she had made a conditional vow to forego meat and to fast on bread and water for the rest of her life. ...

This witness observed her abstinence when she lived in his house, during which time even when she had a fever and her doctors and confessors ordered her to eat meat, she would not do it. Her

Source: Kenneth Mills and William B. Taylor, eds., *Spanish America: A Documentary History* (Wilmington, Del.: Scholarly Resources, 1998), 197, 199-200. Excerpted and translated from "Declaración de don Gonzalo de la Maza (o do la Masa) año 1617. Procesos de beatificación y canonización de Santa Rosa de Lima," published in *Una partecita del cielo: La Vida de Santa Rosa de Lima narrada por Don Gonzalo de la Maza a quien ella llamaba padre*, ed. Luis Millones (Lima: Editorial Horizonte, 1993), from the answers to questions 4, 6, 7, and 29 on pp. 149-52, 153-56, 156-59, 207-8. Reprinted by permission of SR Books, an imprint of Rowman & Littlefield Publishers, Inc.

fasts on bread and water were continuous. . . . [In fact,] this witness saw that she would go a day or two or more without eating or drinking anything, particularly on the days when she took Holy Communion, because at certain times of the year confessors granted permission for one to take Communion every time one went to church, and this is what she did with much modesty and without drawing attention to herself. During these fasts and abstinences, [when] she left the church or her secluded room in his house, she had such color [in her face] and showed such health [that it seemed] as if she was fortifying herself with plenty of nutritious dishes. Worrying over her stomach pains and all that she suffered, one would ask her why she did not eat anything, to which she ordinarily responded that Holy Communion made her feel full to bursting and that it was impossible for her to eat [even] a bite. [. . .]

The said Rosa de Sancta María sometimes told this witness and his wife and daughters that from an early age she had greatly detested putting on a good appearance for people and the care taken by her mother in arranging her hair, face, and clothes. Seeing that she was not getting very far [toward the realization of her ascetic designs] with her mother, at the age of twelve years she cut off her very blonde head of hair, at the sight of which her mother scolded her harshly. [But her quests continued.] Feeling that her fasts and mortifications were not sufficient to drain the color from her cheeks, she poured pitchers of cold water over her chest and back even when she was dressed. Because of this, or because of divine will and providence, she contracted an illness at the age of thirteen years and became crippled and [had to be] clamped to a bed by her hands and feet for a long time. [She suffered] a great pain over her entire body that could not be explained, but, in bearing it, a very great relief and comfort came to her, in [knowing] that on account of Heaven her patience and compliance with the divine will had never faltered.

49. A Black Holy Woman in Seventeenth-Century Lima

Diego de Córdova Salinas, O.F.M. (b. 1591), included a biography of the mulatta holy woman, Estefanía de San José (1561-1645), in his Chronicle of the Order of Our Holy Father Francis in the Most Religious Province of the Twelve Apostles of Peru *(1651).*

What does this brief text reveal about the kind of piety encouraged by the colonial church and about the social reality and political culture of seventeenth-century Peru?

In the heavenly court, where only merits count, all are equally rewarded when their deeds deserve it: the noble and he who is not; the rich and the poor; the black and the white, because, as Saint Paul stated when writing to the Romans (Romans X), God does not make any exceptions, He does not exclude anybody; He calls all to His mansion and to His wedding. . . . This was verified in the case of Sister Estefanía de San José, who being of tawny color, daughter of a slave woman, dressed in rags and often disdained, offered herself to God, endeavored to observe His holy law, loved Him with all her might, and the Lord gave her, while still living, a certain lustre and splendor . . .

SOURCE: Fray Diego de Córdova Salinas, O.F.M., *Crónica Franciscana de las Provincias del Perú*, new edition with notes and introduction by Lino G. Canedo, O.F.M. (Washington, D.C.: Academy of American Franciscan History, 1957), 949-52. Translated by and quoted in Asunción Lavrin, "Women and Religion in Spanish America," *Women and Religion in America*, vol. 2: *The Colonial and Revolutionary Periods*, ed. Rosemary Radford Ruether and Rosemary Skinner Keller (San Francisco: Harper & Row, 1983), 2:58-60. Copyright © 1983 by Rosemary R. Ruether and Rosemary S. Keller. Reprinted by permission of HarperCollins Publishers and the Academy of American Franciscan History.

enriching her with celestial blessings, guiding her to such a holy life, that even in life, she seemed like a Seraphim, burning in the love of God. So much did her exercises spiritualize her. . . .

Relation of her Life by Canon Avila. Sister Estefanía de San Joseph was a native of Cuzco, daughter of a black woman called Isabel the Portuguese (because she was born in Portugal), slave of Captain Maldonado, the rich. After his death, as he had set her free, she entered the convent of Saint Clare of that city as a *donada* (lay sister). There I met her and talked to her many times. She professed and died with a saintly reputation around 1580. This was, then, her mother. Her father was a Spaniard. Estefanía remained in the house and with the family of her master. She was a good looking girl, and in his last will her master set her free. However, his heirs tried to retain her as a slave, which obliged her to flee Cuzco for Lima to defend legally the cause of her freedom. And God was served that she succeeded in gaining it from the Royal Audiencia. Our Lord was thus disposed that she should achieve her salvation, and free her soul, as He had freed her body. . . .

She was very compassionate, and out of charity she raised four poor Spanish children, two boys and two girls, who, with such good breeding, indoctrination and example, became members of the Church. One boy became a priest and the other a Jesuit. The girls went to the cloisters to serve God as nuns. One professed in the monastery of La Encarnación, of Augustinian nuns, and the other in the Dominican convent of Saint Catherine.

She [Sister Estefanía] was very devoted to the Seraphic Father Saint Francis. She professed in his Third Order, and was among those who fulfilled her obligations with the greatest fervor and observance. She helped the abbesses in the administration; collected alms for masses and the saints' feasts. She lived from the work of her hands, making mattresses for four reales, and with this and some alms, she sustained herself in her poverty.

Very Charitable with the Sick. She visited the sick, especially those of her Order, and with great charity cared for them, giving them the remedies they required. She collected old linen rags, and after having them washed clean, she made bandages. These she took to the hospitals, to minister to the sick, whom she continuously visited with the greatest charity.

Exercised Her Weakened Body in Penitence. She exercised herself in all kinds of penitences and asperities, *cilicios* [hairshirts], and disciplines. She fasted on Mondays, Wednesdays, Fridays and Saturdays of every week with rigor and abstinence, and especially on Advent and Lent. She showed no anger for any offense. She was always peaceful and patient.

Very Fervent on the Churches which She Continuously Visited. She visited all churches, and attended all sermons and feasts, jubilees and religious celebrations with such fervor and spiritual joy that she edified all who saw her. . . .

And as this blessed woman loved and feared God so much, she strove by all means feasible to her person and humbleness to attract all whom she could, to the exercise of virtues. She was happy, affable, humble, gracious, and these qualities paved her way into the homes of the principal and richest ladies of the city. . . .

She had several grave diseases, and the last, which was very grievous, with fever and acute pains, she endured with much patience and good example. She asked to be taken to the Hospital of Charity, a very well served women's hospital. . . .

One day, when the Most Excellent Don Pedro Toledo, Marquis of Mancera, Viceroy of these kingdoms, was visiting the sick of the hospital with My Lady the Marchioness, as they often did, they both came to Estefanía's bed, and talked to her with great love, and asked her to commend them to God. Estefanía, who was already very weak, became animated and answered: "My Lord, is not Your Excellency the Viceroy? Why are you visiting a poor mulatto, as myself?" She made them pray a prayer on their knees, and asked them to give alms to the poor, and bid them good-by, begging God to confer His grace on them. The Marquis asked for her hand, and she stretched it, and they both kissed it, and asked her for blessing. And the poor woman gave it to them, making the sign of the cross over their Excellencies. All those present, and I among them, were very edified by the strength of the virtue which made possible such actions: giving valor to a humble woman, a former slave, to talk to such high persons, who, recognizing the sanctity of the sick woman, would kiss her hand and ask for her blessing. . . .

Of Her Blessed Death. On the following day, having received the Extreme Unction, she gave her soul to God at three o'clock in the morning of 9 May, 1645, at age 84. . . . The following day she was given solemn burial in the convent of our Father Saint Francis, which all religious communities attended, as well as the clergy of the Cathedral and many priests . . . the brothers of the Third Order, and a great multitude of people, who accompanied her body . . . with the veneration owed to a saintly woman. . . .

50. A Unique Holy Woman from Seventeenth-Century New Spain

Sor Juana Inés de la Cruz (1658-1695), illegitimate daughter of a Creole family, became a Hieronymite nun in Mexico City and in 1691 wrote her famous Reply *(actually an* apologia pro vita sua) *to the bishop of Puebla, who is here addressed as "Sor Filotea." This work could justly take its place among the works of such early modern European thinkers as Francis Bacon, John Donne, René Descartes, and Blaise Pascal.*

The following excerpt may be divided into three parts: (1) an account of Sor Juana's passion for learning; (2) an outline of the actual subjects of her interests ending with a brief account of her encounter with the bishop of Puebla ("I obeyed her" [the bishop, Sor Filotea]); and (3) a catalog of some outstanding women.

Is there any common denominator in the understanding of Christianity between this highly intellectual woman and her two contemporaries from Lima described in the previous two documents?

Characterize her writing in part 1. Would a consideration of René Descartes' Discourse on Method *(1637) help to place Sor Juana in mainstream European intellectual concerns of the seventeenth century? Evaluate her rationale for the reading program she delineates in part 2. What does she endeavor to establish in part 3? Do the sentiments expressed there suggest why this woman had no choice but to enter a convent? How do the concerns expressed in her* Reply *contribute to an understanding of the vibrancy of the Christian humanist tradition which was always a part, sometimes controversial, of Catholic Christianity?*

[1]   I was less than three years old when my mother sent an older sister to be taught reading at a school for small children, of the kind called *Amigas*. Moved by sisterly affection and by a mischievous spirit, I followed her; and seeing her receive instruction, I formed such a strong desire to learn to read that I tried to deceive the school mistress, telling her that *my mother wanted her to give me lessons*. She did not believe me, since it was incredible; but to humor me she acquiesced. I continued to come and she to teach me, no longer in jest but in earnest; and I learned so quickly that I already knew how to read by the time my mother heard about the lessons from the teacher, who had kept them secret in order to break the pleasant news to her and receive her reward all at once. I had concealed it from my mother for fear that I would be whipped for acting without permission. The lady

SOURCE: Sor Juana, *Carta atenagórica: Respuesta a Sor Filotea*, ed. Ermilo Abreu Gómez (Mexico City: Ediciones Botas, 1934), 54-58, 66-70. Translated by Benjamin Keen, in Robert Buffington and Lila Caimari, eds., *Keen's Latin American Civilization: History and Society, 1492 to the Present*, 8th ed. (Boulder, Colo.: Westview Press, 2004), 190-93. Copyright © by Westview Press. Reprinted by permission of Westview Press, a member of Perseus Books, L.L.C.

who taught me still lives—God keep her—and can testify to this.

I remember that at that time, although I had the healthy appetite of most children of that age, I would not eat cheese because I heard that it made one dull-witted, and the desire to learn prevailed more with me than hunger, so powerful in children. Later, at the age of six or seven, when I already knew how to read and write, as well as to sew and do other women's tasks, I heard that in Mexico City there was a university, and schools where the sciences were taught. No sooner had I heard this than I began to badger my mother with pleas that she let me put on men's clothing and go to Mexico City, where I could live with some relatives and attend the university. She would not do it, and quite rightly, too, but I satisfied my desire by reading in a large number of books that belonged to my grandfather, and neither punishments nor rebukes could stop me. Hence when I came to Mexico City men wondered not so much at my intelligence as at my memory and knowledge, at an age when it seemed I would do well to know how to talk.

I began to study Latin, in which I had barely twenty lessons; and so intense was my application that although women (especially in the flower of their youth) naturally cherish the adornment of their hair, I would cut it off four or six fingers' length, making it a rule that if I had not mastered a certain subject by the time it grew back, I would cut it off again . . . for it did not seem right to me that a head so empty of knowledge, which is the most desirable adornment of all, should be crowned with hair. I became a nun, for although I knew that the religious state imposed obligations (I speak of incidentals and not of the fundamentals) most repugnant to my temperament, nevertheless, in view of my total disinclination to marriage, it was the most becoming and proper condition that I could choose to ensure my salvation. To achieve this I had to repress my wayward spirit, which wished to live alone, without any obligatory occupation that might interfere with the freedom of my studies or any conventional bustle that might disturb the restful quiet of my books. These desires made me waver in my decision, until, having been told by learned persons that it was temptation, with divine favor I conquered and entered the state which I so unworthily occupy. I thought that I had fled from myself, but—wretched me! —I brought myself with me and so brought my greatest enemy, that thirst for learning which Heaven gave me—I know not whether as a favor or chastisement, for repress it as I might with all the exercise that the conventual state offers, it would burst forth like gunpowder; and it was verified in me that *privatio est causa appetitus* [deprivation is the cause of appetite].

[2]   I renewed or rather continued (for I never truly ceased) my labors (which were my rest in all the leisure time that my duties left me) of reading and more reading, of studying and more studying, with no other teacher than the books themselves. You will readily comprehend how difficult it is to study from these lifeless letters, denied the living voice and explanation of a teacher, but I joyfully endured all this labor for love of learning. Ah, if it had been for love of God, as was fitting, how worthy it would have been! True, I sought to direct it as much as possible to His service, for my aspiration was to study theology, since it seemed a notable defect to me, as a Catholic, not to know all that can be learned in this life about the Divine Mysteries; and since I was a nun, and not a lay person, it seemed to me an obligation of my state to study literature. . . . So I reasoned, and convinced myself—though it could well be that I was only justifying what I already wanted to do. And so, as I have said, I directed the steps of my studying toward the heights of Sacred Theology; it seemed to me that in order to arrive there I should climb the stairway of the human sciences and arts; for how should I understand the language of the Queen of Sciences if I did not know that of her handmaidens? [. . .]

At one time my enemies persuaded a very saintly and guileless prelate, who believed that study was a matter for the Inquisition, to forbid me to study. I obeyed her (for the three months or so that she had power over me) in what concerned my reading, but as for the absolute ban on study, this was not in my power to obey, for although I did not study in books, I studied everything that God created, and all this universal machine served me as a textbook. I saw nothing without reflecting upon it; everything I heard moved me to thought. This was true of the smallest and most material things, for since there is no creature, however lowly, in which one does not recognize the *me fecit Deus* [God made me], so there is no object that will not arouse thought, if one considers it as one should. Thus I looked at and wondered about everything, so that even the people I spoke to, and what they said to me, aroused a thousand speculations in me. [. . .]

[3]   I have seen a Deborah giving laws, both military and political, and governing a people in which there were so many learned men. I read of that sage Queen of Sheba, so learned that she dared to test with enigmas the wisdom of the wisest of men, and suffered no reproof for it but instead was made the judge of unbelievers. I observe so many illustrious women—some adorned with the gift of prophecy, like Abigail; others, with that of persuasion, like Esther; others with piety, like Rahab; others with perseverance, like Anna, mother of Samuel; and an infinite number of others, endowed with still other kinds of graces and virtues.

If I turn my gaze to the pagans, I first encounter the Sibyls, chosen by God to prophesy the principal mysteries of our faith, in verses so learned and elegant that they arouse our wonder. I see the Greeks adore as goddess of learning a woman like Minerva, daughter of the first Jupiter and teacher of all the wisdom of Athens. [. . .]

I see a holy mother of my own order, Paula, learned in Hebrew, Greek, and Latin, and most skillful in interpreting the Scriptures—so much so, in fact, that her biographer, the great and saintly Jerome, declared himself unequal to his task. He said, in his usual serious, forceful way: "If all the members of my body were tongues, they would not be enough to proclaim the wisdom and virtue of Paula." He bestowed the same praise on the widow Blesilla and the illustrious virgin Eustoquio, both daughters of the same Paula; for her learning the latter won the name "Prodigy of the World." Fabiola, a Roman lady, was also most learned in the Sacred Scripture, Proba Falconia, a Roman matron, wrote an elegant work in Virgilian measures about the mysteries of our sacred faith. It is well known that our Queen Isabel, wife of Alfonso XII, wrote on astronomy. And . . . in our own time there flourishes the great Christina Alexandra, Queen of Sweden, as learned as she is brave and magnanimous, and there are also the excellent Duchess of Abeyro and the Countess of Vallambrosa.

PART VI
Education

Several religious orders, most notably the Jesuits and Franciscans, established *reducciones* or missions in frontier areas. The Jesuits, for example, organized ninety-nine missions in the viceroyalty of New Spain alone, several others in the viceroyalty of Lima, and nearly four hundred in Brazil. The thirty missions for the Guaraní Amerindians of Paraguay, Argentina, and Brazil are perhaps the best known of all, with a total population of about 90,000 inhabitants in 1767. Both state and church promoted the founding of missions, though for different reasons. Royal officials recognized the value of establishing missions in strategic outposts in order to extend the frontier, prevent encroachment by other European powers, and serve as a first line of defense against warring Amerindians. Churchmen sought to protect Amerindians from exploitative Spanish *conquistadores* and Brazilian *bandeirantes,* or slave raiders, and believed that the Amerindians would better grasp the ideals of Christianity if free from observing and imitating the vices of Iberians. Frontier Amerindians' responses were different from the responses of non-frontier Amerindians to missionary activities. The Guaraní seem to have appreciated the Jesuits' presence, whereas Pueblo Amerindians in the present-day American state of Colorado tortured and killed twenty-one of thirty-three Franciscan missionaries in 1680. Mission Amerindians lived regimented lives that included morning and evening prayers, classes in catechism, and training in specialized tasks by gender; men generally dedicated working hours to agricultural and manufacturing chores; women engaged in domestic work and weaving. Mission priests coordinated daily activities in such a paternalistic and methodical manner that they were sometimes accused of having stifled Amerindians' ability to fend for themselves. Most missions became self-sufficient and created surplus products such as yerba maté, wax, honey, corn, and wheat for sale to outsiders. These well-structured and successful agricultural enterprises led to the mistaken belief that missions possessed tremendous wealth, perhaps hidden within the walls of their churches and residences. Jesuit missions were secularized after the expulsion of the order in 1767, and the Amerindian communities quickly disintegrated. Most Amerindians either returned to the forest or used their manufacturing skills to find employment in cities.[1]

Church and state relations began to change significantly with the ascent of the Bourbons to the Spanish crown at the conclusion of the War of the Spanish Succession (1713). Whereas the Habsburgs had viewed the church as an integral partner and a bulwark of social control, the Bourbons viewed that institution as a threat to the political and economic power of the state. The Crown ended tax-exempt status on church endowments in the 1730s, and properties were generally taxed at 15 percent by the end of the century. Decrees limited the construction of new monasteries and the number of men who could enter religious orders. As Latin America's richest institution, the church had frequently acted as a moneylender. In 1804, however, Charles IV (1788-1808) issued the Act of Consolidation, which required the amortization of these loans and ultimately hindered credit opportunities for the Creole economic elite. In that same year the state filled its own coffers by expropriating certain church properties such as chantries and endowments for pious works. Furthermore, the Crown abolished the ecclesiastical *fuero* in 1812, which had given clerics special privileges such as the right to have their cases heard before church courts rather than criminal courts.[2]

José de Carvalho e Mello, Marquis of Pombal and prime minister to King José I (1750-1777), convinced the Portuguese monarch to expel the more than five hundred Jesuits from Brazil in 1759. King Charles III (1759-1788) followed suit and expelled over 2,200 Jesuits from Spanish America in 1767.[3] The Jesuits' success as educators in cities, ranch owners in coastal areas, and missionaries for Amerindians on the frontier contributed to their demise. Crown officials had always been suspicious of the Jesuits' vow of obedience to the pope and had questioned their allegiance to the goals of royal absolutism. Jesuit high schools and universities catered to Creole youth, whom the Crown feared might someday justify their latent desire for autonomy with the enlightened principles of Descartes and Bacon that they had learned from their Jesuit teachers. Jesuit influence and protection of Amerindians and their lands in border areas such as Paraguay annoyed Portuguese and Spanish monarchs, and they blamed the priests and brothers of the order for having encouraged the Guaraní rebellion of 1754-1756. The expulsion of the Jesuits triggered

---

1. Diana Hadley, "Missions," in *Encyclopedia of Mexico: History, Society & Culture*, vol. 2, ed. Michael S. Werner (Chicago and London: Fitzroy Dearborn Publishers, 1997), 923-26; Margaret E. Crahan, "Missions (Spanish America)," in *Encyclopedia of Latin America*, ed. Helen Delpar (New York: McGraw-Hill, 1974), 379; Nicholas P. Cushner, "Jesuits," in *Encyclopedia of Latin American History and Culture*, vol. 3, ed. Barbara A. Tenenbaum (New York: Charles Scribner's Sons, 1996), 318-19; Nancy M. Farriss, *Crown and Clergy in Colonial Mexico, 1759-1821: The Crisis of Ecclesiastical Privilege* (London: Athlone Press, 1968), 4; David J. Weber, *The Spanish Frontier in North America* (New Haven: Yale University Press, 1992), 134-37.

2. Sarah L. Cline, "Church and State: Habsburg New Spain," in *Encyclopedia of Mexico: History, Society & Culture*, vol. 1, ed. Michael S. Werner (Chicago and London: Fitzroy Dearborn Publishers, 1997), 250-52; Margaret E. Crahan, "Catholic Church (Colonial Period)," in *Encyclopedia of Latin America*, ed. Helen Delpar (New York: McGraw-Hill, 1974), 121; John F. Schwaller, "Catholic Church: Colonial Period," in *Encyclopedia of Latin American History and Culture*, vol. 2, ed. Barbara A. Tenenbaum (New York: Charles Scribner's Sons, 1996), 33.

3. Magnus Mörner, *The Expulsion of the Jesuits from Latin America* (New York: Alfred A. Knopf, 1965), 11, 16.

Amerindian revolts and Creole resentment. By this time the majority of the Jesuits were actually Creoles, and their expulsion meant permanent separation from their families and the removal of the finest educators in Latin America. The Crown sold the Jesuits' lucrative sugar haciendas, mule ranches, and mills and kept the proceeds.[4]

51. Renovation or Tradition in the Late Colony?

Manuel Guirior (1708-1788), a nobleman from Navarre, was appointed viceroy of New Granada in 1772, after a distinguished naval career. His extensive experience in the eighteenth-century Mediterranean world made him the perfect candidate to evaluate the educational system of the colony and propose much-needed reforms.

What conflict that dominated intellectual life in Catholic Europe and the Americas is clearly depicted here between the viceroy and the "regular clergy"? Who are these "regular clergy" and what is their educational regimen? What does the viceroy's statement that the "true principles" of theology are found in the "Church Councils, the ancient canons, Sacred Scripture, and the Church Fathers" suggest about the regular clergy's source for those "true principles"?

The instruction of youth and the encouragement of the sciences and arts are among the fundamental principles of good government and are the source of the happiness and prosperity of a state. . . . Conscious of this fact, and of the zeal with which our prudent king and his government have worked to establish sound methods of instruction, I determined to make my contribution to the worthy project begun by his Excellency, my predecessor, of founding a public university. . . . By this means, at a small cost, the kingdom could make happy its young men, who at present are denied instruction in the useful sciences and the sound methods and good taste introduced by Europe in the study of belles-lettres, and are occupied in futile debate of the abstract questions posed by Aristotle.

Knowing that His Majesty had been informed of this project, and that a decision had been delayed by the opposition of the Dominican convent in this city, which at present enjoys the sole right of granting degrees, and wishing to put an end to this unhappy state of affairs before its evil effects become incurable, I determined in consultation with the illustrious prelate and the ministers who composed the *junta superior de aplicaciones* to commission the attorney of the *audiencia*, Don Francisco Antonio Moreno y Escandón, a man of sound training and one who had all the necessary qualifications for the task, to prepare a plan of study, adapted to local conditions, that might serve as a model for other educational establishments and help to eliminate existing abuses. After he had drawn up this plan,

---

4. Nicholas P. Cushner, *Jesuit Ranches and the Agrarian Development of Colonial Argentina, 1650-1767* (Albany: State University of New York Press, 1983), 5, 159; Asunción Lavrin, "Jesuits, Expulsion of (Spanish America)," in *Encyclopedia of Latin America*, ed. Helen Delpar (New York: McGraw-Hill, 1974), 310; Víctor Gabriel Muro, "Catholic Church: Mexico," in *Encyclopedia of Mexico: History, Society & Culture*, vol. 1, ed. Michael S. Werner (Chicago and London: Fitzroy Dearborn Publishers, 1997), 219; Cushner, "Jesuits," 319.

SOURCE: "Relación del Excmo. Sr. de Guirior," in *Relaciones de los virreyes del Nuevo Reino de Granada*, ed. José Antonio García y García (New York, 1867), 144-47. Trans. and ed. Benjamin Keen, in *Latin American Civilization: The Colonial Origins*, 3rd ed. (Boston: Houghton Mifflin, 1974), 1:314-15.

very intelligently and in entire conformity to the royal intentions, it was examined by the same *junta superior* and approved with universal acclaim and expressions of gratitude to Don Francisco for his zeal. It was also ordered that the plan should be carried out without delay, with the said Moreno acting as royal director of education, until such time as His Majesty . . . should make known his sovereign will.

Despite the opposition of some persons educated in the ancient fashion — notably that of the regular clergy (who were aggrieved because they had formerly monopolized education in their cloisters and were conscious of their inability to teach certain subjects which they would have to learn anew), a beginning was made with the new method in the two *colegios* of this city. . . . This has had such happy results that one year sufficed to demonstrate the progress made by the students in arithmetic, algebra, geometry, and trigonometry, and in jurisprudence and theology, whose true principles they found in the Church Councils, the ancient canons, Sacred Scripture, and the Church Fathers. . . . I am confident that your Excellency, moved by zeal in this cause, will not heed the appeals and clamors of the abovementioned convent, supported by the regular clergy, but will firmly insist that this reform be carried forward, demonstrating to His Majesty and the Royal Council of the Indies the advantages to the kingdom and monarchy of continuing this method and the urgent need for a university, a workshop in which could be formed heroes capable of making this nation happy. . . .

To this end, I have proposed to His Majesty that a beginning, at least, should be made of the university establishment, with the well-founded hope that time and circumstances will bring it to a state of greater perfection, meantime endowing it with many of the revenues of the Jesuit temporalities. . . . I have also informed His Majesty that all the books found in the *colegios* of the defunct Jesuit Society have been taken to form a public library in this capital, to which persons of literary tastes may come to obtain instruction in all subjects. A spacious room has been set apart for this worthy purpose. . . . In times to come this library can be enriched with new books, and with machines or instruments of which men of science will make profitable use.

52. Educating the Guaraní

Félix de Azara (1746-1821), military engineer and scientist, traveled extensively in South America as a participant in expeditions of varying purposes. He gathered information about the life and government of the famous Jesuit "reductions" (missions) in Paraguay in 1781, fourteen years after the expulsion of the Jesuits.

The following excerpts come from his Description and History of Paraguay and Río de la Plata *(published 1847) and demand these questions: (1) From de Azara's description of the Jesuits' duties and activities and those that they required of the Guaraní, determine how the Jesuits understood their mandate as missionaries. (2) How did the Jesuits view the Guaraní? (3) For the Jesuit, what defined a Catholic Guaraní, that is, what was sufficient for a Guaraní to be considered a Catholic? (4) What was Féliz de Azara's evaluation of the Jesuit achievement in the reductions? Did his enlightened and scientific character enhance or detract from his ability to evaluate that achievement?*

SOURCE: Félix de Azara, *Descripción y historia del Paraguay y del Río de la Plata* (Asunción: 1896), 1:338-52. Trans. and ed. Benjamin Keen in *Latin American Civilization: The Colonial Origins*, 3rd ed. (Boston: Houghton Mifflin Company, 1974), 1:270-73.

Having spoken of the towns founded by the Jesuit fathers, and of the manner in which they were founded, I shall discuss the government which they established in them. . . .

In the town of Candelaria there was a father, a kind of provincial, named *Superior of the Missions*, who had authority from the Pope to confirm the Indians and was the chief of all the curacies or towns. In each one resided two priests, a curate and a sub-curate, who had certain assigned functions. The sub-curate was charged with all the spiritual tasks, and the curate with every kind of temporal responsibility. Since the latter required much knowledge and experience, the curates were always priests of notable gravity, who had earlier been provincials or rectors of their colleges; whether or not they knew the language of the Indians was not considered important. Their predecessors in office left them copious diaries, with directions for the management of labor, workshops, and so forth. The curates, in sum, were masters of all. Although each town had its Indian *corregidor, alcaldes*, and *regidores*, who comprised a municipal council like that of a Spanish town, they had no jurisdiction, and were in effect nothing more than the executors of the orders of the curate, who invariably handed down mild judgments in all cases, civil and criminal, but did not permit an appeal to other Spanish judges or *audiencias*.

The curate allowed no one to work for personal gain; he compelled everyone, without distinction of age or sex, to work for the community, and he himself saw to it that all were equally fed and dressed. For this purpose the curates placed in storehouses all the fruits of agriculture and the products of industry, selling in the Spanish towns their surplus of cotton, cloth, tobacco, vegetables, skins, yerba maté, and wood, transporting them in their own boats down the nearest rivers, and returning with implements and whatever else was required.

From the foregoing one may infer that the curates disposed of the surplus funds of the Indian towns, and that no Indian could aspire to own private property. This deprived them of any incentive to use reason or talent, since the most industrious, able, and worthy person had the same food, clothing, and pleasures as the most wicked, dull, and indolent. It also follows that although this form of government was well designed to enrich the communities it also caused the Indian to work at a languid pace, since the wealth of his community was of no concern to him. . . .

It must be said that although the fathers were supreme in all respects, they employed their authority with a mildness and restraint that command admiration. They supplied everyone with abundant food and clothing. They compelled the men to work only half a day, and did not drive them to produce more. Even their labor was given a festive air, for they went in procession to the fields, to the sound of music and carrying a little image in a litter, for which they always constructed a bower; and the music did not cease until they had returned in the same way they had set out. They gave them many holidays, dances, and tournaments, dressing the actors and the members of the municipal councils in gold or silver tissue and the most costly European garments, but they permitted the women to act only as spectators.

They likewise forbade the women to sew; this occupation was restricted to the musicians, sacristans, and acolytes. But they made them spin cotton; and the cloth that the Indians wove, after satisfying their own needs, they sold together with the surplus cotton in the Spanish towns, as they did with the tobacco, vegetables, yerba maté, wood, and skins. The curate and his companion, or sub-curate, had their own plain dwellings, and they never left them except to take the air in the great, enclosed yard of their college. They never walked through the streets of the town or entered the house of any Indian or let themselves be seen by any woman — or, indeed, by any man, except for those indispensable few through whom they issued their orders. If some ailing person required spiritual aid, they brought him from his miserable dwelling to a clean room near the college that was set apart for that purpose, and the sub-curate, carried in a sedan with great pomp, administered the holy sacraments to him there.

When they appeared in the church, although it was only to say mass, it was with the greatest ceremony, wearing costly garments, surrounded and assisted by about a hundred sacristans, acolytes, and musicians. All their churches were the largest and most magnificent in that part of the world, filled with great altars, pictures, and gilding; the ornaments could not be better or more costly in Madrid or Toledo. All this is convincing evidence that the Jesuits spent on churches and their accessories, and in attiring the actors and municipal officers on festival days, the vast sums that they could have appropriated for themselves if they had been ambitious.

The streets of their towns were five paces wide. The buildings were one-story structures, each consisting of a long hall that originally housed all the subjects of a chieftain; they were later divided into little rooms, each seven *varas* long, one to each family. These rooms had no window, chimney, or kitchen, and their entire furnishings consisted of a cotton hammock, for the master of the house; the others slept on skins on the floor, without any partitions between them. The food of the Indians cost the priests little or nothing, since they had a surplus of meat from the increase of the herds on their estates. For clothing they gave each man a cap, a shirt, stockings, and a poncho, all made of cotton cloth, a thick, coarse, light-colored material. They made them shave their hair, and did not permit them to wear anything on their feet. The women also went barefooted, and their only garment was a *tipos* or sleeveless shirt of the same material as was described above, girdled at the waist. . . .

From what I could learn, in visiting all the towns, none of the Indians understood Spanish, nor could they read or write, except for a few who were taught to read and write in Guaraní in order to keep accounts of what was taken into and out of the storehouses and so forth. They had no scientific knowledge and only a few crafts, since they only wove cloth for their own garments and for

slaves or very poor people; but some were taught the trades of ironsmith and silversmith and painting, sculpture, music, dancing, and so forth, in which they were instructed by Jesuits brought especially for this purpose.

All were baptized and knew how to say their prayers, which all the boys and unmarried girls had to recite in a chorus under the portico of the church at dawn. Yet those who have replaced the Jesuits assert that there was little true religion among the Indians. This is not strange, in view of the fact that the Indians themselves say that there were few Jesuit curates capable of preaching the gospel in Guaraní. . . . As a partial remedy for this deficiency, the Jesuits had certain clever Indians learn a few sermons, which they preached in the town square after some festival or tournament; I have heard some of these, and they contained a good deal of nonsense which the orator drew out of his head. . . .

In the year 1769, the Jesuits turned their towns over to an equal number of friars; but theirs was only the spiritual power, while the temporal power formerly enjoyed by the Jesuit curate was entrusted to a secular administrator. There was also established a military governor of all the missions of the Paraná and Uruguay rivers. It could be said that these towns only changed hands, but the Jesuits were more able, moderate, and frugal, and regarded their towns as their own handiwork and private possession, and so loved them and worked for their good. The secular governors, on the other hand, and the administrators whom they appointed, not only lacked the intelligence of the Jesuits, but regarded the wealth of the communities as a mine which was theirs to exploit for a short time. It is not strange, therefore, that the towns have grown poor, and that the Indians are compelled to work harder and are more poorly fed and clothed.

53. Jesuits Must Leave the Country ... Where Is the Treasure?

The expulsion of the Jesuits from Portuguese and Spanish domains in 1759 and 1767, respectively, and the suppression of the order by Clement XIV in the bull Dominus ac Redemptor Noster *(1773) are two major events of the eighteenth century. They had highly detrimental effects on the universities, colleges, missions, and cultural and economic life of the New World. The highly organized, efficient, and self-contained Jesuit order aroused the suspicions of the Iberian kings whose pretensions to absolutism included submission of the church to the Crown. The order's enormous economic success and ability to thrive even during economic downturns, combined with the impressive edifices it built—churches, colegios, missions, cloisters—caused enormous envy and resentment, especially among the landowning colonial elites.*

Once again Joseph Och's journals provide an eyewitness account by one of the Jesuits directly affected by the Crown's decree. Taking into consideration that this eyewitness report on this momentous moment in Jesuit history was written by a Jesuit whose devotion to duty was unquestionable, does his account suffer from self-righteousness or is it credible and accurate? Evaluate (1) his portrait of the visitador real, *don José de Gálvez; (2) the comportment of the king's soldiers; (3) the behavior of all classes of the populace; and (4) the manner in which he introduces the Dominican friar, Francisco León, and in which he reports León's oration.*

It was the twenty-fourth of June in the year 1767, the day of St. John the Baptist, when our fortunes changed. [...]

[T]he Jesuits were all in their houses and up to no mischief. Most of them were in the house garden about three in the afternoon, and were partaking very quietly of their vesper drink [...]

[W]hen, behold! there strode suddenly into their midst a Captain who was at other times cordially known to the community. His expression was serious. He looked about him with sharp eyes, spoke no word, and withdrew. Before this he had searched through all the passages of the large college which counted about ninety to one hundred Jesuits. The gist of his orders was to spy out how many men we had garrisoned in the garden as soldiers, how many bulwarks had been thrown up behind the garden walls, with how many pieces these were equipped, whether the expected number of hundreds of powder kegs, weapons, and

other war equipment could be determined, and so on. [...]

At nightfall all of us retired without any cares or worries, nay without even the slightest thought or suspicion of imminent misfortune. [...]

The men marched at eleven o'clock, being deployed to all streets where there were churches or cloisters. Men's cloisters in Mexico [City] numbered thirty; women's cloisters, twenty. All these communities were invested with twenty or more troops. The five Jesuit establishments were, however, completely surrounded with soldiers. Cavalry drew up before the palace of the Viceroy where also forty small field pieces were aimed down all streets. [...]

The other officers and royal commissioners stood by until early morning at about four o'clock. At the stroke of four on the twenty-fifth of June, a loud shout was heard at the door of the great college. When the porter asked through a

SOURCE: Theodore E. Treutlein, translator and annotator, *Missionary in Sonora: The Travel Reports of Joseph Och, S.J., 1755-1767* (San Francisco: California Historical Society, 1965), 49-53, 57-58, 62-69. Reprinted by permission of California Historical Society.

little window who was there and what was wanted, he got the reply that he should open immediately, that on superior orders certain evildoers who were in the college were to be sought out. Señor Don José de Gálvez, Royal Visitor of the entire Mexican empire, used this sharp duplicity to avoid telling as big a lie as the other officer. Truly, all Jesuits were considered impious delinquents to be seized by this gentleman who had been sent out from Spain a half year earlier for this purpose. [...]

The porter became very frightened when he heard the murmuring of so many armed men and ran hurriedly to get the portal keys from the Father Rector, to whom every night they had to be given, and to ask how he should behave in this situation. He was ordered to open the gate without hesitation or resistance, which he then did. It was still quite dark (for in Mexico day and night are almost equally long). Amid much noise three hundred men entered the college with fixed bayonets and heavily loaded muskets, each man being provided with twenty-five cartridges. They took control of the belfry and, for fear that the alarm would be rung, immediately cut the bell ropes. Two hundred men remained in the court and at the portal, the others occupied the large halls and staircases of the extensive college. Almost every room had a guard. The Señor Visitor came to the room of the Father Rector with the command that he assemble all Jesuits without exception to hear a royal decree. The Rector was not permitted to leave his room. Most of us were up, and when we wished to go through the hallways to the choir, as was our custom, to visit the Blessed Sacrament in the church, we were everywhere stopped by soldiers and ordered to gather in the great house chapel. We Jesuits did not know whether all this was fact or fancy. [...]

When all were assembled they were ordered to surrender their keys, which was immediately done. Next, a briefly worded royal decree was read by a quivering and weeping secretary. "Because of weighty considerations which His Majesty keeps hidden in his heart, the entire Society of Jesus and all Jesuits must leave the country, and their establishments and properties must be turned over to the Royal Treasurer."

What manner of emotional manifestations now occurred can more easily be imagined than described. Some stood there quite dumbfounded and immobile; tears streamed from the eyes of others. Some lifted their hands and eyes passively to heaven while others sobbed. One became insane on the spot, and another had a fit of apoplexy. Most, however, stood there with well-controlled feelings and expressions. [...]

That which happened to us occurred also in other colleges in the city, and all within an hour. Elsewhere soldiers forced their way into cloisters with orders that none be permitted to leave or enter for half a day. They seized all bell towers so that in the event of a possible general alarm they could control the movements of the multitude. Also on this day not a bell was tolled, all churches remained locked, and it is not known whether a single Mass was said by any of the total of approximately two thousand priests distributed among all the orders in Mexico.

Then came the first question: "Where is the treasure?" for these gentlemen imagined and had noised it about that we possessed many kegs of gold, and that many millions would fall to the royal exchequer. However, they were astonished when they examined the books of receipts and expenditures which were placed before them in the procuratory. [...]

The lust for money with their failure to find any put the señores commissioners almost out of their minds and led them to unreasonable undertakings, some of which I shall describe. [...]

When day broke and the townspeople opened doors and windows, they were astonished and dumbfounded to see soldiers everywhere. Those who had planned to go out turned right around at their doors and went back in. Others, however, who for reasons of business were already in the streets and were talking with each other were separated by nudges in the ribs and were told not to walk along the streets except singly. [...]

In the meantime, the greatest and first concern was to have books collected from all rooms and brought to the library. On this occasion I lost all the books I had brought with me to the Indies from Germany, Italy, and Spain, contrary to all laws and contrary to the intent of the royal decree wherein it was ordered that none be deprived of his personal property. They left us only our breviaries and the little book of Thomas à Kempis. [. . .]

Meanwhile, it had become apparent to the city that everything was being directed against the Jesuits. The lamentations, weeping, and wailing were general. Some of the most noble and wealthiest people who had sons, brothers, or friends in the Society were beside themselves, and I know of three who grieved to death in eight days. No one was master of himself. At seven o'clock after trumpet call there was publicly read the royal decree, already read to us, telling of the confiscation of our properties and about our banishment. [. . .]

On the twenty-sixth of June everything went along as the day before. [. . .]

In the afternoon still another decree was issued which forbade each and everyone to wear Jesuit clothes (many clergymen, children and others wore such) under pain of punishment for high treason. [. . .]

Our Señor Visitor was not very talkative because of the rebuffs he had received from all and sundry in the city. He wished very much as soon as possible to remove the Jesuits from their haunts, take them elsewhere, and lock them up in a narrow cell; all this to happen *bello motu*. To effect this he requested many fine carriages from wealthy merchants who refused his request. [. . .]

Such loyalty greatly incensed the Visitor. He issued a new decree threatening with capital punishment any who would decline to surrender carriages needed to convey the Jesuits. [. . .]

Coachmen were seized, coaches were brought out of their stalls, and all available mules were taken to be used either as draft or pack animals. [. . .]

As the first four Jesuits stepped into their carriages a general wailing, crying, and lamentation filled the air. The grief displayed by the womenfolk was most extraordinary. Countesses and marquises, some recognizable, others disguised in poor clothing, fell in crowds upon the reins and harness of the six mules and held the wheels of the coaches, thus to be able to say a few words of farewell. The soldiers noted that it was inadvisable to use much force, for had they done so all would

have been buried beneath a hail of stones from the roofs. As it was, several soldiers had to make a bloody withdrawal because of a few well-aimed stones. All persons who had been confounded yesterday and the day before were now aroused and angry. An uprising would indubitably have occurred had not we Jesuits called out from the carriages and prayed that in the name of God they retire and not oppose the King's orders. These words accomplished more than did muskets, bayonets, and sabers.

The procession finally started. The lamentations were renewed and many ran alongside and followed the carriages for a distance of two hours. Those who were left behind on the streets were inconsolable. To assuage their grief, a certain philanthropist, Father Francisco León, of the Dominican Order, came forth in the square and announced there would be a farewell address delivered from the Jesuit pulpit. This beloved and fine man, possessed of a courage worthy of his name, stepped forth to lay balm upon the wounds with his consolatory speech. His style of oratory was concise, natural, and not exaggerated.

"How long," said he, "shall this, our unavailing grief, endure? Cease weeping! You have no reason to do so. You are bewailing an imagined misfortune of the Jesuits. These people you know not, but the King knows them well. I admit they were your friends and acquaintances, father-confessors and counselors, but stop crying. Their fortune and yours will improve. Do you think that these good people will be led to slaughter, or will have to languish in gloomy prisons? You are very much mistaken. Don't you see the splendid carriages in which they were driven away like cavaliers? You were apprehensive that they would all be sentenced to death, and have their throats cut or worse.

"They will be well settled, cared for, and splendidly fed for the rest of their lives. The King will grant them handsome pensions, and they will live in the papal states. The Jesuits have known for quite a while that their intrigues could not be continued much longer. Their intentions were discovered. To anticipate the misfortune which would sooner or later overtake them they have provided for themselves. All of their estates have long been sold and transferred into astonishing sums of money. This money, many millions, they have already sent overseas and placed in safety. Their accounts lie as credit in Rome, Genoa, Amsterdam and London, perhaps by the hundreds. Hence, they will not be in want. They have enough for their livelihood and will be well off. Therefore, do not bewail them as future martyrs; rather congratulate them, as great gentlemen who have been removed to your material and spiritual advantage. Dry your tears!" and so on.

These were the comforting, pain-allaying, and honeyed words which issued from the Samson-like lion's maw. The clerical gentleman wished to continue but no longer had auditors. All had taken leave of this exortation because they already knew this clever bird. The monk departed and had no difficulty moving along the street through the throng of admirers. Perhaps he fancied he was already wearing the bishop's miter which he hoped to press upon his brow as a reward for merits—a people pacified, an uprising neutralized, and a conspiracy destroyed—to be reported to the court at Madrid which would then be indebted to him for the preservation of such a precious pearl, New Spain. This was the wish of the cowl-bearer. But we were soon to find the fox in his trap, and instead of the miter there was bestowed upon him the *sambenito* (a yellow Inquisition robe). [...]

On the thirtieth of June things went according to plan in our college. We were now only eighty in number; forty had to leave this day at three in the morning. [...]

With three others I constituted the vanguard. It was in the dark of night. All the rest were provided with carriages, and two accompanying horsemen with bared sabers and torches. A coach was not allowed to follow until the one preceding it had gone a distance of six or seven musket shots. Also the most complete silence had to be maintained; the coaches had to proceed very cautiously. It took us two hours to reach the first village called Guadalupe (about which I will speak elsewhere). The entire trip seemed like a funeral procession of mourning coaches.

Many of the most aristocratic ladies walked to Guadalupe dressed in Indian costumes, and disguised gentlemen rode at a gallop from coach to coach until they found the right opportunity to throw into each twenty-four pesos (convention-coins) wrapped in paper. The womenfolk removed precious rings and even their ear pendants and threw them into some of the coaches with the cries: "God be with you, dearest fathers!" It is certain that had we been permitted to talk with anyone and to take leave, we would have received astonishing sums of money for alms. These condolences moved us greatly. For while we were already assured of the friendly feelings of most people, it would never have occurred to us that all classes would have revealed, under such circumstances, the deepest feelings of esteem, love, sympathy, and exceptional generosity toward the Jesuits.

PART VII

The Church and Slavery

The church was neither as strong nor as influential in Brazil as it was in Spanish America. Brazil remained of secondary importance to the Portuguese monarchs during much of the sixteenth century because they preferred to exploit their colonial advantages in Africa and Asia. If the Dutch had not snatched a significant portion of northeastern Brazil from 1630 to 1654, the Portuguese may have paid even less attention to their New World colony. Nor did the Portuguese place the same emphasis on the conversion of Amerindians to Catholicism or express as much angst over the legitimacy of conquest and the treatment of New World peoples. This is not to say, of course, that some sensitive individuals did not attempt to defend Brazilian Amerindians and black Africans from enslavement and exploitation. The Jesuits, under the leadership of Tomé de Souza, arrived in 1549 to undertake the evangelization of Amerindians on the coast. António Vieira, S.J., condemned Amerindian slavery in sermons delivered in both Brazil and the royal chapel in Lisbon. His Jesuit brethren constructed hundreds of missions to protect Amerindians from the constant abuse and repeated slave raids that they suffered. African slaves in the Americas generally received less religious instruction than the Amerindians, especially in Brazil where slave owners enforced a particularly brutal plantation slavery. In addition, the more than four million slaves who arrived in Brazil from the sixteenth through the nineteenth centuries ensured a continuous strengthening of African religious traditions, which significantly shaped the development of Afro-Brazilian religions. The first diocese, Salvador de Bahia, was founded only in 1551, with the other dioceses coming much later: Rio, Olinda, and São Luís de Maranhão (1676), Pará (1719), and São Paulo and Marina in 1745. A seminary to train ecclesiastics was not created until 1739.[1]

---

1. Enrique Dussel, ed. *The Church in Latin America, 1492-1992* (Maryknoll, N.Y.: Orbis Books, 1992), 5, 8; Margaret E. Crahan, "Catholic Church (Colonial Period)," in *Encyclopedia of Latin America,* ed. Helen Delpar (New York: McGraw-Hill, 1974), 120-21; John F. Schwaller, "Catholic Church: Colonial Period," in *Encyclopedia of Latin American History and Culture,* vol. 2, ed. Barbara A. Tenenbaum (New York: Charles Scribner's Sons, 1996), 31; Nicholas P. Cushner, "Jesuits," in *Encyclopedia of Latin American History and Culture,* vol. 3, ed. Barbara A. Tenenbaum (New York: Charles Scribner's Sons, 1996), 317; Hugh Thomas, *The Slave Trade: The Story of the Atlantic Slave Trade, 1440-1870* (New York: Simon & Schuster, 1997), 804.

54. Restoring the Well-Being of the Blacks

Alonso de Sandoval (1577-1652) joined the Jesuit order in Lima, Peru, and, having been ordained a priest, was sent to Cartagena, Colombia, to establish a Jesuit presence in that important depot for enslaved Africans.

In an age of furious competition for social mobility in a profoundly hierarchical and caste society, Sandoval became a remarkable "apostle" to the negros bozales, *that is, blacks born in Africa and completely alien to all things Spanish, and who were consequently shunned by the entire populace.*

This reading from Sandoval's enormous anthropological, historical, and mission-minded work, De instauranda aethiopum salute: Naturaleza, policia sagrada i profana, costumbres i ritos, disciplina i catechismo evangelico de todos etiopes *(Restoring the Well-Being of the Blacks: Nature, Sacred and Secular Policy, Customs and Rites, Discipline and Evangelical Catechesis of All African Nations) beautifully represents both the thinking that dominated and animated the Spanish colony and the commitment of a truly holy man to what was the sole concern of his Jesuit order: to evangelize the human species.*

The passage must be read a number of times in order for the reader to enter the world of this by no means brilliant man who, nevertheless, went further in his understanding of and commitment to the black slave than any other individual of the colonial era—including some outstandingly compassionate members of his own order, for example, Saint Peter Claver (1580-1654).

Sandoval's thinking is buried in a style that at times may seem awkward, cumbersome, and pietistic, yet, with study, reveals passion. Is there evidence that Sandoval is juggling a number of roles that may involve contradictions? Is he aware of the tensions involved because of these roles, which may be delineated as (1) that of the missionary whose prime concern is to baptize, shrive and anoint; (2) that of the highly trained Jesuit who believes that God's love and Christ's salvific death are still operative despite the enslavement of Africans by Europeans, and the latter's absurdly cruel treatment of the former which defies both economics and human instinct; and (3) that of the man whose human sensitivity remains vibrant? Does the Christian humanist element, so much a part of the Jesuit vision, seep through the pious text? What is the significance of the phrase "still some solace in life"?

Once the blacks are captive with the justice that God knows about, they are later thrown into very harsh prisons from whence they do not leave until they arrive at this port of Cartagena or other places [. . .]

[T]hey arrive like skeletons; they are then taken onto land, put into a large patio or yard, [and] innumerable people then arrive, some out of greed, others out of curiosity, and others out of compassion, and from among them those of the Society of Jesus, in order to catechize, indoctrinate, baptize and confess those who are at the time dying. They prepare them for extreme unction; they negotiate that they be brought to them and

SOURCE: Alonso de Sandoval, S.J., *De instauranda aethiopum salute: El mundo de la esclavitud negra en América* (Bogota: Empresa Nacional de Publicaciones, 1956 [1627, rev. 1647]), 107-9, 197-98, 335, 339-40, 378, 584-85, 587. Translated from the Spanish by Lee M. Penyak.

administered it. And although they do their utmost to tend to them on time, they always find some of them already dead without the benefits of the holy sacraments, and others whom they barely reach on time; [the priests] come laden with cloth with which to cover them decently, because otherwise they would look very bad to chaste eyes, and they also bring them something sweet and a gift with which to nurture them and in this way make them sympathetic to the things of God. If in this place the healthy ones do not get sick, there is still some solace in life during the time they are here because they are ordered to be fattened up in order to sell them more advantageously; but since these poor people have suffered so much, nothing keeps most of them from getting sick upon arrival. [. . .]

There was a time when I was going to tend to one of these poor people so that he would die in the Lord, and on my way to help him prepare for death, I discovered that he had already died in the middle of a patio where many people were gathered; he was naked, lying face down on the ground, covered with flies that made it appear as if they wanted to devour him, and there they left him without paying any more attention to him than if he were a dog. I pleaded and requested to the person in charge to cover his body and to do so with the decency suited to Christianity; what they did was take a mat from another poor slave who was dying nearby, half a straw mat that fortune had provided him with, and covered the deceased with it, leaving the other one naked. [. . .]

What happens with these people regarding supernatural things makes one rather want to cry than explain it; and to say it in one word, God gave them [slaves] to them [slavers] so that they could be taught the road to heaven and be guided by their good example (and the one and main reason they [slaves] give for tolerating their captivity is precisely that), although it only seems that they were given to them for the opposite reason and that the devil has convinced the owners of most of these slaves [. . .] which they affirm and hold to be very true [. . .] that those who are already baptized and instructed are worth less than those yet to be baptized; that is, that if they are baptized and have a Christian name and know the prayers and things

of God, they consider them acculturated and versed in our ways, and thus are less valuable. [. . .]

[W]hy don't they look after their blacks? Why don't they give them necessary sustenance? Why don't they clothe and cover them? Why don't they cure and treat their sicknesses? Tell me: just because a moneybag is broken, do you throw it in the mud? You abandon it as a lost cause? A beast of burden because it's been worked to death, do you abandon and forget about it? Well, woe is me, is a slave not a moneybag? Is he not worth more than a beast? Then, why isn't he cared for? Why don't they look after his well being, health, and comfort? Surely this seems the product of fantasy, and no one will believe it if they are told it, that men who plough the seas and traverse lands and put at risk their fortunes, honor, lives and souls, in order to bring and have blacks and get rich off them and by them, [would] treat them so poorly when they are healthy and worse when they are sick [. . .]

I say, then, to those of us who are in charge of such an apostolic work, we should, by way of being faithful to that which to the glory of God and the good of our fellow man we take by the hand, travel by foot, go out to look for native speakers and interpreters for them on days on end, because if this difficulty is not overcome, the entire structure of this elevated enterprise will fall to the ground, since it is an established fact that when tongues are foreign between one man and another, it is as if each did not exist.

With the esteem that God our Lord, the Catholic Church, the Pope, the kings of Castile and Portugal, and the Society of Jesus have afforded the blacks, not only those from Ethiopia, but in particular those from Guinea, Congo, the Philippines, and other parts, pertaining to their conversion and salvation, we will strive to see that they have the capacity [. . .] to receive the sacraments, [and] give them knowledge of the law of God, if they didn't already understand it. In no way is this lost time; rather it is the greatest advancement that any worker could make [. . .] since working with them just a little will suffice for their obligation to know and understand the things of heaven, since it is certain that God obliges consistent with one's capacity [. . .] the

Lord makes each accountable according to the talent he has given him. [. . .]

If it is true, as it is, that our principal vocation in the Indies is to work with the Indians [. . .] then, in the same way, without any difference, we will have to help the blacks, especially in those places and lands where there are no Indians. [. . .]

Spanish merchants discovered the Indies in order to make profits for themselves; they sent large shipments, they set-up companies and have backers, all with the goal of extracting gold, silver, pearls, and precious stones. And Christ, supreme merchant, discovered these same Indies, desirous to enrich his court with something even more precious than gold, silver, and stone: that is, with her native [Indian] souls and the naturalized ones [souls] of the blacks. And for that reason he sent to these parts his agents, stewards, and representatives, who are the religious from so many and such holy religious orders, filled with virtues, holiness, and learning. But seeing that the riches were many and his ministers few, he made and established a Society with men whose goal is to search out souls for him, and for that reason traverse all parts of the world, no matter how remote they be [. . .] What excuse could we possibly have if we did not with the utmost diligence look after the races which in these parts he has put in our hands?

55. A Brotherhood of Black Creole Slaves

The following reading is an excerpt from a sermon delivered to a religious brotherhood of black Creole slaves by António Vieira, S.J. (1608-1697, biography provided in reading 24), in the mid-seventeenth century. What is Vieira at pains to convey in the first three paragraphs? What is the effect of the comparative couplings in the first two paragraphs and the rhetorical questions at the end? In the third paragraph, Vieira attempts to reconcile his Christian belief in the spiritual equality of all mankind, all of whom are equally called to salvation, with the brutal and unequal nature of their physical existence. How successful is he?

One of the remarkable things witnessed in the world today, and which we, because of our daily habits, do not see as strange, is the immense transmigration of Ethiopian peoples and nations who are constantly crossing over from Africa to this America. The fleet of Aeneas, said the Prince of Poets, brought Troy to Italy . . . and with greater reason can we say that the ships which one after the other are entering our ports are carrying Africa to Brazil. . . . A ship enters from Angola and on a single day unloads 500, 600, or perhaps 1,000 slaves. The Israelites crossed the Red Sea and passed from Africa to Asia, fleeing captivity; these slaves have crossed the Ocean at its widest point, passing from that same Africa to America to live and die as slaves. . . .

Now if we look at these miserable people after their arrival and at those who call themselves their masters, what was observed in Job's two conditions is what fate presents here, happiness and misery meeting on the same stage. The masters few, the slaves many; the masters decked out in courtly dress, the slaves ragged and naked; the masters feasting, the slaves dying of hunger; the masters swimming in gold and silver, the slaves weighted down with irons; the masters treating them like brutes, the slaves adoring and fearing them as gods; the masters standing erect, waving their whips, like statues of pride and tyranny, the slaves prostrate with their hands tied behind them like the vilest images of servitude, spectacles of extraordinary misery. Oh God! What divine influ-

SOURCE: Robert Edward Conrad, *Children of God's Fire: A Documentary History of Black Slavery in Brazil* (University Park, Pa.: Pennsylvania State University Press, 1994), 164-65, 167, 170-71, 173-74. Copyright 1994 by The Pennsylvania State University. Reproduced by permission of the publisher.

ence we owe to the Faith You gave us, for it alone captures our understanding, so that, although in full view of such inequalities, we may nevertheless recognize Your justice and providence! Are not these people the children of Adam and Eve? Were not these souls redeemed by the blood of Christ? Are not these bodies born and do they not die as ours do? Do they not breathe the same air? Are they not covered by the same sky? Are they not warmed by the same sun? What star is it, so sad, so hostile, so cruel, that decides their fate? . . .

There is not a slave in Brazil—and especially when I gaze upon the most miserable among them—who for me is not an object of profound meditation. When I compare the present with the future, time with eternity, that which I see with that which I believe, I cannot accept the idea that God, who created these people as much in His own image as He did the rest of us, would have predestined them for two hells, one in this life and another in the next. But when today I see them so devout and festive before the altars of Our Lady of the Rosary, all brothers together and the children of that same Lady, I am convinced beyond any doubt that the captivity of the first transmigration is ordained by her compassion so that they may be granted freedom in the second. [. . .]

The second section—the next four paragraphs (ending with "make use of it to gain that which you deserve")—may be understood as a theology of slavery by a Christian pastor who was fully aware of the injustice and horrors of slavery but who also believed in divine providence, the promise of salvation to all humans, and God's special desire for that of the slaves ("that which you deserve"). Outline that theology briefly.

Behold in the following, black brothers of the Rosary, . . . your present condition and the hope it gives you for the future: "and Josias begot Jechonias and his brethren" [Matt. 1:11]. Your [sic] are the brothers of God's preparation and the children of God's fire. The children of God's fire of the present transmigration of slavery, because in this condition God's fire impressed the mark of slavery upon you; and, granted that this is the

mark of oppression, it has also, like fire, illuminated you, because it has brought you the light of the Faith and the knowledge of Christ's mysteries, which are those which you solemnly profess on the rosary. But in this same condition of the first transmigration, which is that of temporal slavery, God and His Most Holy Mother are preparing you for the second transmigration, that of eternal freedom.

It is this which I must preach to you today for your consolation. Reduced to a few words, this will be my topic: that your brotherhood Our Lady of the Rosary promises all of you a Certificate of Freedom, with which you will not only enjoy eternal liberation in the second transmigration of the other life, but with which you will also free yourselves in this life from the most terrible captivity of the first transmigration. . . .

Although banished Children of Eve, we all possess or all expect a universal transmigration, which is that from Babylon to Jerusalem, from this world's exile to our true home in heaven. You, however, came or were brought from your homelands to these places of exile; aside from the second and universal transmigration, you have another, that of Babylon, in which, more or less moderated, you remain in captivity. [. . .]

Therefore, black brothers, the slavery you suffer, however hard and grinding it may be, or seems to be to you, is not total slavery, or the enslavement of everything you are, but rather only half slavery. You are slaves in your exterior part, which is the body; however, in the other interior and nobler half, the soul, . . . you are not a slave, but free. This first point accepted, it follows that you should know a second and more important point, which I now put to you: whether that free part or half, the soul, can also in some way be enslaved, and who can enslave it. I say to you that your soul too, like anybody's, can be enslaved; and he who can enslave it is not your master, not the king himself, not any other human power, but only you yourself, and this only by your own free will. Fortunate are those of you who can so adapt yourself to the condition of your half slavery that you can take advantage of your own servitude and may know how to make use of it to gain that which you deserve! [. . .]

The next four paragraphs then demonstrate how these mostly Creole slaves (those born in Brazil and socialized to Portuguese colonial culture) may achieve that promise of Salvation by adopting those principles that would be pertinent to all Christians who are not masters of others, free or slave. What are these principles and do they serve for comfort and consolation or for abjection and exploitation?

The Apostle Paul spoke to the slaves in two places as follows: "Servants, obey in all things your masters according to the flesh; not serving to the eye, as pleasing men, but in simplicity of heart, fearing God. Whatsoever you do, do it from the heart, as to the Lord, and not to men. Knowing that you shall receive of the Lord the reward of inheritance. Serve ye the Lord Christ" [Col. 3:22, 23, 24; Eph. 6:5, 6, 7, 8, 9].

When you serve your masters, you are neither their heirs, nor do they pay you for your labor. You are not their heirs because the inheritance belongs to the sons and not to the slaves; and they do not pay you for your labor, because the slave serves through an obligation and not for wages. A sad and miserable condition, to serve throughout life without hope of reward, and to work without hope of rest except in the grave! But there is a good remedy, says the Apostle (and this is not exaggeration, but Catholic Faith). The remedy is that when you serve your masters, you do not serve them as someone who serves men, but rather as someone who serves God; . . . because then you do not serve as captives, but rather as free persons, nor do you obey as slaves, but as sons and daughters [of God]. You do not serve as captives, but as free men, because God will pay you for your labor; . . . and you do not obey as slaves, but rather as sons and daughters [of God], because God, to whom you are similar in that fate which He gave you, will make you his heirs. . . .

Thus far according to St. Paul. And what does St. Peter say? . . . "Servants, be subject to your masters with all fear, not only to the good and gentle but also to the froward" [1 Pet. 2:18]. This is the . . . advice which the Prince of Apostles gives you, and later he adds reasons worthy of being given to the noblest and most generous spirits. Firstly, because it is the glory of patience to suffer without guilt. "For what glory is it, if committing

sin, and being buffeted for it, you endure?" Secondly, because this is the way in which men make themselves more acceptable to God. "But if doing well you suffer patiently; this is thankworthy before God." Thirdly, and truly stupendous: because in that condition in which God has placed you, your vocation is similar to that of His Son, who suffered for us, providing you the example which you are to imitate. "For unto this are you called; because Christ also suffered for us, leaving you an example that you should follow his steps" [1 Pet. 2:20, 21].

I most justly called this reason "stupendous" because who will not be amazed by the low condition of the subjects with whom St. Peter speaks, and by the highness of the most lofty comparison to which he raises them? He does not compare the slaves' vocation to another grade or condition of the Church, but to Christ Himself. "For unto this are you called; because Christ also suffered." More still: the Apostle does not stop here, but adds another new and greater prerogative of the slaves, declaring for whom Christ suffered, and why: "leaving you an example that you should follow his steps." [. . .]

The powerful rhetoric of the last two paragraphs is addressed to those in command of slaves, more the overseers of the plantations than the masters. Those listening to Vieira's sermon, slaves and overseers (the latter uneasy about what Vieira might say) would react quite differently to each of the last two paragraphs of the excerpt, would they not?

But what theology could justify the inhumanity and brutality of the exorbitant punishments with which these same slaves are mistreated? "Mistreated," I said, but this word is totally inadequate. . . . Tyrannized, one might say, or martyrized; because they injure these miserable people, drop hot fat or wax on them, slash them, cudgel them, and inflict many other kinds of excesses upon them, of which I will not speak, these deserving more the name of martyrdoms than of punishments. Well, be certain that you should not fear such injustice less than the slaves themselves; I say rather that you should fear them more, because God feels them much more. As long as the Egyptians only enslaved the children of Israel, God accepted their captivity; but in the end Divine Justice cannot abide its own dissimulation, and after the ten plagues with which the Egyptians themselves were punished, he totally finished with them, and he destroyed them and laid them waste. And why? God Himself says it: "I have seen," says God, "the affliction of my people in Egypt, and I have heard their cry; because of the rigor of them that are over the works" [Exod. 3:7].

Observe two things: first, that God does not complain about the Pharaoh, but rather about his overseers; . . . because the overseers are often those who cruelly oppress the slaves. Secondly, that he does not give slavery as the reason for his act of justice, but rather the oppression and hardship which they inflicted upon the slaves. . . . "I have seen the affliction of my people." And God adds that he had heard their cries, which for me is a cause for great pity, and for God must be a circumstance that greatly arouses His anger. The miserable slave is being whipped, and with every lash he cries out: "Jesus! Maria! Jesus! Maria!"— and the reverence that these two names deserve is not enough to arouse pity in a man who calls himself a Christian. And how do you expect these two names to respond to you when you call upon them at the hour of your death? Know full well that God hears these cries for help which you do not hear; and though they do not touch your heart, you should know that they make your own punishment certain. [. . .]

56. Evangelizing Enslaved Africans in Bahia

The following reading consists of excerpts from an instruction (1707) by Sebastião Monteiro DaVide, archbishop of Bahia, on the method of evangelizing enslaved Africans and their Creole descendants.

How apt is the church's understanding of the attitudes and psychology of the newly arrived "slaves" and how solid is the preparation of the evangelizers for their task? What is the nature of the catechetical exercise and how suitable is that exercise for the Africans to understand and embrace its teachings?

4. We order all persons, ecclesiastics as well as secular, to teach or have taught the Christian doctrine to their families, and especially to their slaves, who because of their ignorance are those most in need of this instruction, sending them to church so that the priest may teach them the Articles of Faith, so that they may know what to believe; the Pater Noster and Ave Maria, so that they may know how to pray; the Commandments of the Law of God and of the Holy Mother Church, and the mortal sins, so that they will know how to behave; the virtues, so that they may recognize good values; and the seven Sacraments, so that they may receive them with dignity, and with them the grace which they give, and the other prayers of Christian doctrine, so that they may be instructed in everything which is important to their salvation. . . .

6. And because the slaves of Brazil are those most in need of Christian Doctrine so numerous are their nations and so diverse their languages, we should search for every means to instruct them in the faith, or for someone who may speak to them in their languages, and in ours, when they can already understand it. And there is no more profitable way than a kind of instruction accomodated to the rudeness of their understanding and the barbarity of their speech. Thus the Parish Priests are required to have copies made . . . of the brief form of the Catechism, which is to be found

SOURCE: Robert Edward Conrad, *Children of God's Fire: A Documentary History of Black Slavery in Brazil* (University Park, Pa.: Pennsylvania State University Press, 1994), 154-55, 157-58. Copyright 1994 by The Pennsylvania State University. Reproduced by permission of the publisher.

in Title XXXII, for distribution to the houses of the parishioners, in order that they may instruct their slaves in the mysteries of the Faith, and Christian Doctrine, in the manner of the said instruction, and so that their questions and answers will be those examined by them when they confess and take Christian communion, and this will be easier than studying from memory the Lord's Creed; and others which those of greater ability learn. . . .

50. And for greater security in regard to the Baptism of the brute and raw slaves, and those of unknown language, such as are those who come from Mina, and many also from Angola, the following will be done. After they have acquired some knowledge of our language, or if there are interpreters, the instruction of the mysteries [special catechism] will be used, which as we said is contained in the third book [Title XXXII] number 579. . . . And aside from this the raw slaves referred to above will be asked only the following questions:

Do you want to wash your soul with holy water?
Do you want to eat the salt of God?
Will you cast all the sins out of your soul?
Will you commit no more sins?
Do you want to be a child of God?
Will you cast the devil out of your soul?

51. And because it has happened that some of these raw slaves have died before it could be learned whether they wished to be baptized or not, the first chance that they may be asked the above questions, either through interpreters or in our own language, they possessing some understanding of it, it is very important for the salvation of their souls that this be done, because then, in the event of death, since they have already expressed their desire, even if this was long before, they may certainly be baptized *sub conditione* or even absolutely, depending upon the assessment of their ability which has been formed up to that time. [. . .]

Brief Instruction in the Mysteries of the Faith, Accomodated to the Manner of Speaking of the Slaves of Brazil, So That They May Be Catechized by It

Questions	Answers
579.	
Who made this world?	God.
Who made us?	God.
Where is God?	In Heaven, on earth, and in the whole world.
Do we have one God, or many?	We have only one God.
How many persons?	Three.
Tell me their names.	The Father, the Son, and the Holy Spirit.
Which of these persons took our flesh?	The Son.
Which of these persons died for us?	The Son.
How is this Son called?	Jesus Christ.
How is His Mother called?	The Virgin Mary.
Where did the Son die?	On the Cross.
After he died where did He go?	He went under the earth in search of the good souls.
And later, where did He go?	To Heaven.
Will He return?	Yes.
What will He come to search for?	The souls of good heart.
And where will He take them?	To Heaven.
And the souls of bad heart, where will they go?	To hell.
Who is in hell?	The devil is there.
And who else?	The souls of bad heart.
And what are they doing there?	They are in the fire, which never goes out.
Will they ever leave there?	Never.
When we die, does the soul die also?	No. Only the body dies.
And the soul, where does it go?	If the soul is good, it goes to Heaven; if the soul is bad it goes to hell.

And the body, where does it go?	It goes to the earth.
Will it leave the earth alive?	Yes.
Where will the body go which had a soul of bad heart?	To hell.
And where will the body go which had a soul of good heart?	To Heaven.
Who is in Heaven with God?	All those who had good souls.
Will they leave Heaven, or will they be there forever?	They will be there forever.

Instruction for Confession

580.

What is confession for?	To wash away the sins of the soul.
He who confesses, does he hide sins?	No.
He who hides sins, where does he go?	To hell.
He who sins, will he sin again?	No.
What does sin do?	It kills the soul.
After confession, does the soul live again?	Yes.
Will your soul sin again?	No.
Because of Whose love?	Because of God's love.

Instruction for Communion

581.

Do you desire communion?	Yes.
Why?	So that Our Lord Jesus Christ may enter my soul.
And when is Our Lord Jesus Christ in the Communion?	When the Father says the words.
Where does the Father say the Words?	In the Mass.
And when does he say the words?	When he takes the Host in his hands.
Before the priest says the words, is Our Lord Jesus Christ already in the Host?	No, there is only bread.
And who puts Our Lord Jesus Christ into the Host?	He Himself, after the priest speaks the words.
And what is in the Chalice when the priest takes it in his hands?	Wine is in it, before the priest speaks the words.
And after he speaks the words, what is in the Chalice?	The blood of Our Lord Jesus Christ is in it.

57. Slaves and Christian Marriage

Jorge Benci (c. 1650-1708), an Italian Jesuit whose missionary assignment was Brazil, published in 1700 Economia cristã dos senhores no governo dos escravos *(A Christian Method for Masters to Manage their Slaves). What do these excerpts on the right of slaves to marry reveal about the nature of the slave system, the mentality of both master and slave, and the role that the church desired to play and actually did play in that system?*

SOURCE: Robert Edward Conrad, *Children of God's Fire: A Documentary History of Black Slavery in Brazil* (University Park, Pa.: Pennsylvania State University Press, 1994), 174-76, 178. Copyright 1994 by The Pennsylvania State University. Reproduced by permission of the publisher.

89. [The Holy Eucharist] is not the only sacrament that masters deny to their slaves; they also prevent them from marrying. The state of matrimony ought to be freely available to the captives, so that no power on earth (says the most learned Father Sánchez) can impede it (Sánchez, Lib. 7, de Matrim, disp. 21, no. 3). And if it is supposed that according to Imperial Law the right to contract marriage is allowed only to free persons. Canon Law in fact revokes this provision of civil law as contrary to the holy and natural law which grants human beings the right to multiply their species, and declares that the marriage of slaves should not be prevented, that their marriages are valid when entered into against the will of their masters. Can that which Emperors are not allowed to prohibit be prohibited by slavemasters of Brazil?

90. I ask you this: For what purpose was Holy Matrimony instituted? Not only for the propagation of the human species, but also (according to the same Sánchez previously cited) as a remedy against lust and as a means of avoiding sin. Is there perhaps a master in existence who has the power to restrain the lust of his slaves so that its effects do not appear, and so that they are not tempted and driven to sin? Certainly not. Therefore, if you cannot suppress your slaves' lust and its results, why must you deny them the remedy that God gave them against it? And do you not see that, aside from subjecting yourself to the excommunication which the Sacred Council of Trent pronounced against those who prevent matrimony, in this way you also make yourselves participants in all the sins which your slaves commit against the Sixth Commandment?

91. You will tell me that marriage is not intended for such brutish people, since as soon as the wedding ceremonies are performed both men and women abandon each other and commit the greatest sins. But if this cause seems reasonable to you, answer the following question: How many masters are there who are married to women gifted with honor and beauty who leave them, perhaps for some enormous, wicked, and vile slave woman? Should we conclude from this that it is also improper for white men and slavemasters to marry? Nobody will say that this rightly follows; because although such licentiousness does exist among the masters after they marry, they should not for this reason be deprived of marriage. Therefore, even if there are individuals among the slaves and blacks, both men and women, who overstep the bounds after they are married, it does not follow that they are therefore not suited for marriage. Allow them to marry, if they wish, because in this way you will meet your obligation. And if, once they are joined in matrimony, they turn to vice, it will be their responsibility, and not yours, to give an account to God of the sins which they have committed.

92. And since it is not right for masters to prevent marriage among their slaves, it is also wrong for them to impede the normal practices of marriage once they have entered into matrimony, separating husband from wife and leaving the one at home and ordering the sale of the other, or forcing him to live in a place so far away that the couple cannot maintain a conjugal relationship. Because, even if by depriving the slave of that which belongs to him according to natural law, you do not sin against justice, as Father Sánchez teaches, it cannot be denied that you sin at least against charity, because by separating married slaves from each other, you deprive them of what is good in marriage, in which case you cause them very serious harm, which charity forbids you to do to another person without a very good cause.

93. And this being the case, it is quite amazing how easily some masters, for insignificant reasons, order the sale to other places of either the slave man or woman, or in some other way separate married couples from each other. Who gave you the power to order these divorces, if the Church, which alone possesses this power, is so careful in this matter that it does not permit a divorce between a man and his wife without quite justifiable and urgent reasons? [...]

Is it not a scandal, and the most hateful in the eyes of God, for the master to establish a friendship with his slave girl? And is it not much worse yet, and more abominable, to compel her by the use of force to consent to her master's sin, and to punish her when she resists and seeks to avoid this offense against God? No Catholic will deny it. And should the master who does this expect to be saved? Such things happen in Mauritania or Bar-

bary, where Mohammed in his sixth command-ment expounded on ungodly people and pro-duced some reasons for pardoning masters who committed such impure crimes. But that this should happen in a Christian land and to Chris-tians who are as Christian as the Portuguese! What can we say except that, aside from the eter-nal suffering with which masters who thus violate and compel their slaves to sin should be punished, they also deserve the temporal death which is imposed by common law and the special laws of Portugal upon all persons who through violence or some other means compel and force women of any quality to sin, even those whom we commonly refer to as worldly. [. . .]

58. São Salvador de Bahia, Shame of Catholic Brazil

Amedée Frezier (1682–1773), "Engineer in Ordinary to the French King," added a brief account of São Salvador to his much longer descriptions of Chile and Peru, where he resided for more than two years. This brief account was published in French and translated into English in 1717. His description of the horrific plight of the enslaved Africans who were brought to this colonial capital of Brazil becomes even more disturbing when it is contrasted with his depiction of the religiosity of the elite inhabitants.

Analyze and evaluate his treatment of the "outward show" of these "Portuguese [. . .] Christians."

Note that the reference to Jews at the end of the document refers to a small number of "converted Jews" in colonial Brazil, some of whom like Luis el mozo in sixteenth-century New Spain (reading 60) desired to recover their original Jewish identity.

The City of *Bahia*, as is well known, is the Capi-tal and Metropolis of *Brasil*, and the usual Seat of a Viceroy; however, the Governor has not always that Title, Witness he that was in our Time.

The Inhabitants have an Outside good enough as to Politeness, Neatness, and the manner of giv-ing themselves a good Air, much like the *French*. [. . .]

19 in 20 of the People we see there, are Blacks, Men and Women, all naked, except those Parts which Modesty obliges to cover; so that the City looks like a new *Guinea*. In short, the Streets are full of none but hideous Figures of Black Men and Women Slaves, whom Delicacy and Avarice, rather than Necessity, have transplanted from the Coast of *Africa*, to make up the State of the Rich, and contribute towards the Sloth of the Poor, who ease themselves of their Labour on them, so that there are always above 20 Blacks to one White. Who would believe it? There are Shops full of those poor Wretches, who are exposed there stark naked, and bought like Cattle, over whom the Buyers have the same Power; so that upon slight Disgusts, they may kill them almost without Fear of Punishment, or at least treat them as cruelly as they please. I know not how such Barbarity can be reconciled to the Maxims of Religion, which makes them Members of the same Body with the Whites, when they have been baptized, and raises them to the Dignity of Sons of God, *All Sons of the most High*; doubtless they will not suffer them-selves to be convinced of that Truth; for those poor Slaves are too much abused by their Brethren, who scorn that Relation.

I here make this Comparison, because the *Por-tugueze* are Christians who make a great outward Show of Religion, even more than the *Spaniards*; for most of them walk along the Streets with their Beads in their Hands, a Figure of S. *Anthony* on their Breasts, or hanging about their Necks, and

SOURCE: Amedée F. Frezier, *A Voyage to the South Sea, And Along the Coasts of Chili (sic) and Peru, In the Years 1712, 1713, and 1714* (London: Jonah Bowyer, 1717), 300, 301–2.

with an extravagant Furniture of a long *Spanish* Sword on their Left, and a Dagger almost as long as a short *French* Sword on their Right, to the end that when Occasion shall offer, neither Arm may be useless towards destroying of their Enemies. In reality, those outward Tokens of Religion are very deceitful among them, not only in regard to true Probity, but even to Christian Sentiments; they often serve to conceal from the Eyes of the World a great Number of *Jews*; an amazing Instance has been seen in that Town. A Curate, after having for several Years behaved himself outwardly to Edification, at last made his Escape with the Sacred Ornaments into *Holland*, to live there as a *Jew*; for which Reason, to be admitted to the Clergy, a Man must prove himself an old Christian, as they call it, that is, of ancient Christian Descent.

59. Slavery and the Political Economy of Portuguese Brazil

The following letter (1794) of the governor of the province of Bahia to the Portuguese secretary of state for the Conselho ultramarino *(Overseas Council) demonstrates the Portuguese church's apparently complete acceptance and promotion of slavery and the slave trade. Some of the rationalizations for this position may be seen as early as c. 1455 in Gomes Eannes de Azurara's* Chronicle of the Discovery and Conquest of Guinea, *in which the author clearly depicts the human tragedy of the capture and enslavement of innocent Africans while simultaneously agreeing that its effect is positive overall because it imparts Christianity to "heathens."*

Does the fact that it is a non-Portuguese Capuchin with fourteen years of experience in Brazilian society, and whom the governor describes as "follow[ing] an opinion" that would "disturb the consciences" of Bahians, suggest something about the relationship between church and state and the political economy of Portuguese Brazil?

Most Illustrious and Excellent Sir:

The Archbishop of this diocese, guided by the vigilance which he always reveals in his efforts to hinder any doctrine of a spiritual nature which might disturb the calm and tranquility of this captaincy, or which might go counter to laws and orders of His Majesty, has informed me that the priest, Friar Joseph of Bologna, an Italian Capuchin missionary, has unwisely and indiscreetly followed an opinion in respect to slavery which, if propagated and adopted, would disturb the consciences of this city's inhabitants and bring future results disastrous to the preservation and welfare of this colony.

This monk had lived in this country for nearly fourteen years with exemplary conduct, complying with the obligations of his ministry—despite some indiscretions and odd behavior which he fell into, and from which he abstained when warned by his superiors—earning the reputation of a virtuous man, eager in the service of God. Later, however, he convinced himself, or was persuaded, that slavery was illegitimate and contrary to religion, or at least, being sometimes legitimate and other times illegitimate, the distinction ought to be made between slaves captured in just and unjust wars. He became so convinced of his belief that, acting as confessor for several persons during the feast of the Holy Spirit, he put this doctrine into practice, making them ponder this very difficult if not unresolvable question, with the purpose of freeing those slaves who were either stolen or

SOURCE: Robert Edward Conrad, *Children of God's Fire: A Documentary History of Black Slavery in Brazil* (University Park, Pa.: Pennsylvania State University Press, 1994), 181-82. Copyright 1994 by The Pennsylvania State University. Reproduced by permission of the publisher.

reduced to unjust slavery. This he did without realizing that whoever buys slaves normally buys them from persons authorized to sell them, under the eyes and with the consent of the Prince, to whom it would be unheard-of, and against the peace of society, to demand of a private person, when he buys merchandise from a person authorized to sell it, that he first inform himself of its source through inquiries not only useless but obviously capable of eliminating every kind of commerce.

In a search for the source of this opinion, which this monk for so long did not follow, it was learned that some conversations that he had with the Italian fathers from the Gôa mission, who are passengers in the ship *Belém* anchored in this port and who were lodged in the Da Palma Hospice, caused the friar to accept this doctrine, not so much because of malice and bad faith, but for lack of greater talents and theological learning, and because of an extraordinary conscience.

To avoid the spread of such a pernicious doctrine, the Archbishop immediately ordered him to suspend his confessions, requesting that I deport him in the same ship, which is continuing its voyage, and that the captain not allow him to go ashore without a positive order from Your Excellency. And, conferring with the Archbishop him-

self on this matter so that I might take further steps which might seem prudent, I judged it convenient to call to my presence the rector of the above-mentioned missionaries from Gôa. I strongly expressed my astonishment at his indiscretion, indicating to him that this matter is extraordinarily delicate and risky, and that it was for the Prince alone to make decisions concerning it, if he should someday judge this convenient; and that finally it was extremely rash and ill-advised, in the opinion of the wise and learned prelate, and of the whole clergy of this city, to bring up such a question. The rector tried to explain himself, telling me that when the priest, Friar Joseph of Bologna, asked his opinion on this point, he had merely responded that there was legitimate and illegitimate slavery, but that he had not encouraged him to do what he did in the confessional. Prior to that he had suggested to him that if there were doubts he should discuss them first with his superior. But, despite this defense, which did not satisfy me, in order to obtain greater security I ordered that the commander of the *Belém* put the said missionaries on board, and not let them set foot on land without a positive order from me.

God protect Your Excellency.
Bahia, June 18, 1794.

PART VIII
The Holy Office of the Inquisition

A few Jewish families arrived in colonial Spanish and Portuguese America despite legislation designed to keep them out. Jews had been under great pressure to convert to Catholicism during the two centuries prior to New World conquest, especially after the 1391 anti-Jewish riots in the Iberian peninsula. Some converted willingly and became known as *converses* or New Christians. Their conversion to Christianity was perceived as suspect, however, and they were usually denied entrance into prestigious state, church, and military positions as well as universities and certain guilds. The vast majority of Jews fled Spain and Portugal for more hospitable areas of Europe after the expulsions in 1492 and 1497. Still others became secret Jews who only outwardly "converted" and who, if discovered, suffered the wrath of the Inquisition. Given these dire circumstances, some escaped to the New World where they hoped to evade the clutches of the Holy Office and wait for the day when they could practice their faith openly. Aware of this possibility, Spanish officials attempted to prevent Jews and other undesirables from reaching the New World and required all emigrants to secure *limpieza de sangre*, that is, "purity of blood" documentation. Some Jews either forged papers or paid bribes to ensure their unfettered passage; thus small communities of secret Jews grew in Lima and Mexico City, though inquisitors continually hunted them down. Secret Jews may have been able to practice their faith more openly in Brazil during the Dutch occupation (1630-1654) but most left for Holland once the colony reverted to Portuguese control. Those who stayed risked having their names registered in the "book of the guilty" or of being sent to Lisbon's inquisitorial tribunal. In all, more than 1,800 individuals in Brazil were denounced as "Judaizers" to the Inquisition, 500 of whom were sentenced to life imprisonment and 21 to death. The tribunal in Mexico City accused 1,300 people of Judaism between 1528 and 1795, including the notorious case of the Carvajal family, whose trials and tribulations are examined in this anthology.[1]

---

1. Anita Novinsky, "Jewish Roots of Brazil," in *The Jewish Presence in Latin America*, ed. Judith Laikin Elkin and Gilbert W. Merkx (Boston: Allen & Unwin, 1987), 35-40, 43; Alicia Gojman de Backal, "Conversos," in *Encyclopedia of Mexico: History, Society & Culture*, vol. 1, ed. Michael S. Werner (Chicago and London: Fitzroy Dearborn Publishers, 1997), 341-43; Morton D. Winsberg, "Jews in Latin America," in *Encyclopedia of Latin America*, ed. Helen Delpar (New York: McGraw-Hill, 1974), 310-11.

Jews were not, of course, the only focus of inquisitors. Established in 1479 by Ferdinand and Isabella, the Spanish Inquisition specifically sought to eliminate heresy and create a country unified by orthodox Catholicism. In 1570, King Philip II established two tribunals of the Inquisition in Mexico City and Lima. A third tribunal was established in Cartagena in 1610. As neophytes to Catholicism, Amerindians were exempt from inquisitorial review; their religious errors and lapses were most commonly dealt with at the parish level. Africans, though equally new to Christianity, were subject to the Holy Office because inquisitors were especially eager to eliminate witchcraft, assumed to be a major component of African religions and a danger to the general populace. With the eradication of Judaism from the empire by the late seventeenth century, inquisitors turned their attention to cases dealing with Protestantism, morals, forbidden books, witchcraft, and, finally, political dissent. People in the viceregal capitals needed to be more vigilant about their activities than those who lived in more remote areas and who were thus outside the immediate reach of inquisitors. But most areas, rural as well as urban, had *comisarios,* or Inquisition officials, as well as *familiares* who acted as informants. People in faraway places such as Nicaragua or Honduras might be arrested and sent to Mexico City to stand trial for serious charges of heresy. Though Portugal never established a tribunal in Brazil, the same general process was at work, and heretics would ultimately be sent to Lisbon.

60. The Holy Office and the "New Christians"

Luis de Carvajal, "el mozo" (1566-1596), was the nephew of one of New Spain's most prestigious and honorable conquistadors, don Luis de Carvajal y de la Cueva (1539-1591). The latter was governor and captain-general of "the New Kingdom of León," a gigantic province consisting of what is today northern Mexico and the southwestern United States. The Carvajals came from a family of Sephardic Jews who had converted to Catholicism. These converts were known as "New Christians," a term used for such Spaniards after the massive persecution of Jews in Spain in 1391. Jewish ancestry was made known only to select members of these families and not to others who fully identified with Catholicism, such as the brother of Luis el mozo *who actually became a Dominican friar.*

This younger Luis, upon learning on his thirteenth birthday that he had Jewish ancestors, became observant, sought to learn all he could about Judaism, and underwent a mystical experience in which he was convinced that God had called him to bring one and all to Judaism.

Calling himself Joseph the Enlightened, Luis wrote his memoirs in 1595 in between prison sentences. He had secretly used the library of a colegio, *in which he served one of his lighter sentences after first being suspected of Judaizing, to deepen his knowledge of Judaism. He had even managed, during one of his heavier sentences after relapsing, to convert an imprisoned friar to Judaism.*

Source: Seymour B. Liebman, trans. and ed., *The Enlightened: The Writings of Luis de Carvajal, el Mozo* (Coral Gables, Fl.: University of Miami Press, 1967), 55-73, passim. Reprinted by permission of University of Miami Press.

The Holy Office and the "New Christians"

His memoirs provide valuable information about this remarkable man, the Jewish presence in New Spain, and the policies of the Holy Office.

The following excerpts allow the reader to enter into the depths of Luis's soul. Who is this man who believed he was "saved from terrible dangers by the Lord" and who spoke of the "sacred seal and sacrament" of circumcision and of his "miserable blind" uncle?

Saved from terrible dangers by the Lord, I, *Joseph Lumbroso* of the Hebrew nation and of the pilgrims to the West Indies . . . in appreciation of the mercies and gifts received from the hands of the Highest, address myself to all who believe in the Holy of Holies and who hope for the great mercies He grants to all sinners awakened by the Divine Spirit which He places in them, and I present this brief history as an account of my life up to my twenty-fifth year of peregrination.

First, I kneel on the ground before the universal God, sanctified by all, and promise to say in the name of the Lord of Truth all the truth and to be exact in all I write, starting [this account of] my life at the very beginning.

Let it be known that I was born in Benavente, village of Europe [*sic*], where I was raised until the age of twelve or thirteen and where I began to learn the principles of the Trinity from a relative. I then continued studying in Medina del Campo, where Divine Mercy found me fitted for the light of its knowledge one certain day which we call [the Day of] Forgiveness, a holy and solemn day among [Jews], ten days away from the seventh moon [according to the Hebrew calendar].

Since the truth of the Lord is so clear and pleasant, it is only necessary to relate that my mother, brothers, sisters, a cousin of ours from that village, and my father, all left with our household for this New Spain. [His brother Gaspar, the Dominican, had preceded them.] Originally we wanted to go to Italy, where the Lord might be served best, because of freedom of religion there. . . . It must have been this moving and coming to this land that was one of the sins for which Justice [God] punished His sons, but with great mercy, as will be seen later on. [. . .]

It is to be noted here, how, from the very day I received this sacred seal and sacrament on my flesh, it served as my armor against lust and as a help for my chastity. As a weak sinner on many previous occasions I now merited the fatal wound that saved me from the same sin my father committed—that of marrying the daughter of a Gentile father [his mother]. But through the sacrament of circumcision I was delivered from this sin and evil thereafter. Meanwhile I was like a sick person who craves what is harmful to him and is offered temptations to offend God. Yet, almost miraculously, the Divine Hand interceded, for God's mercy is infinite. Trust in God, because He is good and His mercy is everlasting.

A year after my circumcision I went, together with my uncle, miserable blind [to Judaism] man, who was governor of that province [the New Kingdom of León] . . . to some newly discovered mines, took along a small book in which I had transcribed the fourth book of the holy priest and prophet Esdras. Esdras' devout lessons had been one of the main reasons for my conversion. Not having the sacred Bible with me I spent my time reading Esdras in that land of savage Chichimecas. [. . .]

I remained in that area of Pánuco for over two years with my mother, my sisters, and my brothers, in exile and in mourning and sadness because of the recent death of our father. Our blind uncle [the governor] tried to marry off the poor orphans, my sisters [Leonor and Catalina], or at least bring them into contact with Gentile soldiers or captains. Our father had opposed such matches during his lifetime. He did so for fear of God, because, as long as he had lived, he obeyed the holy commandment that forbids it [Jewish maidens marrying non-Jews].

What insight does the following section afford about Luis, the larger Jewish community and "New Christians" such as Luis' brother, Gaspar, the "narrow-minded Dominican friar?"

While my elder brother [Baltasar, *Jacob Lumbroso*] and I in Mexico were still poor, we heard about a Hebrew cripple, an older man [Antonio

Machado], who was also in great need and had suffered much, being confined to his bed for thirteen years. While visiting the man (as everybody should perform deeds of mercy), we learned much about God, whose divine generosity provided us there with a book the good Licenciado Morales had left to the cripple for his comfort. This doctor had kept the cripple for many days in his home, trying to cure him; and seeing that the body did not profit from the cure [he was beyond medical skill], he wrote a book for him in order to heal his soul. He [Morales] transcribed Deuteronomy into the vernacular. [. . .]

After the Lord in His immense mercy provided for the needs of the soul, He then provided for corporal needs. In one year, without our having any money or ways of getting it, or even imagining how it would happen, the Lord gave us a fortune that exceeded seven thousand pesos; blessed be He forever who provides for the hungry ones. Finding ourselves in this position, we both decided to leave with the first fleet to sail for Italy, where we could best serve the Lord. However, we considered it regrettable to leave our other elder brother [Gaspar], a narrow-minded Dominican friar who was already a preacher and teacher in his Order.

With a strong and loving hope we went to see him in his monastery, which was near the Inquisition prison. He was a teacher of novices at that time. We intended to try to show him the truth of the Lord and of His holy law. After the three of us had sat in his cell and conversed for a while, I said in a casual manner, "I think that I heard somebody say that when Moses held the Tablets of the Law God wrote on them His holy Commandments." To this the friar answered, "Yes, it was as you heard it said." Then he took a sacred Bible which he had among his books and looked for the chapter in Exodus. He gave it to me and I said, "Blessed be the Lord; so this is the law that should be guarded." Thereupon the unfortunate friar arose and spoke a great blasphemy, saying that it was good to read it but not to observe it. He added that, even if that had been the law of God once, it was old and outdated. [. . .]

Given the ways in which the Holy Office operates—and it is important to note that "ways" is indeed plural—how might the life of a "New Christian" who was actually a secret Jew be described? What are some of the ways in which the Holy Office operates? Note that Luis and his brother, Gaspar, the Dominican friar, were both "New Christians" but only Luis a secret Jew.

Since the fleet was to leave soon, we started our preparations. However, for the benefit of us all, the Infinite Mercy and Divine Wisdom decreed that, about this time, the Inquisition should take prisoner one of my sisters, a widow [Isabel], who was accused by a heretic [Felipe Núñez], one of our own nation [a Jew], to whom she had tried to teach the divine truths a year earlier. [. . .]

Two or three days after my return, I went to see my mother during the night, for I dared not visit her or be with her during the day. When we were about to sit at the table for supper, the constable and his assistants from the Inquisition knocked on the door. Having opened it, they placed guards on the stairs, and doors and went to take my mother prisoner. Although deeply shaken by this blow from such a cruel enemy, my mother accepted her fate with humility; and crying for her sufferings but praising the Lord for them, she was taken by these accursed ministers, torturers of our lives, to a dark prison.

My mother's two unmarried daughters who were with her [Mariana and Anica], seeing that their mother was being taken from them, let forth with such painful and sad wailings that even the worst enemies would be moved to pity. They held onto their mother, shouting, "Where are you taking her?" What the grief-stricken mother must have felt is left to the imagination of the reader. After they took her away, they arrested me, finding me behind the door where, for fear of those cruel tyrants, I had hidden myself. Those cruel beasts grabbed me with great force and took me to the cold and dark prison. I said nothing except, "O Lord, reveal the truth." [. . .]

One day they seized and brought to jail a Franciscan friar. [. . .]

On one of those Saturdays they [the inquisitors] visited the friar first, asking him if there was anything he needed, to which he replied that he wanted only a breviary to comfort himself in his cell by saying the prayers of the Divine Office, as he customarily did.

They next visited me and, on finding me very frail and sad, they ordered the friar to keep me company in the same cell. So it was that on the same holy Sabbath they brought him to my cell. They ordered him not to reveal that he was a friar. After we had been talking for a while during the early evening of that same Sabbath, rejoicing in our mutual companionship, the warden [of the prison] came in with the breviary and, opening the door of the cell, gave it to my companion. I felt great joy and pleasure, for I saw how the Lord had sent me, through this means, that which I desired so much—to pray and read the Psalms as I used to. I thanked the Almighty for this special token of His mercy. [...]

While my mother and I were in prison and in the hands of such cruel beasts, fear made us hide and deny our true beliefs and we did not confess publicly to being keepers of the sacred law of the Lord. [...]

In order to investigate our denials one Friday they called my mother to the audience chamber just as they had done so many other times. Through a small hole that my companion and I had dug in the door to our cell with the help of two lamb bones, I watched her being taken in and out. Seeing that she still denied the charges, those tyrants decided to subject her to torture. Thus they led the gentle lamb to the torture chamber, preceded by the wicked judges, the warden, and the guard. The executioner was already in the torture chamber, completely covered from head to foot with a white shroud and hood. They ordered her to undress and directed that the gentle lamb lay down her pure body on the torture rack. Then they tied her arms and legs to it. As they turned the cruel cords in the iron rings, they tightened the flesh, making her cry out with agonizing wails that everyone heard. I knelt in my cell, for this was the most bitter and anguished day of all that I had ever endured. [...]

[W]e were released from prison with the customary penances and garments assigned in such cases in the name of the law of God by the enemies of that law. [...]

I was put into a hospital apart from them and assigned to work as sexton to idols [images of Christ and the saints]. This mortified me much. [...]

Not wanting to leave my mother and sisters alone my brother-in-law begged the inquisitor the favor of letting me be their companion while he went and came back. This was God's way of taking me out of my second captivity, in which I had lived painfully, being forced to eat prohibited food.

When I was restored to the company of my mother and sisters, I noticed that they bought and ate food prohibited by the Lord. They did this because of fear of their enemies and on account of bad advice from some friends. I forbade this and gave them, as an example, all the saints who had consented to be torn into pieces in cruel torments rather than eat prohibited food or even pretend that they ate it. Although they had acted out of fear, their hearts being with the Lord, I did not have trouble persuading them. In tears and fear they returned to their God and laid aside all these impurities and foods. When the time came for me to go back to the hospital where I had served, an old friar came to visit my mother. He was a man of great virtue, to whom the inquisitor had committed my family for confession and to be guarded. My mother begged him to get permission for me to remain in her company and that of my sisters. This was granted on condition that I stay during the day in a school for Indians [El Colegio de Santiago], which the friar conducted. I was to teach grammar to the Indians. I was also to write letters for the friar and transcribe his sermons.

God's mercy to me was very great through this friar who loved me and all my family so dearly. Since the carnivorous wolves had confiscated all our property, leaving us destitute, every day the friar gave us food from his own plate and table. Thus, through his hand as well as through that of the enemy, God nourished us with great miracles for over four and a half years in the den [or lake]. [...]

Whenever the friar went to have dinner and the pupils went home, I carefully took the keys of the school and locked myself in, reading and transcribing into Spanish many things from the sacred

Bible which I stored up for my soul. . . . Whatever free time I had left was used by the friar, who requested me to make an abstract of the doctrine in Oleaster's *Commentaries on the Pentateuch*. . . . This was a task that was compatible with my inclinations and liking. I so greatly desired to do this that I would have given my life for it. Blessed and praised be the Lord, who complies with our worthy desires.

In these books the Lord unveiled to me the thirteen articles and principles [Maimonides'

Creed] of our faith and religion, things I had not heard of in this land of captivity. [. . .]

When my mother, my sisters, and I came out of prison [February, 1590], our elder brother [Baltasar], seeing the outcome, decided to start on his way. [. . .]

My elder brother and the younger one [Miguel] left Mexico one night for fear of being discovered and caught by the Inquisition. [. . .]

They were determined to die for the Lord if they were caught.

61. Harder, Harder on These Lutheran Heretics! Enemies of God!

Miles Philips was one of a group of English sailors who in 1568, after a severe defeat of their expedition by the Spanish in the harbor of Veracruz, asked to be left ashore in Mexico, fearing the return trip home on two very badly damaged ships commanded by John Hawkins.

According to Philips, after six years of desultory imprisonment, harassment, and workfare, the newly established Holy Office of the Inquisition hit upon ingratiating the populace by making the now numerous shipwrecked English sailors its first victims.

How reliable is this account by an Englishman who saw his compatriots cruelly treated by the Holy Office and who himself suffered from its strictures? How did the Holy Office operate, what were its goals, procedures, and rationales? What distinctions about heresies or testimonies did it endeavor to make? Is it significant that the Office operated in a leisurely way with long gaps between procedures? Note that some of these sailors, after having been whipped through the streets of Veracruz, opted, once their sentences were finished, to stay in New Spain rather than go back to early-Elizabethan England.

As concerning those Gentlemen which were delivered as hostages, and that were kept in prison, in the Viceroy his house, after that we were gone from out the garden to serve sundry gentlemen as aforesaid, they remained prisoners in the said house for the space of 4 moneths after their comming thither, at the end whereof the fleete being readie to depart from S. John de Ullua, to goe for Spaine, the said Gentlemen were sent away into Spaine with the fleete, where as I have heard it credibly reported, many of them died with the cruell handling of the Spaniards in the Inquisition house, as those which have bene delivered home after they had suffered the persecution of that house can more perfectly declare. Robert Barret

also master of the [ship] Jesus, was sent away with the fleete into Spaine the next yeere following, where afterwards he suffered persecution in the Inquisition, and at the last was condemned to be burnt, and with him one more of our men whose name was John Gilbert.

Now after that six yeeres were fully expired since our first comming into the Indies, in which time we had bene imprisoned and served in the said countreys as is before truely declared, In the yeere of our Lord one thousand five hundred seventie foure, the Inquisition began to be established in the Indies, very much against the mindes of many of the Spaniards themselves: for never untill this time since their first conquering and planting in the

SOURCE: Richard Hakluyt, *Voyages* (London: J. M. Dent & Sons, 1907), 6:318-23.

Indies, were they subject to that bloodie and cruell Inquisition. The chiefe Inquisitor was named Don Pedro Moya de Contreres, and John de Bovilla his companion, and John Sanches the Fischall [prosecutor], and Pedro de los Rios, the Secretary: they being come and setled, and placed in a very faire house neere unto the white Friers, considering with themselves that they must make an entrance and beginning of that their most detestable Inquisition here in Mexico, to the terror of the whole countrey, thought it best to call us that were Englishmen first in question, and so much the rather, for that they had perfect knowledge and intelligence that many of us were become very rich, as hath bene already declared, and therefore we were a very good booty and pray to the Inquisitors: so that now againe began our sorrowes a fresh, for we were sent for, and sought out in all places of the countrey, and proclamation made upon paine of loosing of goods and excommunication, that no man should hide or keepe secret any Englishmen or any part of their goods. By means whereof we were all soone apprehended in all places, and all our goods seized and taken for the Inquisitors use, and so from all parts of the countrey we were conveied and sent as prisoners to the citie of Mexico, and there committed to prison in sundry darke dungeons, where we could not see but by candle light, & were never past two together in one place, so that we saw not one another, neither could one of us tell what was become of another. Thus we remained close imprisoned for the space of a yeere and a haife, and others for some lesse time, for they came to prison ever as they were apprehended. During which time of our imprisonment, at the first beginning we were often called before the Inquisitors alone, and there severely examined of our faith, and commanded to say the Pater noster, the Ave Maria, & the Creed in Latin, which God knoweth a great number of us could not say, otherwise then in the English tongue. And having the said Robert Sweeting who was our friend at Tescuco always present with them for an interpreter, he made report for us, y^t in our own countrey speech we could say them perfectly, although not word for word as they were in Latin. Then did they proceede to demand of us upon our othes what we did beleeve of the Sacrament, & whether there did remaine any bread or wine after the words of consecration, yea or no, and whether we did not beleeve that the host of bread which the priest did hold up over his head, and the wine that was in the chalice, was the very true and perfect body & blood of our Saviour Christ, yea or no: To which if we answered not yea, then was there no way but death. Then they would demand of us what we did remember of our selves, what opinions we had held, or had bin taught to hold contrary to the same whiles we were in England: to which we for the safety of our lives were constrained to say, that we never did beleeve, nor had bene taught otherwise then has before we had sayd. Then would they charge us that we did not tell them the truth, that they knew the contrary, and therfore we should cal our selves to remembrance, & make them a better answer at the next time, or els we should be rackt, and made to confesse the trueth whether we would or no. And so comming againe before them the next time, we were still demanded of our beliefe whiles we were in England, and how we had bin taught, & also what we thought or did know of such of our owne company as they did name unto us, so that we could never be free from such demands, and at other times they would promise us, that if we would tell them trueth, then should we have favour & be set at libertie, although we very wel knew their faire speeches were but means to entrap us, to the hazard and losse of our lives: howbeit God so mercifully wrought for us by a secret meanes that we had, that we kept us still to our first answer, & would stil say that we had told the trueth unto them, and knew no more by our selves nor any other of our fellows then as we had declared, and that for our sinnes and offences in England against God and our Lady, or any of his blessed Saints, we were heartily sory for the same, and did cry God mercy, and besought the Inquisitors for God's sake, considering that we came into those countreys by force of weather, & against our wils, and that never in all our lives we had either spoken or done any thing contrary to their lawes, and therfore they would have mercy upon us. Yet all this would not serve; for stil from time to time we were called upon to confesse, and about the space of 3 moneths before they proceeded to their severe judgement, we were al rackt, and some enforced to utter that against themselves, which afterwards cost them their lives. And thus having gotten from our owne mouthes matter sufficient for them to proceed in judgement against us, they caused a large scaffold to be made in the middest of the market place in Mexico right over against the head church, & 14 or 15 daies before the day of their judgement, with the sound of a trumpet, and the noise of their Attabalies, which are a kind of drummes, they did assemble the people in all parts of the citie: before whom it was then solemnely proclaimed, that whosoever would upon such a day repaire to the market place, they should heare the sentence of the holy Inquisition against the English heretikes, Lutherans, and also see the same put in execution. Which being done, and the time approching of this cruell judgement, the night before they came to the prison where we were, with certaine officers of that holy hellish house, bringing with them certaine fooles coats which they had prepared for us, being called in their language S. Benitos, which coats were made of yellow cotten & red crosses upon them, both before & behind: they were so busied in putting on their coats about us, and bringing us out into a large yard, and placing and pointing us in what order we should go to the scaffold or place of judgement upon the morrow, that they did not once suffer us to sleepe all that night long. The next morning being come, there was given to every one of us for our breakfast a cup of wine, and a slice of bread fried in honie, and so about eight of the clocke in the morning, we set foorth of the prison, every man alone in his yellow coat, and a rope about his necke, and a great greene Waxe candle in his hand unlighted, having a Spaniard appointed to goe upon either side of every one of us: and so marching in this order and maner toward the scaffold in the market place, which was a bow shoot distant or thereabouts, we found a great assembly of people all the way, and such a throng, that certain of the Inquisitors officers on horseback were constrained to make way, and so comming to the scaffold, we went up by a paire of stayres, and found seates readie made and prepared for us to sit downe on, every man in order as he should be called to receive his judgement.

We being thus set downe as we were appointed, presently the Inquisitors came up another paire of staires, and the Viceroy and all the chiefe Justices with them. When they were set downe and placed under the cloth of estate agreeing to their degrees and calling, then came up also a great number of Friers, white, blacke and gray, about the number of 300 persons, they being set in the places for them appointed. Then was there a solemne Oyes made, and silence commanded, and then presently beganne their severe and cruell judgement.

The first man that was called was one Roger the chiefe Armourer of the Jesus, and hee had judgement to have three hundred stripes on horsebacke, and after condemned to the gallies as a slave for 10 yeeres.

After him were called John Gray, John Browne, John Rider, John Moone, James Collier, and one Thomas Browne: these were adjudged to have 200 stripes on horsebacke, and after to be committed to the gallies for the space of 8 yeeres.

Then was called John Keyes, and was adjudged to have 100 stripes on horsebacke, and condemned to serve in the gallies for the space of 6 yeeres.

Then were severally called the number of 53 one after another, and every man had his severall judgement, some to have 200 stripes on horsebacke, and some 100, and condemned for slaves to the gallies, some for 6 yeeres, some for 8 and some for 10.

And then was I Miles Philips called, and was adjudged to serve in a monasterie for 5 yeeres, without any stripes, and to weare a fooles coat, or S. Benito, during all that time.

Then were called John Storie, Richard Williams, David Alexander, Robert Cooke, Paul Horsewell and Thomas Hull: the six were condemned to serve in monasteries without stripes, some for 3 yeeres and some for foure, and to weare the S. Benito during all the said time. Which being done, and it now drawing toward night, George Rively, Peter Momfrie, and Cornelius the Irishman, were called and had their judgement to be burnt to ashes, and so were presently sent away to the place of execution in the market place but a little from the scaffold, where they were quickly burnt and consumed. And as for us that had received our judgement, being 68 in number, we were caried backe that night to prison againe. And the next day in the morning being good Friday, the yeere of our Lord 1575, we were all brought into a court of the Inquisitors pallace, where we found a horse in a readinesse for every one of our men which were condemned to have stripes, and to be committed to the gallies, which were in number 60 and so they being inforced to mount up on horsebacke naked from the middle upward, were caried to be shewed as a spectacle for all the people to behold throughout the chiefe and principall streetes of the citie, and had the number of stripes to every one of them appointed, most cruelly laid upon their naked bodies with long whips by sundry men appointed to be the executioners thereof: and before our men there went a couple of criers which cried as they went: Behold these English dogs, Lutherans, enemies to God, and all the way as they went there were some of the Inquisitors themselves, and of the familiars of that rakehel order, that cried to the executioners, Strike, lay on those English heretiks, Lutherans, Gods enemies: and so this horrible spectacle being shewed round about the citie, they returned to the Inquisitors house, with their backes all gore blood, and swollen with great bumps, and were then taken from their horses, & carried againe to prison, where they remained untill they were sent into Spaine to the gallies, there to receive the rest of their martirdome: and I and the 6 other with me which had judgement, and were condemned amongst the rest to serve an apprentiship in the monastery, were taken presently and sent to certaine religious houses appointed for the purpose.

62. The Power and Reach of the Holy Office

There are two separate documents in this section on the Holy Office, one from Mexico City in 1736 and the other from Lima, Peru, c. 1800.

Does the first document by Louis Ramé, an eighteenth-century survivor of the rigors of the Holy Office, written some 160 years later than Miles Philips's report, reveal any changes in the goals, methods, and rationale of the Holy Office? Have its severities softened? Keep in mind that this later account concerns one individual, with only glancing references to "others [who] had abjured . . . and run down the Protestant religion."

The second document, a passage from Travels in South America *by François Raymond Joseph de Pons, published in English in 1807, offers an excellent insight into the power and reach of the Holy Office. Control over the reading materials available to subjects residing within the Spanish empire was simply a logical extension of the Office's jurisdiction over the individual's adherence to orthodox Catholic doctrine.*

Accepting de Pons's accuracy concerning the Holy Office's interest in the title and whereabouts of every book that entered the Spanish empire, what conclusions can be drawn about the agenda of church and state officials, the effectiveness of their intentions, and the ultimate impact on colonial society of their stipulations about printed matter?

Source: Louis Ramé, cited in Reverend Mr. J. A. Baker, *Complete History of the Inquisition* (Westminster: O. Payne, 1736), cited in Abel Plenn, ed., *The Southern Americas: A New Chronicle* (New York: Creative Age Press, 1948), 194-98; François Raymond Joseph de Pons, *Travels in South America* (London: Longman and Orme, 1807), in Plenn, ed., *Southern Americas*, 204-5.

[Ramé]

The chief Inquisitor visited me every Saturday during three months, pressing me every time to abjure my religion; but I would neither hearken nor obey to his urging solicitations. They proceeded then to give me such violent sort of victuals, which turned my head and brains in such a manner that I knew not what I either did or said—insomuch that in one of these fits I had like to have thrown myself out of a window. This lasted a whole year, during which I pulled to pieces a pair of silk stockings which I had, and with the silk and some of the boards of my bed I contrived a sort of harp—which I having been heard to play upon, they took it from me. [...]

The second year being at an end, they carried me before the Tribunal, where, instead of seeing the Inquisitor and the Fiscal [prosecutor], as I had before, I found a great many ecclesiastics and lawyers. A Jesuit, who was the nearest to me, began to speak, and bestowed on me the title of "brother"—telling me that God had made use of all these ways to open my eyes, and had brought me into their power for the salvation of my soul.

I answered him that it had been God's will to let all these punishments and afflictions fall upon me in order to awaken me, and to make me consider the many sins which I had committed against his Divine Majesty, and to try in a greater measure the resolution and constancy which I had shown at the same time that others had abjured their religion, for the sake of some conveniences of this world—and that I prayed God to fortify me in this trial. [...]

Therefore, I say that our Savior Jesus Christ called the people to him by his preaching and admonishing of them, and that he never made use of secret prisons, fetters, etc....

The others began to talk and run down the Protestant religion, saying that it had been invented by one Calvin, who was a very ill man, and had been whipped, etc. To which I answered that I knew of no such religion as the religion of Calvin, but that my religion was that of Christ. [...]

After all this they sent me back again to my secret prison, where I immediately kneeled down, returning God most hearty thanks for his assistance in my past trials, begging at the same time the continuance of it in those which I was likely still to undergo. After which I sang a psalm.

The chief Inquisitor, Don Juan de Miel, came to visit me every Saturday, and always asked me how I did. I generally answered him, as well as I could in this place. [...]

In this manner did I pass the third year, being pretty well used in the beginning. But afterwards they gave me such unwholesome food that it bought upon me a violent and continual looseness, which lasted between three and four months, and I became as lean and as dry as a red herring. I sang, cried, and fought with the Fiscal—as if he had been with me—telling him that he was worse than an infidel. However, I escaped these three years without falling sick. I was troubled with the toothache, and I had one tooth pulled out.

The fourth and last year passed with very little solicitation from my enemies, the Inquisitors, but with great torments caused by the bad victuals which were given me during five months. In the month of November, they carried me before the Tribunal, where the first Inquisitor said to me: "By virtue of the oath which you have taken of speaking the truth, I command you to tell me whether you continue in the same mind and sentiments as before."

I answered, yes I did, with tears in my eyes, believing that the time of my death was at hand. After which my sentence was read in these words; viz.:

"We have found that we ought to condemn, and we do by this actually condemn, the aforesaid Louis Ramé, to be banished out of this Kingdom of New Spain, and to that effect he shall be delivered into the Officer of War's hands, and put into the Royal Prison." [...]

After this they carried me into another prison in the first court, from whence I could see the people that walked in the street. And they gave me good victuals during seven or eight days in which time my sight became stronger—having almost lost it before through the ill food which they had given me. I was then carried into the aforesaid Royal Prison. [...]

The Viceroy with all the Judges came to visit the prisons at Christmas. I begged of him that I might have some ease from the hardships I endured, telling him at the same time how much I had suffered, and the extreme want of necessaries I was now brought to.

After this I was transferred from the Royal Prison to Mixcoac, which is a village about four or five miles from Mexico City. I was put there in a manufacture of cloth, which is the place where all the thieves and malefactors that are condemned by the justice, are bought and sold. . . .

From this manufacture I was carried back into the Royal Prison, where I continued six months longer with fetters on. . . . After these six months they took me out of the prison, and sat me on a mule, to carry me to Vera-Cruz, having two guards along with me, and fetters on which weighed at least five and twenty pounds. They made me get up and down with all this weight, and the mule was so vicious and full of tricks that I believe they gave it to me in hopes that she would break my neck.

[de Pons]

Such is the vigilance of the Inquisition that this regulation concerning the policing of books is more rigorously executed both in Europe and America than any other regulation appertaining to the Spanish regime. From whatever part books may come, in whatever language they may be written, neither the entrance, circulation, nor use, are permitted, until they have been judged orthodox by the commissaries of the Holy Office. Every bookseller in the Spanish dominions is bound to furnish, in the first two months of every year, an inventory of the books he exposes for sale. To this must be subscribed his oath that he has no others than those contained in the inventory.

He is forbidden to purchase or sell any book prohibited by the Inquisition, under penalty, for the first offence, of interdiction from all commerce in books for two years; banishment, during the same term, to twelve leagues distance from the place in which he was established; and a fine of two hundred ducats to the profit of the Inquisition. Repetitions of the offence are proportionally punished.

The book forming the substance of the crime may have been already sold, and in the hands of a third person; but the declaration of the purchaser suffices to subject the bookseller to all the penalties specified.

Every bookseller must have in his store a catalogue of the books censured by the Inquisition, under penalty of forty ducats. It is even necessary that the catalogue should be his own—for if it is borrowed, he is equally liable to the fine, as if he has none.

No bookseller may proceed to the inventory, estimate, purchase, or sale of private libraries, without furnishing to the commissary of the Inquisition a statement containing the names and surnames of the authors, the titles of the books, the subject matter, and the place and year of the impression, under penalty of fifty ducats.

Every person who enters the country with books, must make a declaration detailed and sworn to, which is sent to the tribunal of the Inquisition or its commissaries, who have the power to permit their introduction or to seize them. The omission, or imperfect execution of this declaration, occasions a confiscation of the books, and a cost of two hundred ducats for the expenses of the Holy Office.

When books, as most frequently happens, are deposited at the custom-house with other effects or merchandise, the officers of the customs cannot release the books but by express permission of the commissary of the Inquisition—which he does not grant till he has previously examined them.

Catalogues, which Spaniards may receive from abroad for the selection of books, must, before any use is made of them, be sent to the Holy Office, which may retain or restore them.

Whoever may have the temerity to elude the vigilance of the Inquisition is not, therefore, in peaceable possession of the proscribed books he has received. He remains exposed to those, domiciliary visits, which the commissioners of the Inquisition have a right to make at any hour either of day or night.

63. Appearances before the Holy Office in the Late Colony

William Bennett Stevenson's ship sailed up the coast of Chile in 1804, leaving Stevenson to spend the subsequent twenty years as secretary to various British officials. This allowed him to travel throughout Spanish America and become thoroughly familiar with its institutions, officials of both church and state, and its elite and folk cultures.

His three-volume account of South America was published in London in 1825 and contains two descriptions of the Holy Office, one of a clearly weakened tribunal that summoned him for an inquisition in 1806 [A], the other of the Office upon its abolition in 1812 [B], when he observed the wrath that the populace of Lima visited upon its vacated chambers.

Note the wit with which he describes what would have been a serious confrontation had it occurred a few years earlier than 1806. What is Stevenson slyly and humorously conveying about the tribunal, its personnel, and the colonial clergy (especially those represented by Bustamante)? Why does Stevenson's second account lack the wit of his first? What does the very last entry suggest about the credibility of Stevenson's account?

[A]   Having one day engaged in a dispute with Father Bustamante, a Dominican friar, respecting the image of the Madonna of the Rosary, he finished abruptly, by assuring me that I should hear of it again. [. . .]

After some hesitation, his lordship informed me that I must accompany him on the next morning to the holy tribunal of the Faith; I answered that I was ready at any moment; and I would have told him the whole affair, but, clapping his hands to his ears, he exclaimed "no! for the love of God, not a word; I am not an inquisitor; it does not become me to know the secrets of the holy house," adding the old adage, "*del Rey y la inquisición, chitón,*— of the King and the inquisition, hush. I can only hope and pray that you be as rancid a Christian as myself." [. . .]

[T]he tribunal: it was small, but lofty, a scanty light forcing its way through the grated windows near the roof.

I turned my eyes to the dire triumvirate, seated on an elevated part of the hall, under a canopy of green velvet edged with pale blue, a crucifix of a natural size hanging behind them; a large table was placed before them, covered and trimmed to match the canopy, and bearing two green burning tapers, an inkstand, some books, and papers.

Jovellanos described the inquisition by saying it was composed of *un Santo Cristo, dos candileros, y tres majaderos*—one crucifix, two candlesticks, and three blockheads. I knew the inquisitors—but how changed from what at other times I had seen them! The puny, swarthy Abarca, in the centre, scarcely half filling his chair of state—the fat monster Zalduegui on his left, his corpulent paunch being oppressed by the arms of his chair, and blowing through his nostrils like an over-fed porpoise—the fiscal, Sobrino, on his right, knitting his black eyebrows, and striving to produce in his unmeaning face semblance of wisdom. A secretary stood at each end of the table; one of them bad me to approach, which I did, by ascending three steps, which brought me on a level with the above described trinity of harpies. A small wooden stool was placed for me, and they nodded to me to sit down; I nodded in return, and complied.

The fiscal now asked me, in a solemn tone, if I knew why I had been summoned to attend at this holy tribunal? I answered that I did, and was going to proceed, when he hissed for me to be silent. [. . .]

I was asked if I knew the reverend father Bustamante? I replied, " I know *friar* Bustamante, I have

SOURCE: William Bennet Stevenson, *A Historical and Descriptive Narrative of Twenty Years' Residence in South America in Three Volumes* (London: Hurst, Robinson, 1825), 1:261-74.

often met him in coffee houses; but I suppose the reverend father you mean is some grave personage, who would not enter such places." "Had you any conversation with father Bustamante, touching matters of religion?" "No, but touching matters of superstition, I had." "Such things are not to be spoken of in coffee houses," said Zalduegui. "No," I rejoined, "I told father Bustamante the same thing." [. . .]

After questions and answers of this kind, for more than an hour, Abarca rang a small bell; the beadle entered, and I was ordered to retire. In a short time I was again called in, and directed to wait on Sobrino the following morning at eight o'clock, at his house: I did so, and breakfasted with him. He advised me in future to avoid all religious disputes, and particularly with persons I did not know, adding, "I requested an interview, because on the seat of judgment I could not speak in this manner. You must know," said he, "that you are here subject to the tribunal of the Faith, you, as well as all men who live in the dominions of his Catholic Majesty; you must, therefore, shape your course accordingly." [. . .]

[B]   The act of the Cortes of Spain which abolished the inquisition [1812], and which, during its discussion, produced many excellent though overheated speeches, was published in Lima just after the above occurrence. The Señora Doña Gregoria Gainsa, lady of Colonel Gainsa, informed me that she and some friends had obtained permission of the Viceroy Abascal to visit the ex-tribunal; and she invited me to accompany them on the following day, after dinner. I attended, and we went to visit the monster, as they now dared to call it. The doors of the hall being opened, many entered who were not invited, and seeing nothing in a posture of defense, the first victims to our fury were the table and chairs: these were soon demolished after which some persons laid hold of the velvet curtains of the canopy, and dragged them so forcibly, that canopy and crucifix came down with a horrid crash. The crucifix was rescued from the ruins of inquisitorial state, and its head discovered to be moveable. A ladder was found to have been secreted behind the canopy, and thus the whole mystery of this miraculous image became explainable and explained a man was concealed on the ladder, by the curtains of the canopy, and by introducing his hand through a hole, he moved the head, so as to make it nod consent, or shake dissent. In how many instances may appeal to this imposture have caused an innocent man to own himself guilty of crimes he never dreamt of! Overawed by fear, and condemned, as was believed, by a miracle, falsehood would supply the place of truth, and innocence, if timid, confess itself sinful. Every one was now exasperated with rage, and "there are yet victims in the cells," was universally murmured. "A search! a search!" was the cry, and the door leading to the interior was quickly broken through. The next we found was called *del secreto*; the word secret stimulated curiosity, and the door was instantly burst open. It led to the archives. Here were heaped, upon shelves, papers, containing the written cases of those who had been accused or tried; and here I read the name of many a friend, who little imagined that his conduct had been scrutinized by the holy tribunal, or that his name had been recorded in so awful a place. [. . .]

Leaving this room we forced our way into another, which to our astonishment and indignation was that of torture! In the centre stood a strong table, about eight feet long and seven feet broad; at one end of which was an iron collar, opening in the middle horizontally, for the reception of the neck of the victim; on each side of the collar were also thick straps with buckles, for enclosing the arms near to the body; and on the sides of the table were leather straps with buckles for the wrists, connected with cords under the table, made fast to the axle of an horizontal wheel; at the other end were two more straps for the ankles, with ropes similarly fixed to the wheel. Thus it was obvious, that a human being might be extended on the table and by turning the wheel, might be stretched in both directions at the same time, without any risk of hanging, for that effect was prevented by the two straps under his arms, close to the body; but almost every joint might be dislocated. [. . .]

Scourges of different materials were hanging on the wall; some of knotted cord, not a few of which were hardened with blood; others were of wire chain, with points and rowels, like those of spurs; these too were clotted with blood. We also found tormentors, made of netted wire, the points of every mesh projecting about one-eighth of an inch inward, the outside being covered with leather, and having strings to tie them on. Some of these tormentors were of a sufficient size for the waist [...]

In a drawer were a great many finger screws; they were small semicircular pieces of iron, in a the form of crescents, having a screw at one end, so that they could be fixed on the fingers and screwed to any degree, even till the nails were crushed and the bones broken. [...]

The rack and the pillory were soon demolished; for such was the fury of more than a hundred persons who had gained admittance, that had they been constructed of iron they could not have resisted the violence and determination of their assailants. [...]

We proceeded to the cells, but found them all open and empty: they were small, but not uncomfortable as places of confinement. Some had a small yard attached; others, more solitary, had none.

PART IX
Church and State in the New America

Internal and external factors contributed to the independence of the "Latin" American colonies at the beginning of the nineteenth century. Creoles resented the continued domination of Iberians in political, economic, and religious life. Some native sons had been instructed by the Jesuits in the ideas of the Enlightenment and became determined to apply the concepts of liberty and equality to their own colonial reality, though very few desired to alter the social fabric to benefit Amerindians and peoples of African descent. The Bourbon reforms of the eighteenth century convinced colonists that Spain's grip on its New World possessions had been strengthened rather than weakened. The expulsion of the Jesuits embittered still others, as did changes in the traditional relationship between church and state. Many were also well aware that English colonists to the north had freed themselves from their mother country and, more importantly, that the French had overthrown their own Bourbon monarch and broken the back of royal absolutism in that country.

Napoleon's invasion of the Iberian peninsula in 1808 and the subsequent imprisonment of Charles IV and his son Ferdinand VII (1808, 1814-1833) encouraged many Creoles and peoples of mixed racial heritage to use this propitious occurrence to end colonialism. The priests Miguel Hidalgo and José María Morelos coordinated military efforts, thus beginning Mexico's independence movement. Vicente Guerrero and Agustín de Iturbide achieved final independence for Mexico in 1821. José San Martín and Antonio José de Sucre liberated Argentina, Chile, and the royalist bastion of Peru by 1824. Simón Bolívar and his troops freed Venezuela, Colombia, Ecuador, and Bolivia by 1825. Events in Brazil were strikingly different. King João VI (1799-1826) and his entire court fled Portugal in 1808 and ruled the empire from Brazil during Napoleon's interlude. João returned to Portugal in 1821, but left his son, Pedro I, with instructions to place himself at the head of the Brazilians' inevitable independence movement, which took place in 1822. Brazil's separation from Portugal, therefore, occurred without significant bloodshed but placed that country under monarchical control until 1889. Spain controlled Cuba and Puerto Rico until 1898.

The independence movements were not anticlerical in nature. In fact, opposing sides in the conflict frequently marched behind symbols of the Virgin, such as that of Remedios for the royalists and Guadalupe for the insurgents. Clerical involvement varied according to both the region and one's position in the Catholic hierarchy. Members of the upper clergy—archbishops, bishops, and other dignitaries—tended to support the Crown, because most of them were Spaniards, were wealthy, and had received their appointments by virtue of royal patronage. Members of the lower clergy, especially parish priests, tended to be Creoles or members of the popular classes and were much more sympathetic to calls for self-rule, particularly if they lived in areas where the rebellion enjoyed widespread support. Nonetheless, there were some notable exceptions, such as Bishop José Cuero y Caicedo, who not only supported independence in Quito but also became president of its revolutionary junta. Those who favored independence constantly reiterated their devotion to Catholicism and the church. Despite measures taken against the church by the Bourbons at the end of colonial period, the hierarchy sided with Spain and equated rebellion with heresy. Pope Pius VII (1800-1823) and his successor Pope Leo XII (1823-1829) encouraged clerics to support the Spanish cause and maintain fidelity to Ferdinand VII. Bishops and archbishops threatened clergy and parishioners alike with excommunication if they participated in the independence movement. As Richard E. Greenleaf suggests, church officials believed that "heretics were traitors and traitors were heretics [which] led to the conviction that dissenters of any kind were social revolutionaries trying to subvert the political and religious stability of the community."[1]

Just as the independence movements were not anticlerical in nature, the newly established republics did not attempt to destroy the church's preeminence in society during the first decades of independence. Some priests, such as Francisco Javier de Luna Pizarro in Peru, participated in the constitutional conventions of their countries. Moreover, open hostility to the church would have been impractical given that ecclesiastics and not civil officials administered hospitals and other charitable institutions and assumed the burden of education. These Catholic-subjects-turned-Catholic-citizens, therefore, could not have imagined a diminished church presence or the granting of equal status to other religions. Accordingly, most constitutions recognized Catholicism as the official and only religion. The Mexican constitution of 1824, for example, began with the preamble "In the name of God Almighty, author and supreme legislator of society . . ." and an additional article asserted, "The religion of the Mexican nation is and will always be Roman Apostolic Catholic. The nation protects it with its wise and just laws and prohibits the exercise of any

---

1. Richard E. Greenleaf, "The Mexican Inquisition and the Enlightenment," in *The Roman Catholic Church in Colonial Latin America*, ed. Richard E. Greenleaf (New York: Alfred A. Knopf, 1971), 164-65; Jeffrey Klaiber, "Catholic Church: The Modern Period," in *Encyclopedia of Latin American History and Culture*, vol. 2, ed. Barbara A. Tenenbaum (New York: Charles Scribner's Sons, 1996), 33; Margaret E. Crahan, "Catholic Church (Colonial Period)," in *Encyclopedia of Latin America*, ed. Helen Delpar (New York: McGraw-Hill, 1974), 122.

other."[2] Some liberal reformers, such as Mexico's Valentín Gómez Farías, tried to disestablish the church as early as the 1830s during his interim presidency, but they generally failed because of weak state institutions and the fact that most people did not support this radically liberal initiative. Not until mid-century and later did the concept of "freedom of worship" begin to take hold in many Latin American countries.

Relations between church and state soured when the newly independent republics tried to exercise the ancient prerogative of royal patronage. Government officials sought to control clerical appointments just as the Crown had done previously. Pope Leo XII held that the *patronato real* was not transferable. The church neither wished to offend Ferdinand VII nor cede parts of its own power. Its refusal to recognize the independence of Spain's former colonies until after Ferdinand's death in 1833 further complicated matters. But the papacy also recognized the need to fill church positions, albeit surreptitiously: as early as 1827 Pope Leo approved candidates for episcopal positions in Colombia and filled sees in Mexico in 1831. Liberals in Spanish America viewed the pope as the spiritual leader of the faithful but resented what they perceived as papal claims to final authority. Conservatives, on the other hand, who had typically been royalists during the wars for independence, recognized the papacy as an ally to maintain the status quo. Papal concessions in the newly independent but still monarchical country of Brazil demonstrated the church's comfortable working relationship with kings as opposed to popularly elected officials: Pedro I and Pedro II (1831-1889) enjoyed the ecclesiastical rights inherent in royal privilege until the monarchy fell in 1889. Brazil's new republican government lost that right.

Parishioners in nineteenth-century Spanish America felt the brunt of all these squabbles. Vocations of native sons declined. Most areas witnessed a growing and acute shortage of priests. As a result, states Jeffrey Klaiber, in areas such as Peru, Bolivia, and Nicaragua about 60 percent of all clergy were foreign born by the middle of the nineteenth century.[3]

Tensions between liberals and the church came to a head by the 1850s. The church remained the most powerful landowner, financier, and educator. Cash-strapped liberals in the chronically bankrupt republics coveted the church's wealth and resented its influence over the popular classes. Many liberals believed that Protestant missionary work could be used as a wedge to weaken the church and its conservative allies. Guatemala's president, Justo Rufino Barrios (1873-1885), hoped that Presbyterians would promote a work ethic and, thus, stimulate the economy. Other countries, such as Argentina, Uruguay, and Brazil,

---

2. Felipe Tena Ramírez, *Leyes fundamentals de México, 1808-1957* (Mexico City: Editorial Porrúa, 1957), 167-68; Nancy M. Farriss, *Crown and Clergy in Colonial Mexico, 1759-1821: The Crisis of Ecclesiastical Privilege* (London: Athlone Press, 1968), 2; Klaiber, "Catholic Church: The Modern Period," 33.

3. Kenneth Scott Latourette, *The Great Century in the Americas, Austral-Asia, and Africa, AD 1800-AD 1914*, vol. 5: *A History of the Expansion of Christianity* (New York: Harper & Brothers, 1943), 73; Jeffrey Klaiber, S.J., *The Catholic Church in Peru, 1821-1985: A Social History* (Washington, D.C.: Catholic University of America Press, 1992), 19; John J. Kennedy, "Catholic Church (National Period)," in *Encyclopedia of Latin America*, ed. Helen Delpar (New York: McGraw-Hill, 1974), 122; Víctor Gabriel Muro, "Catholic Church: Mexico," in *Encyclopedia of Mexico: History, Society & Culture*, vol. 1, ed. Michael S. Werner (Chicago and London: Fitzroy Dearborn Publishers, 1997), 219; Klaiber, "Catholic Church: The Modern Period," 33-34.

actively encouraged European immigration in an attempt to "whiten" and "civilize" their populaces. While most arrivals were Catholic, they viewed Protestantism as a component of modern and progressive societies. Liberals in Mexico, El Salvador, Venezuela, Chile, and Ecuador, for example, envisioned a progressive and more egalitarian society unfettered by privilege and, they would have said, by backward institutions like the church. Generally speaking, therefore, liberals sought to increase the power of the state, permit freedom of worship, create civil registries, expropriate ecclesiastical lands and buildings, and diminish the constant celebrations of saints' days, festivals, and religious holidays. While some liberals such as Argentina's José Manuel Estrada (1842-1894) viewed the church as a necessary moral force and partner for a new progressive society, others such as Chile's Francisco Bilbao (1823-1865) viewed Catholicism as the main culprit for societal ills. Benito Juárez (1806-1872) and Melchor Ocampo (1814-1861) led their generation of Mexican liberals to enact reforms that ultimately sparked a civil war (1858-61) over the role of religion. The liberal agenda went so far as to dissolve monastic orders, to deny clergy citizen's rights, and to forbid government officials from attending religious services.[4]

64. Excommunication by a Former Friend

The following extraordinary document, coming from the last days of the colonial era, captures to perfection the bond between church and state and their complete agreement concerning the permanent and hierarchical nature of the sacred and secular institutions that had arisen in Europe in the fifteenth century and were just beginning to be eroded under the influences of the sixteenth-century Dutch, seventeenth-century English, and eighteenth-century American and French revolutions.

Manuel Abad y Queipo (1751-1825), nominated to be bishop of Michoacán in 1810, was, ironically, one of the finest representatives of the European Enlightenment in Spanish America. He proposed progressive reforms to raise the Amerindians out of poverty, eliminate onerous taxation, and end their general marginalization. At the same time, of course, he was a highly committed churchman, advocating the church as the only institution the Amerindians could trust. He was a close friend of the equally enlightened former university professor turned parish priest, Miguel Hidalgo, who was profoundly committed to social reforms that would benefit his poor parishioners and to political reforms that would benefit middle-class Creoles such as himself.

---

4. Pamela Voekel, *Alone before God: The Religious Origins of Modernity in Mexico* (Durham, N.C.: Duke University Press, 2002), 222; Timothy J. Henderson, "Church and State: 1821-1910," in *Encyclopedia of Mexico: History, Society & Culture*, vol. 1, ed. Michael S. Werner (Chicago and London: Fitzroy Dearborn Publishers, 1997), 253-55; Kennedy, "Catholic Church (National Period)," 123; Muro, "Catholic Church: Mexico," 220; Virginia Garrard-Burnett, "Protestantism," in *Encyclopedia of Latin American History and Culture*, vol. 4, ed. Barbara A. Tenenbaum (New York: Charles Scribner's Sons, 1996), 476.

SOURCE: "Decreto de excomunión dado por el Obispo Abad y Queipo [1810]" in José María Luis Mora, *México y sus revoluciones*, vol. 3 (Mexico City: Porrúa, 1950), 57-62 (n.2). Translated from the Spanish by Lee M. Penyak.

Hidalgo, forced by a traitor who divulged the plans of the Creole conspirators into commencing a rebellion before there was time to forge a real coalition between social groups, found himself at the head of a huge number of the underclass. Angry, violent, and destructive, these rebels brought down upon them the fear and wrath of their "betters." His excommunication by his former friend, Abad y Queipo, is a perfect expression of the attitudes of the elites and that of the whole Spanish colonial authority.

Abad's description of the revolution in France is not exceptional, being maintained by such notable historians as the late François Furet (1927-1997). But note carefully his description of the revolution in Santo Domingo. Where could Abad's description be subject to criticism? What would be a fair criticism of Abad's account of the cause of the September 16 insurrection? What, even as a member of the responsible elite, does he not take into account? What would be a reasonable alternative to Abad's understandably hostile reaction to the inscription Hidalgo placed upon the banner of Our Lady of Guadalupe?

Abad further suggests that the Crown appointed him bishop by the people's request ("your request"). He is, therefore, able to claim that he is acting to protect his flock and "your true happiness," and to emphasize his thirty-one-year residence in New Spain as proof of his commitment and devotion to its people. Again, this is a reasonable position, but could it not also be criticized for what it fails to take into account?

The third-to-last paragraph ("On this account") of the edict clearly demonstrates how religious authority becomes political: every political order necessarily possesses means to defend and perpetuate itself, and Abad uses those means. How would these goals be accomplished in the modern nation-state?

"Europeans neither have nor could have other interests than the same that you the natives of this country have. . . ." What is compelling about Abad's declarations in this penultimate passage and what must be subject to criticism?

Don Manuel Abad y Queipo, penitenciary canon of this Holy Church, bishop elect and governor of this bishopric of Michoacán: peace and good health to all of its inhabitants, in our Lord Jesus Christ.

Omne regnum in se divisum desolabitur. Every kingdom divided against itself will be divided and destroyed, says Jesus Christ, our example. Chapter XI of Saint Luke, verse XVII. Yes, my beloved faithful, the history of all centuries, of all peoples and nations, that which has passed before our eyes during the French Revolution, that which presently occurs on the Peninsula, in our beloved and unfortunate homeland, confirms the infallible truth of this divine oracle. But the most analogous example to our situation we have nearby on the French part of the island of Santo Domingo [Haiti], whose owners were the richest, most accommodated and happy men known on earth. Its population was comprised almost like that of ours, of French Europeans and French Creoles, of native Indians of that country, of blacks and mulattoes, and of castes resultant of the first classes. Division and anarchy entered as a result of the aforementioned French Revolution, and everything fell into ruin and was completely destroyed. Anarchy in France caused the death of two million French, that is, close to two-twentieths, the cream of both sexes that existed; it ruined its commerce and marine, and set back its industry and agriculture. But the anarchy in Santo Domingo butchered all of the white and Creole French, without leaving even one behind, and butchered four-fifths of all of the remaining inhabitants, leaving the fifth part comprised of blacks and mulattoes in eternal hatred and deadly warfare, in which they will completely destroy themselves. It devastated the entire country, burning and destroying all possessions, all the cities, villas and localities, so that the best populated and cultivated country in all of the Americas is today a desert, a den of tigers and lions. Here, then, is the horrendous but faithful picture of the anarchistic destruction in Santo Domingo.

New Spain, which had admired Europe through its most brilliant demonstrations of loyalty and patriotism to the mother country, helping and sustaining her with its treasures, with its views and its writings, maintaining peace and harmony despite the maliciousness and schemes of the world's tyrant [Napoleon], finds itself today threatened with discord and anarchy, and with all of the subsequent misfortunes that follow, and which the aforementioned island of Santo Domingo has suffered. A minister of the God of Peace, a priest of Jesus Christ, a shepherd of souls (I wished not to mention that), the priest of Dolores, don Miguel Hidalgo (who had deserved until now my confidence and my friendship), in partnership with the captains of the Crown's regiment, don Ignacio Allende, don Juan de Aldama, and don José Mariano Abasolo, raised the banner of rebellion and ignited the torch of discord and anarchy, and seducing a sector of innocent laborers, had them take up arms; and descending with them on the town of Dolores on the 16th of the current [month of September] at dawn, he surprised and arrested its European residents, looted and robbed their possessions; and going later at seven o'clock at night to the town of San Miguel el Grande, he carried out the same, taking possession of each and every part of governmental authority. On Friday the 21st he occupied Celaya in the same way; and according to our information, it [the rebellion] appears to have already extended to Salamanca and Irapuato. He takes the Europeans under arrest with him, among them the sacristan of Dolores, the priest of Chamacuero, and various religious Carmelites from Celeya, threatening the townsfolk with decapitation if they put up any resistance. And, insulting religion and our sovereign, don Fernando VII, he painted on his banner the image of our illustrious patron, our Lady of Guadalupe, on which he made the following inscription: *Long Live Religion, Long Live Our Holy Mother of Guadalupe. Long Live Fernando VII. Long Live America and Death to Bad Government.*

Since religion condemns rebellion, assassination and the oppression of the innocent, and the mother of God cannot protect these crimes, it is clear that the priest of Dolores, painting on his seditious banner the image of Our Lady, and placing on it the aforementioned inscription, committed two grave sacrileges, insulting religion and Our Lady. He likewise insults our sovereign, scorning and attacking the government he represents, oppressing his vassals, disturbing public order, and violating the oath of fidelity to the monarch and to the government, being equally guilty the aforementioned captains. Nonetheless, confusing religion with crime and obedience with rebellion, he has been able to seduce innocent people, and he has given substantial weight to the anarchy he wants to establish. Evil will rapidly progress if the vigilance and energy of the government and the enlightened loyalty of the people do not stop him.

I, by your request, and without ambition on my part, find myself elevated to the high post as your bishop, as your shepherd and priest; I must go to confront this enemy, in defense of the flock that is entrusted to me, using reason and truth to counter deceit and the terrible recourse of excommunication against obstinacy and wickedness.

Yes, my dear and beloved faithful, I have indisputable rights to your respect, to your submission and obedience in this matter. I am of European origin, but I am an American by voluntary adoption, and by residence for more than thirty-one years. There is not one among us who takes more interest in your true happiness. Perhaps there will not be another who is so painfully and profoundly affected as I am in your misfortunes, because there might not have been another who has been so occupied and occupies himself so much with them. No one has worked as I have to promote the public good to maintain peace and harmony among all of the inhabitants of America, and in preventing the anarchy that I have so feared since my return from Europe. My character and zeal are well known. Therefore, you must believe me.

On this account, and using the authority vested in me as bishop elect and governor of this miter, I declare that the said don Miguel Hidalgo, priest of Dolores and his three accomplices, the aforementioned captains, are disturbers of the public order, seducers of the people, sacrilegious, perjurers, and that they have incurred in grave excommunication of canon law: *Siquis suadente Diabolo* [if persuaded by the devil], for having assaulted the person and liberty of the sacristan of Dolores, of the priest of Chamacuero, and of several religious from the convent of Carmen in Celaya, taking them prisoner and keeping them under arrest. I declare them excommunicated pariah, prohibiting as I do prohibit, that anyone give them aid, assistance and favor, under the penalty of grave excommunication, *ipso facto incurrenda* [by the very nature of the deed incurred], this edict serving as an admonition, in which from now and forever I declare the infringers guilty. At the same time I exhort and order the sector of the population that he has seduced with titles of soldier and comrade-in-arms to return to their homes and desert him within the following three days of receiving notice of this edict under the same penalty of grave excommunication, from that time forward and forever, I declare guilty anyone who voluntarily enlists under his banner or who in any way gives him aid and assistance.

Item [Similarly]. I declare that the said priest Hidalgo and his accomplices are seducers of the people and slanderers of Europeans. Yes, my beloved faithful, it is a notorious slander. Europeans neither have nor could have other interests than the same that you natives of this country have, that is, to aid the mother country as much as possible, defend these dominions from every foreign invasion in favor of the sovereign to whom we have pledged [Ferdinand VII], or any other of his dynasty, under the government that he represents, in accordance and form that the nation resolves as resolved in the assemblies that, as is known, are being held in Cádiz or the island of León, with the interim representatives of the Americas, until the owners return. This is the aegis under which we must resort. This is the unifying bond of all the inhabitants of this realm, placed in the hands of our worthy head, the current excellent Señor Viceroy who, instilled with military and political knowledge, with energy and proper authority, will make the most convenient use of our resources for the preservation of the tranquility of public order and for the external defense of the entire realm. With all classes of the State unified with good intentions, in peace and harmony, and under such a leader—great are the resources of a nation like New Spain in which we can achieve everything. But, separated, unchecked by laws, the public order disturbed, anarchy introduced, as the priest of Dolores desires, this beautiful country will be destroyed. Theft, pillage, fire, assassination, vengeance will set ablaze haciendas, cities, villas, localities and exterminate its inhabitants, and [New Spain] will be left a desert ripe for the first invader who presents himself on our shores. Yes, my dear and beloved faithful, such are the inevitable and necessary effects of anarchy. Loathe it with all your heart: arm yourselves with the Catholic faith against diabolical seditions that disturb you: strengthen your heart with evangelical charity, which bears and conquers all. Our Lord Jesus Christ, who redeemed us with his blood, take pity on us, and protect us in such times of tribulation, we humbly beseech.

And so everyone takes notice and no one feigns ignorance, I have ordered that this edict be published in this Holy Cathedral and be posted on its doors as is customary, and that the same be done in all the parishes of the bishopric, implementing this order with the corresponding copies. Given in Valladolid on the 24th day of September of 1810. Sealed with the stamp of my coat of arms and countersigned by the secretary.

Manuel Abad y Queipo, bishop elect of Michoacán. . . .

65. The Liberator and Religion

Simón Bolívar (1783-1830), the scion of a wealthy slaveowning family of Caracas, as a young man spent several months in Europe where he came to know and admire the works of the philosophes, *the great propagandists of the European Enlightenment. After 1810 he became a major participant in the political and military struggle for the independence of Spanish America. His greatest military achievement came in 1819 with the impossible trek of his poorly equipped army across the formidable Andes mountains. He achieved the goal of taking the Spanish by surprise, defeating them at the critical battle of Boyacá. In the last ten years of his short life, Bolívar devoted his energies to finding a form of government that would foster the progress of a society that he believed was almost entirely unfit for self-government, owing to its colonial heritage and numerous underclass citizens.*

The following excerpts are taken (1) from a private letter (1823); (2) an address to legislators (1823); and (3) a letter to a general (1826) who is a provincial governor.

What does Bolívar fear, and what role does religion play for him? Does it allay his fears, increase them, or work both ways?

Bolívar was baptized a Roman Catholic and was brought up in colonial Spanish America where the Catholic Church was a powerful institution closely allied with the colonial government. Explain how he completely rejected the entire colonial conception of Catholicism, of the church, and of the relation between church and state despite being a believer who unhesitatingly acknowledged a place for "spiritual pastors" in society.

Does the instruction that Bolívar gave to Bishop Torres contradict the social role of the church suggested by the prelate Abad y Queipo in the previous reading? In this letter Bolívar was not concerned with establishing political distinctions about the role of religion in society but with the relationship between the actual Catholic clergy of 1826 and "the civil establishment." Do the same fears Bolívar expressed in the letter (1823) reappear in this passage? What do the last three sentences ("Let us not quarrel") reveal about Bolívar's experience with and understanding of the Catholic clergy?

[1] Religion has lost much of its power, which, perhaps, it will not regain for a long time, since customs now differ from the sacred doctrines; hence, unless society establishes a new system of penalties and chastisements, of sins and transgressions, to improve our moral behavior, we shall doubtless move headlong toward universal dissolution. All the world knows that religion and philosophy restrain men; the former by punishment, the latter by patience and persuasion. Religion has her thousand indulgences for the wicked, and philosophy offers many diverse systems, each favoring some particular vice. The one has binding laws and fixed tribunals; the other has only exponents with no codes or enforcement agencies empowered by political institutions. From this I conclude that we must seek a mean between these two extremes and create an institution authorized both by fundamental laws and by the overwhelming force of public opinion.

On another occasion I shall have more to tell you about this. At present, I have no time for more, and what I have said is of little value. Meanwhile, I am sending you a letter from De Pradt to

SOURCE: Vicente Lecuna, ed., *Selected Writings of Bolívar*, trans. Lewis Bertrand (New York: Colonial Press, 1951), 381-82, 604-5, 616-17.

me, together with my reply, which must not be printed on any account. Be so kind as to present my compliments to the Arboleda and the Mosquera families. I am your most devoted. Bolívar [...]

[2] Legislators, I shall mention one item which my conscience has compelled me to omit. A political constitution should not prescribe any particular religion, for, according to the best doctrines, fundamental laws guarantee political and civil rights, and, since religion has no bearing upon these rights, it is by nature indefinable in the social organization, because it lies in the moral and intellectual sphere. Religion governs man in his home, within his own walls, within himself. Religion alone is entitled to examine a man's innermost conscience. Laws, on the contrary, deal with surface things; they are applicable outside the home of a citizen. If we apply these criteria, how can a state rule the conscience of its subjects, enforce the observance of religious laws, and mete out rewards and punishments, when the tribunals are in Heaven and God is the judge? Only the Inquisition could presume to do their work on earth. Would you bring back the Inquisition with its burnings at the stake?

Religion is the law of conscience. Any law that imposes it negates it, because to apply compulsion to conscience is to destroy the value of faith, which is the very essence of religion. The sacred precepts and doctrines are useful, enlightening, and spiritually nourishing. We should all avow them, but the obligation is moral rather than political.

On the other hand, what are the religious rights of man on earth? These rights reside in Heaven where there is a tribunal that rewards merit and dispenses justice according to the code laid down by the great Lawgiver. As all this is within divine jurisdiction, it would seem to me, at first sight, to be sacrilegious and profane for us to interfere with the Commandments of the Lord by enactments of our own. Prescribing religion is therefore not the task of the legislator, who, for any infractions, must provide penalties, not mere exhortations. Where there are no temporal punishments or judges to apply them, the law ceases to be law.

The moral development of man is the legislator's first concern. Once such a growth has been attained, man bases his morality upon the truths so revealed and acknowledges religion *de facto* and all the more effectively for having come to it by personal experience. Moreover, heads of families cannot neglect their religious obligations to their children. The spiritual pastors are obliged to teach the Gospel of Heaven. The example of all the true disciples of Christ is the most eloquent teacher of his divine doctrine. But doctrine cannot be commanded, nor is one who commands a teacher, for force can play no part in the giving of spiritual counsel. God and his ministers are the authorities on religion, and religion exerts its influence solely through spiritual means and bodies, never through instruments of the nation's body politic, which serves only to direct public energies toward purely temporal ends. [...]

[3] Dr. Torres is about to undertake the administration of the diocese in your department, having been appointed by Orihuela to take charge during his absence. Dr. Torres is a churchman especially noted for his high principles and abilities, for he has a broad knowledge of the fine arts and sciences. He is a particular friend of mine, and he earnestly desires to contribute to the welfare of Peru by strengthening her regime and improving her institutions. Imbued with these sentiments, he is bound to be of great help to you in your department. He has my express instructions to cooperate with you in all that has to do with religion and to bring the civil authority into complete harmony with the ecclesiastic, by inducing the curates and other clerics and agents of the church to lend their positive support to the civil establishment, and by establishing a complete understanding between them and yourself, placating also those who may have had their differences with you. Since Dr. Torres is as discreet as he is affable, he is eminently fitted to accomplish these objectives, which I greatly desire to see realized, for, in Peru's present condition, only the closest cooperation among all public officials can create a solid front capable of withstanding the large number who seek to create disorder and anarchy for motives of personal ambition. I recommend that you listen to Dr. Torres' suggestions, for he is thoroughly versed in my ideas as to how to preserve the work which has entailed so many sacrifices. Let us not quarrel with

the churchmen, as they can always call religion to their aid and induce others to make common cause with them. Misunderstandings with them are always futile; friendly relations with them are always beneficial. They do their persuading in secret and manage men's consciences; whoever possesses these weapons is certain of victory.

66. Church and State in the Sovereign Republics of Spanish America

The new republics of nineteenth-century Spanish America had to come to grips with the institution of the Roman Catholic Church, which, over the three hundred years of the colony, had grown rich, powerful, and arrogant. In most cases, the church was better organized and wealthier than the republics in which it existed. The following readings consist of legal declarations about church and state that represent the different solutions to the problems of the rights and powers of the Catholic Church in republican Spanish America.

They range from the strongly nationalist approach of Colombia in 1824 (1), through the moderate approaches of Venezuela in 1841 (2) and Chile in 1925 (3), and from the highly clericalist approach of Ecuador in 1862 (4) to the fiercely anticlerical approach of Mexico in the 1910s and '20s (5 and 6).

How does the congress of the sovereign republic of Colombia deal with the traditional right of the patronato real *(royal patronage) by which the Spanish Crown had appointed all the archbishops and bishops of the colony? What was the position of the church in the new republic under this legislation?*

Why may the oath required of all Venezuelan bishops appointed by the pope after 1841 be considered a "moderate" solution to the state-church problem, that problem in this case being which institution, church or state, was superior and answerable only to God?

Similarly, article 10 of the Chilean constitution of 1925 may be considered a "moderate" solution to problems growing out of the traditional prerogatives of the Church in Spanish America. Why? What prerogatives of the church are recognized, denied, or modified?

A few clauses from the concordat of 1862 between the Vatican and the sovereign state of Ecuador demonstrate the ideal solution, from the Vatican's point of view, to the issue of church-state relations. Why? Why would this solution ultimately evoke strong opposition?

The revolution that commenced in Mexico in 1910 was by no means focused or characterized by coalitions with coherent programs for change, despite the Plan of San Luis drawn up by Madero and the Plan of Ayala drawn up by Zapata. But there was one constant cry, which cut through all the incoherence and fratricidal factions: denunciation of the power, prerogatives, and possessions of the Catholic Church. The 1914 Carranza and Villa accord and the Villa telegraph are clear examples of this hostility. How do the principles listed in the 1925 circular of the "National Catholic" Church of Mexico illustrate the depth of the revolutionaries' disdain for the historic "Roman Catholic" Church in Mexico? How do the

SOURCE: Lloyd J. Mecham, *Church and State in Latin America: A History of Politico-Ecclesiastical Relations* (Chapel Hill: University of North Carolina Press, 1934; reprint 1966), 112-13, 125, 176-79, 181, 269, 271, 463-64, 470-71, 477-78, 496. From *Church and State in Latin America: A History of Politico-Ecclesiastical Relations* by J. Lloyd Mecham. Copyright © 1966 by the University of North Carolina Press. Used by permission of the publisher.

provisions of articles 24 and 27 of the 1917 Mexican Constitution (an aggressively updated version of La Reforma *of the nineteenth century) respond to the historic position that the Catholic Church held in New Spain? What kind of church would emerge from the implementation of these constitutional provisions?*

Under President Plutarco Elías Calles (1924-1928) the anticlerical provisions of Mexico's 1917 Constitution and the legislation to implement them were systematically and ruthlessly enforced. President Emilio Portes Gil (1928-1930), without admitting to any mistakes on the part of the state or to any excessiveness in the anticlerical laws, made a verbal gentleman's agreement with protesting Mexican prelates, of which this is the only record. What is the thrust of this statement regarding the laws that deal with religion? Could it be subject to different interpretations by the Catholics and the anticlericals?

[Colombia, 1824]

The Senate and Chamber of Representatives of the Republic of Colombia in Congress assembled:

Decree:

Article 1. The Republic of Colombia ought to continue in the exercise of the right of patronage, which the kings of Spain had over the metropolitan churches, cathedrals, and parishes in this part of America.

Article 2. This right is a duty of the Republic of Colombia and of its government, and it demands that the Apostolic See do not change or alter it; and the Executive Power under this principle will celebrate with His Holiness a concordat which will assure for all time, and irrevocably, this prerogative of the Republic and avoid conflicts and claims for the future.

Article 3. The right of patronage and protection are exercised, first, by the Congress; second, by the Executive Power with the Senate; third, by the Executive Power alone; fourth, by the intendants; and fifth, by the governors.

The High Court of the Republic, and the Superior Courts will hear cases that arise out of this matter. [...]

Article 4. The Congress is empowered to:

1. Erect new dioceses or reorganize old ones, to designate their territorial limits, and assign funds to be employed in the building and repairing of metropolitan and episcopal churches.
2. Permit, or even summon, national or provincial councils or synods.
3. Permit or refuse the founding of new monasteries and hospitals, and to suppress those existing if deemed advisable, and to assume control of their property.
4. Draw up tariffs of parochial fees.
5. Regulate the administration of the tithes.
6. Grant or refuse the exequatur to bulls and briefs.
7. Enact legislation deemed necessary for the vigorous maintenance of exterior discipline of the Church, and for the conservation and exercise of the ecclesiastical patronage.
8. Nominate those to be presented to His Holiness for the archiepiscopal and episcopal sees.
9. Enact legislation for the establishment, rule, and support of the missions for the Indians.

Article 6. The Executive is empowered to:

1. Present to the pope for his approval the actions of Congress on the erection of new dioceses and the alteration of old ones.
2. Present to the pope the nominees of Congress for the archiepiscopal and episcopal positions. [...]

[Venezuela, 1841]

oath: "I,_____, Archbishop or Bishop of _____, swear that never will I consider the oath of obedience to the constitution, the laws, and the government of the republic, which I swore to prior to my presentation to His Holiness, directly or indirectly annulled nor in any part diminished by the oath of obedience to the Apostolic See which I must take at the time of my consecration; nor by any later act under any motive. So help me God." [...]

[Ecuador, 1862]

Concordat between Pius IX and the Republic of Ecuador.

September 26, 1862

In the name of the most holy and indivisible Trinity, His Holiness the Supreme Pontiff Pius IX and the President of the Republic of Ecuador name as their respective plenipotentiaries. His Holiness, his eminence the Sig. Jacobo Antonelli, Cardinal of the Holy Roman Church, Deacon of Santa Ágata de Suburra and Secretary of State and Foreign Relations.

And His Excellency the President of the Republic, the most excellent Señor Don Ignacio Ordoñez, Archdeacon of the Cathedral Church of Cuenca in the same republic and Minister Plenipotentiary near the Holy See.

Who, after having exchanged their respective plenary powers, agree on the following articles:

Article 1. The Roman Catholic Apostolic religion will continue to be the only religion of the Republic of Ecuador, and it [the State] will always protect all the rights and prerogatives, which it ought to enjoy according to the laws of God and canonical dispositions. Consequently there will never be permitted in Ecuador a dissident cult or any society condemned by the Church.

Article 2. In each one of the present dioceses, and in those which will be erected later, there will be a diocesan seminary whose direction, régime, and administration belong freely and exclusively to the diocesan ordinaries according to the dispositions of the Council of Trent and of the canonical laws. Rectors, professors, and others employed in the instruction and direction of said establishments will be freely nominated and removed by the ordinaries.

Article 3. The instruction of the youth in the Universities, colleges, faculties, and public and private schools will in all things conform to the doctrine of the Catholic religion. The bishops will have the exclusive right to designate texts for instruction in ecclesiastical sciences as well as in moral and religious instruction. In addition the bishops and the ordinaries will exercise freely the right to prohibit books contrary to religion and good customs, and to see that the government adopts proper measures to prevent the importation or dissemination of said books in the Republic.

Article 4. The bishops, in accordance with the duties of their pastoral ministry, will take care that there shall be no instruction contrary to the Catholic religion and proper customs. With this aim no one can instruct in any public or private institution in the subjects of theology, catechism, or religious doctrine without having obtained the authorization of the diocesan prelate, who can revoke the permit if he deems it opportune. For the examinations (of teachers) in the primary institutions the diocesan will always name an assistant to examine in religious and moral instruction. He cannot assume the discharge of this duty without the consent of the said diocesan.

Article 5. Since by divine right the primacy of honor and jurisdiction in the Universal Church belongs to the Roman Pontiff, all bishops, as well as clergy and the faithful will have free communication with the Holy See. Consequently no secular authority can place obstacles in the way of the full and free exercise of this right of communication by obliging the bishops, clergy and people to submit to the government as an intermediary in their communications with the Roman See, or by subjecting bulls, briefs, and rescripts to the exequatur of the government.

Article 6. The ecclesiastical ordinaries of the Republic can govern their dioceses with full liberty, convoke and celebrate provincial and diocesan councils, and exercise the rights which belong to them by virtue of their sacred ministry and current canonical provisions approved by the Holy See, without being interfered with in the performance of their duties. Thus the government of Ecuador will dispense with its patronal power, and will assist the bishops when solicited, particularly when they are confronted with the evil works of those people who seek to pervert the spirit of the faithful and corrupt their customs. [...]

Article 8. All ecclesiastical causes and especially those relating to faith, the sacraments (which includes matrimonial causes), customs, holy functions, sacred rights and duties whether by reason of persons or subject, excepting the major causes reserved for the Holy Pontiff . . . will be heard in the ecclesiastical tribunals. The same will be tried as civil causes of ecclesiastics, and other matters included in the penal code of the Republic will be tried as crimes. To all ecclesiastical judgments the civil authorities will lend aid and protection, so that the judges can enforce the execution of penalties and sentences pronounced by them.

Article 9. The Holy See consents that persons as well as ecclesiastical properties shall be subject to the public imposts on a par with persons and properties of other citizens. The civil authority should enter into an agreement with the ecclesiastical to obtain the corresponding authorization whenever co-action is necessary. Excepted from said imposts are seminaries, properties and things immediately destined for the cult, and charitable institutions.

Article 10. Out of respect for the majesty of God who is the King of Kings and Lord of Lords, the immunity of churches will be respected in so far as public security and the exigencies of justice permit. In such event the Holy See consents that the ecclesiastical authority, the parish priests, and prelates of the regular houses, permit the extraction of refugees on the request of the civil authorities.

Article 11. Since the income from the tithes is devoted to the support of the divine cult and its ministers, the government of Ecuador is obliged to maintain Catholic instruction in the Republic, and His Holiness consents that the government continue to receive a third part of the tithes. For the collection and administration of the tithes the two authorities, civil and ecclesiastical, will enter into an agreement.

Article 12. By virtue of the right of patronage which the Supreme Pontiff concedes to the President of Ecuador, the latter can propose for archbishops and bishops clerics, qualified in the sense of the sacred canons. [. . .]

Article 20. In addition to the orders and religious congregations which now exist in the Republic of Ecuador, the diocesan ordinaries can freely and without exception admit and establish in their respective dioceses new orders or institutes approved by the Church in conformity with the necessities of the people. To facilitate this the government will lend its aid.

Article 21. After the divine offices in all the churches of the Republic of Ecuador, the following prayer will be said: *Domine salvam fac Rempublicam; Domine salvam fac Praesidium ejus.*

Article 22. The government of the Republic of Ecuador is obligated to employ all proper measures for the propagation of the faith and for the conversion of people found in that territory; and in addition, to lend all favor and aid to the establishment and progress of the holy missions, which with laudable purpose, have been undertaken under the authority of the Sacred Congregation of Propaganda. [. . .]

[Chile, 1925]

Article 10. The Constitution insures to all the inhabitants of the Republic:

Practice of all beliefs, liberty of conscience and the free exercise of all religions that may not be contrary to morality, good usage and public order. Therefore, the respective religious bodies have the right to erect and maintain houses of worship and accessory property under the conditions of security and hygiene as fixed by the laws and regulations.

The churches, creeds, and religious institutions of any ritual shall have those rights in respect to their property as the law now in force may stipulate or recognize; but they will be subject, under the guarantees of this constitution, to common law in the exercise of ownership of their future acquired property.

Churches and accessory property intended for the service of any religious sect are exempt from taxation. [. . .]

[Mexico, Carranza and Villa Accord, 1914]

The present conflict being a struggle of the impecunious against the abuses of the powerful, and understanding that the causes of the evils that bear down the country spring from pretorianism, plutocracy, and clericalism, the Divisions of the North and of the Northeast, solemnly pledge themselves to fight until complete banishment of the ex-Federal army, which shall be superseded by the Constitutional Army, to set up democratic institutions in our country, to bring welfare to labor, financial emancipation to the peasant by an equitable apportionment of land, and other means tending to solve the agrarian question, to correct, chastise, and hold to their responsibilities such members of the Roman Catholic clergy as may have lent moral or physical support to the usurper, Victoriano Huerta. [...]

[Mexico, Pancho Villa Telegraph to State Governor of León]

I sincerely and enthusiastically felicitate you on the decree which you have just published imposing restrictions on the clergy in the State which you govern with such dignity. I also am inclined to follow your wise example because I, like you, think the greatest enemy to our progress and liberty is the corrupting clergy, who for so long have dominated our country. (Signed) Francisco Villa. [...]

[Mexico, Original Art. 24, Constitution of 1917]

Every one is free to embrace the religion of his choice and to practice all ceremonies, devotions, or observances of his respective creed, either in places of public worship or at home, provided they do not constitute an offense punishable by law.

Every religious act of public worship shall be performed strictly within the places of public worship, which shall be at all times under governmental supervision. [...]

[Mexico, Original Art. 27, Constitution of 1917]

II. The religious institutions known as Churches, irrespective of creed, shall in no case have legal capacity to acquire, hold, or administer real property or loans made on such real property; all such real property or loans as may be at present held by the said religious institutions, either on their own behalf or through third parties, shall vest in the Nation, and any one shall have the right to denounce property so held. Presumptive proof shall be sufficient to declare the denunciation well founded. Places of public worship are the property of the Nation as represented by the Federal government, which shall determine which of them may continue to be devoted to their present purposes. Episcopal residences, rectories, seminaries, orphan asylums or collegiate establishments of religious institutions, convents or any other buildings, built or designed for the administration, propaganda, or teaching of the tenets of any religious creed shall forthwith vest, as of full right, directly in the Nation, to be used exclusively for the public services of the Federation or of the States, within their respective jurisdiction. All places of public worship which shall later be erected shall be the property of the Nation.

III. Public and private charitable institutions for the sick and needy, for scientific research, or for the diffusion of knowledge, mutual aid societies or organizations formed for any lawful purpose shall in no case acquire, hold or administer loans made on real property, unless the mortgage terms do not exceed ten years. In no case shall institutions of this character be under the patronage, direction, administration, charge or supervision of religious corporations or institutions, nor of ministers of any religious creed or of their dependents, even though either the former or the latter shall not be in active service. [...]

[National Catholic Church of Mexico, Circular of 1925]

I. Our Church does not constitute a sect but it is based on the real religion, which was founded by our Divine Master and Redeemer.

II. The Holy Scripture of the Old and New Testaments are the headstone of our church, and they can be freely interpreted by the members, as can also tradition and the liturgy.

III. The purity of the most Blessed Virgin Mary, Our Mother and Mistress, is an article of faith with us and no one can belong to the real religion without this belief. The saints also ought to be venerated.

IV. The power of ruling and governing the Catholic Apostolic Mexican Church resides in its primate or patriarch, independent of Rome, the Pope, or authority of the Vatican, and it has no relation to it. The Mexican Patriarch is the only one who will have power to order the ministers and confer on them the power to administer the Holy Sacraments.

V. The Holy Sacraments ought to be administered without any charge in order to end the practice of simony which exists in the Church of Rome, and only for the intention or application of the Holy Sacrifice of the Mass can alms be received, and then they must be freely given by the one who makes the request; the members of the Church are not required to pay tithes or primacies.

VI. The priest of the Mexican Church ought to be a useful member of society, obedient to the laws and institutions of our Fatherland, and not a person who is supported by the labor of someone else.

VII. Ecclesiastical celibacy is abolished as immoral and unnatural; the priest ought to make a home and by respecting it learn to respect that of others.

VIII. All the services and liturgical books ought to be in the Castilian language.

IX. The clergy of the Mexican Church do not pretend to exercise temporal or spiritual dominion over those adhering to it.

X. Our God is a perfect Being without anger or vengeance, thus He does not condemn for all eternity man made in his image and likeness. Punishment for sin is in direct proportion to the act, and its duration is determined by the degree of culpability." [...]

[Mexico, Settlement of Religious Issue, Portes Gil, 1929]

I take advantage of this opportunity to declare publicity and with all clarity that it is not the spirit of the Constitution, nor of the laws, nor of the government of the Republic to destroy the identity of the Catholic Church, nor of any other cult, nor to intervene in any manner in its spiritual functions. According to the Oath which I took when I assumed the Provisional Government of Mexico to obey and cause to be obeyed the Constitution of the Republic and its laws, my purpose has been at all times to comply honestly with this oath and to see that the laws are applied without sectarian tendency and without injury to anyone. . . . With reference to certain articles of the law which have not been clearly understood, I take advantage of this opportunity to declare:

I. The provision of the law which required the registration of ministers does not mean that the government can register those who have not been named by a hierarchical superior of the religious creed in question or in accordance with its regulations.

II. With regard to religious instruction, the constitution and laws in force definitely prohibit it in primary or higher schools, whether public or private, but this does not prevent ministers of any religion from imparting its doctrines within the church confines to adults and their children, who may attend for that purpose.

III. The Constitution as well as the laws of the country guarantee to all residents of the republic the right of petition, and therefore the members of any church may apply to the appropriate authorities for amendment, repeal or passage of any law.

PART X

Catholicism in the New America

The upheavals caused by the wars of liberation (1810-1825) in Spanish America nearly destroyed the fabric of the Roman Catholic Church, whose bishops and priests were bitterly divided over the issue of independence. It is surprising, perhaps, that some bishops supported independence, as did the majority of the secular clergy. Many of the latter suffered imprisonment, exile, or execution (e.g., 125 priests were executed by royalists in New Spain). Some priests remained politically active after independence and did not return to their parishes. Seminaries were closed, bishoprics became vacant, and the number of priests declined (e.g., Venezuela had two hundred fewer priests in 1837 than in 1810). The new republican regimes were mostly anticlerical and resentful of the church's wealth, political influence, and control over education. The church was unable and often unwilling to respond to the new secular order and was unaware of any responsibility to address new spiritual needs generated by the era of national republicanism. Thus the religious practices and attitudes of the colonial era remained intact, and in general religious life became mechanical and jejune. It remained so throughout most of the nineteenth century.[1]

67. A Shrewd Young Briton Comments on Religion in Brazil, 1810s

After residence in Lisbon, Henry Koster (c. 1793-c. 1820), son of a British merchant, moved to Pernambuco (Brazil) for his health, where he managed a sugar plantation on the island of Itamaracá and traveled in the little-known provinces of northern Brazil. His five-hundred-page account, Travels in Brazil, *was published in 1816. In the excerpts below,*

---

1. Enrique Dussel, *A History of the Church in Latin America: Colonialism to Liberation* (Grand Rapids, Mich.: Eerdmans, 1981), 87-91.

SOURCE: Henry Koster, *Travels in Brazil* (London: Longman, Hurst, Rees, Orme and Brown, Paternoster-Row, 1816), 408-10, 411; 249-50, 252; 264-65.

Koster deals with three different aspects of the Catholic religion in late colonial Brazil: (1) the manner and results of converting Negro slaves to Catholic Christianity; (2) the blessing of an engenho, *a sugar mill; (3) the vicar of the parish of Itamaracá, don Tenorio.*

Readings 1 and 2 go together well. What may be concluded about the slaves' understanding of Catholicism? Is there evidence that it differs from that of the general population of Brazil? From reading 3, is it possible to draw any larger conclusions about the Catholic clergy in Brazil, bearing in mind that it is but a single portrait by a lively English Protestant? Compare his portrait with that in the next reading by Robert Walsh.

[1] All slaves in Brazil follow the religion of their masters and not withstanding the impure state in which the Christian church exists in that country, still such are the beneficent effects of the Christian religion, that these, its adopted children, are improved by it to an infinite degree; and the slave who attends to the strict observance of religious ceremonies invariably proves to be a good servant. The Africans who are imported from Angola are baptized in lots before they leave their own shores, and on their arrival in Brazil they are to learn the doctrines of the church, and the duties of the religion into which they have entered. These bear the mark of the royal crown upon their breasts, which denotes that they have undergone the ceremony of baptism, and likewise that the king's duty has been paid upon them. The slaves which are imported from other parts of the coast of Africa, arrive in Brazil unbaptized, and before the ceremony of making them Christians can be performed upon them, they must be taught certain prayers, for the acquirement of which one year is allowed to the master, before he is obliged to present the slave at the parish church. This law is not always strictly adhered to as to time, but it is never evaded altogether. The religion of the master teaches him that it would be extremely sinful to allow his slave to remain a heathen; and indeed the Portuguese and Brazilians have too much religious feeling to let them neglect any of the ordinances of their church. The slave himself likewise wishes to be made a Christian, for his fellow-bondmen will in every squabble or trifling disagreement with him, close their string of opprobrious epithets with the name of *pagam* (pagan). The unbaptized negro feels that he is considered as an inferior being, and although he may not be aware of the value which the whites

place upon baptism, still he knows that the stigma for which he is upbraided will be removed by it; and therefore he is desirous of being made equal to his companions. The Africans who have been long imported, imbibe a Catholic feeling, and appear to forget that they were once in the same situation themselves. The slaves are not asked whether they will be baptized or not; their entrance into the Catholic church is treated as a thing of course; and indeed they are not considered as members of society, but rather as brute animals, until they can lawfully go to mass, confess their sins, and receive the sacrament.

The slaves have their religious brotherhoods as well as the free persons; and the ambition of a slave very generally aims at being admitted into one of these, and at being made one of the officers and directors of the concerns of the brotherhood; even some of the money which the industrious slave is collecting for the purpose of purchasing his freedom will oftentimes be brought out of its concealment for the decoration of a saint, that the donor may become of importance in the society to which he belongs. The negroes have one invocation of the Virgin, (or I might almost say one virgin) which is peculiarly their own. Our Lady of the Rosary is even sometimes painted with a black face and hands. It is in this manner that the slaves are led to place their attention upon an object in which they soon take an interest, but from which no injury can proceed towards themselves, nor can any through its means be by them inflicted upon their masters. Their ideas are removed from any thought of the customs of their own country, and are guided into a channel of a totally different nature, and completely unconnected with what is practised there. The election of a King of Congo [. . .] by the individuals who come from that part of Africa, seems indeed as if it would give them a bias towards the customs of their native soil; but the Brazilian Kings of Congo worship Our Lady of the Rosary, and are dressed in the dress of white men. [...]

I doubt not that the system of baptizing the newly-imported negroes, proceeded rather from the bigotry of the Portuguese in former times than from any political plan; but it has had the most beneficial effects. The slaves are rendered more tractable; besides being better men and women, they become more obedient servants; they are brought under the controul of the priesthood, and even if this was the only additional hold which was gained by their entrance into the church, it is a great engine of power which is thus brought into action.

But in no circumstance has the introduction of the Christian religion among the slaves been of more service than in the change which it has wrought in the men regarding the treatment of their women, and in the conduct of the females themselves. [...]

The slaves of Brazil are regularly married according to the forms of the Catholic church; the banns are published in the same manner as those of free persons; and I have seen many happy couples (as happy at least as slaves can be) with large families of children rising around them. The masters encourage marriages among their slaves, for it is from these lawful connections that they can expect to increase the number of their Creoles. A slave cannot marry without the consent of his master, for the vicar will not publish the banns of marriage without this sanction. It is likewise permitted that slaves should marry free persons; if the woman is in bondage, the children remain in the same state, but if the man is a slave, and she is free, their offspring is also free. A slave cannot be married until the requisite prayers have been learnt, the nature of confession be understood, and the Sacrament can be received.

[2] I had had some intention of leaving Jaguaribe, owing to the turbulence of the neighbourhood, to my ill-health, and to some disagreeable occurrences which had taken place between my landlord and myself. However, as this would

have been very inconvenient, I resolved to stay, notwithstanding all these and other disadvantages.

Preparations were made in the month of August for setting the mill to work; the cane had not attained this year its accustomed growth, in most parts of the country, and that which I possessed was particularly stinted in size, for I had not commenced planting until it was almost too late. Everything being ready towards the end of the month, I sent for a priest to bless the works. Unless this ceremony is performed, every person who is to be employed about the mill, both freeman and slave, would be afraid to proceed to his destined labour, and if any accident happened it would be ascribed to the wrath of heaven, for this breach of religious observance. The priest arrived and said mass, after which we breakfasted and then proceeded to the mill. The manager and several other freemen and the negroes stood around the works; a quantity of cane was placed ready to be thrust in between the rollers, and the four negroes whose part it was to feed the mill stood at their posts. Two lighted candles were placed close to the rollers, upon the platform which sustains the cane, and a small image of our Saviour upon the cross stood between them; the priest took his breviary and read several prayers, and at stated places, with a small bunch of weeds prepared for the occasion, which he dipped in a jug of holy water, he sprinkled the mill and the persons present. Some of the negroes sprang forward to receive a good quantum of this sanctified water; and then the master of the sugar boiling-house led the way to the portion of the works of which he had the direction; and here there was another sprinkling. When we returned to the part of the mill in which the rollers stood, the priest took a large cane, and I did the same; then the signal being given the flood-gate was opened and the works were soon in motion, and according to rule the two canes which the priest and I held in our hands were the first to be ground. I had heard much of this ceremony from persons of the country, and I cannot avoid saying, that although something of the ridiculous may by many persons be attached to it, still I could not help feeling much respect for it. The excitement of devout feelings among the slaves, even of those feelings which are produced by the Roman Catholic religion, cannot fail to be serviceable, and if men are to exist as slaves this is doubtless the religion which is the best adapted to persons in a state of subjection. Slavery and superstition are however two evils which when combined, are surely sufficient to cause the misery of any country.

The carts, the oxen, and their drivers had not received the priest's benediction; they arrived some time afterwards, bringing loads of canes, and the carts were ornamented with the longest that could be picked out placed as flag staffs, and bearing upon them handkerchiefs and ribbons. Each cart in succession stood before the door of the dwelling-house, and the priest complied with the wishes of the drivers.

[3]   I happened to arrive at Conception upon the day of the festival, the 8th of December, however as I had many matters to arrange, I did not see the ceremony in the church, but was invited to dine with the vicar. I went at two o'clock, and found a large party assembled, to which I was happy in being introduced, as it consisted of several priests who are the men of most information in the country, and of some of the first laymen of the island. The dinner was excellent and elegant, and the behaviour of the persons present was gentlemanly. I was placed at the head of the table, as being a stranger; and a friend of the vicar took the opposite end of it, whilst he himself sat on one side of me. I never met a pleasanter dinner-party, there was much rational conversation and much mirth, but no noise and confusion. The company continued together until a late hour, and indeed the major part of the priests were staying in the house.

The parish of Itamaraca has now for some years enjoyed the blessings which proceeded from the appointment of the present vicar, Pedro de Souza Tenorio. His merit was discovered by the gover-

nor, whom he served as chaplain, and by whose application to the Prince Regent was obtained for him his present situation. The zeal of the vicar, for the improvement of the districts over which he has controul is unremitted; he takes pains to explain to the planters the utility of the introduction of new modes of agriculture, new machinery for their sugar-mills, and many alterations of the same description which are known to be practised with success in the colonies of other nations; but it is not every novelty which meets with his approbation. It is no easy task to loosen the deep-rooted prejudices of many of the planters. He is affable to the lower ranks of people, and I have had many opportunities of hearing persuasion and entreaty made use of to many of his parishioners, that they would reform their habits, if any impropriety of behaviour in the person to whom he was speaking had come to his knowledge. His occasional extempore discourses on subjects of morality when seated within the railings of the principal chapel, delivered in a distinct and deep-toned voice, by a man of commanding person, habited in the black gown which is usually worn by men of his profession, were very impressive. He has exerted himself greatly to increase the civilization of the higher orders of people in his parish; to prevent feuds among them;—to persuade them to give up those notions of the connection between the patron and the dependant, which are yet too general; he urges them to educate their children, to have their dwellings in a state of neatness, to dress well themselves, their wives and their children. He is a good man; one who reflects upon his duties, and who studies to perform them in the best manner possible. He has had the necessity of displaying likewise the intrepidity of his character; his firmness as a priest, his courage as a man, and he has not been found wanting. He is a native of Pernambuco, and has not degenerated from the high character of his provincial countrymen; he was educated at the university of Coimbra in Portugal.

68. A Shrewd British Gentleman Comments on the Church in Brazil, 1820s

Robert Walsh (1772-1852), curate in the Anglican Church of Ireland, was made chaplain to the British embassy in Constantinople in 1820, thereafter traveled through Turkey and Asia, obtained a medical degree, practiced medicine in remote parts of Asia, was appointed chaplain to the embassy in St. Petersburg, and, in 1828, was appointed chaplain to the British embassy in Rio de Janeiro.

Walsh's two-volume account of the status of the institutions and people of Brazil is certainly systematic and scientific. His treatment of slavery, a serious issue in Britain at this time, compares Brazilian slavery with the slave and serf systems in Turkey and Russia.

But it is his thoughtful treatment of the Catholic religion, church, and culture of Brazil that is relevant to our concerns. We will consider four disparate issues: (1) the status of the hierarchy and of the religious orders; (2) the extent of learning among the clergy; (3) the problem of tolerance for non-Catholics; and (4) the ceremony of the profession of a nun.

Walsh's description of the church—the bishops, the religious orders, their wealth or lack of it, the problem of celibacy, and the attitude of the important minister of the interior toward the clergy—is highly nuanced and all the more impressive because of Walsh's Protestant status. Elaborate on his achievement. Note especially his description of the numerous poor and homeless in Rio (the "mendicity," i.e., the beggars).

His favorable treatment of Brazil's Catholic culture continues with his description of the brotherhoods and concludes with an extraordinary analysis of the lack of learning among the clergy. Why may this analysis be considered highly sophisticated and an outstanding example of the technique of social science? Why may it be perceived as a compliment to the Catholic Church? What does Walsh's portrait of the bishop of Rio de Janeiro reveal about the bishop and about Walsh?

Characterize Walsh's account of religious tolerance in Brazil and the remarks he attributes to his friend, the bishop of Rio (see number 3 below).

Given Walsh's status as Protestant chaplain, his excellent education, and his extensive travels and experiences in the world, what conclusions about Walsh himself might his description of the profession of a nun elicit? What about his final remarks?

When all of the previous analyses and portraits by Robert Walsh are considered together, what conclusions can be drawn about the health of the church in the Brazil of the 1820s?

[1] When Brazil was first colonized, the ecclesiastic establishments were supported, as in the mother country, by tithes; but from the scantiness of the population, and the small quantity of produce raised in an infant colony, the tithes were found entirely inadequate to support a church, the number of whose ecclesiastics bore a large proportion to the inhabitants. An agreement, therefore, was entered into between the court of Portugal and that of Rome, which gave the whole of the tithe to government, on the condition of their paying the clergy. Instead, therefore, of the laity giving a tenth of the produce of the soil, to support the church, they paid it in for the support of

SOURCE: Robert Walsh, *Notices of Brazil in 1828 and 1829* (Boston: Richardson, Lord & Holbrook, William Hyde et al., 1831), 1:200-204; Robert Walsh, *Notices of Brazil in 1828 and 1829* (Boston: Fredrick Westley and A. H. Davis, 1830), 1:367-71; Robert Walsh, *Notices of Brazil in 1828 and 1829* (London: Frederick Westley and A. H. Davis, 1830), 1:322-24, 326-27, 329-30, 332-34, 351-57.

the state, and government allowed the ecclesiastic who was entitled to receive it, a regular stipend of two hundred milreis or dollars, at that time equivalent coin. This at the time was an excellent bargain for the church; the stipend was a very ample one, and the government lost considerably by the exchange, while the parochial clergyman, who received besides his fees for baptisms, burials, marriages, Easter dues, and daily masses, lived in considerable comfort, and even opulence. But now the order of things is reversed. From the increase of population and produce, the tithes amount to an enormous sum, while the stationary stipend of two hundred dollars is a comparative trifle, and insufficient to procure the common comforts of life, so that the state of the clergy in Brazil is, generally speaking, a state of poverty.

The episcopal establishment consists of one archbishop, six bishops, and two prelates, who are bishops *in partibus*. Nor are these dignitaries of the church more amply provided for. The bishops, who are all suffragans of the archbishop of Bahia, the primate, are also paid by government on the same economical plan; and were it not for the fees, arising from the ecclesiastical tribunals in their respective dioceses, they would find it difficult to support, with decency, the dignity of their station. Such of them as I had the pleasure to know and visit, appeared to me to live with great moderation and simplicity; and, so far from abounding in superfluities, did not seem to me to enjoy even what, in England, would be considered necessaries to men of their rank in life.

The regular clergy in Brazil are not numerous. They are Benedictines, Carmelites, Franciscans, ancient and reformed, with Capuchin missionaries. Of these orders the richest are the Benedictines and the ancient Carmelites. The others make vows of poverty, and neither do nor can possess any property.

But the wealthy orders are just now in imminent danger; from the very reputation of their wealth, the present feeling of the country is not in their favor, and they seem to be held in the same estimation as they were in France at the commencement of the revolution. It is therefore generally spoken of, as a thing just and necessary, that their property should be applied to the necessities of the state. The chamber of deputies have already passed a vote to that effect, and it is imagined, that many persons about the throne are equally disposed to the measure, in the hope of annexing some of the confiscated lands to their own estates, as is notoriously the case in every reformation, particularly in our own. The people of Brazil have always been hostile to monastic institutions in the country, either male or female, and for the same reason—the impediment it throws in the way of population; and this feeling extends even to the secular clergy. On the 24th of October, 1827, Senhor Fiego, a member of the ecclesiastical committee, and himself a priest, I believe, moved in the chamber, "that it would be proper to apply to the pope, to relieve the clergy from the penalty annexed to marrying," and at the same time to notify to his holiness "that the assembly could not avoid repealing the law of celibacy." The motion did not then pass, but it is expected to be brought on again with success. In the meantime, the regular clergy, the Benedictines and Carmelites, have been prohibited from taking novices, an interdict which is believed to be preparatory to their total extinction.

It is supposed, however, that their loss, at least for a time, will be very severely felt, not only by the poor, but by many respectable families of decent appearance, but very scanty income. The whole mendicity of Rio is supported at their convents. A beggar is rarely or ever seen in the streets; and at first I supposed no such class of persons existed in the country, till I saw the steps and platform of the convent of S. Antonio crowded with the lame, the halt, and the blind, and all receiving their daily portions of meat and soup. With respect to persons of a better class, great numbers are tenants to those convents, who with considerate humanity take very low rents, and exact them with great indulgence and forbearance. The Benedictines alone are proprietors of seven hundred houses in Rio. They are, I am told, exceedingly kind landlords to their tenants, who are generally of the humble, but respectable class I have mentioned.

Besides these regular societies, there are various *irmandades*, or brotherhoods, which seem to be on the plan of our benefit societies, but on a more extended scale. They take the name of Carmelites,

Franciscans, Minims, and are called "Third Orders," though they consist entirely of the laity, and are composed of trades-people, and such of a higher class as may be disposed [. . .]

[2]   The native clergy are not, generally speaking, learned men, for they have not the means of being so. The poverty of the bishops, is an impediment to the establishment of ecclesiastical seminaries, on a scale sufficiently extensive or liberal to give the candidates the means or opportunities of a learned education. The inducements to enter the church also are so small, and its stipend so limited, that men of opulent families or brilliant abilities always prefer some more attractive or profitable avocation; and none but persons in the lowest ranks of life devote their children to it: the resources which it affords in other countries, to the younger members of respectable families, not being thought of in this. The candidate, therefore, is a person whose parents are unacquainted with liberal education, who has no knowledge of, nor desire for it himself, and who, even if he had, does not find the means of acquiring it, in the seminary to which he is sent.

To this cause perhaps may be attributed, in some measure, the admission of negroes to holy orders, who officiate in churches indiscriminately with whites. I have seen myself three clergymen in the same church at the same time; one of whom was a white, another a mulatto, and the third a black. The admission of the poor despised race, to the highest functions that a human being can perform, strongly marks the consideration in which it is held in different places. In the West Indies a clergyman has been severely censured by his flock, for presuming to administer the sacrament to a poor negro at the same table with themselves. In Brazil a black is seen as the officiating minister, and whites receiving it from his hands.

Notwithstanding the humble ranks from which the clergy are raised, and the insufficient means of education afforded them, they have already felt the effects of that influx of light and knowledge, which an intercourse with strangers and free institutions, has spread through the country. [. . .]

Among the many exceptions I have met with to the charge of want of learning or information

among the Brazilian clergy is the excellent José Caëtano da Silva-Coutinho, Bishop of Rio, than whom a more learned or, I believe, a more amiable man does not exist. He is by birth a Portuguese, and intended to have embarked with the royal family, but could not obtain a passage in any ship of the crowded squadron. He was watched by the French, but contrived to elude their vigilance, and arrived at Rio in April, 1808. He landed at night, and immediately proceeded to the palace, where he was kindly and gladly received by the Prince Regent, who highly esteemed him, and by the clergy of Rio, who had been for three years without a bishop. In June following, by an alvará [permit] of the prince, he was appointed capelão mor, or chaplain-in-chief to the royal palace. He is now about fifty, or a little more. He is well versed in ancient and modern languages; speaks French and English, not fluently, but reads them both with facility, and is well acquainted with the literature of both countries.

He is not only capelão mor, to the court; but his talents and integrity are so appreciated, that he was recently appointed president of the senate in the present sessions. He is a man of very liberal opinions, perfectly and sincerely tolerant of every sect, while he is warmly attached to his own. He was a strenuous advocate for building the Protestant church, and is fond of the society of English clergymen, and pays particular attention to the British chaplain. He is exceedingly charitable to the poor, even beyond his limited means, and anxious to promote every project which he thinks will benefit the country. He is a man of strict observance and blameless life himself, and exceedingly temperate in his habits. He fasts all the year on one meal a day. He is anxious to effect a reformation among such of his clergy, as he thinks require it: but unfortunately for the cause of morality and religion, the court party has been for some years in open hostility with him; and some clergymen, whom he would have compelled to live more according to their canonical rules, have been so protected, that he has not been able to effect his purpose. [. . .]

The library is a fine spacious apartment, containing about four thousand volumes in different languages, ancient and modern, with a large proportion of French and English. Among the latter he showed me "Southey's History of Brazil," which he said was a standard work, highly prized as one of great research and impartial detail; in the compilation of which, he knew the author had access to the most authentic documents through his uncle, the respectable chaplain at Lisbon.

[3]   The bishop of Rio [. . .] is not only a tolerant and liberal man, but a man of excellent good sense and knowledge of the world. He advocated the cause, in a characteristic manner, with the prejudiced few who opposed it.

"The English," said he, "have really no religion; but they are a proud and obstinate people. If you oppose them, they will persist, and make it an affair of infinite importance; but if you concede to their wishes, the chapel will be built, and nobody will ever go near it." This argument had its weight, and the Brazilians say he was right; for the event has verified the prediction. All opposition was, therefore, withdrawn, and the treaty was signed in a tolerant and liberal spirit, as creditable to the disposition of the king, as of his American subjects. [. . .]

A guard of police was ordered to attend, as a matter of precaution against any bigoted or evil-disposed persons who might be inclined to interrupt the service, or disturb a congregation introducing a new religion, to which their prejudices were supposed to be greatly hostile; but no disposition of the kind occurred. On the contrary, the common people conducted themselves with great propriety abroad, and the interior of the church was filled with a numerous assemblage of very respectable Brazilians, who equaled the Protestants, as well in numbers as in reverence for the place, by a serious and devout demeanour. [. . .]

There is nothing which more strongly marks the growing feeling of toleration in the world, than this concession among a people, formerly distinguished for their spirit of persecution. It is creditable to the good sense and kindly feelings of the Brazilian Portuguese, and the press of the country is continually employed in extending it. [. . .]

[4]   The young lady about to be professed was the daughter of one of the rich proprietarios d'En-genho, or owners of a sugar plantation, who are generally the most opulent people in the country. Her name was Maria Luzia, aged twenty-two. She resolved to take the veil entirely against the wishes of her friends, who were anxious to establish her respectably in life, in a rank to which her expectations entitled her; but she resisted the attractions, and voluntarily renounced the world in the prime of youth, and possessed of considerable beauty and fortune. This propensity in Brazil is not at all uncommon. In the convent of the Ajuda, were two sisters of the same family, already professed, and two more as novices, immediately to take the veil.

This young person had been previously examined by the bishop; whether she had completed her twenty-fifth year, for then she would have been of a competent age to decide for herself, without the intervention of friends; whether it was with her own free consent that she proposed to renounce the world; and whether she designed rigidly to observe her vows, and preserve her chastity. Having answered all these things in the affirmative, certain of the sisterhood, and of her own relations, were appointed as her sponsors, to accompany her during her profession.

The novice professes in two ways; either behind the grating, or by advancing up the church to the altar. The former mode is the rule of this convent. The archpresbyter appeared with the bishop, attended by other clergy, at the altar; and at the same time the nuns entered their apartment below the grating. The archpresbyter then advancing down the aisle to the grating, applied himself to the wicket, and said, "Prudent virgin, trim your lamp: behold your Spouse approaches; come forth and meet him." The novice hearing the words of the archpresbyter, lighted a torch which she held in her hand, and, accompanied by two nuns already professed, advanced to the wicket, while the bishop in his robes at the same time approached from the altar, with his mitre and crozier, and sat on the low throne placed before it. The archpresbyter then said: "Most reverend father, our holy mother, the Church, demands that you should bless this virgin, and espouse her to our Lord Jesus Christ, the Son of God." The bishop demanded, "Is she worthy?" the archpresbyter replied, "As far as human frailty permits me to know, I believe, and certify, that she is worthy."

The bishop then turned to the congregation, and said with a loud voice, "God and our Saviour aiding, we have chosen this present virgin, to bless and consecrate her as the spouse of Christ." The archpresbyter now chanted *Veni*—"Come," and the virgin advanced to him singing, "and now I follow with my whole heart": she then came forward between her sponsors, and knelt at the aperture before the bishop.

She seemed very lovely; with an unusually sweet, gentle, and pensive countenance. She did not look particularly, or deeply affected; but when she sung her responses, there was something exceedingly mournful in the soft, tremulous, and timid tones of her voice. The bishop now exhorted her to make a public profession of her vows before the congregation, and said, "Will you persevere in your purpose of holy chastity?" She blushed deeply; and with a downcast look, lowly, but firmly answered, "I will." He again said, more distinctly, "Do you promise to preserve it?" and she replied more emphatically, "I do promise." The bishop said, "Thanks be to God": and she bent forward and reverently kissed his hand, while he asked her, "Will you now be blessed and consecrated?" she replied, "Oh! I wish it."

The habiliments in which she was hereafter to be clothed, were brought forward, and were sanctified by the aspersion of holy water: then followed several prayers to God, that, "As he had blessed the garments of Aaron, with ointment which flowed from his head to his beard, so he would now bless the garment of his servant, with the copious dew of his benediction." When the garment was thus aspersed and blessed, the girl retired with it; and having laid aside the dress in which she had appeared, she returned, arrayed in her new attire, except her veil. A gold ring was next provided, and consecrated with a prayer, that she who wore it "might be fortified with celestial virtue, to preserve a pure faith, and incorrupt fidelity to her spouse, Jesus Christ." He last took the veil, and her female attendants having uncovered her head, he threw it over her, so that it fell on her shoulders and bosom, and said, "Receive this sacred veil, under the shadow of which you may learn to despise the world, and submit yourself truly, and with all humility of heart, to your spouse": to which she sung a response, in a very sweet, soft, and touching voice: "He has placed this veil before my face, that I should see no lover but himself."

The bishop now kindly took her hand, and held it while the following hymn was chanted by the choir with great harmony:—"Beloved Spouse, come—the winter is passed—the turtle sings, and the blooming vines are redolent of summer."

A crown, a necklace, and other female ornaments, were now taken by the bishop and separately blessed; and the girl bending forward, he placed them on her head and neck, praying that she might be thought worthy "to be enrolled into the society of the hundred and forty-four thousand virgins, who preserved their chastity, and did not mix with the society of impure women."

Last of all he placed the ring on the middle finger of her right hand, and solemnly said, "So I marry you to Jesus Christ, who will henceforth be your protector. Receive this ring, the pledge of your faith, that you may be called the spouse of God." She fell on her knees, and sung, "I am married to him whom angels serve, whose beauty the sun and moon admire:" then rising, and showing with exultation her right hand, she said, emphatically, as if to impress it on the attention of the congregation, "My Lord has wedded me with this ring, and decorated me with a crown as his spouse. I here renounce and despise all earthly ornaments for his sake, whom alone I see, whom alone I love, in whom alone I trust, and to whom alone I give all my affections. My heart hath uttered a good word: I speak of the deed I have done for my King."

Having thus renounced all earthly attachments, and laid aside all human objects of affection, she stood before the congregation dressed in her wedding robes, the garb of her celestial Spouse. The bishop then pronounced a general benediction, and retired up to the altar; while the nun professed was borne off between her friends, with tapers lighting, and garlands waving. The curtain was then drawn, and the ceremony ended.

I thought this whole service exceedingly affecting and beautiful; and it left a strong impression on my mind, notwithstanding the many circumstances attendant on it, which weakened the character of its solemnity.

69. *Son Mui Buenos Catolicos, pero Mui Malos Cristianos*

Henry George Ward (c. 1796-1860), son of a British writer, entered the English diplomatic service in 1816 and in 1823 became chargé d'affaires in the infant republic of Mexico. Britain was, of course, greatly interested in the economic possibilities of the new Latin American republics and demanded thorough reports on their institutions, laws, customs, and economies.

Below are Ward's pages from his Mexico in 1827 *on the condition of the Catholic Church in the new republic.*

What had the era of intermittent wars for independence (1810-1821) and the chaos of the ensuing two decades done to the church in New Spain/Mexico? According to Ward, how did both the state and the church respond to Pope Leo XII's monarchical presuppositions contained in his encyclical of 1824? What does the fact that only "two old Spaniards" among all the Spanish residents (all of whom had lost their superior status with the advent of a republic) favored the bull suggest about the existence of a Mexican nation in 1824? Might Ward's English Protestant sensibility have prevented him from giving an "objective" account of the church in Mexico? Are his comments biased on the "very exorbitant" fees set by the clergy? How common among the clergy might be the cathedral canon's estimate of Mexicans as "very good Catholics, but very bad Christians"?

A short view of the present state of the Ecclesiastical establishments of New Spain will place this point in a clearer light.

The Republic is divided into one Archbishopric, (that of Mexico,) and the nine Bishoprics of La Puebla, Guadalajara, Valladolid, Durango, Monterey, Oaxaca, Yucatán, Chiapas, and Sonora. [. . .]

Seven of the Bishoprics, and *Seventy-nine* of the benefices attached to the Cathedrals, are now vacant. Some of the Chapters are reduced to two or three individuals; many of whom are old, and unable to execute the duties of their situations. Of the three remaining Bishops, (those of La Puebla, Yucatán, and Oaxaca,) One (the Bishop of Yucatán), is absolutely in his dotage; and the other two, from their position in the Southern part of the Republic, are unable to ordain those who wish to enter into orders in the North, without compelling them to undertake a journey of three or four hundred leagues, in order to undergo the necessary examinations. [. . .]

The Parochial Clergy distributed amongst the 1194 parishes, into which the country is divided, are those who suffer most severely from the present disorganization of the Church. They are not only deprived by it of the preferment to which their services entitle them, but many, who accepted in 1821, livings in *Tierra Caliente*, or other unhealthy districts, upon an understanding that they were to be held, (as before the Revolution) for a short term of years, are compelled still to retain their situations, until the exercise of the right of Patronage enables the Government to relieve them. [. . .]

The total inefficacy of Spiritual arms in the New World has been very recently proved by the reception given to the Circular Bull or *Enciclica*, addressed by the Court of Rome to the Archbishops, Bishops, and Clergy in general of the Americas, on the 24th of September, 1824, exhorting them, "to be silent no longer; but to unite in leading back their flocks to the path of the commandments of that Lord, who places Kings upon their thrones, and connects, by indissoluble ties, the preservation of their rights and authority, with the welfare of His Holy Church."

The Government of Mexico, convinced that, in

SOURCE: Henry George Ward, *Mexico in 1827* (London: Henry Colburn, 1828), 1:326, 327-28, 328-30, 333, 335-36, 336-38.

a discussion of this nature, reason and common sense were in its favour, was not deterred from entering upon it by any fears of the intrigues of the Old Spaniards, the prejudices of the people, or the supposed infallibility of the Pope. The Bull was communicated to the nation at large, as soon as received, in the Government Gazette; and there was certainly nothing that savoured either of bigotry, or superstition, in the notes by which it was accompanied. They contained no affectation of humility, no expressions of an eager desire to be reconciled to the Holy See, but entered boldly into the question of the Pope's Spiritual and Temporal Sovereignty; declared the two to be incompatible; and even hinted, very distinctly, that any farther attempt, on the part of his Holiness, to exercise authority in the affairs of this world, would not only prove unsuccessful, but must lead to the loss of his Spiritual jurisdiction likewise. This manly stand, on the part of the Government, against the encroachments of the Holy See, was received with universal approbation. The Legislatures of the States, the Bishops, and the Cathedral Chapters, all expressed their concurrence in the doctrines laid down in the Circular of the Minister for Ecclesiastical Affairs: Pastorals were addressed by them, upon the subject, to their respective flocks; and as the influence of the Government and the Church were thus thrown into the same scale, the *Enciclica* not only failed in creating the desired impression, but produced an effect diametrically opposite to that which was intended.

Not the slightest difference of opinion appeared amongst the natives; and as the President, (who was then armed with extraordinary powers) took advantage of the most critical moment to banish to California two old Spaniards, (the Editors of the Filantropo newspaper at Tampico,) who had endeavoured to circulate, surreptitiously, copies of the Bull amongst the inhabitants of New León and San Luis, the other Spanish residents were effectually deterred, by this rigorous measure, from making any attempt to excite the lower classes, in the name of Religion, to rebellion against the constituted authorities.

The work of Baron Humboldt, and the admirable reports presented to Congress in 1826, and 1827, by the Mexican Minister for Ecclesiastical Affairs, Don Miguel Ramos Arizpe, enable me to institute a comparison, founded upon the most authentic data, between the condition of the Mexican Church before the Revolution and at the present day.

In 1802, the number of Ecclesiastics, Secular and Regular, in New Spain, was estimated at ten thousand, or at thirteen thousand, including the lay-brothers of convents, and other subordinate hangers-on of the Church. The Secular Clergy was composed of about five thousand Priests (Clérigos); the Regulars, wearing the habits of different Orders, of nearly an equal number. [. . .]

In 1826, the number of the Secular Clergy was estimated at 3473, and in 1827, at 3677. The number of those who took orders during each of these years is not supposed to have amounted to one-fourth of those who were ordained in 1808.

The Regular Clergy is divided into fourteen Provinces, possessing 150 Convents, which contained, in all, 1918 Friars; so that the whole of the Secular and Regular Clergy of the present day does not much exceed *one-half* of the number known to exist in 1803. [. . .]

A more equal distribution, at least, of the wealth now engrossed by a few, will be one of the first consequences of the interference of the Congress in Ecclesiastical affairs; and it is highly to be desired that, in this respect, some reform should take place; for in many Dioceses, where the revenues of the Bishop amounted to 100,000 or 120,000 dollars, there were *Curas* (Parish priests) who vegetated upon a pittance of 100, or 120 dollars in the year.

The sources from which the incomes of the Parish priests are derived likewise require investigation, and reform.

No provision being made for them by the State, their subsistence depends upon the contributions of their parishioners; which, in general, are regulated by custom, and not by law: they consist of marriage and baptismal fees and other dues payable on burials, masses, and other church ceremonies, most of which are very exorbitant, and produce a most demoralizing effect amongst the Indian population. For instance, in States, where the daily wages of the labourer do not exceed two reals, and where a cottage can be built for four dollars, its unfortunate inhabitants are forced to pay twenty-two dollars for their marriage fees; a sum which exceeds half their yearly earnings, in a country where Feast and Fast days reduce the number of *días útiles* (on which labour is permitted) to about one hundred and seventy-five. The consequence is, that the Indian either cohabits with his future wife until she becomes pregnant, (when the priest is compelled to marry them with, or without fees,) or, if more religiously disposed, contracts debts, and even commits thefts, rather than not satisfy the demands of the ministers of that Religion, the spirit of which appears to be so little understood. [. . .]

The fees on baptisms, and burials, are likewise very high. In the Mining districts, each miner pays *weekly* to the Church, half a real (a medio), in order to provide for the expenses of his funeral; and on the day of the *Raya* (the weekly payment), an agent of the Cura is always present to receive it. Thus twenty-six reals, or three dollars and two reals (thirteen shillings English money), are paid annually, by each mining labourer, in full health and employment, in order to secure the privilege of a mass being read over his body upon his

decease. An Indian, who lives ten years under such a system, would pay six pounds ten shillings for the honour of a funeral; and yet would not be exempt from continuing his contributions, although the amount paid in one year, ought more than to cover any fees that could reasonably be claimed by the Church.

I do not fear being accused of an uncharitable spirit in these remarks, for I have heard many of the most enlightened of the Mexican Clergy deplore the existence of such a state of things, and admit, that the want of a moral feeling amongst the lower classes, is the natural fruit of a system, under which such abuses have been suffered to prevail.

One of the most distinguished members of a Cathedral Chapter, while lamenting, in a conversation with me, the debased state of the people of his diocese, used this remarkable phrase: "*Son mui buenos Catolicos, pero mui malos Cristianos;*" (They are very good Catholics, but very bad Christians;) meaning, (as he afterwards stated,) that it had been but too much the interest of the lower orders of the Clergy, to direct the attention of their flocks, rather to a scrupulous observance of the *forms* of the Catholic Church, than to its moral or spirit, from which their revenues derived but little advantage.

70. The U.S. Establishment in Amerindian Guatemala

John Lloyd Stephens (1805-1852), graduate of Columbia University, lawyer, and author of two accounts of his extensive world travels, was appointed by President Van Buren in 1839 as special ambassador to the United Provinces of Central America to negotiate a treaty with that federal republic (then nearing dissolution). His Incidents of Travel in Central America, Chiapas, and Yucatan *was published in 1841.*

What does this extraordinary account of Good Friday services in Quetzaltenango, Guatemala, reveal about the status of Catholicism there: the quality and commitment of the clergy and the Indians' understanding and practice of Catholicism? How much does the author's liberal, Protestant, and U.S. background, despite his knowledge of and interest in non-European cultures, color his account of his experience?

Note that the ladino guerrilla leader Rafael Carrera could not always control all his antiliberal followers, resulting in the violence referred to in the reading.

SOURCE: John L. Stephens, *Incidents of Travel in Central America, Chiapas, and Yucatan*, 12th ed. (New York: Harper & Brothers, 1867), 2:209-14.

To return to the cura: he was about forty-five, tall, stout, and remarkably fine-looking; he had several curacies under his charge, and next to a canónigo's, his position was the highest in the country; but it had its labours. He was at that time engrossed with the ceremonies of the Holy Week, and in the evening we accompanied him to the church. At the door the *coup d'œil* of the interior was most striking. The church was two hundred and fifty feet in length, spacious and lofty, richly decorated with pictures, and sculptured ornaments, blazing with lights and crowded with Indians. On each side of the door was a grating, behind which stood an Indian to receive offerings. The floor was strewed with pine-leaves. On the left was the figure of a dead Christ on a bier, upon which every woman who entered threw a handful of roses, and near it stood an Indian to receive money. Opposite, behind an iron grating, was the figure of Christ bearing the cross, the eyes bandaged, and large silver chains attached to the arms and other parts of the body, and fastened to the iron bars. Here, too, stood an Indian to receive contributions. The altar was beautiful in design and decorations, consisting of two rows of Ionic columns, one above another, gilded, surmounted by a golden glory, and lighted by candles ten feet high. Under the pulpit was a piano. After a stroll around the church, the cura led us to seats under the pulpit. He asked us to give them some of the airs of our country, and then himself sat down at the piano. On Mr. C.'s suggesting that the tune was from one of Rossini's operas, he said that this was hardly proper for the occasion, and changed it.

At about ten o'clock the crowd in the church formed into a procession, and Mr. C. and I went out and took a position at the corner of a street to see it pass. It was headed by Indians, two abreast, each carrying in his hand a long lighted wax candle; and then, borne aloft on the shoulders of four men, came the figure of Judith, with a bloody sword in one hand, and in the other the gory head of Holofernes. Next, also on the shoulders of four men, the archangel Gabriel, dressed in red silk, with large wings puffed out. The next were men in grotesque armour, made of black and silver paper, to resemble Moors, with shield and spear like ancient cavaliers; and then four little girls, dressed in white silk and gauze, and looking like little spiritualities, with men on each side bearing lighted candles. Then came a large figure of Christ bearing the cross, supported by four Indians; on each side were young Indian lads, carrying long poles horizontally, to keep the crowd from pressing upon it, and followed by a procession of townsmen. In turning the corner of the street at which we stood, a dark Mestitzo, with a scowl of fanaticism on his face, said to Mr. Catherwood, "Take off your spectacles and follow the cross." Next followed a procession of women with children in their arms, half of them asleep, fancifully dressed with silver caps and headdresses, and finally a large statue of the Virgin, in a sitting posture, magnificently attired, with Indian lads on each side, as before, supporting poles with candles. The whole was accompanied with the music of drums and violins; and, as the long train of light passed down the street, we returned to the convent.

The night was very cold, and the next morning was like one in December at home. It was the morning of Good Friday; and throughout Guatemala, in every village, preparations were making to celebrate, with the most solemn ceremonies of the Church, the resurrection of the Saviour. In Quezaltenango, at that early hour, the plaza was thronged with Indians from the country around; but the whites, terrified and grieving at the murder of their best men, avoided, to a great extent, taking part in the celebration.

At nine o'clock the corregidor called for us, and we accompanied him to the opening ceremony. On one side of the nave of the church, near the grand altar, and opposite the pulpit, were high cushioned chairs for the corregidor and members of the municipality, and we had seats with them. The church was thronged with Indians, estimated at more than three thousand. Formerly, at this ceremony no women or children were admitted; but now the floor of the church was filled with Indian women on their knees, with red cords plaited in their hair, and perhaps one third of them had children on their backs, their heads and arms only visible. Except ourselves and the padre, there were no white people in the church; and, with all eyes turned upon us, and a lively recollection of the fate of those who but a few days before had occupied our seats, we felt that the post of honour was a private station.

At the steps of the grand altar stood a large cross, apparently of solid silver, richly carved and ornamented, and over it a high arbour of pine and cypress branches. At the foot of the cross stood a figure of Mary Magdalene weeping, with her hair in a profusion of ringlets, her frock low in the neck, and altogether rather immodest. On the right was the figure of the Virgin gorgeously dressed, and in the nave of the church stood John the Baptist, placed there, as it seemed, only because they had the figure on hand. Very soon strains of wild Indian music rose from the other end of the church, and a procession advanced, headed by Indians with broad-brimmed felt hats, dark cloaks, and lighted wax candles, preceding the body of the Saviour on a bier borne by the cura and attendant padres, and followed by Indians with long wax candles. The bier advanced to the foot of the cross; ladders were placed behind against it; the gobernador, with his long black cloak and broad-brimmed felt hat, mounted on the right, and leaned over, holding in his hands a silver hammer and a long silver spike; another Indian dignitary mounted on the other side, while the priests raised the figure up in front; the face was ghastly, blood trickled down the cheeks, the arms and legs were moveable, and in the side was a gaping wound, with a stream of blood oozing from it. The back was affixed to the cross, the arms extended, spikes driven through the hands and feet, the ladders taken away, and thus the figure of Christ was nailed to the cross.

This over, we left the church, and passed two or three hours in visiting. The white population was small, but equal in character to any in the republic; and there was hardly a respectable family that was not afflicted by the outrage of [General Rafael] Carrera. We knew nothing of the effect of this enormity until we entered domestic circles. The distress of women whose nearest connexions had been murdered or obliged to flee for their lives, and then wandering they knew not where, those only can realize who can appreciate woman's affection.

I was urged to visit the widow of Molina. Her husband was but thirty-five, and his death under any circumstances would have been lamented, even by political enemies. I felt a painful interest in one who had lived through such a scene, but at the door of her house I stopped. I felt that a visit from a stranger must be an intrusion upon her sorrows.

In the afternoon we were again seated with the municipality in the church, to behold the descent from the cross. The spacious building was thronged to suffocation, and the floor was covered by a dense mass of kneeling women, with turbaned headdresses, and crying children on their backs, their imaginations excited by gazing at the bleeding figure on the cross; but among them all I did not see a single interesting face. A priest ascended the pulpit, thin and ghastly pale, who, in a voice that rang through every part of the building, preached emphatically a passion sermon. Few of the Indians understood even the language, and at times the cries of children made his words inaudible; but the thrilling tones of his voice played upon every chord in their hearts; and mothers, regardless of their infants' cries, sat motionless, their countenances fixed in high and stern enthusiasm. It was the same church, and we could imagine them to be the same women who, in a frenzy and fury of fanaticism, had dragged the unhappy vice-president by the hair, and murdered him with their hands. Every moment the excitement grew stronger. The priest tore off his black cap, and leaning over the pulpit, stretched forward both his arms, and poured out a frantic apostrophe to the bleeding figure on the cross. A dreadful groan, almost curdling the blood, ran through the church. At this moment, at a signal from the cura, the Indians sprang upon the arbour of pine branches, tore it asunder, and with a noise like the crackling of a great conflagration, struggling and scuffling around the altar, broke into bits the consecrated branches to save as holy relics. Two Indians in broad-brimmed hats mounted the ladders on each side of the cross, and with embroidered cloth over their hands, and large silver pincers, drew out the spikes from the hands. The feelings of the women burst forth in tears, sobs, groans, and shrieks of lamentation, so loud and deep, that, coming upon us unexpectedly, our feelings were disturbed, and even with sane men the empire of reason tottered. Such screams of anguish I never heard called out by mortal suffering; and as the body, smeared with blood, was held aloft under the pulpit, while the priest leaned down and apostrophized it with frantic fervour, and the mass of women, wild with excitement, heaved to and fro like the surges of a troubled sea, the whole scene was so thrilling, so dreadfully mournful, that, without knowing why, tears started from our eyes. Four years before, at Jerusalem, on Mount Calvary itself, and in presence of the scoffing Mussulman, I had beheld the same representation of the descent from the cross; but the enthusiasm of Greek pilgrims in the Church of the Holy Sepulchre was nothing compared with this whirlwind of fanaticism and frenzy.

71. A Scots Woman from Boston in a Convent in Mexico City

Frances Erskine Inglis (1806-1882), more widely known as Fanny Calderón de la Barca, was the Scots-born and Boston-bred wife of the first minister of Spain to the independent republic of Mexico. Of boundless curiosity about and sympathy for all things Mexican, she traveled extensively in Mexico City and its environs between 1839 and 1842, describing them in detailed letters to friends, which were published in book form in two volumes in 1843.

What does Madame Calderón's loving description of this "most splendid and richest convent in Mexico" reveal about the nature of the evolution of Mexican—and Latin American—society since the establishment of New Spain?

Friday: April 24th, 1840
San Fernando, Mexico
The Archbishop has not only granted me permission to visit the convents, but permits me to take two ladies along with me—of which I have been informed by the minister, Señor C—o, in a very amiable note just received. [. . .]

Monday: April 27th, 1840
Accordingly, on Sunday afternoon, we drove to the *Encarnacion*, the most splendid and richest convent in Mexico, excepting perhaps La Concepcion. If it were in any other country I might mention the surpassing beauty of the evening, but as except in the rainy season, which has not yet begun, the evenings are always beautiful, the weather leaves no room for description. The sky always blue, the air always soft, the flowers always blossoming, the birds always singing; Thomson never could have written his *Seasons* here. We descended at the convent gate, were admitted by the portress, and were received by several nuns, their faces closely covered with a double crape veil. We were then led into a spacious hall, hung with handsome lustres, and adorned with various Virgins and Saints magnificently dressed; and here the eldest, a very dignified old lady, lifted her veil, the others following her example, and introduced herself as the *Madre Vicaria*; bringing us many excuses from the old Abbess, who having an inflammation in her eyes, was confined to her cell. She and another reverend mother, and a group of elderly dames, tall, thin, and stately, then proceeded to inform us, that the Archbishop had, in person, given orders for our reception and that they were prepared to show us the whole establishment.

The dress is a long robe of very fine white cassimere, a thick black crape veil, and long rosary. The dress of the novices is the same, only that the veil is white. For the first half-hour or so, I fancied that along with their politeness, was mingled a good deal of restraint, caused perhaps by the pres-

SOURCE: Frances Calderón de la Barca, *Life in Mexico during a Residence of Two Years in That Country* (London: Chapman and Hall, 1843), 114-17.

ence of a foreigner, and especially of an English-woman. My companions they knew well, the Señorita having even passed some months there. However this may have been, the feeling seemed gradually to wear away. Kindness or curiosity triumphed; their questions became unceasing; and before the visit was concluded, I was addressed as "*mi vida*," my life, by the whole establishment. Where was I born? Where had I lived? What convents had I seen? Which did I prefer, the convents in France, or those in Mexico? Which were largest? Which had the best garden? &c., &c. Fortunately, I could, with truth, give the preference to their convent, as to spaciousness and magnificence, over any I ever saw.

The Mexican style of building is peculiarly advantageous for recluses; the great galleries and courts affording them a constant supply of fresh air, while the fountains sound so cheerfully, and the garden in this climate of perpetual spring affords them such a constant source of enjoyment all the year round, that one pities their secluded state much less here than in any other country.

This convent is in fact a palace. The garden, into which they led us first, is kept in good order, with its stone walks, stone benches, and an ever-playing and sparkling fountain. The trees were bending with fruit, and they pulled quantities of the most beautiful flowers for us; sweet peas and roses, with which all gardens here abound, carnations, jasmine, and heliotrope. It was a pretty picture to see them wandering about, or standing in groups in this high-walled garden, while the sun was setting behind the hills, and the noise of the city was completely excluded, everything breathing repose and contentment. Most of the halls in the convent are noble rooms. We visited the whole, from the refectory to the *botica*, and admired the extreme cleanness of everything, especially of the immense kitchen, which seems hallowed from the approach even of a particle of dust; this circumstance is partly accounted for by the fact that each nun has a servant, and some have two; for this is not one of the strictest orders. The convent is rich; each novice at her entrance pays five thousand dollars into the common stock. There are about thirty nuns and ten novices.

The prevailing sin in a convent generally seems to be pride; "the pride that apes humility;" and it is perhaps nearly inseparable from the conventual state. Set apart from the rest of the world, they, from their little world, are too apt to look down with contempt which may be mingled with envy, or modified by pity, but must be unsuited to a true Christian spirit.

The novices were presented to us—poor little entrapped things! who really believe they will be let out at the end of the year if they should grow tired, as if they would ever be permitted to grow tired! The two eldest and most reverend ladies are sisters, thin, tall, and stately, with high noses, and remains of beauty. They have been in the convent since they were eight years old (which is remarkable, as sisters are rarely allowed to profess in the same establishment), and consider *La Encarnacion* as a small piece of heaven upon earth. There were some handsome faces amongst them, and one whose expression and eyes were singularly lovely, but truth to say, these were rather exceptions to the general rule.

Having visited the whole building, and admired one virgin's blue satin and pearls, and another's black velvet and diamonds, sleeping holy infants, saints, paintings, shrines, and confessionals, having even climbed up to the Azotea, which commands a magnificent view, we came at length to a large hall decorated with paintings and furnished with antique high-backed armchairs, where a very elegant supper, lighted up and ornamented, greeted our astonished eyes; cakes, chocolate, ices, creams, custards, tarts, jellies, blancmanges, orange and lemonade, and other profane dainties, ornamented with gilt paper cut into little flags, &c. I was placed in a chair that might have served for a pope under a holy family; the Señora and the Señorita on either side. The elder nuns in stately array, occupied the other armchairs, and looked like statues carved in stone. A young girl, a sort of *pensionnaire*, brought in a little harp without pedals, and while we discussed cakes and ices, sung different ballads with a good deal of taste. The elder nuns helped us to everything, but tasted nothing themselves. The younger nuns and the novices were grouped upon a mat *à la Turque,* and a more picturesque scene altogether one could scarcely see.

The young novices with their white robes, white veils and black eyes, the severe and dignified *madres* with their long dresses and mournful-looking black veils and rosaries, the veiled figures occasionally flitting along the corridor; —ourselves in contrast, with our *worldly* dresses and coloured ribbons; and the great hall lighted by one immense lamp that hung from the ceiling—I felt transported three centuries back, and half afraid that the whole would flit away, and prove a mere vision, a waking dream.

A gossiping old nun, who hospitably filled my plate with everything, gave me the enclosed *flag* cut in gilt paper, which, together with her custards and jellies, looked less unreal. They asked many questions in regard to Spanish affairs, and were not to be consoled for the defeat of Don Carlos,

which they feared would be an end of the true religion in Spain.

After supper we proceeded upstairs to the choir (where the nuns attend public worship, and which looks down upon the handsome convent church) to try the organ. I was set down to a Sonata of Mozart's, the servants blowing the bellows. It seems to me that I made more noise than music, for the organ is very old, perhaps as old as the convent, which dates three centuries back. However, the nuns were pleased, and after they had sung a hymn, we returned below. I was rather sorry to leave them, and felt as if I could have passed some time there very contentedly; but it was near nine o'clock, and we were obliged to take our departure; so having been embraced very cordially by the whole community, we left the hospitable walls of the Encarnacion.

72. Church, State, and Social Welfare in Late-Colonial Cuba

Richard Henry Dana (1815-1882), Harvard graduate, rugged seaman (his classic, Two Years before the Mast, *was published in 1840), lawyer, and Free Soiler, spent several months in Cuba in 1859, which he described in his* To Cuba and Back: A Vacation Voyage. *What can be learned about the nature, health, and practice of Catholicism in this description of a tiny place and moment in the history of the church and the state in late-colonial Cuba?*

While waiting in the sacristy, I saw the robing and unrobing of the officiating priests, the preparation of altar ceremonials by boys and men, and could hear the voices and music in the church, on the other side of the great altar. The manner of the Jesuits is in striking contrast with that at the Cathedral. All is slow, orderly and reverential, whether on the part of men or boys. Instead of the hurried walk, the nod and duck, there is a slow march, a kneeling, or a reverential bow. At a small side altar, in the sacristy, communion is administered by a single priest. Among the recipients are several men of mature years and respectable posi-

tion; and side by side with them, the poor and the negroes. In the Church, there is no distinction of race or color. [...]

The whole floor is left to women. The men gather about the walls and doorways, or sit in the gallery, which is reserved for them. But among the women, though chiefly of rank and wealth, are some who are negroes, usually distinguished by the plain shawl, instead of the veil over the head. The Countess Villanueva, immensely rich, of high rank, and of a name great in the annals of Cuba, but childless, and blind, and a widow, is led in by the hand by her negro servant. The service of the

SOURCE: Richard Henry Dana, Jr., *To Cuba and Back: A Vacation Voyage* (Boston: Ticknor and Fields, 1859), 179-81, 183-85.

altar is performed with dignity and reverence, and the singing, which is by the Jesuit Brothers themselves, is admirable. In the choir I recognized my new friends, the Rector and young Father Cabre, the professor of physics. The "Tantum ergo Sacramentum," which was sung kneeling, brought tears into my eyes, and kept them there. [...]

The Casa de Beneficencia is a large institution, for orphan and destitute children, for infirm old persons, and for the insane. It is admirably situated, bordering on the open sea, with fresh air and very good attention to ventilation in the rooms. It is a government institution, but is placed under charge of the Sisters of Charity, one of whom accompanied us about the building. Though called a government institution, it must not be supposed that it is a charity from the crown. On the contrary, it is supported by a specific appropriation of certain of the taxes and revenues of the island. In the building, is a church not yet finished, large enough for all the inmates, and a quiet little private chapel for the Sisters' devotions, where a burning lamp indicated the presence of the Sacrament on the small altar. I am sorry to have forgotten the number of children. It was large, and included both sexes, with a separate department for each. In a third department, are the insane. They are kindly treated and not confined, except when violent; but the Sister told us they had no medical treatment unless in case of sickness. (Dr. Howe told me that he was also so informed.) The last department is for aged and indigent women.

One of the little orphans clung to the Sister who accompanied us, holding her hand, and nestling in her coarse but clean blue gown; and when we took our leave, and I put a small coin into her little soft hand, her eyes brightened up into a pretty smile.

The number of the Sisters is not full. As none have joined the order from Cuba, (I am told literally none,) they are all from abroad, chiefly from France and Spain; and having acclimation to go through, with exposure to yellow fever and cholera, many of those that come here die in the first or second summer. And yet they still come, in simple, religious fidelity, under the shadow of death.

The Casa de Beneficencia must be pronounced by all, even by those accustomed to the system and order of the best charitable institutions in the world, a credit to the island of Cuba. The charity is large and liberal, and the order and neatness of its administration are beyond praise.

PART XI
Enter Protestantism

By law, colonists in Spanish and Portuguese America could not practice any religion except Catholicism. Amerindians, secret Jews, and Africans who practiced their traditional beliefs risked persecution. Protestant arrivals usually suffered a similar fate. Protestant sailors and merchants who traded their wares in port cities ran the risk of imprisonment and flogging. An Englishman and a Frenchman were burnt at Mexico's first auto-da-fé in 1574. Organized Protestant groups proved to be short lived. For example, France's King Henry III (1574-1589) commissioned Huguenot leader Gaspar de Coligny to establish a colony in Rio de Janeiro in 1557. John Calvin (1509-1564) volunteered more than three hundred settlers, including two ministers, to join this effort, which ultimately failed in 1568 because of Amerindian attacks, harsh weather, and Portuguese resolve. Protestants arrived in 1630 during the Dutch occupation of Brazil, but little or no Protestant influence remained when the Portuguese recaptured Pernambuco in 1654. The only incursion of Protestants into Spanish-controlled areas during the sixteenth century occurred in 1528 when Charles I (1516-1556) ceded control of part of Venezuela to the German financial House of Welser. German Protestants may have accompanied representatives of this banking family, but these merchants never attempted to establish settlements or undertake missionary activities prior to their expulsion in 1556. The seventeenth- and eighteenth-century English colonies of British Honduras (Belize), Jamaica, and Guyana welcomed Protestant missionaries, of course, as did Netherlanders in Dutch Guyana (Suriname).[1]

The independence movements and the growing influence of liberalism in Latin America created opportunities for Protestant merchants and missionaries to trade their wares and introduce their understanding of Christianity in this Catholic stronghold. Free trade among nations necessitated that foreign Protestants temporarily residing in Latin America

---

1. Enrique Dussel, ed., *The Church in Latin America, 1492-1992* (Maryknoll, N.Y.: Orbis Books, 1992), 7; Donald Edward Curry, "Protestantism," in *Encyclopedia of Latin America*, ed. Helen Delpar (New York: McGraw-Hill, 1974), 501.

travel throughout the region without fear of reprisals. As early as 1810, for example, Brazil granted English merchants exemption from the Inquisition and also the right to establish an Anglican church, which was built in Rio de Janeiro in 1819. Mexico extended the same privileges in the 1830s to traders from England, Germany, and the United States. Two British organizations, the British and Foreign Bible Society and the Society for the Propagation of the Gospel, sent colporteurs, or Bible salesmen, to Latin America in the 1820s. Members of "mainline" or "historic" Protestant churches such as Anglicans (Episcopalians in the United States), Presbyterians, Methodists, Lutherans, Baptists, Congregationalists, Waldensians, and Mennonites founded churches and built schools and hospitals. Anglicans built chapels in Argentina in the 1820s, as did the Methodists, Lutherans, and Waldensians by the 1840s. Anglicans sent missionaries to Brazil in the 1830s and were particularly successful along the Misquito coast of Central America, as were the Moravians. Presbyterians evangelized in Brazil, Argentina, and Mexico after 1860. Methodists arrived in Mexico in 1871 and Brazil in 1876. Baptist missionaries arrived in Argentina, Brazil, and Chile in the 1880s. Some Protestant missionaries, such as Allen Francis Gardiner, made extraordinary efforts to preach and convert non-Christian Amerindians in areas largely untouched by Catholic society, though with varying degrees of success. Gardiner and other members of his South American Missionary Society explored regions in Argentina, Chile, and Bolivia. Several Society missionaries died of starvation and exposure; inhabitants of an island near the Tierra del Fuego killed eight others in 1859. As Jean-Pierre Bastian notes, however, Protestantism in Latin America was not simply fomented and imposed by foreigners or perceived as a quick fix by disgruntled Catholic liberals and social Darwinists. "Social actors" in Latin America such as teachers and small landowners resented their perennial poverty, marginalization, and alienation and viewed Protestantism as more responsive to their needs. These "social sectors in transition," states Bastian, found Protestantism "a means for individuating oneself and inculcating democratic practices and values. . . ."[2] Though Protestant congregations flourished, membership in absolute numbers remained low by the end of the nineteenth century. Mexico's 385 Protestant congregations in 1892, for example, represented less than 1 percent of the population.[3]

---

2. Jean-Pierre Bastian, "The Metamorphosis of Latin American Protestant Groups: A Sociohistorical Perspective," *Latin American Research Review* 28, no. 2 (1993): 38; Kenneth Scott Latourette, *The Great Century in the Americas, Austral-Asia, and Africa, AD 1800-AD 1914,* vol. 5, *A History of the Expansion of Christianity* (New York: Harper & Brothers, 1943), 105.

3. Jean-Pierre Bastian, "Protestantism," in *Encyclopedia of Mexico: History, Society & Culture,* vol. 2, ed. Michael S. Werner (Chicago and London: Fitzroy Dearborn Publishers, 1997), 1197; Latourette, *Great Century in the Americas,* 102-3; Virginia Garrard-Burnett, "Protestantism," in *Encyclopedia of Latin American History and Culture,* vol. 4, ed. Barbara A. Tenenbaum (New York: Charles Scribner's Sons, 1996), 475-76; Curry, "Protestantism," 501; Dussel, *Church in Latin America,* 12; Colin M. MacLachlan and William H. Beezley, *El Gran Pueblo: A History of Greater Mexico* (Upper Saddle River, NJ: Prentice Hall, 1999), 176.

73. Mission: Reconnaissance

John Clark Brigham (1794-1862), a young Protestant missionary from the United States, traveled through Mexico and South America in 1824-1825 to determine prospects for missionary activity there. His report concentrates on each newly independent republic's relation with the church, the quality of the clergy, and the religious practices of the common people.

The South American colonies won their independence from Spain between 1810 (Argentina) and 1825 (Bolivia). Brigham's observations are made toward the end of this heady period when liberal ideas seem to be in the ascendancy.

Is his description of the nature of South American Catholicism biased, as might be expected of a U.S. Protestant missionary, or are his observations restrained, contextual, and sympathetic? Does he see liberal and anticlerical attitudes becoming dominant, though he is aware that class determines these attitudes? What does his final recommendation reveal about Brigham, South American elites, and the populace?

In placing their religious condition before you, it will be well, perhaps, that I first give a concise view of the state of the church, and its connection with government, in each of the Republics separately; and afterwards describe some of the religious practices and ceremonies common to their churches generally.

Taking the places in the order, in which I visited them, the first to be noticed is

Buenos Ayres

That country has been free from the Spanish yoke for more than fifteen years, and has, on this account, been more enlightened and liberal than any of the sister nations. The bishop, who was formerly placed over them, being attached to the Royal cause, as the South American bishops generally were, left, at the time of the revolution, for the mother country. The secular clergy then assembled, (some of whom were able and patriotic,) formed an ecclesiastical council, elected one of their own number to act in place of bishop, and who, with the council, still continues to manage the spiritual affairs of the church.

The tithes, which were formerly controlled by the Viceroy, now come under direction of the new government, and are annually divided, in part, among the 18 or 20 canons and other dignitaries of the cathedral, a part given to the thirty or forty curates of the different parishes, a part to the public schools, and the remainder used for political purposes.

As the secular clergy are not very numerous, and are always men of public education, and live in their own private houses, the government still continues to pay them from the tithes a competent salary.

But the regular clergy, the cloistered monks of all classes, have met with a different fate. Their houses, lands, and funds at interest, have all been seized by the new government, and they secularized, or persecuted, till none of their six or seven orders yet remain together, except that of St. Francis, and this under a threat of dissolution, when their present number, twenty-eight, is reduced to less than eighteen. The spacious convents of St. Dominic, of Mercy, the Recoleta, and several others, are now converted into hospitals, barracks, and other secular uses, and their few scattered for-

SOURCE: John C. Brigham, "Mr. Brigham's Report Respecting the Religious State of Spanish America: To the Prudential Committee of the American Board of Commissioners for Foreign Missions," *The Missionary Herald* 22, no. 10 (October 1826): 298-99; John C. Brigham, "Mr. Brigham's Report Respecting the Religious State of Spanish America," *The Missionary Herald* 22, no. 11 (November 1826): 337-41.

mer occupants paid but a mere pittance from their old funds. Enough is intended to be given them to prevent suffering, but not enough to afford any temptation for more to assume the monastic habit.

Two houses of nuns, or religious women, still continue there, though the one has now but twenty-two inmates, the other but half that number.

In some of the interior provinces of Buenos Ayres, the church funds have also been seized by the local governments, in others, they are threatened; and in all the number of devotees of both sexes is fast diminishing, and their influence still faster. In almost every circle where you go, monks and nuns, among all classes, have become objects of ridicule.

Chili

Passing over the mountains to the republic of Chili, you find the same state of things in regard to the church, as in Buenos Ayres, only not in so advanced a state, as they have there been a shorter period free from Spanish blindness and oppression. The secular clergy, there about as numerous as in Buenos Ayres, are paid an annual salary from the tithe fund, though only about a fourth part of its former amount.

The government, too, have diminished the number of feast days to eleven, about one sixth of their former number; they have ventured also, the last year, to expatriate their seditious monarchical bishop; and to send back a special envoy from the Pope, who proved to be a political intriguer. A law, too, is enacted for seizing the funds of the convents, though from the great number of existing monasteries, and the feebleness of the new government, it has been thought prudent, as yet, not to put that law in execution. There are yet in the central province of Chili, that of *Santiago*, no less than six houses of monks, and seven of nuns, containing from twelve to a hundred and twelve inmates. These houses, too, are unusually wealthy. Many of the most valuable estates in the country are theirs, and it is thought that, for loaned money, they have claims, to a greater or less amount, on nearly one half of the dwelling houses

in the capital. As you may perhaps wish to inquire how these establishments became so wealthy, I will remark, in passing, that they became so from the funds, which the devotees brought with them, and placed in common stock, at the time of taking the habit; and also from numerous donations, in former times, from superstitious misers, who could not, or *might* not, die in peace, without bequeathing something to the church.

The threatening of these church possessions has given a deathblow to the monasticism of Chili, although it may long continue to struggle before it entirely expires. Formerly, the convents were crowded with youth and children, training for the service of the altar; now, you scarcely see one within their walls below the middle age, and generally they are much above that period.

These regular orders, moreover, are now confined almost entirely to the central province of that country. In the south province, that of *Concepción*, their spacious and costly houses yet stand, but not a monk is found within them. They are all desolate. Their former tenants have died with grief, or fallen in opposing the revolution, or fled to the old world where the evils of liberty cannot molest them.

One nunnery of twenty-eight women still continues, but it is poor, and is all that remains of the many religious establishments, which were once the pride and the terror of Conception.

In the north province, that of *Coquimbo*, other religious houses are yet standing, some of them built in the best style, by the Jesuits, before their expulsion. But these houses are now all empty, or used for schools, hospitals, and other purposes of government. Not a monk, or nun, is found in the place, and the services of the church are performed wholly by the secular clergy. [. . .]

Go into one of those dark temples at the time of vespers; see a few feeble lamps on the far distant altar, throwing their pale rays on the image of a bleeding Saviour, and the long rows of apostles and martyrs; see the numerous paintings of saints and angels staring from every column, and looking down from the high arches above; hear the deep slow tones of an unseen organ, mingled with the mournful prayers of an aged monk, in a tongue long since dead;—and you have at once the feelings, which they mistake for the purest devotion.

When the mass is ended, the congregation retire, each dipping his hand in the vase of holy water at the door, and crossing himself. On reaching their dwellings, which, on feast days, is generally before the hour of breakfast, the black dress of the church is exchanged for one the most showy and extravagant, and they are prepared for visiting the coffee house, the promenade, the cockpit, the bull fights, or for a drive in the country, as fancy may suggest, and in the evening they go to the theatre. Thus passes the Sabbath throughout Spanish America, both with the priest and the people, and at night they lie down, thinking that they have served God faithfully in the morning, and afterwards had much innocent enjoyment.

With all their numerous ecclesiastics, preaching is seldom heard among them, unless during the forty days of Lent, and on the anniversary days of some distinguished saints.

The season of Lent is with them the solemn season. Throughout this period, the theatre is closed, most of their diversions suspended, and some are seen going about the streets with a cross of ashes on their foreheads to remind them of their mortality. If they have obtained no indulgence, they are, too, through this period, to abstain from animal food, and in the course of it, to make their annual confession to the priest. Sermons are now delivered in some of the churches every day, and during the last three of the forty, when they suppose the Saviour lay in the tomb, they are clothed in black, all business is stopped, the streets are empty and still, and silence and gloom pervade every object.

At the close of the third day, the tomb is burst, the Saviour rises, the bells begin to ring, guns are discharged, and rockets, rising from every quarter, seem to fill the air. In the evening, images of Judas are brought out, and publicly hung in the streets, beaten and stoned by the boys, and all their mourning is turned into joy. Now they begin again their suspended pleasures, all exulting that the days of Lent are over.

As I have said, they observe, also, as feast days the anniversaries of some distinguished saints. Formerly these were far more numerous than the Sabbaths, but are now reduced in most places to eleven or twelve.

On the anniversary day of any particular saint, for instance, that of St. Agustin, his image is brought out from the convent bearing his name, clothed in the habit of that order, is placed erect on something resembling a bier, and thus bourne on the shoulders of men through the streets. Following this image, is an immense concourse of people, the high clergy in robes of white satin and gold lace, the lower clergy in black, the various orders of monks in their peculiar habits, a train of youth in scarlet, bearing a tall silver cross and censer, then a retinue of laity with burning candles—a full band of music, playing the while, and priests singing hymns in Latin.

In one part of the procession, is carried also, under a silk canopy, the sacred wafer, or host, which represents the Deity. In another part is sometimes borne the Virgin Mary, clothed in the manner of the richest princess, with numerous jewels, and a crown of gold.

In some places I have seen carried four or five images of the same saint, exhibiting him at different periods of his life. The first which passed represented him as an infant with its mother, the next as a gay thoughtless youth, the next as a penitent, then he passes by as a priest in his robes, and lastly as a canonized saint with a crown of silver.

In the festivals of the patron saints (the supposed local guardians or protectors,) that of St. Martín, at Buenos Ayres, St. Rosa, at Lima, and St. Gaudeloupe, at Mexico, the public authorities on foot, with their six mule coaches trailing empty behind, also join the procession, attended by several regiments of infantry and mounted cavalry in full uniform. At this time the streets, where the procession passes, are hung with flags, cloths of crimson velvet, paintings, mirrors, and various other ornaments; all the bells are ringing, cannon roaring, and rockets bursting in every direction.

I almost fear that you will think this picture, looking at it on paper, exaggerated; but you can be assured that it conveys no full idea of those gorgeous processions, so common in Spanish America.

But what, you may well say, has all this to do with the religion of the heart? How can the splendid bauble think to please that infinite God, who declares he "is a Spirit, and that those who worship him must worship him in spirit and in truth?"

It is indeed a mystery, how the simple religion of Christ, the most simple of all systems, was ever transformed into such an unmeaning show. But through pride and wealth it has undergone changes, until Christianity with them, has become nothing but a system of outward forms, without connexion with the feelings or general conduct. A religious man is made to signify a practical observer of ceremonies, let his life in other respects be what it may.

Having few or no Bibles to go to for correction, they seem to have lost sight, not only of the nature of spiritual worship, but of the proper method of gaining divine assistance. If they are in danger, or distress, the idea of penitence, submission, and future obedience, seem never to be thought of, but the grand inquiry is, what sacrifice can be made to obtain relief?

The dying miser, if conscious of guilt, bequeaths a sum to the church; the lady of rank, if sick, will vow, that if restored, she will wear a garment of sackcloth for half a year; the gay youth for restoration, will promise, perhaps, that she will as long a time abstain from dancing, or going to the theatre. Sometimes when exposed to sudden danger, or in times of earthquakes, they will apply tortures to their arms or feet, and place a crown of thorns on their heads. Some will fall down on the ground, beating their breasts, and calling on saints; others go through the streets, bearing a huge cross, and confessing their sins aloud.

I would not be understood as saying, that these are daily occurrences, or are practiced by all persons; still they are practices, which do exist in almost every place, and to a great extent, and show us, how totally the nature of the Christian system is mistaken and abused. [. . .]

I might also describe their marriage ceremonies, the baptism of their infants, and their funeral solemnities, if solemnities they can be called; but enough is already said, to show you their general religious character, and lead you, I trust, to pity their condition.

After this long history of abuses, which the dark ages originated, and Spanish tyranny has perpetu-

ated, you will wish, probably, to ask whether there is no prospect, under their new governments, that these abuses will be corrected. I answer, there is a *Prospect of Correction*, although its progress must be gradual.

A wise observer of society has remarked, "that a strictly Roman Catholic religion, and a free civil government could never long exist together."

The wide difference which is found between the character of this religion, as it exists in our country, and that which it exhibits in monarchical countries, goes to confirm the truth of the remark quoted, and to give us pleasing hopes as to our new sister republics at the south. Indeed the change this system has undergone in those republics themselves, since their emancipation, and the great reforming principles, which are now at work, go to show, that, in the footsteps of their liberties, a religious reformation must follow. [. . .]

One, who watches the signs of the times, may see, too, that causes are beginning to operate, which must make the secular clergy truly tolerant, or deprive them both of their influence and their living. The government in all those places are themselves disposed to be liberal. I do not believe that one man in ten, in civil authority, would now oppose a perfect toleration of religion, if the common people were thought prepared for such an event. [. . .]

Think, for a moment, how their character has already been changed since the Revolution, not so much in their little religious ceremonies, as in the great principles of action.

Their inquisitions are now changed into school-houses, and the peaceful halls of legislation; the number of feast days is diminished; the practice of selling indulgences stopped; the wealth and power of the priesthood lessened; in one country there is already a free religious toleration, and in all, Protestants live and die undisturbed; the Scriptures too are now freely circulated; and in some instances their children are instructed by Protestant teachers.

Protestant Preachers not yet Admissible

The question might be suggested, for it is often asked, whether Protestant preachers could not now be usefully sent to those countries.

The answer is, that they could not at present. Such a measure, in most places, would be opposed, as yet, to articles of their constitution, and would create such excitement among the lower orders, that the most liberal enlightened statesmen would discourage it.

Although there are many individuals in South America, who have noble and expanded views on all subjects, men who are up with the spirit of the age, still there is in that field a putrid mass of superstition, on which the sun of liberty must shine still longer before we can safely enter in and labor.

In a few places, a Protestant preacher could labor profitably among foreigners collected there, and by private intercourse, if judicious, be widely useful to those of the country. But these places are yet few; as are those where one could be successful in procuring a school; and those are mostly occupied.

We must wait patiently a little longer, till the Ruler of nations, who has wrought such wonders in those countries the last ten years, shall open still wider the way, and bid us go forward.

74. Distributing the Bible

James Thomson, the first Scottish Baptist missionary to arrive in South America, was sent by his church in 1818 as representative of the British Foreign School Society for the purpose of setting up schools to teach reading and writing and to circulate the scriptures.

How does Thomson's experience compare with Brigham's? What is the significance of the enthusiastic commitment of General José de San Martín, the liberator of Peru, to support Thomson and his program? Why introduce the "Scriptures . . . by stealth"?

Santiago de Chile, 8th October, 1821

I wrote you a few lines on the 26th February, and then mentioned that it was my intention to visit Chile. Through the gracious providence of the God of the Bible Society, I have now effected my intention. I left Buenos Aires on the 30th May, and sailing round Cape Horn, arrived safely at Valparaiso, after a voyage of forty-four days. [. . .]

In getting my luggage through the customhouse, I was told, that the books must be inspected by the Bishop. I wished this might be dispensed with, but it was insisted on. I then told the officers, that I was engaged to come here by the Government to establish the Lancasterian schools. That alters the case, said they, and immediately the papers for despatching my books, &c. were signed, and not a single book was so much as looked at either by the Bishop, or by any of the custom-house officers. I was told, before coming here, that there was much less liberality in Chile, as to the circulation of the Scriptures, than in

Buenos Aires. I was, therefore, anxious to avoid the inspection of the Bishop above noticed. I understand he has it in his power to prohibit what books he chooses, and that his prohibition holds, unless the Government give, in the individual case, an order to the contrary. [. . .]

Notwithstanding what I have said above, no interruption to the circulation of the Spanish New Testament has yet been experienced. Soon after my arrival, I gave to an Englishman, who has a shop here, some copies to sell. This man is a Roman Catholic, and I am happy to say, he recommends the Scriptures to the natives of this country, who are of his own religion. He has already sold about twenty. [. . .]

I consider the word of God to have fairly got an entrance into Buenos Aires; and that its prohibition, or any material hindrance to its circulation, is not only unlikely, but, one might say, impossible. I give you this as my opinion, after a residence in that place of more than two years and a half,

SOURCE: James Thomson, *Letters on the Moral and Religious State of South America Written during a Residence of Nearly Seven Years in Buenos Aires, Chile, Peru, and Colombia* (London: James Nisbet, 1827), 34-37, 111, 114-19, 122.

and an intercourse with various classes of society during that time.

I shall now mention some things not formerly noticed, regarding the circulation of the Scriptures in Buenos Aires, and in the surrounding country. A military officer, commanding on a station a short distance from the city, has been greatly delighted with the New Testament, and in consequence, very anxious to make others acquainted with it. He recommended the reading of it to several poor people who were unable to purchase it, and requested to have copies to give them, which he obtained. In this way he has distributed a number of copies. Besides those given to the poor, some have been sold by him to those able to pay for them. [. . .]

A Patagonian chief, called Cualli Piachepolon, in the very centre of Patagonia, is in possession of one of your Testaments. This man has been in the habit of visiting Buenos Aires for some years, in order to exchange the few commodities which his country at present produces, for those of Europe. He has hence acquired some knowledge of the Spanish language. Upon hearing some passages of the New Testament read to him, he requested to have the book, that he might, on his return, explain it to his people.

Should the Lord spare me ten or twenty years, I have no doubt I shall see wonderful and blessed changes on this continent. It is my intention, through the grace of our Lord Jesus Christ, to spend my life (long or short as it may be) in South America; probably not in any fixed place, but residing from time to time wherever I may most effectually promote the work of the Lord, in establishing schools, in circulating the Scriptures, and in the use of such other means as circumstances may direct.

On the day on which I arrived in this city, I called on San Martín, and delivered him the letters of introduction which I had brought from Chile. He opened one of the letters, and observing its purport, said, "Mr. Thomson! I am extremely glad to see you;" and he rose up, and gave me a very hearty embrace. He would not, he said, be lavish in compliments, but would assure me of great satisfaction at my arrival; and said, that nothing should be wanting on his part to further the object

which had brought me to Peru. Next day as I was sitting in my room, a carriage stopped at the door, and my little boy came running in crying, San Martín! San Martín! In a moment he entered the room, accompanied by one of his ministers. I would have had him step into another apartment of the house more suited to his reception; but he said the room was very well, and sat down on the first chair he reached. We conversed about our schools, and other similar objects for some time; and in going away he desired me to call on him next morning, and said he would introduce me to the Marquis of Truxillo, who is at present what is called the Supreme Deputy or Regent. I called on him accordingly next morning, and he took me with him and introduced me to the Marquis, and to each of the ministers.

From all the members of the government I have received great encouragement. On the 6th current an order was issued relative to our schools, and published in the Lima Gazette of the same date. [. . .]

By this order one of the convents is appropriated to the schools, and is now in our possession. I believe the convents here will decrease in number as the schools multiply. There is no contest or balancing of powers between the civil and ecclesiastical powers in this place. The former has the latter entirely at their nod. The case in regard to this convent is a proof of what I have said. The order for the friars to remove was given on Saturday, on Monday they began to remove, and on Tuesday the keys were delivered up. [. . .]

What an immeasurable field is South America; and how white it is to the harvest! I have told you this repeatedly, but I have a pleasure in telling it to you again. I do think that, since the world began, there never was so fine a field for the exercise of benevolence in all its parts. The man of science, the moralist, the christian, have all fine scope here for their talents. God, who has opened such a door, will surely provide labourers. [. . .]

I have said that we have got the New Testament introduced into our school *undisguised*. You probably perceive what I mean by using the word undisguised. The truth is, the New Testament, in one sense, has all along been used in our schools in South America, not however in the open manner we now use it in Lima, but, as I may say, disguised; that is, we have used for lessons extracts from it, printed on large sheets, and in little books, thus introducing the Scriptures as it were by stealth. Each part of these lessons I cause to be read repeatedly in the classes, until the children can read them readily. By the time they can do so, the substance of what they have read, and the instruction contained in it, is tolerably imprinted on the memory. Children, you know, have a habit of repeating to themselves what they have been saying or reading frequently. In consequence of this, what portions of Scripture they have read in the school, they repeat in this way at home.

75. A Presbyterian Botanist in the Wilds of Colombia

Isaac Farwell Holton (1812-1874), graduate of Amherst (B.A., M.A.), licensed Presbyterian churchman and professor of botany from 1848 to 1852, spent two years in Colombia, 1852-1854, taking 1,800 botanical specimens back with him on his return to the United States. His acute observations and commentary make his New Grenada: Twenty Months in the Andes *(1857) a major source for understanding life in mid-nineteenth-century Colombia.*

Does Holton's Presbyterian wit prevent the reader from attaining an objective insight into the state of the mid-nineteenth-century church, clergy, Catholic practice, and class and race in the remote Cauca valley of Colombia?

On Saturday night the bells of the chapel rung a little—just enough to say that there would be mass in the morning. The good Cura leaves San Vicente occasionally for a day, and comes and spends the Sabbath with us; and well he might, for more than half his salary comes from this hacienda. I went to church in the morning as I always do when I have the opportunity. Well, in the first place, we had one baptism and two fractions: that is, two of the babes had received just enough baptism to save them from hell had they died before this time, but not enough for decency.

The priest met the unbaptized at the door of mercy, or side door of the church. One assistant held a little plain wooden cross, and another a lighted candle. After the prayers he put salt in the babe's mouth, and went to the font, an excavated stone, on a pedestal, with a hole for the water to run off. Here awaited the other two babes. One was held on the *left* arm. "Put the head *there*," said the priest. The woman turned herself, so as to bring the head to the required spot; the feet of the babe were more out of their place than ever. An exclamation of impatience from the fasting Cura led an assistant to aid in placing the babe on the

right arm. [. . .] The dress of one [of the babes] tried the Cura's patience again. He exclaimed, amid his prayers, "Better bring your babe naked than with a dress tight at the neck." I held it away with two fingers as well as I could. Then the babe's head was held over the font, face downward [. . .] These prayers would occupy a Protestant clergyman about two hours, but our curate dispatched them very soon. If he skipped a word, or pronounced it wrong, he left it for next time.

He went back to the vestry, put on different robes, and, again accompanied by the cross and candle, met a marriage party at the door of mercy. These were more awkward than the mothers. First, the groomsman, who happened to be the husband of the bridesmaid, placed himself next the bride. The bridegroom tried to insinuate himself between the bride and bridesmaid, apparently intending to be married to one of them at least. When the parties were placed aright, the priest read them a long address, telling them, among other things, that it was their duty to endeavor to raise up heirs, not so much to their goods as to their religion, their faith, and their virtue. The bride, though never married before, need not

SOURCE: Isaac F. Holton, *New Granada: Twenty Months in the Andes* (New York: Harper & Brothers, 1857), 180, 184, 477-79.

excite his anxiety on that point. Not only were two of her children witnesses of the ceremony, but, besides, she was visibly in a state which is here designated by the word *embarazada* [pregnant]. I am aware that this detracts materially from the poetry of my picture, but I cannot help it; the sole merit of my sketch is its fidelity. I must add, then, that the older of her two children appeared to be three fourths black, and the younger three fourths white. The mother was a mulata, the other three adults of pure African blood. All were barefoot; the females wore that plain dress which alone is permitted to rich or poor in church—the head covered with a shawl, the body with a dark-colored skirt (saya). [. . .]

Many intelligent persons are but little acquainted with the Romish religion. We propose to take a view of it as observers, not as theologians. It shall be by a candid statement of facts without comments, which here would be out of place; and if the reader charge me with irreverence, my plea is that I find no reverence among the faithful here, and the less can therefore be expected in me. [. . .]

I have said nothing of confession. It is a rare practice, and I have never seen it but once, although I have been in Bogotá at a time of year when the most confess. Few, indeed, of the more intelligent class ever confess, and, of course, these cannot commune, neither do they fast. In fact, religion is in a great degree obsolete, especially with men. There is nothing to captivate the senses,

no splendor, no imposing spectacles in the richest of their churches. It is simply ridiculous, like a boy's training with sticks for guns. [. . .]

Mass over, every one is at liberty to amuse himself as he pleases, for Sunday is a holiday, and it is a sin to work more than two hours, but no sin to play. At night I found that an extraordinary activity had prevailed in the kitchen; fresh pork and chicken appeared on the dinner-table, and a bottle of aguardiente. At the head sat the Cura, and a vacant space opposite me was at length filled by the four who had figured so conspicuously in the morning. I was not prepared for this. If I must eat with negroes, I will do it with a good grace, but I could well have spared the company of an "*embarazada*" bride. During the dinner we had the music of two octave flutes and a drum.

This was ominous of the evening; in short, bad as was the weather, we had a ball. When I went for my chocolate, I found the good Cura, with his gown tucked up, dancing the bambuco with unusual grace with one of the nymphs of the pastures. As I was making my retreat, young Carlos, about 16, was waltzing with an aged manumitted slave that had been his nurse, and that of all his brothers and sisters before him. Later in the night was a scene yet more curious, as I am told. The pretty little Mercedes, of 17, the white man's daughter, waltzed with the negro blacksmith, Miguel. He appears over 70, is very tall, very grim, and is the most pious man on the plantation.

76. Protestant Missionaries in Catholic Brazil

Presbyterian D. P. Kidder (1815-1891) and Methodist J. P. Fletcher (1823-1901) were U.S. missionaries and indefatigable travelers in mid-nineteenth-century Brazil when that nation was under the aegis of Emperor Pedro II (1831-1889), freemason and liberal. Fletcher traveled two thousand miles up the Amazon in 1862 collecting rare objects in natural history for the great American naturalist Louis Agassiz. Together, Kidder and Fletcher spent a total of eight years in Brazil. Their enormously popular Brazil and the Brazilians Portrayed in Historical and Descriptive Sketches *reached its seventh edition in 1867. Keeping in mind the enthusiastic progressive Protestantism of the two missionaries, what does their account reveal about the institutional Catholic Church, clergy, and laity of the era?*

SOURCE: James Fletcher and D. P. Kidder, *Brazil and the Brazilians Portrayed in Historical and Descriptive Sketches*, 7th ed. (Boston: Little, Brown, and Company, 1867; reprint New York: AMS Press, 1973), 140-44, 146-47, 150, 153-54 n. 160.

Brazil is in every respect the superior State of South America just so far as she has abandoned the exclusiveness of Romanism. Since the Independence, the priest-power has been broken, and the potent hierarchy of Rome does not rule over the consciences and acts of men as in Chili or Mexico. On numerous occasions, measures have been taken in the Assemblea Geral to curtail the assumptions of the triple-crowned priest of the Eternal City; and once, at least, it was proposed to render the Brazilian Church independent of the Holy See. [...]

In Brazil, however, other than political views must be taken of the present freedom from bigotry. The priests, to some extent, owe the loss of their power to their shameful immorality. There is no class of men in the whole Empire whose lives and practices are so corrupt as those of the priesthood. It is notorious. The *Relatórios* (messages) of the Minister of Justice and the Provincial Presidents annually allude to this state of things. Every newspaper from time to time contains articles to this effect; every man, whether high or low, speaks his sentiments most unreservedly on this point; no traveler, whether Romanist or Protestant, can shut his eye to the glaring facts. In every part of Brazil that I have visited I have heard, from the mouths of the ignorant as well as from the lips of the educated, the same sad tale; and, what is worse, in many places the priests openly avow their shame. Dr. Gardner, the naturalist, lived in Brazil from 1836 to '41, and the greater part of that time in the interior, where foreigners are very rarely found. In speaking of the banishment of the laborious and indefatigable Jesuits, whose lives in this portion of America were without reproach, this distinguished botanist says, "What different men they must have been from the degraded race who now undertake the spiritual welfare of this nation! It is a hard thing to say, but I do it not without well considering the nature of the assertion, that *the present clergy of Brazil are more debased and immoral than any other class of men.*"

Though we should lament immorality in any man or class of men, yet the combination of circumstances mentioned has had its effect in rendering the people, as well as the Government, tolerant.

A few years ago, Monsignor Bedini (Archbishop of Thebes, and late Pope's Legate in the United States and in other *partibus infidelium*) was the Nuncio of Pius IX at the Court of Brazil. In July, 1846, the nuncio went to the mountain-city of Petropolis, (about forty miles from Rio), where are many German Protestants, who have a chapel of their own, which, as well as the chapels in other colonies, is protected under the broad shield of the Constitution, and receives a portion of its support directly from the Government. There had been certain mixed marriages; and Monsignor preached a furious sermon, in which he declared that all Romanists so allied were living in concubinage,—their marriages were void, and their children illegitimate. A storm of indignation, both at Petropolis and Rio, fell upon the head of the nuncio, whose arrival in Brazil had been preceded by the rumor of an assurance to the Pope that he would bind this Empire "faster than ever to the chair of St. Peter." The *Diário do Rio de Janeiro*, a conservative journal always considered the *quasi* organ of the Government, denounced M. Bedini in firm but respectful language, and insisted that it was the highest imprudence thus to kindle the fires of religious intolerance. Its columns contained sentiments in regard to this subject of which the following is a specimen:— "Propositions like those emitted from the Chair of Truth by a priest of the character of M. Bedini are eminently censurable."

The nuncio was put down, but not until one of his friends published what were probably the sentiments of Monsignor, in which he complains of the Emperor for "not taking sides in the controversy and using his influence to prevent the spread of Protestant heresies."

There is no country in South America where the philanthropist and the Christian have a freer scope for doing good than Brazil. So far from its being true that a Protestant clergyman is always *tabooed*, and that the people "entertain a feeling toward him bordering on contempt,"—as one writer on Brazil has expressed it,—I can testify to the strongest friendship formed with Brazilians in various portions of the Empire,—a friendship which did not become weakened by the contact of years or by the plain manifestations and defense of my belief; and I can subscribe to the remark put forth by my colleague in 1845, when he says,—

"It is my firm conviction that there is not a Roman Catholic country on the globe where there prevails a greater degree of toleration or a greater liberality of feeling toward Protestants.

"I will here state, that in all my residence and travels in Brazil in the character of a Protestant missionary, I never received the slightest opposition or indignity from the people. As might have been expected, a few of the priests made all the opposition they could; but the circumstance that these were unable to excite the people showed how little influence they possessed. On the other hand, perhaps quite as many of the clergy, and those of the most respectable in the Empire, manifested toward us and our work both favor and friendship.

"From them, as well as from the intelligent laity, did we often hear the severest reprehension of abuses that were tolerated in the religious system and practices of the country, and sincere regrets that no more spirituality pervaded the public mind."

To one who looks alone at the empty and showy rites of the Roman Catholic Church in Brazil, there is no future for the country. But when we consider the liberal and tolerant sentiments that prevail,—when we reflect upon the freedom of debate, the entire liberty of the press, the diffusion of instruction, and the workings of their admirable Constitution,—we cannot believe that future generations of Brazilians will retrograde. [. . .]

It is particularly observable that all the religious celebrations are deemed interesting and important in proportion to the pomp and splendor which they display. The desirableness of having all possible show and parade is generally the crowning argument urged in all applications for Government patronage, and in all appeals designed to secure the attendance and liberality of the people.

The daily press of Rio de Janeiro must annually reap enormous sums for religious advertisements, of which I give one or two specimens. [. . .]

The following is the advertisement of a *festa* up the bay, at Estrella, and is as clumsily put together in Portuguese as it appears in the literal English translation which I have given:—

"The Judge and some devout persons of the Church of Our Lady of Estrella, erected in the village of the same name, intend to hold a festival there, with a chanted mass, sermon, procession in the afternoon, and a *Te Deum*, — all with the greatest pomp possible, — on the 23d instant; and at night there will be a beautiful display of fireworks. [. . .]

Note for 1866.—There are several native Protestant churches now in Brazil. The regularly ordained pastors of these churches are legally authorized to perform the marriage ceremony. The clause of the constitution in regard to religious toleration has been fully tested on three different occasions, and is shown to be a "living letter."—The *Imprensa Evangélica* is the bimonthly religious journal of the Protestants at Rio, and is reasonably successful. Several faithful preachers of the gospel from Europe and North America are now laboring with encouraging success. In Appendix I will be found a remarkable article from the Roman Catholic editor of the "Anglo-Brazilian Times," on the necessity of removing from Brazilian law disabilities in regard to civil and mixed marriages, and to Protestant representation in Parliament.

77. No Protestant Temples Here

The following letter (1864) from the archbishop of Lima to the Peruvian minister of justice and worship is a wonderful example of the position on the Protestant presence taken by the

SOURCE: José Sebastián, "To Mr. Minister of Justice and Worship," *South American Missionary Magazine* 1 (July 1, 1867): 97-100. Reprinted by permission of Brown University Library.

most traditionalist members of the Catholic hierarchy in Latin America, and of the Vatican itself. Pope Pius IX (1846-1878), for example, would be in complete accord with José Sebastián's position. Is the archbishop's rationale theological or political?

Archiepiscopal Palace, Lima, 29th September, 1864. To Mr. Minister of Justice and Worship.

Mr. MINISTER—

I transmit to you the letter (of the 12th inst.) which the Vicar of Callao has addressed to me informing me of the building of a Protestant Temple and School which are soon to be opened in that city.

The work appears sufficiently advanced, and its originators doubtless pretend to ridicule our worship and show the want of respect which they have to our Constitution and the laws of our country.

I will not stop to offer any remarks on the fundamental principles of which the 4th Article of our Constitution is a corollary. God alone can prescribe the worship with which He seeks to be adored, to Him alone it is directed, and He alone can command it. Since we recognize the Catholic faith as the only true one, it is deduced by legitimate consequences that the exercise of the Catholic worship is that alone which can be offered to the Divinity. Our legislators had considered these principles well, and established in all our political institutions, that the religion of the Peruvian nation was the Catholic, Apostolic, Roman, without permitting the public exercise of any other.

But, laying aside reasons so palpable, it is sufficient to consider that the diversity of worship destroys in a nation the unity of thought, of traditions, and of customs, in which national power principally consists. The toleration of different forms of worship is not an advantage in politics, but an inconvenience, or rather an infirmity, which affects nations whose religious opinions are divided.

Religious toleration is only granted in nations where the dissidents from the established religion are numerous, and form a considerable part of that great family called a nation. Then the evil, which divides the worship and the religious opinions, is tolerated, to avoid a greater one, viz., that a

great number of individuals be in want of a worship and of rules of morality which may guide their conduct. In that case, it is better that a people should have some worship, however mutilated, which may preserve some notions of revelation, and of morality purified by the Gospel.

But the Peruvian nation is not in this condition. The people, without an exception, is Catholic. There does not exist the lamentable germ of religious discord. Perhaps all are not members of the Church, as they ought to be; perhaps there are men who have scarcely the smallest tincture of religion; there may be others in whom the corruption of manners has blotted out the religious feeling which is innate in man, which grows and becomes strengthened by education. But the existence of such persons is not a sufficient reason why our laws should be infringed, or our Constitution changed. Those persons, if not good Catholics, will not be Protestants. Their tendency is to have no religion, to renounce all forms of worship, and in short to forget the Divinity. For those toleration is an absurdity, and any worship whatever is an act of fanaticism. With their manners and theories they undermine the fundamental laws of society, of the family, and of the individual, and, consequently, for such as these we should not infringe the laws which we obey in this matter.

Unity, Mr. Minister, in matters of doctrine, religious or political, is a great blessing to nations; all try to obtain it by means of laws, more or less repressive, each one according to the special circumstances and conditions in which it is found. When there is unity in a nation, its thoughts are noble, its force compact, and its action vigorous.

Religious unity produces great effects. It is the germ of charity; it is the principle of love, pure and disinterested, towards our country and our fellow-beings. The religious man works conscientiously, and not for individual interest or base designs.

To permit then, that the public exercise of a new religion be established in a land which has preserved the benefit of its unity, is to sow the seed of discord in our country, and reap, at a future period, too bitter fruits. [...]

It is no answer to say that there is a considerable number of Protestant residents in Callao. These persons have come to our country to make a fortune, and that once acquired they bring their wealth to their own country. This resolution does not arise from the want of religious toleration; it proceeds from the innate love which everyone bears to the land of his birth, acquired in early years, and which is never forgotten; also from a regard to the higher grade of civilization which the European nations have reached, and the greater means of enjoyment which the man of fortune can obtain there. Those, then, who come to Peru to acquire wealth, ought, in compensation, to subject themselves to our laws, and treat them with respect.

Governments are obliged to satisfy the requirements of their subjects; but not to agree to the capricious wishes of anyone whose country is situated in another hemisphere. However great and inviolable the rights of hospitality may be, a foreigner has no right to demand that a people should deny its faith, habits and traditions, violate its own laws, and alter its national character. Neither England, nor any other nation, knowing their true interests, would permit that.

Peru is tolerant to excess, as far as true charity, religious feeling, and national honour demand. She persecutes no one because he may hold a different belief, and in return for that toleration, demands, with right and justice, that her religion be publicly respected and honoured.

But now they do not desire to observe this just measure. They seek to dogmatize in public, to place in open contest the faith and religion of the Peruvians with the beliefs of other nations. They ask for the public exercise of the Protestant worship, in order that Protestantism may be propagated, its errors preached, published, and communicated to the ignorant, to the curious, to the friends of novelties, to the weak in the faith, and to the poor who may be under the protection or influence of dissidents. Protestantism seeks public exercise of its worship, in order, with that pretext, to propagate its doctrines, and diffuse its erroneous instruction among the masses, not only by means of preaching, but also by education in Schools and Colleges.

Since a Protestant temple is established in Callao, there is no plausible reason to hinder the establishment of houses and Colleges of the same kind. What difference can there be between teaching in a temple, and teaching in a room with a few benches? The difference consists only in the number and in the class of the hearers. In the temple are taught small and great, the ignorant and the instructed; in the School and Colleges only weak and ignorant children.

So lamentable are the consequences of an ill-understood toleration. [...]

As Catholic Bishop, I am obliged to preserve from irreligious and heretical contagion the souls redeemed with the blood of the Saviour, and forming part of the flock of our Lord Jesus Christ, which have been confided to my charge. It is my duty, then, to give the cry of alarm against those attacks which are so imprudently made against the purity of the holy religion which we possess; and to demand the fulfillment of the laws of our Fatherland. [...]

May it please your Lordship to bring this reclamation under the notice of His Excellency, &c., &c., &c.

Signed, José Sebastián,
Archbishop of Lima

78. No Protestants in My Parishioners' Homes

Anthony Graybill (1841-1905), a Presbyterian minister from the United States, spent many years as a missionary in late nineteenth-century Mexico, then ruled by Porfirio Díaz (1876-1911). One of Díaz's goals was to reduce the power of the Catholic Church and create a

Source: Mr. [Anthony] Graybill, "Linares," *The Missionary* 21 (1888): 67-68.

modern, secular, liberal nation. His friendliness toward the tiny Protestant presence (385 churches by 1892) was in keeping with that aspiration. What characteristics of the actual religious situation throughout Mexico may be revealed by Graybill's detailed account of this one, specific event?

After much delay and difficulty I succeeded in effecting an entrance with my family into Linares on the 30th último, last Thursday. The first delay was one week at Monterey, on account of impracticable roads caused by excessive rains. We arrived at Montemorelos in our hired hack, drawn by four mules, on the 23d, where we were cordially received and entertained by Rev. Leandro Garza y Mora and his amiable wife. On the 25th, he and I went on horseback to Linares, thirty miles, to secure a house, before taking my family to the place, which turned out to be a more prudent precaution than we had suspected. On the night of our arrival, two houses were offered us, and the owners were anxious to rent. Next morning they informed us very unexpectedly that they were not ready to rent.

We were taken by a friend to another house. The owner, a polite old lady of one of the first families, showed me a very suitable house for fifteen dollars per month. I agreed to the price. She handed me the key, and told me to return at 3 p.m. for the written contract. I did so, but she shook her head, and said she had learned we were Protestants, and she could not rent her house to us; whereupon Leandro preached her a good sermon. But she pointed to an image of the Virgin, and said, "We are all under her care here." I returned the key. A friend told us that the priest had been there after our departure in the morning.

Another house was offered to us the same day. We told the owner we were Protestants, and we had learned that that was a difficulty to proprietors of houses in Linares. He replied that it was none with him; but in an hour he was visited by a commission of señoras, and repented. The priest was now fully aroused, and determined to keep us out of the city. Another house was offered for twenty-five dollars per month by a physician. He assured us that he would make out the papers on the following morning, that he wanted the money, and was not afraid of the priest. At 12 o'clock the next day he said there were difficulties, but that he would have the papers ready by Monday. We had to return to Morelos Saturday night, as Leandro had communion the following Sunday. On Monday a telegram announced that we could not get the house.

I immediately accepted, by telegram, three lower rooms of a house belonging to the city, which was the only resort. And we arrived here on last Wednesday. The house has no windows or fireplace. There is a big family over head; several families use the same yard, as also horses, mules and hogs, all with rights and privileges that we have no power to dispute. But it is the best we can do, and the priest is beaten, so far as his effort to keep us out of the city is concerned.

But on Sunday (yesterday) we were greatly cheered by the spiritual outlook. In the first place, we had no sort of insult offered us as we went to the hired room on the edge of the city, in which Leandro has been holding services monthly for a year—the only permanent Gospel work ever done in Linares. A believer, who had helped us to hunt a house, had the room opened and in order, and about fifty persons assembled and listened attentively to the Word. Mrs. Graybill organized a Sunday school of ten children. At night, we had about fifty again, including those that stood at the doors. We have not benches to seat more than thirty. I announced regular preaching four times a week— Sunday morning and night, Tuesday and Thursday nights. The people are of the poorer class, and many seemed to hear the word gladly, whereat our hearts rejoiced. We feel that the Lord has a people here, and we desire the prayers of His people at home for His blessing on the work.

My furniture and books reached here, by a good providence, the same day we arrived. The mud was so deep that two yoke of oxen had to be hired for most of the way, to supplement the horses, so that the expense of moving has been increased in several ways by the excessive rains.

79. The Eternal Western Missionary Experience

D. B. Grubb, superintendent of the South American Missionary Society of Paraguay, submitted the following brief report to the Ecumenical Missionary Conference in New York, 1900. He had served in Paraguay since 1889. Could this report have been written by a Portuguese Jesuit missionary in mid-sixteenth-century Brazil or by a missionary Franciscan in New Spain during the 1530s? What passages especially suggest that perceptions of the "other" in 1900 differ little from those of 1600? Are there positive as well as negative sides to this quintessentially Western endeavor of "converting the heathen"?

Indians of South America

Rev. D.B. Grubb, Superintendent, South American Missionary Society, Paraguay.

I have been laboring since 1889 in the Republic of Paraguay. The western portion of the Republic of Paraguay is called the Chaco. It is a region rather larger than the whole of France, and it is populated, as far as I can tell, by nearly a quarter of a million of heathen Indians. These Indians have maintained a virtual independence of the neighboring republics ever since the first Spanish conquerors landed in that country; and there are no civilized residents among them except the mission party.

The people we are working among at present comprise three nations, among whom we find some tens of thousands of a very fine class of savage, men who are brave, who are skilled in pottery, and in weaving wool and cotton, and who have a certain knowledge of agriculture. These people have a most interesting religion. They believe in a creator, in the immortality of the soul, in ghosts, and devils.

The country which they inhabit is a great, level plain, stretching for hundreds of miles in two directions; in some places covered by dense forests, abounding in huge swamps, and jungle lands covered with tall grass. When we landed there in 1889, almost nothing was known about the country; we had to explore that whole region for ourselves. Not a single word was known of the language. We had no interpreter; we had to begin by going among the people, living with them, and learning their language by means of signs, step by step. In the Chaco you live, if possible, in rough huts. The huts are infested day and night by insects of all kinds. At night goats and sheep continually prance about, and lucky you are if you do not have the wind knocked out of you two or three times during one night. The food is not choice! A very favorite dish in that country is a mashed up mess of beans. They mash the bean in a native mortar, and then put it in a gourd, and put in a little water and stir it around with their fingers. This thing you are supposed to take up in your hand and suck, and when you are done with it, it is passed on to another, a little more water put in, and the next man takes his turn.

The people live in constant dread of devils. They are afraid to go at night to the swamp, because they say these swamps are the homes of devils. They live in constant dread of their lives, on account of the witch doctors. Witch doctors might send cats or rats, or snakes, or beetles into the body, and only by the help of a friendly witch doctor can one get rid of them. Then they believe in dreams. The Indian believes that when he is dreaming, his spirit really leaves his body and wanders far away; and while his soul is away, another wandering soul may enter in and take possession, and then his own soul cannot get back. Another serious thing is that they hold you responsible for what they dream. If they dream of being killed by a certain man, they hold that man responsible, and think they are justified in killing

SOURCE: D. B. Grubb, "Indians of South America," in *Ecumenical Missionary Conference, New York 1900: Report of the Ecumenical Conference on Foreign Missions* (New York: American Tract Society, 1900), 1:480-82.

him in return. They also bury people alive and practice infanticide. It is not done out of cruelty, but simply from a religious motive.

But these savages are capable of improving. We have a good school among them. Some of them have learned to read and write, some are making progress in the Scriptures, and some of them are truly converted. The natives themselves have built a little church, and we have native teachers there, men and women, who are doing good work among their countrymen. Through the instrumentality of these native teachers we hope to reach 300 heathen tribes in the interior of the land.

80. Hunger for the Scriptures

Hugh Tucker, a lay Protestant agent of the American Bible Society and a lively observant traveler in Brazil from 1886 to 1900, had his The Bible in Brazil: Colporter Experiences *published in 1902. Tucker's observations permit several tentative conclusions about Brazilians' understanding of Christianity, but the problem is, which Brazilians, since consideration of class is essential?*

(1) What kind of Italians, for example, fight for unification of Italy, are exposed to Protestant evangelization there, and later emigrate to Brazil? (2) What kind of old Brazilian men were literate? (3) Why could the "negro boy" not fathom reaching Christ without money? (4) What class of people is able to travel by train? (5) What is significant about the army officials' change of mind? What might Tucker have said to them to achieve this change of mind? (6) Why would it be so easy to sell Bibles? Who would buy them? (7) Why might Protestant churches flourish in the state of Rio Grande do Sul (whose capital is Porto Alegre)?

We next stopped at the small town of Sumidouro; and, following what I have thought to be a wise plan, I first called on the priest and offered him a Bible. He had but little to say, and seemed quite satisfied with his surroundings and the condition of the people. He said the only difference between our Bible and his was that his had notes and explanations while ours had none. As we canvassed the town I met a soldier of the great Italian General, Garibaldi, who had heard the Gospel in Italy. He had wandered off to Brazil and settled in this town among the hills. He gave us a warm welcome into his humble home and there we had very delightful conversation about things pertaining to the Christian warfare and the Captain of our Salvation. In the afternoon I went along a country road leading from the village and by the roadside I sold a Bible to an old gray-haired man. When I was returning to the town about sundown I saw him sitting outside his cabin door with his family and two or three neighbours all gathered around listening as he read aloud the wonderful Words of Life. I did not dare to disturb them, but prayed that the Spirit might help them to understand the truth. At night I preached to a number of attentive listeners in a room hired for the purpose. Among the auditors were the members of this household and at the close of the sermon, I had an interesting conversation with the old gentleman and others. A negro boy came up and asked what I charged for confessing a person. I asked him what he wanted to confess. He said that about fifteen days before he had confessed to the priest all the bad things he had done; but since then he had done a number of evil things, and if it would not cost him too much money he would like to confess them all to me that I might obtain pardon for him. I tried to point him to Christ, but he seemed so ignorant and so fixed

SOURCE: Hugh C. Tucker, *The Bible in Brazil: Colporter Experiences* (New York: Fleming H. Revell, 1902), 91-92, 281-82.

in his idea of confessing only to a priest, and thus with money buy absolution, that he could not grasp the truth. We left in that town more than a score of Bibles, talked with many persons of Jesus and his salvation, preached to them the Gospel and prayed for them. As we journeyed by train the following day we sold more than twenty copies of the Scriptures, and had several interesting conversations with fellow-passengers. [. . .]

I was impressed on my first arrival that the community furnished a rich field for Bible distribution, and while I was awaiting the arrival of a delayed colporteur I improved the opportunity of making an effort in that direction. My custom was to go, early in the morning, into the streets with as many Bibles, Testaments and Gospels as I could carry. I usually sold out by nine or ten o'clock: then returned for breakfast, a rest and some reading. In the afternoon I would go again loaded down with Scriptures, which I generally disposed of by five o'clock in the afternoon, when I returned for dinner. Occasionally a second supply had to be sought, and sometimes I made large sales in the market. I was much encouraged by the wide-open door for the entrance of the truth and found the people ready to listen to words of explanation and commendation of the Bible. In passing

a house one day I saw a number of army officials at the window. When I offered them the Bible they began to make fun of religion. I made no reply till they had said their say, and then entered into conversation with them, which resulted in the sale of sixteen copies before I moved from the window. Incidents of like character occurred almost daily while I was in the city. [. . .]

[T]housands of copies have gone out into all directions through the State, and the reading of them has stirred up much interest. Both the Methodist and Episcopal Missionaries and their helpers are following up the colporteurs, establishing regular services in many places and gathering in the fruits. On my second visit to the State I made a trip on horseback one hundred and twenty miles to get an insight into the needs of the Italian and German colonists north from the city of Porto Alegre and was gratified to find that the work done by our colporteur in these colonies some years ago had developed into regularly organized churches.

With some aid from abroad the people have built comfortable churches, and in the lack of well prepared and ordained ministers one of the Italian colporteurs of the Bible Society, Rev. Matteo Donatti, is now serving in the pastoral office.

81. Woman's Work in Latin Lands

Carrie Carnahan, of the Women's Board of Missions of the Methodist Episcopal Church, presented her report on her church's presence in Latin America to the Conference on [Protestant] Missions in Latin America in 1913. Carnahan's description of the Methodist missionaries in Uruguay portrays a spirit and approach that contrast sharply with those of traditional Catholicism.

(1) What are the three specific characteristics that illustrate this contrast? Explain what she means by the important concept of "self-support." (2) What does her comment on "Anglo-Saxon human nature" reveal about her and about the typical North American missionary? (3) Why is it "not always possible to do as direct and aggressive Christian work . . . in Latin lands as . . . in some parts of the Orient"? (4) Given the nature of the Methodist missionary schools being established in Latin America, why would the Peruvian government ignore article IV of the Peruvian constitution, which restricts mission work to Catholicism?

SOURCE: Carrie Carnahan, "Woman's Work in Latin Lands," in *Conference on Missions in Latin America, 156 Fifth Avenue, New York, March 12 and 13, 1913* (New York: Committee of Reference and Counsel of the Foreign Missions Conference of North America, 1913), 125-28.

We believe that if a stable form of government could speedily be restored in Mexico, Protestant mission work would go forward more rapidly than ever in the past. [...]

Our society has schools in but three of the South American republics—Uruguay, The Argentine, and Peru.

Thirty-five years ago the founder of our school in Montevideo, Cecilia Guelphi, a talented woman of Argentine birth, inaugurated an educational system which encouraged self-support and included a systematic and thorough normal course. Students of this course were required to pass the government examination, thus taking rank with teachers of the same grade in government schools. Miss Guelphi was not only a progressive educator, but a woman of evangelistic spirit. The seven schools which she organized in those early days, had a little army of over 500 pupils and became centers of Christian activity. In most of them, Sunday-schools were held, and several preaching services and prayer meetings were conducted.

This whole work is now centralized in a boarding school, occupying a fine modern building.

The improvement of the Government schools and the opening of private schools in which the Bible is not taught, have somewhat affected our attendance; nevertheless, the school is very strong in its influence and maintains a high standard. One of the school girls, without making her plans known, recently took the entrance examinations in the new Government University for Women and passed brilliantly, to the delight and surprise of her teachers, as the girl was by no means a prize pupil. Every once in a while someone comes over from the Roman Catholic Church to membership in ours, due more or less directly to the Bible instruction quietly and faithfully given in the school. The temperance work being done is accomplishing a great good. There is a growing sentiment in favor of total abstinence among the young people of the city which has as its center a group of our own graduates. When the best man at a fashionable wedding refuses to drink to the bride's health in anything stronger than lemonade, as happened recently, surely things are taking strides in the right direction.

This school emphasizes three things to our Board: the advisability of putting responsibility upon competent, faithful native workers just as soon as they are equal to it—a lesson which Anglo-Saxon human nature does not too readily learn; the wisdom of encouraging self-support from the very inception of a work; the necessity of an administration up-to-date and progressive in educational lines and at the same time deeply spiritual and aggressively evangelistic.

Our school at Rosario in The Argentine, founded thirty-nine years ago, has had the Holyoke plan for its aim. The school is located in a modern building and is always full. The self-support of this school goes toward the upkeep of a large charity or free school in another part of the city. Former students are today the influential wives and mothers of Rosario. [...]

Our Board is becoming more and more strongly convinced that if our schools are to become most worthwhile, if they are to justify the large expense they entail upon us, they must be in charge of those women who are deeply spiritual and who are equipped with the most modern educational methods. It is not always possible to do as direct and aggressive Christian work in the schools in Latin lands as we can do in some parts of the Orient, but with a sufficiently strong missionary force it is possible to create a Christian atmosphere which must tell vitally upon the lives of the students. Our aim is to have in each of these institutions a young woman of culture and tact who shall be able to give her time entirely to the teaching of the Bible and to visiting in the homes of the students. She must be especially fitted for this kind of work, but we believe such a missionary would be worth many times her salary in the results brought to pass.

In Peru we touch one of the neediest fields in all the Continent. The reports of Consular agents for Great Britain and the United States have called the attention of the world to the Putumayo atrocities.*

---

* Severe mistreatment and massacres of local Amerindians in northeast Peru, especially between 1900 and 1910, by rubber magnate Julio Arana.

The Protestant Church of Great Britain—particularly the non-conformist bodies—has been greatly stirred by the claim that Article IV of the Peruvian Constitution prohibits any but Roman Catholic mission work. Years of experience have shown that, while for political reasons effecting the peace and harmony of the country, this article remains in the Constitution, it is practically a dead letter and Protestant Missions are not only tolerated but receive the fullest protection from the government and its officials. We rejoice that this stirring of the British Church has led to the financial and numerical strengthening of the Evangelical Union of South America—an interdenominational organization—and already three picked men, one a physician, have gone to work in the Putumayo district. Our hearts long that scores of workers may soon be sent to the millions of Indians in different parts of the Continent who are as yet untouched by the gospel.

PART XII

Amerindian- and
Afro-Christian Culture

Estimates of indigenous populations in Spanish America vary. Bolivia, Guatemala, and perhaps Peru may be 50 percent indigenous, while Ecuador and Mexico are approximately 25 percent. These populations have never overcome the effects of the Conquest; the national governments, the ruling elites, the imposed new religion, and the dominant materialist, individualist culture remain alien. But most of these populations, save those in the most isolated villages of the Sierra Madre and the Andes, are not locked in time. Despite marginalization, they have survived as distinct societies, have sometimes thrived, and have always taken from the alien culture what seemed appropriate and capable of enhancing their well-being. Such is especially the case in religious concerns.[1]

82. Celebrating the Holy Cross in Yucatan

Alfonso Villa Rojas (1897-1998), born in Mérida, Yucatan, met the great U.S. anthropologist Robert Redfield (1897-1958) in 1930 when Villa was a teacher in the rural community of Chan Kom. He did ethnographic research under Redfield's direction and co-authored Chan Kom: A Maya Village *(1934) with Redfield. Later Villa became director of anthropological research in the Interamerican Indigenous Institute (Mexico City) and researcher at Mexico's prestigious National Autonomous University. The following excerpt is Villa's*

1. Randall Hansis, *The Latin Americans: Understanding Their Legacy* (Boston: McGraw-Hill, 1997), 48; Paul B. Goodwin, Jr., *Latin America*, 11th ed. (Dubuque, Iowa: McGraw-Hill/Dushkin, 2004), 7, 36, 67, 90, 100.

SOURCE: Robert Redfield and Alfonso Villa Rojas, *Chan Kom: A Maya Village* (Chicago & London: University of Chicago Press, 1962, first published by the Carnegie Institution of Washington), 153-55. Reprinted with permission of The University of Chicago Press.

account of the celebration of the Feast of the Holy Cross in the town of X-Kalakdzonot on April 30, 1930.

What are the religious (Christian) components at the heart of this fiesta? What are the other components (note the references to the cargador*)? How might they be explained? What might be the explanation for the revelry, boisterousness, intoxication, and feasting that surround the religious component? What might be the psychology operating here? Note the date of the fiesta.*

It is four o'clock in the afternoon. After four hours of travel by a narrow and rocky path, I have arrived at X-Kalakdzonot. The teacher tells me that X-Kalakdzonot is a *pueblo*, but in truth it can hardly be called a *ranchería*. In the center of a clearing which forms the plaza is erected the kax-che—a rude enclosure of sticks and vines. At one side, on a little eminence, is the school. There are no streets; small paths lead crookedly to the ten or twelve houses hidden in the foliage.

The place has a holiday appearance. [. . .] In a moment appear a number of half-drunk and sweating men, their faces contorted by happy shouts; they are carrying on their shoulders the great trunk of a ceiba tree. This is made firm in the center of the kax-che; it will serve to tie the bulls to. By the shouting and clamor which the act occasions one can tell that the bringing of this tree from the bush to the enclosure is an interesting and important part of the fiesta.

My attention is drawn to the house of the *cargador*, the principal organizer of the fiesta. It is the principal center of activity. [. . .]

Evening is coming. The excitement increases. Every moment one sees little lights coming down the paths; these are the dancers and other celebrants who are arriving on foot or on horseback from the surrounding *rancherías*. With hardly a pause, rockets shatter into space. Every family has brought a dozen or more of these rockets which they set off when it pleases them.

In the house of the *cargador* a supper has just been served. Everyone present has been fed. One table is reserved for the visiting teachers and merchants—*los principales*, the people call them.

From the supper the people move in a procession to a little *oratorio*. There they celebrate the last night of a *novenario* held in honor of the Holy Cross. A *maestro cantor* is in charge; he recites the prayers, and the congregation makes the responses.

During the novena the men have withdrawn a little from the women. Now the men of X-Kalak-dzonot, accompanied by a few male friends, go to the house of the man who has promised to be *cargador* next year. The future *cargador* asks the help of those present to organize the next fiesta, and offers them cigarettes and rum.

The sacred ritual is over; next the Holy Cross will be honored with a dance. The *cargadores*, present and future, go over to the *oratorio*. They are followed by the crowd, and their passage takes place to a great burst of rockets, the playing of music by the little orchestra, and the shouts of the people. The *cargadores* take the Holy Cross from its place on the altar and carry it to a special hut erected in front of the *enramada*. The *santo* is now present at the dance arranged in its honor. [. . .]

Round about the *enramada* people are selling candies, chocolate, bread, drinks, and even ice brought from Valladolid, 65 kilometers away. [. . .] Groups of young fellows excited by alcohol, move about shouting, "Yauti! Yauti! Palalee-ee-eex!" (Hurray, Hurray, boys!) [. . .]

The girls take seats under the *enramada*. They do not dance—not yet. They remain grave, immutable. One would say that they are not enjoying it. On the contrary it is the moment they have been dreaming of all year. At last the brassy notes of the cornet arouse them to activity. The drums begin their stirring beat; the first couple is led out on to the wooden platforms; these resound with the heel-taps of the dancers. The *jarana* has begun.

Dawn comes, and with the crowing of the cocks mingle the last notes of the *torito*—that air with which *jaranas* always end. The last couples leave the dance-platform. Many of the dancers, overcome with fatigue, are already sleeping in hammocks tied to trees, out in the open—for the shelters here are not enough to give lodging to all.

Their repose is brief. At eight o'clock in the morning there is a bustle of activity at the house of the *cargador*. His two assistants, the kulelob, take no rest at all. Now they are busy distributing plates of turkey seasoned with toasted chili (*relleno negro*) to the various groups into which the celebrants have gathered. Gourd dishes of *atole* pass from group to group. [...]

At noon, the present *cargador*, together with his wife and his associate organizers, the nakulob, go to the house of the future *cargador*, whom he thereupon invites to his house, that he may deliver to him the *carga*, or cuch. This is the essential part of the fiesta and gives its name (cuch) to the whole. On a table the kulelob place a cross, a clay vessel containing the cooked head of a pig, a pile of tortillas, several bottles of rum, and on a little plate some cigarettes. The present *cargador* carries the cuch: a decorated pole from which hang many-colored paper streamers, packages of cigarettes, cloth dolls and loaves of wheat bread made in the form of an eagle. He addresses the *cargador* of the fiesta to be celebrated next year, saying:

"In the name of the Father, the Son and the Holy Ghost, I deliver to you this charge (cuch), and that which is upon this table, so that next year you may make your fiesta to the Holy Cross."

To this the other replies: "Thanks, sir; if the Lord God gives us life and health, I promise to do this." [...]

The crowd then moves off to the kax-che, where the bull-fights begin. [...]

The sun, with its fiery rays, moves along its path unnoticed by the crowd, who for the moment have shaken off their habitual melancholy. [...] Moments of excitement, for long periods of hereafter to be the themes of talk for old and young! Moments to become nostalgic recollection for young women, keeping their finery in a trunk not soon to be opened!

83. On the "Indian" in Guatemala

Erna Fergusson (1888-1964), born of a distinguished family devoted to the political, social, and environmental well-being of New Mexico, became interested early in her life in the Hopi and Navajo reservations and in the three cultures of New Mexico—Amerindian, Spanish, and Anglo.

During the 1930s and '40s she published well-informed accounts of her travels throughout Latin America. Typical of her thoughtful contributions toward an understanding of the reality of Latin America are the excerpts below from her Guatemala *(1937), written when Jorge Ubico (president, 1931-1944) was still regarded positively by some progressive political observers. In the brief excerpt below, each spokesman—the educated Guatemalan, the Protestant missionary, and the Catholic priest—expresses his view of the Amerindian and his religiosity. They are very different. Compare the three perceptions.*

Young Guatemalan Educated in the States:

Indians, I tell you, are dangerous. They have to be kept under with force. This is not like your country, where men are equal. I'll tell you.

A few years ago some young men made an excursion to climb Santa María, the volcano by Quetzaltenango, you know. Well, they came to a place where the Indians had been making their *brujería* [witchcraft]. It was just a pile of stones and broken pottery — nothing, dirty. The young men looked at it, moved the things with their sticks and their feet, maybe. I don't know. Then

SOURCE: Erna Fergusson, *Guatemala* (New York: Alfred A. Knopf, 1942), 292-93, 296-97.

they went on. Well, the next week another party came by, different young men, and they didn't touch the things; but the Indians, watching, thought they were the same young men, and they just killed them. Killed them. I tell you, they are dangerous, these Indians.

Well, the government went after them. They knew what village it was, but not what man. But they did enough, I'll tell you, to that village so they'll never bother white men again. They killed about ten men, I think.

Protestant Missionary:

One man, I'm sure he was a Christian man, but these people never understand the morality of the sexes as Anglo-Saxons do. . . . Well, maybe lots of Anglo-Saxons don't either, but at least they don't pretend; they are honest about it. But this man, after his wife died, he just said he had to have a woman, and he is absolutely brazen about how he lives. We talked to him. He was an elder in the church, and we explained that he could not continue in that position, living in sin as he did. We tried to give him some sense of responsibility, of Christian shame, but he just said:

"Well, God made me, and He knows how I am. He knows I can't live alone." [. . .]

The Padre: [. . .]

My people bring me food. And they leave a few coppers in the church, poor things, but they cannot leave much, they who are so poor too.

Do you see my Indians there now? Such devotion! We, with all the wisdom we have, and of course, being from the United States, we are very wise, very superior, very learned people; but even we do not have such devotion as these people. Did you go into the church to see? When you do, go, please, by the side door and sit very still so they shall not notice you. For they are very intent, my poor people there, on their prayers, very close to God they are. For they come there in perfect faith. They have been robbed, you see, for generations, robbed and exploited, their women violated, their little children loaded like beasts. They have been beaten. It is getting different now, with the fine new President we have. But still they have much that is wrong, my poor people. And so they come to church, as you see, each one with his pitiful little candle. Maybe what they do is not quite orthodox, you see. Some people may criticize that I allow it. But that Indian, he talks straight to God, as maybe you and I dare not do, even if we do come from the States and know everything. He talks to his God, telling Him everything, asking help. I know because I understand his language. How could I help these people if I did not? Often I hear what they say.

"Lord and Master," they are saying, "this is not just, this is not right, that he should take my land I have worked so hard to till. Lord, I ask You now to help me, to help my children." And he knows, friends, that the Lord will help him. That is faith, friends, yes, that is faith.

84. The Mystical Chimaltecos

Charles Wagley (1913-1991), noted anthropologist who taught at Columbia University for twenty-five years, is known for major research among the inhabitants of lowland Brazil but did his first studies in the late 1930s on a Maya Amerindian community in Chimaltenango, Guatemala.

Why should Wagley's conclusions about the religious understanding and attitudes of the Chimaltecos prompt the reader to review earlier readings that deal with the "conversion" of the Amerindians at the time of the conquest and early colony? How does Thomas Gage's

SOURCE: Charles Wagley, "The Social and Religious Life of a Guatemalan Village," *American Anthropologist* 51, no. 4, pt. 2 (October 1949): 50.

The Mystical Chimaltecos

description of Amerindian Christianity (reading 31), for example, compare with Wagley's? How does Wagley's footnote concerning the Spanish padre contribute to an understanding of the nature and quality of the Amerindians' "Catholicism"?

Wagley does not provide much information about the daily lives of the Chimaltecos, but in the last part of the excerpt he describes "the local religion." What reality of the Chimalteco does it reflect?

Ostensibly Chimaltecos are Catholic and they are recognized as such by the Roman Catholic Church. Obviously, their religion is not Catholicism as we think of it. Their entire culture is a fusion of Maya and European cultures and this fusion is perhaps most striking in their religion. In prayers, for example, Christ, a Catholic saint, an aboriginal day deity, and a Guardian of the Mountain may be appealed to in that order. Their concept of any one of these deities, whether it be of Catholic or aboriginal origin, is a blend of European and Maya beliefs. One cannot say that the Chimalteco concept of Christ is Catholic nor that the Guardian of the Mountain is a Mayan deity, for the fusion of aboriginal and foreign elements is complete in each detail. The result is not an American Indian religion with a veneer of Catholicism nor is it Catholicism with many aboriginal appendages. Chimalteco religion is a new form—a new religion—arising out of a historical merging of two religions. Their religion is different from each original ingredient and particular to Chimaltenango.

Nevertheless any Chimalteco will tell you that he (or she) is a *muy buen Católico*; to be a good Catholic is to be respectful of all religious forms whether Catholic or aboriginal in origin. In Chimaltenango there is no recognition or memory of any separateness in origin. In fact, Chimalteco religion does not have much contact with the Catholic Church. The Catholic Padre from Huehuetenango visits the village every year or two to baptize children and to perform mass in the church.[1] The mass, however, is unimportant for the Chimalteco. Catholic confession is unknown, and there are no church weddings. The local religion is normally in the charge of the local village functionaries. Indian men who have learned Latin chants by rote from previous *cantores*, direct burials, chanting for the wake and in the burial procession. The *sacristanes* take care of the church and the *mayordomos* arrange the celebrations for the Saints. In the sphere of individual and family religion, the native soothsayers or priests (*Mam chimanes*) are the mediators between the layman and the supernatural. In 1937, there were eleven of these, all past middle age, and the most renowned of them was the municipal priest (*Chimán del Pueblo*) who directed his activities toward public ritual.

---

1. Until the Fiesta of Corpus Christi in 1937 a priest had not visited Chimaltenango in over two years. The Padre at Huehuetenango has more than twenty *municipios* under his care. (Only the government health officer has more.) When the Padre visited Chimaltenango in 1937, he charged seventy-five cents for a baptism and in this manner he took in about ten dollars. The Padre, who was Spanish by birth, complained bitterly of his fate, of the sad state of the church in Chimaltenango, of the impossibility of making good Catholics out of barbarians and brutes. His greatest dream was a wealthy parish in Chicago "where people are rich."

85. Male and Female Concepts of Christ in Bahia

Marvin Harris (1927-2001), cultural anthropologist of Columbia University and the University of Florida, controversial author of seventeen books, including Cows, Pigs, Wars and Witches *(1974), was also an advisor to the ministry of education in Brazil. His* Town and Country in Brazil *(1956) is the result of Harris's meticulous, scientific fieldwork in 1950-1951 in Minas Velhas, a small town in the northeast state of Bahia. The excerpts below deal with the townspeople's religious attitudes.*

How does Harris account for the differences between men's and women's concepts of Christ?

Note that, on the one hand, the men believe in miracles and are devoted to their patron saint, while, on the other, they show a clear lack of deference toward the priest, refusing to see anything sacred in him or to put themselves in a supplicant position toward him (they reject confession, for example). What is the explanation for this seeming paradox?

At best, the people of Minas Velhas exhibit but a mediocre concern for the formal aspects of their religion. The priest and the rituals he performs inside the church—confession, communion, mass—are regarded with emotional disinterest. On any given Sunday, the majority of adult townspeople do not attend mass. [...]

In Minas Velhas the men expect to see the women in church, and the women do not expect to see the men there—much as it is the women who wash clothes and carry things on their heads and not the men. This difference in roles is perhaps rooted in the symbolic structure of Catholicism. Psychologically, Christ, the central figure in the pantheon, would appear to be of little use to the male in Minas Velhas. He represents qualities which in real behavior the culture classifies in a hundred different ways as effeminate. His ministers are denied the male function. He is the idol of the meek and the poor—groups which simply are not idolized in the urban context where the rich and the powerful and the un-modest inherit the visible earth from generation to generation. Moreover, the story of the Crucifixion, the Western world's great tradition of suffering and redemption, is meaningful to the women in a sense in which it is not equally meaningful to the men. Among the men, even among the economically marginal, a sense of oppression does not exist. As long as he has a wife and children, there is an excellent chance that the male's dominating domestic role more than compensates for whatever oppression he may experience at the hands of others. The women, however, do often exhibit a sense of oppression, and are in fact subject to greater and more frequent duress than their husbands, especially if one considers the prolific rate at which they keep bringing children into the world. [...]

The priest's income derives principally from baptisms, marriages, funerals, and special masses. The fees for these services are variable and depend upon the amount of pomp involved and/or the degree of inconvenience to which the priest is subjected. [...]

In the memory of the community, however, it is unknown for a priest to confine himself to an income derived exclusively from religious functions. Some sold religious pictures, others were rich landholders, almost all of them were important financiers for the local gold miners. Throughout the old mining region, priests are associated with real and legendary mining activities. The priest, while not the richest man in the community, enjoys one of the highest regular cash incomes, and cash is the *sine qua non* of serious mining. [...]

SOURCE: Marvin Harris, *Town and Country in Brazil* (New York: Columbia University Press, 1956), 211-14, passim, 219, 221-24, passim, 241. Copyright © 1956. Columbia University Press. Reprinted with permission of publisher.

It is not strange, therefore, that the men of Minas Velhas do not place much importance upon having their sins absolved by the priest. They do not feel sinful and the priest is scarcely the person who can convince them that they should. [. . .]

In keeping with the weak role of official Catholic dogma, the concepts of heaven and hell are not vital issues to the average townsman. The threat and promise of otherworldly rewards make little impression upon the sophisticated, materialistic urbanites. Some of the perfunctory performance of church ritual is undoubtedly maintained, especially among the men, by force of this dogma. In most instances, however, the threat is too ironic, and the promise too remote, to really make an impression on anybody. Eunice, a townswoman deserted by her husband and left alone to bring up six small children by working in a leather shop, expressed the viewpoint typical of many of the inhabitants of Minas Velhas: "I am not afraid of hell," she said, "because I am in it right here and now. I don't believe there is any place where you suffer more than you do on earth."

The ascetic spirit does not exist in Minas Velhas, except among a few individuals—mostly women—who are considered to be fanatics and a little queer. But Catholicism has more to offer than otherworldly heavens and hells. The townspeople are only mildly concerned about the spiritual future, but the material present is of vital interest to all. Hence, wherever Catholicism brings its promise to the present, therein is to be found its greatest affective force in both town and country.

Informal Catholicism

The principal agency available to the villagers and townsmen by which a religiously mediated influence may be brought to bear upon the immediate material world is individual prayer. The belief that events may so be influenced is held by most townspeople and all villagers. Miracles are accepted by the villagers as not only possible but also as relatively frequent; the townsmen regard them as possible but rare. It is this accessibility of supernatural assistance which marks the vital core of Catholicism in Minas Velhas.

The efficacy of prayer depends upon the devotion and faith of the suppliant. It is the general tacit assumption of both townsmen and villagers that the efficacy of prayer does not depend upon a pure moral condition or upon formal religiosity. Anyone who has good reason to be heard and who manifests enough devotion may be successful. In the villages and to a lesser extent in the town, this devotion usually exists as a long-established relationship with a saint, i.e., the deity most likely to be appealed to is the individual's patron saint. This relationship is marked by pictures or images representing the saint which the suppliant keeps in his house; by the observance of the saint's day as a holiday, on which he does not work, has paid for a novena, and perhaps sets off some skyrockets; and possibly by the name of the saint which he has been given by his parents and which he, in turn, will pass on to his offspring. [. . .]

A man whose wife is sick, for example, prays to his favorite saint: "Misericordia. Hear a humble voice. Grant my wife health and I will set off a half-dozen skyrockets in front of the main door of the church on your day." If the wish is granted, the man carries out his promise. This is the basic type of *promessa*—a prayer which contains a bribe in the form of a promise to express devotion and gratitude if the prayer's wish is granted. [. . .]

During a thunderstorm the roof tiles crashed down into the room where a brass-smith's children were sleeping. When the debris was pulled off the bed, the children were found to be unhurt; one of them, in fact, was still sleeping. The father decided that a miracle had been performed by his patron saint, Bom Jesus. He had a photograph taken of the children in the ruined bedroom and said he was going to leave it at the shrine of Bom Jesus. [. . .]

Considering the town's total cultural edifice, we can safely say that Catholicism, even in its folk aspects, is not the keystone in the arch. Far from constituting an important cohesive force, formal religion itself suffers from a series of internal tensions that result from its inability to be reconciled with the institutions which provide its setting. It is at a tangent to the whole complex of masculinity and hence is deprived of the full support of the sex whose participation would be most important in this outspokenly male-dominated culture. It is partisan to the leisure class, maintaining economically based criteria of association which tend to exclude at least one quarter of the population from active participation. Its priests have been caught in the web of political intrigue and have been forced to choose among the local political parties. Its forms of religious association are senescent and secondary to political parties and purely social clubs. The entire edifice is impregnated with a type of philosophy sufficiently materialistic to convert its holy days into occasions for making money.

86. The Pragmatic Tepoztecans

Oscar Lewis (1914-1970), another major anthropologist trained at Columbia University, specialized in studying the culture of poverty in Mexico, Puerto Rico, and among "Hispanics" in the United States. The following excerpts are taken from Life in a Mexican Village: Tepoztlan Restudied *(1951), one of Lewis's many successful books. Tepoztlan (Morelos) is a small town at the base of an enormous sierra some thirty miles south of Mexico City.*

(1) What aspects of Catholicism did the "church," that is, the clergy and the nuns, emphasize in the 1940s, the period when Lewis studied Tepoztlan? (2) How did the "mainstream" majority of Tepoztlan perceive that "church"? (3) How may Lewis's assertion that "the people do not know how to improvise prayers" be explained? (4) The Tepoztecan dislike of confession really reflects on whom? (5) How do the deities and other supernatural figures in the Tepoztecan religion compare with those in the religion of the Chimaltecos (reading 84)? (6) How does Lewis explain the Tepoztecan understanding of the god of Christianity? (7) How do Lewis's considerations reflect on previous accounts of Amerindian "conversion"?

Are there any major differences in religious comportment between the inhabitants of Chimaltenango, Tepoztlan, and Minas Velhas, Bahia?

Just as the cycle of religious fiestas in Tepoztlán follows Catholic practice, with some local modifications, so does the individual Tepoztecan. Only a few persons, mostly women, in the village fulfill all the ritual and other obligations set by the priest and church. These people are looked upon by the rest as fanatics who are "always dressing the saints." The priest does not consider his flock to be "good Catholics." The older people maintain a respectful passivity toward most church activities, while the adult males and many older youths, although not irreligious, tend to scoff at the nuns, the Acción Católica [see Part XXII] and other "fanatics." Among these recalcitrants there is much more interest in the barrio fiestas and one or two of the nearby village fiestas than in the regular daily and weekly religious acts which are required of them. On the other hand, the nuns and the religious associations tend to emphasize the latter. The school, too, so far unsuccessfully, discourages attending fiestas because of the disastrous effects upon school attendance. Regular participation in church ritual is associated with becoming "more cultured." Those who go to boarding schools or who have occasion to live in Mexico City for some time learn to attend Mass, to confess, and to take communion more often than is customary in the village.

SOURCE: Oscar Lewis, *Life in a Mexican Village: Tepoztlán Restudied* (Urbana: University of Illinois Press, 1963), 273-76, 276-77. Reprinted by permission of Ruth Maslow Lewis.

Prayers for various occasions are memorized by Tepoztecans. The older generation learn them in Náhuatl, the younger in Spanish. The people do not know how to improvise prayers, and when their memory fails they prefer to keep silent, or merely cross themselves, or kiss a scapulary to invoke the protection of the appropriate saint. The obligatory morning prayers are seldom said with regularity. Some of the old people still say a prayer at noon when the bell of the municipal clock strikes; the men remove their hats and give thanks to God because they still have strength to work. When the evening church bell rings, the men are again supposed to take off their hats and the women to kneel to give thanks because the day has passed without mishap. We cannot estimate the number of people who fulfill the latter obligation, but in all the time we were in the village we never observed anyone kneeling in prayer outside the church. But men returning home from the fields lift their hats respectfully whenever they pass a cross, and on the bus from Tepoztlán to Cuernavaca all hats go up in unison each time a church is passed. Some Tepoztecans recite prayers on special occasions, such as planting corn, lighting a charcoal furnace, or pruning a tree.

As indicated earlier, most Tepoztecans do not feel strongly the need to attend Mass every Sunday or even on holy days. On the basis of our own observations and informants' estimates, it appears that, on the average, about two hundred, mostly women, attend church on Sundays. The 6:00 A.M. Mass is preferred; those who attend the 8:00 A.M. Mass risk being called lazy. Mass, like older public gatherings, is a welcome form of diversion. It is one of the opportunities for sweethearts to see one another; young people are said to attend not out of devotion but to flirt. Everyone puts on his best clothes for Mass. The older men wear huaraches, white *calzones*, and shirts; the youths wear trousers and modern shirts, and many wear jackets. The women use *rebozos* to cover their heads. Upon entering the church, the women cross themselves with holy water and take seats up toward the front. The men generally do not cross themselves and remain in the rear. Some of the youths stand at one side of the nave, leaning against the pillars so as to be able to see the girls

during the service. The children sit with their mothers and sisters. Five- and ten-centavo pieces are dropped into the plate passed by the sacristan.

After Mass the young men are the first to leave. They remain at the church door, talking, joking, and laughing quietly among themselves, until the girls appear. The older men are the next to leave the church, and then the women. Most of the men go off to drink, while the women go home in little groups of relatives.

Tepoztecans do not rigorously observe Sunday or other holy days as days of rest. During planting and harvesting, everyone works in the fields, and the storekeepers in the center who profit by the week-end tourist trade always work on Sundays and holidays. Informants say, "It is no sin to work on Sunday when it is done out of necessity." Some of the very old people believe that he who works on Sunday ruins himself economically for the rest of the week.

Tepoztecans do not like to confess; the majority do so only once a year. Not giving much importance to sin, Tepoztecans do not regard confession as necessary. Most men consider confession important only when one is about to die but "with the pangs of death, who's going to remember to confess properly?" Women, particularly married women, are less reluctant to confess, and about fifty women are known to take communion and confess quite often. Through the Acción Católica the number of young people of both sexes who do this has increased. Perhaps the most important deterrent to confession, especially among the older people, is that the priest may exact from the confessor the recitation of certain prayers which most people cannot say accurately. Fearing a scolding from the priest, they prefer to avoid the situation. There is no such difficulty with communion. "We would all take communion more often if we didn't have to confess; that we always avoid."

In general, the Tepoztecan feels obliged to contribute to the church and does so by paying *limosnas*. There is a belief that he who refuses to give alms will find that no one receives his soul in heaven and that therefore he must go to hell. He who always gives alms finds that when he dies and his soul goes to heaven, "the Saint to whom he has given alms comes to receive the soul and intercedes with God to allow him to enter, and so he gets to heaven." Thus, when a Tepoztecan lights a candle to some saint or deposits a coin or two in the box, he considers himself deserving of the protection of that saint.

Tithes, which were obligatory and were collected by the government for the church before the Revolution, no longer exist. The local priest, however, hires a *limosnero* at harvest time to go about the fields, riding on a mule, to collect contributions from the farmers. As a rule, each farmer gives about twelve ears of corn, so that the priest collects a good amount for his stores.

Religious beliefs in Tepoztlán reflect Tepoztecan social character and world view. The profoundly practical nature of Tepoztecans precludes religious fantasy, mysticism, and any preoccupation with metaphysics; they seek from religion concrete solutions to problems of daily life and go about it in as direct a manner as their religion permits. Their religious world, like the world in which they live, is full of hostile forces and punishing figures which must be propitiated to secure good will and protection. The act of propitiation is direct and simple, consisting of giving something or doing something which is known to please a particular saint, such as lighting a candle, giving a few coins, offering flowers, burning incense, reciting a special prayer, or performing a certain dance; these offerings incur an obligation on the part of the recipient to favor the donor.

As in most mestizo communities in Mexico and Central America, Tepoztecan religious beliefs represent a fusion of Catholic and pagan elements. The people's concept of God is vague at best; the one characteristic which is clear to Tepoztecans is that he is a punishing God who acts in ways hostile to men. Most misfortunes are ascribed to him; good fortune rarely.

The Holy Trinity is viewed as consisting of three distinct gods. One is God the Father, who is usually pictured with a long, white beard and a large ball in his hand, "that one is the Lord of the World." The second is "the one who died for us, the one who was crucified." The third is "the Holy Ghost or the Holy Dove," who is frequently depicted with the symbol of a dove to which Tepoztecans give divine attributes.

El Tepozteco occupies a special place in Tepoztecan religion and is unique to this community. The process by which he was deified and confused with Catholic figures was paralleled in localities all through Mexico during the colonial period. He continues to play an important role in Tepoztlán, is constantly evoked, and is one of the few legendary figures in the village. He is described to the children in the following manner:

Tepozteco cannot be known; his house is on the hill near El Parque. There he has his *comal*, his *metate*, and everything which he needs in his house, but he himself does not appear. He always lives far off among the clouds. When they don't give him a good celebration on the eighth of September he sends a great wind; when the celebration is a good one then he does nothing, he is content. Tepozteco is a god who is lovable and cruel. He has only one punishment for the village—he takes away the water. He makes *los aires* and they cause illness. He has a mother who is in the church. We say a Mass for his mother. His mother is named *Tonantzin* and also *Natividad*. [...]

Tepoztecans do not distinguish clearly between those misfortunes which might be considered punishments of God, or the work of the devil. Tepoztecans believe firmly in the devil, who is generally called *el pingo*, and to whom is attributed many of the evils which befall them. The powers of the devil, however, are relatively few; he cannot cause drought but he can cause harm to a person, making him an idiot or carrying him off bodily. The devil always appears dressed as a Mexican horseman or as "a tall gentleman, dressed in black like respectable people, with a suit of fine cloth." He is almost always met on lonely roads or in the woods during the night. To combat his evil influence, Tepoztecans recite a prayer to some saint, especially to St. Michael and St. Gabriel. When a Tepoztecan brings an offering to St. Michael he considers it necessary to light a candle to the devil as well, even though it be a small candle, so that he will not be angered.

87. Child of the Dark

Carolina Maria de Jesus (1914-1977), a great-grandchild of slaves, left her life of destitution in the rural interior of Brazil to seek a better life in São Paolo. After a little schooling she taught herself to read and write and kept a diary in which she recorded her feelings and the vicissitudes of her hard life. In 1958 a reporter discovered Carolina and her diary, which became the best-selling book in Brazilian history. The excerpts clearly define the misery and desperation of the poor and make the difficulty of her life palpable.

She makes matter-of-fact references to God, believers, Mass, Jesus Christ, and Sunday. What role does religion play in senhora Carolina's life? What is her understanding of Christianity? Is she "religious" and, if so, in what sense? What do religion and belief mean to her?

When I was a girl my dream was to be a man to defend Brazil, because I read the history of Brazil and became aware that war existed. I read the masculine names of the defenders of the country, then I said to my mother:

"Why don't you make me become a man?"

She replied:

"If you walk under a rainbow, you'll become a man."

When a rainbow appeared I went running in its direction. But the rainbow was always a long way off. Just as the politicians are a long way off from the people. I got tired and sat down. Afterward I started to cry. But the people must not get tired. They must not cry. They must fight to improve Brazil so that our children don't suffer as we are suffering. I returned and told my mother:

"The rainbow ran away from me."

We are poor, and we live on the banks of the river. The riverbanks are places for garbage and the marginal people. People of the favelas are considered marginals. No more do you see buzzards flying the riverbanks near the trash. The unemployed have taken the buzzards' place.

When I went out to look for paper I met a black. He was ragged and dirty and I felt sorry for him. In his tattered clothes he could pass for the president of the Unfortunates' Union. In his eyes there was an anguished look as if he had seen all the misery of the world. He was unworthy of being human. He was eating some candy that a factory had thrown into the dirt. He wiped off the mud and ate the candy. He wasn't drunk but staggered when he walked. He was dizzy from hunger. [. . .]

I'd like to see how I'm going to die. Nobody should feed the idea of suicide. But today he who lives till the hour of his death is a hero. Because he who is not strong gives in.

I heard a woman complaining that the bones she got at the slaughterhouse were clean.

"And I like meat so much!"

I got nervous listening to the woman complaining because it's hard enough for people just to live on this earth, not having sufficient food to eat. For as I've noted, God is the king of the wise men. He put men and animals on the earth. But what the animals eat, nature supplies. If animals had to eat like men, they would suffer greatly. I think of this because when I have nothing to eat I envy the animals.

When I was waiting in line to get some crackers, I listened to the women complaining. One told of stopping at a house and asking for a handout. The lady of the house told her to wait. The woman said that the housewife came back with a package and gave it to her. She didn't want to

SOURCE: David St. Clair, *Child of the Dark: The Diary of Carolina Maria de Jesus* (New York: E. P. Dutton, 1962), 62-63, 69, 97-98, 113, 125-26, 152, 163, 188. From *Child of the Dark* by Carolina Maria de Jesus, trans. David St. Clair, copyright © 1962 by E. P. Dutton & Co., Inc. New York and Souvenir Press, Ltd., London. Used by permission of Dutton, a division of Penguin Group (USA) Inc. and Souvenir Press Ltd. Publishers.

open the package near her friends, because they would ask for some of it. She started to think. Is it a piece of cheese? Can it be meat? When she got back to her shack, the first thing she did was tear open the package. When she unwrapped it, out fell two dead rats.

There are people who make fun of those who beg. [. . .]

The afternoon went by slowly. The Believers are coming with their musical instruments and praising God. Here in the favela there is a shack on "B" Street where the Believers come to pray three times a week. Part of the shack is covered with tin and the rest in tile. There was a day when they were praying and the bums of the favela threw rocks on the shack and broke the tile. Those that hit the tin made a loud noise. Even being insulted they don't give up. They ask the *favelados* not to rob, drink, and to love your neighbor as yourself. The Believers don't permit women to attend their services who are wearing slacks or low-cut dresses. The *favelados* scorn their advice. [. . .]

July 11. I got out of bed at 5:30. I was tired from writing and sleepy. But here in the favela you can't sleep, because the shacks are humid and Neide coughs a lot and keeps me awake. I went to get water and the line was enormous. What an unpleasant thing to wait at that spigot. There's always a fight or someone who wants to know all about the private life of another. In the morning the area around the spigot is covered with shit. I am the one who cleans it up. Because the others aren't interested.

When I got back to the favela I was ill and had a pain in my legs. My sickness is physical as well as moral. [. . .]

The people of the favela know that I'm ill. But nobody shows up here to help me out. I didn't let João go out and he spent the entire day reading. He talks to me and I tell him of the unfortunate things that exist in the world. My son now knows what the world is; between us the language of children has ended.

José Carlos went to the street market. I boiled the bones to make soup. Vera didn't want any. Brother Luiz is putting up the screen to show a movie. I'm not going to go because I'm sick. João asked me to go. I told him that as long as we con-

tinue to live in the favela he was not to play with anybody. I don't want another incident like the first one. Before I used to speak and he would get angry. Now I speak and he listens. I'm going to tell my son about the really serious things in life only when he comes of age.

My son, at 11 years, has already wanted a woman. I explained to him that he must graduate from school, then study even more because a primary school education is not really very much.

July 13. The nurses are coming with Brother Luiz, they are going to cure the sores of the *favelados.* They are teaching the children to pray. I'd like to know how Brother Luiz discovered that the *favelados* have physical sores. [. . .]

I went to wash clothes. At the lagoon was Nalia, Fernanda, and Iracema, who were arguing religion with a woman who said that the true religion was that of the Believers.

Fernanda said that the Bible doesn't order anybody to get married. That it only orders you to increase and multiply. I told Fernanda that Policarpo is a Believer and has many women. Then Fernanda said that Policarpo wasn't a Believer—"he's just hot!"

I thought that was funny and I gave out a whoop. Something I don't discuss is religion. [. . .]

August 9. I got out of bed furious. With a desire to break and destroy everything. Because I only have beans and salt. And tomorrow is Sunday.

I went to the shoemaker to collect his waste-paper. One of them asked me if my book was communistic. I replied that it was realistic. He cautioned me that it was not wise to write of reality.

Today the favela is spinning. Deputy Francisco Franca gave material to finish the clubhouse of the Blacks and Reds. He gave roof tiles and shirts and the people of the favela talk about this Deputy daily. They're going to give a party in his honor.

August 10. Father's Day. What a ridiculous day! [. . .]

I slept and had a marvelous dream. I dreamt I was an angel. My dress was billowing and had long pink sleeves. I went from earth to heaven. I put stars in my hands and played with them. I talked to the stars. They put on a show in my honor. They danced around me and made a luminous path.

When I woke up I thought: I'm so poor. I can't afford to go to a play so God sends me these dreams for my aching soul. To the God who protects me, I send my thanks.

September 3. Yesterday we ate badly. Today worse.

September 8. Today I'm happy. I'm laughing without any reason. [...]

September 14. Today is the Easter of Moses. The God of the Jews. The same God who keeps the Jews free even today. The black is persecuted because his skin is the color of night. And the Jew because he's intelligent. Moses, when he saw the Jews barefoot and ragged, prayed asking God to give them comfort and wealth. And that is why almost all the Jews are rich.

Too bad we blacks don't have a prophet to pray for us.

September 18. Today I'm happy. I'm trying to learn how to live with a calm spirit because for these last few days I've had enough to eat. [...]

[W]e started to talk about prejudice. She told me that in the United States they don't want Negroes in the schools.

I kept thinking: North Americans are considered the most civilized. And they have not yet realized that discriminating against the blacks is like trying to discriminate against the sun. Man cannot fight against the products of Nature. God made all the races at the same time. If he had cre-

ated Negroes after the whites, the whites should have done something about it then. [...]

I got out of bed at 4 a.m. and went to carry water, then went to wash clothes. I didn't make lunch. There is no rice. This afternoon I'm going to cook beans with macaroni. The boys didn't eat anything. I'm going to lie down because I'm sleepy. It was 9 o'clock. João woke me up to open the door. Today I'm sad.

January 4. In the old days I sang. Now I've stopped singing, because the happiness has given way to a sadness that ages the heart. Every day another poor creature shows up here in the favela. [...]

May 3. Today is Sunday. I'm going to spend the day at home. I have nothing to eat. I'm nervous, upset and sad. There is a Portuguese here who wants to live with me. But I don't need a man. And I have begged him not to come around here bothering me.

Today the Father came to say Mass in the favela. He gave the favela the name of "The Rosary District." Many people came to the Mass. In his sermon the priest asked the people not to rob. [...]

I returned and heated some food for the children. Rice and fish. The rice and fish didn't go very far. The children ate and were still hungry. I thought: "If Jesus Christ would only multiply these fish!"

PART XIII

Protestants in
the Twentieth Century

The historic Protestant churches became established throughout Latin America by the beginning of the twentieth century despite discrimination and hostility from governments, the Catholic hierarchy, and Catholic zealots. Membership usually remained confined to upwardly mobile urban dwellers whose precarious economic status tended to make them liberal, democratic, and anticlerical. They resented episcopal interference in temporal affairs, rejected the pope as spiritual leader, minimized the role of saints and the Virgin Mary, and preferred to rely on the written word of the Bible rather than on priests for their personal salvation. But Protestant missionaries never convinced significant numbers of traditional elites, the working class, or indigenous peoples to abandon Catholicism and join their ranks. In fact, by the mid-twentieth century, mainline Protestant churches only represented about 2 or 3 percent of the population. To some Latin Americans, the differences between Catholicism and mainline Protestantism were too insignificant to justify such a radical change of allegiance, especially since Catholicism was so closely linked to Latin American culture and identity. For others, mainline Protestantism seemed even more elitist in membership than traditional Catholicism. In other words, as David Martin suggests, "What historic Protestantism has lacked and still lacks is precisely the capacity to 'go native.'"[1]

The same cannot be said of Pentecostal and neo-Pentecostal Protestant churches, which have grown exponentially in Latin America and in other parts of the globe during the past thirty years. Pentecostals sometimes refer to themselves as evangelicals; for them these terms denote someone who is Christian but not Catholic or mainline Protestant. Pente-

---

1. David Martin, *Tongues of Fire: The Explosion of Protestantism in Latin America* (Oxford: Basil Blackwell, 1990), 282; Jean-Pierre Bastian, "The Metamorphosis of Latin American Protestant Groups: A Sociohistorical Perspective," *Latin American Research Review* 28, no. 2 (1993): 39, 53; Jean-Pierre Bastian, "Protestantism," in *Encyclopedia of Mexico: History, Society & Culture*, vol. 2, ed. Michael S. Werner (Chicago and London: Fitzroy Dearborn Publishers, 1997), 1198.

costal congregations of Hispanics, blacks, and whites emerged in the United States at the beginning of the twentieth century. While Pentecostal churches vary with regard to baptism, church authority, organization, and governance, most emphasize a direct line to God, the gifts of the Holy Spirit, faith healing, speaking in tongues, and as literal as possible reading of the Bible. Frequent migration of Mexican laborers to and from the United States helped to establish Pentecostal churches in Mexico, most notably the Church of God and the Apostolic Church of Faith in Jesus Christ. The largest and fastest-growing Pentecostal church, especially in Brazil, is the Assembly of God.

Unlike Pentecostal churches, whose members come from poor urban and rural areas, members of neo-Pentecostal churches (sometimes referred to as neo-charismatic), such as the Universal Church Kingdom of God (Brazil), the Church of Christ Ministry Elim and the Christian Fraternity (Guatemala), and even some which began as movements within charismatic Catholicism (discussed below), such as Agua Viva (Peru), Ecclesia (Bolivia), and Ondas de Amor y Paz (Argentina), typically espouse a theology of prosperity.[2] Anne Motley Hallum suggests that, in general, members "believe that God rewards good Christians with material wealth. . . ."[3] Professional and business classes who are more educated, entrepreneurial, and politically conservative tend to follow these churches. R. Andrew Chesnut points out that some governments, such as Brazil's, have fostered relations with evangelical communities precisely because they tend to be conservative and, unlike participants in Christian base communities, not radical.

During the past forty years, overall membership in Protestant churches has doubled in Panama, Venezuela, Paraguay, and Chile, tripled in the Dominican Republic, Nicaragua, and Argentina, quadrupled in Puerto Rico and Brazil, quintupled in El Salvador, Costa Rica, Peru, and Bolivia, and sextupled in Honduras, Colombia, and Ecuador. Approximately one-third of Guatemalans are now Protestant. Given current growth rates, Brazil may likely have a Protestant majority by 2030. Some ecumenically minded "mainline" Protestant churches, usually working under the umbrella of the World Council of Churches and the Latin American Council of Churches, maintain active dialogue with the Catholic Church. Many Pentecostal churches are linked in fellowship through the Confraternity of Evangelical Churches.[4]

---

2. Samuel Escobar, *Changing Tides: Latin America and the World Mission Today* (Maryknoll, N.Y.: Orbis Books, 2002), 81.

3. Anne Motley Hallum, "Taking Stock and Building Bridges: Feminism, Women's Movements, and Pentecostalism in Latin America," *Latin American Research Review* 38, no. 1 (2003): 173; Amy L. Sherman, *The Soul of Development: Biblical Christianity and Economic Transformation in Guatemala* (New York: Oxford University Press, 1997), ix-x; Bastian, "Protestantism," 1200.

4. R. Andrew Chesnut, *Born Again in Brazil: The Pentecostal Boom and the Pathogens of Poverty* (New Brunswick, N.J.: Rutgers University Press, 1997), 6, 171; Virginia Garrard-Burnett, "Protestantism," in *Encyclopedia of Latin American History and Culture*, vol. 4, ed. Barbara A. Tenenbaum (New York: Charles Scribner's Sons, 1996), 477; Somini Sengupta and Larry Rohter, "Where Faith Grows: Fired by Pentecostalism," *The New York Times*, October 14, 2004, A:1; J. Samuel Escobar, "The Promise and Precariousness of Latin American Protestantism," in *Coming of Age: Protestantism in Contemporary Latin America*, ed. Daniel R. Miller (Lanham, Md.: University Press of America, 1994), 9-10.

Urban Pentecostal churches usually flourish in poor and marginalized areas where people are overwhelmed with the devastating effects of alcohol, drugs, violence, and crime. Many converts are recent arrivals to the megacity from the countryside, and their "loss of all ties that bind," suggests Martin, may have predisposed them to undertake such a radical shift in their religious affiliation. Newcomers to the faith, notes Juan Sepúlveda, "who have been scarred by neglect, powerlessness, and loneliness find in Pentecostal communities full acceptance and togetherness without preconditions."[5] One's ability to read and analyze text is not a precondition to full-fledged membership and intense participation since, states Phillip Berryman, "illiterates often feel more at home in Pentecostal churches, where the accent is on oral testimony, emotional prayer, and singing—and the ability to read is therefore less important." Through faith healing, Pentecostalism offers its adherents immediate solutions to the grinding problems of poverty, especially those adherents who do not have access to health care. Petitioners accept Jesus as their personal savior in return for a restoration of their health. Religious instruction by community leaders helps the convert learn appropriate codes of conduct and beliefs such as that baptism by healing waters cleanses the soul and alleviates sickness. Devotees provide continuous emotional support. Most Pentecostal churches prohibit alcohol, drug use, and illicit sexuality under penalty of censure and expulsion. Women, who comprise about two-thirds of this movement, benefit greatly once their male relatives cease their abusive behavior. Pentecostal youth who form new social networks are relieved of societal pressures that emphasize consumption and unbridled sexuality. One's decision to join a Pentecostal church, therefore, has little to do with its doctrine. As José Luis Pérez Guadalupe states, "many people first join these groups for a series of reasons, primarily experiential, and later on learn just what this group thinks."[6] Rural Pentecostal churches tend to grow and develop in Amerindian villages where government repression has not been matched by adequate concern from the local priest or the Catholic hierarchy. Frequently, members of an entire community make a collective decision to embrace Pentecostalism rather than Catholicism, and thus preserve group identity. Nearby Pentecostal communities typically ease this transition by helping their neighbors to build a church, school, and hospital.[7]

---

5. Juan Sepúlveda, "The Pentecostal Movement in Latin America," in *New Face of the Church in Latin America: Between Tradition and Change*, ed. Guillermo Cook (Maryknoll, N.Y.: Orbis Books, 1994), 73; Martin, *Tongues of Fire*, 283-85.

6. Quoted in Escobar, *Changing Tides*, 44.

7. Phillip Berryman, "Is Latin America Turning Pluralist? Recent Writings on Religion," *Latin American Research Review* 30, no. 3 (1995): 110; R. Andrew Chesnut, *Competitive Spirits: Latin America's New Religious Economy* (Oxford: Oxford University Press, 2003), 128-46; Elizabeth Brusco, "The Reformation of Machismo: Asceticism and Masculinity among Colombian Evangelicals," in *Rethinking Protestantism in Latin America*, ed. Virginia Garrard-Burnett and David Stoll (Philadelphia: Temple University Press, 1993), 147; Chesnut, *Born Again in Brazil*, 5, 167-70, 173; Hallum, "Taking Stock and Building Bridges," 176, 178; John Burdick, *Looking for God in Brazil: The Progressive Catholic Church in Urban Brazil's Religious Arena* (Berkeley: University of California Press, 1993), 15.

88. Presbyterians in Guatemala

The following reading is a selection from "The Ninety-Sixth Annual Report of the Board of Foreign Missions of the Presbyterian Church in the United States of America" (1933). This account may best serve as an illustration of (1) the quality of the Catholic Church (in this case in Guatemala) and (2) church-state relations, that is, the government's attitude toward the powerful Catholic Church and the new Protestant churches. President Jorge Ubico (1931-1944) may be characterized as an economically progressive, paternalist dictator. A presbytery is an ecclesiastical court consisting of all the ministers and one or two elders from each congregation in a given area (here all of Guatemala) to decide church issues.

Describe the two considerations mentioned above. Why are all foreign and missionary physicians refused licenses by the doctors of the capital city? What is the best use that may be made of the brief "History" that ends the report?

In common with the whole world, the Guatemala Mission has suffered from the depression, but while the effect has been to cripple our efficiency seriously and cramp our ability to use opportunities and to direct religious growth, yet its effect upon the progress of evangelization has been rather favorable. People in distress and desperation think seriously and that favors our work.

The Roman Church is becoming much more active in Guatemala of late, yet the general political situation remains favorable. General Ubico makes a fine president, backed as he is by a vigorous party that stands for toleration, so that we are not thwarted by intolerance either of the Roman or the communistic type.

Organized Churches Evangelistic

The great advances the Mission is making and the yearly increasing activity in native evangelism are leading us to believe that we now have such a planting of the Gospel in this country that, no matter what happens, it can never be eradicated, though it will still need cultivation. Where the first missionary, fifty years ago, had to walk the streets between policemen to be sure of life and limb in this then fanatical city of 100,000 souls, there are now over 1,500 people meeting freely to study the Bible in Evangelical Sunday schools each week, besides a whole army of others in all stages of persuasion. It is now actually easier to establish a presbytery than it used to be to establish a church, or to convert and organize a whole congregation than it was to convert and reform a single member. The Roman renaissance referred to has not retarded our progress in the least, on the contrary, our presence here seems to have had a very purifying effect on that Church, whether this be due to absorption, evangelization, ocular demonstration of the good we are doing, the healthy influences of a liberal Government that protects us, or more likely, to all combined. [...]

In education we have done well, though the attendance has been more limited, owing to the inability of parents to meet expenses. The schools have done good work, the departments are becoming more efficient, the teachers more evangelical, the equipment more satisfactory. Our grade and normal school for girls in Quezaltenango in its ample new building gave good

SOURCE: "Guatemala Mission," in "Minutes of the General Assembly of the Presbyterian Church in the U.S.A.," *The Ninety-Sixth Annual Report of the Board of Foreign Missions of the Presbyterian Church in the United States of America: Presented to the General Assembly, May, 1933* (Philadelphia: Office of the General Assembly, 1933), 134-37, passim. Reprinted by permission of Office of the General Assembly, Presbyterian Church USA.

account of itself, and the Norton School of the capital, though financial conditions were of the worst, under active principalship and faithful teaching and excruciating economy, did a fine year's work. The Boys' Industrial College by its very nature has felt the depression most directly, not being able to market its products when unemployment was so general. Still it did a good year's work, its pupils being highly approved by government examiners in the main. [. . .]

The most satisfactory development of the year has been in the medical department. The fifty-bed hospital has been working to capacity. With this central base of operations, the plan contemplates an extensive outwork with ambulance, corps of workers including nurses, literature distributors, evangelists, etc., making stands for days or weeks at important locations where the sick are many and there is no medical assistance. Such places abound, as most of the doctors are bunched at the capital where alone they can make a living and where they refuse to license missionary physicians or any foreigner. But at last our problem has been solved. One of our own people, a native born, though of Italian parents, has been licensed after a fine medical education in Germany, and he has now been employed by the hospital and the itinerary clinic plan has become possible. It is giving astonishing results and bids fair to take the country by storm. [. . .]

History—Early in 1882 the attention of the Presbyterian Board was called to the fact that in all Guatemala there was not one Protestant church service held, while in the capital were many Europeans and Americans. Assurances were given of the sympathy of the president of the republic, and of freedom of religious belief. The first missionary reached *Guatemala City* toward the end of 1882. The plan adopted was to gather an English-speak-

ing congregation and organize a Protestant church. Services were held in private residences. By April, 1883, the missionaries were fully established. A Sunday school was organized and attended by the children of the president and others in high positions. By the close of the year the new chapel was filled. Spanish work was established and a chapel built in 1891. Two churches were organized in 1892, one of Spanish-speaking and the other of English-speaking people. In 1894 the English church became independent.

A mixed school was established in 1883, but closed in 1889; a boys' school was opened in 1888, but closed at a later date; a girls' school was opened in 1884, but closed in 1891. At the beginning of 1913, another school for girls was opened in a fine new building. Medical work was begun in 1906, and in 1913 the hospital was opened. In connection with the hospital was a training school for nurses. On December 25, 1917, the Guatemala station was entirely destroyed by earthquake, but rebuilding was at once begun. In 1918 the manse and printing house were rebuilt, and in 1921 the church, girls' school and hospital. A boys' school was opened in 1925.

In 1896 a lot was purchased in *Quezaltenango* and a church and parsonage built largely with funds raised on the field. The station was occupied in 1898. In 1902 a terrible earthquake nearly destroyed the town, and great loss of life occurred. A volcanic eruption followed, which ruined the plantations around the city. These calamities interrupted all progress for a time. In 1912 a church building was dedicated. When the building was proposed, contractors refused to undertake the building of a Protestant church, and the work was performed by day labor under the constant supervision of the missionaries. Both of these stations are now rebuilt, and pioneer work is being carried on among the Indians.

89. Mexican Evangelicals, 1935

Statistical information about the evangelical churches in Latin America, even in the recent past, is difficult to obtain. Thus, figures for 1935 gathered by Kenneth G. Grubb, author of Religion in Central America *(1937), and Professor G. Baez Camargo, secretary of the National Evangelical Council of Mexico, joint authors of* Religion in the Republic of Mexico *(1935), are quite valuable. Their data was derived from responses to the following questions: Who constituted the Mexican evangelicals? What class did they represent? Where did they fall within the general population? From the excerpts below, what were those responses?*

The data presented in this chapter represents the experience and opinion of many local pastors and their congregations upon a large number of questions related to the life of their churches. [...]

In 1935 there were, according to Kenneth Grubb and Baez Camargo, 584 organized churches, 1,205 congregations holding weekly services, 259 ordained ministers, 44,113 communicant members and an evangelical community of 89,750 Christians. In the five years which have elapsed since the publication of these figures, there has been an approximate increase of about 25 percent in the evangelical movement, so that there are now about 700 churches, 324 ordained ministers, 1,440 congregations, 53,000 communicant members and an evangelical community of 108,750.

The actual increase has been greater than these figures indicate, but it has been offset by the loss of scattered and un-led congregations and the steady process of attrition of individuals and families that is ever present in the evangelical community.

Social and Economic Status of Evangelicals

The Evangelical Church membership represents a wide cross-section of the occupations and professions of the community in Mexico. A majority of the members, — in many cases a very large majority, — come from the humblest of circles. In the rural churches, day laborers, tenant farmers and farm hands are mostly in evidence, with a sprinkling of artisans, shopkeepers, machinists, teachers and transport workers. In the semi-urban churches, the proportion of small tradesmen, factory hands and clerical workers rises, while in the urban churches, a fair cross-section of the varied activities of the city is represented in the membership, with a number of professional people and petty officials and a very few men of some financial means. Even in the city church, however, the majority of the members come from the humbler walks of life, with a comparatively low earning power. [...]

About 38 percent of evangelical Christians of the churches answering the questionnaire are in debt, with an average debt of 200 *pesos*. The chief causes for indebtedness, given in their order of frequency, are:

> Rising cost of living.
> Poverty.
> Bad management.
> Low salaries.
> Unemployment.
> Inadequate tools and equipment.

However, the economic and social status of evangelicals as contrasted with their non-evangelical neighbors is illuminating and points to the possibility of a sound and expanding evangelical group of the future. Of the churches replying to this question, 57.1 percent stated that their members were in better economic circumstances than non-evangelicals of the same classes and occupa-

SOURCE: J. Merle Davis, *The Economic Basis of the Evangelical Church in Mexico: A Study Made by the Department of Social and Economic Research of the International Missionary Council* (London and New York: International Missionary Council, 1940), 45-47. © World Council of Churches. Used by permission.

tions, 33.3 percent rated their members as equal to the average in economic strength, and only 9.6 percent rated them as inferior.

The health of the evangelicals showed about the same ratio as the foregoing: 66.6 percent of the pastors who replied, rated the members of their churches as superior in health; 22.2 percent rated their members as equal and 11.2 percent considered their members inferior in health to the general community.

The incidence of literacy among evangelicals is very high, estimated at 90 percent among the churches answering. This is contrasted with the 40.7 percent literacy ratio for the entire nation. One third of the churches represented in the answers to the questionnaire have one or more members who are occupying superior positions in the community. Only 13.3 percent of the churches report that commercial or business leaders are among the membership. One or more Government officials and members of the learned professions are found in 20 percent of the churches reporting.

The sanitary and housing conditions of the homes of the evangelicals are reported to be somewhat better than with the average of the population. The absence of heavy drinking, gambling and general loafing in the evangelical community, together with their greater literacy, helps them to make better use of their spare time.

90. Religious Liberty in Latin America?

Here are two analyses of a difficult and unfortunate moment concerning religion in U.S. relations with Latin America. The first is by the great U.S. Protestant theologian, missionary, and spokesman, John A. Mackay, president of Princeton Theological Seminary from 1936 to 1959. Dr. Mackay was writing in 1944, a time when U.S. Catholicism was still suspect by Protestants (see the vehement criticisms of Paul Blanshard in the trenchant American Freedom and Catholic Power *[1949]) and when Catholics were likewise suspicious of the motives and initiatives of Protestants. Mackay succinctly describes the crisis within Latin American Catholicism and the threat of a politically powerful U.S. Catholic clericalism.*

How does Dr. Mackay diagnose the sickness of Latin American religious culture in his "third question"?

Two problems then emerge in two paragraphs, as Mackay responds to his "fourth question": (1) In the first paragraph he actually anticipates a movement that will burgeon in Latin America some quarter century later and which will specifically address his description of the utter failure of Latin American Catholicism to respond to the harsh realities of Latin American society and culture. What are the "two main springs" to which that church should resort for its healing? (2) Second paragraph—What is the "new portent" that Mackay perceives arising in North America, which, however, is centuries old in Latin America?

Note that one caveat is called for when Mackay refers to the Protestant "stainless record" on "bigotry or intolerance." That comment dismisses a major strain in nineteenth-century U.S. history and one still strong in much of the U.S. evangelical movement to this day.

The second analysis consists of a personal statement, interviews, and contextual commen-

---

Sources: John A. Mackay, "Foreword," in George P. Howard, *Religious Liberty in Latin America?* (Philadelphia: The Westminster Press, 1944), xi-xiv; George P. Howard, *Religious Liberty in Latin America?* (Philadelphia: The Westminster Press, 1944), 1-15 passim, xvii-xix.

tary by George P. Howard, who was born to U.S. parents in Argentina in the late nineteenth century, was educated there and later at Northwestern University, Garrett Biblical Institute, and Union Theological Seminary, New York. He was sometime pastor in the United States, an official of the Methodist Mission Board in Argentina, and spent more than thirty-five years in Latin America, mostly in Argentina, as a "Christian apostle to the classes and masses" (Mackay). He also taught at Union Theological Seminary, Buenos Aires. It is remarkable to have a Latin American who is thoroughly acquainted with the United States in all its aspects present his account of a startling religious development (which he studied) taking place in the United States in the 1940s. Howard prefaces his remarks about that development by quoting misconceived, inaccurate, and insulting statements by the U.S. bishops and other clerics. These statements betray an ignorance about the complex realities of Latin American culture that was almost universal then among all U.S. citizens—and is unfortunately still true today. What is that religious development which Howard so severely criticizes?

Howard then gives a full statement of a political development (Mackay's and Howard's Catholic "clericalism") involving the U.S. Catholic Church and the U.S. State Department. What is that development, that is, what policy, formulated by the U.S. Catholic Church, did the U.S. State Department accept and execute?

The excerpt continues with Howard's inclusion of statements by Dr. Armando Solano, by "one of Peru's really great men [unnamed]," and by Dr. Fernández Artucio. It must seem confusing at first that Latin American "liberals" would embrace "American imperialism" and "conservatives" would decry it. What do these "liberals" see in U.S. culture that they want all Latin Americans to experience? What is the dramatic answer to the question posed by Howard in the last three paragraphs of the reading?

John A. Mackay: A third question arises: *What is the crucial problem of Latin-American culture?* According to the best and most thoughtful men and women in the Southern continent, it is this: a religious sense of life — that is, a spiritual inwardness, in which religious faith is correlated with moral action and cultural expression. Their complaint is that Latin-American life has lacked a form of spirituality, which would give it a sense of wholeness, fullness of meaning, and ethical direction.

The truth is that religion and life have never been closely related in the Latin-American spiritual tradition. Religion has been divorced from culture and ethics by a great unbridged chasm. That chasm, according to representative Latin Americans, has also been the tragedy of Spain. How vehemently have eminent men like Miguel de Unamuno, the Spaniard, and Ricardo Rojas, the Argentinean, indicted the religious tradition of the Spanish and Latin-American people

because it has failed to produce true spirituality. Both these great men have given classical formulation to the idea that what Spain and Latin America need more than anything else is a popular and intimate knowledge of the Bible and a reinterpretation of the figure and significance of Jesus Christ. The traditional attitude of the Roman Catholic Church in Spain and Latin America toward the popular reading of the Scriptures has been one of the greatest cultural tragedies in all history.

The fourth question, therefore, is this: *How adequate is Latin-American Catholicism to deal with the cultural situation in the continent which it serves?* The answer is simple. It is utterly unequipped to deal with a problem so difficult and vast.

Up to the present time the record of this Church has been, as North American Catholics know perfectly well, one of the major spiritual derelictions in the history of Christianity. Neither in spiritual resources nor in insight into the true problems of men and nations, nor in the number or prestige of its leaders, can Roman Catholicism in Latin America be looked to for the solution of the crucial cultural problem of these great countries. Nor can it ever have the necessary spiritual equipment to do so until Roman Catholic leaders throughout the Iberian world pick up a lost tradition in Spanish religious history where alone can be found an indigenous fountain of spiritual life. That tradition is discoverable in two main springs: in the work of the great Spanish mystics whom the Church persecuted, but who never broke with the Church — Santa Teresa, John of the Cross, Luis of León; and in the great Spaniards of the sixteenth century who embraced the principles of Evangelical Christianity, especially the famous laymen Alfonso and Juan de Valdés. These men are recognized today by authorities on Spanish literature and history as princes of Spanish letters, and peaks of Spanish moral grandeur. They are, in a word, expressions of the type of Spanish personality that Evangelical Christianity can produce. Juan de Valdés, more than any other figure in Spanish history, is the true point of departure for the religious reformation which is needed by the Church in Spain and Latin America. [. . .]

For one who knows the Latin-American tradition it is abundantly plain that there is emerging in North American life, in both the United States and Canada, a new portent. That portent the people of the Latin world have known for centuries. They have called it "clericalism," the organized political power of the higher clergy of the Roman Catholic Church, as distinguished from the Catholic religious tradition and the mass of the Roman Catholic people. "Clericalism" has emerged at last in two hospitable Protestant countries in the Western world. Its political pressures and international schemes are becoming perfectly plain. Protestants who have a stainless record of anything that might be regarded as bigotry or intolerance, who will stand for the principle of religious freedom to the last, and will even fight for the rights of Roman Catholics, are now bracing themselves to deal with a new portent in Anglo-Saxon America: the portent, the sinister portent, of Roman Catholic "clericalism." This portent is the source, among other

things, of the specious lie that Protestant missions in Latin America are subversive of the Good Neighbor policy.

George P. Howard: I was born in Argentina and have lived nearly all my life in South America. I came to the United States in June of 1942 to engage in an extensive program of addresses on Latin America and the Good Neighbor policy [. . .] I was suddenly face to face with a campaign that was almost as brazen as it was unfair. Statements in the American press so intemperate, even insulting to Protestantism and certainly untrue in many respects, had aroused my audiences and I was compelled to yield to their demand that I answer their questions and meet their interest in this matter. [. . .]

A campaign is evidently on for a postwar program that will grant religious freedom wherever the Roman Catholic Church is in a minority and religious monopoly wherever it has the power to suppress competition. The fight against Protestant missions in Latin America is the first stage of that campaign. Our Protestant representatives in the southern lands are the present victims of the bludgeoning blows of misrepresentation and the quick darts of a mocking wit which have been hurled upon them. The discriminatory attitude of the American press in favor of Catholic interests would lead one to plead: If these Catholic interests are allowed to express themselves without the restraints that even pagan courtesy would dictate, surely we Protestants have the right to present our case. [. . .]

The Roman Catholic agitation against Protestant missions in Latin America was brought out into the open by a manifesto entitled *Victory and Peace*, issued in November of 1942 by Roman Catholic bishops meeting in Washington. It read as follows:

"We send our cordial greetings to our brother Bishops of Latin America. We have been consoled by recent events, which give a sincere promise of a better understanding by our country of the peoples of Mexico and Central and South America.

"Citizens of these countries are bound to us by the closest bond of religion. They are not merely our neighbors; they are brothers professing the same faith. Every effort made to rob them of the Catholic religion or to ridicule it is deeply resented by the peoples of these countries and by American Catholics. These efforts prove to be a disturbing factor in our international relations.

"The traditions, the spirit, the background, the culture of these countries are Catholic. We Bishops are anxious to foster every worthy movement, which will strengthen our amicable relations with the republics of this continent.

"We express the hope that the mistakes of the past which were offensive to the dignity of our Southern brothers, their culture and their religion will not continue. A strong bond uniting in true friendship all the countries of the Western Hemisphere will exercise a most potent influence on a shattered post-war world."

Through such periodicals as *The Catholic Digest*, *Extension*, and *America*, an active campaign was conducted, designed to set the public mind against the idea of Protestant missions in Latin America. Thus the Roman Catholic Church has openly entered the field in an aggressive effort to deprive the Protestant Churches of their right to propagate their faith in the lands to the south.

The gist of the argument is that Latin America is soundly Catholic; that the activities of Protestants there are a "work of pure destruction"; that the presence of missionaries is an obstacle to the Good Neighbor policy; and that they are "the strongest reason why South Americans do not like us." It is alleged that "the great damage done by the American missionaries is in the field of politics. Their work arouses even more enmity against the United States than did the activities of American big business in the old days of dollar diplomacy." *Extension*, the Chicago diocesan paper, in a particularly vituperative editorial said: "There can be no freedom of religion where malevolent interference with the beliefs of Catholic peoples is allowed to run rampant."

These are grave accusations. If true, no one should be more interested in knowing it and acknowledging it than the Protestants. Protestantism makes no claim to "infallibility" and so does not have to save its face by defending its weaknesses. It can admit its blunders and correct its practices. But would it be fair to direct our critical attention only toward the Protestants in Latin America without considering whether the representatives of the Roman Catholic Church have not also made mistakes? [...] A false conception of the spirit of Christian charity has been invoked. One cannot but admire the straight-out-from-the-shoulder attitude of Catholic writers. Take this paragraph, for instance, from an address by Msgr. John P. Treacy, of Cleveland, Ohio, to the Catholic Daughters of America convened in Washington, D. C., during July, 1943, and published in *The Evening Star* (July 14):

"The American Protestant churches exported missionaries into Latin America to convert the natives who were 100 percent Catholic whether they practiced their religion or not. These people wanted their one true faith or no religion and the United States had little or no faith to offer and about 200 so-called religions. Naturally these people resented the colonists from the United States."

This is plain talk. There is no mincing of words here, no false sentimentalism. We know where Msgr. Treacy stands. I cannot believe that when he says that "the United States had little or no faith to offer and about 200 so-called religions" to export, he was representing the best and most enlightened Roman Catholic opinion in America. But he does represent a most aggressive pressure group within that Church and a group that enjoys much power and favor at present in Washington. [...]

[W]hen Catholics ask the American Government to refuse permission to new Protestant missionaries to go to Latin America or to those on furlough to return to their long-established home and work on the southern continent, then they are claiming the right of persecution. Will the people of the United States approve of their State Department's deciding whether properly qualified Protestant missionaries shall be sent to carry on their missionary work in the countries to the south of us?

Roman Catholic emissaries to South America move freely, while passports for Protestant missionaries are hard to get. The necessity for restricting travel on account of war conditions is not the reason why the State Department discriminates against Protestant missionaries. That difficulty exists and is recognized by the Protestant mission boards, who have been parsimonious in their requests for passports.

Nor does the difficulty lie primarily with the South American Governments. With two or three exceptions, countries where military dictatorships keep themselves in power against popular will by the support of the Roman Catholic hierarchy, there are no more restrictions on entrance into those countries than are natural during wartimes. [...]

Latin Americans coming to the United States are kept within Roman Catholic auspices. In his interviews with South Americans who had come to the United States, in most cases as guests of honor of the American Government, the writer constantly discovered perplexity and even resentment created in the minds of these distinguished visitors by this policy of the State Department. [...]

Dr. Gil Salgueiro, of Uruguay, was invited to lecture in the United States; he is not a Roman Catholic and has been nurtured in the anticlerical tradition which is particularly strong in Uruguay. Yet he was sent to lecture exclusively in Roman Catholic institutions of the United States. A former Uruguayan minister of education, whose name I shall omit, was invited by the American Government to come to the United States in 1943. When I interviewed him recently in Montevideo, he said to me: "On my first Sunday in Washington I asked what there was to see and do in that city on Sunday. They gave me the address of a famous Roman Catholic Church! And I, who would not be seen entering a Catholic Church in Uruguay, took the suggestion and went to Church! I was surprised to see how many people attended mass." [...]

South Americans know what it is to be 'protected' from outside and so-called dangerous ideas or relationships. The reaction against this policy of paternalistic manipulation has swung them fiercely toward the opposite tendency of an almost passionate cult of freedom.

Hence the rise of anticlericalism in Spanish America. That term means little or nothing to the average American unless it be to imply something discreditable. "Clericalism" is the priest stepping out of his high function as a representative of spiri-

tual values and using religion itself for the worldly ends of the Church. South America knows it well and has suffered under its handicap for centuries. On that continent will be found many anti-clericals who are good Roman Catholics. In a copy of a leading daily published in Bogotá, Colombia, and which I have before me. Dr. Armando Solano, a great liberal and sincere Catholic, says: "Popular belief in and support of a creed may be weakened not only as a result of anti-religious propaganda, which I dislike immensely, but also as a consequence of the anti-national and unwise attitudes of the clergy. I think that it is possible to be a Catholic and at the same time be anticlerical." [...]

[O]ne of Peru's really great men, whose name I [Howard] shall omit for obvious reasons [made the following statement] . . . "Most of the exchange students chosen to go to the United States are Roman Catholic. So are the professors. Many of these are out-and-out Fascists. And they have come back from the United States more confirmed in their Fascism. I have heard them say: Democracy is a myth in the United States. There is the same attitude in that country toward race that the Fascists have. Others have said: If the democracies win, 'American imperialism' will be more dangerous than ever, for the United States will come out of the war a mighty military power.

"The liberals don't talk this way," he explained; "only the conservatives. 'The United States is meddling in everything,' say these conservatives. 'They distribute newsprint; they are the providers of many things we need; they have even helped to keep certain books out of Peru.' Many of these Conservative Catholics who work in harmony with the coordinator's office are using this relation to keep themselves in power politically." [...]

It was a red-letter day when I was ushered into the private study of Dr. Hugo Fernández Artucio, a distinguished lawyer, member of the Uruguayan Legislature, university professor, and member of "The Free World Association." Dr. Artucio became famous three years ago when he exposed the Nazi spy system in South America. He is the author of *The Nazi Underground in South America.* [...]

"The influence of Catholic intolerance reflected in the foreign policy of the United States is considered by people of liberal spirit in this country as a dangerous symptom of the totalitarian leanings of the United States. Therefore, there is a feeling of resentment among liberal sections of Uruguayan public opinion because of this surprising aspect of American policy." [. . .]

[W]ould the Roman Catholic Church in South America be rid of all religious rivals if the foreign missionaries were withdrawn? Not at all. Protestantism in Latin America is no longer an exotic minority; it has become an indigenous movement that is very largely self-governing and self-propagating. In Chile the largest Protestant group is that of the Pentecostals, who number 30,000 and among whom there is not a single foreign missionary. Their pastors are Chilean. In Uruguay and Argentina, which together constitute what the Methodists call an 'Annual Conference,' this governing body has a native-born bishop, seventy-six national (or native) workers and pastors, and only four foreign missionaries. What would be achieved by withdrawing these four missionaries? In Uruguay the strong Waldensian Church is

entirely autonomous and has no foreign missionaries. The same is true of the Peruvian Evangelical Church. In Brazil there are two independent and completely autonomous Churches: the Congregational and an Independent Presbyterian organization. It can also be said of the Methodist Church in Brazil that it is independent and autonomous. It elects its own bishops and determines its own program and policies. [. . .]

In view of the significance of this whole question, the reply of the Federal Council of Churches to the pronouncement of the Roman Catholic hierarchy against Protestant missions in Latin America was very timely:

"We deplore the pretension of the Roman Catholic hierarchy to circumscribe the religious freedom of Protestant Christians in the proclamation of their faith, while by implication reserving for themselves the right to universal proclamation of their own. We can imagine no policy more certain to project into the New World the baneful intolerance which is now producing such tragic consequences in the contemporary life of Spain."

91. A Protest for the Peruvian Senate

The following excerpt consists of two parts: (1) an introductory statement by George P. Howard, which raises questions about how Latin Americans react to the presence of U.S. Protestant missionaries in their country, and (2) one such typical reaction, made in the Peruvian Senate. Given the statement of the Peruvian senators, how would Howard himself respond to the queries he raised in his introduction?

[Howard's introduction]

Is it true, as critics of Protestant missions allege, that the presence of American missionaries "is resented throughout the continent [South America]"? Is it true, as one critic says, that "the South Americans, being innately polite and kind, especially toward foreigners, try to keep up an appearance of courtesy toward the American missionaries who live among them, but inwardly

their resentment boils like a volcano?" Is it only toward American missionaries that "resentment boils?"

I have lived all my life among these people; I am one of them; I was born in South America; but I never discovered any such general attitude of resentment on the part of the people. Certain individuals, especially those who fear the common people, who have no use for democracy, and who hate everything American — they, of course, "boil

---

SOURCE: Quoted in George P. Howard, *Religious Liberty in Latin America?* (Philadelphia: Westminster Press, 1944), xviii-xix, 53-54.

like volcanos." And they are not very polite about it either!

Nevertheless, I began to wonder. Was I mistaken? Had I been living in a fool's paradise? Was Protestantism hated or resented? How could this doubt be dispelled? There was only one answer. I would return to Latin America and interview leaders of thought, writers, educators, prominent businessmen as well as labor leaders, and ask them candidly and frankly: What do you think of the Protestants? Are they an obstacle to the Good Neighbor policy? Should missionaries be recalled? [...]

[Howard quotes five members of the Peruvian Senate who signed a letter of protest on October 5, 1943]

"Mr. President: In the session of August 27 of 1940 of this Senate it was agreed to communicate with the Minister of Government, asking him to reprimand and punish the subordinate police authorities who had exceeded their authority in their relations with the Protestants. He was also asked to protect the latter in the exercise of the rights which our Constitution affords them. Since that date unfortunate incidents have continued to occur with disconcerting frequency. This makes it necessary for us to act again; not in defense of a religious creed, but in behalf of such elementary principles as freedom of expression and of conscience." [...]

"While millions of men are sacrificing their lives on fields of battle in defense of liberty and democracy, and when declarations like the Atlantic Charter, to which our Government has expressed its adherence have been made, we cannot believe that the time is favorable for inciting religious strife. Concerned as we all are in the great task of uniting mankind to face the disastrous consequences which war produces, the present is surely no proper time to deny to foreigners

or nationals the most elementary human rights. It is certainly not the wisest time in which to expose ourselves to the severe and justifiable criticism of this attitude which has already been made by the press in some of our neighboring countries.

"Let it not be said in defense of this persecution, that Protestant activity is inimical to the country's best interests or distasteful to its people. It has been and is, on the contrary, most beneficial. Up in the mountain regions and especially in the Department of Puno, many are the Indians whom the Protestant missionaries have led out of the most abject ignorance, weaning them from the vices of alcohol and the use of the coca leaf. In other sections of the country also their work is worthy of the highest praise. If our government is not able to support and help such valuable work, it, at least, should feel deeply grateful for what it has accomplished, and that gratitude should express itself in granting these missionaries every possible guarantee of freedom of expression, of reunion and of conscience.

"These considerations oblige us to request the Honorable Senate to communicate to the Ministry of Government our desire that immediate and energetic steps be taken to prevent subordinate authorities from continuing to commit these abuses against the Protestants, and that the latter be given full guarantees for the free execution of their religious acts; and furthermore, that the Minister of Foreign Affairs be requested to send out instructions that the passports of persons desirous of coming to Peru, receive the necessary consular visa without any reference to the religious creed which said persons may profess."

Lima, October 5th, 1943
(Signed) Paul A. Pinto
Pedro Ruiz Bravo
Francisco Pastor
Carlos A. Barreda
Víctor F. Baca

92. Protestantism: Positive or Negative for Latin America?

following two perspectives on Protestantism published in 1944 as contradictory as they might seem on first reading? Both authors, Peruvian Luis Alberto Sánchez and Brazilian Manuel Carlos Ferraz, are men of law and public intellectuals who are vitally concerned with the welfare and integrity of their respective nations.

(1) Would Sánchez refute Ferraz's evaluation of the contributions of Protestantism to Brazil? (2) Would he reject Ferraz's characterization of Protestantism as "a democratic-federative movement"? (3) Would Ferraz deny Sánchez's insistence that the U.S. government sees in every Protestant missionary another possible means of advancing U.S. interests, or even U.S. "imperial penetration" in Latin America? (4) On the basis of his estimate of the state of Roman Catholicism in Brazil, would he find Sánchez's estimate of its status in all of Latin America too positive? (5) Are the two essays mutually exclusive? (6) Given the U.S. government's support of U.S. evangelist campaigns, especially in Central America during the tumultuous 1980s, which of the two writers might be considered the more perspicacious?

Luis Alberto Sánchez, lawyer, author, and lecturer: We Latin Americans will always be suspicious of those who come to us clothed in extraordinary powers and privileges, which we interpret as revealing some definite, ulterior purpose. No Latin American will accept with sincerity religious missions that are supported by regimented "priorities" of the State Department. To our Creole spirit of distrust, a factor which is not reckoned with by Washington's political strategists, every missionary "made in USA" is looked upon as an insurance agent, or a banker who wishes to place a loan, or an employee of the Coordinator of Inter-American Relations, or a member of the FBI. If what Washington officials want is to discredit religion *per se*, they have already made some progress. Let it be clear: everything that comes to us stamped with an official *made in USA* seal suggests self-interest or some ulterior purpose. Implicitly it links itself with the dollar sign. It is worth so much; it is an object of barter. It can be of use. I know that there are many things—and ideas—in the United States, that represent high value in themselves. But you cannot expect those who have known only the overwhelming material power of the United States to believe that those other values exist. Yesterday, in

an economy of peace, they knew the United States through her capitalistic enterprises established with full autonomy and a management independent of the countries in which it functioned. Today, in a war period, they see her through trade organizations eager to be ahead in any deal. Religious propaganda regimented from Washington will lead to a weakening of religious ties and, soon or late, will be considered an ally of imperial penetration. Then it will be that Christianity will end up by appearing to be an expression of imperialism. For the good of all concerned, it were well to avoid this confusion. The days that are ahead will bring us much pain. Men should be able to find somewhere a firm wall against which to lean their weary, sweaty heads. And that support must continue to come from Christianity.

Furthermore, there could be no error more grievous or more un-brotherly than that of thinking that, as far as Christianity is concerned, we are on the same level as the Africans and Asiatics. That is, to consider us as "infidels" or "pagans." They who so think forget that in relation to Christianity we do not need colonizers; we have moved ahead; we could do some colonizing on our account. It hurts our religious consciousness and our civilized self-respect that any one should pre-

SOURCE: Interviews of Luis Alberto Sánchez and Manuel Carlos Ferraz, in George P. Howard, *Religious Liberty in Latin America?* (Philadelphia: Westminster Press, 1944), 152-53, 167-68.

tend to teach us as they would the natives of Mozambique or Tibet what the Christian religion is and even more so, when they pretend to teach us what Catholicism is. We have experts in these subjects who could do honor to a university course in the United States. The organization of a systematic Catholic crusade in the United States to work upon Latin America is equivalent to our launching a movement to Protestantize the United States. [...]

Manuel Carlos Ferraz, distinguished Brazilian jurist and President of the Appellate Court of Brazil: [...] Protestantism has served as a stimulus to Roman Catholicism. It is a warning to that Church that it must awaken from the sleep of indifference into which it had been lulled as a result of its isolation from other currents of Christian thought. When Roman Catholicism was our State religion and other religions were prohibited in Brazil, Catholicism entered a period of decay. The freedom which was later granted to other religions and the separation of Church and State, have been helpful to the Roman Church itself. It has been compelled to open more schools, create more parishes and dioceses and build more churches.

Protestantism has given Brazil upright and honest men who have been of great service to our country. It has awakened in its followers a sense of responsibility and developed in them a staunchness of character that has become a veritable national asset. It has stirred up in its people a hunger to know and given them a taste for reading. One of Brazil's greatest grammarians was a Protestant.

I give no weight to the fear that Protestant pro-

paganda may weaken the political unity of our country. There are countries of solid national unity whose population professes a variety of creeds; Switzerland, Holland, Canada, Prussia and even France are examples. On the other hand there are many Catholic countries whose national unity is weak, as in Spain, torn by internal dissension; Italy, whose lack of national cohesion explains, in large part, its misfortunes; Central America, Catholic and divided into a number of small republics. There does not seem to be any necessary relation between national cohesion and the creed professed by the majority. And if there were, then the facts would favor the Protestant countries where a great and more perfect political unity exists. Incidentally, there is no doubt that in the present war Catholic countries reveal a notable weakness in their spirit of resistance and combativeness, due, no doubt, to their internal divergences.

Protestantism is a democratic-federative movement. The Christian Protestant world is a vast federation of churches, governed democratically in conformity with the model laid down by the primitive church. The life of the local congregations is intense and greatly contributes to the incorporation of evangelical ideals into the life of the community. It tends to the creation of a people who themselves become priests and kings. The people themselves exercise the ministry of the altar.

Roman Catholicism, in its organization, follows the model of an absolute monarchy with accentuated political activities. And be it remembered: in the field of politics men will always be divided. The doctrine of Christ, on the other hand, is a power which makes for solidarity.

93. A Radical Brazilian Pentecostal

The "Assemblies of God," the original Pentecostal churches in Brazil, were founded by two Swedes from the United States, Daniel Berg and Gunnar Vingren, who had arrived in Brazil in 1911 and experienced "the baptism of the Spirit" in 1918. Manoel de Melo (1929-

SOURCE: Harding Meyer, "Die Pfingstbewegung in Brasilien," *Die Evangelische Diaspora: Jahrbuch des Gustav-Adolf-Vereins* 39 (1968): 43f., trans. and quoted in W. J. Hollenweger, *The Pentecostals: The Charismatic Movement in the Churches* (London and Minneapolis: SCM Press and Augsburg Publishing House, 1972), 100-101. Reprinted by permission of SCM Press.

1990), a construction worker from Pernambuco with little formal education, became the first native Brazilian to found a Pentecostal church. De Melo, previously pastor at Assembly of God and Foursquare Gospel, founded the "Evangelical Pentecostal Church Brazil for Christ" in 1955. He estimated the church's rate of growth to be about 80,000 members each year, "the fastest in the world." Shortly after his death The Encyclopedia of Pentecostal and Charismatic Christianity *suggested that "Brazil for Christ" had about five thousand congregations, one million members, and two million adherents.*

A typical weekend service, presided over by de Melo, was observed and described in the late 1960s by Harding Meyer, a German Lutheran professor of systematic theology in São Leopoldo (Rio Grande do Sul). According to Meyer's description of the response of the congregation to the service, how would the congregants define religion? What would they perceive to be its proper function? What Brazilians might attend Brazil for Christ?

From Pernambuco, where he was active as pastor of the Assembléias de Deus, his course took him to São Paulo. A few years later, he broke away from the Assembléias there and put his extraordinary gifts as an evangelist, his famous oratorical talent and his inexhaustible capacity for work at the service of the Cruzada Nacional de Evangelização. There were gigantic attendances at his evangelization meetings in tents, in open places and in parks, which often resulted in astonishing cures of the sick. All he needed for such meetings was an easily transportable loudspeaker system and a couple of musicians, whose songs first attracted the attention of the people. It is said that meetings with an audience of 100,000 were by no means rare and he himself estimated the audience for his morning radio programme at five million. [...]

I was there when one Thursday he had to bring forward the regular service in his provisional main church in São Paulo, a former market hall, from its appointed time on Saturday to Friday evening. Despite this, the church was packed with more than five thousand believers so that there was not even standing room; people were left outside the doors and even on the streets. The two-hour service had all the marks of Brazilian Pentecostal services with their lively, joyful, even hilarious mood: there was vigorous and extremely rhythmical singing emphasized by hand-claps and accompanied by an *ad hoc* 'orchestra' of violins, flutes, clarinets, horns, etc.; all five thousand joined in loud spontaneous prayer which went on for minutes and swelled to a crescendo, suddenly dying away at a sign from the preacher. (Individuals who seemed to have lapsed into speaking with tongues were silenced with an imploring yet sharp 'silêncio!') The sermon—about the parable of the five foolish and five wise virgins—was very emotional and had a strongly admonitory tone, but it was an extraordinarily clear, concrete and attractive exposition of the biblical text. The attention of the congregation did not slip for a moment, and their intensive preoccupation could be seen and heard in movements, laughter, loud interjections and—above all after certain key expressions—cries of 'Glória a Deus', 'Alleluia' or 'Louvada seja o nome do Senhor!'

Without question this temperamental, dark Pernambucan with his squat figure and harsh voice is one of the most popular figures in Brazil and surely the best-known evangelist in the country, admired by some, attacked and criticized by others. When he founded his own movement, a large number of his adherents from the Cruzada Nacional de Evangelização followed him. His own estimate of the annual rate of growth is about 80,000. Of course, it is impossible to confirm that for the moment. Nevertheless, his church may be the fastest growing in Brazil. His own verdict goes even further: 'This work grows faster than any other in the whole world.'

94. Participation Is Everything

In 1971, pastor Manoel de Melo, at the time building the largest church edifice in the world, seating 25,000 people, granted an interview to the editor of the evangelical journal O expositor Cristao (The Christian Expounder). *What is remarkable about the first two paragraphs below? Consider the era, for Brazil and all of Latin America, in which he makes his remarks, as well as the essential thrust of evangelical and Pentecostal Christianity at that time. Why would the World Council of Churches be "under such attack" and who would execute that attack? In what area does de Melo perceive his church to be far ahead of the World Council of Churches? Why, then, does he commit his church to membership in the World Council of Churches? How might de Melo's fellow evangelicals and Pentecostals receive his call to ecumenism in 1971?*

I think that the most important task of the Church is to evangelize. This I understand in the following manner. There is a type of evangelism that produces bigots. But there is also the kind of evangelism that creates a new perspective in the individual. This second form of evangelism does not produce a Sunday Christian, but rather a believer who is able to witness in the society in which he lives. It creates a new consciousness. The Gospel of the Kingdom of God is here and now. It involves the people in concrete living. Take Bishop Hélder Càmara, for example. He is winning people because his message makes men conscious. I see the Church as very complacent. The Church is greatly compromised with the power structure in the nation, and it is a structure which the people no longer accept. The Church that fails to heed this creative message of a new consciousness can prepare its own funeral within the next thirty years.

I believe that the Gospel is more than sufficient for this task of creating awareness. Actually I do not see a single preacher who is proclaiming the Gospel in all its fullness and purity, because the Gospel has a revolutionary content that is violently opposed to injustice.

My attitude to the World Council of Churches

I was present at the Fourth Assembly of the World Council of Churches, in Uppsala. I accepted the invitation because I had heard some of the most barbarous remarks made against the World Council. Anything that is so strongly opposed becomes a star attraction, so I accepted the invitation in order to see for myself. I only accept things and talk about them after knowing them personally. I needed to know the Council which came under such attack. I arrived there and felt like an Ezekiel in the valley of dry bones. We are in the jet age and, from the religious point of view, the World Council of Churches is riding a bicycle. However, it is doing tremendous work such as we are not able to do with all our religiosity: a gigantic work of social action.

What is the use of converting a person only to send him back to the rotten Brazilian society? "Brasil para Cristo" has already called together its team of directors and advisers, and we are going to become members of the World Council of Churches. We are planning on membership, but on one condition: since, on the religious level,

SOURCE: Manoel de Mello (*sic*), "Participation Is Everything: Evangelism from the Point of View of a Brazilian Pentecostal," trans. World Council of Churches Translation Section, *International Review of Mission* 60 (April 1971): 246-48. © World Council of Churches. Used by permission.

they are not at the level which we have already reached, we will not join to receive a religious orientation but rather a social orientation. While we convert a million, the devil de-converts ten millions through hunger, misery, militarism, dictatorship — and the churches remain complacent. Atheism is on the increase due to the conditions of injustice and misery in which the people are living. Preachers are preaching about a far distant future and forget the fact that Jesus valued and gave close attention to the time in which people lived.

The World Council of Churches concerns itself with the contemporary life of people. "Brasil para Cristo" will join the World Council of Churches because of its social mission in today's world. But, there is another reason, namely, that we must get rid of the small-mindedness that divides men into denominations. The World Council is accomplishing this. Ecumenism is another good thing the World Council of Churches offers us. [...]

The [Catholic] Church has arrived at the point where, in the present situation, it has nothing more to offer. It brings people together, sings a hymn, prays, delivers a sermon and then lets people go their own way. That is to say, the people are not challenged to undertake a serious task within the structures of society.

95. Pietism in Brazil

The co-authors of this article, "The Devotional Life of Student Protestantism" (1956) were two Presbyterians laboring in Brazil. Rubem Alves (b. 1933) is a native Brazilian, ordained minister, pastor, theologian, and author. Richard Schaull (1933-2002) was an ordained minister, missionary, professor, and author who had earned a doctorate in theology from Princeton University. The article consists of two mini-essays in sociology and theology, the latter being critical of evangelical Protestantism's pietist tradition, which emphasizes a personal relationship with Jesus Christ. Describe the sociological and theological insights of the article.

When Christians of other lands visit Brazil, they are amazed, and at times somewhat confused, by the type of devotional life, which they find in the Protestant churches. They are impressed by the extraordinary vitality of the simple piety of the average Christian. Here are people for whom the experience of a personal relationship with Jesus Christ is the very centre of life, people who read their Bibles and pray daily. Churches are filled, not only on Sunday morning, but also Sunday evening and at the midweek services. [...]

[P]ietism and revivalism brought to Brazil by the early missionaries ... has now been taken over and made an integral part of modern Brazilian Protestantism. [...]

They produced the dynamic expanding Christian Church that we have today throughout Brazil.

They have raised up several generations of Christians for whom the experience of salvation and of the new life in Christ has been a powerful transforming reality. [...]

It is the product of a type of Protestantism, which has given a central place to the reading and study of the Bible. One hundred years ago the Bible was practically an unknown book in Brazil. Thanks to the unceasing efforts of the Protestants, it is now widely known and read. Even the Roman Catholic Church has reacted to this emphasis by organizing a Bible Correspondence Course and sponsoring Bible Weeks throughout the country. [...]

The Protestant churches in Brazil live on a missionary frontier, the existence of which is taken very seriously. This fact has a tremendous influ-

SOURCE: Rubem Alves and Richard Schaull, "The Devotional Life of Student Protestantism," *The Student World* 49 (1956): 360-66. Reprinted by permission of the World Student Christian Federation.

ence on the devotional life of Brazilian Protestantism. It means that the church is constantly being stimulated by the influx of large numbers of first-generation Christians, who bring with them the intensity of life and the awareness of the radical power of the Christian faith, which is always so evident to the convert. The church is constantly engaged in evangelistic and mission work. The number of new people coming to the church is so large that the weekly Sunday evening service in most Brazilian churches is evangelistic in character. Laymen and pastors are constantly occupied in opening and developing new missions. All this not only tends to maintain the devotional life of the church at a high pitch, but also creates a certain openness to change that is characteristic of a church on the move. [. . .]

One of the most serious weaknesses of our pietist heritage is its inability to show the relevance of the believer's experience of Jesus Christ to the problems which he faces in his life in the world. We are living in a situation in Brazil today in which the problems of the world are very near to us and cannot escape our attention. But if we cannot relate them to our faith, we tend to feel that Christianity is quite irrelevant. Nothing could be more disastrous for our devotional life or contribute so much to the tragic division we often see in the church between those who pray and concern themselves with their soul's salvation, and those who act in the world without the sustaining strength of vital devotional life and worship.

96. Mexican Presbyterians

This wonderfully generous article, "Some Convictions of a Young Church" (1967) by U.S. anthropologist William Wonderly and Jorge Lara-Braud, a Mexican Presbyterian theologian and professor, is based on a survey (1962) and consists, as did the previous reading, of valuable mini-essays in sociology and theology.

What sociological information does it provide? Formulate the theology that is implied in the penultimate paragraph and first sentence of the last paragraph. Keeping in mind that the data available for the article date to 1962, why is it not surprising that the Roman Catholic Church came in third in the area of "the responsibility of the church in social and religious matters"?

[T]he problem is that the differences in *basic* moral and social attitudes among Protestants as compared with non-Protestants are not as sharp as the former have generally assumed. Furthermore, it should be cause for concern among serious-minded Protestants to realize that the attitudes where they do differ from the rest are not always the most positive manifestations of the gospel message. There is a tendency to interpret the "new life" or salvation in negative terms, and consequently to weaken both the internal spiritual vitality of the church and its witness to the non-Protestant world. [. . .]

Two findings seem on the whole to be encouraging. The first relates to the position of women. In their replies to several questions, Protestant women expressed a greater degree of emancipation from family and household and a greater desire for personal progress than did their non-Protestant counterparts. [. . .]

The second encouraging finding came in response to questions that had to do with the responsibility of the church in social and civic matters, namely: (1) Should the church offer orientation in the resolution of labor-management problems? (2) Does the church actually orient its

---

SOURCE: William L. Wonderly and Jorge Lara-Braud, "Some Convictions of a Young Church," *Practical Anthropology* 14 (January-February 1967): 1, 4-6, 12-13. Reprinted by permission of American Society of Missiology.

members in their rights and duties as citizens? (3) Should the church give such orientation in the rights and duties of citizens?

Responses to all three questions suggest a greater emphasis on social and civic matters on the part of the Pentecostal churches than on the part of the historical denominations, with the Roman Catholic Church in third place. [. . .]

But the positive results outlined above are more than counterbalanced by a pattern of negative results in at least two important and related areas. These are a high degree of superficiality in the understanding and application of Christian principles, and a strong tendency to become needlessly isolated from the national culture and society. [. . .]

[F]or many Mexican Protestants religion has become largely a system of morality defined in terms of specific vices overcome and even of taboos, rather than of a life inwardly transformed by the power of the gospel.

It is worthy of note, in contrast, that in reference to matters of personal peace, security, and satisfaction, as well as to family stability and the ability to live in peace with others, Protestants showed no significant difference from non-Protestants. [. . .]

It is undeniable that in this survey there emerges the dichotomy "church" (good) vs. "world" (bad), which tends to lead to complete rejection not only of those aspects of the old life that are harmful, and sinful, but also of those that are morally neutral or even of positive value. Instead of carrying out the admonition to "test everything; hold fast what is good," the "world" is rejected (at least in theory) *in toto*, cutting off at the same time the lines of effective communication with the very relatives and friends to whom, if the Protestants had shared their problems and concerns, it might have been possible to present with greater relevance Christ and his gospel. At the same time, insistence upon a radical break with the "world" leads to danger of an ambivalent attitude—to say nothing of schizophrenia—since in actual practice such a break can be only partial as long as the Christian is still physically present in the world and in his society. [. . .]

If our study has any validity, it would seem to be imperative that those responsible for Christian education and for teaching in the seminaries adopt a less naive position with regard to the sinlessness of the church, and a less extreme position with regard to the sinfulness of the world. In other words, the situation calls for a reconsideration of the sovereignty of Jesus Christ not only in the church (where it is explicitly confessed) but also in the world (where it is not explicitly confessed).

This opposition of "church" vs. "world" becomes especially complicated in view of the fact that the average Mexican Protestant equates "church" with the Protestant community, and "world" with the rest of society, which is predominantly Roman Catholic. Most Protestants make no distinction between orthodox Catholicism (with which, in spite of the basic differences, Protestantism has a great deal in common) and folk Catholicism (that "Christo-paganism" which has resulted from a syncretism of Christian concepts and elements from the Indian religions). They tend to see in every Catholic, even the best instructed, a polytheist who follows the syncretized religion of the Indians; although sometimes, after some courses in a Bible institute, they tend to interpret the gospel message to everyone, including the Indians, as though they were orthodox Catholics. One crucial consequence of all this is that most Mexican Protestants are unable to see the elements of genuineness that are present in the current renewal in the Roman Catholic Church, which is potentially one of the most hopeful developments toward the improvement of that "world" rejected as hopelessly sinful.

97. Who Converts to Pentecostalism?

For fifteen months, in 1959 and 1960, Professor Emilio Willems (1905-1997) conducted and supervised the research on which he based his Followers of the New Faith: Culture Change and the Rise of Protestantism in Brazil and Chile *(1967). He had served as professor of sociology and anthropology at the University of São Paolo before becoming professor of anthropology at Vanderbilt University in 1949. What conclusions about religion in general, Protestant Pentecostalism in particular, and about humanity, human nature, and human needs may be drawn from this little model of social scientific inquiry?*

The rapid expansion of the Pentecostal sects, especially in comparison with the historical Protestant churches, justifies the assumption that these sects meet certain needs, or perhaps correspond to certain aspirations of the people exposed to the brunt of cultural changes, which they neither control nor understand. [. . .] The Protestant congregation with its strong accent on intimate co-operation, personal responsibility, mutual as well as self-help, provides opportunity for the individual whose personal community has been destroyed, to "find himself."

Three aspects of this problem should probably be pointed out at this juncture. Above all, joining a Protestant congregation is by no means the only alternative open to those in search of a social identity. Competitive religious groups such as the various spiritualistic sects, the Umbanda (a fusion of African cult forms and spiritualistic beliefs) and a number of local African cult centers variously named *candomblé, macumba*, or *xangô* have attracted the masses in Brazil, and in both countries the social gospel of political radicalism has served as a rallying point for the masses. Conversion to Protestantism ranks as only one alternative among several, and there is of course a considerable amount of shifting from group to group. Official Brazilian computations, which are notoriously incomplete, report 66,335 exclusions from Protestant churches in 1956, 84,814 in 1957, and 116,975 in 1960 (*Estatística do culto Protestante* 1956:1, 1957:1). Our informants were virtually unanimous in that the turnover within the Pentecostal sects is particularly high.

Secondly, the search for a social identity can be fully appreciated only if the peculiar position of the lower classes is taken into account. In contrast to their highly articulate and well-led counterparts in Europe and the United States, the lower classes of Chile and Brazil are only now emerging from a state of social anonymity. [. . .]

Thirdly, the attractions Pentecostalism holds for the underprivileged masses are multifarious and rather complex. The felt need to rebuild a meaningful system of primary relations (the personal community) in an atomized society may be satisfied, in some way at least, by the Pentecostal sect as well as any other church or sect, provided it meets certain organizational prerequisites which are found in the Catholic parish organization only under exceptional circumstances.

Like other Protestant bodies, the Pentecostal sect offers "redemption" from certain forms of habitual behavior which are defined as sinful and therefore "degrading." According to many of our life histories, the convert feels dissatisfaction with his way of life, even before conversion took place. Although previous religious and moral enculturation may have contributed to those feelings, it became apparent that several other factors played a decisive role in determining a radical change of personal habits. In the first place, many of our informants associated vice with sickness and conversion with health. A Pentecostal pastor in Chile

SOURCE: Emilio Willems, *Followers of the New Faith: Culture Change and the Rise of Protestantism in Brazil and Chile* (Nashville: Vanderbilt University Press, 1967), 122-23, 125-26, 129-31. Reprinted by permission of Vanderbilt University Press.

told us about his unhappy youth which he had spent in the "pursuit of sexual pleasures" and alcoholic excesses. Eventually he contracted a serious venereal disease, which "no doctor was able to cure." When he finally "accepted Christ," his ailment miraculously disappeared and his health became excellent. "Before my conversion," another member of a Pentecostal sect confessed, "my wife was very sick, and I lived without God and hope. Now we all enjoy good health." A woman left her husband because she wanted to live a "purer and more Christian-like life." She was convinced that "vices are bad for the organism." Several interviewees affirmed that they "gained health through faith." [. . .]

Furthermore, our life histories reveal a great deal of "unhappiness" with a life of "vice and sin," even if the person is *not* afflicted with physical maladies. [. . .]

All subjects expressed dissatisfaction with their way of life before conversion. "I drank a lot and was very unhappy." "I accepted the faith because I want to live a better life." "Before conversion I felt emptiness in life which only the church could fill." "I sought peace and happiness and was tired of vices." "Because of my vices we lived in poverty." (Now he owns a small factory.) "I drank so heavily that my wife deserted me, but I felt dissatisfied with my licentious life." "I joined the church because I had a revelation in a dream. Before I led a very disorderly life." "I was in search of something that would change my life of a drunkard." "Before conversion I had no religious ideals whatever; I was vain, egotistic and had terrible family problems." These are typical statements of Chilean converts who are now members of a variety of different churches and sects (Temuco and Concepción). [. . .]

There is little doubt that the troubles preceding conversion were manifestations of personality disorders of varying intensity. [. . .] Drunken bouts, tavern brawls, wife-beating, illegitimacy, neglect of children and a disorganized home life, personal appearance suggesting neglect and un-cleanliness, failure to improve poor housing conditions, and similar traits are often held against the lower classes. One may say, they are identified with lower-class behavior and therefore looked upon with a mixture of moral indignation and amused contempt. It seems that the Protestant convert is particularly sensitive to such criticism, for henceforward he carefully avoids "disreputable" forms of behavior. [. . .] *The desire to become respectable*, that is, to adopt middle-class behavior, obviously plays no minor role as a determinant of conversion.

98. Mormon Missionaries and Mormon Scholars in Mexico

The following reading is an extraordinary account of the Mormon Church in Mexico written by Mormon twin brothers, Gary and Gordon Shepherd, some thirty years after their two years of missionary work there, by which time both had become sociologists and university professors (at Oakland University, Michigan, and the University of Central Arkansas, respectively).

What aspects of the Shepherds' account clearly denote their status as sociologists? Are there any aspects that suggest their commitment to their own church? How might the rapid growth of the Latin American Mormon Church in the late twentieth century be explained? Does that explanation accurately reflect contemporary developments in all of the churches of Latin America? (LDS = Church of Jesus Christ of Latter Day Saints, i.e., the Mormon Church)

Source: Gary Shepherd and Gordon Shepherd, *Mormon Passage: A Missionary Chronicle* (Urbana and Chicago: University of Illinois Press, 1998), 97-99, 100-101, 112. From *Mormon Passage: A Missionary Chronicle*. Copyright 1998 by Board of Trustees of the University of Illinois. Used with permission of the University of Illinois Press and A. Gary Shepherd.

In 1964 the LDS Church in Mexico had approximately forty thousand members. [. . .] By 1996 there were approximately 735,000 Mexican Mormons, the majority of whom had been converted since the 1980s. [. . .]

Culturally, Mexico has been unified by the glorification of its Indian heritage and assimilation of indigenous culture in the institutions and traditions of the Catholic Church. Mexico is still overwhelmingly Catholic, but systematic government secularization of public institutions since the revolution of 1910-20 has led to a loosening of absolute Catholic domination. [. . .]

Mormonism has become an important part of the religious movements that now represent a major challenge to traditional Catholic hegemony. While in Mexico, we struggled to win Catholic converts and often found ourselves in direct competition with Protestant clergy and other lay evangelists in Mexico's expanding religious economy. Our mission leaders encouraged us to concentrate on converting Mexican men and not just their wives or children. This we tried to do, with some success. But often we were frustrated in our attempts and, in many cases, came to view recalcitrant adult males as the primary obstacle to our proselyting efforts.

F. LaMond Tullis, a political scientist at Brigham Young University, has written (1987) that the earliest Mormon converts in Mexico were drawn primarily from the rural poor and, subsequently, the urban lower class. More and more converts, however, now come from the emerging Mexican middle class in metropolitan centers. Many are still relatively poor, but their children are encouraged to rise socially and economically. Tullis reports that the LDS Church has acquired a positive image and government support in Mexico due to the reputation of its schools and its progressive social ethic. Mormonism—with its emphasis on sober striving, performance of civic duty, and providential guidance—appears to resonate with many Mexicans' upwardly mobile social aspirations during a period of national growth, stress, and uncertainty. Perhaps most important, the Book of Mormon's ideology concerning the chosen status and divinely appointed destiny of Native Americans dovetails with Mexi-

can nationalism and has become an exceptionally important pillar of the Mormon faith in Mexico. [. . .]

Difficulties for Mormon missionary activity mounted in 1926 when the government prohibited foreign clergy from entering Mexico to engage in any religious work. Thus, staffing and day-to-day administration of the LDS Mexican Mission was placed temporarily in the hands of a small nucleus of Mexican converts. [. . .]

This administrative hiatus contributed to the growth of a nativistic movement of Mexican converts, who eventually posed a serious challenge to the ecclesiastical authority of the LDS Church in Mexico. [. . .]

At their third convention in 1936 the dissidents broke ranks with church leaders in Salt Lake City and declared the formation of an all-Mexican mission presidency for the governance of church affairs in the Republic. Salt Lake authorities responded to the schism with firmness and a certain amount of patience. They had no intention of allowing local leaders to circumvent the centralized governing procedures of the church, but they also wanted to minimize the institutional damage caused by the breach. Unrepentant leaders of the "Third Convention" were quickly excommunicated while simultaneously being invited to return to the good graces of the church. For more than a decade, effective missionary work in Mexico was severely hampered as World War II intervened and Mexican members were confused by conflicting claims of ecclesiastical legitimacy.

After the war, LDS authorities made a concerted effort to restore religious unity among the faithful. In 1946 a majority of Mexican *Convencionistas* were reconciled to Mormonism's hierarchical authority through the negotiation efforts of mission leaders and an important symbolic visit by church president George Albert Smith. [. . .]

In 1992 the Mexican government adopted [. . . changes in the] constitution that nullified many of the country's formerly anticlerical statutes. The following year—114 years after arriving in Mexico—the LDS Church was formally registered as a legally recognized religious organization with the right to own property in the Republic of Mexico. [. . .] By then, church growth had been so great that Mexico was virtually self-sufficient in supplying its own missionary force. [...]

After more than three generations of religious struggle, Mexico rapidly was becoming one of the LDS Church's premier proselyting areas. Although related to companion compatibility and mutual effort as a team, our success in attracting converts was primarily a function of location. Thus, when paired with motivated companions in Mexico City, Gary enjoyed a good deal of success. In contrast, Gordon spent much of his time during this period working in smaller towns, where people were more closely attached to their tradi-

tions and kinship groups and the Catholic Church was better able to mobilize anti-Mormon resistance campaigns. As a result, even when matched with highly motivated companions, Gordon's success at attracting converts generally was much less than that which Gary and his companions achieved in Mexico City, where many inhabitants were uprooted from traditional ways of Mexican life. Consequently, more individuals in the capital city were open to investigating new meanings, new forms of faith, and a new system of religious authority.

99. Protestant Pastors and Marxist Leninism in Cuba

During the early years of the Cuban revolution, when it was essential to increase the annual income derived from Cuba's basically monoculture economy, volunteers were called to "cut sugar cane." The shortage of machinery and spare parts made human volunteers necessary. Joaquín Andrade, the author of the article below and about whom no information is available, exaggerates the negative role of the churches, not only during the insurrection but afterward, when it might be expected that the churches would become skittish. Nevertheless, it is necessary to remember the criticism, by all kinds of churchmen throughout Latin America, of their own churches' failure to confront the harsh social realities that the Cuban revolution was attempting to address.

Some Cuban churchmen had been sympathetic to the 26th of July movement (J-26, 1953-1958), and Archbishop Enrique Pérez Serrantes of Santiago had actually saved the lives of several rebels and Castro himself by his heroic confrontation with officers of dictator Fulgencio Batista's army. But after mid-1961, when Castro declared the revolution to be Marxist-Leninist and nationalized the means of production, most churchmen were either hostile to or wary of the revolution, and many Catholic clergy fled the country. By the late 1960s, however, because of increased popular pressure, government propaganda, and the palpable needs of society, some Christian laypeople and Protestant ministers volunteered in the cane fields.

The conversation reported below by Andrade took place in 1970, the year when all healthy Cubans were expected to participate in the sugar harvest.

What is the concept of these pastors' Christian duty as they state their own criticisms of their churches' failure to come to terms with the Cuban revolution? How astute is their grasp of politics, decision making in politics, the problems faced by the underdeveloped

SOURCE: Joaquín Andrade, "Protestant Ministers in the Canefields," trans. Latin American Documentation—U.S. Catholic Conference, quoted in Alice L. Hageman and Philip E. Wheaton, eds., *Religion in Cuba Today: A New Church in a New Society* (New York: Association Press, 1971), 50-52, reprinted from Cuba International (Havana), August 1970. Reprinted by permission of Department of Social Development and World Peace: United States Conference of Catholic Bishops.

world, and the possible role of socialism and Marxist-Leninism in the solutions to those problems? Are these pastors aware of developments taking place elsewhere in Latin America at this moment in history (1970)?

Note, in particular, "What is happening in Peru these days": progressive army officers took over the government in 1968 in order to implement radical reforms demanded by divergent sectors of the population.

The rapid change that Cuba is undergoing is shaking up its entire society. Between the inertia of the old oligarchies and the present collective effort of a whole people, there is a chasm that those of the past, who used to live heedless of our country's true interests, can cross only with difficulty. Much of the church, with its creaking bureaucracy and superannuated bishops, never followed the bulk of its ministers and people across that chasm. ("The church," Pastor Israel Batista was to say toward the end of the interview, referring to the Protestants, "has a very important contribution to make. If it doesn't make it; well, that's another matter. We are old men. There is a phrase to describe us: 'we are yesterday's children.'") The hierarchy stayed aloof during the bloody fight against Batista—and then took on a censorious attitude when the first revolutionary measures began to touch their interests.

"One of the great mistakes that we believers were guilty of in the Cuban process," said Pastor Piedra, "was precisely in not standing up to be counted when we should have involved ourselves and risked our necks. Even now, we are quick to criticize on any occasion. That is to say, the church will criticize today, but didn't have the courage to roll its sleeves up and make sacrifices at the crucial moments. I can never forget those words of Martí: 'Those who aren't brave enough to risk their lives should at least be modest enough to stay silent in the presence of those who are taking the risks.' Anyone who remembers how little the church did in those days of insurrection knows that it can hardly condemn anyone today."

Only a tiny minority of Cuban believers could sense what was happening, joined in the process, and went the full road with the rest of Cuban society.

Q. What was your reaction, you believers who are now wholeheartedly with the Revolution, when it swung to the left and openly chose social-ism? Did you hesitate? Did you think you might have to break with the movement?

"Not exactly," replied Piedra. "I don't think that just because the Revolution is Marxist, we who are loyal Cubans have to remain outside the mainstream of its evolution. I'm sure there were good reasons, justifications for going socialist. We're not very much up on international politics. But just seeing what was going on made us think it was inevitable."

Pastor Naranjo would go farther: "Look," he breaks in, "the only way that poor countries can get out of their underdevelopment is by a completely socialist revolution. Besides if you look at how so much of humanity is underdeveloped, that's the only practical, viable hope the people have."

In the group around me was Sergio Arce, rector of the Matanzas seminary, a doctor in philosophy and letters from the University of Havana and holder of a theological degree from Princeton. He had kept silent, listening to his comrades and apparently absorbed by the cadenced wave of workers attacking the canefield. "I look on Marxism," he said, "as basically a science, or, if you like, a scientific way to analyze reality in order to solve the problems facing society. Well, then, if it is the science of society, why not use it? Don't we turn to medical science when we are sick? In other words, Marxism is a science, so we use it as such. To get out of our underdevelopment, we have to use that science. I don't think there is any reluctance on our part to admit that."

Q. But how do you conciliate your faith with Marxist materialism? Comrade Naranjo has just told us very explicitly that Marx's socialist road is the only one for getting out of underdevelopment. Still, how is Marxist materialism compatible with the religion you profess?

"Let me put it in simple terms," Naranjo broke in. "You know that Cuban Governments prior to the Revolution were quite deferent to religion. Today, though, the Revolution we are going through is a Marxist-Leninist one. The problem is not just one of words, however, but of substance. We can't blot out the facts of history. Those old governments had no time for the people's plight, whereas the one we have now is very interested in it, and in producing a new man. As I see it, this new man"—and here he quoted from Brunel—"is a life completely dedicated to one's neighbors. I think that if we have to choose, and if we are honest, even though the Revolution is a Marxist-Leninist one with no place for religion, we still ought to choose that system, because somehow or other it seems to promote all the objectives in the social order that the church, here in Cuba, never managed to achieve."

Only Castellanos, the oldest in the group, seemed to disagree. "I wouldn't say that socialism is the only way that underdeveloped countries have of liberating themselves. I would concede, however, that experience has so far shown us no other way. But it's my fond dream that another way will be found to get all the peoples of Asia, Africa and Latin America out of their underdevelopment. Such a way may turn up: just look at what is happening in Peru these days. That is very interesting. But in the long run I suppose that, whatever the way, it will have to be violent, radical and revolutionary, on the Marxist-Leninist pattern. I am firmly convinced, though, that the contribution of Christian witness is indispensable. That's the responsibility that we who live immersed in this Revolution feel weighing on us."

PART XIV
The Troubled Twentieth Century

In 1891, Pope Leo XIII (1878-1903) responded to the problems of the working classes by asserting in his great encyclical *Rerum novarum* (*On the Condition of Labor,* 1891), that property was a natural right of everyone, including workers, for whom it could mean decent wages, and who therefore had the right to form responsible unions. The encyclical eschewed socialist concepts of class war, on the one hand, and relentlessly profit-seeking capitalism, on the other. This and later progressive encyclicals such as *Pacem in terris* (*Peace on Earth,* 1963), *Populorum progressio* (*On the Development of Peoples,* 1967), and *Solicitudo rei socialis* (*On Social Concern,* 1987) encouraged strategies to improve working and living conditions for laborers, ameliorate tension between social classes, and achieve a more equitable distribution of wealth. These goals, sometimes referred to as "social Catholicism," inspired a new generation of committed Catholics in Latin America to promote the church as an institution that fostered rather than impeded progress and modernization. They viewed Leo's challenges as an invitation to form Catholic labor unions, lay associations, and even political parties. Workers in Mexico and Colombia, for example, formed the National Catholic Workers' Confederation (1921) and the Colombia Workers' Union (1946). The former grew to more than 80,000 members by the mid-1920s; the latter is still that country's largest union.[1] "Catholic Action" lay organizations were formed in nearly every Latin American country during the first decades of the twentieth century, such as in Argentina and Chile (1931), Colombia (1933), Peru (1935), and Bolivia (1938). These lay movements and the church hierarchy helped to found several Catholic universities: Bogotá (1937); Medellín (1945); São Paulo (1947); Porto Alegre (1950); Buenos Aires and Córdoba (1950);

---

1. Robert E. Curley, "Social Catholicism," in *Encyclopedia of Mexico: History, Society & Culture*, vol. 2, ed. Michael S. Werner (Chicago and London: Fitzroy Dearborn Publishers, 1997), 1347-49; Víctor Gabriel Muro, "Catholic Church: Mexico," in *Encyclopedia of Mexico: History, Society & Culture*, vol. 1, ed. Michael S. Werner (Chicago and London: Fitzroy Dearborn Publishers, 1997), 220; Virginia Garrard-Burnett, "Introduction," in *On Earth as It Is in Heaven: Religion in Modern Latin America*, ed. Virginia Garrard-Burnett (Wilmington, Del.: Scholarly Resources, 2000), xx; Enrique Dussel, ed., *The Church in Latin America, 1492-1992* (Maryknoll, N.Y.: Orbis Books, 1992),12.

and Valparaiso (1961). More politically minded members of Catholic Action formed Christian Democratic parties, such as Chile's National Phalanx Party (1938) and El Salvador's Christian Democratic Party (1960). While these associations and parties helped a new generation of Catholics to defend and promote both Catholicism and social justice, their agenda was usually inspired by their own middle- and upper-middle-class backgrounds. Their vigorous defense of the church and private property helped them to receive the backing of bishops and papal nuncios, and they ultimately proved to be strong defenders of a "reformed" status quo. Nevertheless, as Jeffrey Klaiber states, Catholic Action "represented the transition from an older, elitist Catholicism to the more modern and pluralistic Catholicism of Vatican II."[2]

While middle-class and working-class Catholics usually promoted Catholicism within the framework of Catholic Action, other priests and laypersons took a more aggressive approach. Some native and foreign-born clergy, for example, such as the Maryknoll Fathers and Sisters who arrived in Latin America in the 1940s, became vocal opponents of civilian and military regimes that violated human rights and stifled the democratic process. They also helped to establish activist student associations, peasant cooperatives, and housing projects. Father Camilo Torres (1929-1966) even joined Colombian guerrillas in 1965 and sacrificed his life to help destroy the corrosive structures that guaranteed permanent poverty for the majority of his countrymen. Secular social revolutionaries in Mexico, however, learned that changes to the existing order, even if intended to help the poor, would not be accepted if they included anticlerical measures that threatened the viability of the church. With the slogan "*Viva Cristo Rey*" (Long Live Christ the King), 40,000 Mexican Cristeros died fighting government troops, 60,000 of whom also were killed in the war between 1926 and 1929. Cristeros and their leaders, such as Miguel Pro, S.J., executed without trial on 23 November 1927, age 36, resented parts of the Mexican constitution (1917) that eliminated church properties, restricted religious orders, and permitted state legislators to limit the number of priests. Though the Cristeros failed to change the constitution, Mexico's revolutionary party was forced to acknowledge that most Mexicans would not tolerate the complete secularization of society.[3]

---

2. Jeffery Klaiber, "Catholic Action," in *Encyclopedia of Latin American History and Culture*, vol. 2, ed. Barbara A. Tenenbaum (New York: Charles Scribner's Sons, 1996), 28, 35; Jeffrey Klaiber, S.J., *The Catholic Church in Peru, 1821-1985: A Social History* (Washington, D.C.: Catholic University of America Press, 1992), 24-25; Dussell, *Church in Latin America*, 13.

3. Jean A. Meyer, *The Cristero Rebellion: The Mexican People between Church and State, 1926-1929*, trans. Richard Southern (Cambridge: Cambridge University Press, 1976), 107, 213; John W. Sherman, "Liberation Theology," in *Encyclopedia of Mexico: History, Society & Culture*, vol. 1, ed. Michael S. Werner (Chicago and London: Fitzroy Dearborn Publishers, 1997), 743; John J. Kennedy, "Catholic Church (National Period)," in *Encyclopedia of Latin America*, ed. Helen Delpar (New York: McGraw-Hill, 1974), 123; Jeffrey Klaiber, "Catholic Church: The Modern Period," in *Encyclopedia of Latin American History and Culture*, vol. 2, ed. Barbara A. Tenenbaum (New York: Charles Scribner's Sons, 1996), 35-37.

100. Pancho Villa

Doroteo Arango (1878-1923), better known as Francisco "Pancho" Villa, was often portrayed as a wanton villain. Despite an early career as a probable outlaw, however, he was an intelligent, thoughtful, and constructive political leader. His memoirs, dictated in 1914, must be read critically. Does the following episode suggest a connection with legislation that would come out of the Mexican revolution (see reading 66)?

I made the trip to Santa Isabel, Bustillos, Guerrero, and other towns in the district, where my sister Martina lived. She wanted me to be present for a baptism, and the priest who, as I said before, was performing the bishop's duties in Chihuahua, went with me. That priest was a man who had his own ideas, though he was also my friend. And knowing that I followed no religion, and was especially opposed to the ways of the Jesuits, he discussed the protective doctrines and teachings of the Church with the intention of influencing me.

"Sr. General, as you have consented to contract the duties of godfather, you do recognize the laws of our Catholic Church, as God disposes [. . .]

I do not deny belief in God. I affirm it and certify to it since it has comforted me and all men in many of life's crises. But I do not consider everything sacred that is covered by the name of religion. Most so-called religious men use religion to promote their own interests, not the things they preach, and so there are good priests and bad priests, and we must accept some and help them and prosecute and annihilate others. [. . .]

The priest said, "Sr. General, the bad priests will be punished in their time, but while they walk on earth they deserve our respect. God puts them here among us, and if He does it, He knows why."

"No, Señor. If I, as a Revolutionary, arise to punish rulers who fail to fulfill their duty to the people, I must extend the punishment to religious men who betray the cause of the poor. And our punishment is beneficial to the churches in warning the clergy to be charitable and useful, not greedy and destructive, just as the punishment of a bad soldier is beneficial to the military. I understand your reasons, Señor, for thinking God has good and bad priests in this world. He knows why, and He will reward them afterward or punish them according to the conduct of each. But you can be sure, Sr. Priest, that God has many ways, as you religious men preach in your sermons, and that one of the punishments He can impose upon bad priests is the punishment we mete out. God has us, too, the Revolutionaries, and if He permits us to struggle for our love of the people in the way we do, He knows why." [. . .]

"Remember, Sr. Priest, that our Revolution is the struggle of the poor against the rich, who thrive on the poverty of the poor. And if in this struggle we discover that the so-called priests of religion, or most of them are on the side of the rich and not of the poor, what faith, Señor, can the people have in their advice? In my opinion, our justice involves such holiness that the priests and the churches who deny us their help have forfeited their claim to be men of God."

On the trip we went to the Hacienda Bustillos, which belonged to one of the richest families in Chihuahua. The owner was a lady by the name of Doña Luz [. . .]

She too spoke for religion, giving me advice on my duties to God. She did it every time she spoke with me, and I consented to it because she was agreeable, and really very kind [. . .]

"[Y]ou have committed many robberies, Sr. General Villa, and God says, 'Thou shalt not steal.'"

I replied, "I have never stolen, Sra. Doña Luz. I have taken from those who had much in order to give to those who had little, or nothing. For

SOURCE: Martín Luis Guzmán, ed., *Memoirs of Pancho Villa*, trans. Virginia H. Taylor (Austin: University of Austin Press, 1965), 284-87, 389. From *Memoirs of Pancho Villa* by Martín Luis Guzmán, trans. Virginia H. Taylor, Copyright © 1965, renewed 1993. By permission of the University of Texas Press.

myself, I have never taken anything belonging to another except in a situation of the most urgent necessity. And he who takes food when he is hungry does not steal, Sra. Doña Luz. He only complies with his duty to sustain himself. It is the rich who steal because, having everything they need, they still deprive the poor of their miserable bread." [...]

A group of religious men and women came to see me; they said, "Sr. General Villa, we know nothing of war or politics or revolution, although we would like to know about these things in order to pray for the triumph of the armies that fight for justice. But, Sr. General, while we do no harm to anyone with our prayers, which are words of love for our fellowmen, as the God who illumines us commands, General Diéguez ordered our churches closed. For that reason, Sr. General Villa, we come to ask you: what harm can the candles on our altars and our sacred images do the cause of the people?"

I answered, "Señores, I agree in general with your reasoning. The relief that the sad implore cannot harm the people. But behind the altars that the poor erect you must admit that bad priests are often hidden. It was wrong for Diéguez to close your churches and I am going to open them, although he closed them to appear a great Revolutionary and by opening them I will appear to be an instrument of reaction. But if I find the clergy exploiting and deceiving the people under the protection of the churches, especially if they are Jesuits, I will not pardon them; I will punish them as I have punished them in other cities, because the church that shelters the poor under its mantle is one thing and the church that shelters itself under the mantle of the poor is another."

101. In Our Own [Land] There Has Never Been a Real Religious Anxiety

Ricardo Rojas (1882-1957) represents a type of intellectual typical of an earlier day in Latin America and untypical of the United States at any time. This is the wide-ranging scholar who is reluctant to confine himself to expertise over one area, problem, or author and demonstrates confidence in his breadth by thorough documentation. Such a typically Latin American scholar would use the vehicle of the essay, somewhat in the manner of the great Montaigne (1532-1592), to address issues he believed important by reference to literature of all kinds, ages, and cultures.

Widely and deeply read in the Western classics and well acquainted with Eastern philosophy, Rojas, like so many fellow Latin American scholars, was historian and essayist, reflecting on a wide range of topics in books published in Spain and Argentina, his home country. After founding many of the scholarly and research institutions of the University of Buenos Aires, he was chosen to be its rector in 1926. El Cristo Invisible was published in 1928.

The brief excerpt below raises many profound questions concerning the evolution of Western ideas and values and the nature of religious commitment. Our more specific concerns are with the following questions: (1) What are the religious views of an outstanding man of letters in twentieth-century Argentina, a traditionally Catholic nation? (2) How does this thoughtful scholar view the Catholicism of the Argentines, both the "common people" and "upper classes"? (3) What does he mean by his insistence that "there has never been real uneasiness in Argentina in regard to the religious problem"? (He is not referring to church-state issues, the status of the clergy, or to any particular pronouncements of the

SOURCE: Ricardo Rojas, *The Invisible Christ*, trans. Webster E. Browning (New York: Abingdon Press, 1931), 237-39, 244-47.

church.) (4) How does this respectful and knowledgeable university professor vie
Why does he think both Catholics and "freethinkers" would be hostile to l
(5) What is the outlook of the bishop on the church and its future in a world of "
or atheistic materialism"? (The "Constituent Assembly" drew up a liberal-federal constitu-
tion in 1853.) The "guest" is Rojas himself.

GUEST: I understand that the Church clings to its strict traditional principles to save itself as a historical institution; but it ought to save mankind also, although this may mean a change in its polity, as it has changed on other occasions.

BISHOP: There have been changes, but they were merely accidental, not essential. The schisms cleansed the Church of heresy. External modifications, including those made in the mass, did not affect dogma. And for this reason the Church of Christ considers itself unchanged through twenty centuries, both in the name of its founder and in its system of faith. This is what I mean when I say that Christian tradition endures among our people.

GUEST: Perhaps; but the fetishism of the common people and the pretense of piety on the part of the upper classes are not Christian. It is true that worship is practiced, but without understanding its significance. Charity among us is nothing more than an egoistic instinct or a worldly vanity. The reconciliation realized by Saint Augustine, between obedience to ecclesiastical discipline and the necessity of understanding God as the highest expression of truth, searching for him in one's own heart— *interiu intimo meo*— is something which in our country is neither practiced nor understood. If I should write a book for the purpose of setting forth my anxiety about this problem of the soul, I would be looked on with suspicion or hostility.

BISHOP: That would depend on what you might say in the book. If it were written for the purpose of saying what we have so far said, there would be nothing scandalous in it. Some Argentine Catholics would consider your attitude with alarm, others benevolently.

GUEST: That is doubtful! Catholics would believe that I had turned Protestant, or would dub me atheist. As for freethinkers, who are even more superficial in their thinking, they would consider me a fanatic and would call me reactionary. In all Spanish America there is no serious study of these problems, no taste for them, no understanding of them. It is possible that in some countries, as in our own, for example, there has never been a real religious anxiety.

BISHOP: In our country, as in others of the continent, the ancient faith has suffered from the coming of international commerce and materialistic education. But the old ember still glows beneath the ashes.

GUEST: I do not know whether the fire on the hearth can be rekindled, but the ashes are without light and heat. Furthermore, I am not referring to the indifferent or lukewarm, but to ordinary believers and the emancipated thinking classes, when I state that there has never been real uneasiness in Argentina in regard to the religious problem. This is serious for a young civilization, because metaphysical transcendence widens and deepens thought, without taking into account that this process might develop a moral content in politics. [...]

BISHOP: We have had religious unrest. The persecutions of the Church by Freemasonry, or during the period of our emancipation, the action taken by the Constituent Assembly in regard to the standing of the Church, and the lay reforms of a later epoch, are sufficient proof of this.

GUEST: Those anxieties were caused by philosophical, economic, or political struggles; but there was no real religious uneasiness, understanding by this term the inner aptitude of the soul to search after God and find him in the paths of meditation and love.

BISHOP: We have had mystical Christians. Saint Francis Solano, Fray Luis de Bolaños, and the mystic Alonzo de Barzana were all eminent in this respect, and in addition they had the multiple virtues of ecstasy, charity, and the performing of miracles. [...]

BISHOP: I suppose that you will not deduce from all this that secularism, or atheistic materialism, as you should rightly call it, is more powerful in our country than Christianity.

GUEST: I believe that both are equally superficial, with the exception of the powerful individualities which you have mentioned, and others that I might cite who fought on the other side, since I maintain that a calm Christian sentiment inspired the democratic attitude of San Martín, Belgrano, and Mitre, leaders of the people, or the liberal doctrine of Echeverría, Sarmiento, and González, educators of the people.

BISHOP: You incur in a contradiction.

GUEST: Not at all: I ignore the various political devices simply to emphasize the importance of lives. It would be easy to show that democracy, liberalism, and public instruction are remote consequences of the Christian spirit in modern society. Sarmiento was educated by Oro, a clergyman, in the reading of the Gospels, and wrote Christian catechisms for the children of the public schools.

BISHOP: Therefore the Spirit of Christ is that which triumphs.

GUEST: Liberalism and romanticism, which constitute the generous background of Argentine civil tradition, spring from Christianity as a sentiment. Those who have been estranged from Christ in our modern epoch belong to a certain group which read the scientific materialism of Comte, and another with atheistic and anti-clerical tendencies which read Renan; but both forgot that Comte founded the religion of humanity, including the saints in his worship, and that Renan, in his *Life of Jesus*, says: "No revolution shall hinder us from following, in religious matters, the intellectual line, at whose front shines the name of Jesus, and, in this sense, we are Christians." All this is definite and proves what I told you: the superficiality of Argentine consciousness in all that refers to the religious problem.

BISHOP: In spite of it all, the Church which the evangelists of the sixteenth century founded here still subsists in its entirety, and we distrust all those who, in the name of Christ, have weakened Catholic sentiment, whether they were violent like Luther or skillful like Renan. For that reason Latin America remains Catholic.

GUEST: But the axis of European civilization, which was formerly Roman, Iberian, French—that is to say, Catholic and Latin—has been displaced toward Protestant Christians, with the capitalist industry of the Saxons, and toward Orthodox Christians, with the proletarian revolution of the Russians. [. . .]

The spread of Christianity in the eastern and southern countries, which, in the sixteenth century, was in charge of Catholic missionaries, following in the track of Gama and Magellan, has come to be an activity of Protestant missionaries who scatter their Bibles in India, China, Japan, Australia and New Zealand. [. . .] Rome cannot believe that she alone directs today the Christian policy of the world.

BISHOP: The dissenting sects are many, Catholicism is one; they are ephemeral, Catholicism is millennial and will be eternal.

GUEST: Catholicity means universality, and universality is today dissident, since there is a free Christianity.

BISHOP: Catholicism makes progress in the Protestant countries.

102. Anti-Kommunism

Juan José Arévalo (1904-1990), reform president of Guatemala (1945-1951), earned his doctorate in philosophy and educational sciences in Argentina where he lived in exile and worked in education during the dictatorship of Guatemala's General Jorge Ubico (1931-1944) (see readings 83 and 88).

SOURCE: Juan José Arévalo, *Anti-Kommunism in Latin America: An X-Ray of the Process Leading to a New Colonialism*, trans. Carleton Beals (New York: Lyle Stuart, 1963), 125-30.

After the 1944 coup led by progressive forces in Guatemala, Arévalo became the first democratically elected president and launched an era of reform (very much in the spirit of Franklin Delano Roosevelt's contemporary New Deal), which brought Guatemala into the twentieth century. Arévalo may be regarded as the archetypical representative of the politically progressive, university educated, twentieth-century Latin American intellectual who was outraged by his nation's retrograde status and determined to end it. His furious Anti-Kommunism in Latin America: An X-Ray of the Process Leading to a New Colonialism *(1959) is a perfect statement of his ethos.*

Witnessing, from exile in Mexico, the United States-led overthrow of the "ten years of spring" (1944-1954), when Guatemala had been dramatically evolving into a modern, democratic nation, and also witnessing the return of the United Fruit Company as a powerful presence in Guatemala, Arévalo laid out in his book the devices through which the United States and its allies among the reactionary elites were able to return Guatemala to colonial status.

Mariano Rossell y Arellano, archbishop of Guatemala (1939-1964), may be viewed as the quintessential Latin American prelate operating in the mid-twentieth century with a nineteenth-century vision (very much like that of Pius IX—see "Ecuador, 1862," p. 156), thus being the perfect foil for Arévalo's anticlericalism (but not anti-Catholicism).

Explain Rossell y Arellano's theological and philosophical outlook, which allows him to conflate liberalism, conservatism, and communism. How could that be?

Note Arévalo's perceptive analysis of economic liberalism and its relation to the policies of the United States; note also his shrewd dissection of the archbishop's contradictions. Note, in particular, that if Arévalo were writing today he would probably include the terms "neoliberalism" and "free market" in his analysis of "English liberalism," which is exactly the same. Explain the contradiction Arévalo points out in his delightedly sarcastic manner.

Why spell communism with a "K"?

Monseñor Rossell y Arellano provides us with even more important documents useful for our investigation of what we should understand by anti-Kommunism.

From an ideological standpoint, the most striking aspect of our observations, when we dissected the Knights of Industry of New York, was the recognizing that all identified Socialism, be it Marxist or not, be it Christian or not, with Communism. A Catholic Church dignitary who has taken courses in sociology and metaphysics, who has received credits in Latin and has been a diplomat in Rome cannot err by being naive. The Knights of Industry are men with only a rudimentary culture and any illiterate can confuse Socialism with Communism. Rossell y Arellano, however, goes even further than the barbarians in his conceptual confusions. For him Kommunism cannot be distinguished from liberalism and conservatism. At the start, he said, "Economic liberalism and conservatism lead to Communism." On July 21, 1954, hundreds of faithful gathered in front of the Archbishop's palace in Guatemala to celebrate his birthday; they applauded him enthusiastically for the liberation of United Fruit.

In order to keep his hand in, the Archbishop made another political address. "My beloved sons," he began. And at once added: Communism is only the third act of the great process of which the first two are liberalism and conservatism. It is impossible to put an end to it, unless the first two are abolished. Liberalism and conservatism carry the same disease germ: the fundamental principle of Communism: atheistic laws. So long as there are atheistic laws there will be Communism. For the orator on his birthday, the Communist problem reduced itself to a problem of God. The kernel of Communism was in the negation of God. Of God and the Fatherland. He had said, ever since his April 4, 1954, pastoral: "The people of Guatemala should rise up as one man against the enemy of God and the Fatherland."

The docile sheep naturally identified the Guatemalan government with the enemy of God and the Fatherland. Rise up against the constitutional government, "rise up as one man," is an incitement usually heard in the mouth of social agitators, of demagogic leaders, but never in the mouth of a spokesman of Christ. Above all when we know that the revolutionary governments of Guatemala, from October 20, 1944 on, had never done anything against the Catholic Church, the religion of the majority of Guatemalans, or against the resident priests or against the customs and observances of Catholic believers. The sole "crime" was that of having legislated in favor of the workers (1947) and agrarian reform (1952), which seriously affected the profit orgies of United Fruit. This is why the Archbishop's voice found no echo whatever among the Catholics of the country, who remained indifferent to his pastorals and his lying tears. Real tears, in contrast, were those of Foster Dulles and of Eisenhower, who glued themselves to the microphone, weeks after the Archbishop, also to invite the Guatemalans to "rise as one man" against the enemies of the Empire and freedom of opportunity. [...]

Clearly the history of Christianity sets forth contradictions that cannot be bridged. A contradiction, for example, into which Rossell y Arellano falls, in theoretically and verbally condemning "economic liberalism" in the same breath that he personally endeavors to help a commercial enterprise recover its political dominion over the Guatemalan nation. For does it not so happen that all this grandiose iron ring of companies, enterprises, and banks with headquarters in New York, is the product of economic liberalism? And is not liberalism, English liberalism, the philosophy of the United States? And is not the United Fruit one of the important suction pumps seated in the Department of State itself? Rossell y Arellano is not ignorant of this. How, then, is it possible for him to fight liberalism as a philosophic "cause" and at the same time permit it to enter the house as a commercial "effect?" If liberalism is the cause of Kommunism, does this not mean that the "freedom of opportunity" predicated by the Department of State is thereby Kommunism?

103. Portrait of a Troubled Church

Leslie Dewart (b. 1922 in Madrid), né Duarte, was raised in Cuba, where he remained until 1942. He earned his Ph.D. in philosophy at the University of Toronto (1954) and taught philosophy, emphasizing his interests in religion, language, and law. Concerns such as "the Christian crisis and the challenge of history," "the political and religious context of the world crisis," and "the political vocation of Christianity today" led him to return to Cuba and to write Christianity and Revolution: The Lesson of Cuba *(1963).*

Is Dewart's explanation of the "stagnation" of the Cuban Catholic Church the statement of an analytical philosopher? Is there anything in this description of the Catholic Church by a Canadian Catholic that suggests Dewart's own commitment to his church (see similar query in reading 98)?

SOURCE: Leslie Dewart, *Christianity and Revolution: The Lesson of Cuba* (New York: Herder & Herder, 1963), 95-99. Reprinted by permission of Leslie Dewart, who is also the author of *Evolution and Consciousness: The Role of Speech in the Origin and Development of Human Nature* (Toronto: University of Toronto Press, 1989).

Immemorially, then, the Church in Cuba thought of itself, correctly, as impotent, as barely surviving under duress, as threatened by secularism, indifference, freemasonry and, in the last twenty years or so by Protestantism as well. To the Cuban high and low clergy this was especially humiliating in view of the privileged position of the Church in Spain. They knew that Cuba would never realize the Spanish ideal, yet this ideal, being a matter of Christian principle, as they thought, was never to be given up in intention. The Church, thus, was caught in a vicious circle: it was discontent with the here and now, but it saw no other solution than trying to hold on to the past. This was the sort of posture that, by its own implications, could not but confirm the stagnation from which the Church suffered.

The problem of the shortage of priests may provide an enlightening instance of how the vicious circle went. For two generations the shortage was made up, as far as it was ever made up, by the massive importation of Spanish regulars. [...] The Spanish as a whole have not yet become quite reconciled to the reality of having lost their Empire, and most especially Cuba. Many still entertain, and voice, thoughts of a possible reversal of history. The Spanish clergy's militant Spanishness toward the former colony, no less than their conception of what the relations between clergy and people should be, operated generally only to the disadvantage of the Church and tended to diminish the appeal that the priestly ministry might have had for Cuban Catholics.

Naturally, with few native vocations the congregations could not very well maintain seminaries and houses of study in Cuba, so Cuban candidates were sent abroad. Until recently that meant, of course, Spain: Thus, even the native clergy became hispanicized. One should not misconstrue this disadvantage of a Spanish clergy as due to xenophobia, from which Cuba is fortunately almost totally free. The difficulty was specifically Spanish. For example, Canadian priests were sufficiently liberal, and up-to-date to earn respect and admiration. And what was probably the most powerful single agency in the Catholic revival of Cuba's middle classes, namely, the Christian Brothers—who established their

first Cuban foundation at the turn of the century—was until very recent times almost entirely French in composition. It should be added that, unlike the Spanish clergy, the Christian Brothers usually became Cuban nationals. In time they attracted native vocations in great numbers. They were also unique in having had a native Cuban provincial. Their contribution to the modernization of the Church in Cuba was as magnificent as it was un-emulated.

Further to compound the sinuosity of the circle, since early Republican times the Church had concentrated its resources in education work for the upper-middle and upper classes, a condition that prevailed without exception until after World War II, when a few schools for the poor began to appear. The hierarchy seem to have reasoned logically, but not necessarily perspicaciously, that the faith of these classes could be built up most easily and quickly, and that once this was accomplished the middle classes would constitute a sort of elite that would help carry the Gospel to the humble and the poor. The plan was successful enough in the first respect, but certain side effects were not foreseen. They may well have been unforeseeable. For instance, the Church lay itself open to the charge that it was neglecting the poor and courting the rich. Worse, it also lay itself open to the temptation of actually doing so. It seems, indeed, that to some extent it did so: And, upon occasion it did so extravagantly and even unnecessarily. [...]

The hope of a native clergy simply did not materialize [...] because pastoral work was being neglected, even in the city, vocations from the sort of people who would ordinarily have considered going to remote and backward country parishes simply were not forthcoming in sufficient numbers. [...]

[I]f the Cuban Church as a whole was poor, the country parishes were indigent. A country pastor would have starved if he had had to depend upon the parishioners' support. The peasants themselves were not only so needy, but generally so indifferent that only a few would have given even if they had been able. Since the end of World War II the situation was alleviated in part when a few sugar mills began to relieve the diocesan burden by paying pastors' salaries and ordinary parochial expenses.

104. The Catholic Who Is Not a Revolutionary Is Living in Mortal Sin

Camilo Torres (1929-1966), scion of an upper-middle-class family of Bogotá, was ordained a Catholic priest in 1954, studied sociology at the Catholic University of Louvain (Belgium), and returned to Colombia, where he taught sociology and served as chaplain at the National University. The concerns of his students, with whom he was quite popular, and his own sociological insights made him increasingly critical of the status quo. He became active politically, worked with Marxists, and was soon required by the church to choose between his commitments to the secular and the sacred. Choosing the former in 1965, he launched a leftist political coalition but soon acknowledged the futility of peaceful radical change, joined the Army of National Liberation, and was killed in his first military engagement.

"Statement to the Press"—How can "love" and "revolution" go together?

"Message to Communists"—Remember that at the time Torres writes this declaration anticommunism is de rigueur among all political establishments in the Americas save Cuba. Torres's politics may be unconventional, but is his theology?

I took off my cassock to be more truly a priest.
The duty of every Catholic is to be a revolutionary.
The duty of every revolutionary is to make the revolution.
The Catholic who is not a revolutionary is living in mortal sin.

Camilo Torres Restrepo [. . .]

Letter to the Cardinal

Your Eminence:

In agreement with our conversation, it seems to me that, as a testimony of loyalty to the church and to what I consider fundamental in Christianity, I must ask your Eminence for reduction to the lay state and for exoneration from the obligations of my status as member of the clergy.

In anticipation that your Eminence will graciously grant this petition, I permit myself to sign myself

Faithfully in Christ . . .

Statement to the Press

When circumstances prevent men from actively consecrating their lives to Christ, it is the priest's duty to combat these circumstances even if he must forfeit the right to officiate at Eucharistic rites, which have meaning only if Christians are so consecrated.

Within the present structure of the church, it has become impossible for me to continue acting as priest in the external aspects of our religion. However, the Christian priesthood consists not only of officiating at external ritual observances. The Mass, which is at the center of the priesthood, is fundamentally communal. But the Christian community cannot worship in an authentic way unless it has first effectively put into practice the precept of love for fellow man. I chose Christianity because I believed that in it I would find the purest way to serve my fellow man. I was chosen by Christ to be a priest forever because of the desire to consecrate my full time to the love of my fellow man.

As a sociologist, I have wanted this love to be translated into efficient service through technology and science. My analyses of Colombian society made me realize that revolution is necessary to feed the hungry, give drink to the thirsty, clothe the naked, and procure a life of wellbeing for the needy majority of our people. I believe that the revolutionary struggle is appropriate for the Christian and the priest. Only by revolution, by

SOURCE: John Gerassi, ed., *Revolutionary Priest: The Complete Writings & Messages of Camilo Torres* (New York: Random House, 1971), xiii, 324-26, 370-72. Reprinted by permission of John Gerassi.

changing the concrete conditions of our country, can we enable men to practice love for each other.

Throughout my ministry as priest, I have tried in every way possible to persuade the laymen, Catholic or not, to join the revolutionary struggle. In the absence of a massive response, I have resolved to join the revolution myself, thus carrying out part of my work of teaching men to love God by loving each other. I consider this action essential as a Christian, as a priest, and as a Colombian. But such action, at this time, is contrary to the discipline of the present church. I do not want to break the discipline of the church, but I also do not want to betray my conscience.

Therefore, I have asked his Eminence the Cardinal to free me from my obligations as a member of the clergy so that I may serve the people on the temporal level. I forfeit one of the privileges I deeply love—the right to officiate as priest at the external rites of the church. But I do so to create the conditions that will make these rites more authentic.

I believe that my commitment to live a useful life, efficiently fulfilling the precept of love for my fellow man, demands this sacrifice of me. The highest standard by which human decisions must be measured is the all-surpassing love that is true charity. I accept all the risks that this standard demands of me.

Last Clarification

The Cardinal reduced me to the lay state by a decree in which he says that this reduction will be in accord with a rescript which will come from Rome; but that rescript has not arrived. In Rome they asked him to speak to me before imposing the sanction on me, and he did not heed that order.

Disgracefully, the Cardinal gives the appearance of continuing in the same key, without explaining or proving that I am against the Catholic church. It seems that he acted under the pressure of the groups who have control of the country.

The public statements of his Eminence the Cardinal are contrary to his private statements. When I spoke personally with him, we saw that the only

way to save his conscience and mine was for me to ask for reduction to the lay state. He told me it was a sad decision for him, but he also hoped that, at the moment I would consider convenient, I could return to the exercise of my priesthood, at which time he would receive me with open arms.

Message to Communists

The relations that have traditionally existed between Christians and Marxists, between the church and the Communist party, may give rise to doubts and misunderstandings about the relations taking shape within the United Front between Christians and Marxists and between a priest and the Communist party. I therefore consider it necessary to make clear to the Colombian people both my relations with the Communist party and its position in the United Front.

I have said that as a Colombian, as a sociologist, as a Christian, and as a priest I am a revolutionary. I believe that the Communist party consists of truly revolutionary elements, and hence I cannot be an anti-Communist either as a Colombian, a sociologist, a Christian, or a priest.

As a Colombian I am not an anti-Communist because anti-Communism hounds nonconformists among my compatriots regardless of whether they are Communists or not. Most of them are simply poor people. As a sociologist I am not an anti-Communist because the Communist theses concerning the fight against poverty, hunger, illiteracy, lack of shelter, and absence of public services offer effective scientific solutions to these problems. As a Christian I am not an anti-Communist because I believe that anti-Communism implies condemnation of everything that Communists stand for.

As a priest I am not an anti-Communist because among the Communists themselves, whether they know it or not, there may be many true Christians. If they are of good faith, they are entitled to receive Holy Communion. And if they receive Holy Communion and if they love their neighbor, they will be saved. My duty as a priest, although I no longer practice the rites of the church, is to bring people nearer to God, and the best way to do this is to try to make people serve their neighbor according to the dictates of their conscience. I do not seek to proselytize my Communist brethren and induce them to accept the dogma and the rites of the church. What I strive for is that people should act according to their conscience, that they should sincerely search for the truth, and that they should truly love their fellow men.

I am prepared to fight together with the Communists for our common goals: against the oligarchy and United States domination; for the winning of power by the people.

I do not want to be identified with the Communists alone and, hence, I have always sought to work together not only with them but with all independent revolutionaries and revolutionaries of other convictions.

That the large newspapers persist in saying that I am a Communist is of no importance. I prefer to follow the voice of my own conscience and not to submit to pressures from the oligarchy. I prefer to live according to the standards of the apostles of the church and not the standards of the apostles of our ruling class. John XXIII allowed me to join in united actions with the Communists when he declared the following in his encyclical *Pacem in terris*:

It must be borne in mind, furthermore, that neither can false philosophical teachings regarding the nature, origin, and destiny of the universe and of man be identified with historical movements that have economic, social, cultural, or political ends, not even when these movements have originated from those teachings and have drawn and still draw inspiration therefrom. Because the

teachings, once they are drawn up and defined, remain always the same, while the movements, working on historical situations in constant evolution, cannot but be influenced by these latter and cannot avoid, therefore, being subject to changes, even of a profound nature. Besides, who can deny that these movements, insofar as they conform to the dictates of right reason and are interpreters of the lawful aspirations of the human person, contain elements that are positive and deserving of approval?

It can happen, then, that a drawing nearer together or a meeting for the attainment of some practical end, which was formerly deemed inopportune or unproductive, might now or in the future be considered opportune and useful. But to decide whether this moment has arrived, and also to lay down the ways and degrees in which work in common might be possible for the achievement of economic, social, cultural, and political ends which are honorable and useful: these are the problems which can only be solved with the virtue of prudence, which is the guiding light of the virtues that regulate the moral life, both individual and social.

When the people take power into their hands, thanks to the cooperation of all revolutionaries, the nation will consider the question of its religious orientation. The example of Poland shows that it is possible to build socialism without destroying that which is basic in Christianity. One Polish priest clarifies this: "We Christians are duty-bound to help build the socialist state when we are permitted to worship God as we wish."

105. In the Favelas of the Brazil Northeast

Paul Gallet, a priest with experience working in rural and urban parishes in France, answered Pope John XXIII's call for clergy to volunteer for work in Latin America. He kept a journal covering the years 1962 to 1969 about the precarious existence of the people of

SOURCE: Paul Gallet, *Freedom to Starve*, trans. Rosemary Sheed (Middlesex: Penguin Books, 1972), 83-89, 165-67. Reprinted by permission of Gill & Macmillan Ltd.

northeast Brazil, the poorest section of the nation and also the area with the largest Afro-Brazilian population.

The reading below offers several revelations: the profound poverty in the favelas, the perceptions of a concerned European, the values and cosmology of the desperately poor urban dwellers, and, once again, the missionary experience. Describe Gallet's estimate of the poor, that is, not his estimate of their dire poverty but his estimate of the poor as part of human existence, as part of human history. Does he idealize the poor or does he describe them objectively? Does he look at them from a particularly Christian view? How does Gallet describe their religiosity? What is the nature of their concept of religion? How thoughtful, how deep is their vision of God, of Christianity, of the church? What is his concept of evangelization? Whom does he seek out and what are his methods?

1 February: I was interrupted the other day. I spent yesterday among the streets of my new neighbourhood. I've changed my method of visiting: rather than going systematically from door to door, I go through as many streets as I can, and whenever I see someone standing outside a door, or a man working inside, I start chatting, and then go inside.

The leader of the Assembleia de Deus (they're Adventists, rather like Jehovah's Witnesses) has asked me to their service this afternoon: 'It will be a great honour for us,' he said.

I was asked for some holy water, which was undoubtedly going to be used as a 'cure' for something. 'I'm afraid I can't bless any water until Easter.' (What a lie!) Further along I came to a household of consumptives, where one old man is gradually dying. Tomorrow I shall take him communion. A *carrosseiro* (driver of a little donkey cart—there are lots of them here) called gaily, 'Yes it is, it's the Father who was in Piraï!' I went into a snack bar to have a 'cola-jesus' – a horrible fizzy drink, but at least it's cold; we chatted. This is my little world; and it's wonderful—I love it. And I think they realize that. These are the kind of simple people Christ must have known in Palestine. [. . .]

Fortunately we did not go to live in the house called *Do Menino Jesus* (The house of the Child Jesus) where we were offered rooms to rent; it's a brothel in fact (but of course that's quite common here). In most such houses there are quantities of pictures of saints, and statues with candles or vigil lights burning in front of them. Some prostitutes even make novenas or 'promises' to our Lady, asking her to get them work! Who would cast the first stone? That is what real poverty means. You exploit every possibility of earning a few cruzeiros rather than starve or let your children starve.

Tomorrow I'm going to an ACO [Workers Catholic Action] study day. Almost every evening there's some group meeting, either an established team, or a group of beginners. This evening I'm going to the meeting of the União dos Moradores (union of neighbourhood communities).

I really must stop. Pray for me. I can't tell you how happy we are, but one must move slowly, which calls for patience and love. These at least the Lord will supply.

DIARY
Reflections on the mentality of the people
I. Signs of paganism:
Stars on the doors of the houses—*Macumbas*.
No fathers—just women bringing up children.
Prostitution.
People throw a spadeful of earth on to the coffin to ward off bad luck.
Pictures of naked women all over the walls.

One day a prostitute asked me, 'Why can't a prostitute be a godmother?' I tried to explain, and she finally said, 'Oh, yes, priests won't allow people to be godmothers with short sleeves, either, they must have long sleeves.'

The kind of devotion to the saints practised here is syncretism. There are many signs that the influence of Africa is still very much alive: for instance, polygamy isn't *just* the effect of poverty.

There's a house where the prostitutes can go to get rid of their babies when they're three or four months pregnant. It costs 5,000 cruzeiros (just over 8 dollars) without anaesthetic, 10,000 with.

You often hear people say, 'Life is just this, life is this world; there is not any other.'

The other day a carpenter said to me, 'After reincarnation (it's the spiritists who believe in reincarnation) I don't want to be a carpenter any more, because I'm always making nice furniture for other people, and I only have rotten stuff at home. And it's a trade you can't practise honestly.'

The other day, we were in the middle of a May procession when we met another procession in the same street: it was the Divino Espírito Santo, the Divine Holy Spirit—a kind of half-pagan, half-folklore society.

In one house where spirits are worshipped this is what I saw: five bowls of water on one table; five other bowls: one in the middle of the room and one in each corner; a mass of white flowers, stars, a big framed picture of a woman with long hair and a star in her hand walking on the sea; in another corner, a framed Sacred Heart. There's syncretism for you! When she came out, the woman who runs this spiritist house, and who the neighbours tell me is a spirit-healer, declared: 'We are Catholics.'

The reason why people ask for holy water (which they do constantly) is to use it for healing as they are taught.

The *Macumba*: one day a woman told me: 'Well yes, in the world there are two spirits at work. The spirit from below who does harm, you've got to watch out for him; the spirit from above who gives us everything good.'

II. Signs of genuine faith:

In 'Brasília' one day I met a mother who was in tears. Her little boy had just died; but her eyes lit up as she added, 'I'm sure he didn't die as a pagan.'

It seems to be quite common for people to see Christ in the person of beggars. You often feel, from their attitude and what they say, that their response to poverty is bound up with love of Christ.

There is an ambivalence in what they call here 'conformism': it means something akin to 'fatalism', but they never actually say 'fatalism', always 'conformism'. For instance when they say, '*E preciso se conformar*,' what they mean is, 'We must accept it.' You often hear them say, 'We must accept, we must conform to the will of God.' But it's an ambivalent expression: there is something pagan in this outlook of passivity, fatality, inertia; yet there is also something Christian that you often sense too—an acceptance of the cross, and a profound faith and hope in spite of everything.

At one time the people of Riobamba thought the priests were going to take away 'their' statue, to which a lot of people make pilgrimages, and they made the most violent efforts to prevent the jeep the priests were in from getting through because they (quite wrongly) thought that was what they had come for. There was certainly an element of the pagan—of superstition and fanaticism—in their behaviour, but there was a Christian attitude too. They were saying, 'No one, not even the priests, can take our statue away. No one can take away our faith.' You really get the impression here that in one sense religion is not the priests, but the people.

One Christian worker says, 'I never used to have time to do anything, to go to mass, or work with my mates. Now I do find the time. Why?'

Another ACO leader: 'When I was at the first meeting of the movement (which took place in my home) I stayed in the hammock complaining that I was ill. It wasn't true. Today I can't bear to miss a single meeting. Christ has beaten me.' (Those were his actual words.)

When there is danger of death and no priest available, the people generally will baptize their dying babies themselves at home. There's usually someone in the street who's recognized as being good at it, and they go to find that person, because everyone says, 'You can't let him die a pagan.'

You often hear something like this: 'I was born in the Catholic faith and I want to die in it.' Quite often the fact of leaving the Catholic Church to join a Protestant Church or sect may well be a tribute to the Catholic Church. A tribute because of the reasons which underlie the act: with a kind of common sense of the faith, they can no longer accept a devotion to the saints which is in fact, though not in theory, false (in fact it is a form of idolatry as practised here). [. . .]

As far as evangelizing the Catholics goes, we have made a change: rather than constantly fighting against their folklore and all that goes with it we are trying to establish more and more links between the gospel and their ordinary life. Are they unhappy? Then that is a reason to cooperate: 'mothers' clubs' are being formed in which they help one another (sewing, cooking, child care . . .). Do they see how poor other people are? Then that is an invitation to join 'neighbourhood communities' and become the leaven in the lump, to develop their missionary concern. These neighbourhood communities have just formed a 'Federation' for the whole city of S. Recently the Federation elected a committee: ACO members form a large part of it, and there is one in particular who was attracted to communism a few years back, but has now, thanks to the ACO, begun to understand all the values of Catholicism. [. . .]

[O]ne certainly finds in the st⌐ young people full of generosity wh deeper vision of the Church, for instance ⌐⌐⌐ ⌐⌐⌐ ers of the university Catholic groups, and of the MEB [Movement for Basic Education].

People sometimes talk to me of the great danger of communism; I prefer to talk of the great opportunities open to Catholicism. There must be a revolution of the gospel wrought by the young people and adults who are becoming leaders, and by a whole people who are spontaneously generous and religious despite not yet being evangelized in the full sense of the word. That at least is my long-term hope.

106. A Devout Christian Takes Up Arms

The Jesuit-educated son of a Bolivian general, Néstor Paz (1945-1970) was an athlete, seminarian, religion teacher, and an organizer of cooperatives. In 1970 at the age of twenty-four and with the full agreement of his wife of two years who shared his understanding of the demands of Christianity, he joined the Bolivian Army of National Liberation (ELN).

Bolivia in 1970 was in a state of agonized upheaval characterized by rebellion, repression, and the growth of the infamous national security state, a universal Latin American phenomenon. The revolution in 1952, led by the tin miners, had achieved major gains, the most important of which were meaningful land reform, the enfranchisement of the Amerindian majority, and the nationalization of the mines, which ended the power of la rosca, *the oligarchy. After 1964, however, under the brutal regime of General René Barrientos, those gains had been seriously compromised, ignored, or obliterated.*

Despite—or because of—the failure of the Ñancahuazú guerrilla campaign of 1967-1968, the execution of Ernesto "Ché" Guevara, and the new manipulative military regime that seized power in 1969, the ELN launched the Teoponte Campaign in 1970. Its manifesto listed some twenty-four multinational corporations that had skewed Bolivian economic life and made outrageous profits. The manifesto also emphasized the strategic sectors of industry held by foreign interests.

What does Néstor "Francisco" Paz's "Message on Leaving to Join the Guerrillas" have in common with the statements made by other activist Christians at the same historical moment? Is there any new insight or slant that reflects the particular experience of a twenty-four-year-old who had been raising his own consciousness for some eleven years? Must this "message" necessarily differ from other Christian confessions because of its author's decision to actually take up arms? If it does differ, is it because of Paz's decision to take up arms? How

SOURCE: Néstor Paz, *My Life for My Friends: The Guerrilla Journal of Néstor Paz, Christian*, trans. and ed. Ed García and John Eagleson (Maryknoll, N.Y.: Orbis Books, 1975), 21-26. Reprinted by permission of Orbis Books.

does his message compare with Camilo Torres's statements? Does his Christian confession constitute a category distinct from Christian confessions made by those who did not take up arms?

"Every sincere revolutionary must realize that armed struggle is the only path that remains" (Camilo Torres, January 7, 1966).

Following the glorious path taken by our own heroes, the guerrillas of the Peruvian highlands, and by the continental heroes, Bolívar and Sucre, and the heroic commitment of Ernesto Guevara, the Peredo brothers, Darío, and many others who lead the march of the people's liberation, we take our place in the long guerrilla file, rifle in hand, to combat the symbol and instrument of oppression—the "gorilla" army.

As long as blood flows in our veins we will make heard the cutting cry of the exploited. Our lives do not matter if we can make our Latin America, *la patria grande*, a free territory of free people who are masters of their own destiny.

I realize that my decision and that of my companions will bring upon us a deluge of accusations, from the paternalistic "poor misguided fellow," to the open charge of "demagogic criminal." But Yahweh our God, the Christ of the Gospels, has announced the "good news of the liberation of man," for which he himself acted. We cannot sit and spend long hours reading the Gospel with cardinals, bishops, and pastors, all of whom are doing fine right where they are, while the flock wanders about in hunger and solitude. Doing this is called "non-violence," "peace," "Gospel." These persons, sadly, are today's Pharisees.

People no longer listen to the "Good News." Man is always betrayed by his "brother."

"Peace" is not something one finds by chance; it is the result of equality among people, as Isaiah says in his chapter 58. Peace is the result of love among people, the result of an end to exploitation.

"Peace" is not attained by dressing up in silk and living in a medieval palace, or by robbing the people in order to have a millionaire's salary, or by playing on the people's religious superstition in order to live at their expense.

"Greater love than this no man has than to lay down his life for his friends." This is the commandment which sums up the "Law."

For this reason we have taken up arms: to defend the unlettered and undernourished majority from the exploitation of a minority and to win back dignity for a dehumanized people.

We know that violence is painful because we feel in our own flesh the violent repression of the established disorder. But we are determined to liberate man because we consider *him a brother*. We are the people in arms. This is the only path that remains. Man comes before the "Sabbath," not vice versa.

They say violence is not evangelical; let them remember Yahweh slaying the first-born of the Egyptians to free his people from exploitation.

They say that they believe in "non-violence." Then let them stand clearly with the people. If they do, the rich and the "gorillas" will both demand their lives, just as they demanded Christ's. Let them take courage and try it; let us see if they are consistent enough to face a Good Friday. But all that is demagoguery, isn't it, you canons, generals, *cursillistas*, priests of the established disorder, you priests of the peace enforced by violence, of the massacre of San Juan, of the complicity of silence, of the 200-peso salaries, of the widespread tuberculosis, and of pie in the sky when you die. The Gospel is not mechanical moralism. It is a shell hiding a "life" which must be discovered if we are not to fall into pharisaism. The Gospel is "Jesus among us."

We have chosen this path because it is the only path left open to us, painful though it may be.

Fortunately, there are some, and their numbers are growing, who recognize the authenticity of our position and who either help us or have joined our ranks. We need only consider what the right-wing "gorilla" government of Brazil does to a committed Church: Father Pereira Neto was assassinated in a most cruel and inhuman manner. Or recall Father Ildefonso, a Tupamaro, assassinated in Uruguay. Or Father Camilo Torres, silenced by the government and the servile church. But Camilo Torres ratified with his blood what he had said about Christianity:

In Catholicism the main thing is love for one's fellow men: " . . . He who loves his fellow man has fulfilled the Law." For this love to be genuine, it must seek to be effective. If works of beneficence, almsgiving, the few tuition-free schools, the few housing projects—everything which is known as "charity"—do not succeed in feeding the majority of the hungry, in clothing the majority of the naked, or in teaching the majority of the ignorant, then we must seek effective means to achieve the well-being of this majority. . . . This is why the revolution is not only permissible but obligatory for those Christians who see it as the only effective and far-reaching way to make love for all people a reality.

I believe that taking up arms is the only effective way of protecting the poor against their present exploitation, the only effective way of generating a free man.

I believe that the struggle for liberation is rooted in the prophetic line of Salvation History.

Enough of the languid faces of the over-pious! The whip of justice, so often betrayed by elegant gentlemen, will fall on the exploiter, that false Christian who forgets that the force of his Lord ought to drive him to liberate his neighbor from sin, that is to say, from every lack of love.

We believe in a "New Man," made free by the blood and resurrection of Jesus. We believe in a New Earth, where love will be the fundamental law. This will come about, however, only by breaking the old patterns based on selfishness. We don't want patches. New cloth can't be used to mend old garments, nor can new wine be put into old wineskins. Conversion implies first an inner violence which is then followed by violence against the exploiter. May both men and the Lord together judge the rightness of our decision. At least no one can imply that we look for profit or comfort. These are not what we find in the struggle; they are what we leave behind. [. . .]

I am certain that we can achieve this goal, for the Lord "is ready to give us far more than all we can ask or think" (Ephesians 3:20).

"The duty of every Christian is to be a revolutionary. The duty of every revolutionary is to bring about the revolution."

Victory or Death. Francisco

107. Evangelization: Obstacles and Rays of Hope

Fredy (sic) Kunz (1920-2000), a French citizen of Swiss origin, experienced the horrors of a concentration camp in Austria where he was imprisoned for most of World War II. Ordained a priest in 1954, he ministered to the poor of Montreal until 1968, when he joined the diocese of Cratéus in the impoverished Brazilian northeast. Headed by a model bishop, the diocese gave birth to the Fraternity of the Suffering Servant (see Isaiah 50:4ff.), which Kunz joined. That Servant was, of course, Christ, in whom Kunz saw the incarnation of the world's poor.

The value of this seemingly innocuous report, written by Alfredhinho (the endearing name by which the passionately committed Kunz was known during his thirty-two years in Brazil) at the request of his bishop, is its straightforward, unemotional narration of the obstacles to evangelization in rural Latin America. The reader should try to see each section as the depiction of an obstacle.

What is the first massive obstacle described in the first two paragraphs? What is the completely different kind of obstacle described in the third paragraph? The obstacle in the fourth

SOURCE: Alfredo Kunz, "A Story of the Progress of the Small Church of Marroás," *International Review of Mission* 68, no. 271 (July 1979): 266-67. © World Council of Churches. Used by permission.

paragraph is different yet again: why would a priest be expelled from Brazil? The story of Adalto Filho introduces both a new series of obstacles and some bright rays of hope, one of which Filho himself represents. What is that new series of obstacles and what are the rays of hope? Be sure to consider the following terms: "chapel council," "animators," "customary . . . gambling and drinking."

The chapel of St Rita, district of Marroás, was founded in 1872. The district, forty-two kilometres long and eighteen kilometres wide, has a district seat of 500 inhabitants and fifty-two other settlements with a total of 8,000 baptized persons. There are two roads which can be used by carts, but which are some distance from the main road. There are five big landowners, several small owners and many landless peasants who have to pay a rent of up to 50% of their production. A power plant furnishes electricity from 6 to 9:30 in the evening.

There are three municipal schools in the region: Marráos, Guaribas, São João. Education goes only as far as the second grade of primary school. At the seat, there are two Mobral (adult education) schools with fifty pupils, but attendance is very poor. There is also a library and one television set for the community. [. . .]

With the arrival of the priests João and Gabriel, and of the layman Joel, there was a change in style. They visited the people in their homes and held meetings to discuss the Church, the Bible and labour unions. They started to celebrate the Word, took a parochial census, and initiated a system of parish contributions in order to avoid charging fees for the sacraments. As a result, a few people had their eyes opened, but the majority of the people could not accustom themselves to these new ideas, and were furious about the meetings. Many people said the priests were false priests.

On 13 October 1972 Father José, who had worked since 1971 in the parish, was taken prisoner to Fortaleza and expelled from Brazil. The mother church was closed down; Father João was named vicar of Ipueiras. Discouragement was great; the animators went away; the celebration of the Word was interrupted. [. . .]

Adalto Filho, born in 1950, graduated from the Technical School in Tauá. When he returned from the army in 1972, he found the stirrings of activity; there were many people in the church, but he did not participate. Once he was invited to read the Scripture in church which he did, but was immediately embarrassed and withdrew from the altar. Church business was not for men: only for women and priests.

In 1973 he was nominated by the Chapel Council to aid in the preparation of engaged couples. He received some training, and was required to read the Bible in order to be able to explain it to the couples. He started to go to Church, noted the weakness of most of the animators who celebrated the Word, and thought he could motivate this group. He noticed that those who were preparing the baptisms were also weak and decided to help them as well. In July he participated in a retreat for clergy and lay persons in Crateús. He discovered the enthusiasm of these people, of youth joyfully participating in the work of the Church. He returned greatly strengthened to continue the job of animating the community.

Noting that the church was looked down upon, he started a cleanup campaign, worked to cement the entrance and to buy 16 benches. The people became more enthusiastic, and began attending mass in greater numbers. In January 1973, he participated in the meeting of the animators to plan the pastoral programme for the year. Now more experienced, he returned to the community and organized with the animators the feast of St. Rita. The people, the businessmen, and the authorities all united to make the feast a strictly religious occasion. (The only person who would not cooperate was Corporal Bezerra; against the will of the people he organized a dance near All Saints Day, on which occasion a young man was killed.) At the hour of mass, the merchants closed their shops; there was no gambling or drinking as had been customary.

108. The Churches and Peasant Leagues

Francisco Julião (1915-1999) was born and raised in Pernambuco in Brazil's northeast (where slavery had existed until 1888), among some of the most impoverished peasants in all of Latin America. After earning his law degree in 1939, he defended his tenant and day-laboring neighbors against continued abuse by the owners of latifundios and engenhos and continued to do so after his election as deputy to Congress in 1950.

Julião was driven to found the Peasant League in 1955, which finally brought to the surface the problem of land in Brazil and the smoldering resentment of the peasantry. By 1964 Peasant Leagues were flourishing all over the vast northeast, striking fear into the landowners, the military, and the church, all of whom anticipated a communist and revolutionary onslaught. At this time, Brazil's constitution (1946) guaranteed political rights such as freedom of speech, freedom of the press, and freedom to organize. Thus, the leagues were legal and complied with all the requirements of the law.

A coup backed by the U.S. CIA in 1964 overthrew progressive president João Goulart and brought in a junta of generals (1964-1985), causing Julião to be exiled. From Mexico he wrote his Cambao—The Yoke: The Hidden Face of Brazil, *published in 1968.*

The excerpt below describes clearly the brutal realities of the structures and institutions of Brazil, the recalcitrance and belligerence of the elites—governmental, economic, clerical, and military—and the near impossibility of even shedding light upon these realities, much less challenging them.

What pressure does Julião see operating on the parish priest that account for the latter's supine behavior? What has to happen, according to Julião, before the Catholic Church takes a moral position on the pressing issues of the day, such as the demands of the Peasant Leagues? What might that "moral" stand be? (See paragraphs beginning with "When the peasant movement . . ."; "Possibly the fact . . ."; "Pope Pius XI. . . .")

Why would Protestant missionaries be sympathetic with the Peasant Leagues?

Denouncing movements for justice and change as "communist" has been the tactic of elites—in the United States, Latin America, and Europe—even before the Bolshevik revolution. What, therefore, is striking about the dialogue between the landowner and the peasant?

Would the bishop from Pesqueira recognize Julião's description of "peace"? Would he agree with Julião's condemnation of this "peace"? Why did the bishop not respond to the letter? What may have been his problem?

In the beginning the League met with systematic hostility from clerical authorities. Knowing the deep religious sentiments of the peasantry and the constant labours of parish priests to stifle the spirit of rebellion among the working masses, the League always avoided open conflict with the church: it would have been easily suppressed had it confronted an institution then still reactionary and insensitive towards the peasants' conditions since its ties were rather with the *latifundio* as they had earlier been with the slave-owners.

I used to think of the complaint of Joaquim

Source: Francisco Julião, *Cambão—The Yoke: The Hidden Face of Brazil*, trans. John Butt (Harmondsworth, England: Penguin Books, 1972), 148-53. Reproduced by permission of Penguin Books Ltd.

Nabuco, a Catholic and liberal, who in the middle of the abolition campaign in the last century declared: 'Unfortunately our movement for abolition owes nothing to the state church. On the contrary, the fact that convents and secular clergy possess slaves completely undermines their religious sentiments, and no priest ever prevented a slave auction or the religious practices of the *senzala*.' This does not mean that all the clergy closed their ears to the clamour of the landless peasantry, just as a few priests raised their voices—even in church—against the evil of black slavery. But the system was well organized and was powerful enough to silence a young priest's romantic Christianity without difficulty, or to suppress any member whose conscience was pricked by years of guilty silence.

It's not easy for a man who has spent ten years under the rigid discipline of a seminary to rebel against the rules when he has sworn to obey them without question; just as it is hard for a professional soldier to break out of the system of barrack-room hierarchies and support a revolt against a dictatorship maintained by force in minority interests. One can thus readily understand why Catholic workmen's circles led by weak-willed priests at first opposed the League: such circles constituted a small and lifeless organization confined to the narrow limits of the parish. The priests feared clashes with the owners who controlled local political life so that the workmen's circle was controlled by a larger, more inflexible organization—the *latifundio*.

When the peasant movement led by the League gained impetus, the cities were invaded by a mass of country people coming not to fairs, masses or burial grounds but to the judges and prefects to demand their rights, or to demonstrate in the streets with banners calling for agrarian reform. As a result the church, concerned by events in the countryside, decided to widen the scope of its activities, and the bishops and priests were split into two clearly divided groups: one reactionary, bent on suppressing the League by denouncing its activities as subversive and dangerous; the other sympathetic to the movement, adopting a courageous, intelligent and progressive attitude towards it. In between these two groups a few priests lit a candle for God and another for the Devil, talking radicalism and revolution to the peasants and secretly collaborating with the *latifundio* and the state's repressive organizations in an attempt to patch up social divisions.

But before things got to this point the League had started out on a difficult path, which brought it into inevitable conflict with the *latifundio*. It is only fair to say that the League was able to count from the start on the steadfast support of a few Protestant missionaries from several sects who went about, bible in hand, delivering sermons about the land, seed, ploughs, sowing, harvesting and work, drawing on symbols and passages from the two Testaments to win followers and widen their field of action. It was only natural that a persecuted religion should seek out the persecuted, and the League welcomed the support of such preachers, but always avoided giving preference to any one sect, just as it always refused to discriminate between Catholics, Protestants or any other faith.

The League's only objective was to win the support of all groups to attack the *latifundio*. Without doubt the Protestant preachers netted many a fish, especially in areas where the Catholic Church was directed by intolerant priests in league with the wealthy landowners: such priests were refusing to marry, baptize or confess League members, on the grounds that membership was a sign of communism. João Pedro Teixeira, for example, who was a Protestant pastor led the Sapé League where the overwhelming majority of members was Catholic. Joaquim Camilo and José Evangelista, both Protestants, led the League at Jaboatão in Pernambuco, one of the most active in the state.

Jaboatão (the only city in Brazil to elect a communist prefect, Dr. Rodrigues Calheiros) was the scene of an episode between a Protestant peasant and member of the League and the vice-prefect of the city, a landowner, and the incident is an indication in itself of the level of politicization and acuteness of the peasantry.

Whenever a League centre was opened in a city or town it was our custom to invite the local authorities to be present at the ceremony; this was a public demonstration of the organization's legality. Some authorities would attend; others found a thousand excuses to keep away; many refused on the grounds that the League was subversive because it aimed at changing existing law and at agitating the peasantry against the landowners. When the vice-prefect of Jaboatão was invited to the inauguration of the Jaboatão League he refused on the grounds that the League was communist. Whereupon the peasant retorted: 'The League's inside the law. It's been registered. It has proper statutes. You can see them.'

The landowner, however, counter-attacked: 'The devil knows what clothes to wear. He puts on pilgrim's clothes to fool you, but the people look at his feet and can see they're goat's feet. Communism is like the Devil.'

'Excuse my ignorance, boss, but I've noticed that whenever something turns up that'll benefit the poor they tell you it's communism. That way they're stoking communism up. It'll end by winning. . . . '

'Do you know what communism is?'

'No. My law is of another kind, Jesus Christ's, our Lord's.'

'Then I'll tell you. Communism is taking other people's goods, outraging other people's wives and daughters and attacking our religion. That is the law of communism.'

The Protestant thought for a while and gave the following reply, which is still remembered in the North-East.

'Well, if that's the law of communism, we're already in it. Look: the poor man rents some land, builds a house, puts up a fence, plants some trees and makes some other improvements. One day the boss goes against him, chucks him out and doesn't give him a penny. So he's taking other people's goods. If the poor man has a pretty daughter, there'll soon be some foreman or plantation-owner or rich man to dishonour her. It's no good his complaining: rich men don't marry poor women. As for the rest, I'm a Protestant myself, and the landowner where I live is a Catholic woman. I can't worship in my own house or sing my hymns because she doesn't like them. She's attacking my religion. . . . There we are, boss. The League came to finish with this law which you call communism and make another, a fair law, to protect the poor.'

Possibly the fact that Protestants joined the League and made inroads among tenants in areas where the priests were most intolerant, put the church on the alert and helped persuade the bishops to look on the agrarian problem in a new light. The fact is that the church could not remain indifferent in the face of a conflict as tense as that which had blown up amongst the now awakening peasants and the enraged and fearful landowners. Faced with this the church could not stay silent, and compromised with the *latifundio* as it had done the previous century during the struggle for abolition of black slavery. The world had changed so radically in the last fifty years that a passive attitude would have been irremediably damaging to the church.

Pope Pius XI had already declared that the greatest scandal of the nineteenth century was the church's loss of the working classes. On the basis of this declaration Father Francisco Lage noted that if the church became isolated from popular movements in Latin America and was turned into an ally of the oligarchies and wealthy classes another later Pope would one day say something similar but more serious: 'The greatest scandal of the twentieth century was the church's loss of Latin America.'

In 1960 a north-eastern bishop from Pesqueira, Pernambuco, alarmed by the advances of the peasant movement, travelled to the South to denounce the misery prevalent in the north-eastern countryside, but also complained that I was disturbing the tranquillity of the region. I replied with an open letter written in a respectful tone to which he never replied. Here is the passage about peace:

There is peace in the countryside. Excellency, I know this. I hate this peace with the same hatred I have for slavery, backwardness, hunger, poverty and the *latifundio*. Of what does this peace consist? The silence of millions of tiny children who instead of being sheltered in healthy homes with clothes for their bodies and milk for their stomachs, find their way into crude wooden coffins in the local cemeteries, all destroyed by hunger. It is a peace based on the silence of the peasant woman who is old at thirty; based on the tears she sheds at the funeral of a peace founded on the silence ... evicted by the *capanga*, by the ...gal authorities from the plot of ...he was born because he ...against *cambão*, rent increases, interest rates and a thousand other cruel kinds of exploitation. I oppose this peace.

That is why I have been agitating in the Pernambuco countryside with the noblest of intentions. I write, speak, indoctrinate. Let Your Reverence read my writings and honour me with listening to my teachings in person; and if any word of them goes against the holy scriptures I too shall fall silent.

109. Becoming Christian after Catholic Education

Marcio Moreira Alves (b. 1936) studied law at the State University of Rio de Janeiro and authored A Grain of Mustard Seed: The Awakening of the Brazilian Revolution *(1973). In this book he stated that he left the church because of the Catholic education he received in his youth. Active in politics as a progressive and defender of human rights (he was elected for a term to the congress that was later emasculated by the military junta), he was forced to go into hiding and exile because of these activities.*

It was during the darkest early years (1964-1968) of the military junta (1964-1985) that he met with Catholics who shared the same concerns he did. He understood those concerns well but not "these strange Christians" who were so full of "humor and optimism," "permanent[ly] questioning," which "provided them with a sense of security," and whose goals were "more exacting and ambitious" than those of "orthodox Catholics."

(See the first half of the paragraph "From politics our talks. . . .") What is the difference between the theology of "these strange Christians" and that of traditionally "orthodox Catholics"? What does the discussion of the compatibility of Marxism and Christianity by these "catacomb Christians" demonstrate about the situation within Latin American Christian churches in the 1960s? Roger Garaudy (b. 1913), a leader of the French Communist Party in the post–World War II era, published Anathema to Dialogue *(1965), initiating an influential exchange between Marxism and Christianity. Luigi Longo (1900-1980), a founder of the Italian Communist Party in 1921 who became its head in 1964, shortly thereafter eliminated the materialist, atheist dogmatism from the party's ideology. Both developments were perceived as groundbreaking possibilities for the future. Alves's account of his discussion with his activist Catholic friends of the church's condemnation of violence (last three paragraphs of the excerpt) demonstrates their intellectual astuteness. What do their specific references and examples force them to conclude about the church as an institution? Do these conclusions agree with the contemporary estimates of the church by church people themselves? What are "sociological churches"?*

Whoever is exposed to a formal Catholic education will later have to overwork the Holy Spirit to become a Christian. Christianity is presented there as nothing but a mediocre set of rules. The brainwashing, dehumanizing teachings inflicted upon defenseless children and adolescents hide Christ's true message. [. . .]

As I went through Recife's jails and gathered

SOURCE: Marcio Moreira Alves, *A Grain of Mustard Seed: The Awakening of the Brazilian Revolution* (Garden City, N.Y.: Anchor Books, 1973), 141-56. From *A Grain of Mustard Seed* by Marcio Moreira Alves, copyright © 1973 by Marcio Moreira Alves. Used by permission of Doubleday, a division of Random House, Inc.

information from political prisons all over the country, I started to stumble upon this unusual group of victims. Their presence puzzled me. It didn't fit into my prejudices or correspond to my knowledge. I had followed with a distracted eye the political evolution of the Church's writings. The accounts a few friends working with JUC, Catholic University Youth, gave me about their revolutionary option had been stored in the back of my mind as something irrelevant and bizarre. I imagined that both the committed statements and JUC's position sprang from the Church's opportunistic tendencies. Left seemed the way of the future. [. . .]

To discover that the change was genuine, that these were people willing to back their commitments with their lives, was something of a revelation. I was attracted by these strange followers of a religion so radically different from the one I had once known and rejected. I tried to understand them. Contacts, discussions, explanations developed into friendships strengthened by common interests, common tasks, and mutual trust. A priest would ask me to negotiate with an embassy the granting of political asylum to someone he was hiding. While we drove from one ambassador to another, trying to keep calm in the face of diplomatic indifference and then sharing the joy of depriving the torturers of another victim, we talked. Or a woman would appear with a text to be published and we would discuss the situation of JOC, the Workers Catholic Movement, or the bishops.

From politics our talks passed on to Church affairs and, finally, to religion. The commitment of this breed of Christians was directly inspired by the Gospels. Christ was to them a very real human being whose insertion in time changed their own lives. They discussed His teachings objectively, using their minds and faith to discern the meaning of each text and its relevance to them. They tried to demystify Christianity by retaining the original values that had been hidden by rules. Theirs was a search for the human dimension of God, the only one they thought capable of enhancing divinity. Their flexible religious procedure seemed, however, to provide them with goals more exacting and ambitious than those set by the "orthodox" Catholics I had known. And though

their choice was one of permanent endless investigation, it provided u. sense of security not common among those v. hide within a closed universe in which all doubts have already been answered by Scholastic philosophy. To be sure of one's choice is a joyful blessing. I found that these strange Christians were some of the gayest people I had ever met. They faced life with humor and optimism, enjoying both its pleasures and its challenges.

I joined these "catacomb Christians" by sharing their political activities and slowly began to get interested in their religious opinions. They guided me through readings of the Gospels. They were extremely discreet and went to great lengths so that I would not feel they were proselytizing. I hesitated, I stumbled, I was terribly afraid of not being able to follow the demands an option of this sort would set for me and I tried to cover up these fears with metaphysical doubts. All the while they amiably stood back, though always ready to discuss any subject which might have become a problem for me.

During the first years of military dictatorship in Brazil radical Christian groups were discussing two theoretical problems which had to be solved in order to give greater effectiveness to their political actions—Marxism and violence. The questions were: Can a Christian be a Marxist? Can a Christian resort to violence in order to achieve social justice? Most of the groups' members gave a positive answer on both counts. They stayed together building structures parallel to those of the Church. Those who refused Marxism and violence either drifted into political inactivity or stayed within the Church's social organizations.

The main arguments for the compatibility between a Christian and a Marxist option were developed by student and worker groups highly influenced by the overtures toward Christianity then being made by two European Communists—France's Roger Garaudy and Italy's Luigi Longo. Both considered the problem of Marx's atheism a false one. Longo held that Marx denounces only alienating religion—the sort of religion existing in his time. Garaudy argued that Marxism is an effort to end man's alienation and that this is precisely the sense of Christ's message before it was deformed by the sociological churches throughout history.

Brazil's radical Catholics argue that the Gospel does not offer an ideology to guide the social and political actions of Christians. What it does is to urge them to be the co-builders of history, a mission to be accomplished through social and political decisions. A Christian therefore must look elsewhere for an ideology, a fact the Catholic Church takes into account when it tries to formulate its "social teachings." [. . .]

The discussion about violence and non-violence flowed from the decision to work for socialism. Once again the groups thought that the Church's recent condemnations of revolutionary violence are not only unsound but hypocritical. Invoked today to disapprove of socialism, traditional theology actually justifies violence in no uncertain terms. Thomas Aquinas listed the conditions that free tyrannicides from sin; crusades were not only tolerated but financed and glorified; and texts about "just wars" abound. Doctrine evolved in a good way when it started to reject wars, but then why not condemn with equal vigor all acts of aggression, every kind of violence? How can the Vatican's resounding declarations against revolutionary struggles bind Catholics when its silence over the massacres of Jews in Nazi Europe and American atrocities in Vietnam still rings so loudly in their memories? Why should priestly service to Christ be better personified by Francis Cardinal Spellman, garbed in combat fatigues blessing an invading army in Indochina, than by Father Camilo Torres, who chose to free his people by grasping a gun, and who paid for his dream with his life? And if non-violence is such a Catholic virtue, where are the Catholic Martin Luther Kings, where are the Catholic Gandhis? In what continent, in what country have cardinals and bishops led marches, strikes, boycotts and sit-ins against racism, imperialism, colonialism, exploitation, all the evils they so eloquently denounce when they issue statements from their palaces? There are many Catholics who are willing to back with their lives and their freedom the

causes their fidelity to Christ dictates. These are laymen, priests, nuns, even some members of the hierarchy, but they almost always taste the bitterness of solitude. When they act they find themselves isolated in their Church, estranged from its leadership, sometimes denounced by it. Hélder Câmara, António Fragoso and the few other bishops brave enough to speak out against the dictatorship's policy of torture and exploitation are unsupported by their colleagues and ignored by Rome. Daniel and Philip Berrigan have no cellmates clothed in purple.

The refusal to condemn the conquering violence of the powerful and the unwillingness to support those who rise up against the colonizers is complemented by the refusal to denounce less visible injustices—"white violence" as it is called in contrast to violence that is bloody. There are, of course, sporadic texts dealing with murders committed by the simple functioning of inhuman structures—the declaration of Medellín, for instance, signed by Latin America's bishops—but they are not tuned to the Church's main preoccupations and doctrinal efforts. [. . .]

At present the chances of changing the Church's political orientation are far-fetched but not inexistent. Brazil has some 250 bishops, one of the world's largest hierarchies. Some forty are progressive though only a handful are truly outspoken. An equal number are rigidly conservative and ready to go to any lengths to please the government—even public defense of torture. The rest are either timid, uninformed, politically aloof men or else they are professional opportunists. Unfortunately the three active cardinals lean to the right. Vicente Scherer, of Porto Alegre, is a sincere reactionary. Rio's Eugenio Sales is an authoritarian opportunist and Avelar Brandão, although sensitive and intelligent, is too much of a diplomat to commit himself to a cause. Only the archbishop of São Paulo, Evaristo Arns, not yet a cardinal, has the guts to protest when his priests are tortured or when the Death Squadron embarks on a bloody spree.

PART XV
Proto-Liberation Theology

Some priests, such as Camilo Torres's friend and classmate, the Peruvian theologian Gustavo Gutiérrez (b. 1928), rejected violence but began to develop a theology of liberation to foster social justice by using scripture and the moral authority of the church. The second conference of the Latin American episcopate, held in Medellín in 1968 following the decrees of Vatican II (1962-1965), adopted the concept of "preferential option" on behalf of the poor as the official stand of the church in Latin America. Influential Protestant theologians, such as Brazilian Presbyterian Rubem Alves (b. 1933), vigorously echoed the plea to eradicate poverty and promote social justice. These theologians emphasized God's plan for liberation in both spiritual and temporal matters. The statement by Argentine Methodist José Míguez Bonino that "the Bible speaks of the mercy and the judgement of God: God's compassion for the poor and oppressed, God's wrath and judgement for a world in which the larger part of God's children are condemned to hunger, deprivation, marginalization and death" is fully representative of the phenomenon known as liberation theology.[1]

110. It Is Good for the Church to Go through Prison

Carlos Alberto Libanio Christo, known universally as "Frei Betto," was a seminarian, born in 1944 to middle-class parents and raised in the conservative state of Minas Gerais, where

---

1. José Míguez Bonino, "Chapter 13: The Struggle for Justice and Peace," in Daniel Chetti and M. P. Joseph, *Ethical Issues in the Struggle for Justice* (Religion Online: www.religion-online.org/cgi-bin/, accessed on 5/14/2004), 5 of 9; Anne Motley Hallum, "Taking Stock and Building Bridges: Feminism, Women's Movements, and Pentecostalism in Latin America," *Latin American Research Review* 38, no. 1 (2003): 174; Jeffrey Klaiber, "Catholic Church: The Modern Period," in *Encyclopedia of Latin American History and Culture*, vol. 2, Barbara A. Tenenbaum, ed. (New York: Charles Scribner's Sons, 1996), 36; John W. Sherman, "Liberation Theology," in *Encyclopedia of Mexico: History, Society & Culture*, vol. I, Michael S. Werner, ed. (Chicago and London: Fitzroy Dearborn Publishers, 1997), 743.

SOURCE: Carlos Alberto Libanio Christo, *Against Principalities and Powers: Letters from a Brazilian Jail*, trans. John Drury (Maryknoll, N.Y.: Orbis Books, 1977), 7, 23-24, 26, 134-37. Reprinted by permission of Orbis Books.

the military initiated the overthrow of the constitutional republic in 1964. He left the university, where he had been studying journalism (a pursuit he later resumed), to enter the Dominican order, and he took his solemn vows in 1968. By that time the antiterrorist division of the special police services had adopted a particularly hostile policy toward the religious orders, especially the Dominicans, who were seen as supporters of the increasingly vocal opposition. The students who made up most of this opposition were of all stripes, including Christian activists. They were all lumped together, branded as terrorists in a nationwide propaganda campaign, and subjected to massive arrests, one of which swept up Frei Betto.

The letters excerpted below come from the first full year of Betto's imprisonment, which lasted for twenty-two months before he was sentenced to four more years in prison "without his guilt having been proven." The letters, subject to prison censorship, were collated by his family in 1971 without his knowledge and published that year.

By the time of his imprisonment in November 1969, the president of the Brazilian Bishops' Conference, Avelar Brandão (later created cardinal by Pope Paul VI), called the government's anticlerical campaign "a premeditated plan to disparage the church," a charge repeated by the bishops of the northeast. In a communiqué, the leaders of the Dominican order in Brazil explicitly recognized the authentic Christian sentiments animating their imprisoned colleagues.

What do the first two entries suggest about Betto's nature, that is, his character and mentality? Does his entry of December 31 a year later confirm or modify this estimate? What does the visit of the papal nuncio reveal about the position of Paul VI and the Vatican on clergy acting on their own Christian consciousness? What do the priests' and Betto's request of the nuncio reveal? Describe conditions for political prisoners using data from all the excerpts, including information about Tito. Betto's entry of March 3, after the first paragraph, constitutes a major indictment of the church and of Betto's own deficiencies and covers a wide range of issues. What is the main focus of the indictment? Does it resemble criticisms of the church considered in earlier readings? Does Betto offer any new insight, perspective, or formulation? (Note especially the last two paragraphs of the entry of December 31.)

São Paulo
December 7

. . . The only news here is my new prison life. Since I only arrived here a week ago, everything is still new to me. It's likely that I will be in Tiradentes Prison for some time. There are about two hundred of us political prisoners here, young people of both sexes. Our cell is big, roomy, and airy. We have two bathrooms with showers, a washtub, and a kitchen with stoves. There are thirty-two people in our cell, almost all of them young. The few older men have adapted perfectly to their new style of life. We have two injured people. One was beaten up by the police when they seized him; the other threw himself out of a fourth-floor apartment window. Both are convalescing now. The group is divided into teams, which take daily turns at housekeeping. Yesterday it was my team's turn. We got up early, swept the cell, and made coffee (with milk and bread and butter). Some members of our team helped bathe the injured, while others did the cooking. I was a cook and by some miracle did not do too badly. [. . .]

To a religious community

February 22

. . . It is a rainy and gloomy Sunday here. Now there are fifty of us in this cell, and we are trying to make the best of it. Many are sleeping on mattresses on the ground because there is no room for more beds. The silence reflects the darkness of this gray day. It is not the silence of tranquility or inner peace; it is a kind of suffocation. So many people together and so little talk. It's as if we wanted to scream but the sound dies in our throat, and we simply keep silent and wait. [...]

What did the Jews think about in the concentration camps, knowing they would soon die in the gas chambers? Perhaps they thought about nothing, just as many of us are doing right now. Perhaps they simply waited in silence, but not for anything in particular—not for death and certainly not for some miraculous release. [...]

To his brother, Luiz Fernando

February 26

... We had a cordial visit from the apostolic nuncio. We priests and religious spoke with him for about two hours. We described our plight, and it made a deep impression on him. We have no guarantees and no security. He pledged his solidarity with us and showed great interest and understanding. He told us that Paul VI knows about our situation and that the Vatican Justice and Peace Commission knows about the tortures. After our conversation he gave us a fine box of chocolates and packs of American cigarettes. He also gave us the papal blessing. We asked him to visit the other prisoners too because the church must concern itself with the plight of *all* prisoners, not just clerics and religious. The prison warden assembled all the inmates in our wing, and the nuncio spoke to them. He alluded to the torture, showing real understanding for all those who fight in the name of justice. Then he gave the papal blessing to all, "even to non-Christians because the blessing of the Holy Father never hurt anyone." We asked him to make sure that the church took an interest in the families of those political prisoners who are really poor. He promised to get in touch with *Caritas Internationalis* concerning their plight. [...]

I know Tito well. He would never become so desperate that he would try to commit suicide. I'm sure they tried to "suicide" him. It has happened to many political prisoners in our great Brazil.

Yesterday the nuncio tried to see him, but they wouldn't permit a visit. [...]

March 3

... Tito is back with us. He stays in bed or drags himself around, limping. He is recuperating from the terrible suffering he endured. He was tortured for three days: parrot-perch, electric shock, whippings, beatings. They even reached new heights of sadism, putting an electrode in his mouth. It was the intention of the army to interrogate all the Dominicans once again, because they felt our interrogators at DOPS had been in too much of a hurry. To escape the suffering they were inflicting on him and to make a public protest against such interrogation of political prisoners, Tito finally resolved to commit suicide. He had a razor blade, and he slashed the veins and arteries on the inside of his left elbow. He lost a lot of blood.

To Sister Ruth, a Brazilian nun

December 31

We have done all we can to get the church to issue a protest. It must take a stand on the grave situation in Brazil before it is too late. But the bishops are used to being on the defensive, and they prefer omission to risk. Maybe someone will have to die before the church will react [...]

Alongside our well-appointed houses we have built schools to educate the bourgeoisie, setting our seal of approval on their right to possess *things* in a world where most people possess nothing but hunger and misery. We have lost the apostles' daring. We have given our blessing to European colonialism in Asia, Africa, and Latin America. Time and time again in mission lands we have tried to proclaim the gospel in French and English, and we have drunk deep at the well of social and racial prejudice. To conceal the fact that the skin of the black is repugnant to us, we have said that he is "not very intelligent," that he practices "evil customs," that he is a "savage." We doubt the honesty of the mulatto; we consider Orientals "primitive." But God is not bound by our classifications, as I have discovered here in prison.

I came here filled with lofty intentions. I was going to bring the gospel to these "creatures"—thieves, murderers, brutes you'd be afraid to meet in broad daylight. *But God was here long before I arrived.* Believe me, it is they who have revealed Christ to me. Before we arrived, he was here with them, accomplishing the redemption of the world. They are crucified alongside Jesus. Whose fault is it? Our fault: because we have closed our eyes to human misery, closed our windows against the sight of the slums, avoided the red-light districts, and adopted the bourgeois lifestyle available only to the privileged few.

Living with these people here, I have learned how despicable are our prudence through which we avoid these people, our customs through which we shirk the radicalism of the gospel, our ever-so-sensible counsels through which we convert no one, our lethargy disguised as patience in the face of oppression and social inequality and institutionalized violence.

We have faith in these new stirrings of the Holy Spirit within the church. Perhaps the Spirit has cast us into the world's darkness so that we may learn to view history differently. This suffering is profoundly redemptive. [...]

To his cousin Maria

December 31

[...] There are more than three hundred political prisoners here, both men and women. For seven months there were forty of us in a cell that had room for twenty. For four months I slept on the floor. In September the inmates organized protest demonstrations against the terrible prison conditions and the excessive slowness of the judicial proceedings. Because Giorgio went on a hunger strike, retaliatory measures were directed against us priests. We were taken from prison and sent separately to different barracks. I spent twenty days in solitary confinement in a cell belonging to the cavalry barracks. It measured one meter by three, with hardly room for a bunk. It had no water or sanitary facilities, and I was only allowed to use the washroom once a day—at 8:00 a.m. I faced total solitude there, surrounded by soldiers but unable to exchange a single word with anyone. My only reading material was my New Testament. I was later transferred to headquarters where conditions were slightly better. There at least I could wash up, because there was a water faucet in the cell. [...]

We spend our time in prison reading, doing calisthenics, and studying theology. We are not idle. Every evening we get together for prayer. We recite the Psalms, chant hymns, and receive the body of our Lord. We have not received permission to celebrate Mass, but the chaplain of the military police comes with consecrated hosts every so often.

For me all this represents a revival of the life lived by the church during the first three centuries of its existence. It would be incredible if the church were not present somehow in prisons under a regime that oppresses the human person. Here we are in fellowship with "the wretched of the earth." We are in communion with those who have been invited to the Lord's banquet. All this is grace, as is any suffering endured in a Christian spirit.

I can assure you that prison has effected radical transformation—a profound conversion—in us. Behind these bars many things lose the value they once had, and new discoveries turn us into new people. It is good for the church to go through prison. There it rediscovers the way that Christ had pointed out, the way of poverty and persecution. (...)

111. A Martyr for the Mato Grosso

Three years after his arrival in Brazil in 1968, Pedro Casaldáliga (b. 1928), a Claretian priest from Galicia, Spain, was appointed bishop of São Félix de Araguaia, a huge diocese that is part of the state of Mato Grosso. He has been an outspoken and courageous defender

SOURCE: Pedro Casaldáliga, "Letter," *International Review of Mission* 66 (July 1977): 263-65. © World Council of Churches. Used by permission.

of his poverty-stricken flock, many of whom are indigenous people who have been histori-
cally subject to wanton abuse by every authority. He has been the object of frequent death
threats.

The letter below constitutes a remarkable insight into the dark reality of interior Brazil,
the demands expected of committed Christians, especially the clergy, and their willingness to
respond to those demands. Elaborate on these considerations.

São Félix, Mato Grosso
October 19, 1976
Dear Brethen,

To all of you, in this one letter, I send a deeply affectionate embrace in the Lord Jesus — in his Passion — because once again the Paschal suffering is definitely with us.

On October 11th, at seven p.m., Fr. João Bosco Penido Burnier, a Brazilian Jesuit priest, was mortally wounded at the local police station. His aggressor was a soldier of the Military Police of the State of Mato Grosso. Shot in the head, the priest died the following day in Goiania.

The repercussion has been widespread and profound. Father João Bosco was a missionary among the Indians in the neighbouring Prelature of Diamantino, on the other side of Xingu. Diamantino, Guirantinga and São Félix made up our regional unit of the Missionary Indian Council (CIMI). Since Fr. João Bosco was a regional coordinator, we invited him to attend our annual Indian Meeting held in Santa Terezinha, October 4th to 6th.

On October 11th, in Ribeirão Bonito, we were taking part in the procession to the river bank where he blessed the baptismal water for the baptisms on the following day.

A little later a boy brought me the message that two women who were prisoners in the police station were being tortured. A police contingent had come from Barra on account of the death of Corporal Félix, well-known in the region for his brutality and even murders. The two women were the sister and the daughter-in-law of Jovino, who killed Corporal Félix, practically out of self-defense . . . With the arrival of the police, terror has again spread in Ribeirão, Cascalheira and the sertão (interior part of the country). The police beat, arrest and torture the people . . . The boy said that the women could be heard from the street crying, "Don't hit me!"

I felt obligated to go to the police station to intercede on behalf of the poor women. The boy wanted to go with me, but I would not let him. He was very young, and afterwards he would be a target of the police. Fr. João Bosco overheard our conversation and insisted on going with me.

We reached the police station yard, enclosed with wire, where two aggressive soldiers were waiting for us. They insulted us when we tried to carry on a calm dialogue. The priest said he would report their arbitrary action to their police superiors when he passed through Cuiaba. One of the soldiers, Ezy Ramalho Feitosa, then slapped him in the face, hit him with his revolver and fired the fatal shot.

Dr. Luis y Bia attended the priest in our small mobile health unit. The doctor, the priest and I, escorted by friends in another car, travelled the road to Xingu by night to find an hacienda which we knew had an air taxi. The next day, before daybreak, we flew to Goiania and took the priest to the Neurological Institute. It was all of no use, as Luis y Bia had already concluded. It had been a soft-nosed bullet and had entered the brain.

The impressive thing is that Fr. João Bosco had been able to talk for more than two hours to those of us who accompanied him. It was a truly Christian death. He repeatedly said that he was offering his life for the Indians and for the people. He called on Jesus. He remembered the CIMI. Repeating the consummatum of the Lord, he said to me, "Dom Pedro, we have finished our task."

He died for justice and charity. In the Amazon region. In a particularly critical hour or, if you wish, a time of martyrdom.

We buried Fr. João Bosco in Diamantino, under the Mato Grosso sun and under the songs of victory of the people. The reporters were impressed. One of them wept.

What more? Pray that we may be faithful, that

the Spirit preserve among us the gift of joy, that the Church be a witness until the end.

Do not be dismayed; help "our people" not to be dismayed. The Lord is the Resurrection and the Life, and the whole Church accompanies us in fellowship. This death and the threats are a testi-mony to others "outside", who are also struggling for the formation of the new man. It is not a sad hour. It is a beautiful hour of the gospel.

I embrace you all in Christ with the most fraternal communion.

Pedro Casaldáliga

112. We Have Had No Democracy for Five Hundred Years

Paulo Evaristo Arns, O.F.M. (b. 1921), archbishop of São Paulo (1970-1998), cardinal, classical scholar, and outspoken opponent of the military dictatorship (1964-1985), was a champion of labor and of human rights, which he stressed emphatically included social as well as the usual civil rights. He remains one of the outstanding prelates of the twentieth-century Roman Catholic Church in Latin America.

In 1986 he granted an interview with a journalist from NACLA (North American Congress on Latin America), excerpts from which follow. He discerns three phases in Brazil's struggle against "imprisonment, torture and disappearances" between 1964 and 1985. He describes specifically the committees, organizations, publications, meetings—in other words the political activities—that were actually able to force a repressive, violent, military regime to abandon its worst apparatuses. Explain how this involvement of the church in such activity must be seen to come within the purview of the gospel.

"Why are human rights only for thieves?"—Why does Arns think it is so easy for people—and not just Brazilians—to forget and distort the real meaning of human rights?

Here in São Paulo, there have been three principal phases. The first was marked by the struggle against imprisonment, torture and disappearances under the authoritarian regime. At that time, we formed a strong group of lawyers and others. There have actually been four important human rights groups. The first was the Peace and Justice Commission, whose task was to inform public opinion. The commission produced publications, gave interviews and investigated human rights abuses.

Later on, when people knew more about the situation, we formed a second group, the Commission for Human Rights. Its goal was to assist people to think through these questions and to organize against further abuses. Then we created regional human rights centers, because many people suffered under the regime. They were sacked from factories and subjected to other injustices. Finally, to coordinate these regional centers and to help solve local problems, we started a main center called the *Centro Santo Días*, in honor of a metal worker who was killed by the police in a 1979 strike.

We also thought that we had to contribute in some way to the rest of Latin America, which was suffering from the effects of repression. This was particularly true in the Southern Cone: Chile, Paraguay, Argentina, Uruguay and Bolivia. So we started an ecumenical group called CLAMOR, which met many times with human rights groups in Argentina. Groups from Uruguay, Paraguay, Chile and even some from Bolivia during the worst repression [. . .] were in contact with us. This, then, was the first phase of our work with the Church during this 20-year period.

SOURCE: Joan Dassin, "Paulo Evaristo Arns: Archbishop of São Paulo, Brazil," *North American Congress on Latin America: Report on the Americas* 20 (September 1986), 67-71, passim. Reprinted by permission of NACLA: Report on the Americas.

A second major phase was the re-establishment of civil rights in Brazil. The Church itself had been severely censored. For example, the government closed down the Church radio station, the *Nove de Julho*, which was the major station in Brazil. There was total censorship. I was able to make public statements only because I had journalist friends. I managed now and then to appear publicly or to make a statement, but it was very difficult. The diocesan newspaper, *O São Paulo*, had to take its page proofs to the police for prior censorship. So we began the struggle for a return of freedom of the press. Later on, we struggled for habeas corpus, then for the right of assembly, then for the reorganization of political parties and, above all, for amnesty for those accused of political crimes. The struggle for amnesty was our greatest battle. [. . .]

My first appeal was here in the São Paulo cathedral. Dalmo Dallari, the president of the Peace and Justice Commission, was in Europe at the time, meeting with more than 10,000 Brazilian exiles in many countries. It was there that he began the amnesty campaign. At the same time, I made an appeal in the São Paulo cathedral for a total, unrestricted amnesty. That was the only place where I could speak openly to the people. The planning for this campaign began in 1974 and 1975 and, in 1976, the movement went public. From there the campaign went forward until amnesty was finally granted by the government in 1979.

The third phase of Church involvement, and a very important one at that, was the struggle for justice for the working class. The working class was the most oppressed—it still is—and it was very difficult for workers to hold a demonstration. Santo Días, as I mentioned, was one of the workers murdered by the police, and many other labor leaders were imprisoned. But the workers did not lose heart, because they had the support of the Church. The movement continued with the leadership of Luís Inácio da Silva, Lula [elected president in 2002], even though he was imprisoned for his role in the massive demonstration. We held a demonstration in the cathedral—it was packed—protesting the imprisonment of the labor leaders. But the most important thing was the logistical support that Catholic community groups gave to the workers, which helped them to organize meetings, receive food, etc. Jaime Wright, our Presbyterian colleague, helped us a great deal at that time.

The community groups also provided moral support which helped people to believe in the workers' movement. Word of what was happening spread and countered what the major media said. The newspapers, magazines and television either remained silent or denounced these efforts as a communist plot. This same workers' struggle, which began in 1977 and 1978, continues now under the leadership of the workers' federation, CUT. So far, there has been no resolution to the struggle, even though workers' rights are so important to democracy. [. . .]

[E]conomic power is another form of dictatorship. The concentration of economic power is the greatest dictatorship in Latin America. In Brazil, this remains as it has always been. [. . .]

[T]he United States has never respected Latin America. That is not the case in Europe. When I speak in Germany, politicians, artists and religious people are in the audience. In the United States, I find only isolated groups interested in Latin America. These groups are very active and understanding, but they are isolated. I never saw any interest among politicians, although I once went to Washington and spoke with some congressmen. This was done only through the intervention of American bishops. All the European ambassadors come here to visit, but an American comes only to say goodbye or to announce he has arrived. The Americans never come to talk. Canadians are better in this regard. [. . .]

The concept of human rights in Brazil was something new, although Brazil had signed the Universal Declaration of Human Rights in 1948. When torture and imprisonment began during the military regime, we published 50,000 copies of the declaration. Our copies had footnotes indicating where to find certain of the declaration's points in the Bible. It also included human rights declarations made by different churches. We eventually distributed a million and a half copies. Students confronted the police with this little book and recited aloud from it, in chorus, against the dogs and tanks.

This was a great struggle in São Paulo, which was really worth the trouble. Afterwards, though, when the opposition movement gained strength, the military government began a defamation campaign against human rights. This still exists. For example, there are some radio programs with a large audience which say that to defend human rights is to defend thieves. In this thinking, human rights guarantees protect criminals, not law-abiding people. Everywhere I go, people always ask, "Why are human rights only for thieves?" This is because human rights have been forgotten again, just as they were when everyone suffered under a regime which made us all into victims. Aside from this, there is also great ignorance in the developed world about human rights, especially when they include social rights. Our book *Brasil: Nunca Mais* was a response to precisely this situation, although the Church had already published many handbooks on citizens' rights vis-à-vis the police, job security, etc. These were written in popular form, with drawings and stories. *Brasil: Nunca Mais* is an examination of the reality we lived for 15 years, from 1964-1979. [...]

I believe that there have been few times in Brazil when there has been so great a possibility that the people will actually influence the course of history. So I am hopeful, although all the forces from the past, from the dictatorship, are still present. I believe that the Brazilian people have become much stronger in these 20 years. They make many wrong choices, but this is natural because we have had no democracy for 500 years.

113. Dom Hélder Câmara

Hélder Pessoa Câmara (1909-1999) was ordained a priest at age twenty-two and immediately committed himself to ministering to the poor and marginalized, who make up the vast majority of Brazil's population. He recognized that the church's policies and programs on charity were utterly inadequate to confront the misery of the masses and that, in fact, the church's position in society could not be reconciled with its moral teaching and mandate to bring "good news" to the poor.

During his some twenty years in Rio de Janeiro he developed social programs geared toward empowering the poor themselves psychologically and economically. He continued to develop such programs as archbishop of Olinda and Recife (1964-1985) in Brazil's impoverished and heavily black northeast.

The following statement, which was made three years earlier than that of Gustavo Gutiérrez (see next reading), demonstrates that a committed Christian pastor could also acutely analyze the dysfunctional nature of Latin American society without having enjoyed advanced academic study. Thus, dom Hélder Câmara was highly critical of his church, the elite establishment that dominated society, and the United States that meddled constantly in Brazilian affairs. He saw the need for radical change and the realistic methods that would bring that change about.

Dom Hélder speaks directly, at the darkest period of the military dictatorship, to those who are writhing under a yoke that is crushing them. Gutiérrez articulates a theology that makes explicit the moral responsibility of every committed Christian at any time to carry out concrete actions.

SOURCE: Hélder Pessoa Câmara, quoted in Paul E. Sigmund, ed., *Models of Political Change in Latin America* (New York: Praeger Publishers, 1970), 146-49. Reprinted by permission of Paul E. Sigmund.

Dom Hélder Câmara

(1) Why does dom Hélder call for "structural" and not just "moral" revolution? Why [rev]olution"? (2) What does "internal colonialism" mean? (3) "We Latin Americans . . . ," [have] we spoken . . . ," etc. Who is "we"? Are not the Amerindians and Afrobrazilians, to w[hom] dom Hélder refers, also Latin Americans? Does he not accept them as such"? (4) What does dom Hélder finally conclude in his minidisquisition on violence? Does his theological conclusion coincide with his political one? (5) How can dom Hélder equate the nonviolent heroism of Martin Luther King with the guerrilla violence of Camilo Torres and Ché Guevara?

It is easy to speak about violence when it is a question of condemning it from afar, without identifying it, distinguishing its various types, or analyzing its deeper causes; or of praising it from afar, in the manner of a living room Ché Guevara. . . .

An initial observation that is fundamental to a real understanding of the problem of violence is this: The whole world is in need of a structural revolution.

In the underdeveloped world, this truth seems evident; but as one examines the underdeveloped world from many perspectives—economic, political, social, and religious—one begins to understand that a superficial alteration will not suffice. We must attempt a total change in depth, a profound, and rapid change, a structural—let us not fear the word—revolution. . . .

From the economic point of view, who is not aware that a system of internal colonialism exists in the underdeveloped countries? That is to say, there is a small group of the privileged in those countries whose wealth is maintained at the expense of the misery of millions of their fellow citizens. It is still a semi-feudal system: In some ways the life appears patriarchal, but in reality the absence of individual rights creates a subhuman condition of real slavery. The rural workers—real pariahs—have no access to most of the land, which the owners of the great estates keep uncultivated for future speculation.

When this situation exists in a continent such as Latin America, which is entirely Christian—at least in name and tradition—one can appreciate the enormous responsibility of Christianity. Without ignoring the great examples of abnegation, of sacrifice, even of heroism, we must recognize that in the past—and this danger persists into the present—we Latin Americans bear a large responsibility for the injustice that exists in this continent. We accepted the slavery of Indians and Africans: And even now, have we spoken in a clear and straightforward fashion to the owners of the large estates, to the great and the powerful? Or have we closed our eyes and helped them to have an easy conscience, so long as they cover up their frightful injustices with alms for the construction of churches (frequently scandalously large and ornate, in shocking contrast with the surrounding misery), or with contributions for our social programs? Have we perhaps made Marx appear to be correct, presenting a passive Christianity to the pariahs—one that is both alienated and alienating, truly an opiate of the masses . . .? [. . .]

What I am saying about Latin America can be said about almost the entire undeveloped world: Everywhere there is real need of a structural revolution. . . .

Now, we ask ourselves if the structural revolution that the world needs necessarily presupposes that violence be exercised at times, even unconsciously, by the same people who condemn it as a plague on society.

Violence exists in the underdeveloped world: The oppressed masses are abused by small groups of the privileged and powerful. It is well known that if the masses try to become human beings and make an effort at education or popular culture, if they organize themselves into syndicates or cooperatives, their leaders are described as subversives and Communists. It has been said very accurately: "They appear to be rebels against the established order—they are put outside the law . . . they must be removed for order to reign." . . . Disorderly order! [. . .]

Violence also exists in the developed world, as much on the capitalist as on the socialist side. In this respect, there are signs of disquiet that speak very clearly.

In the face of this threefold violence—in the

underdeveloped countries, in the developed countries, and by the developed countries against the underdeveloped countries—one can understand why people think, talk, and act in terms of liberating or redeeming violence. [. . .]

Allow me the small favor of expressing my position:

With respect to those who, in conscience, feel obliged to opt for violence, not the easy violence of the guerrillas of the living room, but the violence of those who have proved their sincerity by the sacrifice of their lives, it seems to me that the memory of Camilo Torres or of Ché Guevara merits as much respect as that of the Reverend Martin Luther King.

I accuse as the real promoters of violence all those, whether of the right or the left, who have hurt the cause of justice and impeded peace. [. . .]

A lifelong effort to understand and live the Gospel has led me to the profound conviction that the Gospel can and should be called revolutionary, in the sense that it demands a conversion in each of us. We do not have the right to enclose ourselves in our own egoism. We should open ourselves to the love of God and the love of mankind. And it is enough to think of the beatitudes—the quintessence of the Gospel's message—to discover that the choice for Christians seems clear: We Christians are on the side of nonviolence, which is a choice neither of weakness nor of passivity. Nonviolence is believing in a higher power than the power of war, of death, and of hate—it is believing in the power of truth, justice, and love.

If this seems moralistic to you, wait one moment. The option of nonviolence is rooted in the Gospel; it is also based on reality. Do they want realism? Then I say to them: If there should appear in any part of the world, but above all in Latin America, an outbreak of violence, they can be certain that, immediately, the great powers will arrive—even without a declaration of war—and we will have a new Vietnam. [. . .]

114. Gustavo Gutiérrez

What does the Christian minister (of any denomination, time, or place) mean when he/she proclaims "God loves you"? Are not the implications of that apparently simple message that each person is worth something, has dignity, can free him- or herself from base instincts, is capable of achievement, even transcendence, and is certainly capable of freeing him-/herself from the snare of "sin," that is, self-indulgence, selfishness, and isolation? But is not this also true of one's neighbor, and of all "neighbors," that is, the entire human community? What, then, is the ultimate implication of these truths? What do they mean for human existence?

Gustavo Gutiérrez, O.P. (b.1928), considered the "father" of liberation theology, ponders these questions in his dense seminal opus A Theology of Liberation: History, Politics and Salvation *(1971).*

Gutiérrez, with many contemporaries in Latin America—Catholic clergy and laity, labor leaders, university professors, Marxists, high school students, communists—realized that their "neighbors" were the vast poor majority of Latin Americans, a permanently depressed, marginalized, oppressed class of humanity who had been set apart from what should be the true human community.

In order for the above-listed groups to help this mass of people to actually become "neighbors" and part of a real human community, those groups had to understand concretely and fully the reality—economic, social, and cultural—that shaped, oppressed, and controlled

Sources: Gustavo Gutiérrez, *A Theology of Liberation: History, Politics and Salvation*, trans. and ed. Sister Caridad Inda and John Eagleson (revised edition, Maryknoll, N.Y.: Orbis Books, 1988), 112-16, 174. Reprinted by permission of Orbis Books.

that mass of people. Social-scientific analysis, including the sociological analysis developed by Karl Marx in the nineteenth century and which twentieth-century scholars further refined into "Marxist analysis," they believed would achieve this.

Gutiérrez, who had earned his B.S. in medicine at the National University of Peru in order to become a psychiatrist, decided shortly thereafter to enter the seminary to become a priest. He also did extensive graduate studies in philosophy, theology, psychology, and sociology at the Catholic University of Louvain, Belgium (1951-55), the University of Lyon, France (1955-59), and the Gregorian University in Rome (1959-60). He was ordained in 1959.

He returned to Peru to teach sociology at the Catholic University and to become pastor of Cristo Redentor parish in Rimac, one of Lima's slums, where he continues to live among his poor parishioners.

Armed with an experiential and analytical knowledge of the poor, Gutiérrez—and fellow Christians who shared his chagrin and outrage at their plight—relied on the scriptures to determine the goals that such a plight demanded of Christians, and the actions necessary to achieve those goals.

Gutiérrez lays out his understanding of that determination in the work referred to above. The best approach to the excerpt below is to consider a key biblical passage analyzed by Gutiérrez, the stunning account of the last judgment: Matthew 25:31-45 (25:35: "For I was hungry and you gave me food; I was thirsty and you gave me drink; I was a stranger and you made me welcome"). From his theological analysis (in the first paragraph of the excerpt) of the passage from Matthew, Gutiérrez draws three concrete conclusions—three moral principles—for the Latin American Christian. (A) The "neighbor," "the least of my brethren," is the mass of Latin American poor. "[C]ommunion and fellowship [with them . . .] constitute the ultimate meaning of human life." (B) "Love" demands concrete actions in their favor. (C) The only way "to reach the Lord" is through reaching out to the poor, that is, through human mediation. In the ensuing excerpts below Gutiérrez further describes these three moral principles.

Is there any doubt that for Gutiérrez there can be only one way for the true Latin American Christian to act? Formulate concretely that way, referring to Gutiérrez's program (see A, B, and C above). What special caveats for Christian behavior does Gutiérrez emphasize in the last three paragraphs of his analysis?

The "conclusion" of Gutiérrez's book is brief, but (a) it enables the reader to view the larger picture that animates Gutiérrez, (b) it reiterates his insistence on relating concretely to one's neighbor, and (c) it suggests that the raising of their consciousness by the oppressed themselves is a major component of developing a theology of liberation. Explain that "larger picture" and the concrete action required of the Latin American Christian. How would Gutiérrez respond to Câmara's paragraph beginning "A lifelong effort . . ." from the previous reading? Would Gutiérrez not make one brief, potent addition?

This is the line of thinking we will follow. The passage [Matthew, above] is rich in teachings. Basing our study on it and in line with the subject which interests us, we wish to emphasize three points: the stress on communion and fellowship as the ultimate meaning of human life; the insistence on a love which is manifested in concrete actions, with "doing" being favored over simple "knowing"; and the revelation of the human mediation necessary to reach the Lord.

[A] The human person is destined to total communion with God and to the fullest fellowship with all other persons. [. . .]

To sin is to refuse to love, to reject communion and fellowship, to reject even now the very meaning of human existence. Matthew's text is demanding: "Anything you did not do for one of these however humble, you did not do for me" (25:45). To abstain from serving is to refuse to love; to fail to act for another is as culpable as expressly refusing to do it. [. . .]

They asked him, "Who is my neighbor?" and when everything seemed to point to the wounded man in the ditch on the side of the road, Christ asked, "Which of these three do you think was neighbor to the man who fell into the hands of the robbers?" (Luke 10:29, 36). The neighbor was the Samaritan who *approached* the wounded man and *made him his neighbor*. The neighbor, as has been said, is not the one whom I find in my path, but rather the one in whose path I place myself, the one whom I approach and actively seek. [. . .]

[B] [C]harity exists only in concrete actions (feeding the hungry, giving drink to the thirsty, etc.); it occurs of necessity in the fabric of relationships among persons. "Faith divorced from deeds is barren" (James 2:20). To know God is to do justice: "If you know that he is righteous, you must recognize that every man who does right is his child" (1 John 2:29). But charity does not exist alongside or above human loves; it is not "the most sublime" human achievement like a grace superimposed upon human love. Charity is God's love in us and does not exist outside our human capabilities to love and to build a just and friendly world [. . .]

The Samaritan approached the injured man on the side of the road not because of some cold religious obligation, but because "his heart was melting" (this is literally what the verb *splankhnizein* means in Luke 10:33 [. . .]

[C] We turn to the third idea [. . .]

It is not enough to say that love of God is inseparable from the love of one's neighbor. It must be added that love for God is unavoidably expressed *through* love of one's neighbor. [. . .]

[T]his conclusion is valid not only for Christians, but for all persons who, in one way or another, welcome the Word of the Lord into their heart. [. . .]

God is revealed in history, and it is likewise in history that persons encounter the Word made flesh. Christ is not a private individual; the bond which links him to all persons gives him a unique historical role. God's temple is human history; the "sacred" transcends the narrow limits of the places of worship. We find the Lord in our encounters with others, especially the poor, marginated, and exploited ones. An act of love toward them is an act of love toward God. [. . .]

Nevertheless, the neighbor is not an occasion, an instrument, for becoming closer to God. We are dealing with a real love of persons for their own sake and not "for the love of God," as the well-intended but ambiguous and ill-used cliché would have it—ambiguous and ill-used because many seem to interpret it in a sense which forgets that the love for God is expressed in a true love for persons themselves. [. . .]

[T]he neighbor is not only a person viewed individually. The term refers also to a person considered in the fabric of social relationships, to a person situated in economic, social, cultural, and racial coordinates. It likewise refers to the exploited social class, the dominated people, the marginated. The masses are also our neighbor. [. . .]

Our encounter with the Lord occurs in our encounter with others, especially in the encounter with those whose human features have been disfigured by oppression, despoliation, and alienation and who have "no beauty, no majesty" but are the things "from which men turn away their eyes" (Isa. 53:2-3). These are the marginal groups, who have fashioned a true culture for themselves and whose values one must understand if one wishes to reach them. The salvation of humanity passes through them; they are the bearers of the meaning of history and "inherit the kingdom" (James 2:5). Our attitude toward them, or rather our commitment to them, will indicate whether or not we are directing our existence in conformity with the will of the Father. This is what Christ reveals to us by identifying himself with the poor in the text of Matthew. A theology of the neighbor, which has yet to be worked out, would have to be structured on this basis.

"Conclusion"

The theology of liberation attempts to reflect on the experience and meaning of the faith based on the commitment to abolish injustice and to build a new society; this theology must be verified by the practice of that commitment, by active, effective participation in the struggle which the exploited social classes have undertaken against their oppressors. Liberation from every form of exploitation, the possibility of a more human and more dignified life, the creation of a new man—all pass through this struggle.

But in the last instance we will have an authentic theology of liberation only when the oppressed themselves can freely raise their voice and express themselves directly and creatively in society and in the heart of the People of God, when they themselves "account for the hope," which they bear, when they are the protagonists of their own liberation. For now we must limit ourselves to efforts which ought to deepen and support that process, which has barely begun. If theological reflection does not vitalize the action of the Christian community in the world by making its commitment to charity fuller and more radical, if—more concretely—in Latin America it does not lead the Church to be on the side of the oppressed classes and dominated peoples, clearly and without qualifications, then this theological reflection will have been of little value.

PART XVI
In Nicaragua

On July 19, 1979, after eighteen years of struggle against overwhelming odds and the deaths of fifty thousand of their supporters, mostly young people, the Sandinistas marched triumphantly into Managua, Nicaragua. They faced an empty treasury, a devastated economy, and the suspicion and hostility of the U.S. government, which during the Cold War consistently saw Latin American revolutionary movements as pro-Soviet threats.

A few months before this defining moment in Nicaraguan history, the Third General Conference of the Latin American Episcopate (the Roman Catholic bishops of Latin America and the Caribbean, meeting in Puebla, Mexico) promulgated its "Final Document" (February 13, 1979). The closing pages of the document include the following:

> *The New Human Being*
> We must create in the people of Latin America a sound moral conscience, a critical-minded evangelical sense vis-à-vis reality, a communitarian spirit, and a social commitment. All that will allow for free, responsible participation, in a spirit of fraternal communion and dialogue, aimed at the construction of a new society that is truly human and suffused with evangelical values.

A significant segment of the Catholic Church in Nicaragua—base communities, most members, male and female, of religious orders, and many diocesan priests—were ardent supporters of the Sandinista revolution, seeing in its program for society an opportunity for the growth of a renewed Nicaraguan church that would be identified with the temporal as well as the spiritual well-being of the heretofore ignored majority of the nation. To this sector of the church the Sandinista's "logic of the majority" coincided with Puebla's "preferential option for the poor" (Final Document, sections 733-35, 1134-52).

The Nicaraguan hierarchy (seven bishops, three of whom were open to the newly emerging order) sent three messages to the Nicaraguan people in 1979: June 2, on the right of armed insurrection; July 30, an unfavorable consideration of the revolutionary project; November 17, a positive view of the possibilities of that project (prompted by recommendations from the religious orders working in the nation). Thereafter, the majority of bishops showed growing hostility to the revolution and to the sector of the church that supported it.[1]

115. The Gospel in Solentiname

Ernesto Cardenal (b. 1925), Catholic priest, major Latin American poet, and minister of culture (1979-1990) in the Sandinista revolutionary government, ministered (1965-1977) to a community of impoverished peasants in the isolated archipelago of Solentiname in Lake Nicaragua.

As pastor he led the community in reading and reflecting on the Bible and transcribed the comments made by members of his flock. The result is the arresting Gospel in Solentiname *(4 vols., 1975). Cardenal wrote an epilogue in 1977.*

"Jesus a Cause of Division"—this section may be characterized as electrifying, because of both Matthew and the peasant respondents. Explain. Characterize the quality of the peasants' comments.

Epilogue A: What is the relationship between Cardenal's brief disquisition on contemplation and Gutiérrez's on Matt. 25:31-45 in the previous reading?

Epilogue B: "Contemplation . . . brought us to the revolution." It is late 1977, the rebellion by the Frente Sandinista de Liberación Nacional (FSLN) is growing and seems able to withstand the assaults of the well-armed Guardia Nacional. Rhetoric? Rationalization? Responsible religious rumination, or rubbish?

Epilogue C: Does this describe a just war waged justly?

In Solentiname, a remote archipelago on Lake Nicaragua with a population of *campesinos*, instead of a sermon each Sunday on the Gospel reading, we have a dialogue. The commentaries of the *campesinos* are usually of greater profundity than that of many theologians, but of a simplicity like that of the Gospel itself. This is not surprising: The *Gospel*, or "Good News" (to the poor), was written for them, and by people like them. [. . .]

Each Sunday we first distribute copies of the Gospels to those who can read. There are some who can't, especially among the elderly and those who live on islands far away from the school. One of those who read best (generally a boy or a girl) reads aloud the entire passage on which we are going to comment. Then we discuss it verse by verse.

We use the Protestant translation entitled *Dios llega al hombre,* which is the best translation of the Gospels that I know. The translation is anonymous, but it was unquestionably made by a poet. It is in the simple language of the Latin American

1. John Eagleson and Philip Scharper, eds. *Puebla and Beyond: Documentation and Commentary* (Maryknoll, N.Y.: Orbis Books, 1979), 222-23, 264; Joseph E. Mulligan, S.J., *The Nicaraguan Church and the Revolution* (Kansis City, Mo.: Sheed and Ward, 1991), 164-69; John M. Kirk, *Politics and the Catholic Church in Nicaragua* (Gainesville: University Press of Florida, 1992).

Source: Ernesto Cardenal, *The Gospel in Solentiname*, vol. 1, trans. Donald D. Walsh (Maryknoll, N.Y.: Orbis Books, 1982), 1:vii-x, 260-65. Originally published as *El evangelio en Solentiname,* vol. 1 (Salamanca: Ediciones Sígueme, 1975). Reprinted by permission of Orbis Books. Ernesto Cardenal, "Epilogue," in *The Gospel in Solentiname* [paperback edition], vol. 1, trans. Donald D. Walsh (Maryknoll, N.Y.: Orbis Books, 1982), 267-68, 270-71. Originally published as *El evangelio en Solentiname,* vol. 1 (Salamanca: Ediciones Sígueme, 1975). Reprinted by permission of Orbis Books.

campesino, but it preserves a maximum fidelity to the Scriptures. [...]

The archipelago of Solentiname has thirty-eight islands; some are very small, and only the largest are inhabited. The population is about a thousand, composed of some ninety families. The houses are usually thatched huts, all spread out, some distance apart, on the shores of the different islands. [...]

Not all those who do come take an equal part in the commentaries. There are some who speak more often. Marcelino is a mystic. Olivia is more theological. Rebecca, Marcelino's wife, always stresses love. Laureano refers everything to the revolution. Elvis always thinks of the perfect society of the future. Felipe, another young man, is very conscious of the proletarian struggle. Old Tomás Peña, his father, doesn't know how to read, but he talks with great wisdom. Alejandro, Olivia's son, is a young leader, and his commentaries are usually directed toward everyone, and especially toward other young people. Pancho is a conservative. Julio Mairena is a great defender of equality. His brother Oscar always talks about unity. The authors of this book are these people and all the others who talk frequently and say important things, and those who talk infrequently but also say something important [...]

I am wrong. The true author is the Spirit that has inspired these commentaries (the Solentiname *campesinos* know very well that it is the Spirit who makes them speak) and that it was the Spirit who inspired the Gospels. The Holy Spirit, who is the spirit of God instilled in the community, whom Oscar would call the spirit of community unity, and Alejandro the spirit of service to others, and Elvis the spirit of the society of the future, and Felipe the spirit of proletarian struggle, and Julio the spirit of equality and the community of wealth, and Laureano the spirit of the revolution, and Rebecca the spirit of Love.

Jesus a Cause of Division
(Matthew 10:34-37)

Before reading the passage we were going to comment on, Oscar had seen the title and exclaimed: "I don't understand this! He came to bring unity. Why does it say here that he's a cause of division. He's supposed to be love!"

I said that first we ought to read it. We read this brief passage from Matthew, four verses, and went on to comment on them: *Do not believe that I have come to bring peace to earth; for I have come to bring not peace but the sword.*

Antenor said: "Injustice had always reigned on earth. He is coming to put an end to that state of affairs. So he's coming to fight. But he's not going to be fighting all alone. He does it with us."

Marcelino: "He brought a very sharp weapon, which is his word. He brought that weapon for us. And it's what we're receiving here."

One said: "Jesus is against being a conformist. That is why he said he didn't come to bring peace."

Another said: "There are people who want to live in peace, to have no problems ... "

And young Armando: "There are two kinds of peace. There's a peace that's simply to accept injustice, to remain quiet while the exploitation goes on. And there's another peace, the one we get after we achieve justice, when things get straightened out."

Laureano: "It seems to me that Jesus is teaching here that just because he was Jesus he wasn't going to change things, bang!, to divide everything up. On the contrary, it's up to us to fight so that we can have peace."

Armando: "Because you have to fight to reach that peace, right?"

Laureano went on: "Yes, you have to fight hard in every country to get justice established throughout the world."

Alejandro said: "Another thing that I see is that you can't have peace if you really love your neighbor. Even when there's peace in a community, like here in Solentiname, where life is peaceful and happy because we're all at peace, even here, deep down you have the great worry, the uneasiness ... because you see injustice more clearly. And the cause of this worry, I think, is love. And you can say, then, that this person is not completely at peace because he is concerned about others. And it would be too bad if we were all calm."

Another said: "Since Jesus has come to bring a change, that is, a Revolution, he wasn't coming to bring peace but war."

I: "It's clear that as long as there is a class of oppressors and a class of the oppressed, you can't want to have peace between oppressors and oppressed, because that means to want to have oppression. But if we want the oppressed class to be freed so that there won't any longer be oppressors and oppressed, then we really do not want peace."

And Oscar said: "Ah, now I understand. What Jesus brought was unity for some but not for all. For some—those who are on the side of love. He's the cause of division because he's the cause of unity." *I have come to set the man against his father, the daughter against her mother, the daughter-in-law against her mother-in-law: so that each one will have for enemies the members of his own family.*

Laureano: "This seems to be against love, but as a matter of fact you shouldn't always be stuck to your family, to your own kind. You should be for everyone, for your blood brothers as well as for those who aren't your blood brothers, because these are your brothers too."

Another of the boys said: "It happens sometimes that the father is an exploiter and the son is a good Christian and the son has to be against him."

Antenor: "This division within families has to happen. And whenever there are new ideas that go against tradition, the parents are almost always in favor of the traditional ways and the new ideas are against them."

Laureano: "As I see it here he's setting the young against the old: the son against the father, the daughter against the mother, the daughter-in-law against the mother-in-law. It seems that Jesus sees that the division he's going to cause in families will be mainly a division between generations. And it's because the young people are the ones who are almost always with the Revolution, and not the old people."

I said that that division in families of which Jesus spoke was seen clearly in Cuba at the time of the Revolution. Many families were divided, and whenever there is a Revolution this has to happen.

Leonel: "How long? Until we've reached unity, right? Because it can't always be like that. Division happens so that later there will be unity, a final peace."

Armando: "But meanwhile Jesus comes to break the unity of the family, which was considered a very sacred thing, and since the family is the basis of society he comes to upset all of society. Here he publicly declares himself a disturber of social peace."

Antenor: "That business about the family I see also as a way of talking about the class struggle." *He who loves his father or his mother more than me is not worthy of me; and he who loves his son or his daughter more than me is not worthy of me.*

One of the young men said: "There are a lot of people here who are too attached to their families."

And Olivia, who hadn't spoken up to then, said: "Jesus isn't saying here that we have to love the God of heaven and forget about people, but that's how it has been understood in our traditional religion. And so for example a man leaves his money to 'God,' as he says, because he'd rather leave it to God than to the poor. No, I think that when Jesus is talking about love for him, he's putting himself in the place of the poor, and of our neighbor in general. And what he means is that we should love all people, all our neighbors, and not just those in our family."

Another added: "To love God is to love your brother, isn't it?"

And Laureano: "Your brother, but not your brother because he's the son of your mother, but because he's your brother who is everybody."

Felipe: "Some think they're pleasing God with prayers or songs, but singing to God is loving your brother."

And one of the girls: "It's a matter of loving not only our family and your friends but of loving everybody, and that's hard."

Armando: "And speaking of the God of heaven—the God of heaven doesn't exist, or at least the only way we can know him is as he is made flesh in other people."

Felipe: "Anyone who loves other people, practically speaking, already knows God."

I said that was exactly what Saint John said.

And Alejandro: "It's because God is love. Anyone who loves knows him because he has known love."

Julio: "The sword splits, divides, and now I see why he says that he brought the sword."

Gloria: "The sword of love."

Epilogue

[A]   Twelve years ago I arrived at Solentiname with two companions to found a small, contemplative community. Contemplation means union with God. We soon became aware that this union with God brought us before all else into union with the peasants, very poor and very abandoned, who lived dispersed along the shores of the archipelago.

[B]   Contemplation also brought us to the revolution. It had to be that way. If not it would have been fake contemplation. My old novice master, Thomas Merton, the inspirer and spiritual director of our foundation, told me that in Latin America I could not separate myself from political strife.

In the beginning we would have preferred a revolution with nonviolent methods. But we soon began to realize that at this time in Nicaragua a nonviolent struggle is not feasible. Even Gandhi would agree with us. The truth is that all authentic revolutionaries prefer nonviolence to violence; but they are not always free to choose.

The gospel was what most radicalized us politically. Every Sunday in mass we discussed the gospel in a dialogue with the peasants. With admirable simplicity and profound theology, they began to understand the core of the gospel message: the announcement of the kingdom of God, that is, the establishment on this earth of a just society, without exploiters or exploited, with all goods in common, just like the society in which the first Christians lived. But above all else the gospel taught us that the word of God is not only to be heard, but also to be put into practice.

As the peasants of Solentiname got deeper and deeper into the gospel, they could not help but feel united to their brother peasants who were suffering persecution and terror, who were imprisoned, tortured, murdered, whose wives were violated and whose homes were burnt. They also felt solidarity with all who with compassion for their neighbor were offering their lives. For this solidarity to be real, they had to lay security, and life, on the line.

In Solentiname it was well known that we were not going to enjoy peace and tranquility if we wanted to put into practice the word of God. We knew that the hour of sacrifice was going to arrive. This hour has now come. Now in our community everything is over. [. . .]

[C]   But now brush will grow once again where our community used to be, just as it did before our arrival. There, there was a peasant mass, there were paintings, statues, books, records, classes, smiles of beautiful children, poetry, song. Now all that is left is the savage beauty of nature. I lived a very happy life in that near paradise that was Solentiname. But I was always ready to sacrifice it all. And now we have.

One day it happened that a group of boys and girls from Solentiname, because of profound convictions and after having let it mature for a long time, decided to take up arms. Why did they do it? They did it for only one reason: for their love for the kingdom of God, for the ardent desire that a just society be implanted, a real and concrete kingdom of God here on earth. When the time came these boys and girls fought with great valor, but they also fought as Christians. That morning at San Carlos, they tried several times with a loudspeaker to reason with the guards so they might not have to fire a single shot. But the guards [the Guardia Nacional, Somoza's army] responded to their reasoning with submachine gunfire. With great regret, they also were forced to shoot.

Alejandro Guevara, one of those from my community, entered the building when in it there were no longer any but dead or wounded soldiers. He was going to set fire to it so that there would be no doubt about the success of the assault, but out of consideration for the wounded, he did not do it. Because the building was not burned, it was officially denied that it was taken. I congratulate myself that these young Christians fought without hate—above all, without hate for the wounded guards, poor peasants like themselves, also exploited. It is horrible that there are dead and wounded. We wish that there were not a struggle in Nicaragua, but this does not depend upon the oppressed people that are only defending themselves.

116. *Misa Campesina Nicaragüense*

Carlos Mejía Godoy (b. 1945) must be considered the Nicaraguan music laureate. He has composed every type of song—romantic, patriotic, religious, and political. Terming his nationality "Sandino-Nicaraguan," he spent 1973-1975 traveling through the entire country listening to the talk, the religious expression, the music, and the stories of the people of the diverse regions in order to capture their spirit and express it in the Nicaraguan Peasant Mass.

The text, written by Mejía and excerpted below (the Meditation Hymn, Offertory, and Farewell Hymn are omitted), may be considered a perfect expression of liberation theology. Why? It is significant that the Mass is based on two years of intimate contact with all types of people throughout Nicaragua, and is not merely the result of professional artistry.

Note that milpa = *corn patch—source of the bread of life.*

Entrance Hymn

You are the God of the poor,
the human and simple God,
the God who sweats in the streets,
the God with the weather beaten face;
therefore I speak to you
just as my people speak
because you are God the worker
Christ the laborer.

You go in hand with my people,
you fight in country and city,
you stand on line there in the field
to get your daily wage.

You eat snow cones there in the park
with Eusebio, Pancho and Juan José
and you even complain about the syrup
when that does not have enough honey.

I have seen you in the general store
ensconced in a shed;
I have seen you selling lottery tickets
without your being ashamed of that job;
I have seen you in gas stations
checking the tires of a truck
and I have even seen you on the highways
with leather gloves and overalls.

Kyrie

Christ, Christ Jesus,
identify with us.
Lord, Lord my God,
identify with us.
Christ, Christ Jesus,
be in solidarity.

Not with the oppressor class
which exploits and devours
the community
but with the oppressed
with my people
who thirst for peace.

Gloria

With the happiest
music of my people I come to sing
this Gloria to Christ
which I prefer to the bullfight music.

I want to sing to Jesus
who is leader of truth
with the overflowing
and explosive joy of the rockets
which illuminate our skies
on our popular *fiestas*.

SOURCE: *Misa Campesina Nicaragüense*. Words and music by Carlos Mejía Godoy and El Taller de Sonido Popular. Translated from the Spanish by Walter J. Petry.

Glory to God in Siuna, Jalapa and Cosigüina,
and Solentiname, Diriomo and Ticuantepe.
Glory to God in Tisma, Waslala and Yalagüina,
and Totogalpa, Moyogalpa and Santa Cruz.

Glory to the one who follows the light of the
    Gospel,
to the one who denounces injustice without fear.
Glory to the one who suffers imprisonment and
    exile
and gives his life fighting the oppressor.
Today we glorify you, Lord, with marimbas,
with violins of *ñámbar*, sonajas and atabales,
with chirimillas, quijongos and sambumbias,
with the indigenous dances of Subtiava and
    Monimbó.

Creed

I firmly believe Lord
that from your generous mind
this entire world was born,
that from your artist-hand
as primitivist painter,
beauty has come to thrive:
the stars and the moon
the little homes, the lagoons,
the little boats sailing
on the river towards the sea,
the huge coffee plantations,
the white cotton plantations,
and the forests hacked up
by the evil hatchet.

I believe in you
architect, engineer,
artisan, carpenter,
mason, shipbuilder;
I believe in you
creator of thought,
of music and of the wind,
of peace and of love.

I believe in you, Christ the worker,
light of light and true
only-begotten son of God
who, to save the world
in the humble and pure womb

of Mary, became incarnate.
I believe that you were beaten
and with jeers tortured,
martyred on the cross,
Pilate being the praetor,
the Roman imperialist
malicious and soulless
who washing his hands
wanted to hide his fault.
I believe in you, compañero,
the Human Christ, the worker Christ,
Conqueror of death,
who with immense sacrifice
engendered the new man
for liberation.
You are resurrected
in each arm that is raised
to defend the people
from exploitative rule,
because you are alive on the ranch,
in the factory, in school;
I believe in your fight without let up,
I believe in your resurrection.

Communion Hymn

Let us go to the *milpa*,
To the Lord's *milpa*.
Jesus Christ invites us
to his harvest of love;
the cornfields shine
in the light of the sun,
let us go to the *milpa*
of Communion.

The people gather themselves
around the altar,
very close to the [divine] fire
the whole community meets together;
I come from the interior,
way beyond Sacaclí;
I bring pretty *mazurquitas* [songs]
and a pretty little tune which I sing
like this.

The little fish of the lake
want to accompany us
and jump around excitedly

as *encalichados* in brotherhood:
Lagoon fish and bass
the Guapote and the Gaspar,
the mojarras, the guabinas
and even the sardines seem to sing.

Communion is not a myth,
inconsequential and banal;

it is commitment and life,
a raising of Christian consciousness;
it is to share the fight
for community,
it says: I am Christian
and on me, brother, you can count.

117. Sandinistas and Christianity I

The literacy workbook (1980) was designed to teach the illiterate citizens of Nicaragua (some 52 percent of the population) both to read and write and also to begin to think in a new, more proactive, progressive manner in keeping with that of the revolutionary regime, which had just come to power. Does Lesson 22 accomplish that goal? How would this new approach affect people's thinking about the church?

The proposed constitution was vetted in multiple town meetings held throughout Nicaragua during 1986. One of the fiercest debates concerned whether it was appropriate to refer specifically to Christianity in a secular political document that guaranteed religious freedom. Does the reference to Christianity compromise the commitment to freedom of religion and to the establishment of a modern secular republic?

Dawn of the People: "Heroes and Martyrs" Sandinista Reading-Writing Work Book

National Literaracy Crusade for the Liberation of Nicaragua, 1980

Lesson 22:

There is freedom of worship for all churches that defend the interests of the people. The true church must be committed to the people. The church cannot be indifferent to the needs of the people. Glory to our martyrs!

Constitution of Nicaragua

18 November 1986
(Extract from the Preamble)

. . . In the name of the Nicaraguan people; of all the democratic, patriotic and revolutionary organizations of Nicaragua; of her men and women; of her workers and peasants; of her glorious youth; of her heroic mothers; of the Christians who, from their faith in God, committed themselves to and inserted themselves into the struggle for liberation of the oppressed; and of all those whose productive works contributed to the defense of the Fatherland.

Source: "Heroes and Martyrs: National Literacy Crusade for the Liberation of Nicaragua, 1980." Translated from the Spanish by Walter J. Petry; *La Gaceta: Diario Oficial*, Año XCI, no. 5. Managua, Nicaragua, January 9, 1987, pp. 33-34. Translated from the Spanish by Walter J. Petry.

118. Sandinistas and Christianity II

The official statement by the national directorate of the Frente Sandinista de Liberación Nacional (FSLN), "On the Role of Religion in the New Nicaragua" (Oct. 1980), was composed when the Sandinista revolutionary regime faced increasing opposition. One of the tactics of that opposition within and without Nicaragua was to brand the revolution as anti-Christian, Marxist, atheist, or all three.

Western revolutions previous to that of the Sandinistas, excepting the seventeenth-century English revolution, were strongly anticlerical and antireligious, perceiving the churches as part of the established order, which had to be removed.

Carlos Fonseca (1936-1976) and the eight other original "founding fathers" of the FSLN arrived at their revolutionary ideology from a variety of perspectives, namely, secular humanism, socialism, Marxism, disillusionment with jejune Catholicism, or simply pure outrage at the Somoza dictatorship. None conceived of the possibility that Christians, out of their Christian commitment, would join the FSLN, which had evolved into three tendencies, two radically Marxist and one flexible and pragmatic. It was the latter tendency that allowed the new nine-man directorate of 1979 (Tomás Borge was the only surviving original member) to draw up, during a time of increasing tensions, uncertainties, and growing opposition to the revolution, the remarkable statement below.

Note that three priests headed ministries in the new revolutionary government: foreign affairs, housing, and culture; and a fourth, the official literacy campaign.

How does the declaration handle religion, the church, the churches, churchmen, believers, and nonbelievers? How does it treat history, especially the ecclesiastical history of Nicaragua? How does it present and define the revolutionary regime, and where does it place that regime politically? Does the declaration represent a serious statement of political philosophy or a clever, manipulative piece of political rhetoric?

Note that the Somoza dynasty ruled Nicaragua from 1934 to 1979.

For some time the enemies of our people — driven from power once and for all — have been carrying on an obstinate campaign of distortions and lies about various aspects of the revolution, with the aim of confusing the people. This campaign of ideological confusion seeks to promote anti-Sandinista fears and attitudes among the people, while at the same time politically wearing down the FSLN through interminable polemics that never seek honest conclusions, but in fact seek precisely the opposite.

The question of religion has a special place in these campaigns of confusion since a large percentage of the Nicaraguan people have very deep-rooted religious sentiments. In this regard, the reactionaries' efforts have been aimed at spreading the idea that the FSLN is using religion now in order to later suppress it. Clearly, the purpose of such propaganda is to manipulate our people's honest faith in order to provoke a *political* reaction against the FSLN and the revolution. [. . .]

Christian patriots and revolutionaries are an integral part of the Sandinista people's revolution, and they have been for many years. The participa-

---

SOURCE: Originally published by the National Directorate of the FSLN in the October 7, 1980, issue of *Barricada* and translated by Intercontinental Press, in Carlos Fonseca, Daniel Ortega, Tomás Borge et al., *Sandinistas Speak: Speeches, Writings, and Interviews with Leaders of Nicaragua's Revolution* (New York: Pathfinder Press, 1986), 105-11 passim. Copyright © 1982 by Pathfinder Press. Reprinted by permission.

tion of Christians — both lay people and clergy — in the FSLN and the Government of National Reconstruction is a logical outgrowth of their outstanding participation at the people's side throughout the struggle against the dictatorship.

Through their interpretation of their faith, many FSLN members and fighters were motivated to join the revolutionary struggle and therefore the FSLN. Many gave not only their valiant support to our cause, but were also examples of dedication, even to the point of shedding their blood to water the seed of liberation.

How could we forget our beloved martyrs Oscar Pérez Cassar, Oscar Robelo, Sergio Guerrero, Arlen Siu, Guadalupe Moreno, and Leonardo Matute, or the dozens of Messengers of the Word [laypeople trained to raise Christian consciousness through readings of the Bible] murdered by the Somozaist [sic] National Guard in the mountains of our country, or so many other brothers and sisters.

We should give special mention to the revolutionary work and heroic sacrifice of Catholic priest and Sandinista member Gaspar García Laviana. He represented the highest synthesis of Christian vocation and revolutionary consciousness.

All these were humble men and women who knew how to fulfill their duty as patriots and revolutionaries without getting bogged down in long philosophical discussions. They now live eternally in the memory of the people, who will never forget their sacrifice.

But the participation of Christians was not limited to serving as fighters in the Sandinista Front. Many Christians, lay people and clergy, who never participated in the ranks of the FSLN although some were linked to it, professed and practiced their faith in accord with our people's need for liberation. The Catholic church and some evangelical churches even participated as institutions in the people's victory over the Somoza regime of terror.

On various occasions the Catholic bishops bravely denounced the crimes and abuses of the dictatorship. Monsignor Obando y Bravo and Monsignor Salazar y Espinoza, among others, were abused by Somozaist gangs. It was a group of priests and monks that exposed to the world the disappearance of 3,000 peasants in the mountains in the north of our country.

Many Christians of different denominations carried a liberating message to the people. Some even gave refuge and food to the Sandinistas who were mercilessly persecuted by Somozaism. [sic] [. . .]

To a degree unprecedented in any other revolutionary movement in Latin America and perhaps the world, Christians have been an integral part of our revolutionary history. This fact opens up new and interesting possibilities for the participation of Christians in revolutions in other places, not only during the struggle for power, but also later in the stage of building the new society.

In the new conditions that are posed by the revolutionary process, we Christian and non-Christian revolutionaries must come together around the task of providing continuity to this extremely valuable experience, extending it into the future. We must perfect the forms of conscious participation among all the revolutionaries in Nicaragua, whatever their philosophical positions and religious beliefs. [. . .]

The FSLN sees freedom to profess a religious faith as an inalienable right which is fully guaranteed by the revolutionary government. [. . .]

Some authors have asserted that religion is a mechanism for spreading false consciousness among people, which serves to justify the exploitation of one class by another. This assertion undoubtedly has historic validity to the extent that in different historical epochs religion has served as a theoretical basis for political domination. Suffice it to recall the role that the missionaries played in the process of domination and colonization of the Indians of our country. However, we Sandinistas state that our experience shows that when Christians, basing themselves on their faith, are capable of responding to the needs of the people and of history, those very beliefs lead them to revolutionary activism. Our experience shows us that one can be a believer and a consistent revolutionary at the same time, and that there is no insoluble contradiction between the two. [. . .]

Outside the framework of the FSLN, Christian activists — whether they be priests, pastors, members of religious orders, or lay people — all have the right to express their convictions publicly. This cannot be used to detract from their work in the FSLN or from the confidence that they have gained as a result of their revolutionary activity. [...]

The FSLN has a profound respect for all the religious celebrations and traditions of our people. It is striving to restore the true meaning of these occasions by attacking various evils and forms of corruption that were introduced into them in the past. [...]

Some reactionary ideologists have accused the FSLN of trying to divide the Church. Nothing could be further from the truth or more ill-intentioned than this accusation. If there are divisions within the religions, they exist completely independently of the will and activity of the FSLN.

A study of history shows that around big political events members of the Catholic church have always taken different and even contradictory positions. Missionaries came with the Spanish colonizers, and they used the cross to consecrate the slave labor that had been initiated by the sword. But against them arose the firmness of Bartolomé de las Casas, the defender of the Indians.

In the beginning of the last century many priests fought for the independence of Central America, some with weapons in hand. And on the other extreme there were priests who defended the privileges of the crown in Latin America with equal vehemence.

After liberation from the colonial yoke, we find the anti-interventionist positions of Monsignor Pereira y Castellón, who called for defense of the nation's interests against the North American invasion. During the Somoza epoch the figure of Monsignor Calderón y Padilla stands out, attacking the Somozas' vice, corruption, and abuse of power against the poor.

And today there is the massive revolutionary commitment among revolutionary Christians.

Earlier we mentioned the participation of many Christians in the people's revolutionary struggle. But we must also point out that some, like León Pallais and others, remained at Somoza's side to the end.

We should not forget that in that period there were priests who proudly paraded their military ranks and official positions — of course no one demanded that they give up their posts. But we should also not forget that in contrast to these sad examples we have the immense figure of Gaspar García L. and so many other Sandinista martyrs of Christian origin. [...]

The priest compañeros who have taken posts in the government, in response to the FSLN's call and their obligations as citizens, have thus far carried out extraordinary work. Facing great and difficult problems, our country needs the participation of all patriots to move forward. It especially needs those who had the chance to receive higher education, which was denied to the majority of our people. [...]

Like every modern state, the revolutionary state is secular and cannot adopt any religion because it is the representative of all the people, believers as well as nonbelievers.

119. Disappointing a Fragile Flock

María López Vigil, a Cuban Catholic whose family left the island with the advent of the revolution, gradually adopted a progressive understanding of the demand for change in Latin America and embraced critically the Sandinista revolution in Nicaragua, where she still resides. She addressed this open letter to Pope John Paul II upon witnessing the disastrous visit he made to León and Managua in March 1983.

The letter both narrates and advocates. The narrative is factual and coincides with

SOURCE: Judy Butler, "The Pope, the Press, and Political Passions," *North American Congress on Latin America: Report on the Americas* 17 (July-August, 1983): 29-31. Reprinted by permission of NACLA: Report on the Americas.

accounts by others. It is the advocacy that needs analysis. What is López's perspective? How does she portray the nature of Nicaraguan women's religiosity? Does she think the Sandinista revolution has affected these women's understanding of Christianity? How may the pope's formality and seeming imperviousness to the mothers be explained?

Holy Father,

For many months the people of Nicaragua awaited you. Those who are poor and find their religious expression among the rockets and rum that come each year with the festivals for the Virgin Mary and for Santo Domingo [patron saint of Managua] awaited you. Also those poor whose faith has matured more and who are organized in base communities, catechumenical or charismatic communities, those who have seen dozens of Delegates of the Word—peasant catechists—die at the border, they too awaited you. For the first time in many months—not without tension, certainly—one event united all of Nicaragua.

Full of hopes, they awaited you. There were peasants who signed up for the journey to the capital three days in advance. The government used up two whole months' worth of gasoline so that all who wanted to hear you in León or Managua could do so. All the impoverished and weak infrastructure of this "small and martyred" country (as Comandante Daniel Ortega called it on greeting you) was put at your service. This was done with pleasure, in the belief that a pilgrim of peace with your social influence would show your solidarity, as so many others have done, with the just cause of a people who have suffered so much.

For a month they studied your orations in other countries and wrote letters to you expressing their problems. They prepared songs, painted signs, organized vigils. On the eve of your visit they prayed that God would enlighten you. The peasants of Jalapa—the war zone on the border—sang on television: "Here all of us love you; speak for Nicaragua."

Holy Father, they needed you to speak for Nicaragua. One day before you arrived in Managua and in the same plaza where you celebrated the mass, they held a service for 17 youths assassinated by *somocistas* on the northern border of the country. Then they dried their tears and went to meet you, certain that your message would help stop the hands that come from Honduras to shoot at Nicaragua.

With microphone in hand I had the opportunity to follow you closely through your stay in this country. I saw you arrive at the airport, a little tired and even cold, despite the heat of this land and the protective warmth of its people.

A group of mothers of "heroes and martyrs" (as they are called here), those mourning women who were at the end of the diplomatic receiving line, were happy with that white rosary that your assistant presented to them after you had already moved toward the helicopter that would take you to León. "Can I put it on now?" one asked me. "Why not? It is for you." The woman's eyes were full of tears as she put it around her neck, over her black dress. She had lost her son. The *somocista* guards killed him. But the Pope had given her a rosary and this consoled her.

When we arrived at the César Augusta Silva Center to broadcast for all Nicaragua the event that was going to happen there—the meeting with the Government Junta and the leadership of the Sandinista Front—we saw again in the entrance a group of mourning women who were anxiously awaiting you. More mothers of more dead. (Every day young people fall on Nicaragua's border, defending this country from those who want to return to the past.) I saw how they handed you a letter, in which they asked from you a word for peace and a condemnation of U.S. aggression. They asked it in the name of Jesus Christ and of the Virgin Mary. I read this letter on the radio. It was one more among the thousands that these people, recently made literate, wrote to their Holy Father. Among the mothers, doña Mercedes was the most forward. With unsure letters she penciled her own letter to read to you personally. And she began to do so. You could scarcely listen to her. With the rush that characterizes these necessarily pressured trips you moved on to the next point of the pre-established agenda. But doña Mercedes was happy. You had smiled at her. She had lost her son. The *somocista* guards killed him, but the Pope at least had looked at her.

At 4:30, under a relentless sun—in which one person fainted per minute, as we could see from the press gallery—600,000 Nicaraguans waited for you in the July 19th Plaza. All who wanted to could come to the plaza. All. Not only the "Sandinistas," Holy Father. That multitude made up the half of this country that was able enough to get to Managua, from little children to pot-bellied women to the old people; all those that you had been told couldn't come.

I found myself, broadcasting on radio, just behind a group of mothers of heroes and martyrs at the left side of the gallery. They were dressed in mourning, and with the photo of their dead children in their hands they were saying the rosary as you arrived at the plaza. "What do you expect of the Pope?" we asked them. "I am hoping for a prayer for our dead." "I hope that he will pray for peace, so that there will be no more deaths on the border." "If the Pope makes such a pronouncement, the U.S. government will not continue carrying on such outrages against us." "The Pope will defend us, he will show solidarity, we are sure of it."

When you got to the plaza, with the staff of the shepherd and the miter of your authority, 600,000 flags waved in the air. There were the blue and white of the Republic, the white and yellow of the Vatican, the red and black of the Sandinistas. Dozens of doves were released and 600,000 voices shouted "Long live the Pope!" "We want peace!"

The mothers in mourning sang and followed the mass attentively, as did all the people. Respectfully and with growing expectation as the homily approached. "Now the Pope is going to speak, now he is going to speak . . . " ("Speak for Nicaragua," resonated silently the eager voices of the peasants on the border.)

You began your homily. The central theme was the unity of the Church. In a language difficult to understand, you spoke of unity around the bishops. You insisted. And unity around the poorest? And unity of all to achieve peace? And unity of all around Jesus, who was assassinated by the Roman empire? In a tone more understandable than your words, you affirmed your authority with disquieting emphasis.

It was at the end of the homily, when, after having heard the word "bishops" fifteen times and never once the word "dead" or "peace," that the outcry began to escape from the hearts of those women. It was a cry which the bishops themselves detected years ago as the identity of the poor of Latin America. It was the cry "ever more tumultuous and impressive," that "growing, impetuous and occasionally threatening cry," that is the "shout of a people who suffer and demand justice, liberty and respect for the fundamental rights of the individual and of the people."

This is the sequence of events as I witnessed them. The mothers first asked for peace and a prayer for their dead. They cried and made their claim in a reasonable voice. Then they began to do it with shouts, with lamentations. Soon thousands and thousands and thousands of voices supported them. ("We want peace!," then "Popular Power!") The spark caught fire and the heat spread.

Finally, the mothers at my side decided to go in front of the rostrum itself, facing the altar, so that you could see them. There, while the mass went on, they raised toward you the photos of their children. "A prayer for our dead!" By then the plaza was already in chaos. It was the shout of the "voiceless" ones who have now been given a voice in this recently liberated land.

I don't know if it is because I live in Nicaragua and love these people, but I couldn't continue broadcasting for the lump in my throat. Perhaps you came from very far and thus were not moved. Perhaps the stones of that old Church you live in have become too hard with age.

A kiss for one of these mothers and an "Our Father" for their fallen—there are so many— would have been enough to end all the "irreverencies." Holy Father, why did you not do it?

Today, the day after your arrival in Nicaragua, Managua seems to have been to another funeral. Tired and aghast, the people's sorrow is indescribable. There is neither peace nor joy. There is neither unity, nor even hope. The divisions have been deepened and an anguished feeling of indignation, of perplexity, of deception—also of shame and guilt—tortures everyone. Why did you do it, Holy Father? Why did you open this wound in a people already so full of pain?

"The Pope said nothing to us, he left us with an emptiness," a peanut vendor near the plaza told me. The plaza was still covered with papers, with the footprints of a multitude of sheep who had sought their shepherd.

God cannot want this huge emptiness that you left in the hearts of these people to be filled with blood, with more blood, by those who today clap their hands with glee for what happened in the 19th of July Plaza in Managua.

With faith in Christ and in his Church,
María López Vigil

120. Letter to My Friends

Fernando Cardenal, S.J. (b. 1932), younger brother of Ernesto, joined the Jesuit order in 1952 and, because of the rigorous seminary system in place at the time, was not ordained until 1970. Like so many others (Torres, Ernesto Cardenal, Gutiérrez, López Vigil), he had had his consciousness raised by the ferment in Latin American society and in the church and pledged, "I will dedicate my life to the full liberation of the poor in Latin America wherever it might be most useful."

He became one of "the Twelve" distinguished Nicaraguan professionals who represented the Sandinista movement to the outside world in the mid-1970s; and when the revolution came to power in 1979 he was appointed head of the literacy campaign and subsequently vice-director of Sandinista Youth, an official organization of the FSLN. He became minister of education in 1984, one of four priests still holding government ministries, which church law (Canon 285) forbids. Pope John Paul II demanded that Cardenal choose between what the pope saw as a political rather than a priestly commitment: leave "politics" or the Jesuits. In the following public letter Cardenal explains his choice to leave the Jesuit order (not the priesthood itself, only the active ministry for a temporary period) because of his commitment to the poor, which he sees as an integral part of his priestly character.

Is this yet another statement of liberation theology? If so, what are the core assertions that make it so? Are there any characteristics not found in other such statements previously read? What characteristics denote his priestly nature? What does Cardenal's analysis contained in the four paragraphs of no. 11 reveal about the theology of the church hierarchy?

In these last years of my life (1979-1984), in particular during the weeks and months of 1984, a good number of friends from various countries, Christians or Christians at heart, cardinals, bishops, priests, brother Jesuits, religious, both men and women and lay friends have written me, have taken an interest in me. In these last months I have not answered these letters. Though grateful, I have kept silent waiting for the time when I could tell the whole truth.

On various occasions the national and international press has referred to me, making affirmations sometimes true and sometimes false. Now is the time to speak. I want to give a simple and fraternal answer (without being antagonistic, for this would be senseless in the present situation of Nicaragua), giving at the same time my honest view of what has happened and is happening. [. . .]

Not long after the triumph of the Sandinista revolution, the Bishops of Nicaragua began to pressure us priests who were part of the revolution to abandon our commitment to it. That meant (Maryknoll) Father Miguel D'Escoto, minister of external affairs; my (Trappist) brother Ernesto,

---

SOURCE: Taken from Fernando Cardenal, "Why I Was Forced to Leave the Jesuit Order," *National Catholic Reporter* 21, no. 11 (January 11, 1985): 1, 6-8. Originally published in Fernando Cardenal M., "Carta a mis amigos," *Barricada* [Managua, Nicaragua] (December 11, 1984), 1.

minister of culture; Father Edgar Parrales, minister of social welfare; and myself in charge of the literacy campaign. After long months of tension, finally, in June of 1981, the conference of bishops of Nicaragua granted us permission to continue in our work as an exception because of the emergency our country was experiencing; on our part, we were to voluntarily renounce celebrating any of the Sacraments in public or in private. Since that time, they have never again granted us a meeting, even though we have asked for one many times.

Before the end of the first year of this agreement, the Bishops once again began to pressure us to completely leave our work in the revolution. They did not pressure us personally but always used the mass media. In these last two years the Vatican also began to participate in the pressure, but it also never did so personally or directly. Ever since I accepted the nomination as minister of education, the pressure through the media has intensified much more, to the point where I see clearly in these last weeks of 1984 that I will now be faced with the final alternative of either abandoning my commitment to the Nicaraguan revolution or being expelled from the Society of Jesus and receiving the ecclesiastical sanctions of suspension from priestly duties and interdict.

I thought that I could nourish the hope that the church would see in my work a missionary type of apostolic service along the lines of gospel presence and inculturation in a new historical process which has taken an option for the poor. Because of this, I thought I would be able to keep hoping that a conflict between a desire and command of the church and my conscience would never arise.

Throughout these last months, I have dedicated a lot of time to discernment and spiritual direction, always involving much prayer for a greater confirmation in my decision. I have reflected on the whole of my situation with people of deep spiritual experience who love the church and know the spirit of the Society of Jesus.

Because of this, I can responsibly state that honestly, objectively and seriously I conscientiously object to the pressures of the ecclesiastical authorities. In all sincerity I consider that, before God, I would be committing serious sin if in the present circumstances I were to abandon my priestly option for the poor, which is presently being concretized in Nicaragua through my work in the Sandinista people's revolution.

My conscience grasps, as if in a global intuition, that my commitment to the cause of the poor of Nicaragua comes from God, and that my desire not to abandon my work comes from God and that for me today to be faithful to the Gospel and to do God's will in my life is to continue with my present responsibilities. I cannot conceive of a God who asks me to abandon my commitment to the people.

But if I do an analysis, I easily discover many reasons which reinforce the conviction of my conscience. Here are a few, briefly stated:

1. This revolutionary process of Nicaragua, in spite of the mistakes inherent in every human enterprise, which I, because I am inside of it see very clearly, is a process which places the interests of the poor above everything else. Politically, therefore, it is a legitimate translation of the Latin American church's preferential option for the poor.

2. I can verify that this process, once again in spite of errors, is trying to create an original model of revolution, one of whose most characteristic features is respect for the Christian religion of the majority of the Nicaraguan people and the active participation of religious leaders in the construction of the new society.

3. I have experienced that, in the midst of tendencies toward unbelief, my priestly presence, as a religious and as a Christian among the revolutionaries, is an important testimony to the value and the role of the faith. I see this activity of mine in the context of Decree IV of the 32nd General congregation and in the special mission against atheism given the Society by his holiness Paul VI.

4. Since the end of my tertianship, in 1970, I promised to live my priesthood in service of the poor, leaving its concrete applications to the impulse of the Spirit. Since then I believe that with the grace of God, I have fulfilled this promise— always in consultation with my Religious Community, in its widest sense, and with my superiors in the Society of Jesus. This promise is radically fulfilled today in Nicaragua by working in the revolution.

5. Since then I encouraged as a priest many, many young people and many adults both from the moneyed as well as from the popular classes that, moved by this faith, they might dedicate themselves in the most efficacious manner possible to the cause of the poor; in Nicaragua, this cause was being carried forward by the F.S.L.N. Not a few of these followed my words and inserted themselves as yeast in the dough and in our history; thousands were assassinated, among whom were my brother-in-law and three nephews. A bond of blood that has been shed also unites me to this cause, to this people.

6. I am convinced that our presence in the Nicaraguan revolution in these times brings a great transcendence not only to this process, but also to all the processes of social transformation which will take place in Latin America. One has to be blind not to see this. We don't believe in models, but these experiences enlighten, and above all, inspire.

7. I am under the impression that our revolutionary process is so novel and original that it is difficult to understand from outside. I sincerely feel that the challenge which (without trying to and without taking personal merit for it) we are carrying forward, the responsibility which weighs on our shoulders and the repercussions this involves in these times in whatever definitive decisions we take, are not well understood. The hundreds of letters written to us from all over are a tangible proof of what we are affirming.

8. Our little Nicaragua is almost totally defenseless against the avalanche of calumny and clever manipulation of every type which try to delegitimize and denigrate it, thus more easily justifying military oppression against it. The cause of the people and the truth of this cause has to face so much mud slinging and infamy. We can do something about this. That is why we are going to accompany the people in the revolution with all our strength, shouting to all who care to listen, with all the force of our priestly credibility and with all the moral authority that we have in the eyes of our friends: "Don't believe the calumnies against Nicaragua; like all human beings we make mistakes as we go along, but not as our detractors claim. Our goals are just, noble, beautiful and holy." Nicaragua, now more than ever, needs qualified witnesses to the truth and justice of its cause. And this is where we should be.

9. To leave the Revolution precisely at this time would be like deserting my commitment to the poor, and I would have difficulty convincing myself that at this time my withdrawal could be anything but a betrayal of the cause of the poor and even a betrayal of my country. A very careful analysis of the international situation indicates to us that any moment we could move from being a nation besieged by contrarevolutionaries officially and publicly supported by the present U.S. government, to becoming a nation suffering more direct intervention by the military forces of the U.S. government, precisely because the present U.S. administration does not want to accept the Sandinista people's revolution.

10. At a time when the whole country is in a state of "general alert" and the Sandinista Army ready for combat and waiting for military aggression, I am ordered to leave the revolution. The task I have been given for the eventuality of intervention is a dangerous one. I know clearly that my life is in greater danger than during the struggle against the dictatorship of Somoza, but I cannot abandon my people. I will never abandon them. I love this cause more than my life, and they are asking me to abandon it precisely when my people are in critical danger, calumniated and accosted by the most powerful country in the world.

11. The order which I am being given obliges me to make conscience [sic] decisions, but I have come to realize that the pressures which are provoking this order don't originate in theological reflection, nor in evangelical inspiration of pastoral necessity. In communion with the church I have the right to say that some bishops of Nicaragua have taken a political stance which yesterday and today continues to show that they are in open contradiction to the interest of the poor majority of Nicaragua.

Also the Holy See, in the case of Nicaragua, appears to be imprisoned by misconceptions in the political sphere that it has received from the traumatic experiences of Eastern European conflicts which have nothing to do with the history of the People of God in our Latin American countries and much less with the revolutionary process in Nicaragua. From our vantage point, the political stance of the Vatican toward Nicaragua coincides with that of President Reagan. With my withdrawal they are trying to deligitimize the revolutionary process. Here, there is no question of a Dogma of the Christian Faith, neither a Catholic doctrine nor any Christian moral imperative: there is only political confrontation. The bishops have publicly shown themselves to be united to those who are attacking the revolution, to those who wish the destruction of this regime in order to return to the past. The rigid application of canon 285-3 cannot help but appear in [Nicaragua as a pretext to use us in an attempt to undermine the Revolution, uniting this] action to a series of all kinds of aggressions which the U.S. government and its allies are directing against our little country. They want to facilitate the work of Goliath in the destruction of David.

Moreover, this whole incident was carried out by the bishops in a manner that is scarcely pastoral. Six times I asked the Episcopal Conference to meet with me in order to dialogue, but they did not even answer my letters. It hurts to feel permanently rejected by one's Pastors.

On July 8 this year, before making public my nomination as minister of education, I wrote the president of the conference (with a copy to each of the bishops) asking that they give me an opportunity to dialogue with them, and I terminated the letter with this paragraph: "Henceforth, I wish to point out that I am more than ready to broach with you or with the whole episcopal conference any concern, problem or perspective that you have on your mind in the area of education."

This letter had the same fortune as the previous ones; it was not answered.

This whole combination of reasons makes up some of the elements that have resulted—for the first time in 32 years of Jesuit life—in my having problems with a command of obedience. In the situation we are considering, I have a serious objection in conscience to obeying . . .

Today, two years after making this testimony, I confirm it with greater conviction.

I believe that canon 285 is valid, and I am not against it. [. . .]

I maintain my objection in conscience. [. . .]

At no time will I ask to leave the Society of Jesus. [. . .]

I will continue to live as a religious, and, with God's grace, I will try to keep my vow of celibacy. No one can take my priesthood away from me. [. . .]

I consider myself to be a sinner. I have a deep awareness of this. I don't want anyone to idealize me, because this would be a big mistake. But the interesting thing in this situation is that they are not punishing me for my sins, but for what I experience as God's call to me, and to this call I cannot say no.

I am grateful for the support, the advice and the deep friendship of the Jesuit Community at Bosques de Altamira, especially of its Superior, Father Peter Marchetti, S.J. All these years they have been my brothers and best friends.

I am grateful to Father Provincial's delegate for Nicaragua, Fr. Iñaki Zubizarreta, S.J., who always took an interest in my situation. A great friend and a man of God.

The Provincial of the Central American Province, Father Valentín Menéndez, S.J., accompanied me with genuine kindness, understanding and support. I would also like to thank Reverend Father Peter-Hans Kolvenbach, S.J. superior general of the Society of Jesus, for respecting my conscientious objection, for his personal appreciation and for the interest he has taken in positively resolving my situation.

The one who has categorically refused to grant an exception to the priests in Nicaragua so that they might continue working in the revolutionary government has been Pope John Paul II. It hurts me to say this, but as a Christian I cannot keep quiet. [. . .]

N.B. The Jesuits, by papal command, expelled Cardenal from the order in 1984. He was reinstated in 1997.

121. Homily on Two Christian Revolutionary Martyrs of Nicaragua

José Llaguno Farías (1925-1992) was born in Monterrey, Mexico, and was ordained a Jesuit priest in 1956. He served the Tarahumaras, a marginalized but united and closely knit indigenous community in a remote area in the state of Chihuahua. He was made vicar apostolic (bishop) of Tarahumara in 1975 and served until his death.

He traveled to Nicaragua in 1988 and delivered the homily commemorating the martyrdom in 1983 of Felipe and Mery Barreda, who were tortured and assassinated by anti-Sandinistas because of their commitment, as Christians, to the revolution. Clearly this is another authentic statement of liberation theology. What especially makes it so?

Estelí, Nicaragua, 9 January 1988

As I said to you at the beginning, we are meeting to celebrate our faith, a faith that is lived—a faith lived, to the point of giving oneself, to total commitment, by the Barredas and by so many other sons and daughters of mothers of heroes and martyrs who are here with us. I come from very far with great love for Nicaragua. For years I lived with the wish of being with you, of sharing your faith, of sharing your giving, of sharing your commitment.

I arrived in Nicaragua the day before yesterday and yesterday I was in Granada for ordinations to the priesthood. I give thanks to God that they invited me to be with you today because my visit to Nicaragua, without being here with you today in Estelí, would not have been worthwhile. I missed the presence of the people yesterday. I missed the music of the base [Christian] communities. I missed the mothers present here with their sorrow, their hope and I want therefore to thank God for this opportunity. Many have already spoken of the faith, of that lived faith, of that giving, of that love of Felipe and Mery [Barreda]. In Mexico we know them. In Mexico we love them. And providentially I also met the group of [Mexican] priests and laymen and women who came to work in the coffee harvest and want, at least I interpret it as their desire, to thank all of you for the example of commitment which Nicaragua is for us and for all of Latin America. I indeed ask you that in spite of your fatigue, in spite of your suffering that you not weaken—you are our hope. If little Nicaragua can move on ahead and seek its liberty, its independence, with dignity, that motivates the remainder of us peoples of Latin America. Truly you are an inspiration for us all.

I didn't want to prepare these words too much because I want to speak with you what I carry in my heart and for that one does not prepare. In September I was here a few days and spent a full morning in Matagalpa also with the mothers [of heroes and martyrs]. I went home converted. I had always loved Nicaragua but with these brief visits what appeared impossible has been realized: each day I love you more. And in Mexico our base [Christian] communities live continually with the image of your efforts and commitment.

Here the faith is lived but it is lived even to the point of martyrdom. Here is lived hope, that hope which is based on the grace of God and human effort. Here is lived charity, love. The love that goes to the point of giving up one's life for one's brothers. And as they, Felipe and Mery, did not give up their lives only at the time of their martyrdom but for many years before. It was a giving of their life for others, to live for those others, to commit themselves to others, and that is being Christian. And your revolutionary process, a Christian process, is an inspiration to us all. Today in the Eucharist I want above all to give thanks to God for the example of Nicaragua. I also want, together with my brother priests from Mexico, to ask the Lord to sustain you in the fight, to sustain your hope so that you continue to be an inspiration for us all.

SOURCE: José Alberto Llaguno Farías, S.J., Homily in Estelí, Nicaragua, January 9, 1988. Recorded on tape, transcribed, and translated from the Spanish by Walter J. Petry.

We are experiencing difficult moments—difficult for you as Nicaraguans and Christians as well. But the hope of better times in which community is fully lived, in which commitment to one's brother is fully lived, I believe that it is not so distant. So much blood of martyrs cannot have been spilled in vain. It was said in the past that the blood of Christians is the seed of life. And here this land soaked with so much blood of the young must bear fruit and must bear the fruit of Christian life of freedom and dignity.

The Lord bless you all, the Lord inspire you all, and [may you all] continue to give these examples. A people poor and powerless which precisely by being poor and powerless can live the gospel. That was the great discovery I made: in Nicaragua the gospel is lived in families, in society, in the government, in the [FSLN] Front the gospel is lived and it is lived because you are poor and powerless. If you were a rich and strong people you would not be, you would not live the gospel.

The Lord bless you, and let us all unite in this Eucharist to remember the fifth anniversary of the Martyrdom of Felipe and Mery and of so many other boys and girls, the blood of young Nicaragua. Giving thanks to the Lord for these witnesses, for these martyrs, and praying to the Lord for them.

José Alberto Llaguno Farías, S.J. Vicar Apostolic (Bishop) of Tarahumara, Mexico.

122. The Easter Pastoral

The pastoral letter signed by the ten bishops of Nicaragua in April 1986 represents the traditionalist hierarchy's understanding of authentic Catholicism, liberation theology, and Sandinista ideology and tactics. The letter was written at a time of fierce conflict when the United States-backed Contras *were using terror tactics to demoralize and destabilize the Sandinistas. At this time there was also an economic downturn, the institution of the draft, and cleavage within the church; hence, the bishops' constant references to "reconciliation."*

How does the hierarchy characterize the "sector of the Church" that is animated by liberation theology? What specific fears does this "popular church" arouse in the traditionalists? Is there evidence in the previous documents of a "beligerent group undermin[ing] the . . . [Catholic Church]," constituting a "popular church"? Do such documents reflect the warnings of Puebla (nos. 535, 536)? See footnote 1 to part XVI (p. 278).

Paragraph A—Are there echoes here of documents previously discussed? Paragraph D— Is there evidence for these assertions in previous documents? Italicized subheading beginning "The church opts for man . . ."—Reference is made here to the censorship imposed by the government in time of war. Given the tensions described above, which were felt by all sides, is it possible to extract some basic facts from the rhetoric of the passage? Italicized subheading beginning "The church, agent of peace . . ."—Ironically, why might the Sandinistas agree with the bishops' wording in the second paragraph in this section?

U.S. Department of State

Subject: Nicaraguan Catholic Bishops Issued Pastoral Letter on National Reconciliation.

1. On April 6, the Nicaraguan Catholic Bishops issued a pastoral letter "on the eucharist, source of unity and reconciliation". Addressed to priests, deacons, monks, nuns, Catholics and "men of good will", the letter urged both spiritual reconciliation of religious in Nicaragua and political reconciliation of all Nicaraguans through dialogue. It strongly denounced the "popular

Source: "Nicaraguan Catholic Bishops Issued Pastoral Letter on National Reconciliation [6 April 1986]," in *Congressional Record-Senate*, 21 April 1986, 8120-8121.

church" and opined that "all forms" of foreign aid "that lead to destruction, pain and the death of our families . . . are condemnable".

2. There follows an informal translation of excerpts from the pastoral letter, the Spanish text of which will be sent to ARA/CEN and S/LPD by Septel:

(Begin translation:)*

The Church, Symbol and Instrument of Unity and Reconciliation

The church in Nicaragua wants to be the symbol and witness that unity among Nicaraguans is possible and wants, besides, to be an efficacious instrument to achieve it. We know that throughout history the church has encountered obstacles in the realization of this mission which are useless to avoid. His Holiness John Paul II, on the occasion of the last Purísima celebration, told us: "You know well, beloved bishops, that specifically to you has been given the ministry and the word of reconciliation (2 Cor. 5, 18 and 19). You, beloved brothers, are particularly conscious of this duty as you have demonstrated, sending to the Catholics of Nicaragua, on April 22, 1984, at Easter, a pastoral letter on reconciliation. I am sure that you will continue undertaking with confident perseverance the mission that Christ has given you."

We are conscious that in order to achieve national reconciliation, it will not be enough to have "simple arrangements—rather, authentic transformations that integrate all the people in the management of their own destiny" are necessary— and that "those rights and aspirations that we want to defend or exalt are of no political group, but of all men and specifically of our Nicaraguan brothers. . . . It is that specific man, our Nicaraguan brother, who is the object of our concern" (see pastoral letter of the Nicaraguan episcopate: "on the principles that direct the political activity of all the church as such." March 19, 1972).

We are convinced, likewise, that reconciliation will only be possible through dialogue. This dia-

logue of which we speak "is not a truce tactic in order to strengthen positions necessary to the prosecution of the fight, but the sincere effort to respond to anguish, pain, exhaustion, the fatigue of so many who long for peace. So many who want to live, to rise from ashes, to seek the warmth of children's smiles, far from terror and in a climate of democratic life together. . . . It is urgent to bury the violence—enough of violence!—which has cost so many victims in this and other nations" (see John Paul II, visit to San Salvador, Central America, March 6, 1983).

Today we want to inspire Nicaraguans to assume the responsibility which each one has to make possible reconciliation, unity and peace in Nicaragua.

Spiritual Unity and Reconciliation
A church lives

We recognize with joy the firmness and depth of the faith of our people in general, who remain faithful to their beliefs and religious traditions, who cultivate the love of the eucharist and the Holy Virgin, who acknowledge and accept their legitimate pastors with proven loyalty toward them and toward the person of the Holy Father, in spite of institutionalized ideological attacks and of the scandalous disobedience of some ecclesiastics.

We live in a privileged time in which the Holy Spirit is renewing the church; it strengthens and prepares it for the fulfillment of its universal mission. We verify an increase in priestly and religious vocations, and the existence of a laity which seeks to live its Christianity with greater fullness and responsibility. We recognize an intense life of prayer and the strengthening of many Catholics who testify to their faith and are even disposed to give their lives for Christ and for their church.

For the love and compassion that the Lord has shed on Nicaragua, we raise our thanksgiving to God, and we encourage the faithful to remain strong in the faith.

There coexists, together with this reality never-

---

* The document was retrieved by the National Security Archives (a private non-governmental organization) and was originally transmitted by the U.S. Bureau of Inter-American Affairs, Office of Central American Affairs. The U.S. State Department's Office of Public Diplomacy for Latin America and the Caribbean (S/LPD) was established in 1983.

theless, a sector of the church, object of our pastoral concern, to which we also direct our call to reconciliation and unity.

A church put to the test

A belligerent group, priests, monks, nuns, and laymen of diverse nationalities, insisting on belonging to the Catholic Church, in reality work actively with their deeds to undermine the same church, collaborating in the destruction of the foundations on which are founded unity in the faith and in the body of Christ.

To this group is added a nucleus of persons, frequently sincere and well-intentioned, but no less mistaken. Together they are known as the "popular church." The Holy Father has pronounced repeatedly concerning its nature and function, pointing out its errors and condemning its positions.

Who makes up this so-called "popular church"

(A) They manipulate the fundamental truths of our faith, arrogating the right to reinterpret and even rewrite the word of God to conform it to their own ideology and use it for their own ends. But, as the Document of Puebla says: "All ideology is partial since no particular group can claim to identify its aspirations with those of the global society" (535). "Ideologies themselves have the tendency to absolutize the interests that they defend, the vision that they propose, and the strategy that they promote. In such case, they are transformed into true 'lay religions.' They are presented as an ultimate explanation sufficient to all, and so is constructed a new idol, from which is accepted, at times without realizing, a totalitarian and obligatory character. In this perspective it should not be strange that ideologies try to use people and institutions to serve the efficacious achievement of their ends. This is the ambiguous and negative side of ideologies" (536).

(B) They try to undermine the unity in the body (of the church), challenging the constituted authorities of the church with acts and postures of frank rebellion, and they protest against the most elemental measures of ecclesiastical discipline.

(C) They try to diminish or remove the confidence and loyalty of the people toward their priests and bishops, toward the church as an institution, and toward the person of the Holy Father, asserting or spreading by various media strongly financed by anti-church groups, or by media which the state itself puts at their disposition, accusations and calumnies of all kinds. With special persistence, they try to present the bishops as persecutors of ecclesiastics and as allies, followers, and supporters of imperialist plans of the United States, and the Holy Father as executor of said plans.

(D) They try to divide the church, its bosom the "class warfare" of Marxist ideology. Therefore, they try to identify the church with the interests of the powerful, while they reserve for themselves the title of "church of the poor." Nevertheless, we note that they applauded the expulsion of priests who gave great parts of their lives to the service and direct coexistence with the most poor and dispossessed.

Ecclesiastical reconciliation

Without any exclusion, we invite these brothers to reconsider their errors and postures, to revise their loyalties and to mend their ways, so that that which today is fragmentation and alienation avoids becoming, one day, total division and schism.

Likewise, we urge all the people of God, priests, monks, nuns, and laymen to congregate in unity with their pastors to celebrate the eucharist and express their communion and love, abhorring negative or indifferent postures that strike at the unity of the church of Christ.

National Unity and Reconciliation
The church opts for man

Why is the church, tested from within, also being tested from without? It is sought to muzzle it and hobble it in order to subjugate it in the midst of the applause that the institutionalized lie and half truths evoke from the unwary. It is accused of remaining silent while it is silenced, depriving it of its only radio station, and all news of aggressions suffered and all words of defense are censored from the communications media. It is asked to raise its voice in favor of peace, but when it seeks it via reconciliation and dialogue it is slandered and fought, since what is sought is not a moral orientation, but the manipulation of a pronouncement. When it does make itself heard, those who would like to dictate its words criticize it, not for what it said but for what it supposedly should have said. It is accused of making politics, while simultaneously it is demanded that it pronounce upon the most delicate matters of national and international politics. In this situation, we insist that our church opt only for man himself, for all Nicaraguans.

The church, agent of peace

It is in favor of this man, and because "we cannot hush that which we have seen and heard" (Acts 3.20), that we lift up our voice to say: enough now, the blood and the death! The blood spilled of so many Nicaraguans shouts to Heaven!

It is urgent and final that Nicaraguans, free of foreign meddling or ideologies, find a way out of the conflictive situation that our fatherland lives.

Today, we reaffirm with renewed emphasis that which already in 1984 we said in our pastoral letter of April 22, Easter. "Foreign powers take advantage of our situation to foment economic exploitation and ideological exploitation. They look at us as objects of support to their power without respect to our person, to our history, to our culture and our right to decide our own destiny. Consequently, the majority of the Nicaraguan people live fearful of the present and insecure in their future, experience deep frustration, cry for peace and liberty; but their voices are not heard, extinguished by the bellicose propaganda of one or another party."

We judge that all forms of aid, whatever be their source, that lead to destruction, pain and the death of our families, or to hate and division among Nicaraguans are condemnable. To opt for the annihilation of the enemy as the only road to peace is to opt inevitably for war. The church is the first to want peace and seeks to build it by means of conversion and penitence.

PART XVII
Later Liberation Theology

By the early 1970s Catholic faithful who accepted the message of liberation theology began to meet in Christian base communities (CEBs) to reflect on how major episodes in the Bible, such as the exodus of Jews from Egyptian slavery, applied to their own reality. These groups typically ranged from ten to twenty persons and met in churches and private homes in both urban and rural areas. Priests and nuns had the expertise to direct group discussion; skilled catechists did so in the many areas without a strong clerical presence. Participants perceived themselves as simply another of those religious groups that flourished in Catholic parishes, such as Catholic Action, sodalities, Legion of Mary, Holy Name Society, and so forth; they had no sense of themselves as independent or autonomous bodies. But some of the hierarchy perceived them as competition, a threat to clerical authority, and accused them of creating a "parallel" church or a popular church. Perhaps some confusion might have been caused by publications such as the booklet issued in 1983 by liberation laity and clergy in Nicaragua entitled *Historia de la iglesia de los pobres* (History of the Church of the Poor). But that history was simply an account of all the missionaries, regular clergy, and bishops who fought for the numbers of Nicaraguans who were poor, uneducated, and marginalized. The same kind of Catholics who were the authors of this solidly researched work had published four pamphlets treating the pope with almost excessive reverence on his impending visit to Nicaragua earlier that year. Nowhere in Latin America was there any threat of a breakaway, schismatic, or unorthodox church that would result from liberation theology. Like secular states, the institutional church ran scared and sought "security." CEBs existed throughout Latin America, though they became and remain especially prominent in such countries as El Salvador and Brazil. More than 150,000 CEBs existed in Brazil alone by the early 1990s. Some bishops, such as El Salvador's Oscar Romero (1917-1980), actively encouraged CEBs as a vehicle to promote political and social consciousness. Others, such as Colombia's Alfonso Cardinal López Trujillo (b. 1935), viewed these groups with suspicion since parishioners sometimes interpreted scripture in ways that, he believed, fostered class conflict and support for socialist regimes.[1]

John Paul II's election as pope in 1978 signaled the beginning of the end of hierarchical commitment to the goals and methods of liberation theology. Conservative forces within the church hierarchy showed their strength at the conference of Latin American bishops in Puebla, Mexico, in 1979 and attempted with some small success to distance the church from the movement. The new pontiff evaluated the movement through the lens of his own experiences in Soviet-dominated Poland and found it problematic. He viewed the Sandinista revolution in Nicaragua (1979) as confirmation that liberation theology promoted radicalism that benefited communism and, ultimately, threatened the church. He supported conservative bishops, such as Miguel Obando y Bravo of Managua (b. 1926) whom he created cardinal in 1985 and who squelched grassroots efforts that disturbed the status quo and involved politically active priests. In 1984 the head of the Congregation for the Doctrine of the Faith, Joseph Cardinal Ratzinger (who became Pope Benedict XVI in 2005), denounced parts of liberation theology that he considered Marxist and believed could lead to totalitarianism and atheism. "Those who, perhaps inadvertently, make themselves accomplices of similar enslavements," he claimed, "betray the very poor they mean to help."[2] The church also silenced one of liberation theology's greatest proponents, the Brazilian Franciscan Leonardo Boff (b. 1938). Despite these events, adherents of liberation theology continued to operate from the rubric of "preferential option for the poor," sometimes paying the ultimate price. In 1980 a right-wing death squad gunned down Oscar Romero, who had become a relentless advocate of justice by his searing three-year experience as archbishop of San Salvador. In 1989 the Salvadoran army shot at point-blank range six Jesuit priests and their two housekeepers in their university residence.

But progressive Catholicism has not declined solely because of papal and episcopal hostility toward liberation theology. Perhaps its message could not be sustained beyond a first generation of devoted adherents who were willing to give so much of their lives to the cause of temporal liberation, seeking the Kingdom of God on earth. As David Martin suggests, the theology of liberation theology may have been convincingly elaborated by leading intellectuals, but it also made liberation theology likely "to pull poor people struggling mainly for survival into much larger and bloodier struggles of which they had often had more than enough."[3] To a certain degree, by the early 1990s progressive Catholics in CEBs

---

1. José Luis Gutiérrez García, *Testimonios: Cárdenal Alfonso López Trujillo* (Bogotá: Plaza & Janés Editores, 1997), 142; John Burdick, *Looking for God in Brazil: The Progressive Catholic Church in Urban Brazil's Religious Arena* (Berkeley: University of California Press, 1993), vii, 2; Anne Motley Hallum, "Taking Stock and Building Bridges: Feminism, Women's Movements, and Pentecostalism in Latin America," *Latin American Research Review* 38, no. 1 (2003): 174.

2. Henry Kamm, "Vatican Censures Marxist Elements in New Theology: Injustice Acknowledged; But in Major Report, Church Says Liberation Doctrine Betrays Catholicism," *The New York Times,* September 4, 1984, 1, 10; Jeffrey Klaiber, S.J., "The Jesuits in Latin America: Legacy and Current Emphases," *International Bulletin of Missionary Research* 28, no. 2 (April 2004): 65-66; John W. Sherman, "Liberation Theology," in *Encyclopedia of Mexico: History, Society & Culture,* vol. 1, ed. Michael S. Werner (Chicago and London: Fitzroy Dearborn Publishers, 1997), 742-44.

3. David Martin, *Tongues of Fire: The Explosion of Protestantism in Latin America* (Cambridge, Mass.: Basil Blackwell, 1990), 270.

had already successfully helped pressure Latin America's brutal military regimes to open up the democratic process, and members of the "popular" church could theoretically work within the political apparatus. Hence, they now had less need to protest against societal abuses through the framework of liberation theology. Others, as José Comblin states, may have grown weary as liberation became "a language, a rhetoric, an ever-repeated discourse ... [that did] not lead to concrete actions and social victories."[4] Since liberation theologians acknowledged an intellectual debt to Marxist analysis, even sympathetic observers who lauded efforts to alleviate poverty and injustice, such as Pedro Arrupe, the Society of Jesus' twenty-eighth general (1965-1983), warned that the emphasis on the economic factor in determining all social reality was, ultimately, "prejudicial to Christian faith."[5] Finally, evangelical Christians and charismatic Catholics rejected liberation theology as belonging to an unsuccessful, confrontational era.

123. A Theology of Women's Ordination

Leonardo Boff (b. 1938), the premier Catholic theologian of Brazil and one of the founding fathers of liberation theology, received his doctorate in theology from the University of Munich in 1970 and taught theology at the Jesuit Institute in Petropolis, Brazil, for the ensuing twenty years. Author of more than seventy books that develop various aspects of liberation theology, he was increasingly subject in the 1980s to censorship by Joseph Cardinal Ratzinger, Vatican Prefect of the Congregation for the Doctrine of the Faith (the former Holy Office of the Inquisition). He left the priesthood and Franciscan order in 1992 and remains a faithful Christian.

The following excerpt from Boff's Ecclesiogenesis: The Base Communities Reinvent the Church *(1977) may be approached as a model of theological reflection in general and of liberation theology in particular. Where does Boff start his reflection? Consider especially the first four paragraphs. Describe the nature and the substance of the fifth paragraph ("if by 'feminism' . . ."). The phrase "Correctly analyze . . ." is the key to Boff's approach in that paragraph and the following one. What does Boff actually do in those paragraphs? Is not the last sentence of the reading a QED—"which was to be demonstrated"—on the legitimacy of women's ordination?*

---

4. Quoted in Phillip Berryman, "Is Latin America Turning Pluralist? Recent Writings on Religion," *Latin American Research Review* 30, no. 3 (1995): 116. For Comblin's own proposal for liberation theology to become a lay movement within the church, see José Comblin, "Brazil: Base Communities in the Northeast," in *New Face of the Church in Latin America: Between Tradition and Change*, ed. Guillermo Cook (Maryknoll, N.Y.: Orbis Books, 1994), esp. 206-9, 213-16.

5. Pedro Arrupe, "Marxist Analysis by Christians," *Origins* 10, no. 44 (April 16, 1981), 691-92; Burdick, *Looking for God in Brazil*, 221.

SOURCE: Leonardo Boff, *Ecclesiogenesis: The Base Communities Reinvent the Church*, trans. Robert R. Barr (Maryknoll, N.Y.: Orbis Books, 1986), 76-77, 79, 93-95. Reprinted by permission of Orbis Books.

church communities constitute a
is not only of the Christian freedom
ut of the liberation of woman, as
well ....d more in the basic communities,
women are assuming functions of leadership. In
this context, the problem of women's priesthood
arises. In view of the frequency of its broaching, in
basic communities as well as outside, we offer the
following theological reflection.

The subject of women's priesthood is part of
the general subject of women's liberation. Today's
world, in varying degrees, but at least in some
degree everywhere, is characterized by a broaden-
ing of the field of individual liberties—along with
the danger of a simultaneous amplification of the
potential for the strangulation of this same area of
liberty. After many millennia of a patriarchal primacy, the present age is host to a notable change
of awareness with respect to the relationships
between man and woman and the roles they play
in human society.

People generally wish that the difference
between the sexes could be acknowledged in a way
that would not involve particular privileges for
either. The tendency of our planetary civilization
is to overcome patriarchalism and matriarchalism
and move in the direction of a society of free persons, freely associated in marriage, and independent when it comes to personal fulfillment, with
respect for the differences between the sexes, and
with every person enjoying the right to live in conformity with this difference. Indeed, we are beginning to see a special human richness residing
precisely in the actualization of what is different
with each sex, understanding this differential in
reciprocity and mutuality. What is being sought is
equality in difference.

Any authority enjoyed by either member of the
human couple with respect to the other is exercised in a framework of personal equality, and
understood not so much as the function of one of
the sexes—this concept having been due to the
matriarchate or the patriarchate, depending on
the case—but as a function freely accepted by
both partners, and liable to be exercised now by
one, now by the other. [. . .]

If by "feminism" we understand whatever
defends the basic equality of women to men, maintains that women are human persons, and opposes
any institutions that seek to reduce them to the status of objects, then Jesus Christ was certainly a
feminist. After all, the general tenor of his ethical
preaching consisted in the liberation of human
beings from a legalistic, discriminatory morality,
in favor of a morality of decision, freedom, and a
communion of sisters and brothers. Just as God
makes no distinction among persons, but loves
them all (cf. Mt. 5:45), so neither should human
beings entertain any "preference of persons."
Human beings ought to love all other human
beings, without distinction and indiscriminately,
as sons and daughters of God and therefore brothers and sisters of one another. This ethical revolution launched by Jesus created a space for the
liberation of woman as a person. [. . .]

Correctly analyzed, ordination does not properly confer a power for worship and consecration.
It is not the priest who consecrates, baptizes, or
forgives. It is Christ who forgives, baptizes, and
consecrates. Priests lend their persons and their
faculties in order that the invisible Christ may
become sacramentally visible. The ministerial
priesthood is not a power to consecrate; it is the
power officially to represent the one, eternal
priesthood of Jesus Christ. The sacrament of order
raises a particular person to the dignity of this
function. [. . .]

The function of the priest in the local church is
the same as the function of the bishop in the
regional church and the pope in the universal
church. Each is constituted *principium unitatis
visibile*. Is it permissible that this function of
procuring unity be exercised exclusively by men?
Modern history and sheer fact have shown us that
women easily have the same capabilities as men,
not only in civil government, but in the experi-
ments, already under way in the church, of religious women who have assumed the direction of a
local church. Women discharge the role of pro-
curer of unity in their own female way—differently from men, but achieving the same reality:
harmony, good functioning, and unity in the
community of believers.

Promotion to the sacrament of order raises a
given person in the community to the assignment
of presiding, in oneness and reconciliation, at the

various services. All should be solicitous for this oneness. But the priest, male or female, is officially thrust forward, set before the community, in order to be head, in the name of Jesus Christ himself, of the *diakonia* of reconciliation and unification in the community. [. . .]

If a woman can be the principle of unity, as she is in so many communities, then theologically there is nothing to stand in the way of her empowerment, through ordination, to consecrate, to render Christ sacramentally present at the heart of the community's worship.

124. More Martyrs for El Salvador

Jon Sobrino, S.J. (see reading 127), escaped death on November 16, 1989, only because he was in Thailand engaged in the work of his order. His reflections on the occasion of the deaths of his six confreres, their housekeeper, and the housekeeper's daughter, at a time when there were already at least some 30,000 martyrs in El Salvador, speaks eloquently the language not particularly of liberation theology but of a profound Christian.

Why does he say: "As you might . . . remember, in El Salvador . . . the poor people decided simply to live"? Why does he put it that way? If the Salvadoran people (and their counterparts throughout our world) are represented by the ugly, faceless Suffering Servant of God (see Isaiah 52:13-15; 53), what must follow? What are the next questions? Why does Sobrino conclude that the Jesuits, in their capacity as university professors, are acting like the "good Samaritans"? What must be the nature of their university? Why do "the poor of the world have everything against them, by definition"? Is Sobrino's statement inspired by Marxist analysis?

I would say first of all that these six Jesuits were human beings. Now you might think one takes that for granted, but that's one thing I've learned in El Salvador — not to take that for granted— that we are human beings.

Maybe you might think that this is a very small compliment, no?, to glorious martyrs, to say that they were human beings. But they lived in the reality of El Salvador, and that's important in the sense of what a human being is. If we don't live in the real reality, it seems redundant, no? — we are not human beings. We are something else.

They incarnated themselves in Salvadoran reality. Words don't communicate Salvadoran reality because it is so absolutely different and distant from your reality that it would be very difficult for you to understand.

What is reality in El Salvador? Poverty. The poverty in El Salvador is not the exception, or the

anecdote. Poverty is reality—80-85 percent of Salvadorans live, survive, in poverty. They are not like myself and yourself — those who take life for granted. All of you and myself take life for granted — the minimum of eating and clothing, the minimum of education . . .

Who are those who do not take these things for granted? [The poor.]

The majorities are poor people. Poverty in El Salvador — also in Guatemala, Haiti, Honduras and Chad, in the world — poverty, and unfortunately this is no rhetoric, means being close to death. Life is the task. Surviving is the task, not getting a degree.

And as you might know, or remember, in El Salvador as in many other countries of Latin America, the poor people decided simply to live. Your politicians and government say they wanted to bring about a revolution. These people simply

SOURCE: Jon Sobrino, "Men of Life: The Martyrs of the UCA," *Central America/Mexico Report: Bimonthly Journal of the Religious Taskforce of Central America and Mexico* (December 1989), www.rtfcam.org/report/volume_1 (retrieved May 10, 2004). Reprinted by permission of Religious Task Force on Central America and Mexico.

wanted to live, to have enough bread and so on. And they organized and they exercised those human rights which again you take for granted.

And when they organized in popular movements, they were killed — by the hundreds and by the thousands. That's what happened. That's the basic reality of El Salvador.

[El Salvador has been compared] to the Suffering Servant of God. Fr. Ellacuría, one of the martyred Jesuits, did that, as did Archbishop Romero. Romero once said in a homily that the Suffering Servant in Isaiah is the best description of El Salvador. And he used to say how good it is that biblical scholars don't say whether this mysterious figure of the Servant of God is one man or a people. Romero said that for him, the Suffering Servant of God is Jesus of Nazareth and the Salvadoran people, the suffering people.

I don't have better words to communicate to you what Salvadoran reality is. Isaiah says that the Suffering Servant — he, or she, or it — had no human figure, and that's the Salvadoran people. Poverty is ugly, it doesn't look beautiful. And when these people get killed, and tortured — it is a people without human face.

Of the Servant of God it is said that those who pass by turn their heads away so as not to look at him face-to-face. Because in a way it is nauseating — to confront ourself with that humanity without human face. I also think that we turn our heads away because, if you look really face-to-face at the crucified peoples of this world, the question is obvious if we have a heart of flesh and not a heart of stone. Are we somehow responsible for that? What have we done?

Of the Servant it is said that he was called impious. What are Salvadorans called, those who do something for the poor, and some of the poor themselves—you know, communists, Marxists. Well, that's the modern word for impious.

Of the Servant it is said that he was buried among sinners, in other words, that not even in death did he have the minimum of dignity. You know how some of the Salvadoran people die — beheaded, tortured, without dignity. Some of them disappear, not even their corpses are found. So this wonderful western democratic civilization dares to do what so-called primitive people never

dared to do — to hide the corpse. At times they are found in clandestine cemeteries, no dignity in that. [. . .]

You have read the parable of the Good Samaritan. The Samaritan found a wounded man in the way and he was moved to compassion, to mercy, and he helped the wounded man. It's very interesting that no reason is given as to why he did that. Did he do that to fulfill the great command? No. Why, then? Because that's the primary human reaction to anybody in need.

What these Jesuits saw was not just a wounded man, but a whole people wounded on the street. And they tried simply to help them. [. . .]

This reaction of mercy and compassion is, I hope, to be human. And I don't take that for granted. It's not easy to be human. Maybe it's easier to be a Jesuit, or a Christian, or a university professor, because we know the rules of the game, basically. But it's not easy to be human, to consider, really, compassion and mercy as that which is first and that which is last.

Being university people, they used words and concepts to describe the type of mercy which is needed in El Salvador today — and that's justice. Justice is love for the majority of oppressed people. That's justice.

And they used the language of radically transforming structures, and at times they even used the language of revolution, which means revolving things [turning things around]. [. . .]

In a country like El Salvador, if we only train students, if we only produce professionals, administrators or lawyers, or economists, what do we do? If we only do that, we reinforce an unjust world, and unjust structures. If we only do that, the university is contributing to evil, to sin.

That was the beginning of the idea of a new university. If we should run a university as Jesuits and as Christians, then we have to re-think what a university is, to see what good it produces, that at least counterbalances the evil, and hopefully, produces more good than evil.

We believe that the Christian university is possible if this university tells the truth about our reality in a way which is appropriate to the university, so analyzing it, but [always based in] reality, reality. Through any of our courses, we have to bring to the fore the Salvadoran reality, and that is so painful. [There are] people who know everything about Napoleon or St. Augustine [. . .] but do not know how many people starve every day in their country — this basic fact of every day reality, of Salvadoran reality, they don't know. [. . .]

It is reality which demands what should be investigated. And then the social projection, when we try to project the university directly to the majorities, to the poor through our publications, public statements, and so on—that's what they tried to do.

Besides that, as you know in this world of ours, it is not only that the university or high school or whatever has to promote knowledge in the presence of ignorance. If that would be the only problem, the solution would be easy. We have to promote knowledge in the presence of life. In the world, there is a gigantic cover-up so that we don't see reality as it is, and as I usually say to my friends, Watergate and Irangate are minor cover-ups compared to the cover-up we exercise towards the whole world, to the Third World, so that peo-

ple in your country and in Europe don't know effectively that there is a Third World. [. . .]

[L]et's be honest, is there any hope for a country like El Salvador? How much more news of war, of atrocities? You know, the poor of the world have everything against them, by definition. Governments, oligarchies, the wealthy, the armies, most of the political parties, very often the churches, at times the universities, at times the theologians. Really, the poor have against them almost everything.

So, is there hope for El Salvador? Is there hope for those of us, really for you—does it make sense to go on working for El Salvador, for Guatemala, or South Africa? Well, I don't have a conceptual answer, but I want to end with this word. When I see a great love on earth, people who really love other people, when the American sisters, Archbishop Romero, and Jesuits, without being able to give a reason, [show us this great love], then I still have hope, and I still try to work and give the best of myself.

125. Don Samuel Ruiz García

Samuel Ruiz García (b. 1924) was appointed bishop of San Cristóbal de las Casas in 1959 and served until 2000. San Cristóbal is part of Chiapas, the southernmost state in Mexico, with a population (2003) of 4.2 million, 80 percent indigenous Maya from three major nations and languages. Forty percent of these Maya are malnourished, the highest rate of malnutrition in Mexico.

Ruiz was typical of Vatican appointments during the Cold War era. He had studied theology and scripture in Rome, been appointed rector of the seminary of León, Guanajuato, and was a thoughtful, bookish, conservative priest whose piety would make him the perfect prelate to thwart any inroads that communism might make in this impoverished and isolated state. His first pastoral letter was on the dangers of communism.

In order to communicate with his flock, this energetic and zealous prelate began to study their languages: Tzeltal, Tzotzil, and Ch'ol. The ability to actually engage his parishioners and the fresh air he experienced at the four sessions of Vatican II made of him a crusading bishop, passionately committed to the evangelization of the Amerindian by Amerindians themselves. He achieved this goal by initiating the diaconate movement—scores of Amerindian deacons catechizing their peers.

Source: Alberto Huerta, "Lawless Roads Still: The 'Red' Bishop of Chiapas," *Commonweal* 120, no. 22 (December 17, 1993), 12-14. © 1993 Commonweal Foundation, reprinted with permission.

In January 1994 an uprising took place in Chiapas—led by the Ejército Zapatista de Liberación Nacional (EZLN)—demanding first-class citizenship for the indigenous: housing, schools, access to medical care, roads, and also an end to the massive human rights violations by landowners supported by local officials of the PRI* (Partido Revolucionario Institucional—Institutional Revolutionary Party) and by members of the military. The rebellion was complicated because of tensions among the indigenous, some of whom supported the PRI because they had included some Amerindians in their favored circle. But the rebels saw the PRI as the primary cause of the miserable conditions suffered by the majority in Chiapas. An additional complication was precipitated by the San Cristóbal diocese's longtime commitment to the poor, which allowed the church to be accused of encouraging and collaborating with the rebels. Empowering the indigenous made Ruiz an enemy of the landowners and of local PRI officials, both of whom prevailed upon the apostolic delegate, Archbishop Girolamo Prigione, to harass Ruiz and force him to resign. Prigione's priority was to encourage the national PRI to repeal the anticlerical legislation arising out of the constitution of 1917 and to recognize the Roman Church as a legitimate institution (see reading 66). Ruiz's mediation between the EZLN and the federal government caused him difficulties with the Vatican, but he maintained his office, resigning (as canonically required) only upon his seventy-fifth birthday and despite enormous protests from the indigenous population. The Vatican accepted Ruiz's resignation posthaste.

The article below, a mixture of interview, historical background, and analysis, presents the reader with an excellent introduction to Chiapas, its contemporary status (1990s), and to the longest-tenured bishop in Mexican history. The author, Alberto Huerta (Ph.D., University of California at Santa Barbara), is associate professor in the department of languages at the University of San Francisco.

What does the article reveal about Ruiz, who (1) himself was on a hit list in 1992, who (2) dismisses talk of liberation theology, and (3) whose diocese houses some 40,000 Guatemalan refugees and (4) boasts 7,000 indigenous catechists working within their respective communities (the Tzeltal, Tzotzil, and Ch'ol). Explain the intimate connection among the four foregoing facts. What is so important about the last section of the article in which Huerta discusses Bartolomé de Las Casas, Graham Greene, Garrido Canabal, and Patrocinio Gonzáles Garrido? What point is Huerta trying to make? What relevance does it have to the thrust of this anthology? May not this interview be considered a direct response to López Trujillo's Declaration of Los Andes? (see reading 128)

Less than a year ago, the name of a Catholic bishop—Don Samuel Ruiz García of San Cristóbal de las Casas, in the southern Mexican state of Chiapas—appeared on a hit list. The assassination plot, traced to a handful of landowners, was foiled by the bishop's supporters, committed like him to defending the human rights of the indigenous peoples who make up 80 percent of the diocese. They are proud descendants of the once powerful Maya civilization. Though the police were given the names of the conspirators, Don Samuel did not file charges. It was characteristic of him, as I later learned, that he forgave the perpetrators and did not wish to "embarrass" those involved. A co-worker, Sister Lucy Jiménez, who is responsible for more than 40,000

---

*The PRI controlled Mexican politics from 1929 to 2000, when Vicente Fox of the PAN (Partido Acción Nacional—National Action Party) assumed the presidency. Fox's influence never penetrated into Chiapas.

Guatemalan refugees housed in the many refugee camps in the diocese, smiled when she said, "Someone would be gunning down Don Samuel, and he would most likely apologize to the assassin for something or other. He is like that, always careful not to offend a person's dignity." At the same time, however, mindful of pastoral implications, the diocese let it be known that the attempt constituted grave sin.

Some members of Don Samuel's flock say he has received thirty or so death threats since he was consecrated bishop by Pope John XXIII at age thirty-five in 1960. When I pressed him on the matter he shrugged his shoulders: "They are exaggerations." But the assassination plot was genuine, and many believe that serious threats against the bishop are routine.

The bishop is less casual about labels pinned on him by elements of the local press and government calling him a "Communist" and a "Red." They are calumnies, he says, attempts to defame his character and undermine his option for the poor. But such name-calling, said the diocesan vicar general, the Reverend Gonzalo Ituarte, O.P., is expected. "Anyone who is concerned for the poor, and especially the indigenous peoples, is labeled a 'Red.' You have to get used to that idea, if you are going to work here."

Close associates of Don Samuel point out that, despite his easy dismissal of the threats, for years he has had a CB radio in his car (which he drives himself); they say the purpose is to keep the chancery informed of his whereabouts as a means of lessening the possibility of his being martyred like San Salvador's Oscar Romero, or of becoming "*un desaparecido*." The bishop explains the matter more prosaically:

"Some years ago I realized that we work generally in the jungle and that priests, religious, and catechists were very isolated from each other. So I thought that CB radios might help to break this isolation. I put it off, however, because I did not want the government, or the local press, to say we were abetting any kind of guerrilla or insurgent groups, either from Guatemala or here in Chiapas. But now everyone has a CB, so I have encouraged our priests and pastoral agents to install them in their cars and jeeps."

At sixty-nine, Don Samuel does not like to aggravate or sensationalize the tense political and religious situations in his diocese. But in the early 1980s, when the Guatemalan-based helicopters harassed the refugee camps in Chiapas and Guatemalan soldiers crossed the border in search of political prisoners, he demanded that the Mexican government protect the refugees and grant them temporary asylum. Along with other Mexican bishops, he helped promulgate the 1984 episcopal statement, "On the Situation of the Refugees."

Five years after Don Samuel became head of the once powerful diocese of Chiapas, the Vatican divided it into three dioceses. "I was the bishop of all Chiapas," he says. "When it was divided into three dioceses, that of Tuxtla Gutiérrez (the capital of the state) and Tapachula on the Pacific Coast, I was left landlocked between the two."

Bishop Ruiz García is a product of the Second Vatican Council, and his diocese reflects its spirit. With eighty-eight priests, many religious women and men, and committed lay workers, he has been generous in delegating authority among a vicar general with seven associates, a chancellor, pastoral agents, and teams of catechists. He recently commented on these teams with childlike enthusiasm: "We have 7,000 indigenous catechists—Ch'ols, Tzotzils, and Tzeltals—working in these communities. They themselves are the autochthonous church of hope that *Gaudium et spes* eloquently affirmed when referring to the poor and those who suffer." [See *Gaudium*, nos. 58-62.]

Asked to elaborate, Don Samuel turned sober, even ponderous. "Beginning with Vatican II, the subsequent various bishops' conferences in Latin America, and the meeting in Santo Domingo last year with the pope, the church has recognized the particular spiritual richness inherent in the expression of faith found among the indigenous peoples of the Americas. Do not forget that it was the African bishops at the Second Vatican Council who demanded recognition for the cultural expression of their faith as a valid interpretation of Christianity. The church has found itself in the enviable position of fostering the discovery of a God incarnating himself daily in the lives of the poor and oppressed. The pope affirmed this spe-

ırch in his addresses recently in

.ıs hardly universal in Chiapas,
...ıc wounds of the conquest still fester in
memory. A colonial-era law in the city of San
Cristóbal required an *indio* to step off the sidewalk
into the street on encountering either a *ladino* [. . .
Hispanized Amerindian or mestizo] or a *coleto* (a
descendant of the conquerors). The law stayed on
the books until the early 1980s.

Yet it is in the heirs of the Mayas that Don
Samuel has invested his fullest confidence. Time
and again, in ordination ceremonies, he has reiterated, "The indigenous people with whom you
work will evangelize you, and not the other way
around." His latest pastoral letter, "In this Hour of
Grace," was issued in August to mark the visit of
Pope John Paul II to Mexico's indigenous peoples.

Don Samuel's respect and concern for the
indios extends beyond his own flock. I talk with
four Tzotzils and Tzeltals—a Catholic, a Presbyterian, an Evangelical, and a freethinker. All spoke
of the bishop with affection and with gratitude for
his defense of their human rights. I asked Don
Samuel whether he was concerned that his ecumenical spirit might lead to defections. "Interest-
ingly," he said, "that is one area where there is
general agreement. The Catholic church and the
mainline Protestant denominations are discovering their option for the poor by working with
them. We are not disturbed with other evangelical
efforts, so long as they address the real needs of the
people, who often are being deprived of their own
lands and harassed indiscriminately by the
landowners and the law enforcement authorities."

Don Samuel looked annoyed when I said I
thought I was hearing echoes of liberation theology, a sometime target of criticism from the Vatican. "You are confusing two different things," he
said. "We are not doing theology in the European
sense where you move through a deductive
process, going from the universal to the particular.
We find ourselves with many pastoral particu-
lars—the poor, the hungry, the oppressed, those
who suffer injustice. The conquest was an imposition of faith, yet every day we see the Incarnation
of Christ in the Americas.

"On judgment day we will not be asked about
our theological speculation. We will be judged on
what we did with those whom God entrusted to
our care. Our concern is pastoral. If theologians
put a label on what is done, that is speculation."

If the evangelical spirit of love and compassion
in the diocese reflects Bishop Ruiz García's commitment to Vatican II, it is also something of a
throwback to earlier times. The first bishop of
Chiapas was the legendary Dominican Bartolomé
de las Casas, who came here in 1545, and whose
presence still permeates like the dense fog that fills
the valleys around San Cristóbal at night. Las
Casas defended the *indios* against colonial oppression, not only in his well-known protest to the
Spanish court but also on the scene—at times
excommunicating *ladinos* and *coletos* who mistreated the indigenous people. I learned from an
American working in Chiapas of a priest who followed in the Las Casas spirit when he refused the
Eucharist to several wealthy women as they
approached for Communion. The night before at
a fiesta he had overheard them speaking about
recruiting their Indian maids to initiate their sons
in sexual adventure. Later he met with the indignant women privately to educate them in the
church's respect for the *indio*. Such pastoral
courage seems common in the diocese.

But life in Chiapas is hardly idyllic. When Graham Greene trekked here on a mule in the spring
of 1938, he was investigating the state of Catholicism ten years after the blood bath of priests and
nuns that resulted from the Mexican government's persecution of the church, an experience
that gave birth to *The Lawless Roads* and *The
Power and the Glory*. Greene also discovered an
interesting syncretism of magic and dogma, and
encountered an emotional depth of faith he had
not previously known. At the same time he
detected a Kafkaesque darkness in the continuing
struggle between faith and ideology, which
included the destruction of churches and the
burning of statues in neighboring Villahermosa
under the ruthless [Governor] Garrido Canabal.

As late as September 1991, the conflict flared
again when a pastor, Father Joel Padrón of Simo-
jovel, was arrested without a warrant and detained
in the state capital, Tuxtla Gutiérrez. The governor—Patrocino González Garrido, a descendant

of the infamous Garrido Canabal—had approved the arrest. The pastor was accused of inciting the *indios* to repossess land to which they claimed title. Immediately Don Samuel, his vicar general, and the diocesan human rights commission denounced the arrest as a flagrant act of oppression directed against the church. Finally, when more than 4,000 *indios* marched on Tuxtla Gutiérrez, Fr. Joel was released. In an irony Greene would have appreciated, the Salinas government then appointed González Garrido minis-

ter of the interior, a post that endows him with considerable power over the Mexican police. Chiapanecos wait to see what vengeance the new minister may exercise against the church and the poor in San Cristóbal and elsewhere.

Don Samuel remains vigilant; the diocesan human rights commission carefully documents every instance of abuse. If that makes him a "Red," it is not because of ideology but because he follows in the long line of Catholics who have risked martyrdom in Mexico.

126. Until I Was Forty Years Old I Never Spoke of Liberation Theology

"You see, as a last resort, until I was 40 years old I never spoke of liberation theology and I think I was Christian. If I could be Christian before liberation theology, I hope to be able to be Christian after liberation theology." (Gustavo Gutiérrez)

For those still perplexed about the nature of liberation theology, this interview (1994) given by its "father," almost a quarter century after the appearance of his book A Theology of Liberation, *will (1) put that phenomenon in context, (2) clarify its point of departure, (3) clarify its relation to Christian commitment, and (4) explain the manner in which it confronts new and contemporary assaults on the poor. Explain each consideration. What does Gutiérrez mean when he says "before . . . [the poor] didn't exist"? (See reading 102 for a definition of neo-liberal.)*

What is the current state of Liberation Theology? How is it situated within the neoliberal context? Can one say that it has been or is being overcome by other theological currents? How would a liberation theologian analyze the 'New World Order' and the perspective from Latin America?

We asked these questions recently to the founder of Liberation Theology, Peruvian priest Gustavo Gutiérrez. What follows comes from this interview. [. . .]

"Well, as is normal, there are important facts that any reflection on the poor must take into account. But they do not imply a very radical change in Liberation Theology, because the poverty of the large majority of Latin Americans, disgracefully, has not changed; indeed it has got-

ten worse. Therefore, there is no radical change. While there are poor people, there will be Liberation Theology. But we have to take into account the new facts of the world economy." [. . .]

"The word accommodate can have negative connotations, a little bit pejorative. But if what it means is that those who defend the poor, those who struggle for justice in Latin America, have to take into account the facts described, if they call this accommodation, then of course there is.

But it would be absurd if, faced with a new political and economic panorama, those who defend and fight for justice do not keep these things in mind, this new situation. That would make them completely ineffective. In this sense, then yes. I would prefer not to use the term accommodate." [. . .]

SOURCE: Interview of Gustavo Gutiérrez by Paulino Montijo, quoted in "Liberation Theology in the Neoliberal Context," *Latin American Documentation* 25, no. 2 (November/December 1994): 17-21. Originally published in Paulino Montejo, "La teología de la liberación en el contexto neoliberal," *Presencia Ecumenica* [Venezuela] (June 1994), 32-34.

"No [Gutiérrez responds to the suggestion that the historical and socio-political method and mediations of Liberation Theology continue to be the same], this is not necessarily so. I believe that the whole idea of science, and the social sciences, which try to be a science, although poorly but nevertheless do try, is to change. A science changes, it evolves by hypothesis. The physics of Galileo is not the physics of Newton, and that of Newton is not that of Einstein. That is, physics changes its hypotheses. And sociology and the social sciences have the right to change their hypotheses in accordance with reality, in order to interpret the situation of poverty in Latin America.

Liberation Theology has not elaborated the social sciences, it finds them in place. And we have to follow the course of the evolution of the social sciences to better understand reality. Besides, in Liberation Theology, even though we were aware from the start of the psychological, cultural and anthropological reality of Latin Americans, we did not study them in depth. This has come about in the last 10 or 12 years." [. . .]

"I would say that the framework of Liberation Theology then was the reality of poverty and the search for its causes. And, in accordance with the social sciences of the era, the main cause was dependence.

Dependency theory today has changed greatly. The dependence of the poor countries is greater nowadays in some aspects, such as technology, and is much greater with respect to the rich countries. This is what is important to us. And, of course, if there is dependency, there are diverse interests. This can be analyzed in the conflict, and ultimately, between social classes, but also at the racial and cultural level. And this is from the start of Liberation Theology, at least in what I have written." [. . .]

"I believe that people think that when something is not on the front pages of the newspapers, it is a thing of the past. And I am glad that Liberation Theology is no longer on the front pages of the newspapers, because we can't do our job then. [. . .]

I think that it is not possible to determine the opinion of Rome from one or two persons. Rome is a very complex world, where many things exist,

I sincerely believe that this is an excellent moment for the perspective opened by Liberation Theology. Because I believe that the poor are more aware of their capabilities every day, of their strength as the poor, as belonging to a culture, indigenous for example, or belonging to the female gender. All this gives them a great strength. I think that today Liberation Theology has a vigor that it did not have 5 or 10 years ago." [. . .]

"I believe that Indian theology, black theology and women's theology, to cover a few different aspects, are deeper expressions of the faith lived by the poor.

From the start, Liberation Theology proposed reflection on practice in the light of faith as a method to be used. The practice, daily life, experience and traditions of the indigenous cultures are confronted by the Christian faith. In that case, they are deepenings. One cannot speak of inclusions as if they were from far away. It is a deepening and enriching of Liberation Theology. And besides, one must not exaggerate the role of Liberation Theology. It is important and we can talk if it is present, if it has disappeared or if another theology is added. The faith of the poor on this continent, their struggle for liberation, is more than Liberation Theology and Indian Theology. The existence of the indigenous people, their contact with nature, with God and with their traditions are much more important. Theology is secondary. To reflect on these realities is much more important.

I often answer questions by saying: You see, as a last resort, until I was 40 years old I never spoke of Liberation Theology and I think I was Christian. If I could be Christian before Liberation Theology, I hope to be able to be Christian after Liberation Theology.

Liberation Theology, Indian Theology, Black Theology, Women's Theology, are not articles of faith. They are intellectual means of analyzing a reality that is really what is important, to be Christian, to be a follower of Jesus and to be a witness to the resurrection." [. . .]

"I said that Latin America is poorer than before. This varies from country to country. It has caused a major crisis, as could be expected. But this crisis has not come from Liberation Theology. But I also believe that the people have more hope. There is a crisis. But why is there a crisis? Why is there a crisis in what we call human life; why are there adolescence or youth crises? Why? Why does the adolescent exist? Why does the youth exist? Why wasn't there a crisis of the poor before? Because they didn't exist. I believe that the poor of today have personality. They struggle because they now have a presence they did not have before. In other words, if there is a crisis today it is because the movement of the poor is stronger in Latin America." [...]

"The 'New World Order' of today is dominated by a liberal or neoliberal mentality. From the Christian side, for example from the side of the Catholic bishops in Santo Domingo, there have been very strong criticisms of neoliberalism. Because neoliberalism tends to exclude from its projects and plans a part of the population that it considers useless, unnecessary to economic development. This is why we talk about the excluded so much today. There is a sector of economy that it is not interested in, not even to exploit it. For this reason, from the human and Christian point of view, we cannot accept an order that is based on the adoration of money, of profit." [...]

["]I do not know what is going to happen in the future. I don't know it. I can say what I want to happen. I can also say that, contrary to what some people say, I believe that Latin America, as well as the Catholic Church, is going through an interesting, rich and vital period. I know the people love to cry and complain about how bad things are. But, truthfully, if we compare how things were 30 years ago in Latin America and the church to things today, we find that we are in a much more interesting situation today.

When I say rich, I do not mean easy. It is very difficult. We know many people who have given their lives for the poor. But I believe that there is a great and important future waiting."

127. The Real Core of Liberation Theology

Jon Sobrino, S.J. (b. 1938), is a Spanish Basque and longtime citizen of El Salvador, to which he made his permanent commitment in the early 1960s, having earned a doctorate in theology in Germany. He has used his expertise in theology to develop a Christology relevant to the oppressed and suffering poor he knows so well from his parish work and university research.

The brief passage below is taken from the final pages of his Jesus in Latin America: The Significance for Faith and Christology *(1982). Perhaps this excerpt could have been placed at the beginning of this section because it makes clear the starting premise of all who may be labeled practitioners of liberation theology. But it also makes clear the ending premise. When the passage is understood, it should startle Christian believers because it clearly differentiates their motivation from that of humane, progressive, or secular humanist activists. Why? What does Sobrino mean by the important first sentence of the penultimate paragraph?*

I am well aware that the situation in El Salvador and throughout Central America is much more a replica of Good Friday than of Easter Sunday and that my theologizing may therefore seem to be making an Easter virtue of a Good Friday necessity, so to speak. Despite all, however, I end where I began: The resurrection of the one who was crucified is *true*. Let it be foolishness, as it was for the Corinthians. But without this foolishness, because it is true—or without this truth, because it is foolish—the resurrection of Jesus will only be one more symbol of hope in survival after death that

SOURCE: Jon Sobrino, *Jesus in Latin America* (Maryknoll, N.Y.: Orbis Books, 1987), 158. Reprinted by permission of Orbis Books.

human beings have designed in their religions or philosophies. It will not be the Christian symbol of hope.

This *truth* is still being historically repeated. An emphasis on the crucified one is not at the service of a conceptual dialectic. It issues from an observation of the historical reality of the crucified. When a pastoral minister in a base community in El Salvador, one suffering extreme hardship in the form of repression, was asked what his community was doing as church, he answered simply, "Keeping up the hope of the suffering. How? We read the prophets, and the Passion of Jesus. So we hope for the resurrection."

No one hopes for the resurrection like the crucified do. They sustain their hope by recalling the life and death of Jesus, seeking to reproduce them actively, or by suffering passively the lot that likens them to Jesus as the disfigured servant of Yahweh. Paradoxically, this gives them hope.

From the midst of history's crucified—without any compact or compromise with their crosses—Jesus' resurrection must be proclaimed. In those crucified, Jesus is present today. In service to them, the lordship of Jesus becomes present today. In the stubborn refusal to strike a pact with their crosses, and in the stubborn, persistent quest for liberation from these crosses, unshakable hope becomes present *in actu*, becomes present historically.

Now we understand a little better what it means to speak of Jesus' resurrection. Our understanding will enable us to correspond, in history, to the reality of the risen one.

PART XVIII
Critiques of Liberation Theology

In his opening address to the Fourth General Conference of Latin American Bishops (Santo Domingo, October 1992), Pope John Paul II unequivocally reaffirmed the church's "preferential option on behalf of the poor" and said that "the genuine praxis of liberation must always be inspired by the doctrine of the church as set forth in the two instructions by the Congregation for the Doctrine of Faith."

The famous "Instruction on Certain Aspects of the 'Theology of Liberation,'" issued on August 6, 1984, by Joseph Cardinal Ratzinger, prefect of the Congregation, was the more definitive of these two instructions and initiated a worldwide debate not yet exhausted.

Despite misleading accounts in the world press that depicted the Vatican as irrevocably hostile toward liberation theology, the latter remained very much alive, its advocates making use of the Vatican's admonitions and also of criticisms from other sectors of the church, including practitioners of liberation theology themselves, to make it more effective. In an interview a month after the "Instruction" was published, Gustavo Gutiérrez said that "authoritative sources have explicitly rejected the possibility of any condemnation [of liberation theology]; Cardinal Ratzinger has been very clear about this in his 'Instruction' which he views as one contribution to the dialogue on this delicate topic."

Alfonso Cardinal López Trujillo's failure to persuade the Puebla conference (1979) to condemn liberation theology constituted a major landmark in the church's continuing attempt to come to grips with the political, economic, and social realities of Latin America. The fact that Leonardo Boff, Brazil's leading liberation theologian and an innovative thinker in the field of ecclesiology, was the only major liberation theologian driven from the priesthood by the continued coolness of the Vatican, suggests that the sector of the church that adheres to this understanding of the Christian mission is fully committed to developing a theology that both remains within the church's guidelines and also responds to the realities it encounters within Latin American society.[1]

---

1. Alfred T. Hennelly, S.J., ed., *Santo Domingo and Beyond: Documents and Commentaries from the Fourth General Conference of Latin American Bishops* (Maryknoll, N.Y.: Orbis, 1993), 50-51.

128. A View from the Hierarchy

Alfonso López Trujillo (1935-2008) is from a staunch Catholic family, and his father was a high official in the national government of Colombia. Alfonso was ordained a priest in Rome in 1960 and earned his doctorate in philosophy from the Angelicum. He returned to Colombia, where he rose rapidly in the hierarchy, culminating in his appointment as archbishop of Medellín by John Paul II in 1979 and as Cardinal in 1983. Previously he had been elected general secretary of CELAM (Conference of Latin American Bishops) by his confreres. The pope appointed him president of the Pontifical Council for the Family in 1990.

The pastoral constitution of Vatican Council II, "On the Church in the Modern World," Gaudium et spes (1965), rejected the ethos adopted by Catholicism as a response to the Reformation and to the secularism arising out of the Renaissance, scientific revolution, and Enlightenment. That ethos, post-Tridentine Catholicism, viewed the world as a snare and threat that should be kept at arm's length, and culminated in Pius IX's "Syllabus of Errors" (1864), which strongly condemned most of the characteristics—political, cultural, and intellectual—of the modern world.

Liberation theology was being formulated at the same time that Gaudium et spes *was adopted and shares the same affirmations that the Christian church must interact with the world and that it has much to learn from and much to teach that world. Concepts such as participatory democracy, political equality, women's rights, and the idea that slavery, economic poverty, illiteracy, torture, religious intolerance, and disease are evils to be combatted were developed by the secular humanists of the European Enlightenment and were only hesitantly embraced by the church.*

The document below, "Declaration of Los Andes" (1985), authored by López Trujillo and signed by twenty-three laymen and clergy, is a vigorous attack on liberation theology, which it portrays as a movement confronting and eradicating social ills rather than emphasizing and strengthening man's liberation from sin under the auspices of the hierarchy of the church.

The post–Vatican II church had called for Christians to be actively involved in the creation of a more just world, which would mean engaging their secular "sisters and brothers" with their Christian understanding of justice and charity. Both López Trujillo and proponents of liberation theology recognized this call for a renewed understanding of the Christian vocation. But López Trujillo's reading of that vocation does not make it central and allows only for reform of existing structures, while that of liberation theology makes it central and demands non-violent but radical or revolutionary change.

Would the numbered paragraphs in the declaration indeed be read the same way by both López Trujillo and any of the liberation theologians discussed earlier? (See no. 9, paragraph 2; first sentence of no. 11; numbers 13, 14, and 15.) What passages exaggerate or caricature the approach taken by liberation theology? Which are merely rhetorical or tend toward the libelous? Is the editors' treatment of this declaration unfair? Explain.

SOURCE: "Communio (Latin American Edition): 'Declaration of Los Andes' (July 1985)," in *Liberation Theology: A Documentary History*, ed. Alfred T. Hennelly, S.J. (Maryknoll, N.Y.: Orbis Books, 1990), 444-50, passim. Reprinted by permission of Orbis Books.

1. We the undersigned are Christian pastors and laity with training in philosophy, theology, and the social sciences. [...]

Our purpose was to investigate the response which the so-called theologies of liberation have made to the serious challenge to the Christian conscience created by the misery and marginalization of vast numbers of the people of Latin America. [...]

2. The common denominator which unites us, which led to our meeting, and which dominated our lengthy meetings is essentially the following: complete fidelity to the gospel, as it is professed by the church's magisterium, by the social teaching of the church, and by the content of the Instruction *Libertatis Nuntius* ["Instruction on Certain Aspects of the 'Theologies of Liberation'"]. [...]

4. The theology of liberation, as the authors just mentioned understand it, claims to be a "new way of doing theology" from the perspective of "the oppressed" and takes a certain interpretation of liberating praxis as its source and as the ultimate criterion of theological truth. This requires an essentially political reading of the word of God, which ends up interpreting the whole of Christian existence, faith, and theology in a political key. This radical politicization is aggravated by the uncritical use of a rationalist biblical hermeneutic, which ignores the basic exegetical criteria of tradition and of the magisterium. [...]

5. (b) In no case can praxis be the first or foundational act of theological reflection. Praxis and experience always arise from a definite and concrete historical situation. Experiences like this can help theologians adapt their interpretation of Scripture to their own time. But prior to praxis is the truth the divine master has entrusted to us. [...]

6. If the above is valid for any type of praxis, it becomes much more problematic in the concrete case of certain theologies of liberation, since their "liberating praxis" acquires a meaning that is clearly derived from Marxism. [...]

7. Theology can and should make use of the social sciences. However, on the one hand it cannot accept the subordination of theological discourse to the discourse of any positive science. On the other hand, it cannot concede scientific valid-ity to the Marxist analysis of society or to the dialectical interpretation of history, since their ideological character is evident. Finally, it must be denied that the Christian people in the name of some science are forced to work in a single socio-political movement, since this ignores their right to legitimate pluralism in temporal matters, where Christian faith does not require only one solution. [...]

9. Jesus Christ is presented as the "subversive from Nazareth," who entered into and deliberately committed himself to the "class struggle" of his time. His life and liberating death are seen as simply that of a martyr for the people, who was crushed by the ruling Judeo-Roman establishment. This is undoubtedly an attempt to manifest the historical, social, and even political dimension of the life of Jesus. It is certain that the Lord did move within the social context of his own time and place. The portrait, however, of a "historical Jesus" who died for the poor classes and against the rich ones is not drawn from the New Testament but rather from an a priori dialectic of conflict, which is profoundly at odds with the faith of the church on fundamental issues. For one thing, the mystery of the incarnate word and of the divine nature of Christ is, if not openly denied, at least so obscured and distorted that in this interpretation the church can no longer recognize its own faith as it was defined in the early councils. Furthermore, the sacrificial and salvific dimension of the Lord's death is dissolved in favor of a political interpretation of his crucifixion, thus bringing into question the salvific meaning of the entire economy of redemption. The profound mystery of the passion and death of Jesus and the unfathomable depths of the love of God the Father revealed therein are thus obscured, as are the radical meaning of sin and the dignity proper to human beings as objects of this boundless divine love.

It is only in the light of these mysteries as proclaimed by the faith of the church that we understand the full meaning of the redemption— namely, that Christ liberated us fundamentally from the radical slavery of sin, and by virtue of this his liberation should extend itself effectively in the effort to remove economic, social, and political forms of slavery, which are derived from sin. [...]

11. The evangelization of the poor is a messianic sign which looks to liberation from all the sufferings and enslavements of human existence. But this statement has on occasion been interpreted in a unilateral way, which distorts its biblical meaning. Poverty is reduced to its material aspect and even more is interpreted by means of a sociology of conflict. The poor are thus identified with the proletariat and are viewed through the lens of class struggle, which involves inevitable partisanship. The result is a kind of theological reflection and ecclesial preaching centered almost exclusively on socio-economic questions, at times bitterly self-seeking and even more frequently overlooking or forgetting essential dimensions of faith and basic features of human experience. We have observed the uneasiness of many persons who feel abandoned and ignored in their aspirations and religious needs because of a mistaken interpretation of the option for the poor. [. . .]

13. [. . .] In communion with the church's hierarchy, we believe that authentic liberation is based on "the truth about Jesus the savior, the truth about the church, and the truth about humankind and its dignity" (Instruction, XI, 5), and that this liberation must be understood in a context that is at the same time perennial, dynamic, and capable of renewing the teaching of the church, especially its social teaching. [. . .]

14. [W]e state that the social teaching offers principles capable of effective guidance in the task of building a society based on justice and solidarity. An adequate solution to the present problems of Latin America will not be achieved by simplistic declarations based on Marxist ideology, but rather by vigorous action based on careful analyses of the multiple causes of the poverty of so many individuals and families. [. . .]

15. Every genuine theology must incorporate this joyous and tremendous truth: what is at stake in our historical existence is eternal life, inasmuch as the total and definitive liberation of the human person will only take place in the consummation of the kingdom in heaven and in the vision of God face to face, to which all of us are summoned. [. . .] [I]t is only in this truth that the supreme dignity of the human person shines forth, that person created in the image of God and summoned to sonship with God; it is this alone that grounds the ethical imperative that never allows the human person to be considered a mere object at the mercy of powerful interests or any kind of ideology.

129. A View from the Academy

David Stoll (b. 1952), a U.S. anthropologist specializing in Central America, takes a highly critical view of the "liberal" consensus about Latin America held by the majority of U.S. university professors who specialize in disciplines that deal with Latin America. The specific comments he makes in the excerpt below on liberation theology and his direct and lively style of delivery are both typical of his approach and apt as criticism.

Note the positive contributions he recognizes in liberation theology before he tackles its negatives. What are those positives for Stoll? The excerpts from Gutiérrez (reading 114) do not explicitly mention "consciousness raising" of the poor majority as a major aspect of liberation theology, although it is implied in the excerpts (especially in the Conclusion) and made explicit elsewhere in his writing. Where have the practitioners of liberation theology gone wrong, according to Stoll? Note his astute analyses of the differing methods by which the poor resist oppression and the consequences that follow therefrom, neither of which he claims are recognized by advocates of liberation theology. Why are the "conservative evangelicals" so successful in reaching the oppressed despite their initial indifference toward the

SOURCE: David Stoll, *Is Latin America Turning Protestant? The Politics of Evangelical Growth* (Berkeley: University of California Press, 1990), 310-14. Copyright © 1990 The Regents of the University of California. Reprinted by permission of University of California Press and David Stoll.

changes so desperately needed in Latin America? (For earlier evangelical Pentecostal perspectives, see readings 93-97. For contemporary perspectives, see readings 148 and 151.) On serious reflection, may Stoll's remarks be considered "pot shot"? The question arises whether specific examples actually exist of this "leap from a religious base into a political disaster" or "safely situated intellectuals hav[ing] had an outsized role in its [liberation theology's] production."

This study has not made a thorough case for why liberation theology may be better at filling faculties, bookshelves, and graves than churches. [. . .]

[I]f I have chosen worst-case situations, they should provide warnings for elsewhere. In revolutionary Nicaragua, the Christians who have identified most strongly with the Sandinistas apparently have not managed to appeal to the poor as effectively as more conservative evangelicals have. In highland Ecuador, the social activism of the most progressive Catholic diocese seems to have been outmatched by an evangelical movement. In Guatemala, my account suggests, certain Catholic clergy practicing liberation theology were partly responsible for the military's identification of church organizations as subversive, which led to a wave of terror from which the Catholic Church may never recover its former stature.

Even in each of these cases, liberation theology could be interpreted in a more favorable light. Perhaps I have placed too much emphasis on the contradictions involved, while discounting the struggle to overcome them. But liberation theology has achieved such paradigmatic status in thinking about the politics of religion in Latin America that I think my pot-shot approach is needed, at least temporarily, to call attention to the possibility that evangelical Protestantism is more successful on the popular level.

I do not wish to deny that liberation theology represents a courageous reformation in church life. It cannot be dismissed as a clerical maneuver to regain popular support or a Marxist front as enemies do. To the contrary, its critiques of church life are penetrating even the evangelical camp, where they could become influential. No one has written its obituary: much more is to be expected of its capacity for self-criticism and change. But while liberation theology is a vital creation of the oppositional culture of clergy and university, its reception among the poor tends to be problematical. In practice, moreover, it has been forced to carry the highest hopes in the most hopeless situations. It has been drawn into merciless crossfires. And in certain situations, it seems to encourage the growth of its nemesis, right-wing fundamentalism. [. . .]

Only in Nicaragua, under the Sandinistas, has liberation theology come to power, so to speak. Now that a new society seems within reach, does a practice of consciousness-raising and dissent become the established faith? At least a few activists talked about maintaining critical distance from the Sandinista state, but others were acting like "court prophets" for it. Against the onslaughts of foreign and domestic enemies, such Christians felt a duty to defend the revolution. But by joining the Sandinista power structure and defending its unpopular measures, they risked distancing themselves from the Nicaraguan people and discrediting their talk of a better world.

The central exercise in liberation theology, consciousness-raising, raises a tangle of issues. To begin with, there is the risk of failing to speak to the actual needs of the poor, as opposed to idealized versions of those needs. Liberation theology endeavors to come out of the day-to-day experience of the poor: when successful, maybe it does. But it also originated in the crisis of the Catholic Church and its attempts to recover a popular base. Despite the struggle to build a grass-roots church, the prophets of the movement tend to be religious professionals with professional interests, a fact dramatized by their disputes with offended laities and anxious hierarchies. Consciousness-raising is supposed to be dialectical, generated out of the interaction between organizer and people. But it began by defining the poor in terms of what they lacked, then presuming that they should become something else through pedagogy.

Such presumptions often become apparent in collisions with popular religion, the folk Catholic traditions that clergy left, right, and middle have often tried to suppress or reform. Under the usual conditions faced by the poor, in which open dissent is followed by punishment swift and sure, folk practices have permitted expression of popular aspirations in ambiguous but sometimes strategic ways. What outsiders interpret as resignation can serve as a protective mantle for vital traditions of cultural resistance. Expressions of subordination mingle with expressions of defiance, in complex forms of ritual communication between dominant and subordinate social classes which, over time, may redefine relations between the two. Practitioners of liberation theology differed widely on how to deal with the dilemmas posed by popular religion, such as its frequent reinforcement of exploitive patrón-client ties. But they often tried to undermine such traditions, for representing a religion of domination, with the result that they alienated the people they were trying to organize.

Perhaps the basic difficulty is that a message centering around "liberation" contradicts how the poor usually prefer to deal with oppressive situations: a subtle combination of deference, foot-dragging, and evasion, as James Scott has pointed out in his work on everyday forms of peasant resistance. The kinds of defiance liberation theology tends to encourage, in contrast, have been suicidal in many times and places. Given this fact of life out in the hard places where liberation theology must prove itself, the frequent assumption of the need for revolutionary upheaval indicates that more or less safely situated intellectuals have had an outside role in its production.

Encouraging the poor to insist on their rights in explicit new ways meant throwing away the protective cloak surrounding religious activities. It meant forsaking the traditional function of religion as a sanctuary from oppression. Once landlords or the state were ready to retaliate, liberation theology demanded life-and-death commitment from the people who were supposed to be liberated. Christianity is about sacrifice, of course. But it is not about putting other people on the line. When situations polarized into violence, outsiders promoting liberation theology tended to be forced out, leaving behind their local allies to relearn an old lesson about the states' ability to put down unrest. One martyrdom after another might seem to justify armed struggle as the only way forward, but most revolutionary uprisings are unsuccessful. It was so easy to leap from a religious base into a political disaster.

In Central America, as revolutionary conflict turned into a war of attrition with no end in sight, conservative evangelicals appealed to the traditional resignation of the poor in ways liberation theology could not. However much liberation theology spoke to aspirations for a better life, the escapism of the evangelical message was more compatible with the usual posture of the poor— fatalistic acceptance of the constraints on their continuous negotiation for survival. Under such circumstances, it was easy for liberation theology to fall out of touch with the people it claimed to represent.

When the revolutionary movement was shattered in Guatemala, evangelicals took the opportunity to invite survivors into their churches. In contrast to liberation theology, evangelicals offered to improve one's life through a simple personal decision, to surrender to Christ. That sounded easier than overturning the social order. Evangelicals provided an ideology, not just of political resignation as so often noted, but of personal improvement. They told the poor not to preoccupy themselves with large events they could not influence in direct, obvious ways. Instead, a person was to concentrate on what he could change, such as his drinking habits. Evangelicals also captured the poor emotionally, in ways highly politicized Christians often failed to.

130. A View from an Activist

Phillip Berryman, a former Catholic priest who served in Panama (1965-1973) and as representative of the American Friends Service Committee in Central America (1976-1980), is thoroughly knowledgeable about the actors on all sides of religious issues in contemporary Latin America. The following excerpts from Religion in the Megacity: Catholic and Protestant Portraits from Latin America *(1996) offer a different perspective on the defects of liberation theologians, some of whom he believes do not live up to their commitment to "critical reflection on praxis." What are the four realities that Berryman says are overlooked by liberation theologians? (He numbers three realities himself, but precedes them by mentioning—almost humorously—yet another important oversight.)*

Latin American feminist theologians frankly admit that they are behind North American feminists. Public discussion of reproductive matters is stifled, not because Latin American women are so different from European and North American women, but because of male power in society, buttressed by periodic ecclesiastical intervention. If there is a distinctive "Latin American perspective" on women's issues, it is difficult to discern, largely because Latin American women—poor and well off, scholars and barrio leaders, nuns and factory workers—are not free to express it. [. . .]

Approximately twenty years ago, the major Latin American male theologians were at least forced to recognize sexism as a particular form of oppression. There is little evidence, however, that they have internalized the critique of patriarchy. In this respect they are little different from other Latin American male intellectuals who show few signs that they have been challenged by the feminist critique. [. . .]

[S]ome of the elements of a Latin American feminist theology [. . .] would take into account women's experience, and in particular that of their bodily experience; their roles as nurturers, breadwinners, and community leaders; abuse against them from rape and domestic violence; their limited presence in public life; and their own meanings of God, cosmos, and human relationships. There were many constraints, however. Forces in society ranging from traditional elites,

the military, and the Catholic hierarchy were largely successful in muzzling public discussion of reproductive issues. Most trained women theologians were either members of religious orders or worked in Catholic institutions, particularly universities, where they enjoyed nothing like the academic freedom found in Catholic universities elsewhere. Nevertheless, a Latin American feminist theology seems destined to be expressed more and more forcefully in the coming years.

A second area largely overlooked in liberation theology is the urban character of Latin American society. One could read dozens of volumes by liberation theologians without realizing that Latin America has made the "urban leap" in the last generation or so. It might be argued that the theologians are not writing about either rural or urban people as such, but in fact one of the volumes in the Theology and Liberation series is entitled "The Indian Face of God" and is composed of case studies of inculturation of Christian faith in indigenous societies. Another, entitled "Theology of Land," is a theological reflection of church involvement in the struggles of the landless, particularly in Brazil. Surely the experience in urban shantytowns (people struggling to survive, to create a community and family life, to deal with social polarization and build base communities) could have been the source of important theological reflections.

Indeed, in *The God of Christians*, the Chilean

SOURCE: Phillip Berryman, *Religion in the Megacity: Catholic and Protestant Portraits from Latin America* (Maryknoll, N.Y.: Orbis Books, 1996), 158-60. Reprinted by permission of Orbis Books.

theologian Ronaldo Muñoz does reflect urban Latin America. For example, he outlines how the image of God changes when peasants migrate to the city, based no doubt on his own decades of experience in the shanty towns of Santiago. Over a decade ago, Clodovis Boff published a theological journal on his pastoral work in the rubber gathering area in the state of Acre near the Bolivian border (where Chico Mendes later rose to fame and was murdered). Some of Ivone Gebara's essays reflect her life in Camaragibe (near Recife). What I am suggesting is that it is time for theologians to write out of experiences, such as those of Matías Camuñas. Pablo Richard has recently spoken of a "breakdown" in cities which "need to be cleansed of the poor. In several countries (e.g., Colombia) death squads maraud nightly, killing off street children, tramps, beggars, prostitutes, homosexuals, the unemployed, the homeless, etc." He goes on to say that the change in the situation of the poor—from being exploited to being excluded and regarded as redundant—challenges liberation theology "radically at every level—terminology and world view, commitment and pastoral practice, as well as moral and spiritual depth."

A related matter is that of the emerging popular culture, which is urban and very much influenced by international (U.S.-led) consumer culture. Minutes after landing in Brazil (and for a few weeks afterward), I heard the piped-in voice of a current hit by Whitney Houston. One finds virtually no sensitivity to this culture in the major theologians, who are quite ready to endorse the need for "inculturation" vis-à-vis indigenous cultures (and those of African origin). Again, Comblin at least puts his finger on matters when he says that in the 1970s it was hoped that popular religiosity could be the link between base communities and the masses. In fact, however, "traditional Catholic religiosity, traditional Catholic customs and practices are also rapidly disappearing. The 1980s were decisive. During that decade television spread everywhere and has gone into almost every house. Today television takes up the time that used to be reserved for traditional culture, for religion, prayers, processions, saints' feasts, and so forth. What is left is a much fuzzier reservoir of religiosity, one almost without beliefs and with few religious practices. The new popular masses have abandoned or are abandoning the traditional ceremonies and religious customs. That is why they are predisposed to any other kind of new religion." [. . .]

[O]ne might read a dozen volumes by liberation theologians without encountering the word "television," let alone a discussion of its implications for today. The same might be true of many North Atlantic systematic theologians, but they are less inclined to claim that their theology arises out of practice.

PART XIX

Diverse Responses to and by the Catholic Church

The final two decades of the twentieth century in Latin America witnessed the same phenomena of change and continuity as do all eras in modern history. In these twenty years, rebellion and revolutionary spirit faded, although resistance to oppression, marginalization, and environmental degradation continued by other means. Cuban president Fidel Castro's addresses, separated by the two decades, may be perceived as emblematic of this era.

131. Fidel on the Church

Fidel Castro Ruz (b. 1926), son of a prosperous hacendado *of Oriente province, is undoubtedly the best-read* guerrillero *and maximum leader in all revolutionary history (see his extraordinary "History Will Absolve Me" speech [1954] in his own defense, written in prison without library privileges). He presided in 1959 over the consolidation of the Cuban revolution which was far advanced by the time of this speech (1980) celebrating the Cuban national holiday (July 26). Castro had just returned from Nicaragua where he had gone to help celebrate the first anniversary of the triumph (1979) of the Sandinista revolution. The speech concentrated on Cuba's economic and international situation and had few theoretical or philosophical concerns, so his lengthy comments on religion were frankly unexpected. What do these enthusiastic and even emotional comments on Christianity in general and the Catholic Church in particular indicate about Castro, Cuba, and this historic time, the late 1970s and early '80s?*

Source: Fidel Castro, *Fidel Castro Speeches: Cuba's Internationalist Foreign Policy, 1975-80*, ed. Michael Taber (New York: Pathfinder Press, 1981), 320-21. Copyright © 1981 by Pathfinder Press. Reprinted by permission.

I also met with a large number of priests and progressive religious leaders who are on the side of the revolution and give it their full support. [*Applause*]

Nicaragua is a country where religious feelings go far deeper than they did in Cuba; therefore, the support given to the revolution by those religious sectors is very important.

In Chile once, and also in Jamaica, we spoke of the strategic alliance between Christians and Marxist-Leninists. [*Applause*] If the revolution in Latin America were to take on an antireligious character, it would split the people. In our country, the Church was, generally speaking, the Church of the bourgeoisie, of the wealthy, of the landowners. This is not the case in many countries in Latin America, where religion and the Church have deep roots among the people. The reactionary classes have tried to use religion against progress, against revolution, and, in effect, they achieved their objective for quite a long time. However, times change, and imperialism, the oligarchy, and reaction are finding it more and more difficult to use the Church against revolution.

Many religious leaders have stopped talking exclusively about rewards in the other world and happiness in the other world and are talking about the needs of this world and happiness in this world. [*Applause*] For they see the hunger of the people, the poverty, the unhealthy conditions, the ignorance, suffering, and pain.

If we bear in mind that Christianity was, in the beginning, the religion of the poor, that in the days of the Roman Empire it was the religion of the slaves, because it was based on profound human precepts, there is no doubt that the revolu-tionary movement, the socialist movement, the communist movement, the Marxist-Leninist movement, would benefit a great deal from honest leaders of the Catholic Church and other religions returning to the Christian spirit of the days of the Roman slaves. [*Applause*] What's more, Christianity would also benefit, along with socialism and communism. [*Applause*]

And some religious leaders in Nicaragua asked us why strategic alliance, why only strategic alliance; why not speak of unity between Marxist-Leninists and Christians? [*Applause*]

I don't know what the imperialists think about this. But I'm absolutely convinced the formula is highly explosive. [*Applause*] It exists not only in Nicaragua but also in El Salvador, where the revolutionary forces and the Christian forces are closely united.

Look how reaction and fascism are constantly murdering priests, how the archbishop of El Salvador was brutally assassinated. This is because reactionaries and fascists—many of whom go to church every Sunday—when they see their interests affected, endangered, do not hesitate to plant bombs in churches and to assassinate priests and bishops. They'd murder the pope if they could. [*Applause*]

But not only in El Salvador; there's Guatemala, where there's also constant repression and murder, including that of priests. There are numerous priests who are on the side of the revolution.

I'm telling you this so you'll have an idea of how situations change, how different they are in each country, and therefore we cannot be thinking of a strictly Cuban formula, because that formula is specifically for us.

132. Chico Mendes

Francisco Alves Mendes Filho (1944-1988), the most courageous labor leader of twentieth-century Brazil, and also a passionate environmentalist, formed the seringueiros *into a union when he realized that their way of life was threatened as well as the very existence of the rainforest. The* seringueiros *were longtime inhabitants of the Amazon rainforest who*

SOURCE: Chico Mendes, *Fight for the Forest: Chico Mendes in His Own Words*, trans. Christopher Whitehouse; ed. Tony Gross (London: Latin America Bureau, 1989), 53.

were able to obtain a subsistence level of life by rubber tapping, collecting Brazil nuts, and other ecologically sustainable activities. He was brutally murdered in 1988 by order of two landowner brothers.

What does the brief excerpt from his Fight for the Forest: Chico Mendes in His Own Words *(1989) say about Mendes's character and about the church he encountered?*

We have had a lot to do with the Church but there have been clashes at times, because although the Church has an important role in our struggle, it is only prepared to go so far. For example it has been very difficult about our interest in linking up with political parties. The political space the Church has given us has been very important and recently things have improved, for example the Pastoral Land Commission (CPT) has been more actively involved in our movement after a period in which it vacillated in its attitude towards us. We have good links with the Prelacy of Acre-Purus, but things are much worse in the Juruá Valley where the Church is very conservative. We have a good relationship with the Church at Carauari, another region in the state of Amazonas. I think the links we've had with the Church have been positive and we've been able to build up a working relationship which benefits both the Church and the rubber tappers. The Church cannot give up on us now, after having worked so hard with us in the 1970s.

133. Guadalupe Sides with the Oppressed

Andrés Guerrero (b. 1943), great-grandson of a Cherokee, graduate of St. Thomas University in Houston, Catholic seminary student, and doctor of theology from Harvard Divinity School, has enjoyed a tumultuous career as a highly qualified, outspoken Mexican-American fighting the anti-Chicano prejudices of U.S. academe and refusing to accept Anglo-Saxon myths and values.

Guerrero's dissection of the Chicano psyche is jarring. How appropriate are these contradictory characterizations in describing the actual behavior of a Chicano/Chicana? By what logic does Guerrero conclude that the Virgin of Guadalupe, a sign of hope and protection for most Mexicans, is a "symbol of liberation" which "gives us [Chicanos] our identity as social and cultural beings in society"? What exactly does that mean? How can Guerrero conclude, for example, that "for Chicanos the symbol of Guadalupe is against the hoarding of material possessions"? What is a "Chicano theology"?

Our *mestizo* ancestry is both Spanish and native American. Historically, then, we are both oppressor (Spanish) and oppressed (native American). Racially, we are both white (Spanish) and red (native American). Economically, the Spanish gained power as they acquired the land; native Americans lost power and became landless. We live in a gringo society, but our culture is Mexican. We have a gringo impulse (learned from the gringo), but our *corazón* is Latino. We relate to the impoverished world because of our oppression, but we live in a technological, industrial, affluent world. We embrace two world views in our reality, the European and the indigenous. We practice *machismo* (male chauvinism), yet our Mexican heritage is woman-centered. Our fathers are the heads of the household, but our mothers are the hearts of it. Some of us feel superior because we

SOURCE: Andrés G. Guerrero, *A Chicano Theology* (Maryknoll, N.Y.: Orbis Books, 1987), 17, 105, 143-44, 146-48. Reprinted by permission of Andrés Guerrero.

are white; some of us feel inferior because we are brown or red. The European in us is individually inclined; the indigenous in us is communally inclined. The Protestant in us is competitive, but the Catholic in us is social. As Protestants we have ecclesiastical leadership but lack social awareness; as Catholics we have a social consciousness, but little ecclesiastical leadership. [...]

Faith is that mystery in us that drives us to believe in something we cherish and hold dearly but do not see. We cannot prove the existence of God or that Jesus Christ is the Son of God. We have faith as Christians that God exists, and we believe that Jesus Christ is God's only begotten Son. We also trust that these articles of faith are true because we have been taught that they are so by our elders, by the tradition of the church, and by our parents who are part of a larger believing community. So the element of trusting in something or someone is included in our understanding of faith. We trust that we are not being deceived. The truth handed down to the Mexican nation was that the miraculous apparition was a revelation.

Guadalupe appeared as an Aztec maiden. No Indian doubted that she was Indian. Moreover, she appeared to an Indian, one of the downtrodden, not to a Spaniard. We could say that, politically, she appeared on the side of the oppressed. [...]

Guadalupe as a symbol of liberation gives us our identity as social and cultural beings in society. In the liberation process the need to know where one's place is under the sun is important. Guadalupe, the Virgin *Morena*, symbolizes our social and cultural specialness. Mexicans and Chicanos are a special people because Guadalupe selected them to bring forth her message to the oppressed and downtrodden [. . .] Socially and culturally, Guadalupe helps to bring the central theme of liberation to fruition by taking on our identity as *mestizos*.

The political significance of the symbol of Guadalupe lies in its unifying strength. Chicanos are all familiar with the image of Guadalupe as the nurturing mother who does not abandon us when we need her. Unity is necessary for organization and for building up a resistance against forces that impede our liberation. No liberation movement can succeed without the unity and cooperation of the group. Both Catholic and Protestant Chicanos can unite and organize themselves using Guadalupe as their symbolic banner. Guadalupe sides with those who are tortured, raped, and murdered by repressive governments. Politically, Guadalupe sides with the oppressed.

Economically Guadalupe is against capitalism. She cannot condone the actions of the growers and multinational corporations. She condemns their actions because of the exploitation and the institutionalized violence they impose upon the wretched of the earth. Because of the inequalities democratic capitalism brings to the different-colored peoples in this hemisphere, she is more apt to choose some type of socialist government as an option for the poor. In terms of the economic margin for Chicanos in the United States, Guadalupe is a symbol of resistance against exploitative and unjust wages. She symbolizes direct action against the unequal distribution of resources and goods. For Chicanos, the symbol of Guadalupe is against the hoarding of material possessions. To share everything we own is imitative of her generosity toward us. She promised that no sigh, no matter how small, would go unheard. [...]

Miguel Hidalgo y Costilla, Emiliano Zapata, and César Chávez have used the symbol of Guadalupe to move the people because they recognized the process of liberation going on and the powerful influence Guadalupe could have in such a process. Guadalupe for them was a powerful symbol to be used to move the oppressed against their oppressors. [...]

[T]he symbol of Guadalupe cannot be used in opposition to the violated mother. Males cannot "hail" Mary and then turn around and oppress women. Chicano theology could not condone this contradiction. In Chicano theology, Guadalupe, as a symbol of liberation, is the Mother of all the oppressed. Women as specific victims in every culture hold a special place and have an important mission to announce their liberation. Guadalupe can be used as a powerful symbol of liberation by women. It is in this direction a Chicano theology ought to develop.

134. Hands Off the Darién!

When Rómulo Emiliani (b. 1948, in Colón, Panama) was appointed vicar apostolic (in effect, bishop) of Darién in 1989, there was one dirt road, impossible to navigate in the rainy season, connecting the neglected, isolated, southernmost state of Panama to the rest of the country. Uncontrolled logging, barely functioning schools, malnutrition, and absence of infrastructure were some of the problems of this forgotten state, which Emiliani forced the nation to confront.

Shortly before he was transferred to the diocese of San Pedro Sula, Honduras, he made the declaration excerpted below. What had Emiliani and those who had been killed or kidnapped been doing to cause the retaliatory crimes Emiliani reports in this declaration? What did these "nationals and foreigners [Colombians]" want?

We are a small but sovereign nation and the Darién is still a region where the poor have land and hope for a better future. But you, whoever you may be, are blocking all these integral development processes, which is why we ask that you take your hands off the Darién. If you are any violent group from Colombia, who come bathed in the blood spilled by so many victims of your cruel and absurd war, or if you are a mix of nationals and foreigners, who are equally bad, we ask that you take your hands off the Darién because we want to live in peace.

Our poverty is enough, we do not need for it to be bathed in innocent blood. Return Domingo Samaniego and Alexis Ortiz, who have been kidnapped and whose families cry uncontrollably for their loss. The family of Antonio "Pipo" González, assassinated when he resisted [being] kidnapped, is in mourning. I will tell you again, take your hands of the Darién, whoever you may be. El Común, a poor, indigenous village along the Chico River, has been attacked twice. Boca de Cupe, along the Tuira River, has been attacked, leaving one police officer wounded and another dead. The Catholic pastoral center in Errebachi, also along the Chico River, was attacked and the missionaries there were temporarily forced to flee. Again along the Tuira River, they attacked the community of Capetí and stole the people's food. They held the entire town, including a Salesian religious sister, hostage for several hours. The following day, they assassinated a resident of Boca de Cupe. On another occasion, they wounded a police officer, shooting him three times in the leg, along the Chico River. They also shot a driver from the Catholic mission in the face. They attacked the town of Canaán Membrillo, assassinating Alberto Choco, an indigenous man. We are asking you, take your hands off the Darién, whoever you may be. Those of you who attacked three trucks on the road to Peñitas and 11 fishermen in Garachiné, stealing their outboard motor, take your hands off the Darién. Those of you who assassinated police officer Branda along the Tuira River, and who kidnapped Monti Ramos for nearly a year, we say take your hands off the Darién.

This is the only province where the poor have land, but they are selling it out of fear. We dream of land, progress, harmony, respect for human rights and dignity for everyone. Do not try to alter this or make the poor suffer even more. In the end, the poor are the ones who are the most affected by social chaos. This is a region where many people are building a better world based on their own efforts and sacrifice. We do not want this to become a no-man's land. The war in Colombia hurts us and we are united with the suffering of millions of Colombians who are tired of so much violence and who no longer want to be in

SOURCE: Rómulo Emiliani, quoted in "Take Your Hands off the Darién," *Latin American Documentation* 30, no. 4 (March/April 2000): 21-22.

mourning. We are in solidarity with all the people displaced by the war, who wander the country and settle along the nation's different borders. They are looking for a little bit of security and bring with them their pots, their clothes and their suffering, accumulated during an absurd war that should stop. We also have them in the Darién, displaced people without home or future, who have been received in this poor but generous land.

Take your hands off the Darién, you Panamanians and foreigners who are against peace, who use the night for protection and launch surprise attacks. We are a poor people, but we are aware of our rights and only those people who want peace and dignified work are welcome here. We do not want war or death caused by hatred and greed. TAKE YOUR HANDS OFF THE DARIÉN.

135. Fidel Welcomes John Paul

Pope John Paul II made a pastoral visit to Cuba in January 1998. With Cuba's slow emergence from the real difficulties of the "special period" (the years following 1990, the era of economic downturn that followed the collapse of the Soviet Union and access to cheap oil), the Cuban government undoubtedly recognized the benefits of such a visit, and so, after a long period of off-and-on negotiations and final agreement on certain concessions on human and civil rights, the Cuban government eagerly extended an invitation. As part of the attempt to lessen the pain of the "special period," the fifth Congress of the Cuban Communist Party (1992) had already abolished all statutes that limited the access of Catholics and other Christians to the rights and privileges available to all Cuban citizens.

The United Nations had condemned the U.S. trade embargo against Cuba every year since 1992 (by a vote of 157 to 2 later in 1998 after the pope's visit). That embargo had been tightened in 1992 and again in 1996. The pope also condemned the embargo during his visit. How might John Paul II respond to Castro's comparison of the persecution of the Cuban people by the trade embargo to the persecution of the early Christians?

In his encyclicals and allocutions the pope had denounced many times the same political, economic, and social evils that Castro included in his address. How might the pope respond to Castro's portrayal of the Cuban church of his youth and to the portrayal of Cuba with which he ended his greeting?

Your Holiness:

The island whose soil you have just kissed is honored by your presence. You will not find here those peaceful and good-natured native inhabitants who populated it when the first Europeans reached this island. The men were almost all exterminated by exploitation and slave labor that they were unable to withstand; the women were converted into objects of pleasure or domestic slaves. There were also those who died under the blade of homicidal swords, or as victims of unknown diseases imported by the conquistadors. Some priests left heartrending testimonies of their protests against such crimes.

Throughout the centuries, more than one million Africans, cruelly uprooted from their distant lands, took the place of the indigenous slaves who had been wiped out. They made a considerable contribution to the ethnic composition and origin of the current population of our country, in which the culture, beliefs, and the blood of all those who participated in this dramatic history is mixed.

SOURCE: Fidel Castro, "Castro Confidently Welcomes Pope to Cuba," *The Militant* 62, no. 5 (February 9, 1998): 9. Reprinted by permission of *The Militant*.

It is estimated that the conquest and colonization of the entire hemisphere cost the lives of 70 million indigenous people and led to the enslavement of 12 million Africans. Much blood was spilled and many injustices were committed, many of which—after centuries of sacrifices and struggle—still persist under other forms of domination and exploitation.

Cuba achieved its nationhood under extremely difficult conditions. It battled alone with unsurpassable heroism for its independence. For that reason, exactly 100 years ago it suffered a genuine holocaust in concentration camps, where a considerable part of its population perished, primarily women, the elderly, and children. This was a crime committed by the colonialists that, although it has been forgotten in the conscience of humanity, has not ceased being a monstrous crime. You, a son of Poland and a witness of Oswiecim, can comprehend it better than anyone.

Your Holiness, another genocide is being attempted today, so as to bring to its knees through hunger, disease, and total economic asphyxiation a people who refuse to submit to the dictates and sway of the most powerful economic, political, and military power in history, far more powerful than that of Ancient Rome, which for centuries threw to the lions those who refused to renounce their faith. Like those Christians atrociously slandered in order to justify the crimes, we, who are similarly slandered, would prefer death a thousand times before renouncing our convictions. Just like the Church, the revolution too has many martyrs.

Your Holiness, we think like you on many important issues of today's world, and that is a source of great satisfaction to us. On other matters, our opinions differ, but we pay respectful homage to the deep conviction with which you defend your ideas.

In your long pilgrimage throughout the world, you have seen with your own eyes much injustice, inequality, poverty; fields without crops and peasants without food and without land; unemployment, hunger, disease, lives that could have been saved by a few pennies but are lost; illiteracy, child prostitution, children working from the age of six or begging in order to live; shantytowns where hundreds of millions of people live in inhuman conditions; discrimination for reasons of race or sex, entire ethnic groups ousted from their lands and abandoned to chance; xenophobia, contempt for other peoples, cultures destroyed or being destroyed; underdevelopment, usurious loans, uncollectable and unpayable debts, unequal terms of trade, monstrous and unproductive financial speculation; an environment mercilessly destroyed, at times beyond repair; unscrupulous arms trading for repugnant commercial ends, wars, violence, massacres; generalized corruption, drugs, vices, and an alienating consumerism imposed as an idyllic model on all peoples.

Humanity has grown almost fourfold in this century alone. Billions of people are suffering hunger and a thirst for justice; the list of the peoples' economic and social disasters is interminable. I am aware that many of them are a constant and growing concern of Your Holiness.

I have had personal experiences that have allowed me to appreciate other aspects of your thinking. I was a student at Catholic schools up until I went to university. I was taught then that to be a Protestant, a Jew, a Muslim, a Hindu, a Buddhist, an animist, or a participant in other religious beliefs constituted a horrible sin, worthy of severe and implacable punishment. More than once, in some of those schools for the wealthy and privileged, among whom I found myself, it occurred to me to ask why there were no Black children there. I have never been able to forget the totally unpersuasive responses I received.

Years later, Vatican Council II, convened by Pope John XXIII, took up some of these delicate questions. We are aware of Your Holiness' efforts to practice and preach respect toward believers of other important and influential religions that have spread throughout the world. Respect for believers and nonbelievers is a basic principle that we Cuban revolutionaries have inculcated in our compatriots. Those principles have been defined and are guaranteed by our Constitution and our laws. If difficulties have arisen at any time, the fault has never been with the revolution.

We cherish the hope that, one day, no adolescent in any school in any region of the world will need to ask why there isn't a single Black, Indian, Asian or white child in it.

Your Holiness:

I sincerely admire your courageous statements on what happened with Galileo, the well-known errors of the Inquisition, the bloody episodes of the Crusades, the crimes committed during the conquest of America, and on certain scientific discoveries that nowadays go unquestioned but which, in their time, were the object of so many prejudices and anathemas. That necessitated the immense authority that you have acquired in your Church.

What can we offer you in Cuba, Your Holiness? A people with fewer inequalities, fewer unpro-tected citizens, fewer children without schools, fewer sick people without hospitals, more teachers and more doctors per inhabitant than any other country in the world visited by Your Holiness; an educated people to whom you can speak with all the liberty you wish, and with the security that this people possesses talent, a high political culture, deep convictions; absolute confidence in its ideas, and all the awareness and respect in the world to listen to you. There is no country better equipped to understand your felicitous idea, such as we understand it, and so similar to what we preach, that the equitable distribution of wealth and soli-darity among human beings and peoples must be globalized.

Welcome to Cuba.

PART XX

Latino Jews, Afro-Latinos, and Amerindians

Political and economic strife combined with anti-Semitism prompted more than 100,000 Jews from Europe, North Africa, and the Middle East to emigrate to Latin America at the end of the nineteenth century and throughout the period of the two world wars. Large urban areas such as Buenos Aires, São Paulo, Rio de Janeiro, Montevideo, Santiago, Mexico City, and Caracas today possess communities large enough to forge strong cultural, religious, and educational associations. Ashkenazim from North Africa and central and eastern Europe arrived first; they and their descendants represent the majority of Jews who reside in Latin America today. Sephardim from the eastern Mediterranean constitute the second largest group. Both adhered to Orthodox Judaism. Lesser numbers following Conservative or Reform rituals migrated later. These groups generally developed independent religious and social organizations with little intermingling between them, although this appeared to change in the late twentieth century. Whatever the country of origin, most Jews formed part of the middle and upper-middle classes and engaged in professions such as merchandising, scientific research, and education. Only a few Jews gained political prominence (most notably in Argentina and Uruguay), due in part to their relatively small numbers and to the misguided belief that they controlled vast economic resources and perpetuated serious social inequalities. The activities of the Inquisition fostered anti-Semitic attitudes during the colonial period, and such attitudes linger in the form of painted swastikas on buildings and acts of terrorism such as the bombing in 1992 of Argentina's Israeli embassy, which killed twenty-nine, and the bombing in 1994 of the Argentine Israelite Mutual Association, which killed eighty-five. The Jewish People Policy Planning Institute estimated the total Jewish population in Latin America for 2005 to be 398,000, down from 514,000 in 1970—the decrease due to economic factors, especially in

Argentina. The three countries with the largest Jewish presence are Argentina (185,000), Brazil (97,000), and Mexico (40,000).[1]

Slaves brought to the New World African traditions which, over time, blended with Christian and indigenous elements. Some followers view these religious beliefs as separate and distinct from Catholicism while others practice both simultaneously, though without church sanction. During the colonial period the Spanish Inquisition actively pursued blacks and others who used witchcraft, but with limited success; one of the reasons for the establishment of a tribunal of the Inquisition in Cartagena in 1610, in fact, was to root out African religious traditions at a major port of entry for African slaves in Spanish America. It is not surprising that African religious influence proved especially enduring in slave areas replenished by frequent arrivals. This was particularly true in Cuba and Brazil, which received more than 800,000 and 4,000,000 slaves respectively—many coming in the nineteenth century before the final abolition of slavery in these areas in 1886 and 1888.

The Afro-Cuban religious traditions of Abakuá, Palo Monte, and Santería have flourished since the early colonial period. All three, notes George Reid Andrews, share common traits: they revere spirits of the dead, acknowledge the power of supernatural forces found in nature, and maintain tightly knit social structures in which members receive select sacred knowledge of rituals and practice as they grow within the religion. But significant differences exist as well. The Abakuá, like those who follow the leopard cult in Africa, are polytheistic. Devotees of Palo Monte believe in one all-powerful creator god, Nzambi Mpungu, but rely on the intercession of the spirits of deceased ancestors in order to resolve conflicts and cure afflictions. Followers of Santería, or "the way of the Saints," accept the Christian God and saints as well as African deities such as Shangó, the god of thunder and lightning. They also use *orishas,* or anthropomorphized natural objects, to effect favors on their behalf, and "feed" these *orishas* with animal sacrifices. Cuban authorities between 1900 and 1920 falsely accused followers of African-based religions of kidnapping and murdering white Catholics, although, as Andrews states, the authorities' real intention may have been to dissuade whites from continuing to join the mostly black- and mulatto-directed religions. The exodus of Cubans since the revolution of 1959 has helped to spread Afro-Cuban religious beliefs, especially Santería, to other countries in Latin America as well as to the United States. In Venezuela, for example, followers of the ancient spiritist cult of María Lionza had previously sought the intercession of Amerindian chiefs, Catholic

---

1. Haim Auni, "Latin America and the Jewish Refugees: Two Encounters, 1935-1938," in *The Jewish Presence in Latin America*, ed. Judith Laikin Elkin and Gilbert W. Merkx (Boston: Allen & Unwin, 1987), 68; Saúl Sosnowski, "Jews," in *Encyclopedia of Latin American History and Culture*, vol. 3, ed. Barbara A. Tenenbaum (New York: Charles Scribner's Sons, 1996), 320-22; Morton D. Winsberg, "Jews in Latin America," in *Encyclopedia of Latin America*, ed. Helen Delpar (New York: McGraw-Hill, 1974), 310-11; Gilbert W. Merkx, "Jewish Studies as a Subject of Latin American Studies," in *The Jewish Presence in Latin America*, ed. Judith Laikin Elkin and Gilbert W. Merkx (Boston: Allen & Unwin, 1987), 5-10. For statistics on Jewish population, see Rami Tal, ed., *Jewish People Policy Planning Institute Annual Assessment, 2005: Executive Report; Facing a Rapidly Changing World* (Jerusalem: The Jewish People Policy Planning Institute, 2005), esp. 12, 29. See also Efraim Zadoff, *A Century of Argentinean Jewry: In Search of a New Model of National Identity* (Jerusalem: Institute of the World Jewish Congress, 2000).

saints, and even national heroes such as Simón Bolívar. With the arrival of Santería devotees, however, these traditional intercessors have been mostly replaced by Cuban *orishas*, and the Venezuelan Santería movement now numbers in the thousands.[2]

Afro-Brazilian religions, mostly Candomblé and Umbanda, have expanded rapidly since the early twentieth century. Candomblé is similar to Santería in that it emanates from the African Yoruba area of southwestern Nigeria and Benin and adopts aspects of Catholic liturgy such as veneration of the saints. Believers might claim to be Catholics simultaneously, though the Catholic Church rejects such dualism and views Afro-Brazilian religions as devil worship. Umbanda, an offshoot of Candomblé, has become the most popular Afro-Brazilian religion since its inception in the 1920s, presently accounting for more than twenty million followers. Its name derives from the Abanheenga language of the Tupi-Guaraní and means "the set of divine laws."[3] John Burdick's work on religions in Brazil includes analysis of the belief system of Umbandistas. *Chefes* and *ogãs*, or revered spiritual leaders, hold rituals that are attended by groups ranging from a few to several hundred members. Umbandistas believe that one's goodness and purity at death determines one's location in the multitiered astral plane. The dead become spirits who wish to become completely pure and to occupy the highest plane. Female and male mediums help contact the spirits. Mediums acquire this ability either through birth or vocation. Novice mediums tend to twitch wildly while they receive spirit possession whereas more skilled and older mediums receive the spirit calmly and naturally. Both humans and spirits need the help of the mediums, since the former seek spiritual healing, medicinal cures, and advice while the latter seek to purify themselves. Reincarnation allows all spirits to improve their place on the multitiered astral plane. Umbandan rituals usually take several hours and include drumming, the aroma of incense, and mediums who smoke cigars and drink alcohol, especially beer and *cachaça*, in preparation for communication with the spirits. "The basic umbandista assumption," notes Burdick, "is that no matter how much faith and love one has in one's heart, one may still be affected by envious or unscrupulous neighbors."[4] So much is outside the control of the poor, marginalized followers of Umbanda that they are undoubtedly comforted by this nonjudgmental religious system, which does not blame them for their own maladies and afflictions or impose rigid codes of conduct that deny the joys of life.

2. George Reid Andrews, *Afro-Latin America, 1800-2000* (Oxford: Oxford University Press, 2004), 69-72, 122, 169-70.

3. Andrews, *Afro-Latin America*, 73-74, 169; "Umbanda: The Cosmic Proto-Synthesis," 1 of 1 <www.umbanda.org/conce_.htm . . . > Accessed on 12/3/2004; "Câmara aprova: Dia da Umbanda," 1 of 1 <www.cmc.pr.gov.br/web/noticias.nsf . . . > Accessed on 12/3/2004.

4. John Burdick, *Looking for God in Brazil: The Progressive Catholic Church in Urban Brazil's Religious Arena* (Berkeley: University of California Press, 1993), vii, 47-56.

136. Argentinian Jews Flourish despite Adversity

The article below, one of hundreds by Daniel J. Elazar (1934-1999), Ph.D., University of Chicago, late professor of political science at Temple University, Philadelphia, and of intergovernmental relations at Bar-Ilan University in Israel, demonstrates one of his major interests: Jewish community organization worldwide.

The following excerpts must be regarded as no longer current because Elazar's data, gathered in Argentina in 1986, allowed for positive conclusions about the future of Argentine Jewry. Then came the bombing of the Israeli embassy in 1992 and the total destruction of the AMIA (Argentina Jewish Mutual Aid Society) building in 1994, which cost eighty-five lives. These anti-Semitic terrorist acts were followed by the catastrophic collapse, in 2001-2002, of the Argentine economy, which wiped out much of the middle-class Jewish community, reducing thousands to destitution. Professor Elazar's article is relevant, however, because it demonstrates that even in the face of long-time Argentinian anti-Semitism (especially during the 1960s and the Dirty War [see reading 158]) the Jewish community was able to maintain and strengthen its identity.

Is the article below merely sociological, with only passing reference to "Jewish religious life . . . becom[ing] more important"? Does it provide any specific insight into the religious dimension of Jewish life in Argentina?

For two decades Argentinian Jewry has been portrayed as a dying community. First there was the collapse of the community's cooperative banking system in the 1960s. Then the disproportionate impact of right-wing counter-terror on the Jewish community. That was followed by a general sense of decline in the commitment of individual Jews to communal institutions as reflected in lower turnout in community elections and less involvement in communal activities other than the sports clubs which were refuges for Jews but not strongholds of Jewishness.

Then in the 1970s came the demographic issue. A Tel Aviv University study of Argentinian Jewry revealed that accepted estimates of half a million Jews in the country were gross exaggerations. Subsequent studies by the Hebrew University demographers dropped the number of Jews to below 300,000, initially 265,000 and most recently less than 235,000, indicating that assimilation and emigration were taking a drastic toll. For most of the Jewish world the verdict was that we are witnessing the effective end of a community once viewed as a model of successful Jewish communal life in the diaspora.

This winter's recent [1986-87] visit to Argentina has left me with the belief that the obituary is premature. The problems of Argentinian Jewry are real enough, whether they are the common problems of assimilation and acculturation shared by all the diaspora or whether they are problems distinctive to the Argentinian situation. But that is not the whole story. My first surprise was with regard to the demographic situation. True, it was not entirely a surprise since I had earlier come to the conclusion that proper scientific caution had led the demographers to somewhat underestimate the number of Jews in Argentina. But there I discovered that the Vaad HaKehilot, the federation of Jewish communities, had begun to conduct sample censuses of its own in smaller provincial communities and in the two just completed they had discovered significantly larger numbers of Jews than they had hitherto estimated.

SOURCE: Daniel J. Elazar, "Are the Jews of Argentina Disappearing," Jerusalem Center for Public Affairs, 1987, http://www.jcpa.org/dje/articles3/argentina.htm. Reprinted by permission of Jerusalem Center for Public Affairs.

If future censuses of this kind follow the same pattern, then we will have to substantially revise our present estimates upward.

My next surprise was to find that Hebrew was still more widespread as the language of the Jewish leadership than in any other diaspora community that I know. I would not like to suggest that it is the common Jewish language in Argentina but it was clearly easier for me to speak Hebrew than English with many of the people that I met. Less surprising but still pleasing was to note that although the old Eastern European-originated institutions of the community have indeed declined, the community is regrouping around others.

Particularly notable in this respect is the revival among the Sephardic Argentinian Jewry. The Sephardim had always been able to better accommodate their Jewishness with integration into larger Argentinian society since they came from similarly Mediterranean civilizations. Nevertheless, their Jewish ways remained private, confined to their homes and synagogues.

Now the Sephardim are undergoing something of a Jewish renaissance, expanding their institutions and most especially their day schools, and undergoing a religious revival as well. In all of this they are helped by the fact that their institutions have more money at their disposal (at least per capita) than those of the Ashkenazi community. The Ashkenazim are still suffering from the failure of their cooperative banks, while the Sephardic Banco de Mayo survived and has subsequently flourished so that it can provide substantial funding and credit for community projects. In addition, the younger generation of Sephardim is more likely to continue in the family business than is the case among the Ashkenazim, where the younger generation tends to go into academic life or the professions, further reducing the disposable wealth that can be tapped for communal purposes.

In general, Jewish religious life in Argentina has become more important. Originally an almost totally secular community with an absolute minimum of traditional Orthodox institutions, maintained principally for appearances sake, today an increasing number of Argentinian Jews are finding out what Jews in other diasporas have discovered, that surviving as Jews requires some kind of religious identification and expression. [...]

Another sign of the new-found energy among Argentinian Jews was to be found at the meeting of the Latin American Jewish Studies Association. That organization, founded originally by North Americans, led by Dr. Judith Laiken Elkin of Michigan, the organization's driving force, could not even meet in Latin America until its fifth conference. This year for the first time its meeting was held outside of the United States, in Buenos Aires with the co-sponsorship of the AMIA, the umbrella organization or kehilla, of Buenos Aires. Even more impressive were the number of young Latin American and particularly Argentinian scholars who presented papers at the meeting, in many cases based upon field research. In other words, Argentinian Jewry is becoming sufficiently mature to begin to examine itself through accepted scientific methods and sufficiently important in the eyes of its younger generation to be considered worth examining. [...]

None of this is to suggest that Argentinian Jewry is not undergoing all the pangs of assimilation or confronting all the elements of anti-Semitism, usually discussed in describing it. What is important to note is that there is another side to the story as well. As always, we have a community of Jews living on the razor's edge, showing signs of both growth and decline. Equally important, no longer is Argentinian Jewry simply a Zionist or Israeli colony. Today it is moving toward a situation where its voice could also be heard in the councils of world Jewry and it will have something to contribute.

137. Future Prospects for the Argentinian Jewish Community

The following reading, published in 2005 by the Department for Jewish Zionist Education, a part of the Jewish Agency for Israel, is obviously a necessary complement of the preceding report by Elazar (1987). What insights does it offer about Jewish religious practice in Argentina? Does it preclude the positive approach of Daniel Elazar?

[I]t is important to understand that—unlike the situation in some other national communities where the principal means to identify as a Jew is through religious affiliation and membership in a synagogue—the situation in Argentina has long been more about affiliating through organizations with a particular cultural and political definition. Organisations such as the Jewish socialist Bund have lasted far longer than in almost any other places in the Jewish world and left-wing political frameworks within the Jewish community have made their mark socially and culturally. [. . .]

Traditionally, there has been a very strong and vibrant cultural and educational life within the Jewish community. In 1999, some 50% of the age group went to Jewish day schools—a very large percentage for any Diaspora country. Today, the numbers and the percentage are lower. There are currently about forty Jewish schools (of which, some thirty are in Buenos Aires), with some 16,000 students, but this is a downward trend.

In cultural terms, the community has developed many vibrant institutions, many of which were connected, in one way or other, to Zionism and Hebrew culture, both of which have left deep marks on the community. There are many competent Hebrew speakers in the Jewish community, as a result of the educational process through which many have passed, such as Bamah—the Jewish Educator House—and Ebraica—the Jewish Community Center. Zionist youth movements are also strong in the community, although they were affected by the recent economic difficulties; they survived the crisis and continue to be an important influence on Jewish youth in Argentina. [. . .]

There has been considerable assimilation in the community. The current estimate for the whole of Argentina stands at about 45% of all marriages.

There are cases of intermarriage recorded in the Jewish agricultural colonies in the early years of the twentieth century, but the numbers went up greatly among the native-born second and third generation. The numbers of out-marrieds today are very high, especially in the smaller provincial towns outside of Buenos Aires. [. . .]

The community at present numbers about 187,000. A generation ago it was over 300,000. Some of the numbers have been lost to Aliyah, while others represent emigration to western countries, but much of the drop in numbers represents assimilation and intermarriage.

To a large extent, the community's future is also linked to Argentina's economic situation and Antisemitism. If the economy continues to improve to the status quo ante, it would be reasonable to assume that most of the Jewish community will prefer to remain in Argentina, and preserve their Jewish identity through the various frameworks and options in the community.

SOURCE: Steve Israel, "Connecting to Communities, Jewish Peoplehood—Belonging and Commitment: Six National Communities—Argentina," The Department for Jewish Zionist Education, The Jewish Agency for Israel (2003, 2005). http://www.jafi.org.il/education/identity/2-4argentina.html. © The Department for Jewish Zionist Education, The Jewish Agency for Israel. Used by permission.

138. Jewish Life in Contemporary Mexico

Shep Lenchek (c. 1920-2004), a U.S. businessman, retired in Mexico in 1991 where he quickly became a writer for El ojo del lago, *the leading English-language monthly of Mexico, staffed by members of the U.S. community. He was treasurer of the Chapala delegation of the Mexican Red Cross from 1993 until his death in 2004. The following are excerpts from the concluding installment of "Jews in Mexico, A Struggle for Survival" (2000). What is the religious dimension of Lenchek's positive portrait of the Mexican Jewish community?*

Most Mexican Jews are well rooted in the society and the younger members of the group are beginning to take part in politics, something the older generations avoided. There is evidence that if Jews do choose to enter Mexican organizations and politics, they have every chance of success. Jennifer Rose Esq., a lifetime resident of Morelia, was kind enough to put me in contact with a website that deals with the Jews of Tijuana. One current story is about the election of David Saul Guakil, a Jew, to the Tijuana City Council. He had previously served as president of the Tijuana Chamber of Commerce. Quoting Sr. Guakil, "Although some questioned how a young man like me could advance so quickly in the ranks of the PRI, not once did anyone comment adversely on the fact that I am Jewish." The same article, mentions a former president of the Chamber of Commerce, Marcos Levy, also a Jew. Thus it is obvious that in Tijuana, a city of more than 2,000,000 people with a Jewish population of approximately 2,000, Mexicans will judge a man by his abilities, not his religion. [. . .]

Attitudes are changing as the generation that lived through the brief 1930's outbreak of anti-Semitism in Mexico, brought on first by a depression and then by Nazi sympathizers, passes away. Jews seem more willing to enter into the mainstream of Mexican life.

Ing. Alberto Varon M., the honorary Israeli Consul in Guadalajara, Mexico's second largest city, confirms this. He points out that Jews serve in high positions in the Federal Government. They are prominent members of the Chambers of Commerce in Monterrey and Guadalajara as well as Tijuana. Mexico and Israel have just concluded a new trade pact.

Increased contact between Mexican and Israeli businessmen bodes well for Jewish Mexicans.

Today, most Mexican Jews can be classified as "upper middle class." Many are professionals, even more are in business. They do not dominate the Mexican industrial complex nor its banking system, despite having founded it. All the original banks were nationalized. Thus the charge that "Jewish bankers" control the economy of a country, a ploy used by anti-Semites to stir up anger against Jews, cannot be used here.

There is a "café society" in Mexico City that has always welcomed Jews, mostly from the arts, fashion industries and entertainment world. A Jew, Jacobo Zabludovsky, has been called "Mexico's Walter Cronkite." Frida Kahlo, flamboyant artist, lover of Leon Trotsky, wife of Diego Rivera, was a pillar of Mexico's "smart set," until her death in 1954. Her father was a Hungarian Jew and she never denied a Jewish heritage.

Still, for most Mexican Jews their social life centers on their family and within Jewish organizations. One such group, named Tribuna Israelita, promotes close ties with Mexican society and monitors anti-Semitism. By and large, groups that promote Zionism and Israel command most community support. Still, the Jewish tradition of helping the less fortunate leads the Jewish community to support Mexican charities. The aforemen-

SOURCE: Shep Lenchek, "Jews in Mexico, A Struggle for Survival (Part 3 of a 3 Part Series)," *Mexico Connect* 4, no. 1 (May 2000), http://www.mexconnect.com/mex_/travel/slenchek?sljews in mexico3.html. First published in *Mexico Connect* (www.mexconnect.com).

tioned Honorary Consul of Israel gives a monthly donation to the Mexican Red Cross.

The chief problem of Mexican Jewry today is intermarriage, especially of young men with Mexican women. This is largely because of the unwillingness of Orthodox Judaism to agree to conversions. They accept only children born of a Jewish mother. Virtual Jerusalem, an internet website at http://www.jerl.co.il/ that monitors Jewish communities around the world, estimates the rate of intermarriage in Mexico to be between 5% and 10%. Most Jews in Guadalajara dispute these figures, claiming they are too high. [. . .]

There is some evidence that the total Jewish population in the country is growing. In 1995 a study by the Hebrew University's Institute of Contemporary Judaism concluded that the Jewish population of the world is growing in only two countries, Israel and Mexico. This is plausible, since Orthodox Judaism encourages large families and the majority of Jews in the country are Orthodox. In Mexico City, it is estimated that over 80% of all Jewish children receive all of their pre-college education in a Jewish educational network. There are "Talmud Torahs" that prepare boys for *bar mitzvahs* and girls for *bas mitzvahs* connected with every synagogue. There are several "Yeshivot" which prepare boys for the Rabbinate and a Hebraic University that turns out Jewish teachers for this educational system. There are more than 16 Jewish youth groups in the city. In the smaller cities, children are also exposed to Judaism as a way of life in a less elaborate Jewish school system. The Catholic Church has long proclaimed, "Give me a child for the first seven years of its life and it will be ours forever." Mexican Jews have adopted their theory.

All cities with sizeable Jewish populations have community centers that combine a place of worship with a cultural center, a private school that offers both religious and secular education, a library, health club and more. Referred to as "the club" it is the focal point of social activities for the entire congregation. Mexican Jews see themselves as "family," even if not actually related. Often a walled compound, open only to members, these "clubs" minimize chances of inter-marriage. Non-Jewish Mexican social life also revolves around the family. Thus, to a certain extent both groups have similar outlooks and attempt to exert control over the social life of their children.

Questioned about their future, most but not all Jews in Guadalajara are optimistic. All agree that the main problem is intermarriage. Those who are optimistic feel that the grip of the Orthodox is loosening. Congregations are moving toward a more liberal conservatism. In 1999, Reformed Rabbis have visited Mexico City with an eye toward starting a reformed congregation. Someday, conversion in intermarriages may become acceptable. This would certainly ease the problem. Also, as the Mexican economy improves, young Jews who sought better opportunities in Mexico City or abroad can stay or return "home." Guadalajara is now the home of high-tech industries, mostly branches of foreign businesses. New opportunities for well-educated people, including Mexican Jews, are opening up. [. . .]

Speaking with a Jewish woman, she pointed out that the desire to live a full Jewish life is another reason young Jews prefer Mexico City to other places in the country. "Kosher foods, kosher restaurants are readily available there. This is not the case in Guadalajara," she said.

As the younger generation of Mexican Jews becomes the majority, they will possibly practice a more liberal Judaism than their forefathers. They may become less religious, which ironically would make it easier for them to live as Jews, no longer attempting to meet all the demands of Orthodox Judaism. If Reformed Judaism gained a foothold in the country, it would ease some of the problems of intermarriage. Also, Jews might begin to accept "*Converso*" groups who have of their own free will already returned to the religion of their ancestors. Again, it is the Orthodox establishment that prevents this.

It is also possible that there are still some latent fears of the Catholic Church that have caused Mexican Jews to maintain a low profile. In early March, 2000, Pope John Paul II laid many of these fears to rest. He called anti-Semitism "a massive sin against humanity" and the Holocaust "an indelible stain on the history of the last century." He continued to seek rapprochement between Catholics and Jews by visiting Israel and again decrying anti-Semitism at Yad Vashem, a memorial to the victims of the Holocaust. He also prayed at the Western (Wailing) Wall, a remnant of Herod's Temple, destroyed by the Romans in 70 A.D. It is the holiest shrine of Judaism. Hopefully, these efforts will have an impact on Catholic attitudes toward Jews and vice-versa.

Actually, Jews have much in common with their fellow Mexicans. Both groups are sincerely religious and family oriented. Both were victims of oppression and have suffered tyranny. Even in modern times, they have felt discrimination, Mexicans in the United States, Jews in Russia. Descendants of survivors, bolstered by strong religious convictions, they are determined to survive. Ultimately, like all those who live in Mexico, their future depends largely on the ability of their homeland to make social and economic progress.

They live with hope.

139. A Jewish Remnant in Central America

Corrie MacLaggan (b. c. 1981) published an article in the Chicago Jewish Community Online *(2003), which described the problems facing young Jews who desired to preserve Jewish life in areas of Latin America where Jews are an especially tiny minority. What are the challenges facing these young people, and what are their responses to them? What are the religious reasons behind their desire "to preserve Jewish life"?*

Young leaders in small Jewish communities throughout Latin America feel a great responsibility to preserve Jewish life in their hometowns—and they're worried about the future. These youths, together with young people from larger communities like Buenos Aires, came together in this town [Antigua] 30 miles outside Guatemala City as part of the Ninth Meeting of Leaders of Latin America and Caribbean Jewish Institutions and Communities. [...]

Of the nearly 600 lay leaders, rabbis, educators and volunteers from 22 countries who gathered to share ideas, about 100 were under age 30. At a time when Latin America's economic problems have caused many Jews to leave for Israel, the United States and other places, young people said they are concerned about maintaining what's left of their Jewish communities.

Daniel Cahen [*sic*], from San Salvador, El Salvador, where there are about 60 Jewish families, said he doesn't know if he'll find a Jewish woman to marry. "I'm worried for myself and my future," said Cahen, 27. "I want my kids to be Jewish." His concerns echo those of young people across the region.

Each Latin American country has distinct political and economic circumstances—making life for a Jew in Monterrey, Mexico, quite different than for one in Havana, for example—the small communities throughout the region face similar struggles. Many of the young people from small Jewish communities grew up in places where there weren't always rabbis and where it could be difficult to connect with other Jews or follow Jewish traditions. Some of them are working to change that.

Here in Guatemala, where there are about 250 Jewish families, it was common for young adults to disconnect from the community after graduating from high school, youth leaders said. Three years ago, a group of young people started the Jewish University Students of Guatemala. The group includes people between the ages of 18 and 30 who aren't necessarily students. Joe Kaire, president of the group, spoke about his organization during the conference. "We didn't have a place to

Source: Corrie MacLaggan, "Latin Jews Confront Challenges" (November 5, 2003), *Chicago Jewish Community Online,* www.juf.org/ (accessed 10/08/2005).

keep developing our Jewish identity," Kaire, 25, told the audience. "Now we do, but it's a slow process." It's hard to form a community, he said, because so many young Jews go to college outside Guatemala City—either elsewhere in Guatemala or in the United Sates. Those who stay don't necessarily join the student group. That worries the group's president-elect, Joseph Mejía.

"We need to unify the community of young people," Mejía, 21, said. "If not, we're going to lose the customs." It's not always easy to live a Jewish life in Guatemala, Mejía and Kaire agreed. "In Mexico, if you want to keep kosher you have several restaurants to choose from. If you don't keep kosher in Mexico, it's because you don't want to," Kaire said. "But here, it's very difficult." Even though Mexico has 50,000 Jews, the overwhelming majority are in Mexico City. Outside the capital, the communities are small and isolated—more similar in some ways to Guatemala City than Mexico City.

Eduardo Berner is from Monterrey, a city of more than 3 million people—including some 120 Jewish families—in northern Mexico. He said that nearly every Jewish person he knows, including his father and uncles, has had to go to Mexico City to find a Jewish spouse. He probably will do the same, said Berner, a 23-year-old student. Maintaining a community of young Jews in Monterrey is a challenge because many young people go to

college in the United States, he said. "I don't know what the solution is," Berner said. [. . .]

According to Bertha Delgado Farin, 23, of Santiago de Cuba, the challenge on her island is how to revitalize a Jewish community that was dormant for years. After the Cuban revolution in 1959, about 90 percent of Cuba's Jews left for economic reasons, and Jewish life in the country further dwindled after the government began discouraging religious practice. There still is no permanent rabbi in Cuba, but Jewish life is thriving again. The synagogue in Santiago de Cuba, located more than 500 miles from Havana on the southwestern part of the island, was rededicated in 1995 after having been closed for 16 years.

Delgado Farin did not learn she was Jewish until she was 12. She remembers her mother lighting a small candle each Friday night, but she didn't know why. Now she attends synagogue on Fridays and studies Torah on Saturdays. She said she worries about how to get those younger than her involved in the community. Intermarriage also is an issue, she noted, since there are only about a dozen Jews between the ages of 13 and 30 in Santiago de Cuba. Though her own husband is not Jewish, Delgado Farin says she is determined to provide a Jewish upbringing for their daughter, Sophia, 2. "We have a lot to learn about Judaism," she said. "But every day I'm determined to learn more—and I feel extremely, extremely proud to be Jewish."

140. Black Religion in Cuba

Esteban Montejo (c. 1860-1973), remarkably, lived long enough to see in the Cuban revolution a meaning and purpose behind his long arduous life. Sought out by Miguel Barnet (b. 1940), Cuban anthropologist and writer, Montejo dictated episodes of and commentaries on his life, which Barnet shaped into a biography of "an authentic actor in the process of history in Cuba" (from "Introduction" to the first edition of Barnet's Biografía de un cimarrón *[1966]). Montejo's long life included working as a slave on a sugar plantation, living as a maroon in the forests of Cuba, fighting (1895-1898) for independence from Spain, and witnessing U.S. occupation of Cuba.*

The excerpts below deal with the whole range of religions in Cuba, during the period of

SOURCE: Miguel Barnet, *Biography of a Runaway Slave*, trans. W. Nick Hill (Willimantic, Conn.: Curbstone Press, 1994), 33-37, 39, 78. Reprinted by permission of Curbstone Press.

slavery (ending in 1886) and up to the 1960s. What is that range of religion? In the syncretic religions, how strong is the African strain? What aspects of Catholicism have been absorbed by those religions in which the African strain predominates?

As I understand it, at that time the guajiros made music using only a guitar. Later, around the year 1890, they played danzones on those pianolas with accordions and gourds. But the white man has always had music different from the black. White man's music has no drum at all. Tasteless.

The same thing more or less happens with religions. The African gods are different although they seem to resemble the other ones, the gods of the priests, which are stronger and less decorated. Right now, if you up and go to a Catholic church, you see no apples, no rocks, no rooster feathers. But in an African household those are the first things you see. The African is more down to earth.

I knew about two African religions in the barracoons, the Lucumí and the Conga. The Conga was the more important. At Flor de Sagua it was well known because the witches put spells on people. They gained the trust of all the slaves with their fortune-telling. I came to know the older blacks more after Abolition. [. . .]

For the work of the Congo religion they used the dead and animals. They called the dead nkise and snakes majases, or emboba. They prepared cazuelas and everything, and that's where the secret to make hexes was. They were called ngangas. All the Congos had their ngangas for mayombe. The ngangas had to work with the sun. Because he has always been the intelligence and the strength of men. As the moon is for women. But the sun is more important because he gives life to the moon. The Congos worked with the sun almost every day. When they had a problem with some person, they followed that person along any path and gathered up the dirt they walked on. They saved it and put it in the nganga or in a secret little corner. As the sun went down, the life of the person would leave him. And at sunset the person was quite dead. I say this because it happens that I seen it a lot during slave times.

If you think about it, the Congos were murderers. But if they killed someone, it was because some harm was being done to them, too. No one

ever tried to work a hex on me because I have always been a loner, and I've never cared to know too much about other people's business.

Witchcraft is more common with the Congos than with the Lucumís. The Lucumís are more allied to the Saints and to God. They liked to get up early with the strength of the morning and look at the sky and pray and sprinkle water on the ground. When you least expect it, the Lucumí is doing his work. I have seen old blacks kneeling on the ground for more than three hours speaking in their tongue and telling the future. The difference between the Congo and the Lucumí is that the Congo does things, and the Lucumí tells the future. He knows everything through the diloggunes, which are snails from Africa. With mystery inside. They're white and a little lumpy. Eleggua's eyes are made from that snail.

The old Lucumís would lock themselves in the rooms of the barracoon, and they would clean the evil a person had done out of him. If there was some black man who had desire for a woman, the Lucumí would calm him down. I think they did that with coconuts, obi, which were sacred. They are the same as the coconuts today, which are still sacred and can't be touched. If someone dirtied the coconut, he would get a severe punishment. I always knew when things were going good because the coconut said so. He ordered Alafia to be pronounced so everyone would know there was no tragedy. All the saints spoke through the coconuts. Now the master of all of them was Obatalá. Obatalá was an ancient, so I heard, who was always dressed in white. They said that Obatalá was the one who created you, and who knows what else. People come from Nature, and so does Obatalá.

The old Lucumís liked to have their figurines, their gods, made of wood. They kept them in the barracoon. All those figurines had a big head. They were called oché. The Eleggua was made of cement, but Changó and Yemayá were made of wood, and the carpenters made them themselves.

On the walls of the rooms they made marks of the saints with charcoal and whitewash. They were long lines and circles. Even though each was a saint, they said the marks were secret. Those blacks kept everything a secret. Today they've changed a lot, but back then, the hardest thing in the world was to get them to trust you.

The other religion was Catholicism. It was introduced by the priests who wouldn't go into the barracoons during slavery for love or money. The priests were very neat and tidy. They had a serious look that didn't sit well in the barracoons. They were so serious that there were even blacks who hung on their every word and obeyed them to the letter. They learned the catechism, and then they would read it to the others. With all the words and the prayers. Those were the house slaves, and they met with the other slaves, the field slaves, in the bateyes. They came to be the priests' messengers. Truth is, I never learned that doctrine because I did not understand it at all. I don't think the house slaves did either but because they were so refined and so well-treated, they became Christians. The household slaves got consideration from the masters. I never seen a severe punishment for a one of them. When they were sent to the fields to cut cane or take care of the pigs, they pretended to be sick and didn't work. That's why field slaves didn't want to see them at all, not even in a painting. Sometimes they went to the barracoon to visit with a family member. And they took back fruits and 'taters for the master's house. I don't know if the slaves made gifts from their conucos or if the house slaves just took them. A lot of problems with fighting in the barracoons were caused by them. The men arrived and wanted to flirt and fool around with the women. That's when the worst pushing and shoving began. I was probably twelve years old, and I figured out the whole mess.

There were other tensions, too. For example, between the Congo witch doctor and the Christian there was no getting along. One was good and the other bad. That still goes on in Cuba. The Lucumí and the Congo don't get along either. They bickered over saints and witchcraft. The only ones who didn't have troubles were the old timers from Africa. They were special, and you had to treat them different because they knew all about religion. [. . .]

If a man went to a witch to ask for help getting a woman, the witch sent him to get some of the woman's tobacco if she smoked. You ground up the tobacco and a bottle fly, those green, stinging ones, enough to make a powder which you gave to the woman in water. That's how the woman was seduced.

Another treatment was taking the heart of a humming bird and grinding it into powder. You put it in the woman's tobacco. And if you wanted to make fun of them, all you had to do was send off to the store for barley. Any woman would die of shame on account of that barley because a man would put a little where she was going to sit down, and no sooner than it touched her behind, the woman would begin to break wind. That was a sight to see—those women farting with their faces all powdered up.

The old blacks entertained themselves with that kind of nonsense. When they were over sixty, they stopped working in the fields. Though, truly, they never knew their real age. But it happened that if a black man got tired and set himself apart, then the overseers said he was ready to be a doorman. Then they put that old man at the gates of the barracoon or at the pig sty, where the big litters were produced. Or, if not that, he helped the women in the kitchen. Some of them had their conucos, and they spent their time gardening. Doing those jobs gave them time for their witchcraft. They weren't punished or paid much attention to. But they had to be quiet and obedient. That's for sure. [. . .]

One should respect religions—even though you might not be much of a believer. In those days even the most clever man was a believer. The Spaniards were all believers. The proof is that on the feast days of San Diego and Santa Ana at Purio there was no work. The mill took a rest. The boilers were cold and the fields were deserted. It made you think of a sanctuary. The priests came in the morning and started to pray. They prayed for a long time. I learned little. I almost didn't even pay attention. And it's because I've never cared for priests. Some were criminals, even. They liked pretty white women and slept with them. They were both lecherous and pious. They had a child, and they called him a godchild or a nephew. They hid them under their robes. They never said, "This is my child."

They kept track of the blacks. If a woman gave birth, she had to call for the priest before the baby was three days old. If she didn't, a serious complaint was lodged with the owner of the mill. That was why all the children were Christians.

When a priest passed by, you had to say to him, "Your blessing, father." Sometimes they didn't even look at you. A lot of Spaniards and Canary Islanders are like that, not the Galicians.

Priests and lawyers were sacred in that period of time. They were highly respected because of their titles. Even a university degree was something special. Blacks were none of these things, least of all priests. I never seen a black priest. That was for the whites, and the descendants of the Spaniards.

141. A Night of Umbanda

In the excerpt below, Lindsay Hale, Ph.D. in anthropology (University of Texas, 1994), describes a ceremony he attended while doing research in Brazil in 1991. He supplies the following contextual orientation:

The pretos velhos—*literally "old blacks"—are of central importance to Umbanda ritual. Said to be the spirits of Afrobrazilian slaves, the* pretos velhos *are revered for their wisdom, kindness, and empathy; millions of Brazilians have sought their advice and spiritual intervention for problems ranging from illness to marital difficulties to loss of employment or business setbacks. And many* Umbandistas, *especially those who identify themselves as Afrobrazilians, feel an ancestral connection with the* pretos velhos *and equate the spirits' stories of suffering in slave times with their own contemporary experiences of racial and class injustice.*

On the Saturday night that falls closest to May 13, Umbanda centers throughout Rio perform the festa dos pretos velhos, *the feast of the old slaves. The date commemorates the final abolition of slavery in Brazil in 1888. The following vignette (1991) comes from the annual celebration of the* pretos velhos *at an Umbanda center that places particular emphasis on its Afrobrazilian heritage.*

Why may this ceremony be considered profoundly spiritual? Does it share any of the characteristics of Catholic or Protestant Christianity? Is there a spiritual dimension to Jorge's emotional response to the somber presence of the hungry Afrobrazilians at the ceremony?

It was three o'clock in the morning. I was tired, and glad for the refreshing cool of the night. Jorge [c. 62 years old, a successful hydraulics engineer, from humble beginnings in Rio] and I stood near the drums, watching as about thirty of the mediums, most in trance and all dressed as old slaves, sat on their little stools around a big rectangle of white sheets on the ground. Leaves were strewn over the sheets, and there were big clay pots full of food—corn, okra stew with peppers and shrimp, boiled eggs, bananas, papayas, pineapples, oranges, even some grapes (an expensive delicacy, imported from Chile), bean fritters, fish, yams, rice, an enormous steel pot of black beans. The food had been brought down from outside in a joyous procession as the drummers played and

SOURCE: Lindsay Hale, vignette provided to editors for inclusion in this anthology.

everyone sang African words of which very few knew the literal meanings. The old slaves circled the food several times, in a hobbling, shuffling dance, bent over on their canes, shaking with palsy. And then they sat to partake of the spiritual essence of the food (being spirits, the old slaves do not physically consume the food). They seemed deep in memories, their eyes were far away. And then I noticed several of them were quietly weeping.

I turned to Jorge. Jorge, at the time in his vigorous early sixties, prized his African roots. Samba and religion were big in his life. Jorge, I said, the old slaves are crying. Why are they crying? He put a hand on my shoulder and leaned close. They're crying, my gringo, because they're remembering. See, when they were in Africa, they never were hungry. There was always plenty, and they were free. When our ancestors were brought over here—those ancestors we represent as old slaves like these—the worst thing about their lives was the hunger. Even worse than the beatings, you recover from those. But the hunger was always there. The food was terrible, just enough to keep them alive from one day to the next, sometimes not that. When they dreamed of freedom, of a good life, they dreamed of food. So they see this, this looks to them like heaven, like home. They cry because they remember how they suffered, and they cry because we remember them and give them this out of love. They cry from pain, they cry from happiness. They cry because they know we are free, not slaves like they were. That we have food, all we need.

Jorge's voice was cracking a bit and I stood silent with a lump in my throat. He went on. See, things have really changed. We're free! We sons and daughters of Africa have plenty! Things have changed, right? Jorge looked at me, and his eyes drew mine to look out at the better than 100 people out there sitting on the benches in the audience, waiting for the old slaves to finish taking in the spiritual essence of the food. Most were not regular visitors to the center. Most I could tell from their clothing were poor; many were too, too thin. Here they were, at three o'clock in the morning; they had sat on those benches for hours. To celebrate their ancestors, yes, but when their ancestors had their fill, they would get theirs, a feast of good, good food, protein and vitamins and fats and fibers which comes very rarely for people in their circumstances. Yes, my gringo friend, Jorge went on, his arm now on my far shoulder, holding me close, things have changed but things have not changed so very much at all.

142. Catholic Mass and Candomblé in Bahia

Kathleen de Azevedo, born in Rio de Janeiro, has taught English for over a decade at Skyline College in California. Her account (1997) of Catholic and Candomblé services in São Salvador, Bahia, suggests the intense yet easy religiosity of Brazilians in the suffering northeast section of their country. She describes a Catholic Mass, an ex-voto devotion (loving depictions of miracles restoring health after sicknesses and accidents), a popular cult of a "martyr-saint" and a Candomblé ceremony.

Her report portrays several significant aspects of popular Brazilian religiosity: (1) Some of those who "followed the Mass with familiar ease" are revealed to be unabashed devotees of Oxalá. What does this dual commitment indicate about Brazilian understanding of religion? (2) Some believe in miracles and express that belief in ex-voto devotion to Our Lord of the Good End (Outcome). What is the relation of that devotion to that of Babalú-Ayé?

Source: Kathleen de Azevedo, "True Believers," *Brazzil Magazine*, April 1997, 24, http://www.brazzil.com/p24apr97.htm (accessed on 10/07/05). Reprinted by permission of *Brazzil Magazine*.

(3) Some "canonize" Anastácia the Slave as "martyred-saint." What does this suggest about Afrobrazilian perception of the Catholic Church in Brazil? (4) Participants in the ceremony, whatever the level of their involvement, leave with a feeling of cleansing, renewal, well-being, and joy. How might these emotions compare with those that might be felt by Catholics after attending Mass?

What are the similarities between the Catholic Mass and the Candomblé ceremony? How apt are Azevedo's final comments about Brazilian religiosity being "the glory of three continents" and her remaining remarks about the inevitable joining of "the white of the Eucharist and the white of Oxalá's robe"? What is the significance of the "white"?

Inside Bonfim, a large crowd for Friday Mass spilled into aisles and doorways. I stood in back of the church and scanned the heads, a sea of *morena* hair, a variety so Brazilian: tight oiled curls, free-flowing waves, straight course manes. Black men and women dressed in white, took the empty seats nearest the altar. These seats used to be reserved for the wealthy, but times have changed. Now in spite of the standing-room Mass, the congregation left these seats vacant on purpose. It was hot. The collective murmur of the Glória mingled with the thick flutter of missals. The worshippers in white followed the mass with familiar ease; the white clothes boldly displayed their devotion to Oxalá, the most powerful Yoruban deity of the *orixá*.

The *orixá* are worshipped by practitioners of Candomblé, the African-Brazilian religion of Bahia. There are many theories of its origin, but one belief is that mankind sprang from a single ancestor, and some of the descendants achieved divinity which enabled them to control natural forces such as disease, thunder, and the oceans. These ancestors with special powers make up the *orixá*, and their spiritual energy, or *axé*, enters their contemporary descendants during a ceremonial trance. [...]

[T]he *orixá* and the saints were honored side by side, each gradually taking on the identity of the other. The official laws forbade the practice of Candomblé, and in an act of resistance that forever affected Brazilian culture, the faithful "hid" their *orixá* in the identity of the saints, and continued practicing their African religion at will. For example, Oxalá is often portrayed wearing white garments and a silver crown. Oxalá's reputation for his beauty, purity and as the creator of man

syncretize him to Jesus Christ/the Lord of Bonfim. When the Portuguese placed O Menino Jesus dressed in a white gown and small imperial crown on their altars, it was as if master and slave ironically spoke in almost the same spiritual tongue.

Historical habits don't survive without present need. Worshippers don't necessary choose between Christ and Oxalá, on the contrary, the two deities are often worshipped together, their divine forces combined. It is a way to "cover your bases" so to speak. Brazil has endured a history of political instability and poverty. The belief in divine intervention, common to both Catholicism and the Candomblé, often provides spiritual sustenance to fragile lives. [...]

The patience of many here put me to shame. The ex-voto room at the side of the main church is an example of this faith. This room, sweetened with the resin smell of incense, filled my ears with pleadings and prayers. On the ceiling hung the ex-votos, molded plastic arms and feet and heads and hearts, translucent and yellow—offered by faithful parishioners whose prayer for cure had been answered. The walls of this chapel were covered with photos and with testimonials on slips of paper thanking Senhor do Bonfim for His miracles. [...]

The portrayal of suffering is prominent in Brazil's churches, but oftentimes, the torment of slavery remains in the periphery. In the cobblestone square of the Pelourinho [a whipping post for slaves] stands the Igreja Nosso Senhor do Rosário dos Pretos [Church of Our Lord of the Rosary of the Blacks] painted in bright porcelain blue. The church was built by blacks for blacks. I stepped into a late afternoon Mass. The congregation clapped and sang to music belting out of an electric organ. [. . .] In a courtyard off to the side of the church, I found the shrine of Anastácia Escrava (Anastácia the Slave). The weathered picture painted on tiles showed Anastácia Escrava with her mouth strapped in a muzzle. Small jars of flowers had been set at [the] foot of the picture and small candles burned in her honor. Anastácia, an Angolan princess, was brought to Rio as a slave and became the mistress of her white master. When his wife found out of the affair, she had Anastácia "silenced" with a ceramic disk secured by a leather strap. This form of torture eroded the mouth which led to starvation. Anastácia is sanctified, though not considered a "saint." In other words, many followers regard her as holy and claim miracles on her behalf, but she has not been canonized by the Catholic church. Nevertheless, Anastácia's attempt to voice her oppression and her martyrdom became an inspiration to other blacks who pay their respects.

To get a sense of the African voice, I needed to step away from the churches and look to the *terreiros* around Salvador, where Candomblé celebrates black heritage and the vigor of their community. [. . .]

From outside, the *terreiro*, was much like other small red brick homes; a small iron gate opened to a porch where everyone removed their shoes. The larger *terreiros* have several rooms, with the *peji*, or altar, being in one room, and the dancing taking place in the adjoining *barracão*. Many poorer communities have the *peji* and dancing in one area. This *terreiro* was one small oblong room. Fringed white crepe paper flags covered the ceiling. The men and women were separated and instructed to sit on the benches alongside two walls, facing each other. Two congo drums stood at one end of the room near the front door. On the other end, the *peji* was covered with vases of flowers, a statue of the Virgin Mary, a brown bottle of water, ceramic dishes and paper bags of bread. Hidden in every *peji* are the stones which contained the *axé*, the spirit of the *orixá*.

The *iaôs*, the young women who have been initiated into the religion, the "brides of the gods," greeted each other before the ceremony. They wore white lacy blouses, colorful graceful skirts that swept just above their ankles, and scarves tightly wrapped around their heads, emphasizing the dark bold beauty of their full faces and graceful cheekbones. Three elderly women, the *equedes*, moved with confidence as they placed their hands on the young women's shoulders, giving advice. The *equedes* act like priests, supervising and protecting the ceremony.

A large man with strikingly white skin worked his way through the crowd a bit clumsily, knelt in front of the altar, and covered his face with his hands. Two young men, drummers, set themselves at the congas and their fingers hit the leather, rolling out a rhythm. The three *equedes* sat together near the drums. One by one, the young *iaôs* reverently bowed low to the ground at the elders' feet, brought their hands to their lips, then with the same hand stroked their own hair as if anointing themselves. With the same motion, they paid respects to the drums.

With the drums' constant rhythm, the younger women began dancing gently, gracefully lifting their elbows so their arms helped to undulate their ribcages. The tall man rose from his meditation, and started dancing. I recognized him to be the *babalorixá*, more commonly called the *pai de santo*, the spiritual leader of the Candomblé. He stamped his feet and lunged forward, hooted and whirled around, his dark loose curls flopping over his eyes and the sweat flinging off his skin. Meanwhile, a young man who had been sitting in the sidelines began to waver, his eyes half-closed. Suddenly he jolted up. An *equede* led him to the floor. He gave another jerk then began spinning, elegantly bent forward and sweeping the air with his curved arm. He stopped, dazed and the old woman gently guided him back to his seat.

The *babalorixá* stopped dancing and went to one of the young *iaôs*, took her face into his hands, and chanted a short incantation. Others, including the practitioners sitting in the sidelines, lined up and he cradled their faces and blessed them as well. The *pai de santo* picked up a small boy and lifted him high. The little one grinned, tickled by the crepe paper fringe on the ceiling.

The *iaôs* began slipping into trances as if falling asleep, some nodded back resisting, while others let themselves be taken by the persistent drums. People broke out singing samba songs; others made the sign of the cross. Remarkably, the dreamy-eyed danced so gracefully, while thrashing and shuddering and sinking down onto their knees. The old *equede* caught the celebrants before they dropped and eased them down. One of the *iaôs*, a beautiful lean woman, collapsed with her head falling forward; her turban slipped off, letting loose beautiful thick wavy hair. An old woman gently picked her up, and pulled her locks away from her sweaty neck, then helped her to the altar. The more lucid celebrants looked at each other knowingly and murmured the names of various *orixás*. The pervasive drums and singing had the strange ability to grow on me, and though I remained un-tranced, I felt cleansed.

The ceremony ended as everyone returned to a waking state. They looked happy, relieved, their faces shiny with sweat. They stroked each other's hair and embraced. As people left the *terreiro*, the *pai de santo* stood at the door with the bags of bread and handed each one a roll, a bit like communion. He was gregarious, if not a bit jolly. I wondered what he did during the day when he was not functioning as a *pai de santo*. Outside, voices coming from the lighted houses on the hill tinged the cool and quiet evening.

The practice of Candomblé and Catholicism varies between Brazilians. Some ignore the African element completely. Others see the African religion as a source of identity, resistance and liberation. In the case of Candomblé, I saw a joy that is a part of worship. The strength and drama of these two religions make the spirituality found in Brazil unique. In a sense, the religious history of Europe and Africa came together and formed a third religion in the New World. The glory of three continents!

No wonder the white of the Eucharist and the white of the Oxalá's robe could not help but come together in celebration of misery and hope, enslavement and freedom, and death and resurrection.

143. Xango and the Holy Ghost

Esther Iverem, journalist, author, and poet, is founder and editor of SeeingBlack.com, *a Web site dedicated to the black perspective. The following brief excerpt concludes her 2001 article on Candomblé.*

Consider carefully Iverem's final sentence, especially the phrase "the Holy Ghost . . . same African spirit." Might the Candomblé Xango indeed be considered the Christian Holy Ghost?

[W]e return to Opo Afonja [a Candomblé compound], again wearing white, for the Xango festival. The main house for ceremonies is packed. Men and women are separated on opposite sides of the seating area. The women from our group stand or squeeze into the upper rafters on the women's side. The members of the terreiro protected by Xango dance in a circular motion around the center of the floor in wide white skirts, some accentuated with bright fabric. Many stop and give honor to the spiritual leader of the compound, Mãe [Mother] Estella, by kneeling before her or kissing her hand. When the dance reaches a crescendo, some of the members get possessed by the spirit and go into a trance. These people eat fire—Xango is the god of fire. They pass a bowl of fire from head to head.

It reminds me of my childhood growing up in the Church of God in Christ [a Black Pentecostal denomination]. Those folks got the holy ghost. These people tonight in Bahia are possessed by Xango. But it looks like the same spirit, the same African spirit, with a different name in a different place on the globe.

SOURCE: Esther Iverem, "Land of the Orishas: Candomblé in Bahía," SeeingBlack.com (April 9, 2001); http://www.seeing black.com/x040901/orishas.shtml. Reprinted by permission of Esther Iverem, author, editor, and publisher of Seeing-black.com.

144. Santería

The charts below use the Spanish version of the names for the orishas *(secondary gods) revered by the Yoruban Africans who were brought to Cuba and Puerto Rico and who maintained their religious beliefs during and after enslavement. Their religion, called Santería, ultimately spread to others in the Caribbean, and is very closely related to the previously considered Candomblé of Brazil. (The Brazilian Portuguese versions of the names of the* orishas *differ slightly.)*

Omitted from the charts is Olodumare, who may be understood as prime mover, ultimate source, first cause, designer of all that exists, neither created nor begotten. Within him are many different facets or persons, one of whom, Olofi, god on earth, serves as humanity's personal god who is worshipped. For believers in Santería, "Jesus Christ is the mask of Olofi" (De la Torre).

How do the Santería commandments compare with the biblical commandments of the ancient Hebrews? Do they suggest that both societies had similar needs?

What does the Greco-Roman-Yoruban equivalency chart indicate about human culture and religion?

Consult the next chart, which delineates the actual function of the Yoruban orishas. *Are they indeed equivalent to Western culture's well-known Greco-Roman deities?*

To be able to judge the equivalencies of the orishas *and the Catholic saints (last chart) knowledge of the lives, legends, and attributes of those saints is necessary.*

The Commandments

1. You shall not steal.
2. You shall not kill, except [in] self-defense.
3. You shall not eat the flesh of humans.
4. You shall live in peace with your neighbors.
5. You shall not covet your neighbor's possessions.
6. You shall not use the name of your God in vain.
7. You shall honor your mother and father.
8. You shall not ask for more than what I have provided, and you shall be content with your fate.
9. You shall neither fear death nor commit suicide.
10. You shall keep and respect my laws.
11. You shall teach my commandments to your children.

Comparison of Yoruba Mythology to Greek and Roman

Function	Greek	Roman	Yoruba
Ruler of the Gods	Zeus	Jupiter	Obatalá
The Gods' Messenger	Hermes	Mercury	Elegguá
God of Divination	Apollo	Faunus	Orúnla
God of Thunder	Gebeleizis	Fulgora	Changó
God of the Hunt	Artemis	Diana	Ochosi

SOURCE: Miguel A. De La Torre, *Santería: The Beliefs and Rituals of a Growing Religion in America* (Grand Rapids, Mich., and Cambridge, U.K.: Eerdmans, 2004), 40, 46, 48-49, 52, 54-55, 124-25. © 2004 Wm. B. Eerdmans Publishing Company, Grand Rapids, Michigan. Reprinted by permission of the publisher; all rights reserved.

Function	Greek	Roman	Yoruba
God of War	Ares	Mars	Oggún
God of Healing	Asklepios	Aesculapius	Babalú-Ayé
God of the Sea	Poseidon	Neptune	Yemayá
Goddess of Love	Aphrodite	Venus	Oshún
God of the Underworld	Hades	Pluto	Oyá
God of Nature	Pan	Inuus	Osain
God of the Volcano	Hephaestus	Vulcan	Aganyú
God of Agriculture	Demeter	Ceres	Oko
God of Science	Athena	Minerva	Inle
God of Wifely Role	Hera	Juno	Obba
Heavenly Twins	Kastor & Polydeukes	Castor & Pollux	Ibeyi

Influence of the Orishas and Corresponding Catholic Saints

Orisha	Has Power Over	Patron of	Personal Characteristics	Corresponding Catholic Saint
Obatalá, Oxalá, Orisainla	All things pertaining to human heads; bones; all things white	Fatherhood	Regal; wise; peaceful; pure; serene; patient	Our Lady of Ransom
Elegguá	Crossroads; fate	Doorways; messengers; tricksters; justice	Playful; unscrupulous; clever; mischievous; childlike	Anthony of Padua; Martin of Porres; Benito, the Holy Infant of Prague; or Holy Child of Atocha
Orúnla	Human destiny	The oracles of Ifá	Wise; sagacious	Francis of Assisi; St. Phillip; St. Joseph
Changó	Fire; thunder and lightning; semen	Revenge upon enemies	Passionate; sensual; risk-taking; arrogant; prone to violence	St. Barbara; St. Mark; St. Jerome; St. Elijah; St. Expeditus; St. Bartholomew
Ochosi	Hunting; jails; courtrooms	Those seeking legal justice	Impartial; quick-witted; alert	St. Norbert; St. Albert; St. Hubert; St. James
Oggún	War; employment; hospitals; minerals; iron and other metals	All human effort	Militant; belligerent; hardworking; strong	St. Peter; St. James (in Santiago); St. John the Baptist; St. Paul; the Archangel Michael

Orisha	Has Power Over	Patron of	Personal Characteristics	Corresponding Catholic Saint
Babalú-Ayé	Smallpox and other illnesses	Beggars; the sick; the disabled	Gentle; compassionate; humble	Lazarus
Yemayá	Ocean	Womanhood; motherhood	Maternal; dignified; nurturing	Our Lady of Regla
Oshún	Gold; rivers; lower abdomen; fertility	Eros; love; marriage	Seductive	Our Lady of Charity
Oyá	Cemeteries; death; wind; human respiratory system	Niger River in Africa; ancestors	Tempestuous; violent; sensual; authoritarian	Our Lady of Candelaria; St. Teresita
Osain	Nature; forests; herbs	Houses	Solitary; rational; chaste	St. Sylvester; St. John; St. Ambrose; St. Anthony Abad; St. Joseph; St. Benito
Aganyú	Volcanoes; earthquakes	Those with high blood pressure and fevers	Fiery; violent; muscular	St. Christopher; Archangel Michael (in Santiago); St. Joseph
Oko	Agriculture	Delicate matters	Peacemaker	St. Isidro
Inle	Fertility of water to produce crops	Fishermen; healing of human illnesses	Studious; scientific; calculating	Angel Raphael
Obba	Oba river	Human ears and bone structure	Neglected wives; virtuous; gullible	St. Rita of Casia; St. Catalina of Siena; the Virgin of Carmen
Ibeyi	Good luck; childhood illnesses	Children	Innocence	Sts. Cosmas and Damian; Sts. Crispin and Crispinian; Sts. Justa and Rufina

145. Affirming Afro-Latin American Identity

Until the very last decades of the twentieth century, Latin American nations virtually denied the role of Afro-Latin Americans in their history and discriminated against them in all areas of life. In countries where their presence was profound—Brazil, Cuba, the Dominican Republic, coastal Colombia, Panama—they were virtually written out of national history (save Cuba after the revolution) and did not appear in school textbooks. For black Latin Americans, to "get ahead" meant to ignore the supposed ignominy of slavery and "act white," marry lighter, and shun black relatives and friends; in other words, to deny black or Afro-Latin American identity.

Melania Cueto Villamán, sister in the Apostolado order, and Emigdio Cuesta Pino, a longtime priest in the Society of the Divine Word, address this historical reality, which has resulted in widespread ignorance of the achievements of slave culture, of the heroism of cimarrones, *maroons, and their* palenques *and* quilombos, *and of the massive contribution by Afro-Latin Americans to the colonial and national economies.*

How do Cueto and Cuesta, in the first half of their article, add to the above description of the plight of Afro-Latin Americans? How do they characterize the church's acknowledgment and treatment of Afro-Latin Americans, historically and in the present? When society at large does actually recognize the Afro-Latin American, how do Cueto and Cuesta characterize that recognition? How do the authors determine that "the right to be different is a mandate from Jesus"? Does their brief treatment of Jesus and the Gospels suggest they are navigating familiar currents?

Affirming our identifies as Afro-Latin American religious men and women is a path that needs to be undertaken. We need time to reflect on concepts that are part of religious life but do not affirm our identity as Afro-Latin American men and women. We can begin discussing elements, recognizing the need to find a way of talking about our reality in a balanced way that identifies, affirms and values us as black men and women, religious men and women descendents of Africans. This is a process that is just now under construction.

Introduction

We begin with some historical considerations, convinced that our own history will let us know who we are and help us identify a profile for our future. We also consider some aspect of history with respect to the Church and religious life as instances that allow us to recognize ourselves and give us more elements to build an Afro-Latin American religious life. As such, we believe that it is necessary to present the fundamentals of all religious life, referring particularly to Jesus in whom we can understand fraternity, apostolic work and the meaning we try to give our lives and our communities. [. . .]

The black population has never fully accepted the fact that our ancestors were slaves, but it [slavery] has influenced us in a significant way. It will take time for black men and women to become aware of this, shake off this historic weight and correct the negative vision that has befallen us in order to [be] seen objectively in Latin America and the Caribbean.

SOURCE: Emigdio Cuesta Pino and Melania Cueto Villamán, quoted in "Elements to Reaffirm our Afro-Latin American Identity in Religious Life," *Latin American Documentation* 32, no. 3 (January/February 2002): 20-26. Originally published in Spanish as "Elementos para reafirmar nuestra identidad en la vida religiosa como afroamericanos y afroamericanas," *CLAR* 4 (July-August, 2001): 55-67. Reprinted by permission of *CLAR* (Confederación Latinoamericana de Religiosos [Colombia]).

In many of our countries the only thing that is truly known about the black population is that our ancestors were brought to this continent from Africa as slaves. The social position of black men and women has been and continues to be on the periphery in Latin America and the Caribbean. This marginalizing periphery [. . .] has not only been geographic, but also social, political and economic. With few exceptions, such as Law 70 [recognizing the ethnic rights of Afro-Colombians] in Colombia, fraternity campaigns in Brazil, the struggles of black men and women in the United States, and organizations in Ecuador and Peru, Afro-Latin Americans have not been accepted, valued or recognized as people capable of contributing to the construction of a new society.

The conquests of black men and women through the histories of our countries have been characterized as destabilizing the dominant system. Expressions of this are the *palenques* in Colombia, *quilombos* in Brazil, *manies* in the Dominican Republic, uprisings against owners, rebellions during Carnival, in the mines and all activities that enriched the slave owners.

In many of our countries there are many towns or communities that are exclusively for black people. In many cases they are the remnants of the *palenques* or the large mines, where it was possible to achieve a certain level of freedom.

The achievements that society recognizes of black men and women in universities, business and even religious life have generally been framed or accompanied by a process of denying our black heritage, a process of becoming white.

Most people are often unaware of this process, which consists of denying our heritage to be considered "someone." We see black people in many social settings, but they have never accepted themselves as Afro-Latin Americans. These people are incapable of looking beyond their personal conditions, using their own experience to say that racism does not exist in Colombia or other Latin American countries. These people generally do not suffer any kind of racial prejudice, because they have been modeled according to the requirements of society and consider themselves to be a "different" kind of black.

Afro-Latin Americans who have gone through this "whitening" process do not see their own socio-cultural, historic or community experience, feeling that they have overcome a painful past, the past of poor blacks in our countries. [. . .]

Many of our honorable representatives, black people participating in the social or political life of the country, are blacks who belong to this group (*mulato*). The debt they have to our people is that they never publicly say they are black and do not identify with us. Nevertheless, whenever there are complaints about racism these people are held up as an example [that] racism does not exist.

It is not hard to find black men and women who accept that they are inferior to others in society and are resigned to accept their situations of poverty, misery and marginalization. It seems that each one of us has learned our role in this historic process. [. . .]

[A]ll the social structures must learn how to coexist with black women and men as part of the societies we want for the future. We cannot continue ignoring the contributions of our presence and participation. Afro-Latin Americans demand being considered subjects in the societies they helped build.

Evidence in religious life

There have been men, women and circumstances in the Church and religious life that have accompanied Afro-Latin Americans. This is the case with St. Peter Claver, S.J., Alonso Sandoval, S.J., St. Martín of Porres, St. Benito, OF [*sic*], Fray Juan of the Cross, Anurite (Sister of the Holy Family) and other men and women of good will who have discovered Jesus where many others did not want to look.

In many cases the only voice of encouragement for our people came from religious men and women committed to the poor. They saw in Afro-Latin Americans a population where they could develop their missionary vocation. [. . .]

Misery and marginalization have existed in our communities throughout Latin America and the Caribbean and religious life [has not made black communities a priority], which are considered the "poorest of the poor."

In Colombia, which is considered to be the Latin American country with the largest [total] black population after Brazil, there are few congregations that work directly with the Afro-Latin American population. [. . .]

A proposal for Afro-Latin American men and women who want to join religious life

Awareness from religious life: The life, history and culture of our peoples have to follow us in evangelization. As such, it is more important than ever to consider:

Intolerance: We cannot deny that we live in a society that is incapable of accepting differences, a process that has been evident since the conquest and colonization of which we are victims.

Lack of commitment: It is no secret that the Church has not assumed a clear position on slavery. It can be claimed that its silence was an accomplice to the abuses that were committed. Furthermore, many men and women of the Church used the Word of God to justify these abuses. Our Church has a historic debt with the black world. The abuses continue in many communities, where Afro-Latin American men and women are forced to deny their black heritage.

Lack of valorization of Afro-Latin Americans: There have been a series of impositions that tend to reduce Afro-Latin Americans to certain cultural elements, such as music, dance and sports, denying other aspects of our identities, including spirituality, wisdom, resistance and willingness to survive. An attitude of rejection continues in our communities where our spiritual expressions are not accepted or respected.

Renew religious life: The lifestyles of the majority of congregations in Latin America and the Caribbean are strongly influenced by western culture. We are aware that the majority of the congregations were founded in Europe or the founders were European. This fact should not be used to justify abuses committed against people born in other cultures, particularly black women and men.

The ideal of religious life proposed by Jesus is not incompatible with being black. Religious life as an option or sign for people in the Church is compatible with all cultures, because it is a Gospel calling and the Gospel is not culturally exclusive. Jesus invited us to live his alternative project, which was life in abundance and an option to free our brothers and sisters who have lived under the dominant, oppressive system for more than 500 years. If we lose sight of this, we lose the legitimacy of the Gospel, which invites us to live the religious life from our own dynamic. We are different, we think differently, have different dreams and our hope and confidence in Jesus is different. The right to be different is a mandate from Jesus, it is an important element for social and personal liberation.

146. A Resurgence of Maya Religion

Marcelino Palax (b. 1970) is one of the youngest men to have become a Maya priest in Guatemala. He has worked as a promoter of Maya spiritual practice and as a consultant to the indigenous human rights organization CERJ (Consejo de Comunidades Étnicas "Runujel Junam").

The interview excerpted below was done by Report on Guatemala, an organ of NISGUA (Network in Solidarity with Guatemala).

Given the nature of the religious cosmology of the Maya described by Palax, what must have been the result of the imposition of clerical Catholicism upon the Maya in the colonial era?

SOURCE: Interview of Marcelino Palax by Report on Guatemala [RG] in "Revival of Mayan Religion," *Latin American Documentation* 24 (January/February 1994): 14-17, passim.

Palax's history of the sodalities is an account by a traditional authentic Maya believer. Could there be another response to his interpretation that "our people agreed . . . because they were threatened"? Note that the sodalities (cofradías) were ecclesiastical institutions of the laity centered around devotion to a saint or the Holy Sacrament. Among the indigenous they evolved into a kind of civic-religious municipal organization permitting men to advance their status in the towns.

How might Palax respond to the extraordinary growth of evangelical Protestantism in his Guatemala over the last quarter century?

MP. My name is Marcelino Palax. I am a Cakchikel Maya from the village of Xacaxac in the municipality of Solola in Guatemala.

R.G. How were you chosen to be trained as a Mayan priest?

M.P. Well, we are not chosen, or elected by the community, rather, we have a sacred Mayan calendar that has 260 days, 13 months of 20 days each. This calendar controls the lives of humanity. When a person becomes a musician, a painter, or a priest, it is very much because of destiny, it is authorized by the Creator, and not chosen by people of the community.

R.G. Does the Mayan family usually consult the calendar when a son or daughter is born in their family?

M.P. This is something our ancestors understood. In order to conceive a child, they used the calendar to look for a day which favored the child becoming a good person. The 260 days of the Mayan calendar, the thirteen months of 20 days, are the same as nine Spanish months, the time until the birth of a child. There are exactly 260 days until the birth of a child.

The child's destiny is governed by the calendar, according to the dates of conception and birth. So the Mayan people look to the calendar to conceive a child.

Some Mayas offered sacrifices of art and also consulted with God through a Maya priest about the destiny of their child, about what work a person would do in life. If a person fulfills his obligations as revealed by the calendar of his birth, things go well for him in life; if a person does not fulfill them, then, things go badly for them. When the Spaniards arrived, they burned all our documents, our Mayan codes of law; so then our grandparents were left in the darkness, they didn't

know how to conceive a child according to the calendar. That's why there are many murderers, there are many thieves; this is what comes to us from not knowing, not understanding our destinies according to the calendar.

R.G. How did you find out that you were destined to be a priest?

M.P. The truth is that I got sick from not working to fulfill my destiny, my obligations. I was a campesino, I worked in the fields, but I encountered many problems, many failures. That is when I had to go to consult with a priest. The priest took me to a Mayan altar, did a reading of my calendar, and he told me that, yes I did have a destiny, to work with the community, with the indigenous people, to serve them as a priest. [. . .]

R.G. Can a woman become a priest?

M.P. It depends on the Mayan calendar. There is a calendar reading which is favorable for a priest, there is another favorable for a priestess, there's another for a midwife, there are others for painters, marimba players and so on. [. . .]

R.G. Perhaps you could give us an example of the problem people might come to you for.

M.P. I don't know if they do this here in your country, but in Guatemala sometimes a couple will go to a Christian priest before they are married and say "We need to know if this couple is related at all." This is because of the children this couple might have. So that's like the work of the Mayan priest. You come with your birth date and your girlfriend's date of birth and ask, "Is it suitable or not for us to marry?" The priest might say "No, she is like this, you're like that, it's not suitable." Or perhaps, "It's suitable but you're going to need a lot of spiritual support." If a person has never-ending failures in life, he can come to me, and I can read the calendar and tell him, "Look your destiny is this and this. Have you complied with this?" Then he must answer that question inside himself. [. . .]

R.G. Is the practice of Mayan rites more widespread now than in recent years, or is it just more public?

M.P. Actually it is both. The Mayan religion has suffered from the invasion of other cultures and religions especially Christianity, which continues to invade us in a variety of ways, particularly now through the communication media. In rural areas the media that reaches most people is the radio, and different Christian sects have their own radio stations. They broadcast not only their preaching, but also music programs that the communities like a lot. So Christianity entered our communities through many means, and many of our youth no longer pay attention to the Mayan religion.

But when Spain and the Latin American countries started to make a lot of noise about celebrating the Columbus Quincentennial, this caused a restlessness, a curiosity, in our people, and an investigation of the Mayan religion began, and more people began to consult with the priests and the elders about what had happened. The message of these elders has been received by the people with much interest, and our Mayan religious practices are being revived publicly, and are being accepted by our people, who understand that what happened 500 years ago was not a conquest nor was it a meeting of the two worlds; rather, it was an invasion. So more people understand now what has happened to our culture and religion, and more people are interested in knowing about it and practicing it.

R.G. What has been the role of the sodalities?

M.P. The sodalities have a very sad history. Many people don't know this history, so they still value the sodalities. Prior to the Spanish invasion, we had our own social structure. Those who guided the people were the elders: for the Mayan people to govern one must have capacity and experience, which depends greatly on age. But the Spaniards changed that social structure, taking out the elders and putting in young men who had no experience or authority in the communities. But when the Spaniards saw that the young people did not have the capacity to guide a whole people they thought, "We'll find those elders some chore to do so they'll be there together when we need them." So they gave the elders a chore. "Take care of this saint. This saint will be your responsibility." And our people agreed to do it, because they were threatened. And this was how the sodalities began.

R.G. Can people practice both Christianity and Mayan religion?

M.P. This is an issue that must be well understood. There are many people who had baptism imposed on them when they were born. All, all the Mayan people have been baptized, but it is an imposition, an invasion of our culture from the 500 years. So now there are all these people who have been baptized but haven't attended church since then and who don't consider themselves Christians. Many of them continue their Mayan customs, but in ways that have been very influenced by Christianity. Some say, "That's good, let's put these two religions together," but the truth is that you really can't do both. Now with this public revival of Mayan religion, the ritual practices are being purified—and the people are being purified—of the Christian influences that have been imposed. People are returning to their religion, they are finally understanding that it is their true religion. We call this "cultural conversion" and it is growing now in Guatemala.

R.G. Is it part of your work to support this conversion?

M.P. Yes, CERJ was the first organization of the popular movement to sponsor a large public Mayan ceremony in Guatemala: we had a conference on Mayan religion on the second anniversary of our organization (1990) and it included the first open public Mayan ceremony. The coalition of Mayan organizations, Majawil Qij, was born out of this revival.

PART XXI

Protestantism into the Twenty-First Century

What accounts for the massive gains made by Protestantism in Latin America, especially in the last three decades? Why is it that the majority of churchgoers in Latin America today are Protestant? Why is it that evangelical Protestantism—especially Pentecostalism—is reaping the fruit of this upsurge, rather than the "mainstream" Protestant churches (Lutheran, Methodist, Presbyterian, Episcopalian)?

Primary reasons for evangelical Protestantism's appeal are its simplicity and accessibility, its biblical base, its sense of the "priesthood" of all believers, the availability of its ministers, the ability of "ordinary" men and women to become ministers, its emphasis on the formation of the individual conscience by the individual's meditation upon the scriptures, its strong sense of the church congregation as community, its lack of intimidating authority, and its flexibility in adapting to specific environments.

Secondary reasons for this appeal are the disarray within the Catholic Church and the latter's inability to find a unified and coherent manner with which to implement the vision enunciated in the documents promulgated by the episcopal conferences held at Medellín and Puebla in 1968 and 1979. In actuality, it is impossible to speak of a "Latin American" church. The seven Meso-American, nine South American, and two Caribbean Spanish-speaking nations, and the one Portuguese- and one French/Creole-speaking nations each possesses an episcopal conference which is answerable only to the Vatican.

Within each of those twenty churches are sectors that may be termed traditional, centrist, and progressive, each with highly contradictory agendas. Differing conceptions about the liturgy, base communities, liberation theology, charismatics, lay involvement, Vatican directives, the social component of Catholicism, ruling elites, authoritarian regimes, human rights, and revolutionary movements have prevented any coherent image of the church from emerging.

The unwieldiness of the traditional parish where the ratio of priests to parishioners is extraordinarily low and the perennial shortage of priests (despite a recent increase in vocations) have become a severe problem inasmuch as the Latin American church has always deemed clerical status mandatory for those initiating and directing church enterprises. Even the diaconate, which was restored to prominence by Vatican II and which allows married men to officiate at certain church functions, has been viewed with suspicion by the majority of Latin American bishops. This deprives the church of relevant insights by men with families who know the realities of living in societies that are largely dysfunctional for the majority of their citizens.

The absence, at least since the birth of the national republics, of an evangelizing tradition within the Catholic Church, together with her historic reliance on state support to uphold cherished church concerns, has prevented her from becoming a dynamic presence in society as the Protestant churches have done. Even after experiencing the ire of anti-clerical regimes, the Latin American church has not overcome her desire for close church-state ties. She has trusted more in the support to be obtained from officialdom than that which she might receive by cultivating the faithful and relying upon their growing loyalty.

Finally, responsibility for the weak responses of the Catholic Church to the needs of the faithful that were necessitated by the turmoil and upheavals of the last decades of the twentieth century also falls on the shoulders of the late John Paul II. His long incumbency as pope (1978-2005) was, on the whole, unfortunate for the church in Latin America. Despite his learning, brilliance, and sanctity, and his progressive encyclicals extolling human rights and acutely analyzing the problems arising from the world's varied political economies, Karol Wojtyla was apparently never fully convinced of the devastating effects that the profoundly cynical and entrenched oligarchical-militarist regimes of Latin America had upon the majorities in their nations. The pope demonstrated a strange misreading of the needs of the Latin American church in his dealing with bishops and priests who, as committed Christians, were actively involved in the search for justice. He canonized (2002) a José María Escrivá (1902-1975), a Spaniard, founder of the clericalist/elitist (despite being 98 percent lay) Opus Dei and virtually ignored an Oscar Arnulfo Romero (1917-1980), archbishop of San Salvador, who was forced by the harsh realities of his flock to challenge the regime that was crushing them and who was ultimately assassinated after calling upon the Salvadoran army to cease killing Salvadoran citizens. He allowed Joseph Cardinal Ratzinger's Congregation for the Doctrine of the Faith to arouse suspicion about theologians (e.g., Leonardo Boff) who were attempting to develop a spirituality relevant to the actual lives of Latin Americans and a "Christology from below" that reflected "the teaching and actions of the Jesus of history." This position of the pope demonstrated a centralizing mentality alien to the much-vaunted concept of "subsidiarity" and thwarted the vitality of the Latin American church.[1]

The episcopal appointments by John Paul's predecessor, Paul VI (1963-78), were cau-

---

1. See Alfred T. Hennelly, ed. *Liberation Theology: A Documentary History* (Maryknoll, N.Y.: Orbis Books, 1990), 122, 159; and David Stoll, *Is Latin America Turning Protestant? The Politics of Evangelical Growth* (Berkeley: University of California Press, 1990). For an understanding of subsidiarity, see David J. O'Brien and Thomas A. Shannon, eds. *Renewing the Earth: Catholic Documents on Peace, Justice and Liberation* (Garden City, N.Y.: Image Books, 1977), 62, 78, 158.

tious (e.g., Romero was a devout, conservative, seminary professor; López Trujillo [appointed bishop in 1971] an articulate intellectual Vatican insider; Aramburu, a prelate with close ties to the Argentine military, when they were chosen) but a good number were willing to listen to grassroots movements of all kinds—theological, charismatic, social, lay, and clerical. Most of the men John Paul appointed as bishops in his twenty-six-year reign—at his death the vast majority of the Latin American hierarchy—were not inclined either to challenge the repressive status quo or to support the clergy who did so. They usually were managers and not imaginative pastors and understood that the pope apparently perceived any deviation from traditional procedure as a threat to the established order of the hierarchical church and to her normal relations with secular regimes.

147. A Sin of Omission by Another Christian Church

Lisandro Orlov (b. 1942), a Lutheran pastor in Argentina, was invited by the Ecumenical Pastoral Commission to Accompany People with HIV/AIDS, of Santiago, Chile, to offer a training program for people who want to do the kind of work indicated by the title of the commission. Pastor Orlov was trained by the Lutheran Church to carry out pastoral work with those who have HIV/AIDS.

The remarkable presentation below may be read in a number of ways: (1) as any professional counselor's approach to dealing with those who are HIV-positive; (2) as the approach of a thoughtful Christian who sees a gap in his/her church's ministry; (3) as the approach of a practitioner of liberation theology; (4) as the approach of one who meditates on the Gospels and asks how Jesus would treat those who endure the stigma of HIV and the pain of AIDS; and (5) as the approach of a Christian who is anxious to make his/her church relevant and truly Christian in the face of lived reality.

Which way(s) is [are] most appropriate? Does Orlov present Jesus as the "subversive from Nazareth," as described by López Trujillo, thereby making Orlov a perfect example of a practitioner of the wrongheaded liberation theology criticized by López Trujillo? (See reading 128.)

Why is a Lutheran pastor involved so closely with an AIDS pastoral when there are other illnesses as serious or more serious [than] this one?

What justifies an AIDS pastoral commission is not the disease itself. An illness is not sufficient enough reason to set up pastoral commission of this kind. All of us working on this issue are clear that we are doing this work because there is a confusion over the diagnosis. [. . .]

When a person is diagnosed as HIV positive or with AIDS the entire solidarity network, both in

the family and at the societal level, breaks down because there is this confusion linking a medical diagnosis with a moral diagnosis.

This does not happen with other illnesses. When someone finds out they have cancer or any other serious illness their solidarity network gets stronger. No one would think of expelling from school or church someone diagnosed with cancer. [. . .]

At one point I thought the conflictive issue was homosexuality, but that's not it. The definite con-

SOURCE: Lisandro Orlov, quoted in "AIDS: The Power of Conversion," *Latin American Documentation* 29, no. 2 (November/December 1998): 23-27.

flictive issue is sexuality. The churches do not have a coherent message in relation to sexuality. They continue to repeat ideas from the 11th and 12th centuries that have never changed.

Today's situation, with its cultural norms, technological changes, the sexual revolution, women's liberation and the liberation of gay communities are forcing a change that is still difficult for the churches to accept.

Their approach to sexuality, despite all the talk about it being a gift from God, continues to be full of dualism. There is a separation between the physical and the spiritual. There continues to be a patriarchal dualism with the masculine valued more than the feminine. [. . .]

The first attitude has been silence. This silence is like an accomplice, because they say that silence equals death, and the churches have been part of this message. Only recently have there been signs of people willing to talk. The churches need to ask forgiveness from society for remaining silent, for taking so much time to speak out, to denounce, to act.

They also have to ask forgiveness because they were quick to condemn, to judge, to offer a negative image of a vengeful God when the Gospel actually talks to us about a loving God.

In many cases health and sickness have been associated with sin. A cheap theology was developed that says people are sick because of something they did. We know, though, that illnesses are caused by a virus not by sin. The same thing was said in earlier times about diseases that were incurable. When a cure was found people stopped thinking about these diseases as a curse from God. [. . .]

[A church that deals with AIDS] becomes a church that decides to bear the cross, because it means taking on the stigma that many people are living with today. It is the same example as Jesus Christ with the lepers. We always talk about how He cured them, but we forget that during Jesus' day lepers were considered liturgically impure, because their illness was associated with sin. They were not allowed to enter the synagogue or the temple. When Jesus Christ touched the lepers He was defying society, questioning all the value structures of the religious leaders of his day.

Touching a leper was the same thing as being a leper. It was so impure that it meant going through an entire purification process in order to reintegrate into society. Jesus touched the lepers, He hugged them and, as such, was considered religiously impure, a leper.

Jesus Christ was a bothersome figure for the religious leaders of His day. He disturbs the tranquility of our religion, because He forces us to open ourselves up to all those who have been expelled from our communities. When Jesus returns He will sit with all those who have been expelled from our churches and not with us because we are like the Pharisees of His time. [. . .]

It is not about compassion or mercy. These principles put us on a plain of superiority. The AIDS pastoral commission has to do with justice and not with the virus, with the dignity of people who have been wounded, many times by society and the church. When we say that the church has to be a community of health, a healing community, we are not talking about the body, but about the dignity of people, which is much more important than simply curing the body.

The Gospel shows us that those who evangelized the church, and the disciples were those who were different: The Samaritan, the foreigner who is looked down upon and who shows us the path to solidarity; the widow, with her example of generosity; the prostitutes are going to show us the path to the Kingdom, because we read that they will be the first to enter. This is very troubling. It changes us. [. . .]

We do not want to continue with the pastoral; we want it to be something provisional until the church and society changes and the doors that are closed today, open. We say: "We are open to the world." That is a lie! We are not open to everyone because we are open with conditions: Come, but be sure you are like the rest. We are not open to sexual minorities, to the majority who are economically poor. There are many people who are not included in our communities.

What would happen with transvestites, with homosexuals, with drug addicts if they were not sick? Would we accept them into our communities? Do we only accept them because they are sick? It is completely incoherent. What are we preaching? We condemn them and then go to the hospital and we want to help them. This is a kind of pastoral that we cannot carry out with mental reservations. We either commit ourselves completely with the people we accompany or we should abstain and stop being hypocritical.

148. A Baptist Pastor Critiques His Evangelical Churches

The reading below written in 2000 by the brilliant Chilean activist Baptist Víctor Rey, director of the Latin American Theological Fraternity and head of the Chilean branch of World Vision, an international Christian relief and development organization, suggests a man of acute intellect, deep Christian faith, and profound honesty and courage.

Nos. 2, 3, 4, 6: What is Rey's most basic criticism of evangelical Protestantism? Do his criticisms resonate with the accounts of evangelical Protestantism that precede this reading? (See readings 93-97.)

No. 6: What does he mean by "the churches should also be questioning and prophetic"?

No. 7: Explain "the identity problem" that he perceives in the Catholic Church. Note that Opus Dei is a conservative, elitist movement within Catholicism, favored by Pope John Paul II, who appointed members to important dioceses in Latin America. It encourages prominent Catholics both to grow spiritually and to convince governmental and other institutions and powerful figures in society to favor the Catholic Church.

"Some positive signs from Protestantism": Nos. 1, 2: Numbers 1 and 2 are reciprocal; one suggests the other. How does Rey's concern here compare with the theology of the evangelical churches expressed in readings 93-97? Whom does Rey echo?

Nos. 3, 4, 5: Numbers 3, 4, and 5 reflect the new positive sense of reality Rey perceives in the evangelical churches. Express that reality (see 4 and 5) in one coherent statement. Note that CLADE 1 = Congresos Latinoamericanos de Evangelización, 1969.

"Conclusion": Emile Cioran and Enrique Rojas have brilliantly characterized the "successful," though empty and unhappy, twentieth-century individual. How does Rey describe the qualities of the only church that can be successful in reaching this person?

2. The massive explosion of Evangelical movements, and Pentecostalism in general, is an issue of the past few decades. Their growth is so great that in some countries they are expanding faster than the population and for the first time in the history of Latin America it is possible to think of a Protestant majority. As theologian René Padilla states: "We continue being a minority today, but we are a visible minority." The numerical growth of Protestantism brings with it certain risks, with superficiality being the most obvious. The megachurches, which convert old cinemas into temples, run the risk of institutionalizing a commercial Evangelical religiosity (water from the Sea of Galilee, soil from Jerusalem, trips to the Holy Land, special scarves and crosses, etc.). A large number of the Evangelical churches are concerned only with increasing their numbers. There now exist certain formulas for trying to calculate how much it costs to bring each new member into the church.

3. We have to admit that the cross has been replaced by a religiosity that does not belong to

Source: Víctor Rey, quoted in "Protestant Churches and the Challenges of the New Millennium," *Latin American Documentation* 30, no. 6 (July/August 2000): 1-7. Originally published in "La Iglesia en América Latina y los desafíos del nuevo milenio," *Presencia Ecuménica* [Venezuela] (January-March 2000): 35-41.

the cross. Many leaders have been tempted by the "theology of prosperity" without troubling themselves about whether or not this is biblical. The relationship with witnessing has been damaged. We are growing used to financial and moral scandals involving pastors and leaders.

4. In many churches we can see that emotions have become more important than the Bible, it is more important how one feels than in what one believes. This is dangerous because an emotion has to be replaced by one that is stronger so that it remains effective. We are no longer "the people of the Bible and the hymnal." The Bible is used only tangentially and services are full of songs that are repeated over and over again. In this new reality, in which feeling is more important than reason, the Gospel preacher must know how to recognize the world we live in and not apply strategies that were used in the past and are no longer efficient. [. . .]

6. Many sectors of the Evangelical churches have grown through the seduction of power. The important Evangelical politicians have not been the best examples. The important battles undertaken by Evangelical leaders have been for privileges. The churches should also be questioning and prophetic. This second dimension should also be present in the Christian message, because the fight for justice is still missing. This is the pending task. Something is wrong when governments feel comfortable with the churches. I think we should declare a moratorium on "presidential breakfasts" in Latin America.

7. The growth of Protestantism in Latin America troubles the Catholic Church and it is willing to do anything to stop its advance. The issue of ecumenism is not on the Catholic Church's agenda. The Catholic Church is focusing on itself and certain sectors within it use the term "sect" to refer to Protestant churches. The Catholic Church is beginning to recognize the importance of the media and Evangelization, while important Pentecostal figures have been using radio and television, and even buying their own networks, for years. All of this shows us that there is an identity problem within the Catholic and Protestant churches. It is no longer possible to talk about one Catholic Church and one Evangelical Church.

Opus Dei has gained importance and leadership within the Catholic Church, while liberation theology is in crisis. The bishops who believe in this current have been replaced and their influence curtailed.

Some positive signs from Protestantism

1. Integral mission is a concept that has been solidifying in Latin America's Evangelical churches. It is now normal to find next to a church, regardless of its size, a health center, a school, a soup kitchen, etc. The majority of the churches have understood that they have an integral mission and that evangelization goes hand in hand with social responsibility. It is their duty to become agents of change, to help transform their community. There is a recuperation of the Gospel social awareness [sic].

2. Some sociologists and theologians maintain that one of the keys to the growth of Protestant churches has been the concept of the "universal priesthood of each believer." Each Evangelical feels that it is his or her mission to spread the message of Christ and that there is a sense of urgency to this task. They are aware that this is their mission and the churches assign this missionary task to pastors, women, children, the laity, Afro-Latin Americans, indigenous people, etc. It is an important axis that aims at involving all members in God's work in the world as an essential aspect of the church's mission, which is the mission of the Kingdom.

3. If we look at a map of the beginning of the 20th century we will see that the majority of the world's Christians were found in Europe and the United States and that the membership was Caucasian. Today, at the end of the century, the situation has reversed. The majority of Christians are found in what is called the third world, in Africa, Asia and Latin America. The face of Christianity has changed. It is now a dark face. An incredible transcultural missionary spirit is rising on these continents. It is not a traditional style, like the one that came from the North with a large dosage of paternalism, but develops with local creativity and in many cases is supported economically by the local population. "Latin America has stopped

being a continent that receives missioners, but has become a continent that sends missioners out into the world." [see reading 155]

4. The search for unity is something we can see in the different congresses, workshops and seminars held in Latin America. [. . .]

5. Theological reflection has been another area that has been growing among Latin American Evangelicals. In 1969, when CLADE I was held in Bogotá, Colombia, it was shown that Evangelicals have their own theology. René Padilla, however, said that, "the theology of Latin American Evangelicals was a theology on loan." Most of what was preached, what was taught in the theological seminaries, what was read and what was published came from the North. Since then there has been a renovation in this area and we now find Evangelical literature and hymnology written by Latin Americans. If we review the declarations made at different congresses we also see contributions that shed important light on different aspects of the challenges facing the region's churches. It is particularly important to highlight the contributions of the Latin American Theological Fraternity (FTL) and the Latin American Council of Churches (CLAI). These organizations are aware that theological work only makes sense if it maintains strict ties to the churches and their work. There is, however, much work still to do, because the word theology is still frowned upon in some Evangelical circles.

Conclusion

The second millennium ended with the churches still on the defensive in the face of the challenges of technology, the secular spirit of the wealthiest classes and the threat of numerous sects, which are trying [to] attract millions of poor people by offering them something that transcends their peripheral neighborhoods. Several years ago Rumanian philosopher [Emil] Cioran spoke of the need of demystifying a rationalism

that only brought misery and totalitarianism. "Everything can be smothered in humankind except the need for the Absolute that will survive the destruction of the temples and the disappearance of religion from the face of the earth." We are witnessing a generation that is more religious than its predecessor. [. . .]

On the personal level, there is the kind of person Enrique Rojas has called the "light person." This is a person who has almost everything and will continue to have even more things because of technology, but at the same time is a person who lacks the beliefs, values and ideals that make life sacred. [. . .]

This kind of successful yet unhappy person, who feels less and less tied to any community, lives for and by a kind of virtual reality offered by computers and television. They connect to operators in other countries while ignoring what goes on in their own neighborhood.

Can the churches offer a way out of this in the third millennium? During the next millennium technology will offer things that are dreams today, like instant transportation and the prolongation of life. Human beings will become increasingly stronger. They will be gods of power. The church that knows how to position itself in the new society, expressing and interpreting this society while offering answers to ethical and existentialist problems, will be the church of the third millennium. There are many churches and sects that want to play this fundamental role. One of these is the Evangelical church.

But it will not be able to take on this new role if it is on the defensive. It will have to do this being a critical friend of the world. It cannot be an adversary, but an understanding friend that questions the new technological world because technology is empty of values. The church's mission in the third millennium is to unite the transcendental with the immanent, the eternal with the daily, in one message.

149. A Presbyterian in Cuba

Raimundo García Franco has been a Presbyterian pastor (since 1953) in Cárdenas, Cuba (hometown of Elián González). He founded the Christian Center for Reflection and Dialogue in 1991. He has served since then as its executive director. The center, an important NGO, offers courses to people from all parts of the island on organic farming, food preservation, the use of medicinal plants, sex education for youth, alternative sources of energy, gender and development, and human rights. Paul Jeffrey, longtime journalist in Latin America, conducts an interview with García Franco in 2004.

Who is Pastor García Franco? What is his concept of the church and its role in society? What are his criticisms of the church, which is enjoying new freedom? How does he view the Cuban government? What is the implication of his reference to the "kind of freedom" existing in the United States? What do his tranquil references to and treatment of the problems he has encountered from the Cuban government suggest about his vision and commitment as a pastor? What does he mean by a "theology of commitment"? Where does his understanding of it place him in the context of developments over the last four decades within the Christian churches in Latin America? Compare his attitude to that of Cuban churchmen in 1971 (see reading 99).

Paul Jeffrey: Why is a church center involved in growing food?

Raimundo García Franco: For many years we've had a crisis with the production of food. The government tries to implement new plans and projects, but we always find ourselves facing problems. So we decided to get involved, to do things in an organic and sustainable manner. And the Ministry of Agriculture has declared our farm a provincial reference center. Last year we produced 108 tons of vegetables. We've got chickens and ducks and pigs and fish, and we're working on increasing production at lower cost. We're trying to develop new ideas and new technologies that can be implemented in the country, especially focused on saving energy. [. . .]

You give away a lot of those vegetables you grow.

Our program of pastoral accompaniment and consolation attends people like the elderly with no family, those who are disabled, and people living with HIV-AIDS. We have personnel who cook and deliver food to 130 people every day. We have three social workers who are helping these folks with their daily problems, whether it's a single mother or a child with different capacities. [. . .]

The many activities you carry out reflect a greater space for the churches and civil society than existed earlier in the revolution.

I've had the privilege of participating in all of the church-state dialogue in Cuba since the 1960s, including direct dialogue with the president. Some will argue that there haven't been big changes in Cuba. Yet from my point of view, there have been. The consciousness of the people and the society has changed. This is not the Cuba of 1970, or 1980. This is a Cuba that started to change in the 1990s, and that change has continued. Although we're still living under the same political and social regime, people today express themselves in a different manner. I'm not saying that socialism will fall tomorrow, but people are provoking a crisis that obligates a response. [. . .]

Despite all the great errors and problems we have here, we're still better off than most of Latin

SOURCE: Raimundo García Franco, quoted in Paul Jeffrey, "Cuba Is Changing: An Interview with the Rev. Raimundo García-Franco," *New World Outlook* [new] 64, no. 5 (May/June 2004): 9-11, passim. Reprinted by permission of *New World Outlook* and Paul Jeffrey.

America. But we need more space for dialogue and for a kind of freedom that's not just something we'd copy from the United States. You've got serious problems in the United States with the kind of freedom you have. How do we go forward unless we expand the commercial relationships we've been developing inside Cuba? Where's the money to invest going to come from?

We need a wider political dialogue at the same time. The United States has to dialogue with this little country. [. . .]

I'm not from the government, nor am I an emigrant, nor am I a dissident. So it's as if I don't exist. We need new space for dialogue, which is what we're trying to do with our center.

An important point here is that whether we agree or not with a government, we've got to respect the government. The fact that some North Americans don't agree with (President George) Bush doesn't mean that he's not the President of the United States. We've got things here that are good, some that are bad, and some things that are very bad, but we've got a government. And it should be present in every dialogue. [. . .]

In the last 15 years the church in Cuba has experienced a lot more freedom than before. But has it responded adequately to the theological and social tasks that come as a result?

This is one of the problems that most worry us. Some of us would have liked to see the church in Cuba recover with strength, but with an awareness of its errors in the past.

Yet what we're seeing rise up now is a church mostly indifferent to these problems and a church leadership that is too interested in comfort, in a certain standard of living, in taking advantage of the fact that they're the church. Because of the new relationships they form with people from outside the country, many aren't worried about social issues. Some are interested only in proselytism, in massive growth without any responsibility. There's no interest in ethical questions or ethics in the society. We're witnessing almost medieval attitudes again in some churches. This is one of the most terrible things happening in Cuba today.

A theology of commitment—a theology of daily life and an ability to see the face of Christ in the needs of the people—is being lost. For those of us who have long struggled for a new vision of the church, we're once again in the minority. We were in the minority until 1990 because of the political dynamics. Now we're in the minority within the churches.

So what do you do in response?

Our center is part of the church, and we're pushing the church to broaden its vision and its responsibility to the people. We do something here that no one else in the church is doing in Cuba: sex education. In many churches that have grown quickly, the leaders have told their members that sex is a sin. Let's talk about responsible sexuality, let's talk about sexual ethics, but please let's not talk about sex as a sin.

150. A Methodist Aymara in Bolivia

Eugenio Poma was born about 1943 on a Bolivian hacienda where his family and some twenty others worked for the landowner without wages, demonstrating the existence of a "thriving" feudal system (until the revolution in 1952 put an end to it). He now works for the World Council of Churches as executive secretary of its Indigenous Program.

The simple, straightforward account by Poma reveals much about the social situation of mid-twentieth-century Bolivia, especially its effects on the indigenous. But our interest concerns religion and the fifty-year presence of the Methodist Church in Sallcapampa, and hence in Bolivia as a whole in the twenty-first century.

SOURCE: Eugenio Poma, "My Story as Part of the Evangelical Methodist Church in Bolivia," *New World Outlook* [new] 64, no. 6 (July/August 2004): 7-8, passim. Reprinted by permission of *New World Outlook* and Eugenio Poma.

How did the church define itself and its mission in 1954? Whom did it seek out? How did it operate? Who were the "operators"? And how did the church relate to the sociopolitical reality of Bolivia?

How would the Methodist Church respond to these same queries today?

Born in Sallcapampa, the seventh child of Gregoria and Pedro Poma, I learned to care for the guinea pigs (a food source), pigs, sheep, and cows; carry water to the house; and assist the priest with the seasonal rituals for planting and harvest. The fundamental lesson in the Aymara indigenous community was that "life is good when everything is in harmony."

Although the families on the hacienda were oppressed, there was hope that the situation would change; and so the parents invited more or less educated people, who knew how to read and write in Spanish, to come to our houses at night. This was done without the knowledge of the landowner or his foreman, who considered these to be subversive visits.

My parents tried to win the landowner's favor by naming him as our godfather. Perhaps the landowner would invite us to the city as his servants.

Bonifacio, my older brother, went to the city of La Paz as the landowner's servant and was able to attend school there. He participated in the popular uprising that led to the revolution in 1952, but he was subsequently murdered in the streets.

I was then taken to La Paz as a replacement for Bonifacio in 1951. I spent one year in the city, learned Spanish, and learned firsthand the racial discrimination practiced by the urban elite toward Aymarans who left the hacienda.

In 1953, I returned to Sallcapampa, where the Agrarian Reform had liberated the laborers and made them owners of the land that they had worked.

Early School Years

In 1954, the Methodist mission had already begun. I entered elementary school in Sallcapampa, where teachers, called preceptors, had been sent by the Methodist Church at the community's request. That school had a budget 50 percent of which was contributed by the Methodist mission and the other 50 percent by the community.

After two years in elementary school in Sallca-

pampa, I moved to the Methodist Central School in Ancoraimes, where I attended fifth and sixth grades. During this process, I was very much influenced by Christian teachings.

For reasons that I still do not understand, I was invited to continue my studies at the Methodist American Institute in La Paz. This was a challenge. The day that I was interviewed by the school principal, I tried to fail. However, it seems that the missionary who brought me to La Paz had already fixed the results.

I remember my first day of classes as my biggest trial because I was not prepared to face a community so different from Ancoraimes or Sallcapampa. The other boys ridiculed me and said things like "There goes the 'Indian.'" Closing myself up in the classroom to do homework, coming early, and leaving classes late were my strategies for avoiding constant discrimination. As the years went by, I excelled in sports. I was the best soccer player in my class. Every time the American Institute played, my name was prominent; but during parties, birthdays, and vacations, I was ignored. [. . .]

Because of social problems and the nationalistic fever of that period in Bolivia, I began to participate with organizations that sought the establishment of a democratic government. I was conflicted about how the role of the church fit into a social movement that sought to change the dictatorial government. Even the Methodist church in Ancoraimes could not understand, which led me to distance myself from church activities for two years. I moved to La Paz to study at Simón Bolívar, the Superior Normal School where I graduated as a Normal Professor of English in 1974.

In 1975, I became a member of the Council of Amautas, which led a movement within the church to change the prevailing church structure. The great majority of the members, who were indigenous, were not allowed to participate in the decision-making process. [. . .]

In 1979, I returned to Ancoraimes, Bolivia, to serve as Director of the Ancoraimes Vocational School.

During the 1980 coup d'état, I was fired by the new military dictatorship and had to leave Ancoraimes. I was elected National Secretary of Services for four years by the General Assembly of the Methodist Church, composed of delegates from all the different Methodist congregations in Bolivia.

In 1986, I was elected as the first lay bishop of the Methodist Church in Bolivia for a four-year term.

Reflection

My formation would have been more complete if my Christian education had integrated the principles, values, and traditions of my indigenous culture. The basic principles of my culture hold the same values Jesus taught, interpreted in a different way.

Today, mission is no longer exclusively carried out by workers from distant lands but also by those who are the fruit of that earlier work. They emerge as the new protagonists in their own lands among Andean or Amazonian souls. They take into account ancestral values, not in opposition to Christian doctrine but as a complement toward our encounter with the true God of life, justice, and peace. All this contributes to the construction of a new world.

151. Pentecostalism Comes of Age in Latin America

The goal of the Latin American Evangelical Pentecostal Commission (CEPLA), founded in 1990, was "to strengthen the ecumenism of the Spirit." This goal was furthered in the meeting in 1994 in Lima, Peru, of pastors, bishops, presidents, and leaders of different Pentecostal churches of Latin America. This gathering was followed up in 2001 by a similar meeting "within the context of the Latin American Consultation of Pentecostal Women," in Barquisimeto, Venezuela, the purpose of which was stated as follows:

To evaluate the Pentecostal process of cooperation and unity led by the Evangelical Pentecostal Latin American Commission (CEPLA), and to make decisions on lines of work for the years to come.

We have come so far, by the convocation of God's spirit assumed by our Pentecostal pioneers, founders of the churches we represent today.

Entrusted in God's hands, we also respond to the historical commitment in search of a Latin American and Caribbean Pentecostal church united, strengthened by and faithful to the Gospel of Jesus Christ. We urge the other churches, members of CEPLA, to respond affirmatively to this call.

For this reason, and in the midst of an intense journey of prayer and reflection, for the decision we assume today, it seems timely to make the following statement:

1. In the last eleven years CEPLA has continued a journey which began in the 1960s, and has been expressed in many encounters, consultations, workshops, intense work, exchanges, courses, ecumenical participation at the local, continental and global levels.

2. During these years we have seen the consolidation of these efforts, which reaffirm and commit our Latin American and Caribbean Pentecostal identity.

3. We have the conviction and urgency to

SOURCE: Consultation with Pentecostal Churches, Lima, Peru, November 14-19, 1994. World Council of Churches. Excerpts from "The Consultation" (Hubert von Beek), "The Pentecostal Identity" (Rev. Dr. Gabriel O. Vaccaro), "Pentecostalism, In the Power of the Spirit" (Bernardo L. Campos M.), "A Pentecostal Perspective on Evangelization" (Maritza León), "Our Vision of Unity and Ecumenism" (Bishop Gamaliel Lugo Morales), www.pctii.org (accessed on 10/03/2005). Reprinted by permission of World Council of Churches, Geneva, Switzerland.

deepen, improve and transform this experience into a more effective service to the Pentecostal people.

4. We feel in our hearts that the decisive moment has come to establish an organism which can represent us and make visible our witness and commitment.

5. Therefore, all Pentecostal churches present agree on:

5.1. The creation of a Latin American and Caribbean Council of Pentecostal Churches. To that end, we initiate a process of consultation, convocation and constitution within the Pentecostal churches.

5.2. We entrust the conduction of this process to CEPLA's director along with the presidents of the churches Brazil for Christ, Pentecostal Church of Chile, The Christian Mission of Nicaragua, and Christian Biblical Church of Argentina so that a charter assembly is held in a period of three to five years.

The announcement of this 2001 statement of purpose was followed by a "Consultation" and six short treatises on various aspects of Pentecostalism which were originally delivered at the 1994 Lima meeting, five of which are excerpted below.

A thorough analysis of the six presentations on Pentecostalism suggests a number of motifs:

1) *Celebration of the continuing growth and strengthening of indigenous (meaning native born citizens, whatever their race or ethnicity) Pentecostal churches, independent of US missionary influence, increasingly manifesting an authentic national culture of strongly popular character;*

2) *Celebration of increasing social commitment and involvement, recognition that the stereotype of "social idleness is out of date today;" recognition of a sympathetic coincidence of Pentecostalism's growth with that of a democratic ethos in Latin American nations and of a "symbolic equivalency" between Pentecostalism and "messianic groups of political or religious persuasion;"*

3) *Recognition of the dangers of "neo-Pentecostalism" and also the dangers of "fundamentalist USA forces," and the spirit of exhibitionism; also recognition of the "fear of deviation from . . . pure doctrine," with the consequent recognition of the need for more biblical training for the ministry and more association with non-Pentecostal churches.*

I. The Consultation

"The Consultation" by Hubert van Beek, executive secretary of the World Council of Churches, constitutes a description, warts and all, of the characteristics of Latin American Pentecostal churches based on the testimonies of the countries represented at the 1994 Lima meeting. .

What are those characteristics? Of what are the Pentecostals especially proud? What are their self-criticisms, chief problems, and their immediate and long-range concerns?

When Latin American Pentecostal Christians meet they share their experiences through testimonies and worship. It was therefore natural that these two expressions of communication and communion were very prominent in the consultation.

Indeed the meeting began with a series of testimonies from various countries. These stories illustrated from the outset that there are Pentecostal churches in Latin America which are deeply concerned with the political, social and economic conditions of the people among whom they witness of their faith. Each story spoke of the hardships caused by the credo of neo-liberalism. Each story was in its own way an account of the hope that these communities of faith bring in the midst of situations of poverty, unemployment, violence, drugs and crime. During the years of violence caused by the Army and the Shining Path in the Ayacucho region of Peru the evangelical and Pentecostal churches were the only ones who stayed with the people. Thus these testimonies, and others given in the course of the meeting, provided the right setting for the discussions throughout the week.

Each day of the meeting opened with a worship

celebration. That in itself is quite normal for WCC events. But it was Latin American Pentecostal worship, not hindered by time limits or well prepared orders of service. It was worship that through prayer, testimonies and comments gave space for dealing with many of the issues that emerged in the discussions during the consultation. Thus there was a constant flow back and forth between celebration and reflection.

Daily Bible studies were another feature that is common to many meetings. In Latin America Bible studies are intimately linked to the context of the people, using popular expressions of music, dance and drama. Thus the scriptures came alive in their relevance for the daily life of the communities back home.

Whether they meet among themselves or with others, *identity and spirituality* are essential for the Pentecostal churches in Latin America. Therefore the consultation started its work with presentations on these central themes, in a variety of forms: a pastoral reflection on Pentecostal identity, a scholarly paper on Pentecostalism in the power of the Spirit, a video in which common people talked about the power of the Spirit in their life. The meeting went on to reflect on evangelism, community, social commitment and unity, gradually widening the scope of mutual listening and dialogue between the Pentecostal participants and those representing other denominations within the WCC and CLAI.

The majority of the Pentecostal participants were representative of what could best be described as indigenous, autonomous churches which are not—or no longer—dependant on foreign mother churches or mission bodies. There is also another manifestation of the Pentecostal movement in Latin America which is known as neo-Pentecostalism. This is characterized by big campaigns and massive use of the media. It is imported from abroad and often portrays the gospel as a message of prosperity and personal fulfillment.

The discussions focussed on indigenous Pentecostalism in Latin America and brought out many of its marks. It is essentially a popular movement among the poorest sectors of society that responds to the spiritual needs of the people. Pentecostal faith offers an intimate personal relationship between the believer and God. The Pentecostal Christian encounters the power of the Spirit in his or her daily life and feels compelled to share that experience of God's presence with others. Evangelism is done in a direct, personal way, and with a sense of urgency. Popular, indigenous Pentecostalism is rooted in the culture of the people. It has a strong sense of community. The faith is personal but not individual; it is lived out and celebrated in the worshipping and serving community. Celebration, care for the neighbour and solidarity with the needy go hand in hand, holding the spiritual and the social together. The Pentecostal message can be a powerful agent of healing and reconciliation in broken communities. The social commitment of these churches of the poor is a source of hope in the midst of hopelessness.

There are various manifestations of Pentecostal ministry, which reflect the variety of gifts of the Spirit: preaching of the word, teaching, intercession, counselling, music, diakonia, etc. Pentecostal churches do have pastors. However the emphasis is not on structures or forms of ministry whereby one person is set apart but on the recognition that the Spirit is free to work in all believers. What counts is the message. Little attention is given to the content of the ministry. There is a great need to improve biblical and theological training.

The Spirit may arouse extraordinary ministries of healing, exorcism or prophecy. Miraculous healing through prayer may be a problem for others, it is not for Pentecostals. In any worship service there will be some manifestation of the Spirit. This understanding of ministry gives much importance to the role of lay persons. There can be abuse. It is the task of the pastor to see to it that everything is done in good order.

When structures are too tight Pentecostalism will always seek to break out and find new ways of expression. It is dynamic movement of continuity, rupture and transformation. The negative side of this strength is that Pentecostal churches fall easily prey to dissent. The scandal of division is particularly obvious in evangelism. The priority of proclaiming the good news is often perverted to become sheer competition for filling the church.

As is often the case in these meetings women were under-represented in the consultation. But those who were present made their voices heard. In the Pentecostal churches the Bible is often used to make women feel they are inferior to men. In some churches women can be pastors, in others not. The women in the barrios of Latin America suffer more from poverty and violence than the men. But it is the women who are involved in community activities. They run the soup-kitchens, care for orphans and street children, organise neighbour help, do door-to-door evangelism. These actions give them space to discuss problems which are not discussed in the church. They become aware of the need to acquire knowledge and skills. This helps them to claim their right and dignity as equal members of the community. For the Andino women the struggle is even more difficult. Many of them do not speak Spanish, they lack biblical knowledge, skills and resources. They are eager to learn but get little support from the church and feel alone. As one participant put it: how can the church evangelize if within its own community the relations between men and women are not sound?

The relations between the Pentecostal churches in Latin American and the Roman Catholic Church are complex. For the latter the rapid growth of Pentecostalism is an enormous challenge. Roman Catholic accusations of proselytism are matched by complaints of persecution and discrimination of Pentecostals. This is aggravated by the influence of conservative Pentecostalism from North America. In some countries there is outright hostility. In other places some cooperation is possible. The international, official Roman Catholic-Pentecostal dialogue may in the long run contribute to a better mutual understanding.

The Pentecostal churches feel the need to develop contacts and exchanges with non-Pentecostal sister churches, in particular with regard to theological and pastoral education for which they need help. In their experience the Pentecostal movement is not taken seriously by most of the Protestant theological seminaries in Latin America. Pentecostals are trying to learn the ecumenical language but they see little effort on the side of their ecumenical partners to understand Pente-

costalism. An example was given of a Pentecostal church in a Latin American country which had had a long-standing relationship with a non-Pentecostal church in the USA and had received many guest preachers from there. But the first Pentecostal pastor to preach in this sister church had yet to be invited. The churches engaged in the ecumenical movement should learn to value the gifts of the Pentecostal churches.

The participants were especially eager to strengthen relations with Pentecostal churches in the USA and in other parts of the world. They hoped that international ecumenical organisations such as the WCC and CLAI could help them in this regard.

The participants in the consultation accepted a proposal to produce and adopt a common statement summarizing their findings and recommendations. A small group prepared a draft which was thoroughly discussed and unanimously agreed upon [. . .]. This document will serve as the basis for further dialogue and cooperation between the WCC and CLAI and the Pentecostal churches through the Latin American Evangelical Pentecostal Commission (CEPLA). [. . .]

II. The Pentecostal Identity

"The Pentecostal Identity" by Dr. Gabriel O. Vaccaro, bishop, Church of God, Buenos Aires, analyzes six characteristics that comprise Pentecostal identity, three of which are excerpted below in a summary made by Pastor Jorge Julio Vaccaro.

The striking nature of his discourse may be described as its combination of biblical fundamentalism and sober critical analysis, the latter a characteristic not usually attributed to evangelicalism.

What animadversions does Vaccaro offer to his fellow Pentecostals?

Let us briefly reflect upon the following doctrinal elements:

1. Evangelization and conversion
2. Baptism in the Holy Spirit—Speaking in tongues
3. The Church as a charismatic and healing community
4. The spiritual world

5. The "surprise" and "expectation" elements in each meeting
6. The paradox of ecumenism and exclusiveness [...]

3. The Church as a charismatic and healing community

"But you are a chosen race, a royal priesthood, a holy nation, god's own people . . . " (I Peter 2:9) [...]

The presence of the Holy Spirit in the body of Christ is not a passive but a very active one. In a world doomed by despair and death, the Church should be, to be faithful to its own nature, the place where human beings find hope and life and the "shalom" they need. This does not mean that the Church should become a refuge for people to withdraw from the world, which would amount to "alienation."

Pentecostal churches have always offered a "milieu" which favours the healing of human beings. What is meant here is the atmosphere which evolves in a worshipping community. The hymns, songs and chorales, testimonies and preaching convey the message of God to the people. In the Pentecostal worship God's victory over evil is lived out and celebrated and this victory is shared with God. This brings about an atmosphere in which healing can occur.

The concept of physical, emotional, spiritual and mental health is typically Pentecostal. God's sovereignty over human beings allows for the supernatural to happen, which is nothing less than the direct intervention of God's power in the life of a human being. [...]

4. The spiritual world [...]

In Pentecostal doctrine, the demonic forces are intelligent spiritual beings determined to destroy human beings and their well-being. Thus they must be fought not with human power but with the power of the Holy Spirit. The manifestations of evil can be seen in the individual as well as in the "unjust social structures". [...]

In a classical manner, Pentecostals have divided the works of Satan in: temptation, oppression and possession. The meaning of temptation is well known to all Christians. We shall focus briefly on the meaning of oppression and demonic possession, and its redemption. [...]

The problem that many progressive and biblical Pentecostal preachers face is that most of these ministries are carried out in the midst of an exhibitionist show. Rightly, a gifted charismatic writer has asked: "Who shall free the exorcists from the spirit of exhibitionism?"

Progressive Pentecostalism insists upon the biblical, theological and spiritual preparation of the servants of God. This is extremely important. When dealing with a victim of oppression or possession, the gift of discernment must be used in order to know the steps to be taken. Some would recommend that the person should first be examined clinically, then psychologically and, as the last resort, to enter into the spiritual realm. [...]

6. The paradox of ecumenism and exclusiveness [...]

The Holy Spirit has not been and is not owned by any particular denomination. Unfortunately, as time went on and the movement expanded, some exclusive spirits became apparent. To be sure, it also came about as a consequence of the persecution that Pentecostals suffered from other churches and denominations. [...]

Other reasons can be found in the "fear of deviation from what is considered the pure doctrine:" this expression, skillfully used by the fundamentalists, inspired fear within the emerging Pentecostal movement about contextual, theological and historical changes during the process of growth and expansion.

The "lack of theological training" should also be mentioned. This was one of the most serious deficits in Pentecostalism in Latin America. The expression "the letter kills" was used and abused and cited out of context for many decades. It was not until the '50s when the Pentecostal churches broke away from their mother churches, especially from the United States, and became self-governing, that they began to see the importance of training and started the creation of many biblical institutes and seminaries.

Regarding social work, the missionary undertaking blocked and alienated the Pentecostal mind by teaching that social involvement had political undertones. It was also in the '50s, when the churches became independent, that their international leadership began to get involved in social and political issues. [...]

Thanks to God many churches are acquiring a social commitment in a world plagued with all sorts of injustices: the Unión Pentecostal Venezolana (Pentecostal Union of Venezuela), the Misión Pentecostal de Chile (Pentecostal Mission of Chile), the Iglesia de Dios en Argentina (Church of God in Argentina), to mention only a few in Latin America, have taken basic steps forward in their commitment to the poor and the disappeared, participating in meetings on development and human rights, attending peace conferences, joining historic churches in the spiritual unity of the people of God and raising their voice against human injustice.

III. Pentecostalism, in the Power of the Spirit

"Pentecostalism, In the Power of the Spirit" by Rev. Bernardo L. Campos M., of the Iglesia Pentecostal "Casa de Oración," Lima, views Latin American Pentecostalism as a concrete and powerful religious movement, part of a world-wide phenomenon, and having four characteristics.

His sociological analysis consistently demonstrates the effects of society upon Pentecostalism and those of Pentecostalism on society. Psychology, economics, U.S. foreign policy, politics, revolution, institutional Catholicism, neo-liberalism, etc.—all affect Pentecostalism.

What are some results of these influences, according to Campos? Do they lead in any specific direction(s)? What is the relationship between Pentecostalism and capitalism?

What does Campos suggest, in his concluding paragraph, about the future direction of Pentecostalism? Does this vision connect with the thrust of liberation theology?

The Pentecostal movement is one of the most important religious experiences of this century.

This has been recognized by Catholicism as well as by the various Protestant families in Latin America and the Christian world as a whole.

Pentecostalism is both a world socio-religious phenomenon and an alternative movement in the life and mission of the Christian church. Pentecostalism is, above all, a religious movement and not a "denomination," not a religious organisation. Although there are religious communities which call themselves "Pentecostals" and religious groups labeled "charismatic" within Catholicism, it is the Pentecostal movement which confers them their vitality and which gives rise to their organic and visible expressions.

The current political juncture in Latin America has generated such a public debate about the Church, the sects and religious freedom, that a description of the diverse religious expressions— among them Pentecostalism—is necessary in order to provide a coherent theological vision and promote the ecumenical dialogue on sounder foundations.

The following four considerations will allow us a first approach to the understanding of the Pentecostal movement as a sign of the power of the Spirit.

1. A movement of spirituality

According to Pentecostals' self-understanding, Pentecostalism is not a simple socio-religious phenomena, or the result of political and religion expansion of North American financial capitalism. [...]

From a theological point of view Pentecostalism, in Latin America and elsewhere, is a religious experience of the divine. As a religious experience, it represents a ritualized enlargement of the original Pentecostal events (Acts 2, 10, 19), with the aim and aspiration to express the very substance of Christianity—in this case, the "foundational Pentecostalism." [...]

[T]he Pentecostal movement has produced a social impact and has adopted cultural forms which threaten to tear down the religious hegemony of the Catholic Church.

The cases of Brazil, Chile and some Central American countries have given a lot of trouble to clergy and politicians. In Guatemala, El Salvador and Nicaragua, for instance, some expressions of Pentecostalism have been used by neo-conservative and fundamentalist USA forces to heighten and/or control the political tensions in that region. What is at stake behind this feigned war of religions? Nothing less than the opportunity to assert social identities and political projects and programmes, as well as the attempts to affirm old and new hegemonies through the use of religion.

2. A movement of protest [. . .]

Pentecostalism, which was born out of a deepening of religious and spiritual life, proscribed philanthropy from its works, and embraced a radical comprehension of the world as the locus of sin, without further discussion. Yet, Pentecostalism was unable to break away from the individualism inherited from the original missionary societies.

Nonetheless, Pentecostal ethics and morals cannot be explained by historical and theological assumptions only. On the contrary, contemporary sociologists of religion are pointing to social and economic factors. [. . .]

For others, Pentecostalism is the religious expression of a particular social and economic ethics. [. . .]

In all these approaches, Pentecostalism is seen as a response to the need of the people to create and structure their own symbolic contexts, which give meaning to the reality and regulate their daily behavior.

Pentecostalism as a "symbolic system"—as was the case for the Catholicisms of Christendom and Neo-Christendom in Latin America, "historic" and missionary Protestantisms, Socialism and Populism—meant and still is for the oppressed people of the continent, an alternative of religious satisfaction for the trauma of the conquest and colonization which destroyed the original social fabric through the use of religion and the manifestations of the sacred that prevailed at that time.

As a form of "social protest" and as an utopia of liberation, the Pentecostal movement reminds us of certain historic movements such as the Taki Onqoy in the Andean society of the 16th century (Huamanga 1560-1570) in Peru. [. . .]

However, the very reality of poverty in Latin America and the new world scenario (globalization, neo-liberalism) have forced Pentecostal communities to face reality. In Peru as well as in other countries, Pentecostals are becoming actively involved in civil society, re-creating ways of participation which had been previously rejected (social action, political engagement).

This rejection of the organized world, this apparent isolation (fugamundi) which takes the form of ethical righteousness (do not drink, do not smoke, do not dance, keep yourself pure, etc.) and of "Substitute societies" to the real society, are the responses that Pentecostals give to the marginalization imposed on them by the dominant religious groups and the economic and political powers. But to characterize Pentecostalism in terms of "social idleness" is out-of-date today. We see that Pentecostalism is coming of age; more and more we are becoming aware that we must be subjects and protagonists of our own history.

3. A popular movement [. . .]

Pentecostalism is characterized by its strong popular appeal, which raises some serious questions about the relevance of traditional religious structures such as the official Catholicism and Protestantism.

Pentecostal denominations, like the Church Base Communities (CBC), are truly popular churches in two ways: in the sense that their social base is the people; and by assuming an identity and a socio-political project in which the people, as an organic unity, are the agent of social change by means of religious structures.

However, the fact that a multitude of peasants, workers, poor students, marginalized people and gypsies convert to God daily through Pentecostalism is not only a matter of percentages, religious conflicts or denominational growth. Rather, it should be seen as the opening of social spaces in which, once a truly popular church is constructed, the affirmation of an inclusive and pluralist national identity and the search for alternative ways of democratic life are made possible; it is also an essential factor of social transformation.

This "popular" character of Pentecostalism has

direct implications for the transformation of the religious field itself. An autonomous financial structure (not depending on resources from Europe, America or Asia); a liturgy in which the elements and cultural mediations of the indigenous religion prevail over the contents of the ancient Christian tradition (Hebrew, Greek, Latin); a community life which favours socialization and personal involvement and facilitates the social participation of its members; and an organic solidarity with the less favoured sectors of society—all of these are essential features of Pentecostalism which are at the basis of a profound social transformation of the continent.

As a mixture of urban proletariat, popular culture and mass movement, Pentecostalism is the only sector of Protestantism which can identify itself with the regional phenomenon known as "popular reality."

4. A movement of social change

In the present composition of the religious field in Latin America, Pentecostalism—as any other religious charismatic expression of renewal—upholds a two-pronged relationship with civil society. On the one hand, it maintains conflicting relationships with the religious establishment (Catholic Church, historical Protestantism). On the other hand, it sustains relationships of compromise with corporate States which are in the process of destructuring, and even with States which undergo processes of re-structuring, as in Nicaragua and Chile during the '70s. [. . .]

It is not too far-fetched to affirm that a symbolic equivalency is possible—on different levels—between Pentecostal and some messianic groups of political or religious persuasion. These are the religious manifestations which promote, in the long run, socialist alternatives and resist, in spite of everything, the "collapse of hope" after lost battles—such as in Nicaragua, where Christians and Sandinistas attempted to recreate hope—or the sense of "loss of hope" created by certain groups which have an interest in the "downfall" of socialism.

Pentecostalism accompanies, permeates and directs ways of being of indigenous groups and of large masses of immigrants who are searching for their identity in Latin America. In the case of Chile, the expansion of socialism and Pentecostalism corresponded chronologically, and also coincided tactically. It should also be recognized that many transactional relationships gave birth to political clientelism on the part of the State with the Church and to religious clientelism on the part of the religious groups with the civil society, through the legitimization of the State.

Of late, some analysts of the Peruvian religious scene have suggested the hypothesis of a possible relationship of interaction and mutual influence between the emerging religious groups and a new type of capitalism. [. . .]

Pentecostalism is far from contributing to so-called "popular capitalism" or to providing a favorable milieu for its development, except in the form of consumers or of available cheap labor. In my view, this is due to a number of reasons: It is not asceticism but "mysticism" that is prevailing among Pentecostals; not saving but "spending" is the cultural pattern—because the little they receive is not enough to make savings and because it represents symbolically in monetary terms the value of their life ("fetichization"). Work cannot be considered as vocation and profession because the overriding situation among the Protestants is one of marginalization and unemployment, which sometimes takes on the form of redeeming self-denial. [. . .]

The transforming capacity of Pentecostalism does not rest upon its doctrinal coherence, but in its openness to new social practices at the critical and decisive junctures of a society in transition.

Therefore, born in the heat of a real and symbolic struggle against official Catholicism and Protestantism, as well as against political and partisan dogmatism, Latin American Pentecostalism has revealed conditions of symbolic mediation for what could be an affirmation of proletarian hope and national ethos. Those who fight Pentecostalism, whether religious people or politicians, do so because they are afraid of Pentecostal competition in the civil society, or because they have realized that Pentecostalism could embody a counter-programme in the political society. To the question of which should be the arena where Pentecostalism should fight its battle, the obvious answer is that Pentecostalism should struggle both in the civil and the political society. Yet, it is in the civil society where Pentecostalism will have the possibility to decide the future of the country and of its social involvement. If this is the vision of Pentecostals with their minimal participation in the political society, they would have understood with clarity where their role is more effective. This is not the time, in my opinion, to join the political class neglecting the need to pass through the social organizations. It is in the participation in the social organizations that maximum use should be made of a historical opportunity of far reaching consequences in our countries in the region. And this is possible precisely in the power of the Spirit, which makes possible the renewal of all things. [...]

IV. A Pentecostal Perspective on Evangelization

"A Pentecostal Perspective on Evangelization" by Maritza León, pastora, of the Iglesia Cristo Viene, Estado Miranda, Venezuela, narrates a brief history of the planting of Pentecostalism in Latin America, mostly by missionaries from the USA. She also explains the problems and schisms this created, especially in her country.

"A Pentecostal leadership of national character"—is that the focus of León's concern? What are "the two dimensions" to which she refers? Why does the Latin American Pentecostal experience, according to León, lead to "ecumenical action"? What does that action entail?

It was under the guidance of the Assemblies of God of the USA that a Pentecostal leadership of national character began to develop which had the opportunity to form itself. This is the aspect of witness of the evangelization in Venezuela. The other aspect or experience was the confrontation within Pentecostalism between Rev. Exeario Sosa, who was inspired with a vision of unity by [Federico] Bender [who first introduced progressive Pentecostalism in Venezuela] and missionaries opposed to interdenominational unity. The last missionaries who arrived in Venezuela brought along a stronger and more restricted doctrinal stance than the original one, which provoked a division in 1957 between the Assemblies of God and a group led by Rev. Sosa and other pastors. The latter gave birth to the Evangelical Pentecostal Union of Venezuela, with Rev. Sosa as its first president. [...]

In our country [Venezuela] as in other countries I have mentioned, it was through faith campaigns accompanied by extraordinary healings that Pentecostalism expanded. Because of our social history, Pentecostalism needed and needs charismatic leaders, men and women of character who put on the sandals of the oppressed and marginalized people, in the manner of Jesus when He accompanied the two men on the road to Emmaus.

We have not abandoned the traditionally integrated way of evangelization but we have enriched it in a contextualized perspective of Jesus Christ in our communities. Thus we can nurture the two dimensions, not from the point of view of a sectarian ecclesiastical organization but deeply rooted in the spiritual, social and cultural structures which form the space of our struggles and victories.

All this has helped us to take the line of ecumenical action. We are aware that Pentecostalism in Latin America is still influenced by the doctrine and praxis of those Protestant societies where it was born but it is taking roots in the culture and identifying itself with the values of our peoples, growing by leaps and bounds as a movement of response in the midst of a society permanently in crisis, providing room for popular sectors to be subjects—because in this type of community there is participation, in terms of the language used as national and regional level as well as the opportunity to give witness of what we have experienced in our life. [...]

V. Our Vision of Unity and Ecumenism

Bishop Gamaliel Lugo Morales, of the Union Evangelista Pentecostal Venezolana, introduces his comments on unity and ecumenism with a profoundly negative characterization of Latin American society. According to Bishop Lugo, what precisely is the burden imposed by the "powers of this world" and "forces opposed to the Kingdom of God"? What is the dilemma which thus confronts the churches that endeavor to lift that burden? According to Lugo, what does Pentecostalism offer those who bear the burden? How may the "living forces of Pentecostalism" begin to lift that burden?

I. What is our understanding of ecumenism?

To speak about unity and ecumenism in our Latin American and Caribbean context is both important and difficult. We live in a context which is so much violated, so much divided, so much penetrated by the individualistic and mercantilistic values of neo-liberalism that it would seem that efforts aiming at unity, dialogue, solidarity and cooperation do not count. Yet it is the culture of solidarity and cooperation which may help to combat the accelerating impoverishment and deterioration of life which the powers of this world have brought upon us.

The terms unity and ecumenism have been misinterpreted in many of our Pentecostal churches, so much so that they have become dirty words. In many cases these terms have been associated with communism, or with the surrender of the Evangelical Church to the Catholic Church. [. . .]

Therefore, to speak about ecumenism is to speak of unity and cooperation. Unity and cooperation for what? How? With whom? Is it meant as unity and cooperation among the Christians or the whole created world? Is it an inclusive or an excusive unity?

There are those who seek unity or encounter with the other in order to confront others, to destroy, annihilate and kill. Some alliances are forged for the sake of killing. That was the case of the Gulf War [1991], or the invasion of Haiti [1994]. It is also the case of large religious sectors in Latin America which conclude alliances with the ruling powers to impose their faith and ideology as the absolute truth, denying the faith of other peoples and other religious groups. [. . .]

The Process of Pentecostal Unity and Cooperation in Latin America [. . .]

a) The Latin American Kairos [the sacred moment when God breaks through time]: A Challenge to the Pentecostal Churches

The major problem that Latin Americans face is the 500 year-long historical crisis, a burden caused by forces opposed to the kingdom of God that has plunged our continent in anguish, despair and misery greater than any force could ever produce. [. . .]

This explains the importance which the analysis of the national and Latin American conjuncture is acquiring in our debates and gatherings and why our pastoral and prophetic work is rooted in the slums, favelas and poor communities of the continent. Our churches are, on the whole, made up of peasants, indigenous people, workers, students, taxi-drivers, women, blacks, youth, etc. In this respect, we are calling on the living forces of Pentecostalism in Latin America and the Caribbean to take on, with renewed urgency, the historical role it must play in favour of the unity of the Church and of the creation [*sic*]* in the current historical juncture of the continent.

b) Pentecostalism and the Disregarded: Women, Indigenous People, Youth, Children, Etc.

In all the countries of Latin America and the Caribbean the blacks, the indigenous peoples, the youth, the children and the women are victims of social, economic, cultural, racial, religious and gender discrimination; they are what we call the disregarded sectors. [. . .]

[T]he forsaken and poorest sectors of the population find in the praxis of Pentecostalism a kind of participation that the dominant society denies them. Thus it is possible that the Pentecostal Church in Latin America is transforming itself into a place where the marginalized resist their marginalization in a society dominated by minority groups which intend to maintain the poorest sectors of the continent in anonymity.

---

*The retrieved text is defective here: there has been an omission. But that provides an opportunity for the reader to fill in the gap: "the creation" . . . of what?

152. A Bolivian Pentecostal in the United States Examines His Church in Latin America

Pedro C. Moreno (b. 1961), a Bolivian lawyer, Pentecostal, and graduate of the Fletcher School of Law and Diplomacy (Tufts University), is the senior director of Justice Initiatives with Prison Fellowship International and editor of the Handbook on Religious Liberty around the World *(Charlottesville, Va.). In 1991 he organized the first chapter of the Rutherford Institute (for religious freedom) on South American soil. His analysis in 1997 of the startling phenomenon of Pentecostalism in Latin America begins with a scathing and ironic portrait of Latin America, which, by now, must seem familiar. He continues his analysis by presenting a positive picture of Pentecostalism, especially its social effects, and slyly suggests that they bode well for "a bright and prosperous future." Certainly the qualities he lists coincide with a democratic ethos and with modernization.*

What are those qualities and why does he state that they are thwarted by "Pentecostalists themselves"? Moreno's caveats about Pentecostalism were the result of his own observation and analysis, but do they not echo the self-criticism contained in the 1994 CEPLA document? What is Moreno's own special concern about Latin American Pentecostalism, despite its "good intentions . . . zeal . . . and passion"? What does he suggest are the remedies?

The region [. . .] still operates in several self-destructive ways. State officials both act and are seen to act as virtual kings and lords, while monopolies are still strong in the economic, political, social, and even religious realms (with an established and, in some cases, official church). Tax evasion, exacerbated by governmental corruption and mismanagement of public funds, has crippled democratic reform and weakened the accountability of public officials. A career in government is still seen primarily as a way to amass a fortune.

Though its people are warm and generous, Latin America is also a continent marked by great social paradoxes. A land of deep religiosity, but little morality (i.e., institutionalized lying and socially accepted adultery); saturated with "macho" types, but not enough responsible men; with a ruling class ethnically "mestiza" (mix of Indian and European), but, out of prejudice, considering itself "white;" where the law is seldom openly challenged, but frequently disobeyed or ignored.

Against this political and social backdrop, a Latin American version of "The Great Awakening" seems to be taking place. One needn't even believe in God to recognize that the historical phenomenon of a spiritual awakening remains by its nature an unpredictable event. But the question nonetheless remains why, of all the forms of Protestant and Catholic Christianity capable of leading such a revival, Pentecostalism is the one to which Latin America seems to have turned. [. . .]

Latin Americans, accustomed to economic and political roller-coasters, seem to be at home with the new Pentecostal spiritual roller-coaster. [. . .]

More important than the elements with which Latin Americans are familiar, however, may be the elements with which they are not. The personalized dedication on the part of the leadership and flexible structure break from the Catholic and even Protestant divisions between clergy and laity. The Pentecostal acceptance of women in leadership, in some cases even at the pastoral level (typically two-thirds of the congregations are women), adds to its popularity. Though most members of

SOURCE: Pedro C. Moreno. "Rapture and Renewal in Latin America," *First Things* 74 (June/July 1997): 31–34, passim. Reprinted by permission of *First Things*.

Pentecostal churches are poor and uneducated, an increase of middle and upper class members has brought the social classes together in a way unfamiliar to Latin American people. Similarly, the services bring together racial castes—descendants of the Native Americans, the European colonists, and the African slaves—in ways rare in some of the more prejudiced Latin countries. White and black, mestizo and Indian, educated and illiterate may be found holding hands and even kissing each other (a very unlikely occurrence in a highly prejudiced society). [. . .]

The Pentecostals find themselves not only questioning existing religious structures (both Catholic and Protestant), but also giving expression to a deep-rooted discontent with existing social and economic conditions—the discontent the Communists were certain existed throughout Latin America, though their revolution failed to spread. This religious dissidence is furthering modernization in Latin America, taking advantage of the new pluralism and democracy the collapse of the Communist threat allowed to develop in political and economic realms.

One might conclude that the "Pentecostalization" of Latin America promises a bright and prosperous future. [. . .] About whether the explosive growth of Pentecostalism will bring forth the long awaited and much needed economic and social transformation of Latin America, however, serious doubts and uncertainties remain. [. . .]

[C]hurch members place great importance solely on "religious" matters at the expense of every other activity or aspect of life. Church takes precedence over family, work, and social life. [. . .]

Caio Fabio, president of the Evangelical Association of Brazil, wonders if the Latin American revival is one "in the manner of God" or if it is a revival "à la latinoamericana." If the latter is the case, Fabio predicts, "it will die in the illusion of a superficial or inoperative evangelical joy." Fabio concludes that "we may simply become the majority in a country of immoral and miserable people, without anything changing substantially in our continent." The pattern of Pentecostals despising or at least minimizing their studies or professions and the value of their work has caused an ecclesiastical atrophy and a lack of growth beyond church activities. It has also diminished other areas of life, such as education, business, and especially politics (seen largely as Satan's domain). [. . .]

The great and ongoing religious revival in Latin America gives Pentecostals (and Evangelicals in general) an unparalleled opportunity to transform the continent in all areas of life. But this enormous spiritual energy could be spent in individual and religious self-gratification if it is not directed properly toward society. The leaders of Pentecostalism in Latin America have good intentions, much zeal for God, and a passion for evangelism. They must consider carefully, however, the fact that they may be helping to breed a generation of frustrated and mediocre students and professionals. "It does not matter that I had poor results in this academic period, as long as I led some people to the Lord" becomes the resulting attitude among Pentecostal students. [. . .]

Pentecostals alone will not be able to have a transforming impact. It is essential that Pentecostals work together with all Latin American Christians. The union of Pentecostal energy with other Protestants' theological training, knowledge of church history, and emphasis on character building would make any social effort all the more effective—particularly when it seeks as well the active participation of God-fearing Catholics. [. . .]

There is no automatic correlation of evangelical growth with economic and social advancement. At the least, it will require that we Pentecostals see all areas of society, not just the church, as part of God's Kingdom; that our emotions be balanced and enriched by reason; that we see ourselves as ministers of God in all that we do; and that while anticipating Christ's prompt return, we are prepared for the long run.

153. Roundtable on the Future of Pentecostalism

José Orozco is a Chicago-born, freelance journalist working in Caracas, Venezuela. His article on the strengths and weaknesses of Pentecostals was written in 2004, ten years after CEPLA Lima and seven years after Moreno's piece. Do the three pastors—Pirela, Olson, and Aguirre—offer any new insights about Pentecostalism or do they echo the strengths and weaknesses described earlier by others? Does the Jesuit, Apolinar Pérez, advance new perceptions about the nature of Pentecostalism? What are Orozco's own conclusions about the future of Pentecostalism and its potential effects on Latin America? Where does he stand vis-à-vis the positive perspective of the pastors and that of Pérez?

The growth of evangelical Christianity in Venezuela, as in the rest of Latin America, begs a few questions: How will this social transformation help or hurt the region? Will evangelical Christianity save the country from its social ills, while spurring tolerance, development and true social justice, as some claim? Or are we in for further disappointment?

The religious marketplace: Most evangelical converts come from the Catholic Church. For those that stay in evangelical congregations, they find their spiritual and material needs met in a way that the Church hasn't learned to do.

The influence of free market capitalism on contemporary religion cannot be underestimated. Based on the idea of choice, and the freedom to pick a product from a variety of competing alternatives, the days of inheriting your parent's religion and passing it down has given way to the religious marketplace. Besides syncretic Roman Catholicism, and cults like María Lionza and Santería, Pentecostals and other evangelicals are marketing their religions to poor consumers, and succeeding.

Pastor Joaquín Pirela thinks that the "inclusive" nature of evangelical churches represents part of its appeal. "We talk to the hookers and the drunks," said Pirela who leads a non-denominational church and doubles as Press Secretary for the Evangelical Council of Venezuela (CVE), an umbrella group which includes over 150 evangelical churches and church organizations. Pirela adds that evangelical churches are more in touch with contemporary life, allowing divorced people to remarry, something the Catholic Church still prohibits.

Along the same lines, Pastor Samuel Olson, head of the Las Acacias Evangelical Pentecostal Church and President of CVE, believes evangelicalism gives converts a new identity. "They feel recognized by God and everyone else. No longer rejected, they feel accepted. They get their personal dignity back."

Evangelicalism's intense religious regimen makes for busy schedules. Unlike Catholics, who are known for low church attendance, Pentecostals demand weekly church attendance as a minimum commitment. Pentecostal churches further involve their members by encouraging them to organize meetings, perform with a church band or choir, participate in Bible study, and volunteer to help and proselytize to addicts, sex workers, and the homeless. Any church member who does half that will naturally feel great attachment to their church.

The change in new converts is sometimes breathtaking. "A new person assumes moral responsibility in his community and family life," said Olson. "Their (religion) gives them a sense of place. That represents a possibility for a better future, for a way out of their situation."

Evangelicalism's marketing approach is direct. Unused to outside concern, the poor are impressed by the ways these religions seek them

SOURCE: José Orozco, "Evangelical Christianity Moves the Masses," VHeadline.com (December 8, 2004): accessed on www.vheadline.com (retrieved on September 23, 2005).

out in the roughest barrios. Seeing a local drug dealer transformed into a bible-thumping preacher further sparks curiosity. Maybe this is a way out, they think.

Going to barrios to preach, feeding the homeless, rehabilitating drug addicts—this approach has helped California's Victory Outreach International grow to over 500 churches in 23 countries. Their strategy is simple and effective. "Where are the drugs?" asks Manuel Aguirre when he arrives at a new place during his missionary trips. "We find these places, and establish ourselves. When you have changed the addict, the whole family follows. That's our strategy." He could have added: show people miracles, and they respond. [...]

The product of defectors from various Christian denominations, Pentecostalism has influenced mainstream Protestantism and even Catholicism. The Catholic Charismatic movement has gained in popularity by emphasizing a similar visceral relationship to God. Where Marxist Catholic liberation theology as a social movement failed, society's most spiritually and materially hungry were left to seek out alternatives like evangelicalism.

Apolinar Pérez, a priest who works at the Gumilla Center, a Jesuit-run social services NGO, suggests that liberation theology failed because it was more political than spiritual. "Marxism was unrealistic," said Pérez. "This revolution within the church was moving so fast that the Church itself pulled the plug on it because these kinds of changes have to take place over time."

Evangelicalism, by contrast, generally sticks to the spiritual, addressing the social indirectly. As a strategy, it seems more effective than talking radical politics to the poor.

Although Latin American evangelicalism has successfully competed against the centuries-old dominance of the Catholic Church, the story of an imminent evangelical takeover of Latin America is more than a little exaggerated.

Evidence indicates that many converts don't last long in evangelical churches, often returning to the Catholic Church. Although the serious commitment that evangelical churches demand attracts converts that require a spiritual boot camp, that very commitment seems to push many to abandon evangelicalism. Edward L. Cleary, a

Latin Americanist and former missionary, wrote on the subject, "living up to the perfectionist character of Pentecostalism is extremely difficult."

"People sometimes look for a light evangelicalism," explained Aguirre, "an easy solution to their problems." Rather than a profound transformation, many converts are moved by a temporary emergency. "Many go to (an evangelical) church looking for a corrective in the middle of a crisis," said Pirela. "When things turn out to be hard, they leave through the back door."

Evangelicalism continues to capture the hearts and minds of Venezuelans and other Latin Americans. But is the sky really the limit for Latin American evangelicalism, or are Catholicism's profound roots too much in the long-term? [...]

There's no doubt that evangelical denominations reach out to Venezuela's most vulnerable people much more aggressively than the Catholic Church. Victory Outreach's Aguirre, himself a former gang member and heroin addict, obviously sees the poor as that untapped target group prime for religious conversion.

Yet it's not just religious marketing, but a genuine desire to change the lives of society's castoffs that motivates these churches. Motivated by evangelical zeal and a belief in God's power to change lives, pastors and church members think evangelicalism has the power to transform the continent.

Besides abstract feelings of belonging, evangelical churches help members to recover from drug addiction, repair family ties, and generally integrate into society. They go further, finding people jobs, and providing daycare, clothes, and other basic needs for members. People find structure and purpose to chaotic and hopeless lives. Ultimately, what they find is not only a reason to live, but a reason to live better.

"We concentrate on the individual's total development," said Pirela. "If we succeed in evangelizing society, we can achieve a social transformation by reducing drug addiction and poverty."

Olson argues that evangelical Christianity has all the ingredients for a social transformation. "It works as a yeast that slowly affects social structures," said Olson. "Ethics, commitment to country, social duty and responsibility, participation, a rejection of social determinism, and the ability to share with others" are no doubt the foundation of democracy. Besides improving economic opportunities, bible study, missionary work, and preaching teach reading [sic], speaking and administrative skills that help people become better citizens.

A social transformation takes place over many decades, however, and requires careful and wise guidance. It also depends on other historical factors, like war and the global economy, which can be unpredictable. Evangelical Christianity's own hopes for wide-ranging social change in Latin America rest on growth [of their church]. [. . .]

Pérez suggests that people seek stability in their churches, and that the variety of evangelical practices goes counter to that need. Perhaps that's what's behind the revolving door effect that brings many converts back into the arms of the Catholic Church.

Aguirre too believes in the importance of structure. According to Aguirre, a "large minority" of evangelical churches "don't know where they're going." He pushes churches to develop mission statements to guide their work. "Without one, you don't have any direction," said Aguirre. [. . .]

Even if evangelical Christianity succeeds in gaining many more Latin American converts, it's obvious that not everyone will change religions, and that many go back and forth anyway. As Pérez suggests, a social transformation, if done right, takes a very long time and a great deal of intelligent stewardship. But perhaps Pérez's most incisive criticism of the evangelical movement is its separation of spiritual and social missions.

"They don't tackle social problems directly," said Pérez. "Social change has to be direct and structured." Pérez argues that in that sense the Catholic Church has been more effective and thus has a better shot of socially transforming the region. Despite Pérez's strident arguments, as a Marxist, he's clearly in the minority. The Church's efforts are [lagging] well behind Pérez's rhetoric.

Still, Pérez is right to indicate that evangelicals conceive of social change on a personal basis. They change many individuals, but disparate efforts don't lead to major social change. Evangelicals also lack the political consciousness that Catholics have developed. If changing minds politically remains a condition for changing lives socially, evangelicals are traveling the wrong road.

Yet continuing social crises promise to further boost evangelical growth in the region. The evangelical appeal to the poor is undeniably strong. Even if evangelicals lack organizational structure, they provide the structure and community individuals need to lead productive lives. An out of touch Catholic Church suggests that at the very least a large evangelical minority will make themselves heard in Venezuelan society for a long time to come.

While evangelical growth might be Latin America's biggest social movement, it's wise not to exaggerate its importance. Fervent believers in miracles, it makes sense that some evangelicals guarantee no less than a radical transformation of the region. But social change requires much more than a religious transformation. If the underlying socio-economic conditions stay the same, the same social ills will remain.

154. A Humanist Nightmare?

What prompted Constantino Urcuyo, a prestigious lawyer, doctor of sociology (University of Paris), university professor, Costa Rican legislator and presidential advisor, to make such pointed and sobering remarks about contemporary religion, especially that characterized by evangelicals? Does Urcuyo accurately depict the characteristics of contemporary religion embraced by the various Latin American churches that have been described in this anthology?

SOURCE: Constantino Urcuyo, quoted in Robert Sabean, "Costa Rica Dialogue: To What Lengths Political Discourse Has Come!" *Latin American Evangelist* 84, no. 3 (November 2004-February 2005): 14. Originally published in Spanish in *La Nación* (Costa Rica) on July 25, 2004. Reprinted by permission of *Latin American Evangelist*.

[. . .] We live in an age in which religions are taking on a new importance. The changes create uncertainty and the search for identity is a refuge against anxiety. The XXI Century begins by mixing God with politics, spiritual power with secular power. [. . .] The theology of dominion rationalizes religious political activism; its central idea is that Christians are obligated to occupy secular institutions until Christ comes. The great ideologue of this doctrine, Francis Schaeffer [1912-1984, a highly influential Swiss Presbyterian minister whose many books outline a biblical-based, Christian world-view], held that the U.S. was loyal to biblical principles, but that the evolution of society replaced these with secular humanism. Christians have a divine mandate to restore morality, the grounds for which are found in Genesis 1:26, that orders them to have dominion over the earth. In addition to a literal reading of the Bible, Evangelicals pay great attention to studying the end times. Some Evangelicals believe that Christ will return before the advent of a 1000-year reign; others are postmillennialists and believe that their task is to establish it now, that Christ will only return once the Christians have reigned for 1,000 years. [. . .] The similarities with the Taliban and jihad are astounding, but the doctrine has been accompanied by growth in adherents. According to the *Le Nouvel Observateur* seminar, Evangelicals have gone from 4 million in 1940 to 500 million. One in every four Christians is today an Evangelical. In accordance with the Institute for the Study of American Evangelicals at Wheaton College, there are in the U.S. 100 million Evangelicals, 35% of the population. The Christian Broadcasting Network (CBN) operates in 180 countries. The expansionist impulse is articulated with similar tendencies in exterior politics. Many have come to see the world conflicts as a religious war, with the disadvantage that there is no conflict harder to manage than that in which both sides are convinced that only they have access to divine truth and that those of the other side are adherents of the devil.

155. Brazilian Missionaries and the 10/40 Window

Oswaldo Prado is vice president of the Global Center of Missions in Londrina, Paraná (Brazil), and a member of the Missions Commission of the World Evangelical Fellowship. He clearly speaks with authority on the evangelical church in Brazil.

Even within the brief autobiography (A) Prado introduces his major theme, the Brazilian evangelical church as the source for missionaries. But he first presents a minihistory of Brazilian Protestantism, which ends with the excerpt below, (B).

(B) "In other words, mission was disconnected from the church" (Prado's final comment in his brief portrait of the evangelical church). How does he characterize that church? Is it possible to discern his own view of the historical church he has described?

(C) How does Prado present the strong missionary movement within the church? How does he explain the phenomenon? Does he suggest what might be its strength and its special character?

Does he make any connection between his description of the nature of the Brazilian evangelical church and the powerful surge in its missionary impulse? Why does he leave the reader with the disturbing phrase "mission was disconnected from the church"?

Note that the 10/40 Window is that part of the world contained in the rectangle formed from 10° to 40° north of the equator, from West Africa to East Asia, peopled by the majority

SOURCE: Oswaldo Prado, "A New Way of Sending Missionaries: Lessons from Brazil," *Missiology: An International Review* 33, no. 1 (January 2005): 48-52, 54-56, 58-59, passim. Reprinted by permission of *Missiology: An International Review*.

of the world's Muslims, Hindus, and Buddhists, who are described by "AD2000: 10/40 Window Overview" (an organization established in 1989 to mobilize and centralize Protestant missionary activity in the 10/40 world) as "spiritually impoverished souls."

[A] I am a fourth-generation "evangelical," (the term we use for Protestants in Brazil). My great-grandfather received the gospel from a foreign missionary at the end of the nineteenth-century. I was raised, therefore, in a Christian environment in a Presbyterian church, and, in my early twenties, I began my theological studies in the Theological Faculty of the Independent Presbyterian Church of Brazil.

After I graduated, I pastored a Presbyterian church in the city of São Paulo for 20 years. That church had the unique experience of sending several young people and couples as missionaries, not only to other places in Brazil, but also to other countries.

In the early 1980s, I and two other pastors had the privilege of initiating a Brazilian transcultural missionary agency, which later was called *Avante* (Forward, Onward, Go Ahead!). This organization, of which I was president for more than ten years, sends Brazilian missionaries to other cultures. [. . .]

I have been a witness to all that the Lord has done in Brazil in recent years, especially in what is referred to as the missionary awakening. I believe that God, in God's sovereignty, has allowed Brazil to be a very blessed nation, making it possible for many Brazilians to be sent as missionaries to different countries around the world. [. . .]

[B] [I]f today we are a church extremely verticalized and with little or practically no inclination to incarnate the Christ of the Gospels, it is because the missionary history written on the Latin American continent was loaded with an ethereal spirituality with no commitment to the challenges of this fallen world. [. . .]

This vision of a nearly total disconnection between the theology of mission and the reality of the world is more evident in the life and ministry of missionary Ashbel G. Simonton, precursor of Brazilian Presbyterianism. At Princeton, where he studied, the conservative tendency adhered to the so-called "Spiritual Church," which practiced a strong dichotomy between the sacred and the profane. Simonton's diary clarifies what we are affirming: "The world appeals to what is sensual. The enmity of the heart inclines us to reject the doctrine of the humility of the Cross. To live it is necessary to elevate oneself to another sphere, absorbing all the power of a world unknown to our sight, and of Jesus, the invisible Savior." [. . .]

This inherited legacy closely accompanied the church in Brazil and in Latin America causing many to feel secure with the promise of eternity in the next world, but ignoring the reconstruction of this world in chaos, but created by God. In other words, mission was disconnected from the church. [. . .]

[C] How could one imagine the Latin American continent immersed in poverty, corruption, dictatorships, and uncontrollable inflation launching a missionary experience like that of the countries in the First World? In the post-Comibam [Cooperación Misionera Iberoamericana] years a missionary awakening took place in Brazil, and, by the grace of God, a new history of mission has been written in recent years.

Naturally there were many struggles and even strong opposition. An old paradigm was being broken and something new was happening. In the 1980s I was pastor of a local church in São Paulo, and I remember a conversation with one of the leaders of that church. He said to me, "Forget this idea, pastor! This business of missions is not for us in the Third World. Mission is for the churches of North America and Europe who have tradition in this area and the financial resources."

As time passed I began to hear repeatedly this type of comment from other Brazilian leaders and pastors, always implying that this new experience occurring in some local churches had nothing to do with our reality. However, at the same time, the Brazilian missionary advance was incredible and even uncontrollable. [. . .]

In light of all of this, the question that we as Christians should ask is: Is there hope that those who live immersed in tragedies, crises, and blunders can be part of the people of God who take the good news of the gospel to unreached peoples? Or is this an exclusive task of the developed nations with more experience of the Christian faith? "Can anything good come out of Nazareth?" as Nathanael once said to Philip (John 1:46). [. . .]

Today approximately 17 percent of Brazilians identify themselves as evangelicals. At the beginning of 2003, thirty million Brazilians were evangelicals. [. . .] How has the Brazilian evangelical church sent its missionaries to other cultures in the midst of this context? [. . .]

Horizon Mission: Radical Project: a Revolutionary Latin American Model [. . .]

In 1999, Horizon Mission decided to recruit dozens of young Brazilians to send to the 10/40 Window. They sent 96 Brazilian missionaries and are currently developing Radical Project II which will send more missionaries in 2004.

Radical Project has several distinct characteristics. The candidates commit to serve at least five years on the field, to receive missiological training, and to raise their own support. The first two and a half years are for training: one year in Brazil, another year in a Latin American country and some months at the headquarters in the country of Gales [Wales]. The other two and a half years the missionaries serve on the field, in a nation within the 10/40 Window.

Why the name Radical Project? David Botelho lists some of the reasons. In the first place, the missionaries should have a radical commitment. Since all of the support is raised in Brazil, the proposal is that each of the missionaries assume a lifestyle very similar to the people they will be serving.

Secondly, those who participate in this missionary project live in a radical community—all the finances are administered in a common pool, which encourages a sense of mutual responsibility and accountability. For example, when a box of chocolates arrives in the mail, even though it was sent to one person, it belongs to the group. The other interesting thing is that the so-called "radicals" visit churches in Brazil to raise their support not individually, but as a team. Furthermore, they are sent as a team to the mission field.

Thirdly, they have a radical partnership. The missionaries come from different denominational

and theological backgrounds. This causes them to respect differences, knowing that they are there to take the gospel of Christ to an unreached people. Also the multi-racial teams are composed not only of Brazilians, but also missionaries from Paraguay, Venezuela, England, and the United States. [. . .]

Today Horizon Mission has 104 Brazilian missionaries in countries of the Middle East, Asia, Niger, and the Latin American countries of Bolivia, Paraguay, and Venezuela.

Antioch Mission: A Pioneer Missionary Organization among Brazilians

A second model comes from a missionary organization that was the first to be established as a genuinely "Brazilian" interdenominational transcultural missionary agency. [. . .]

Potential candidates are those who have a call to transcultural mission, are experienced Christians, and are connected to a local church in Brazil. They must be aware that they will raise all of their spiritual and financial support and that they are responsible for their own physical and emotional well-being. [. . .]

The Antioch Mission demonstrates much care in the preparation of the future Brazilian missionaries. The missionary preparation is divided into three parts: theoretical studies of anthropology, contextualization, mission principles; travel to a Latin American country for practical training; and serving as a missionary in Bolivia, as an intermediary field before going to the final destination. [. . .]

Today the Antioch Mission has 72 Brazilian missionaries in diverse countries, including Albania, Ukraine, Spain, Mozambique, China, and others. [. . .]

I recognize that God has done something supernatural in Brazil, especially in relation to the sending of missionaries to other peoples. It would have been impossible to imagine this 20 years ago. I remember hearing some pastors and leaders saying when all of this was beginning, "Soon this will end. It is only a wave that came and soon will go away." But, by the grace of God, none of it ended. To the contrary, this missionary movement has grown greatly in these last years, and it seems that it will continue to grow, in spite of the difficulties we face.

PART XXII

Roman Catholicism into the Twenty-First Century

The Catholic charismatic revival is an important development in Latin American Catholicism during the past thirty years. Perhaps as many as twenty-five million Catholics in Latin America now consider themselves charismatic, ten million of whom reside in Brazil. The movement was originated in 1967 by students from Duquesne University (Pittsburgh, Pennsylvania), a Catholic institution founded by members of the Congregation of the Holy Ghost. These students claimed that they had received an effusion of charismata by the Holy Spirit. Charismatics, like Pentecostals, give particular attention to the gifts of the Holy Spirit, emphasize praise singing, intense Bible study in prayer groups, speaking in tongues, faith healing, and appeals for deliverance from demonic possession. Most participants aspire to lead ascetic lives, though failure to abide by strict moral codes does not result in banishment from the church. Unlike Pentecostals, charismatics maintain firm allegiance to the pope and venerate the Virgin Mary and the saints. While also popular in other parts of the world, the Catholic charismatic revival seemed a perfect vehicle for Latin Americans who sought exciting and innovating ways to express their religiosity without leaving the church. Support is especially strong from both the middle and popular classes, as well as from women: that is, from the very same groups that might otherwise have joined Pentecostal churches. Participants prefer a spiritual and individual relationship with God and hope to cure personal afflictions, such as illness, alcoholism, drug abuse, and domestic violence. Many are unconvinced that the Catholic Church can or even should endeavor to alter the social and economic structure of their respective countries. If the charismatic movement initially gave pause to some members of the church hierarchy because of its potential to diminish ecclesiastical authority in favor of direct reliance on the Holy Spirit, most bishops subsequently recognized its important role in stemming the growth of Pentecostalism. Others, perhaps, viewed this form of worship as more attractive and comfortable than the "preferential option" of the poor espoused by liberation theologians.[1] R. Andrew

---

1. R. Andrew Chesnut, "A Preferential Option for the Spirit: The Catholic Charismatic Renewal in Latin America's New Religious Economy," *Latin American Politics and Society* 45, no. 1 (spring 2003): 78, 55-72; R. Andrew Chesnut, *Born Again in Brazil: The Pentecostal Boom and the Pathogens of Poverty* (New Brunswick, N.J.: Rutgers University Press, 1997), 3, 174.

Chesnut's use of instructions from Guatemalan bishops (1997) highlights both the promise and threat of this form of Catholic worship for the church hierarchy:

> In Charismatic Renewal groups massive assemblies are often organized at which the sick are prayed for in a special way. These assemblies must be under the responsibility of a priest, authorized for such an event by the bishop, so that everything develops according to the spirit of our Catholic tradition for the greater glory of God and for the good of the infirm who with faith come to receive the healing power of Jesus in his church.[2]

Students of religions in Latin America will undoubtedly witness important changes and continuities as the twenty-first century advances. During the past fifty years, there has been a slow decoupling of national and religious identity. No longer can it be assumed that to be Latin American is to be Catholic.[3] By the church's own admission, the percentage of Catholics in South America has decreased from 92.2 percent in 1965, to 90 percent in 1975, to 90.7 percent in 1985, to 89.1 percent in 1995, to 86.2 percent in 2005.[4] Despite the recent gains by Protestant groups, especially Pentecostals, the power, prestige, influence, and even adaptability of the Catholic Church cannot be discounted. The number of seminarians in Latin America suggests that young Catholics continue to view a life dedicated to serving parishioners and the church as a worthy pursuit. Contrary to popular perceptions, the number of seminarians in South America rose from 17,475 in 1995, to 19,409 in 2000, to 23,378 in 2005.[5]

There is general acknowledgment by Latin Americans that religious pluralism will continue to grow. Peoples of various faiths and traditions now share the same social space. Mormon missionaries dressed in Western attire seem commonplace on city streets and country lanes. Orthodox Jews in their own distinct clothing walk to and from synagogues on Saturdays. Indigenous peoples and others decorate altars and churches with symbols and images reminiscent of the pre-Hispanic past. Pentecostals fill soccer stadiums to empower themselves with the gifts of the Holy Spirit. Religious movements of Eastern ori-

---

2. From Conferencia Episcopal de Guatemala, 415, quoted in R. Andrew Chesnut, *Competitive Spirits: Latin America's New Religious Economy* (Oxford: Oxford University Press, 2003), 89.

3. Chesnut, *Competitive Spirits*, 18.

4. Felician A. Foy, O.F.M., ed., *1965 National Catholic Almanac* (Patterson, N.J.: St. Anthony's Guild, 1965), 397; Felician A. Foy, O.F.M., ed., *1975 Catholic Almanac* (Huntington, Ind.: Our Sunday Visitor, 1974), 438; Felician A. Foy, O.F.M. and Rose M. Avato, eds., *1985 Catholic Almanac* (Huntington, Ind.: Our Sunday Visitor, 1984), 379; Felician A. Foy, O.F.M., and Rose M. Avato, eds., *1995 Catholic Almanac* (Huntington, Ind.: Our Sunday Visitor, 1994), 368; Matthew Bunson, ed., *2005 Our Sunday Visitor's Catholic Almanac* (Huntington, Ind.: Our Sunday Visitor, 2004), 333. Statistics are typically two years old at time of publication and include percentages of all persons baptized, not necessarily church attendees. Mexico is sometimes included as part of North America and sometimes with Central America in these almanacs, and, for that reason, only statistics on South America are consistent.

5. The population explosion, however, has concurrently meant that the number of Catholics per priest has risen dramatically: there are 6,382 Catholics per priest in Mexico (compared to 1,311 in the United States) and 7,112 Catholics per priest in South America (compared to 1,342 in Europe). See Bryan T. Froehl and Mary L. Gautier, "Latin American Catholicism," *International Bulletin of Missionary Research* 28, no. 2 (April 2004): 68-69; Felician A. Foy, O.F.M., and Rose M. Avato, eds., *1995 Catholic Almanac* (Huntington, Ind.: Our Sunday Visitor, 1994), 368; Matthew Bunson, ed., *2000 Our Sunday Visitor's Catholic Almanac* (Huntington, Ind.: Our Sunday Visitor, 1999), 345; Matthew Bunson, ed., *2005 Our Sunday Visitor's Catholic Almanac* (Huntington, Ind.: Our Sunday Visitor, 2004), 333.

gin such as the Hare Krishnas and the Moonies sing, chant, and proselytize in city squares and on university campuses. Muslim communities slowly grow in strength and build mosques. Umbandan mediums shake uncontrollably as they receive spirit possession and help heal afflicted souls. The more eclectic pay close attention to the zodiac, have their palms read, cross themselves whenever they pass before a church or shrine, listen attentively as psychics reveal the importance of tarot cards, and pray and light candles to saints, guardian angels, and protective spirits.

Meanwhile, Catholics continue their pilgrimages to la Vírgen de Guadalupe, la Vírgen de la Caridad (El Cobre, Cuba), and Nuestra Señora de Copacabana (Bolivia). Charismatic leaders, after attending church-sponsored orientations, continue to animate their lively brethren. Other traditional parish organizations pursue their work. The CEBs (Christian Base Communities), so productive in Brazil and Chile in the '60s and '70s, in El Salvador and Nicaragua in the '70s and '80s, and active constructively in most areas of Latin America during the post–Vatican II/Medellín era, have been marginalized by both positive political and negative economic developments and by most of the bishops. Many of the new cohort of parish priests do not view the poor as a priority and resent active involvement by the laity. Despite meetings of CELAM (Conference of Latin American Bishops) at Medellín, Puebla, and even Santo Domingo in 1992, the vision of the Latin American church seems to be: "the pope in Rome, the bishop in his diocese and the priest in his parish."[6] And the laity, obedient, quiescent, invisible.

156. Testimony of Juan González ("Jany"), Charismatic

The address given by Juan González ("Jany") in 2005 to young Catholics in Puerto Rico has all the spontaneity and fervor of a person who has had a profound conversion experience. It characterizes the Pentecostalism that was declared, analyzed, and criticized by Protestant Pentecostals themselves in several previous readings (Manoel de Melo in nos. 93 and 94; Alves and Shaull in no. 95; Víctor Rey in no. 148; and Vaccaro and Campos in no. 151 ["Pentecostalism Comes of Age"]).

Consider Jany's address and his 2002 minihistory of Pentecost in the Catholic Church in responding to the following queries: What is the element in Jany's Pentecostalism that differentiates it from that described and analyzed by the aforementioned authors? Is Jany's Pentecostalism vulnerable to any of the criticisms made by those authors? May it be said that Jany's Pentecostalism also "responded" to some of those same criticisms?

---

6. Barbara Fraser and Paul Jeffery, "Base Communities, Once Hope of Church, Now in Disarray," *The National Catholic Reporter* 41, no. 4 (12 November 2004), 16. See editors' introduction to Part XXI (pp. 355-57) for a delineation of the problems that characterize the Catholic Church today.

Source: Juan A. González Rivera, "¿Qué es la Renovación en el Espíritu Santo? (March 19, 2002)," and "Testimonio del Joven Predicador Puertorriqueño Juan González (July 24, 2005)." Renovación Carismática Católica de Habla Hispana, www.rcc.org. Translated from the Spanish by Lee M. Penyak and Walter J. Petry. Reprinted by permission of Juan A. González.

[Address given by Jany to young Catholics on Sunday, July 24, 2005]

At 11 am on 7 February 1999 in the small town of Aibonito on the island, Jesus came into my life.

Blessings to all. I begin by saying proudly that I am a son of the Catholic Charismatic Renewal. I am now 23 years old, and I serve the Lord full-time. I would like to share with you young people what God did in my life. Not to glorify myself, nor for anything like that, only so that this testimony may edify the lives of others. This is my testimony, without much detail, short and precise.

I attended Catholic schools all my life, but my family was not active in the church. I went to Mass once a month since it was a school requirement. When I was sixteen, I was one of the most popular kids in school. Bright, athletic, and preoccupied with girls—that's how I would describe myself. I began to try drugs and tried them all. I joined a dance group that specialized in Regaeton concerts. What happened was that all this went to my head.

When I still had two years left to finish high school, one of my religion teachers, for the final assignment of the year, asked us to summarize each chapter of a book entitled "To the God of My Youth." I spoke with the teacher, and told him that I had no intention of reading that book because it was boring, clearly an excuse since I did not want to read it because it was about God. The teacher made me an offer and said to me: if you go on a three-day retreat next week, I'll give you an "A" for the final assignment, and you won't have to read it. An irresistible offer I couldn't refuse. I said to myself, three days are not that much, and for a good grade—I'm going to go. Already, I had fallen into the nets of the ship JESUS, and already I had bitten the lure.

On the fifth of February, I got to the retreat house of the Salesian Fathers of Puerto Rico. Some [participants] had brought marijuana to the retreat, and I was smoking it. Whatever anyone had to say didn't really matter to me, and I ignored them. It was soon Sunday, February 7th, and the retreat ended at noon. With one hour left for everything to end, Jesus called to me. It was the time for the manifestation of the Holy Spirit, and every one was praying, crying, speaking in tongues, falling down backward—for me complete madness. I said: you're all crazy and I went to the back of the chapel. And there, in a little corner of that little chapel in the center of the island, Jesus touched me, called to me and spoke to me.

I could hear his voice, which said to me: you are mine, I have chosen you for myself, you are going to work with young people and you are going to become a preacher, a prophet for the nations.

I answered him: but, I, how? I don't know anything about you, I don't even know you. And I can't preach because I'm a stammerer.

Jesus [said]: Don't worry. You are going to preach my word and shout (expulsarás) my words out of your mouth. I thought I was going crazy, that the drugs were killing my brain, because I was hearing things and voices. I still couldn't believe what was happening to me.

And at a certain moment, I became paralyzed by an image of a person in front. I could only see eyes looking at me. I felt that look was coming to me little by little. It penetrated my eyes, ran through my body until it got to my heart. When I felt that sensation that struck my heart, it was like an exploding tire. Jesus had penetrated my heart and had enthroned himself in it. He was healing me, he healed my wounds, he healed the wound from my parents' divorce, he healed the damage done by drugs, he healed the wound of my loneliness, he healed the wound from a father who never sought me out. It was no longer I, it was Jesus in me.

I left that retreat a new man, renewed, changed and transformed. With nothing in my hands, but with my heart full to capacity and with a promise made by God. I did not begin to preach right away. I had to go through a process of conversion, slowly and effectively. And don't forget that I was a STAMMERER.

One year after this, it occurred to me that I had to decide to study and go to the University. After a long period of discernment, I enrolled in the school of Theology. When I acquired a little more knowledge, I again felt in my being that promise of God in my heart. The word of God held me captive, and God wanted to open my lips to proclaim it. I couldn't resist any longer, the fire of Jesus in my heart was burning me up. I had to preach. But I was a Stammerer.

On one occasion, some preachers from a Puerto Rican movement called the Cheo Brothers were at my parish. One preached while the other interceded for the preacher. That day I arrived late with a friend and the parish church was very full. We had to stay outside, and I took advantage of the opportunity to reveal to my friend what was happening to me.

He told me: Jany, you are a stammerer, you can't preach. I answered: I know, I'm aware of it; if it were solely on my account, I wouldn't preach. But it's something stronger than I. He kept on saying: Jany, you can't, you can't and you cannot.

But for the Glory of God, one of the Cheo Brothers was close by and heard part of the conversation; he approached me and put his hand on my shoulder and said to me

Don't worry, you're going to preach.

My friend said to him: for him to preach, God will have to cure him first.

The Cheo Brother turned to him and told him: NOOO, God is not going to heal him. Smart and clever guys like YOU will go crazy in the face of the power of God when you hear him preach. You will say: How is it possible that when he preaches he doesn't stammer? This will make it clear (para que quede garantizado) that it is not HE [Jany] but rather GOD in HIM. [sic].

He turned to me and said: CONGRATULATIONS, today begins your ministry.

And from that day, God sent me to different places to preach, and now the stammerer can't keep his mouth shut, so that it's open to the four winds, proclaiming the grandeur of Jesus.

And it's amazing; many times I cry after I preach because it is humanly not possible, humanly it is impossible for me to speak that way. I realize that without him I am nothing.

Now I have a degree in theology and am studying for a master's in divinity and theology. Everything, my life, my future, my studies are about the Lord and for the Lord.

[I am] a young layman who serves the Lord and will serve him forever until he calls me. I am a member of Catholic Charismatic Youth of the Archdiocese of San Juan, Puerto Rico. I am coordinator of the prayer group of my parish. I conduct workshops and bible courses and [I am a] preacher full-time.

I don't consider myself worthy of any of these honors. I only say all this so that you can see that

God can indeed make use of a stammerer to proclaim his word. HE CAN USE YOU.

Put yourself in the hands of God and he will make powerful use of you.

[Mini-history of Pentecost in the Catholic Church by Jany on March 19, 2002]

What Is Renewal in the Holy Spirit?

On the day of Pentecost, the promise of Jesus was fulfilled; the Holy Spirit was poured out over the disciples, who, in the company of Mary, the mother of Jesus, were gathered in prayer.

From the beginning of the Church, the Spirit is the force that moves her and which gives her power to do the things that Jesus did in his Name and enables her to accomplish her mission.

Through the entire history of the Church, the Holy Spirit has directed her development and path, renewing her and revivifying at distinct moments the spirit of that first Church born on the day of Pentecost. [. . .]

Jesus continues to enrich his Church with his gifts and charisms. The first and most important of all gifts is the Holy Spirit himself. The Church is enriched with these gifts and charisms to transform the face of the earth.

Birth and Expansion of Renewal

On January 29, 1959, Pope John XXIII made a surprising declaration. The Holy Spirit had inspired him to convoke a council, the Second Vatican Council. On Pentecost of that same year, he ended his elocution with this prayer: "Oh Holy Spirit! Your presence leads the church infallibly. Spread, we ask you, the fullness of your gifts over this Ecumenical Council. Renew your wonders in our days as in a new Pentecost."

On December 8, 1965, the Council ended. The events that happened after have been variously appraised. The program of renewal proposed by the Council began to be enacted, not without serious difficulties, which brought doubt and anguish to many.

In 1966, several Catholic men of Duquesne University of the Holy Spirit, Pittsburgh, met frequently to converse about the vitality of their life of faith and to pray in common.

Those professors had dedicated themselves for

many years to the service of Christ, giving themselves over to various apostolic activities . . . In spite of all that, they felt that something was lacking in their personal Christian life.

Although they could not specify why, each one recognized that he had a certain emptiness, a lack of dynamism, a spiritual weakness in their prayers and activities. It was as if their Christian life depended too much on their own strengths, as if they advanced [primarily] under their own power and motivated by their own will . . . They decided to make a commitment: every day they would pray for each other with the Sequence (liturgical poem) of the Mass for Pentecost: "Come Divine Spirit . . . "

It was during the month of February, 1967, when they saw their desires realized, when they received a new outpouring of the Holy Spirit.

Charismatic Renewal or Renewal in the Holy Spirit had been born. [. . .]

Renewal in the Holy Spirit, as a current of graces, raised by the Holy Spirit in the Church of our time, exists and lives for the Church and in the Church, from which [derives] the strong bond with its legitimate Pastors and the desire to serve together with them, to achieve the renewal of Catholic communities. Renewal, then, is situated within the Church, in the very heart of the Church.

157. Perón and the Church

Juan Perón (1895-1974) became the real power in the Argentine government (1943) and actual president (1946-1955; 1973-1974) because of strong support from the powerful labor unions, which he fostered. Immensely popular with the descamisados *(shirtless ones), the urban proletariat, he proclaimed* justicialismo *(a mixture of nationalism, corporate capitalism, and populism) as Argentina's path to the future.*

Meanwhile, Catholic Action, a movement fostered by Pope Pius XI (1922-1939) and whose purpose was to organize Catholic laymen to fight for the church and Catholic values against the pernicious "-isms" of the contemporary world, had became a visible presence in European and Latin American societies by the 1950s.

Note that there are a number of interest or "power" groups referred to in the following address (1954) by Perón to Argentinian provincial governors and representatives of provincial labor organizations.

Is it possible to distinguish between how Perón perceives these groups, including his own, and how these groups might actually perceive themselves? Where do the bishops stand? Distinguish between Catholic Action as a whole and "the twenty or thirty . . . opponents [of Perón]." If there are 16,000 clergy in Argentina and only 20 or 30 "opponents" among them, why does Perón make so big an issue of them?

Note that the next reading explains the placement of this mid-twentieth-century document in Part XXII, which is devoted to currents that flow in the twenty-first century.

The organization "Catholic Action of Argentina," which is international in character, includes among its members certain anti-Peronists. In fact, the anti-Peronists control this organization. They act with suave hypocrisy. It is their custom to attend meetings and to talk like this: "I do not

SOURCE: Juan Domingo Perón, "La intromission del clero en la política gremial: Discursos del presidente Perón y declaraciones del partido peronista," *Hechos e Ideas: Publicación de cuestiones políticas, económicas y socials* (Buenos Aires) 27:126-27 (October-November 1954): 387-97. Excerpted and translated by Fredrick B. Pike, ed., *The Conflict between Church and State in Latin America* (New York: Alfred A. Knopf, 1964), 184-87. Reprinted by permission of Fredrick B. Pike.

come here in the name of Catholic Action. . . ." Yet, in reality, they are operating in its name. We must subject this type of Catholic Action member to our careful scrutiny. It is often the same with the clergy. [. . .]

This has nothing to do with the Church in itself, and I want to make this point quite clear. I have talked with high dignitaries of the Church, with bishops and archbishops, who are simply men like any of the rest of us. I presented to them the problems now being encountered by those organizations that are suffering injury because of the attitudes of several Catholic groups. And I confronted the prelates in the presence of the representatives of those organizations that are being injured. I had received urgent notice that restlessness was mounting not only in the small syndicates but also in the General Confederation of Labor, in the Confederation of Professionals, in the General Confederation of University Students, in other student organizations, and in many other groups. So, I told the prelates:

I do not understand why they are being organized, these groups of Catholic laborers, Catholic lawyers, Catholic doctors, and Catholic farmers. We are Catholics too! But to be Peronists we do not have to proclaim that we are Catholic Peronists. We are simply Peronists, and within this context we can be Catholic, Jewish, Buddhist, Orthodox, or what have you. It is not necessary for us to ask a Peronist which God he prays to. For us, the faith that a person professes is irrelevant, so long as the person is a good human being. That is all that counts!

The prelates agreed with us, and before all those representatives of the victimized organizations who were present as witnesses, they—the bishops and archbishops—were the first to condemn those priests who were not faithful to their duties. They added that they not only condemned such men, but declared them enemies against the ecclesiastical dignity. This was said by the prelates, and certainly I ought to honor and place credence in the voice of the prelates! [. . .]

I trust the word of those men who represent the Church in Argentina. And consequently, we must take appropriate measures when we encounter men who have failed to fulfill their duties as Argentine citizens and as priests. They are operating beyond the laws of their country, and beyond the laws of God as well. Therefore, we know already what we are going to do with them. [. . .]

For us the situation is absolutely clear. It belongs to us, as civil authorities, to see that these men fulfill their duties at least to the state. The prelates will provide for taking the necessary means to make them fulfill their religious duties, and this problem is no concern of ours. [. . .]

Córdoba, unquestionably, is the place where the most unusual occurrences have taken place. There, one encounters a certain Father Bordagaray, associated with the University of Córdoba, who says that we have to make a choice between Christ and Perón. I have never had a conflict with Christ. Precisely what I am trying to do is defend the doctrines of Christ, which for over two hundred years priests of this type in Argentina have sought unsuccessfully to destroy.

I also believe that a certain Father José V. López, a Spaniard, is in Córdoba. We are about to take the necessary measures against him. There also is Father Julio Treviño, who claims that we are promoting delinquency by having swimming pools in the jails. I do not know what this has to do with Christian piety, but I do know that it has a great deal to do with sanitation. Whether or not this priest bathes in the swimming pool does not concern me.

For us, this is simply a matter of individuals. There are approximately 16,000 members of the clergy here. We will not raise a problem with the Church because twenty or thirty among them are opponents. It is natural that among such a large number there should be some who are against us. What must we do? Simply take measures against those few. The hierarchy is eminently correct when it tells me that the matter does not pertain to the Church, but only to some of its misguided priests. We are going to help the Church put them in their proper place. That is all!

158. The Church Is Going to Be Pilloried for This

The role of the church in Argentina probably represents the Roman Catholic Church at its political worst in twentieth-century Latin America. This was made abundantly clear by its role in the "Dirty War" (1976-1983), when Argentina was governed by a military dictatorship that engaged in state terrorism and massive violations of human rights, culminating in the infamous "disappearances" of some 13,000 to 30,000 citizens.

All Latin American nations inherited the colonial era's close ties between state and church (the patronato real), which had included the nomination of bishops, payment of salaries, and expenditures for the establishment of schools, hospitals, and orphanages by the state (i.e., the Crown through the Council of Indies). This colonial legacy was one of state superiority and church subservience. All of this suggests that the state's goals were paramount and the church's subordinate.

This legacy carried over into the nineteenth-century republican era, but by the twentieth century most Latin American nations had separated church and state. Nevertheless, the state, despite moments of fierce anticlericalism (as in the extraordinary case of Mexico), respected the historic role of the church and Catholicism in the nation.

The Argentinian church, however, never broke away from a subordinate position vis-à-vis the state, which continued to pay the salaries of the clergy and subsidize seminaries, chancery offices, and the social and educational work of the church, and also required (until 1994) the president to be Catholic (while guaranteeing freedom of worship).

The church's acquiescence to and legitimization of the military junta in Argentina are partially explained by this history. But the establishment in 1905 of military chaplains and in 1957 of the Military Vicariate (a diocese comprised exclusively of military personnel and their families, headed by its own archbishop, staffed by chaplains holding officer rank, all receiving comfortable salaries) inevitably compromised the church in relation to secular authorities.

The powerful fear of communism among Latin American elites together with the Cuban revolution, the military coup (1964) in Brazil, and the turmoil leading up to and including the new Perón era (1973-1974 [see previous reading]), all contributed to the scandalous role of the Argentinian bishops during the Dirty War. Only four out of eighty active bishops openly denounced the regime, which was characterized by a national security ideology, as terrorist. The extraordinary failure of those shepherds to protect their flocks occurred after the strong injunctions on human rights pronounced by Vatican II and Medellín (1968). Even the declarations of Puebla (1979) failed to influence the bishops (whose salaries had been augmented munificently by the junta), and neither did the murder of twelve priests, the disappearances of five, the jailing, torturing, and exiling of some twenty-one others, the murder and/or disappearances of eleven seminarians, the murder of one of the four outspoken bishops (Enrique Angelelli of La Rioja), and the probable murder of another bishop (Carlos Ponce de León of San Nicolás de los Arroyos) between 1974 and 1980.

Source: Emilio F. Mignone, *Witness to the Truth: The Complicity of Church and Dictatorship in Argentina* (Maryknoll, N.Y.: Orbis Books, 1986), 2, 5, 6, 36, 66, 67, 98-99, 101. Reprinted by permission of Orbis Books.

THE CHURCH IS GOING TO BE PILLORIED FOR THIS

The reports of international human rights organizations detailing the torture and killings had no influence on the bishops. Nor did Pope John Paul II's reference in 1983 to the "painful drama of the disappeared in Argentina" change the bishops' defense of the junta's final rationalization of the "disappearances." (Sadly, this reference was the only time the pope referred to the human rights abuses although he had been asked to do so by faithful Catholics since Puebla in 1979.)

The following is a sampling of the hierarchy's reaction to the military junta. For the full context of these quotations, see Emilio F. Mignone, Witness to the Truth: The Complicity of Church and Dictatorship in Argentina *(Maryknoll, N.Y.: Orbis Books, 1986). See also Penny Lernoux, "Blood Taints Church in Argentina,"* National Catholic Reporter *21, no. 24 (April 12, 1985), 1ff.*

What is the lesson that might be learned by the church in Latin America from the extraordinary lapse in Christian comportment by the hierarchy and the majority of the clergy in Argentina during the military regime? Does the behavior of the clerical sector of the Argentinian church—and much of the lay sector as well—suggest that churchmen cannot extricate the church from its history or from the values of its contemporary brutal environment?

"May not Christ someday want the armed forces to go beyond their normal function? [1975]"

"Providence entrusted the army with the duty to govern, from the presidency all the way to intervening in a union [1976]."

"Christ has entered with truth and goodness [1976]."

"Malevolent Argentinians who leave our country are organizing against our country from outside, supported by the forces of darkness, and they spread news, and from outside carry out campaigns in combination with those who are working in the shadows within our borders. Let us pray, that the arduous labor of those who govern us spiritually and temporally may be successful. Let us be children of a nation in which the church enjoys a kind of respect that does not exist in all countries under the curse of Marxism [1977]."

"[T]he best defense is to attack rather than show patience and tolerance [1977]."

"If I could speak with the government, I would tell it that we must remain firm in the positions we're taking: foreign accusations about disappearances should be ignored [1977]."

"I believe the ICHR [The Inter-American Commission on Human Rights] should not have come. The government very generously allowed them. Thus, I also respect the commission, but there was no reason why a foreign commission should come to examine us. I believe that the government is now doing things well and all this was unnecessary. In any case, now that the commission has come, I pray to God that they may be objective and not be influenced by those who have created this problem in Argentina: the families of those guerrillas who engaged in killing, kidnapping, and robbery [1979]."

"The members of the military junta will be glorified by generations to come [1981]."

"In Argentina there are no common graves; each body has its own casket. Everything was registered in the proper books. The common graves are of persons whom the authorities were unable to identify after they died. Disappeared? Things should not be mixed up. Do you know that there are some 'disappeared' persons who today are living quite contentedly in Europe? [1982]"

"The Mothers of the Plaza de Mayo must be eliminated [1984]."

[Archbishop Vicente Zaspe of Santa Fé, 1977] "At one particular moment he [Zaspe] stopped, lowered his head thoughtfully, and said, 'Look,

Mignone [author of book], some years down the road, the Church is going to be pilloried for this.'"

[Father Rubén Capitanio, 1983] "I am in the church because of Jesus Christ, not because of de Neveres [one of the four outspoken bishops against the Junta] or Plaza [one of the bishops most supportive of the Junta]. I love this church and hence I must acknowledge that it is in very grave sin, starting with the pope and coming down through the nuncio, bishops, priests, nuns, and Christian communities. The Church is responsible for millions of lives lost, not for hav-

ing killed them, but because it did not save them. When the bishops realized they might be accused of omissions, they brought out a book recounting all the efforts they made. But this book that tried to justify them is nothing but a proof of guilt, for it shows they knew what was happening. . . . I wonder what would have happened if, in April 1977, when their first letter was sent to the military junta, there had been a threat to excommunicate the junta, and that the military vicariate was going to resign, that all the military chaplains would resign, and there would have been a complete break with the government."

159. Mea Culpa Lite

Washington Uranga, born in Uruguay and longtime resident of Argentina, is a journalist, and also a teacher and researcher in communications at the National University of La Plata, Argentina. He wrote the following analysis in 1996 immediately after the publication of the long-awaited document of the Argentine Conference of Bishops (1996) in which the latter were expected to respond to their position during the massive human rights violations sponsored and directed by the Argentine military from 1974 to 1983.

Uranga's reference to 20,000 disappeared must be considered as a moderate estimate. Violations included kidnapping of infants after one or both of their parents were murdered or "disappeared," their bestowal on families or friends of the military, and the torture of both those who were later murdered and those who survived.

Are there any aspects of Uranga's analysis of the document that may be criticized as unfair, too weak, or too strong? What do the passages from the document reveal about the nature of the church in Argentina in the 1990s? Given the position of the church vis-à-vis the terrorist regime from 1976* to 1983, does the hierarchy in 1996 address the position of its embodiment during that regime? Is the hierarchy evasive, hypocritical, contrite, unrepentant? What has the Argentine hierarchy—many of whom were not yet bishops during the era of the junta—learned?

"Without admitting to responsibilities the Church did not have in these events (in the 1960s and 1970s, characterized by guerrilla terrorism and repressive state-sponsored terror), we must recognize that there were Catholics who justified and

participated in systematic violence as a means of achieving 'national liberation' through the taking of political power and establishing a new form of society, inspired by Marxism, that unfortunately swept up many young people. And there were

---

* Isabel Peron was technically president until she was ousted by the military.

SOURCE: Quoted in "Mea Culpa Light," *Latin American Documentation* 27, no. 1 (September/October 1996): 19-21. Originally published in Spanish in Washington Uranga, "Mea Culpa Light," *Pastoral Popular* [Santiago, Chile] 47, no. 252 (May-June 1996): 11-12.

other groups, in which many of the children of the Church participated, they illegally responded to the guerrillas in an immoral and atrocious manner, which is an embarrassment to all of us."

The Argentine bishops used these words to characterize the tragic period in the history of this South American country and, at the same time, to release a timid self-criticism of the Church in general, but not the hierarchy in particular, without taking responsibility for these actions.

After a year of arduous internal discussions and debates, on April 27 the Argentine Conference of Bishops (CEA) approved and distributed the document in which the hierarchy reiterated the fundamental thesis that it has maintained over the past few years: The Church denounced violations of human rights through documents and chose to use private contacts to talk with the military authorities.

The document states that, unfortunately, "what was done did not stop the horror." Addressing the accusations directed against the hierarchy during the past few years, principally from human rights organizations, that it did nothing to stop the terror or participated directly with the military, the bishops said that "if some member of the Church, regardless of his position, approved through his recommendation or had a role in these events (human rights violations), he did so under his own responsibility, gravely erring or sinning before God, humanity and his own conscience."

The Argentine bishops' "examination of conscience" came within the framework of the preparations for the Great Jubilee of the year 2000 and in response to Pope John Paul II's "Before the Arrival of the Third Millennium," a document that calls on the entire church to reflect on the actions of the past. The Pope's call, however, "fit like a ring on a finger," because a self-reflection by the bishops was always being demanded by the Argentine society. [. . .]

The bishops finally reached an agreement to say very little and basically not admit to having made mistakes. "We feel profoundly that we were unable to mitigate further the pain produced by this drama. We are in solidarity with the many who feel hurt by it and sincerely lament the participation of members of the Church in the violation of human rights," they stated.

Further on, in the only section where they actually ask for forgiveness, "the bishops, invoking the words of Paul VI, ask humbly for forgiveness from God, our Lord, for the sins that can be attributed to us." They add, "we beg our brothers and sisters who feel offended by us that they too forgive us. We are willing to forgive the sins that were committed against the church." [. . .]

The bishops' statement has provoked differing opinions in Argentine society. The majority of the political parties were pleased with the limited self-criticism of the bishops, seeing it as a sign for the rest of Argentine society. Human rights organizations, for their part, criticized the statement and reminded the bishops once again of the different "manner" in which they received the military officers who were ruling at the time, hearing their explanations while refusing to meet with the Mothers of the Plaza de Mayo and hear their complaints about human rights violations. [. . .]

Two of the most important gaps in the "examination of conscience" are the lack of reference to the disappeared (more than 20,000 in Argentina during the 1976-83 military government) and the people who were killed, including figures such as La Rioja Bishop Enrique Angelelli, assassinated in 1976.

160. The Mexican Bishops and the EZLN

On March 28, 2001, the Mexican bishops addressed the National Congress, offering their reflections on the recent march of Zapatista leaders from Chiapas to Mexico City. The recognition of the multiethnic and multicultural nature of Mexico, the affirmation of racial

SOURCE: Quoted in "Peace and Reconciliation in Chiapas," *Latin American Documentation* 31, no. 6 (July/August 2001): 11-14.

equality, and repudiation of continued injustice to the indigenous is an understandable priority of the bishops. But most of their address is devoted to the EZLN (Zapatista National Liberation Army), with whom the bishops are clearly sympathetic now that the EZLN has affirmed its political and nonmilitary nature after being in arms for seven years. The bishops admonish both leaders of the EZLN and members of congress about their proper duties and the correct position they should embrace.

Is this intense involvement in politics a legitimate aspect of the pastoral duties of bishops? Does it raise any problems? What is immensely significant about the bishops' reference (see no. 1) to "God's plan for humanity"? Evaluate the quotation in no. 1 of the communiqué: "The Catholic Church, which is an expert on humanity. . . ." How might the varied Amerindian nations of Mexico, large and small, respond to this resounding affirmation of the integrity of indigenous peoples? How credible might they find the bishops' two declarations? What must have happened both to the Mexican church and to the congress that permitted the clergy to promulgate documents such as these and the congress to consider them?

Note that the 1917 Mexican Constitution contained draconian clauses that disenfranchised the clergy, forbade them to speak on politics, and prohibited Catholic schools. Until the last decade of the twentieth century, a good-standing member of the Partido Revolucionario Institucional (PRI) had to espouse anticlerical rhetoric.

On the occasion of the Zapatista leaders' march to Mexico City and other states in the country, we offer the following reflections:

1. Mexico is a pluri-ethnic and pluri-cultural nation. Our roots are as much in the millenary indigenous cultures as they are in European cultures, and the mix teaches us that our humanity is formed by the actions of the Creator and all the migrations over time. Our country cannot overlook what we have received from our indigenous cultures as an ingredient of our national identity.

As such, it is necessary that the laws and the attention of the government and civil society focus on our indigenous brothers and sisters. Refusing to pay attention to them is unjust and racist, and goes against fundamental human rights and God's plan for humanity. Jesus Christ taught us to love with a preference for the poorest of our brothers and sisters, the marginalized and excluded, because we are all children of the same God and, as such, brothers and sisters.

Our indigenous brothers and sisters and all Mexicans carry within us the dignity of the human person, by nature intelligent, free and open to the transcendental, the principle, subject and end of all intellectual and collective activity.

2. The EZLN (Zapatista Army for National Liberation) has decided to no longer use weapons, making them unnecessary through political dialogue. They are a political force and no longer a military option. As such, we respectfully call on the representatives and senators in Congress to listen closely to them. Listening to them is part of the dialogue as a privileged way to deactivate war. This is, then, an opportunity that we cannot miss in order to consolidate paths to peace in Chiapas and the rest of the country.

After listening to the proposals of the EZLN and the valuable contributions of other groups, the legislators will proceed with the responsibility and representative quality that the nation has conferred on them to make the necessary constitutional changes, taking into account the supreme good of the homeland. In addition, they need to begin a reform of the state, because some of the issues are still pending from the San Andrés dialogue (when the Zapatistas and government of former President Ernesto Zedillo sat down to talk).

3. For their part, the EZLN representatives need to be aware that the country is made up of very diverse groups and ways of thinking. The construction of democracy demands respect for

diversity and living together with people who act and think differently.

As such, they cannot impose on the nation the criteria of one group, even if these criteria are reasonable and offer elements that need to be considered. This means that once they have been heard by the legislators they need to accept the laws that are freely adopted.

If they modify the so-called "COCOPA [Comisión de Concordia y Pacificación (established 1994)] Proposal" taking into account other rights, they need to accept the law as it is approved with the cooperation of all sectors and not prolong the conflict.

Just as there is dialogue to favorably resolve the legislation on indigenous rights and cultures, there also needs to be dialogue by both sides to deal with the Zapatistas who are in prison and remove the 3,000 soldiers still in the area. The conditions for dialogue cannot be efficient if they are set only by one side.

4. We call on the general population to listen to the proposals the EZLN leaders will offer to society in the different states included along their march. Their way of dressing (ski masks and bandanas covering their faces) is only symbolic — and mystical — but what is important is the content of their demands and the peaceful way they have chosen to present them. We need to analyze their words, understand their ideologies and accept the just causes that gave rise to the conflict so that they are not repeated again.

We need to have a critical attitude so that we are not surprised by the magic of language or advertising, but also humble as we begin to understand how we have failed our indigenous brothers and sisters. In particular, we ask that discriminatory and racist attitudes, particularly any violent provocation or aggression that damages the peace process, be avoided. We all need to cooperate to rebuild peace.

5. Christianity, being an essential ingredient in our roots, is a necessary element in finding solutions to this situation. As such, we invite all those who believe in Jesus Christ to intensify their prayers so that God will give us the gifts of the Holy Spirit, above all wisdom, prudence, truth and love, so that Chiapas and Mexico give way to

the construction of justice and peace that culminate in fraternity and reconciliation. We ask our mother, Our Lady of Guadalupe, who wants to see all the peoples of this land united, to intercede on our behalf.

Communiqué from the Mexican Bishops' Indigenous Commission on the EZLN March

1. Everything that affects humankind interests the Catholic Church, which is an expert in humanity. As such, given that "being human necessarily means existing in a determined culture" (John Paul II, Message Jan. 1, 2001, #5), the church is very interested in everything that refers to indigenous peoples, because "embracing culture as an element that shapes the personality is a universal experience whose importance is priceless. Without being rooted in a definite culture, the person runs the risk of being exposed to an excess of contradictory stimuli that will not contribute to a balance and calm development" (John Paul II, #6).

2. The church is particularly interested in the legal and juridical development to establish a more just order for indigenous peoples in the country, without forgetting that "a culture, in the sense that it is truly vital, should not fear being dominated. In the same sense, no law can maintain it alive if it has died in the soul of the people" (John Paul II, #15).

3. We perceive that many protagonists in society have shown themselves open to the proposals that lead to peace. We perceive a new environment and mentality, with concrete steps taken by a government that is open and willing to dialogue.

4. Hopefully the EZLN is also willing to show signs of co-responsibility. We Mexicans are convinced that society will not be built by the barrel of a gun, and we live together each day showing our faces.

5. The EZLN march that begins today, despite the negative statements because of the International Red Cross' decision not to accompany the leaders, will be carried out in a climate that will allow all Mexicans to freely travel the country with the guarantee of our laws. Many opinions have

been aired through the use of freedom of expression, which is not strange given the diversity of ideas and facets that are complementary to this issue. We need to learn how to listen without disqualifying what the other says.

6. Last July 2 (2000), we Mexicans showed our civic pride, peacefully taking a democratic step (with the presidential elections). If we did this, strengthened by our confidence, today we can take a new step that will put us on the path to peace. All Mexicans are interested in and concerned about the conditions of our indigenous brothers and sisters. In the climate of democracy that we are living, God wants the EZLN march through the states to proceed with peace, respect and civility for the authentic good of indigenous peoples.

7. A possible fruit, which we are all searching for, is to mature in our appreciation for indigenous dignity. Almost all Mexicans, to greater and lesser extent, have some indigenous blood, the root of our idiosyncrasies, religiosity and identity as a nation. We hope for the recognition of the indigenous peoples as persons and children of God. If we know each other better, we will know ourselves better.

8. Along the same lines, another fruit we need to search for in our pluriethnic and pluricultural nation is that the San Andrés Accords be received, studied and discussed in the Congress to achieve a more just and equitable legislation that respects the rights of all the minorities within our nation.

9. Without overlooking underlying ideologies, we believe that the EZLN position looks for so-called integral reform of the state to achieve greater dignity, justice and development for all people. Their march must help us become more aware of the importance of the time in which we are living, which calls for the participation of all people to build a Mexico that is more just, dignified and developed.

10. Beyond the spectacle or euphoria, and without falling into the superficiality of the march, it is important that it wakes the awareness of Mexicans to the urgency of the Gospel principles to build the Mexico that we want, which is more just, dignified and developed. For this reason, to the indigenous call, "never again a Mexico without us," we want to add, "never again a Mexico without Christ, never again a Mexico without the Gospel, never again a Mexico without the serious and responsible contribution of its faithful."

11. As such, it is urgent that as Christians we raise our petitions for Mexico, because God does not build a house in vain.

161. San Juan Diego Cuauhtlatoatzin

Pope John Paul II canonized more saints than all his predecessors together, attempting to find exemplary candidates from every nation and culture. As a special gesture to Guatemala, he traveled there on July 30, 2002, to canonize Pedro de San José de Betancourt (1626-1667), a poor shepherd who became apostle to the underclass and abandoned of that country. The very next day as a special gesture to the Mexican nation he traveled to its capital to canonize Juan Diego. His homily at the ceremony made clear the purpose of the canonization and the benefits to the church, nation, and faithful that would redound from it. What are those benefits? Given the recent growth—in Mexico and elsewhere in Latin America—of movements expressing pride in indigenous culture and demands for equal rights and even autonomy, how might indigenous peoples react to the portrayal of Juan Diego as saint? Might John Paul's choice indicate the political approach he felt appropriate for contemporary Latin America?

SOURCE: John Paul II, "Canonization of Juan Diego Cuauhtlatoatzin: Homily of the Holy Father John Paul II, Mexico City, Wednesday July 31, 2002," www.marianland.com/guadalupe002.html (retrieved on May 5, 2003). Reprinted by permission of marianland.com.

"I thank you, Father . . . that you have hidden these things from the wise and understanding and revealed them to babes; yea, Father, for such was your gracious will" (Mt 11:25-26).

Dear Brothers and Sisters,

These words of Jesus in today's Gospel are a special invitation to us to praise and thank God for the gift of the first indigenous Saint of the American Continent.

With deep joy I have come on pilgrimage to this Basilica of Our Lady of Guadalupe, the Marian heart of Mexico and of America, to proclaim the holiness of *Juan Diego Cuauhtlatoatzin*, the simple, humble Indian who contemplated the sweet and serene face of Our Lady of Tepeyac, so dear to the people of Mexico. [. . .]

Today I address a very affectionate greeting to the many indigenous people who have come from the different regions of the country, representing the various ethnic groups and cultures which make up the rich, multi-faceted Mexican reality. The Pope expresses his closeness to them, his deep respect and admiration, and receives them fraternally in the Lord's name. [. . .]

What was Juan Diego like? Why did God look upon him? The Book of Sirach, as we have heard, teaches us that God alone "*is mighty; he is glorified by the humble*" (cf. Sir 3:20). Saint Paul's words, also proclaimed at this celebration, shed light on the divine way of bringing about salvation: "*God chose what is low and despised in the world . . . so that no human being might boast in the presence of God*" (1 Cor 1:28, 29).

It is moving to read the accounts of Guadalupe, sensitively written and steeped in tenderness. In them the Virgin Mary, the handmaid "*who glorified the Lord*" (Lk 1:46), reveals herself to Juan Diego as the Mother of the true God. As a sign, she gives him precious roses, and as he shows them to the Bishop, he discovers the blessed image of Our Lady imprinted on his tilma.

"The Guadalupe Event", as the Mexican Episcopate has pointed out, "meant the beginning of evangelization with a vitality that surpassed all expectations. Christ's message, through his Mother, took up the central elements of the indigenous culture, purified them and gave them

the definitive sense of salvation" (14 May 2002, No. 8). Consequently Guadalupe and Juan Diego have a deep ecclesial and missionary meaning and are a model of perfectly inculturated evangelization. [. . .]

"*The Lord looks down from heaven, he sees all the sons of men*" (Ps 33:13), we recited with the Psalmist, once again confessing our faith in God, who makes no distinctions of race or culture. In accepting the Christian message without forgoing his indigenous identity, Juan Diego discovered the profound truth of the new humanity, in which all are called to be children of God. Thus he facilitated the fruitful meeting of two worlds and became the catalyst for the new Mexican identity, closely united to Our Lady of Guadalupe, whose mestizo face expresses her spiritual motherhood which embraces all Mexicans. This is why the witness of his life must continue to be the inspiration for the building up of the Mexican nation, encouraging brotherhood among all its children and ever helping to reconcile Mexico with its origins, values and traditions.

The noble task of building a better Mexico, with greater justice and solidarity, demands the cooperation of all. In particular, it is necessary today to support the indigenous peoples in their legitimate aspirations, respecting and defending the authentic values of each ethnic group. Mexico needs its indigenous peoples and these peoples need Mexico!

Beloved brothers and sisters of every ethnic background of Mexico and America, today, in praising the Indian Juan Diego, I want to express to all of you the closeness of the Church and the Pope, embracing you with love and encouraging you to overcome with hope the difficult times you are going through. [. . .]

Blessed Juan Diego, a good, Christian Indian, whom simple people have always considered a saint! We ask you to accompany the Church on her pilgrimage in Mexico, so that she may be more evangelizing and more missionary each day. Encourage the Bishops, support the priests, inspire new and holy vocations, help all those who give their lives to the cause of Christ and the spread of his Kingdom.

Happy Juan Diego, true and faithful man! We

entrust to you our lay brothers and sisters so that, feeling the call to holiness, they may imbue every area of social life with the spirit of the Gospel. [...]

Beloved Juan Diego, "the talking eagle"! Show us the way that leads to the "Dark Virgin" of Tepeyac, that she may receive us in the depths of her heart, for she is the loving, compassionate Mother who guides us to the true God. Amen.

162. First among Equals among the Bishops

First among equals among the Catholic bishops of Latin America, Francisco Javier Cardinal Errázuriz Ossa (b. 1933), archbishop of Santiago de Chile, was in 2003 elected president of CELAM (Consejo Episcopal de Latinoamérica), the organization to which all Roman Catholic bishops of Latin America belong. Soon thereafter, he was interviewed by the journal 30 Days in the Church and in the World, *published in Rome, by director Giulio Andreotti. Cardinal Errázuriz, the spokesman for the hundreds of bishops of Latin America, describes the status of the church in basically positive terms, but that of Latin America in negative ones. What movements, events, or teachings may have influenced Errázuriz's thinking in each area? Has he echoed any of the previous analyses contained in this anthology? Where does his response to the three questions on "social commitment," "spiritualizing," and "preferential option" place him on the spectrum of "traditional versus progressive Catholicism"? How might the Pentecostals and other evangelicals respond to Errázuriz's comments on the "sects"? Are his references to the latter accurate and fair? How apt is his response to the question on "the situation of the indigenous populations" in Latin America?*

[Question] Your Eminence, from the privileged standpoint of the presidency of CELAM, how do you see the situation of the Latin-American Church?

FRANCISCO JAVIER ERRÁZURIZ OSSA: The seeds of the Gospel spread by the first evangelization are still giving their fruits. The Catholic substratum of our culture is a living reality. The phenomena of secularization are not present to the same degree and aren't making ground at the same pace as they are elsewhere. Even the sociologists are surprised at the faith in God of the immense majority of the population, at the popular religious sentiment and its expressions, such as devotion to the Virgin Mary, the admiration for the person of the Pope, to be found in Latin America. The growth and multiplication of Church movements is an encouraging phenomenon, and the evangelizing presence of permanent deacons, who are doing valuable work especially in situations where priests are not plentiful and the influx of men and women religious, from Italy for instance, that was once significant, now no longer happens. Nevertheless, we are working hard at training qualified catechists, one of the more frequent forms of voluntary work with us, in pastoral work with the young and in the field of vocations, but in that field it's clear we must trust in the Lord. The faith and the heart of the Christian communities beat in liturgical celebrations. [...]

[Question] Your Eminence, how do you instead see the social situation of the continent?

ERRÁZURIZ OSSA: In recent decades unfortunately social problems have grown sharper. In many countries poverty has grown, and deprivation also. There is also a lack of trust in public ser-

SOURCE: "Interview with the New President of the CELAM [Cardinal Francisco Javier Errázuriz Ossa]," September 2003, www.cardinalrating.com/cardinal_30_article_959.ttm (accessed on 9/28/2005).

vices, above all among young people, not least because of the disrepute into which the political parties have fallen, something that has brought about ungovernable situations in several countries on the continent. It's true that we have many committed lay people, many well-trained, but there is a lack of figures of high moral and religious stature to act as leaders and moral and political guides for the younger generations.

[Question] Is this critical situation due to internal problems or is responsibility to be sought elsewhere?

ERRÁZURIZ OSSA: To both of those factors. A large number of builders of society have no professional ethics, and when they lose credibility because they don't do their job properly, they don't react in time. On the other hand the means to give impetus to rapid productive and human development are missing. Some countries don't have them because paying off their foreign debt is strangling them. But where has all that loaned money gone to? Unfortunately many times the flood of money has financed corruption instead of economic development. So it happens that there are countries on the verge of bankruptcy in which there are some very rich characters who live thanks to money pocketed immorally.

[Question] Those [are] the internal causes. And the external ones?

ERRÁZURIZ OSSA: The globalization of the economy, as it was done, has determined the fact that the poorest countries and peoples are sidelined by development. Globalization is a fact of life, inevitable, but it's not inevitable that it should lower the standard of living of the people already with very little. It depends on the model of globalization that is applied. We can and must hope that there is real globalization of solidarity, the criteria for which are not only economico-financial [sic] but also create space for respect of the dignity of the economically underdeveloped.

[Question] Among the causes of the impoverishment of the continent there is also the "free market" policy that has reigned over the last decade . . .

ERRÁZURIZ OSSA: Let's take the case of

Argentina: they say that it has plummeted into this terrible crisis precisely because it followed free-market doctrine to the letter, applying the recipes prescribed by the international financial bodies. Unfortunately this "free market" system has been set up within a relationship of inequality among the various nations, with the weaker countries unable to escape the diktats of the more powerful. The problem, however, doesn't concern only the model but the people who apply it, their honesty, their sense of justice, their concern for the weak and the dignity of the peoples and their cultures. That is why I believe that only a pastoral of sanctity, linked to greater attention to the social doctrine of the Church, can bring about change. But it will take decades. [. . .]

[Question] At the May Assembly Cardinal Giovanni Battista Re stated that a bishop's concern "will always be the proclamation of the Gospel, but he must also help human progress and the good of all." The Latin-American Church is sometimes accused of being unbalanced in its social commitment . . .

ERRÁZURIZ OSSA: According to the times and circumstances, greater value is set at times on certain aspects of the Christian life. It's obvious that when there are priests who are in contact every day with situations of great poverty, there may be the temptation to a more unilateral commitment in the social sense. That happened in part after the CELAM General Conference held in 1968 in Medellín. Liberation Theology also arose out of an awareness of the enormous injustices present on our continent. Today instead importance is also given to other aspects of the Christian faith, for example the *lectio divina* [prayerful reading of the Bible] that has spread almost like a new thing, although the monastics have always practiced it. And almost all the new ecclesial movements have at the core of their charism the school of sanctity and communion. It's clear, however, that they mustn't lose social perspective.

[Question] Isn't there a danger of a spiritualizing Church that is unconcerned by social questions?

ERRÁZURIZ OSSA: It's almost impossible for that to happen. [It] Could be that a group, a community, even a diocese, concentrates for a certain period of time only on the spiritual training of their members; however, that will be the point of departure for the whole Christian commitment, and it's almost impossible to live without seeing the plight of the poor who surround us. And one can't forget the Lord's attitude towards the poor, widows, the sick.

[Question] In what way do liberation theology and the preferential option keep their relevance?

ERRÁZURIZ OSSA: Preferential concern for the poor remains an absolute priority throughout the Latin American Church. The issue of Liberation Theology is different since, though setting out from just exigencies, it offered a partial and reductive vision of the Gospel message, even through an arbitrary selection of the books of Holy Writ. In the same way it isn't allowed to study the word of God only from one perspective, that of the poor in the socio-economic sense, keeping silent on the preferential option of Jesus for the poor in spirit, with which he built his Church. Albeit the two options frequently coincide, it is not always so. At times it happens that the poor from the material point of view, are not poor in spirit. Many Pharisees come from poor sectors of the population. [. . .]

[Question] The Pontifical Commission for Latin America devoted [a] good part of its last plenary meeting, held last March in Rome, to the problem of the sects. Is it a very alarming phenomenon for the Church?

ERRÁZURIZ OSSA: Yes and no. It's less alarming than was feared. Up to a short time ago it was thought that most of Brazil would be Pentecostal in the arc of a few years. And that has not happened. Nevertheless the whole phenomenon is worrying. It's true, membership of the sects has increased in a notable fashion. Without counting then that in some countries certain groups and sects conduct their proselytism aggressively against the Church and without any ecumenist spirit. For the Church the growth of these groups entails the challenge of approaching in merciful spirit and with missionary ardor, holding out the Bible and the image of the Virgin Mary, to the very many people who have left it, eager to encounter the brotherly support of Christians, and thirsty for communion and the Gospel.

[Question] Behind this expansion do you glimpse a design for dominance by the US or do you think nothing similar is involved?

ERRÁZURIZ OSSA: One sometimes notes, in effect, an extraordinary multiplication of missions and preachers coming from the United States without there being that many believers. But there are now also fully home-grown bodies.

[Question] The situation of the indigenous populations is another delicate issue for Latin America . . .

ERRÁZURIZ OSSA: These populations have a stronger awareness of their identity than they had in the past, and also the cultural world tends to have greater respect for minorities. Within the Indio world, however, there are different tendencies. There are native groups, the Mexican ones for example, who want to recover their traditions without giving up the Christian faith. Elsewhere instead there are even people who want to return to Pre-Columbian paganism. To avoid that involution I think it's important to pay attention to the figure of the Indio Juan Diego whom the Pope canonized just a year ago [2002] in Mexico.

Index